# Brokers of Empire

*Japanese Settler Colonialism in Korea, 1876–1945*

Harvard East Asian Monographs 337

# Brokers of Empire

## *Japanese Settler Colonialism in Korea, 1876–1945*

Jun Uchida

Published by the Harvard University Asia Center
and distributed by Harvard University Press
Cambridge (Massachusetts) and London, 2011

Printed in the United States of America

The Harvard University Asia Center publishes a monograph series and, in coordination with the Fairbank Center for Chinese Studies, the Korea Institute, the Reischauer Institute of Japanese Studies, and other faculties and institutes, administers research projects designed to further scholarly understanding of China, Japan, Vietnam, Korea, and other Asian countries. The Center also sponsors projects addressing multidisciplinary and regional issues in Asia.

Publication of this book was partially underwritten by the Academy of Korean Studies Institutional Grant at the Korea Institute, Harvard University.

Library of Congress Cataloging-in-Publication Data

Uchida, Jun.
Brokers of empire : Japanese settler colonialism in Korea, 1876–1945 / Jun Uchida.
p. cm. -- (Harvard East Asian monographs ; 337)
Includes bibliographical references and index.
ISBN 978-0-674-06253-5 (hardcover : alk. paper)
ISBN 978-0-674-49202-8 (pbk : alk. paper)
1. Korea--History--Japanese occupation, 1910–1945. 2. Korea--History—1864–1910. 3. Korea--Colonization--History. 4. Japanese--Colonization--History. 5. Japanese--Korea--History. 6. Colonists--Korea--History. 7. Japan--Colonies--Administration. I. Harvard University. Asia Center. II. Title.
DS916.54.U32 2011
951.9'03--dc23

2011019693

Index by the author

♾ Printed on acid-free paper

First paperback edition 2014

Cover illustration: (top) Detail from "Japanese Empire—Political," *Times Survey Atlas of the World*, ed. John Bartholomew and Edinburgh Geographical Institute (London: The Times, 1922), plate 65. © 2005 David Rumsey Historical Map Collection, www.davidrumsey.com. (bottom) "Kyoryū mindan teppai tōji no giin" (Japanese leaders of the Seoul Residents' Association at the time of its abolition). Ōmura Tomonojō, *Keijō kaikoroku* (Keijō: Chōsen Kenkyūkai, 1922).

Last figure below indicates year of this printing
21 20 19 18 17 16 15 14

*To my mother,*

*Keiko Uchida*

# *Acknowledgments*

This book is a product of a long intellectual journey that began as a dissertation project, coursed through the shifting currents of scholarship on empire, and has left me with still more questions to explore. In the course of this decade-long endeavor, I have accumulated enormous debts to my teachers, colleagues, and friends who have given me support, criticism, and inspiration that are etched on the following pages.

Andrew Gordon guided my project through the dissertation phase as the most generous reader as well as the most perceptive critic. His keen analytical mind penetrated my writing at various stages of its evolution and nurtured my overall sensibilities as a historian. For his unflagging support and mentorship, I am forever in his debt. During my two-year fieldwork in Japan and Korea, I was blessed to have another mentor, Kimura Kenji, a pioneering scholar of Japanese settlers in Korea. Kimura sensei took me under his wing and shared with me his wisdom and expert knowledge of the sources and archives that were all indispensable to my research. In the course of writing, I received further support and inspiration from scholars who have opened new lines of inquiry into the history of colonial Korea. Peter Duus, whose study of the Japanese activities in pre-annexation Korea serves as a guidepost for this book, read and commented on my entire dissertation draft despite its volume. Carter Eckert, though his seminars and his work on colonial capitalism, taught me the complexities of Korean history and the importance of engaging with Korea in order to understand the rise of modern Japan.

During my fieldwork in Japan and Korea, I had the opportunity to immerse myself in a diverse network of professional historians, independent researchers, and graduate students who shared their ideas and in-depth knowledge of local archives with me. I owe special thanks to Yoshizawa Kayoko for her friendship and introduction to her scholarly circles. My research and analysis of primary sources benefited greatly from the guidance and criticism of Hashiya Hiroshi, Higuchi Yūichi, Itagaki Ryūta, Kamiya Niji, Hyung-gu Lynn, Sin Chang-gon, Sŏn Chae-wŏn, Takasaki Sōji, Yi Hyeong-nang, and Yoshida Mitsuo. For enlightening me with their own work and knowledge, I must also thank Mark Caprio, Kasuya Ken'ichi, Ōhama Ikuko, Ōkubo Yuri, and Ken Robinson.

My archival "dig" was supported by a more extensive list of individuals and institutions. In Japan, I would especially like to thank Kawa Kaoru, Tsuji Hironori, and the staff of the Yūhō Archive at Gakushūin University for introducing me to rare and unpublished sources on settlers and transcriptions of recorded interviews of former colonial bureaucrats. I am equally grateful to Pak Chae-il and Kōno Yasunori of the Cultural Center Arirang, another archival gem, for letting me stay in the stacks for extended hours. I thank the Institute for Social Science at the University of Tokyo for hosting me as a visiting researcher and allowing me access to the university's various libraries. I was also glad to use the National Diet Library, Yokohama National University Library, and Waseda University's Central Library.

In Korea, I owe special gratitude to Hŏ Yŏng-nang and the staff of the Kuksa P'yŏnch'an Wiwŏnhoe for introducing me to its enormous digital archive and allowing me to use uncataloged materials especially police reports. In exploring the colonial documents housed at Korea Central National Library, Seoul National University, and Korea University in Seoul, I obtained generous help and guidance from Anzako Yuka, Chŏng Chae-ch'ŏl, Chŏng Chae-jŏng, and Pak Sŭng-jun. The kind staff of the Naksŏngdae Archive and the Seoul City Research Institute at Seoul City University provided service and assistance beyond the call of duty. And I wish to express my heartfelt thanks to Ms. Yi Suk-cha for her tremendous hospitality in hosting my research stay in Seoul.

In the United States, the staff at Harvard-Yenching Library, Stanford University's East Asian Library (especially Kyung-mi Chung and Naomi Kotake), and C. V. Starr East Asian Library at the University of California, Berkeley (especially Hisayuki Ishimatsu) made themselves available to help me even at short notice. I also thank Christine Cho and Tsūdō Ayumi for helping me complete my bibliography, and David Fedman for reading over the proofs.

I owe a particular debt of gratitude to the many individuals who agreed to meet with me for interviews and respond to my questionnaires. I would like to thank members of the Chūō Nikkan Kyōkai especially Fujimoto Hideo, Aoki Etsuko, and Kudō Masumi, all of whom sadly passed away before this project saw completion. Nakao Minoru, who over many years headed the umbrella organization of settler school alumni associations, helped me circulate my questionnaires and put me in touch with a variety of settler repatriates' organizations. For facilitating my interviews in Korea, I am grateful to Yi Po-hye and Sasaki Kuniyuki who invited me to attend the school reunion of his alma mater, Seoul Industrial School. I would like to thank his former Korean classmates for taking the time to meet with me and sharing their colonial experiences anonymously.

In the course of transforming my dissertation into a book, I produced multiple iterations of the manuscript that were read by still more individuals who offered me invaluable comments and criticisms. I would like to thank Miranda Brown, Caroline Elkins, Julian Go, Thomas R. H. Havens, and Louise Young for reading some revised chapters of my dissertation. Lieba Faier and Theodore Jun Yoo, as well as my current and former JFRoG comrades (David Como, Zephyr Frank, Sean Hanretta, Yumi Moon, Tom Mullaney, Caroline Winterer) kindly read and helped me rewrite the introduction. And I am deeply grateful to Carol Gluck, Yoshihisa Tak Matsusaka, Andre Schmid, and Eiko Maruko Siniawer for reading and commenting on all or parts of my book manuscript just as it began to take shape.

In the final stage of my serial revision, many colleagues and friends at Stanford came to my aid to ensure the book's timely completion. The entire cohort of historians of East Asia—Mark Lewis, Yumi Moon, Tom Mullaney, Gi-Wook Shin, Matt Sommer, and Kären Wigen—read and critiqued the final version of my manuscript by organizing a workshop for me. Kären Wigen, who has guided me with grace and intellectual generosity since my arrival, went out of her way to comment on my writing at the sentence level. Richard Roberts also read my manuscript in its entirety and provided me with critical feedback that helped me clarify and deepen my comparative observations on colonial Africa. And Allyson Hobbs frequently let me brainstorm with her about key passages in the text. My gratitude to these colleagues and friends is beyond words.

This book also builds on valuable insights and feedback I gained from conversations with the following people: my fellow dissertation writers Marjan Boogert, Michael Burtscher, Matthew Fraleigh, Chong Bum Kim, Yōichi Nakano, Izumi Nakayama, Jin Kyu Robertson, Hiraku Shimoda, and Karen Thornber; my fellow post-docs, Jessie Abel, Jonathan Abel, Chelsea Foxwell, Todd Henry, Ayu Majima, Trent Maxey, and Se-Mi Oh; and scholars I met at conferences and workshops, especially Alexis Dudden, Henry Em, and Erik Esselstrom. Moreover, I frequently bounced my ideas off Cemil Aydin, Kyu Hyun Kim, Hyung Gu Lynn, and Yōsuke Nirei, each of whom has provided me with a model of transnational scholarship to which I aspire. And to Sue Jean Cho and Joe Wicentowski, my sincere thanks for giving me moral as well as intellectual support when I needed it the most.

I am extremely grateful to William Hammell of the Harvard University Asia Center for his care, expertise, and patience with which he guided me through the entire process of publication. I must also thank two anonymous reviewers, one of whom, in a 30-page report, painstakingly combed through my long-winded manuscript to point out what did and did not belong in this book. I have done my best to incorporate their most pointed criticisms, which helped me to trim the manuscript and bring it back to my original focus and question.

Although I relied heavily on the help of many individuals as noted above, I take the sole responsibility for all flaws and shortcomings in this book. If one of them may still be its length or level of detail, it reflects my on-going struggle to contribute to the divergent scholarly worlds of Japan, Korea, and North America.

The research and writing of this book were generously funded by the Social Science Research Council, the Korea Institute and the Reischauer Institute of Japanese Studies at Harvard University, the Matsushita Foundation, the Northeast Asia Council of the Association for Asian Studies, the Harvard Academy for International and Area Studies, and the Center for East Asian Studies at Stanford University. In particular,

I wish to thank Ruiko Connor, Stacie Matsumoto, and the staff of the Reischauer Institute and Suzan Laurence and Myong-suk Chandra of the Korea Institute for offering me every means of assistance during my postdoctoral stay in Cambridge.

My last words of thanks are reserved for my family and parents, who have directly or indirectly shaped the conception and thrust of this book. The topic of colonialism was too close to home especially for my grandparents; like many former settlers I met, they remained all but silent about their own experience as repatriates, and their historical view of Asia, to the end, differed considerably from mine. But in their silence I discovered my own ignorance, even parallels between their colonial past and my adolescence as a Japanese expatriate in Southeast Asia. From its inception, moreover, I have had an indispensable supporter of my project, Keiko Uchida, my mother. In serving as my constant listener and interlocutor, she has imparted to me not only her faith in my abilities, but her *mondai ishiki* without which this book would have been spineless. I dedicate this book to her with love and gratitude to everything that she has done for me.

Parts of Chapters 5 and 6 appeared in a preliminary and abridged form in "Brokers of Empire: Japanese and Korean Business Elites in Colonial Korea," in *Settler Colonialism in the Twentieth Century: Projects, Practices, Legacies*, ed. Caroline Elkins and Susan Pedersen, 153–70 (New York and London: Routledge, 2005).

# *Contents*


| | | |
|---|---|---|
| | *Maps, Tables, and Figures* | xi |
| | Introduction | 1 |
| Part I: Emergence | | 33 |
| 1 | The World of Settlers | 35 |
| 2 | Settlers and the State: Uneasy Partners | 96 |
| Part II: In Action | | 141 |
| 3 | Building an Empire of Harmony | 143 |
| 4 | The Discourse on Korea and Koreans | 188 |
| 5 | Industrializing the Peninsula | 227 |
| 6 | In Search of a Political Voice | 263 |
| Part III: Organs of the State | | 305 |
| 7 | The Manchurian Impact | 307 |
| 8 | Citizens and Subjects under Total War | 355 |
| | Conclusion | 394 |
| | Appendixes | |
| | 1. Settler Leaders in Seoul, 1910–1930s | 404 |
| | 2. Oral Sources | 409 |

## *Reference Matter*

*Bibliography* 415

*Index* 459

# *Maps, Tables, and Figures*

## *Maps*


| | | |
|---|---|---|
| 1 | Northeast Asia | xviii |
| 2 | Distribution of Japanese Population in Korea, 1914 | 63 |
| 3 | Seoul, circa 1930 | 75 |
| 4 | "Twelve-Year Plan on Korean Railroads," August 1927 | 251 |


## *Tables*


| | | |
|---|---|---|
| 1 | Growth of Japanese Population in Korea, 1880–1944 | 65 |
| 2 | Growth of Japanese Population in Cities, 1890–1940 | 65 |
| 3 | Occupations of Japanese Residents in Korea, End of 1907 | 67 |
| 4 | Occupations of Japanese Residents in Korea, 1910–1940 | 68 |
| 5 | Main Pro-Government Organizations, 1915–1925 | 159 |


## *Figures*


| | | |
|---|---|---|
| 1 | Honmachi in Seoul, circa 1930 | 74 |
| 2a–b | Autumn Festival at the Keijō Shrine | 81 |
| 3 | Governor-General Saitō Makoto | 147 |
| 4 | Research Committee on Education | 150 |
| 5 | Dōminkai Leaders: Sin Sŏng-nin, Nakamura Kentarō, and Satō Torajirō | 167 |

| | | |
|---|---|---|
| 6 | Advertisement for the Dōmin "Mail-Order Lectures" | 174 |
| 7 | Class of the First Dōmin Summer University, August 1925 | 175 |
| 8 | Aoyagi Tsunatarō (Nanmei) | 192 |
| 9 | Chōsen Kenkyūkai (Korea Research Association) | 193 |
| 10 | Watanabe Sadaichirō | 245 |
| 11 | A Scene of a Provincial Council (North Kyŏngsang province) | 271 |
| 12a–b | Female Leaders of the Ryokki Renmei | 371 |

# Brokers of Empire

*Japanese Settler Colonialism in Korea, 1876–1945*

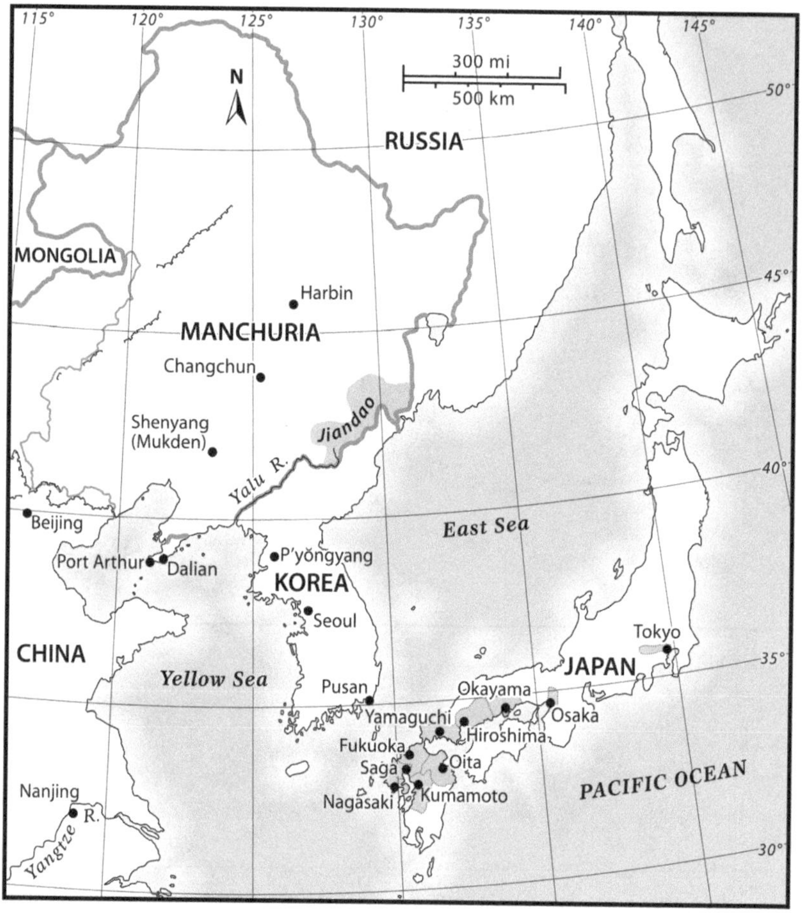


Map 1 Northeast Asia

NOTE: Prefectures highlighted on the map of Japan indicate the main origins of Japanese migrants to Korea.

# *Introduction*

In 1904, when the Imperial Japanese Navy launched a surprise attack on the Russian Pacific Fleet at Port Arthur to settle their contest over Korea and Manchuria, a stream of Japanese merchants and camp followers crossed the Korea Strait. Amid the wave of migrants was Kobayashi Genroku (1867–1940), a scion of a merchant family from the southeastern shore of Lake Biwa. Hauling a cargo of merchandise and accompanied by some twenty clerks and factory hands, Kobayashi boarded a ship for Pusan to "seize this golden opportunity" to expand his family's business, Chōjiya, which he had recently inherited at the age of 24. On the eve of the Meiji Restoration, Chōjiya had switched its product line from samurai armor to Western clothes, which the young emperor would shortly declare the new "national dress." And just as imperial Japan shed the "flimsy" garb of the Orient, Chōjiya provided officers and bureaucrats stationed on the peninsula with Western caps and uniforms—a trade that Kobayashi would pursue for the rest of his life with the singular resolve to "bury his bones" in the Korean soil that fell under Japanese control in 1905.[1]

Chōjiya's fortunes closely followed the trajectory of Japan's new empire. Through a combination of business acumen, official patronage, and sheer luck, Kobayashi transformed Chōjiya into a first-class clothier, known throughout the empire for its leadership in Western tailoring and

1. The biographical details on Kobayashi Genroku and Chōjiya come from Chōjiya Shōten 1936.

its efficiency in mass production.[2] He also did much more. A devout Buddhist, Kobayashi supported local charities, nurtured native monks, and educated the poor, in addition to hiring an unusually large number of Koreans at his main store in Seoul. Embracing what he called the "Buddhist commercial way" of wedding business to philanthropy, Kobayashi built a sizable Korean clientele based on Chōjiya's reputation as a "conduit of *naisen yūwa* [harmony between Japanese and Koreans]."

By 1930, Chōjiya was expanding its business on a continental scale. With a sales network that stretched to what would become the Japanese-dependent state of Manchukuo, Chōjiya refashioned itself from a clothier into a department store in 1929. And when the colonial state soon afterwards launched efforts, in the name of industry and labor, to encourage Koreans to wear colored (rather than traditional white) dress, Chōjiya was among the first to seize the business opportunity. But while it was happy to oblige the state's call, the store also claimed the campaign had been its own. Back in the late Meiji period (1868–1912), when Chōjiya first "introduced Japan-made woolen fabrics to Korea," according to its self-edited history, the company "took the initiative in calling for the improvement of Korean dress by promoting the use of colored clothes," decades before the state began to pay the subject any attention.

Mapping its "70 years of experience" onto Japan's global emergence, Chōjiya, at the peak of success, painted itself not only as a humble servant of the emperor, but as a harbinger of modernity that helped build the nation's status in the world.[3] Such a claim was not hyperbole. For his patriotic "contribution to Korean development," Kobayashi received numerous official honors, including a blue medal of merit conferred by Emperor Hirohito. Yet keeping the store's name alive among residents of Korea—and years later in the memories of former settlers—was not so much these official accolades as its founder's legacy as "a self-made man": a powerful fiction that lay at the heart of settler lore, and one that outlived the demise of Chōjiya's business empire in 1945.

Buried in the colonial archives of Korea are portraits of hundreds of Japanese men and women like Kobayashi. Between 1876 and 1945, a wide array of people journeyed across the sea—not only soldiers and

---

2. Kageyama 1921, 211.

3. Keijō Shinbunsha 1930, 48–50.

officials, but merchants, traders, prostitutes, journalists, teachers, and continental adventurers who, in remaking their lives on the peninsula, also helped to make their nation's empire. Although most migrants were driven primarily by personal profit and only secondarily by national interest, their mundane activities and the state's ambitions were inextricably entwined.

While empire wrought sweeping and often devastating changes to the Korean people, it brought opportunities for Japanese to transform ordinary lives into extraordinary careers. The life of emigrants was uncertain and many returned home empty-handed, but many others did well, amassing personal fortunes while supporting the empire. The career of Kobayashi reveals the diverse ways in which settlers shaped the local contours of colonialism—business, industry, religion, social work, and print—with effects that directly or indirectly reverberated in the metropole. Above all, his career shows that settlers not only cooperated with the state, but also pursued colonial projects of their own—projects that did not always coincide with official policies, but had lasting consequences for Japan's empire as well as for its Korean subjects. That overseas settlers formed an important, and independent, vector of influence in all phases of colonial rule is a central argument of this book.

The presence of these settlers in Korea, like the story of Kobayashi, has remained largely unknown. By 1945, Korea was home to over 700,000 Japanese civilians, joined by 300,000 army personnel. Comparable in number to the *colons* in French Algeria, they formed one of the largest single colonial communities in the twentieth century. Following Japan's surrender, at the behest of the victorious Allied powers, all but a handful of the one million Japanese nationals were repatriated to the home islands by the end of 1946. The sudden displacement of such a large and entrenched settler population is in itself a striking phenomenon, but this physical retreat following their nation's defeat is less surprising than their near disappearance from history. Having been uprooted from Korean soil, settlers like Kobayashi have not only receded from Japanese history, they have almost vanished from Japanese public memory.

Only against the backdrop of a complex intersection of history-writing and memory-making does this paradox become fathomable. In postwar Japan, public attention—including the attention of the political left—has long focused on those held accountable for the war and colonial aggression: servants of the state. Ordinary Japanese enter the story chiefly as victims rather than perpetrators of violence.[4] Although scholars have contested this trend, as Lori Watt points out, the overseas experience and its aftermath—the metamorphosis of colonists into repatriates (*hikiagesha*)—has failed to find a place in either narrative, their culpability paling next to that of the men who drove the machinery of the state, while their suffering has been deemed "not equivalent to the suffering of people in the metropole."[5] And settlers have not simply fallen off the radar. The politics of memory among former colonists themselves are also implicated in the way the Japanese remember (or forget) their colonial past.[6] Most settlers repatriated from Korea have lived in self-imposed silence or have kept their memories private, out of shame or fear of association with the militarist past—a position no doubt encouraged by their own government's failure to take a clear and consistent stance on "war responsibility."[7] The testimonies they have left in memoirs, autobiographies, and school albums relate their struggles as overseas pioneers of humble origins, while separating them from high imperialist politics. The effect is to draw an artificial division between state and commoners (*shomin*) and create parallel archives—one chronicling official repression, the other nostalgic innocence—that barely speak to one another.

This historical and historiographical displacement behooves us to reexamine the conventional narrative that equates Japanese colonialism with the rule of the Governor-General (*sōtoku seiji*) in Korea. No doubt the Governor-General was the central player in each phase of Japanese rule. The authoritarian nature of his power was unquestionable, as was the harsh and repressive character of his regime. Yet this colonial governance was less unitary and autocratic in practice than historians have

---

4. Kajimura 1992 [1974]; L. Young 1998, 7–8, and n. 5; Takasaki 2002.

5. Watt 2009, 54. As I will explain below, conventional studies on the Japanese empire have either ignored settlers or conflated them with the state as "the colonizer," another factor that accounts for the absence of settlers in both public memory and scholarship.

6. For a critical analysis of the memories of settler repatriates from Manchukuo, see Tamanoi 2009.

7. See Seraphim 2006, Part II.

assumed.[8] Despite being the font of authority, the Governor-General was not the only wielder of power in the colony. Numerous civilians helped maintain and expand Japanese hegemony on a daily basis, while pursuing interests and ambitions of their own.

Why did so many Japanese move to Korea? How did they interact with Koreans? What was the relationship of the settlers to the colonial state? And how do we reconcile their modest power with their weighty numbers? To answer these questions we must retell the colonists' story from the beginning: the moment when Kobayashi, along with thousands of Japanese migrants, first set foot on the peninsula. By putting these settlers squarely into the picture—and Japan into comparative discourse on empire—this book aims to reexamine Korea under colonial rule from its foundation. More than eyewitnesses or bystanders of the Governor-General's rule, it contends, settlers shaped how the Japanese empire began as much as how it ended, and indeed, how it fared during the 36 years of its existence.

## *Brokers of Empire*

In this book, I refer to settlers like the merchant Kobayashi as "brokers of empire." The following chapters cover multiple generations of Japanese who made Korea home, but their focus lies chiefly on the first generation, who settled in Korea before or immediately after the beginning of the Governor-General's rule in 1910, and who led the Japanese resident community through the late 1930s. My account highlights the activities of a diverse cast of characters—entrepreneurs, essayists, political fixers, educators, social reformers, religious leaders, and other non-governmental actors—who not only oversaw their communities but actively mediated the colonial management of Korea as its grassroots movers and shakers.

At an abstract level, the term "broker" captures the profit-oriented mentality that guided settler activities, from daily commercial endeavors

8. From old to new works on colonial Korea, it is common to describe the Governor-General's rule as a military dictatorship, or a form of "colonial totalitarianism," in the most powerful image offered by Gregory Henderson (1968). A few works that have challenged this image of the colonial state by illustrating its limits and internal workings include a dissertation by Hyung Gu Lynn (2001) and a comparative study of colonial bureaucracies in Taiwan and Korea by Okamoto Makiko (2008).

to large-scale petition movements. The role of settler leaders ranged from advancing their interests to negotiating among competing factions to maintain settler unity. More important, the concept underscores how settlers, as conduits of metropolitan capital and culture, mediated Japan's rise as a modernizing nation and empire. A central task for the brokers of empire was to remind fellow Japanese of this role by stressing the links between their activities and the struggle of empire. (And one of the greatest obstacles facing settler leaders was the apathy of their countrymen, in the colony as well as in the metropole.) In addition to educating the general public about Korea's conditions, the brokers of empire spoke tirelessly of settlers' duty to civilize Koreans and above all to civilize themselves as respectable colonists—a task that proved no less vexing than combating metropolitan ignorance.

The term "brokers" also captures the intermediary position of settlers, who operated simultaneously as agents and pawns of colonial power. The concept highlights their agency without losing sight of the overweening power of the colonial state, which placed a host of limits and constraints on the settlers' ability to govern their own affairs, or to constitute a viable civil society.[9] Moreover, it calls attention to the way the line separating the state and settler society continually shifted and blurred, which itself was an important function of colonial power.[10] Settlers operated on the porous edges of empire, where their practices sometimes merged and mixed with those of government and metropolitan agents. Identities and backgrounds of settler leaders—who included some former bureaucrats and many who worked for the Government-General in semiofficial capacity—also attest to how the distinction between officials (*kan*) and civilians (*min*), drawn and manipulated by both parties, was not as fixed as it appeared.

This elusive boundary between settlers and state was precisely what gave the brokers of empire a measure of influence in colonial governance. Lacking meaningful local or metropolitan representation in the administration of Korea, these men found other ways to bring their voices to bear on the regime. Not only did they utilize the press, they

---

9. See Chapter 2 for information on the early period of settlers' self-government.

10. For this point, I draw on the critical insight provided by Timothy Mitchell, who showed how state-society boundaries are produced as an aspect of power relations and as a technique of modern governance (1991, 77–96).

worked through existing parastatal institutions such as chambers of commerce and city councils, as well as new organizations of their own devising, with the aim of codifying their interests into policy. To *mediate* is both to act as a connecting link and to intervene in a process, in ways that can change the terms for all involved. Through an arsenal of strategies, often behind the scenes and at the grassroots level, the brokers of empire sought to influence Korean governance, making sure they would not remain on the sidelines of colonial politics.

Finally and most significantly, I deploy the concept of brokers to show, as Albert Memmi has written, how settler power and colonialism itself were shaped in engagement with the "colonized."[11] At each stage of colonialism, Koreans both constrained and channeled settler agency. If the Japanese colonists intruded upon Korean society in violent and exploitative ways, their activities did not go unchallenged by traditional social structures, commercial customs, and other aspects of local culture. The strength and resilience of local responses, indeed, reminds us of the fact that in fin-de-siècle Korea the rise of nationalism preceded the onset of formal colonial rule.[12] Devoid of the political power and resources of white colonists in Africa (of which more later), Japanese settlers in Korea were often compelled to enlist the cooperation of local elites—aristocrats, bureaucrats, entrepreneurs, landlords, religious leaders, and "pro-Japanese" elements—who shared similar, though not identical, stakes and class interests in the colonial project. Settlers' growing interactions with Koreans, in turn, produced assimilation anxieties, raising not only the specter of "Japanized" natives or "Koreanized" Japanese, but fundamental questions of nationhood. Ambivalence underlying the border-crossing activities of the brokers of empire deepened over time, as the state redrew and broadened the boundaries of citizenship to accommodate colonial subjects. Assimilation was as much about Koreans as it was about Japanese.

In documenting the role of Japanese settlers as brokers of empire, this book moves between two levels of analysis: the making of Korea as a colony of settlement, and settlers' agency within that project. The former refers broadly to the way Korea was conquered, settled, and governed

---

11. Memmi 1965, ix.
12. See Schmid 2002; and Duncan 1998, 198–221.

by and for the Japanese—and the impact of the Japanese community as a whole on Korean society. The latter refers more specifically to the activities and aspirations of settler leaders under the Governor-General's rule. The individual actions of brokers and the collective impact of settlers represented the articulated and unarticulated, the conscious and unconscious modalities of domination, where agency intersected with structure in the operation of colonial power. They demonstrate not only how a select group of aspirants aggressively pushed the empire from below, but how ordinary settlers consolidated imperial control when they were excluded from colonial governance, how they became drawn into colonial politics when they were preoccupied with daily commerce, and how they served as local conduits of assimilation when their intention was quite the reverse. It was this dynamic—that settlers became the crux of empire as well as the crucible of encounter *in spite of themselves*—that gave Japanese colonialism in Korea its intense yet fragile character. Throughout the book, my analytical lens will alternately zoom in for a close look at individual settler profiles and zoom out for a wider view of the colonial topography of power.

## *Between Nation and Empire*

Japan's modern quest for wealth and power overseas began in the closing decades of the nineteenth century, at a time when the Meiji leaders quickly came to conclude that a nation could not be imagined without an empire. Japan's emergence as a modern state coincided with the revolutionary transformation of imperialism from a mission delegated to a few chartered companies into a project undertaken by a nation-state and fueled by industrial capitalism. The Japanese aim to build a "rich nation and strong army" (*fukoku kyōhei*) thus entailed not only Westernization at home but also imperialism abroad. In the words of Peter Duus, "the pursuit of an expansionist agenda was part and parcel of the larger mimetic project of the Meiji elites."[13]

Yet in comparison with its European predecessors, Japan's path to modernity and empire traced an unusually steep trajectory. In the late nineteenth century, most European powers were already centuries into the business of exploring the globe and were driven by at least a hundred

13. Duus 1995, 12.

years of industrial revolution, when Japan launched both processes more or less simultaneously.[14] Single-minded as it was in its pursuit of parity with the West, Meiji imperialism was guided neither by a blueprint for conquest nor by an inevitable law of monopolistic capitalism. The process was messier and more complicated. While aggressively seeking economic rights and concessions vis-à-vis Western rivals, the infant imperial state with a meager home market struggled even harder to persuade domestic capitalists and financiers to invest in distant, and politically unstable, lands. If classic theories of J. A. Hobson and Lenin fail to explain Meiji imperialism, its sources must lie elsewhere. We need to look, first of all, at the motley crew of ordinary Japanese who first crossed the waters with modest capital or none at all.

Overseas settlers were a critical link between national formation and imperial expansion in the rise of modern Japan. Nations project their power, politicians and propagandists argued, not only by arms but by "peaceful methods" of commerce and emigration.[15] What the countrymen earned abroad enriched the state's coffers and helped solve its balance-of-payments problem, in addition to enhancing Japan's power and prestige in the world. Korea lay at the center of such official imagination at the turn of the century. Separated from the archipelago by only 120 miles, the Korean peninsula, as the Meiji leaders repeatedly declared, was a "dagger thrust at the heart of Japan" and therefore critical to national security. Korea was also a gateway to the Chinese continent, where imperial Japan could emerge onto the global stage, and a strategic territory abutting Manchuria, a buffer against Tsarist Russia. Peopling the peninsula in this context became the key to Japan's national and imperial construction. The government and promoters envisioned this as the work of hardy agrarian pioneers much like those who had settled on Hokkaido, Meiji Japan's first site of mass colonization. Although Korea was far more densely populated than Hokkaido, it was also viewed as "a colony of settlement" where excess farm labor would be exported.[16]

---

14. The exception among the European imperialists is Germany, which, like Meiji Japan, modernized and expanded overseas more or less simultaneously. On the German empire, see Smith 1978 and Wehler 1985.

15. L. Young 1998, 312–17. Also see Azuma 2008.

16. This vision was made explicit in the Japanese cabinet's 1904 decision to transform Korea into a protectorate (Duus 1984, 141).

But long before the state articulated a formal policy, scores of humble Japanese from the southwestern prefectures in the 1880s and 1890s began to flock to the ports of Pusan and Inch'ŏn in search of profit, adventure, labor, land, or simply a better life. Driven by divergent motivations, the lives of these mostly voluntary migrants came to be entangled with the state's broader ambitions, as demonstrated by their support for the Japanese troop operations during two imperialistic wars fought over Korea, against the Qing dynasty in 1894–1895 and Tsarist Russia in 1904–1905. Each war bound migrants closer to their nation as Japanese, while producing colonial nouveau riche like the clothier Kobayashi. And victory in each war, accompanied by a further wave of migration from home, consolidated Japanese state control over Korea as much as it expanded the settler community, knitting the young nation into the social fabric of empire.

But this synergy between state and society wore increasingly thin in the course of protectorate rule, which began in 1905. After all, local settlers did not merely feed and clothe their empire's soldiers and bureaucrats; they became aggressive builders of empire in their own right. Disregarding official caution, migrants seized Korean land while betraying the government's vision of farm colonization. Merchants and fortune seekers continued to stream into Korea, pursuing aggressive commercial tactics that often tarnished the national image. Settlers also launched their own projects to "civilize" Korea: educators and Buddhist priests engaged in a mission to spread Japanese language and culture; continental adventurers sought opportunities to intervene in Korean politics; and journalists infused with the spirit of the popular rights movement joined local Korean reformers and leveled sharp attacks on Japanese state policies. As they grew in size and influence, settlers not only developed a sense of solidarity vis-à-vis Koreans, but also modes and ideologies of expansion quite different from those of their own government—a recipe for conflict with the state.

By the time Korea was formally annexed in 1910, what was once a tiny enclave of merchants and sojourners confined to a few treaty ports in the 1880s had grown into the largest overseas Japanese community in the empire, numbering over 170,000.[17] The physical entrenchment

17. Chōsen Sōtokufu Shomu Chōsaka 1924, 1–5.

of Japanese in Korea, as demonstrated by their ubiquitous presence in cities, itself became a form of domination.[18] Yet the forces that gave rise to this community were diverse, multiple, and internally conflicting. And the next 36 years of Japanese rule in which the settler community continued to grow, albeit more slowly—through such transformative events as the March First Movement of 1919, the Manchurian Incident of 1931, and the onset of total war in 1937—were driven by forces similar in complexity to those that had laid its foundations. Broadly put, colonialism in Korea entailed two distinct processes of expansion. On the one hand, the colonial government, a local representative of Tokyo, built an infrastructure of formal administration and imposed new economic and social systems on the Korean society. On the other hand, ordinary Japanese migrated and settled in Korea largely of their own volition, dominated urban commerce and trade, and pressed further into the interior. They did so by capitalizing on the enlarging framework of Japanese hegemony, but mostly while operating outside the purview of officialdom. Japan's colonial empire in Korea was forged in the context of fluidity and plurality, where the state's goals meshed only imperfectly with the interests and aspirations of its citizens. Analyzing this dynamic process is one of the central aims of the present book.

## *Writing Settlers into the History of Empire*

Given their sheer number, their significance to imperial strategy, and their impact on colonial rule and local communities, the relative absence of settlers from the history of the Japanese empire is striking. By opting to focus solely on the colonial state, historians have long assumed, as one leading scholar wrote, that "the overseas settlement of Japanese . . . never became the dominant activity of the Japanese colonial empire."[19]

18. In 1935, when the number of Japanese in Korea totaled 583,428 (the largest figure in the colonial empire), settlers formed fully 30 percent of the local population in Seoul and Pusan, and 25 percent in satellite cities such as Taegu and Kunsan (Chōsen Sōtokufu, *Chōsen Sōtokufu tōkei nenpō* 1935, 22–30).

19. Myers and Peattie 1984, 11. Although mass colonization of Korea was not consistently or vigorously pursued as state policy following the failure of the Oriental Development Company's farm colonization program (see Chapter 1), it is significant that *in spite of* the lack of direct state support Japanese men and women continued to migrate to the peninsula in large numbers. Mark Peattie correctly points out that "overseas Japa-

A more careful look at historical records suggests a different picture. The study of settlers enables us to rethink the formation, impact, and internal dynamics of Japanese colonialism from a new vantage point—"from within"—and to deepen our understanding of empire in critical ways.

A focus on settlers, first of all, allows us to disaggregate colonial power. In most conventional accounts, Korea under Japanese control—from "military rule" in the 1910s, through a "liberal" interlude in the 1920s, to the wartime policy of *naisen ittai* ("unity between Japan and Korea")—was virtually the Governor-General's imperium. Historians have focused on the interactions between this powerful ruler and Korean people of diverse backgrounds, interests, and ideological persuasions, who made colonial space, to the end, a site of deep contestation. Although their interactions merit further analysis, in this narrative settlers remain either ignored or lumped together with the colonial state. Assumptions that underlie most studies on Japanese colonialism are, first, that the towering figure of the Governor-General overshadowed the presence of settlers and their influence in colonial politics, and, second, that settlers were mere lackeys of the state, cogs in its vast ruling machinery.

In challenging a simple conflation of state and settlers, and the static image of colonial power it has generated, this book builds on the pioneering work of a few historians. Since Kajimura Hideki in a series of articles in the 1970s proposed a "bottom-up" approach to the history of Japanese colonialism,[20] the studies by Kimura Kenji and Peter Duus provided the first vivid portraits of settler communities in the period before Japan's annexation of Korea in 1910.[21] For the colonial period, Takasaki Sōji more recently offered the first comprehensive survey of the history of settlers—although his narrative, aimed at a general audience, reads less as an analysis than as an exposé.[22]

---

nese in Asia never attained the political importance of the French settlers in Algeria or the whites in Rhodesia," but I would not discount their importance and influence so readily to conclude that "the Japanese colonials were seldom influential in shaping colonial policy" (Peattie 1988, 262).

20. Kajimura 1992 [1974].

21. Kimura 1989; and Duus 1995. Kimura has also authored many articles on settlers' economic activities in the colonial period (1993, 1997, 2001a, 2002, 2004).

22. See Takasaki 2002; and my review of this work (Uchida 2003b).

Rather than documenting the role of settlers as perpetrators of colonialism (an obvious facet of a complex history), this book is concerned with exploring the intricate and contradictory ways—coercive as well as persuasive, accommodative as well as discriminatory—in which settler power operated on the Korean peninsula. On the one hand, settlers' commercial activities helped to integrate Korea into Japan's imperial economy, and in their political vision the peninsula remained yoked to the metropole. Their communities also served as mundane conduits for Japanese culture and modernity, reaching into many aspects of Korean lives where official policies could only go so far. On the other hand, settlers spread inequalities and fueled social discontent by dominating opportunities in enterprise, education, and bureaucratic employment. Their widely reported abuses and practices of exclusion ran counter to the official rhetoric of assimilation and hobbled state efforts to finesse a delicate balance between control and legitimacy. In exerting constructive as well as corrosive influence over Korean rule, settlers revealed the brunt of Japanese colonialism in all its contradictions.[23]

Settlers developed their own ideas about how best to govern and develop Korea. As the following chapters will illustrate, they vigorously sought to translate their visions into policy by sending letters and petitions to colonial officials, publishing opinions in the local press, and holding meetings and rallies under the watchful eyes of the police. The tentacles of settler influence extended beyond Korea to the heart of metropolitan politics. With the support of "Korea hands" in the Diet, settler leaders sought to influence their nation's policies on issues ranging from Korean industry to suffrage. And in so doing they not only defended their projects and presence in the empire, but also tried to reshape colonial issues into matters of national power. Far from remaining submissive, settlers actively fought their way into colonial and national politics, at times inserting themselves between the Japanese state and the Korean people.

Nor did settlers speak with one voice. Their political activities often reflected profound divisions and disagreements among the local Japa-

23. In the context of colonial Africa, scholars have similarly noted how settlers—especially in Algeria and Southern Rhodesia where they were numerous—could impose serious limits on the state's autonomy (C. Young 1994, 161–62), much as they could enhance its ability to extend the reach of its power (Herbst 2000, Chapter 3).

nese community over the nature and form of governance, the colony's relationship to the metropole, and the meaning of Japanese citizenship—divisions that Koreans could also exploit to their own ends. Indeed, to recognize the multiplicity of settler positions is to gain an important insight into the Korean side of the experience. At the local level, the Korean people encountered under Japanese rule not a colonial monolith, but different and often quarrelling groups of Japanese competing for power and influence.

Settlers also offer a window into the nature of the colonial state and the internal mechanism of colonial power more generally. In a spectrum of colonial states in the twentieth century, the Government-General of Korea appears to stand out in its scope of power, its commitment to rule, and its autonomy from the metropolitan legislature.[24] Yet if the colonial state by nature, as historians of Africa have debated over the decades, exhibited both "strong" and "weak" facets of authority, so too did the rulers of Korea operate in such contradictory guises, as they straddled the demands of the metropole and those of the colony as well as conflicting interests of local groups within the colony. Taking for granted the dominance of the Governor-General, historians have especially missed the state's struggle to anchor its authority in the multiethnic polity and its continual efforts to rule through local actors, practices, and institutions.[25] Rather than rely solely on its massive police force and bureaucracy, the colonial government worked with local men and women of influence, often taking care not to alienate voices of dissent but instead to co-opt them into its ruling structure. Along with Korean elites, settlers assisted the state in governing Korea and overcoming its limits

24. When compared to the colonial states in Africa, which constantly jostled between the metropole and local settlers (Lonsdale and Berman 1979, 80; Berman 1990, 424–25) or among indigenous and expatriate groups on the ground (R. Roberts 1996, 18–24), the Government-General of Korea was relatively "stronger" in both developing and implementing policies, though its control over the local population was by no means complete, as later chapters will show.

25. A number of historians have stressed the centrality and competence of Japanese bureaucrats in governing their colonies (Kublin 1959; Peattie 1984a, 26). For an insightful study of the effort of the Tsarist Russian empire to embed its authority in the local Muslim communities across Central Asia, see Crews 2006.

to "broadcast" power over a vast geography.[26] As later chapters will make clear, the colonial state relied on settler initiatives at critical turning points—from Japan's early penetration into Korea, to the reconstruction of empire in the aftermath of the March First Movement, to the mobilization of the colonial population for total war. More than mere policy shifts, passage from one phase of colonial rule to another was often a product of deepening engagement with local society, with each instance exposing the limits and the malleability of state authority under the guise of control. What we know as the "Governor-General's rule," this study contends, was less a competent dictatorship than an improvised form of governance that involved frequent, if unequal, dialogue with local actors.

Paying attention to settlers also allows us to enter spaces of local encounter between Japanese and Koreans that remain largely unexplored. Much of the literature on the Japanese empire has been either top-down, focusing on the colonial state and its policies, or bottom-up, focusing on local nationalism and the growth of Korean subjectivities. In between those two levels existed complex zones of experience that a new generation of scholars is now beginning to unearth. Since Gi-Wook Shin and Michael E. Robinson proposed the concept of "colonial modernity," scholars in recent years have approached Korea as a fluid and contingent space of encounter shaped by a global framework of modernity and not reducible to a simple dialectic of rule and resistance.[27] At the same time, a caveat has arisen against the danger of conflating colonialism with

---

26. In colonial Africa, the presence of settlers strongly influenced the state's ability to "broadcast power." This ability, according to Jeffrey Herbst (2000), depended on how invested the state was in extending its control over the territory, which, in turn, depended on how densely it was settled. Apart from settler colonies like South Africa, Herbst argues (in contrast to C. Young 1994 and Mamdani 1996) that the European powers were not all that committed to extending their territorial control over most of colonial Africa where settlers' presence remained minimal. The Japanese rulers in Korea—whose ambitions were reflected in their massive administrative presence, security forces, and financial investment—were far more committed than the European empires "on the cheap." Nevertheless, this did not mean that the reach of state power was absolute (especially over the rural areas where the majority of Koreans lived), nor did it preclude the need for local collaborators and intermediaries (including settlers).

27. For seminal works that have engaged and interrogated the concept of "colonial modernity" in a variety of ways, see Kim and Chŏng 1997; Shin and Robinson 1999; Kim Chin-song et al. 1999; Yun Hae-dong 2003; Namiki 2003; Itagaki 2004; Matsumoto 2005; Chang et al. 2006; Yoo 2008; and Itagaki 2008.

modernity, or the tendency to inflate the reach of colonial authority over the local population.[28] Our understanding of colonial modernity can be further enriched by examining how settlers, in their fraught relationship with the regime and Koreans, extended as well as limited its hegemonic operation on the ground. Joining the ongoing efforts launched by Todd A. Henry, Yi Sŭng-yŏp, and others,[29] I approach the contact zone from the vantage point of settlers, whose role and significance can be fully appreciated only when placed in the context of their interactions with Koreans.[30] My analysis focuses on encounters within what might be called the colonial "middle"—Japanese settlers and the bourgeois or upper-class Koreans they most frequently engaged—whose power and influence placed them below colonial officialdom, but most certainly above the majority of the Korean population as owners of business, land, and capital.

---

28. See To 2001; and Cho Kyŏng-dal 2005, 2008. Noting the arbitrary nature of colonial power, these scholars have called into question the notion of "hegemony" to explain Japanese colonialism (as applied, for instance, to the period of "cultural rule" in the 1920s by Shin and Robinson 1999). Itagaki Ryūta (2008) has also recently warned against the general tendency to assume a unilinear transition from premodern exclusion to full participation in modernity.

29. I place my work particularly within a cohort of scholars who have focused on the lived experience of Japanese colonists—including Todd Henry's (2006) critical and multilayered analysis of the spatial construction of colonial Seoul, Helen Lee's (2003) study of race relations between working-class settlers and Koreans through the popular media, Nicole Cohen's (2006) historical ethnography of the colonial education and upbringing of Japanese children, and Mark Caprio's (2009) timely reexamination of assimilation policies. Outside of the English-language scholarship, I have drawn on the pioneering scholarship of Kimura Kenji, as well as the recent works of Yi Sŭng-yŏp (2001, 2003, 2005, 2008), who shares a similar approach to settlers and their politics. Japanese settlers are also treated in a rapidly growing Korean-language literature on the history of colonial cities and urban spaces (see, for instance, Hong Sun-gwŏn 2006, 2008; Kimura and Sakamoto 2007), some of which are cited in Chapter 2.

30. For the notion of "contact zone," see Pratt 1992. While refraining from treating settlers as sole agents of history, this book is about a story of Japanese colonialism in Korea that places settlers at the heart of analysis. Thoughts and actions of Koreans (or policy-makers), examined in greater depth by scholars cited throughout the book, will be treated only as they intertwined with those of settlers who remain the central characters of my story. My methodology here is informed by comparative studies that have approached settlers as a way of understanding colonial encounters and the internally contested nature of colonial power (including Comaroff 1991; Russell 2001; Stoler 2002a; Elkins and Pedersen 2005; and Coombes 2006).

The presence of this "middle" group made the dynamic of local encounter more complex than suggested by the image of intractable confrontation (or passive submission in the case of elites). Nor did settlers' interactions with Koreans or with the colonial state fit neatly in the conventional picture of "collaboration," a concept this study seeks to complicate further.[31] To be sure, settlers reflexively stood on the state's side of the divide when faced with Korean defiance. But the settlers, too, often found their economic and political aspirations denied by the Governor-General's repressive policies. In such a situation, the same settlers who petitioned the authorities on their own (as they did in lobbying for settler self-government) might also align themselves with like-minded Koreans vis-à-vis the colonial and metropolitan governments (as they did in lobbying for greater local autonomy and industrial subsidies). Just as many Koreans found it expedient to work with Japanese to advance their interests, settlers often found it advantageous to make common cause with indigenous elites. Yet a closer look at the interactions among these elites reveals that their motivations for joining hands were scarcely identical. As the book's core chapters will demonstrate, although settlers and Korean elites worked together in agitating for economic and political freedom, more often they collided with each other over agendas to advance the lot of their respective communities. Even as the two groups began to collaborate with the state more boldly during the 1930s, Korean elites did not cease to think of their actions in terms of ethnic interests nor did settlers cease to seek local supremacy.

---

31. In the existing historiography, the term "collaborators" has been primarily used in the context of World War II, such as Vichy France's collaboration with Nazi Germany and the Chinese collaboration with wartime Japan. Its usage is conventionally limited to members of the subjugated population, who voluntarily offered their labor and resources to serve the interests of an imperialist or totalitarian regime, at the expense of the interests of their own national community. In the recent scholarship on this topic, Timothy Brook (2007) has significantly challenged the assumed coherence of a nation and broadened the parameters of scholarly debate by showing how nation became a shared locus of struggle for both nationalists and collaborators in wartime China under Japanese occupation. Throughout this book, I propose to further complicate the definition and usage of "collaboration" by treating settlers, as scholars of colonial Africa have done, as a distinct category of local allies to the state, and by analyzing their interactions with Korean bourgeois elites, which represented another form of "collaboration" in the colony.

The politics of collaboration were shaped by contingency, and spanned a range of interests including class, nation, and personal gain.

### *Japanese Settler Colonialism in Comparative Perspective*

Writing settlers into colonialism creates a new way to write Japan into a comparative history of empires. In Japanese colonial parlance, Korea was "Japan's Algeria" just as Algeria was "France's Korea."[32] Although such a perception was widespread at the time, the full implications of Korea as a colony of settlement have not been probed. A number of historians have classified colonial Korea as an "occupation" or "exploitation colony," without taking account of the presence of an unusually large number of settlers.[33] Colonial Korea defies a clear typology. It stood somewhere between an "exploitation colony" and a "settlement colony," effectively comprising a mixture of the two.[34]

Settler colonialism is a term that has conventionally been applied to the British white dominions of Canada, Australia, and New Zealand, or such African colonies as Kenya, Rhodesia, Algeria, Tunisia, and South Africa.[35] The former were "neo-Europes,"[36] where a sparse indigenous population was displaced or decimated by colonists from across the sea. Each operated as an autonomous state under the British crown, where white settlers who constituted self-governing civil societies essentially morphed into modern nation-states. By contrast, settler colonies in Africa were distinguished by dependence on indigenous labor and admin-

---

32. Zeitaya Gorō, "Aruzeria jijō (1)," *Chōsen* (Chōsen Sōtokufu), January 1921, 82.

33. Myers and Peattie 1984, 11. For a typology of colonies, see Osterhammel 2005, 10–12.

34. Delissen 2000, 132. Alternatively, Korea under Japanese rule may be conceptualized as a form of "peripheral colonization," as Mark Caprio (2009) argues, which refers to the colonization of contiguous territories (including Okinawa and Hokkaido).

35. For works on settlers in colonial Africa, see Lustick 1985; Kennedy 1987; Berman 1990; Prochaska 1990; Comaroff 1991; and Berman and Lonsdale 1992. For works on settlers in the British white dominions, see Wolfe 1999; and Pearson 2001. Studies that examine these settler colonies in a comparative framework include: Denoon 1983; Stasiulis and Yuval-Davis 1995; Coombes 2006; and Goldstein and Lubin 2008. For studies that have analyzed the formation of the state of Israel in terms of settler colonialism, see Shafir 1996; and S. Robinson 2005. For an intriguing discussion of how the Zionist model of collective agricultural settlement in Palestine informed the Japanese colonial thinker, Yanaihara Tadao (1893–1961), see de Boer 2006.

36. Crosby 1996.

istrative ties to the metropole.[37] The latter offer many useful insights for colonial Korea, where Japanese settlers faced similar circumstances as well as peculiar constraints under the Governor-General's rule.

As a starting point for analyzing the power of Japanese settlers, it is useful to compare them with their better-studied counterparts in colonial Africa. I am concerned here not with demonstrating the comparability of Korea to these colonies as a polity,[38] but with gaining specific insights into settlers as a distinct locus of power (separate from the state). My comparison, in other words, approaches Korea from a different analytical angle by using settlers as a conceptual prism to rethink Japanese colonialism. The point of the exercise is not to fit Japanese settlers into European models, but to complicate the model itself: to think about settler colonialism, as a global formation shaped in locally specific contexts, and to push the growing scholarly discourse on settlers beyond European examples.[39]

---

37. Osterhammel 2005, 7. We must also note some important differences among the settler colonies in Africa. British Kenya, for instance, was less autonomous than South Africa, which received dominion status (equivalent to independence) in 1910, and Southern Rhodesia, which obtained self-government in 1923. The internal administration of each colony was also complex. In the case of Algeria, the colony in the nineteenth and early twentieth centuries was divided into three administrative zones: "civil territories" where European settlers concentrated, "mixed territories" ruled by the military with limited autonomy for local settlers, and the "Arab territories" subject to complete military control (Ruedy 2005, 73).

38. Apart from French Algeria, a more appropriate comparison in this regard might be made with the British territories of Scotland, Wales, and Ireland, as Mark Caprio (2009) has recently shown. Of all settler colonies in Africa, French Algeria was perhaps most comparable to Korea in terms of the physical proximity of colony to metropole, density and pattern of settlement, and the policies of assimilation. In each case, empire-building was seen as an extension of nation-building, marked by a commitment to the permanent integration of the territory into the national domain. The massive investment of capital and resources in Korea underscored the official intention to transform Korea into an "outer province" of Japan in much the same way that the French saw Algeria as "an unincorporated extension of France." In each case, migration from the metropole was a central strategy of colonization and consolidation of metropolitan state authority (Lustick 1985, 7).

39. A few exceptions to this model include Elkins and Pedersen 2005 (which brings European and East Asian examples into dialogue), and Fujikane and Okamura 2008 (which conceptualizes the Asian, including Japanese, settlement of Hawai'i in terms of settler colonialism).

When thinking about the "typical settler" in each colony, Japanese in Korea bear closer resemblance to the French in North Africa than to the British in East Africa. Compared to the gentlemen farmers who settled on the Highlands of Kenya or their lower-class counterparts in Southern Rhodesia,[40] the men and women who migrated to Korea were a more motley group—almost as diverse as the home communities they left behind—not unlike the *pieds noirs* who settled in Algeria.[41] Settlers in both Korea and Algeria also formed a substantial urban presence, at their most numerous constituting 3 percent and 13 percent of the total population in the colony, respectively.[42] By contrast, settlers reached barely half a percent of the local population in Kenya, where the size and scale of settlement had less to do with control over the colonial political economy.

Nonetheless, Japanese and European settlers of all places and periods shared the "demographic imperative": being a tiny minority, they lived in fear of being "swamped" by the natives who vastly outnumbered them.[43] This became a pretext for insisting on strict racial classifications, mobilizing against the enfranchisement of indigenous peoples, and resisting miscegenation,[44] even when such segregationist practices were at odds with state policies. Being alluring targets of anticolonial resistance, settlers developed a siege mentality, which fed into highhandedness, racism, and occasional violence toward natives that often surpassed the level of official coercion. These propensities were found among Japanese in Korea as much as among white colonists in Kenya

40. Kennedy 1987, 92–99. "Rhodesian settler society was . . . more complex and stratified than its northern counterpart. But it was, nevertheless, demographically dominated by settlers of lower-class origins" (94).

41. Stora 2001, 22. Non-French settlers—the Jewish, Italian, Maltese, Spanish, and other Mediterranean peoples—made up half the European community in Algeria in the 1870s.

42. Tange 1943, 2–3; Charrad 2001, 116.

43. The "demographic imperative" was harbored by European settlers at some points in Australia and New Zealand and continually in South Africa (Evans et al. 2003, 178–79).

44. More than a reflection of settler paranoia, the fear of miscegenation was real in Portuguese Mozambique, where, as of 1940, "of the more than a quarter of all live births among the so-called civilized population that were illegitimate, fully 96 percent were of mixed race" (Penvenne 2005, 88).

or Southern Rhodesia, where settler power was "matched by fear, arrogance by anxiety, disdain by suspicion."[45]

Japanese settlers' attitudes toward the metropole also exhibited many similarities with those of white settlers in Africa. In gauging their relationship to the homeland, Japanese colonists constantly oscillated between assimilation and autonomy in order to safeguard their local dominance over the natives—what Ian Lustick identified as "the peculiar predicament of a certain type of settler colony."[46] To be sure, Japanese settlers never attempted to seek local autonomy to the extent that their British counterparts did in Kenya and Rhodesia or that the *colons* in Algeria did in the 1920s and 1930s.[47] Too weak to cut their ties to the imperial core, Japanese settlers sought instead to bind Korea more closely to the home country in keeping with the official policy of *naichi enchō* (extending the mainland). Yet at the same time, they saw no contradiction in insisting on the autonomy of the colonial governor from Tokyo and stressing the special importance of Korea relative to other colonies. This duality also characterized the settlers' industrial vision of Korea as an auxiliary as well as autonomous part of Japan's imperial economy.

If settlers had mixed feelings about the metropole, they harbored still more ambivalence about the colonial state. Just as the British farmers accused Kenyan administrators of "indigenophile" tendencies, and the *colons* abhorred the paternalistic "native policy" in Algeria (even as they relied on the state to promote their economic interests at the expense of native welfare),[48] Japanese settlers resisted the official policy of Korean accommodation and constantly intervened against signs of Korean advancement. Where colonial officials spoke of assimilation, settlers often loathed the idea of ethnic unity and dreaded the prospect of sharing power with Korean elites. And Japanese colonists, like Europeans, justified their dominance by evoking the low "cultural level" (*mindo*) of natives, although the claim to civilizational superiority was dubious. The lower-class origins of many Japanese migrants made them particularly prone to subvert any policy measures that dared to narrow the gap be-

45. Kennedy 1987, 187.

46. This characteristic was found in Algeria from the 1830s to the early 1900s and Ireland from the early sixteenth to the end of the seventeenth century (Lustick 1985, 8).

47. Good 1976, 610.

48. Lustick 1985, 48.

tween the two peoples, let alone treat them on the same administrative level. Because cultural and racial affinities also marked their relationship to Koreans (as was well understood and manipulated by the state authorities), maintaining difference from the natives became the foremost priority of settlers, who saw that distinction as a key source of their power.

Upon closer scrutiny, differences between the Japanese and European settler colonial states seem compelling. In colonial Africa, settler power was defined first and foremost by control over land and labor. This was unequivocally demonstrated by extensive land expropriation in Algeria and South Africa, and by territorial segregation in Kenya and Southern Rhodesia, where white farmers appropriated the best spreads in the Highlands while herding Africans into native reserves. The settler estate, the economic basis of these European colonies, depended on government services that furnished capital and facilitated the transfer of resources from surrounding African areas. The colonial regime, in turn, was structurally dependent on settler accumulation for revenue and political order. This interdependence between state and settlers, as much as their conflict over native policy, drove the colonial political economy in Africa.[49] In Korea, by contrast, Japanese settlers' activities—mostly in commerce, trade, and service—constituted a much smaller part of the revenue structure, and in terms of capital participation, they played only a supplementary function in the state-led development of the colonial economy.[50] Moreover, although many lived off the rents of Korean tenant farmers, Japanese settlers never completely moved the native inhabitants off their land the way European settlers did in "the *pulverization* in Algeria and the violent depopulation in Kenya."[51]

Such economic weakness of Japanese settlers directly translated into political meekness—unlike European farmers in Kenya who enjoyed political power disproportionate to their often unprofitable enterprise. Through representation in local colonial councils and in the metropoli-

---

49. Berman 1990, 174.

50. Fiscal sources in the metropole, channeled largely through bureaucratic investment, accounted for the bulk of capital formation in the colony (for further discussion, see Chapter 5).

51. Good 1976, 611; Evans et al. 2003, 11. We might also note the annihilation of the Aborigines in Australia (Wolfe 1999).

tan assembly, European settlers exerted political pressure on the state authorities much more successfully than their Japanese counterparts. By the 1920s, the settlers in Algeria filled the ranks of colonial bureaucracy and the *colons* later became an important element in the breakdown of the Fourth Republic in France. The settlers in Southern Rhodesia successfully clamored for and obtained self-government within the British crown in 1923. In these territories, indeed, the colonial state became "often little more than an instrument of the settlers."[52] By contrast, Japanese settlers in Korea, shorn of the right to self-government after annexation, lacked the representative levers through which to assert control over colonial politics. Although they were granted some legislative power in the 1930s, it was far from sufficient for local Japanese to seek autonomy from the metropole or to take control over the colonial state apparatus—prospects that remained too unlikely for most settlers to entertain seriously.[53]

Part of the explanation for this disparity lies in the enormous presence of the Japanese state in colonial Korea. If there were numerous settlers, there were also numerous bureaucrats dispatched from the metropole. Whereas a mere 80 colonial administrators governed a country of 5 million Africans and 40,000 settlers in Kenya in the early 1950s,[54] nearly one-quarter of the approximately 700,000 Japanese in Korea had some form of governmental employment in 1940.[55] Backed by this vast civil service, the Governor-General succeeded, more often than did European colonial administrators, in shunning metropolitan intervention from above and settler interference from below. This, in turn, made Japanese settlers relatively more dependent, even parasitic, on the state, which was the major source of protection, privilege, and patronage in the colony. Although Japanese generally enjoyed greater social status and privileges than Koreans, the presence of a strong state apparatus blocked their political ascendancy.

---

52. Osterhammel 2005, 75.

53. The ability to govern themselves—an important measure of civil society—seems to be the most compelling difference between European and Japanese settler societies, which I will address in Chapter 6.

54. Elkins 2005, 18.

55. See Chapter 1, Table 4.

The Japanese settlers' relative weakness also points to a predicament issuing from their legally ambiguous status. In colonial Africa (especially in Algeria, South Africa, and Rhodesia), European settlers enjoyed full citizenship rights while natives were institutionally and racially excluded from civil society.[56] This equation of "settlers" with "civil society" diminishes significantly in the case of colonial Korea. Japanese settlers from the bourgeoisie down to petty merchants similarly derived their wealth and power from the exploitation of local labor and the suppression of indigenous rights, but their status was a far cry from that of rights-bearing citizens. Suspended between the colonial and metropolitan legal systems (which only partially overlapped), residents overseas, while subject to national duties of conscription and taxation, were denied the fundamental, if limited, civic rights such as suffrage and the freedom of assembly enjoyed by Japanese at home.[57] Furthermore, in contrast to the European colonies in Africa, where whites and natives were often administrated separately, the Governor-General of Korea placed both settlers and Koreans under his uniform legislative authority. If Japanese people were "citizen-subjects" (*kokumin*)[58] in the metropole, they were "more subjects than citizens"[59] in the colony.

Given the low degree of incorporation into governance and the equally low degree of institutionalization of privilege, the paramountcy of settlers over "natives," on the whole, was far more tentative in Korea than in the colonial states of Africa. This relative disenfranchisement of Japanese settlers highlights their ontological condition of being neither completely "the ruler" nor "the ruled"—or, to borrow the observation of John and Jean Comaroff on the English missionaries in southern Africa, their subaltern status as "the dominated fraction of the

56. C. Young 1994, 118–20, 151, 161–62. Mahmood Mamdani notes that "civil society" in colonial Africa "was first and foremost the society of the *colons*" (1996, 13–19). Although this may be true for most settler colonies, it is important to note that in Algeria, non-French settlers from Europe were granted French citizenship status only starting in 1889 (C. Young 1994, 80, 120).

57. See Chapter 2. For a detailed explanation of the application of metropolitan and colonial laws to Japanese settlers and colonial subjects in the empire, see Asano and Matsuda 2004.

58. For the translation of *kokumin* as "citizen-subjects," see Kyu Hyun Kim 2007.

59. Delissen 2000, 134.

dominant class."[60] Rather than equal partners with the state, Japanese settlers were positioned ambivalently in the colonial order, at once the objects and the subjects of the Governor-General's rule. Like overseas settlers elsewhere, they occupied the liminal or "in-between" space of colonial encounter, with racial anxieties similar to those found among Europeans in the Dutch East Indies,[61] but without the apparent constitutional and civilizational security of their counterparts in Africa. Such ambivalence, which I propose to call "liminality,"[62] created a significant ideological gulf between settlers and the colonial state. It was precisely the settlers' efforts to negotiate their condition of uncertainty—their continual struggle, in the absence of legal or political guarantees, to maintain local dominance—that gave rise to their role as brokers of empire.

## *Three Phases of Settler Colonialism*

In all phases of Japanese rule, the brokers of empire operated within a complex geometry of power characteristic of twentieth-century settler colonialism at large: a quadrangle of relations among local settlers, the colonial administration, the indigenous population, and the imperial

---

60. Comaroff 1991, 59. In studies on empire, the term "subaltern" has acquired a specific meaning to apply almost exclusively to the colonized (since the rise of "Subaltern Studies"). But here (and elsewhere in this book), I recuperate the term's original meaning to refer to the "lower" and "inferior" status the Japanese settlers occupied vis-à-vis the colonial state (*The Concise Oxford Dictionary of English Etymology*, s.v. "subaltern.").

61. Stoler 2002a.

62. In colonial and postcolonial studies, the concept of the liminal is more commonly used to explain an "in-between" space in which hybrid identities may form as a cultural effect of colonization on the colonized (see Bhabha 1994). In the context of colonial East Asia, and in a slightly different usage, Ming Cheng Lo has described Taiwanese doctors under Japanese rule as cultural "in-betweens" (2002, 7). Drawing and departing from these studies, I approach this in-between space from the perspective of the colonizer, but without assuming its coherence or stability. By liminality, I refer to the settlers' ambivalent, interstitial, and marginal condition of being "in between" (or being "neither nor"): in between Japan and Korea, state and society, subjects and citizens, colony and metropole. The brokers of empire operated on ever shifting boundaries that separated these categories. This ambivalence, or "growing up Japanese in colonial Korea" according to Nicole Cohen (2006), also shaped the "culturally hybrid" identity of settler children. For a similar discussion of Japanese in America occupying the interstitial space between the United States and the Japanese empire, see Azuma 2005.

metropole.[63] The activities of the brokers of empire also spanned a wide array of domains. Less institutionalized than most European variants, Japanese settler colonialism operated through interpersonal networks, in forums as diverse as the market, local politics, the press, social work, and everyday life practices. Consequently, settler power was multifarious, manifesting itself in economic dominance, political intervention, social control, cultural representation, and ideological manipulation. This book explores each of these loci through three distinct phases of Japanese rule on the peninsula.

Part I examines the formative period of Japan's expansion into Korea, from the closing decades of the nineteenth century to the first decade of Governor-General's rule in the 1910s. Chapter 1 shows how ordinary Japanese were transformed into subimperialists, situating their history of migration within the two revolutionary contexts of Chosŏn Korea and Meiji Japan. The nascent character of Japan's informal empire allowed various non-governmental actors, from merchants to "men on the spot,"[64] to intervene in its process of expansion at the local level. From these early crude endeavors there gradually emerged communities of Japanese expatriates who forged their own cultural world, through which colonial power came to be woven in the fabric of everyday life.

By the time of protectorate rule in 1905, settlers not only became physically entrenched in Korea, but began to assert their own voice in imperial politics, which increasingly ran up against the state's effort to centralize control and maintain order. Tension reached its peak following the annexation act of 1910, as Chapter 2 shows, when the new Governor-General of Korea, Terauchi Masatake (1910–1916), abolished settlers' self-government as part of his policy to bring all residents under his uniform authority. Out of this atmosphere of discord emerged the first generation of brokers of empire, bent on recovering autonomy and resisting assimilation policy. They set the pattern for decades of settlers'

---

63. Elkins and Pedersen 2005, 4. See also Berman and Lonsdale 1992, which adopts this basic formulation for analyzing the relationship between settlers and state in British Kenya.

64. The term "men of the spot" refers to a motley group of "subimperialists," including merchants, settlers, soldiers, missionaries, and diplomats, who provided the initial impetus for imperial expansion. See Fieldhouse 1973.

struggle for citizenship and their ambivalent relationship with the colonial government.

Both the state and settlers, however, were compelled to retool their strategies of expansion in response to a sudden outburst of Korean demonstrations for independence in March 1919. Focusing on the ensuing decade of "cultural rule" under Governor-General Saitō Makoto (1919–1927, 1929–1931), Part II examines how the brokers of empire, from men of letters to businessmen, joined officials in rebuilding the shaken colonial enterprise while striving to expand their own leverage over Korean governance. Through the four key domains of their activity—ideology, press discourse, economy, and local politics—around which Chapters 3–6 are organized, I illustrate the Janus-faced character of settlers as allies of the colonial government and agents of their own interests. In addition to serving as informal advisors to Saitō, on the one hand, settlers helped counter local nationalism by co-opting a variety of influential Koreans into "pro-Japanese" organizations, and propagating the Pan-Asianist ideology of *naisen yūwa*, a new watchword for assimilation (Chapter 3). Journalists and scholars also guided the officials by making Korea intelligible and manageable through the production of knowledge about Korea and investigation of Korean ethnic character (Chapter 4). On the other hand, the settler leaders, by taking advantage of the new climate of opportunity under Saitō, pursued their economic interests and pressed their political demands ever more aggressively. While prominent businessmen took part in economic policy-making, merchants and contractors lobbied the authorities in Seoul and Tokyo, asking them to relax control on local enterprise and nurture Korean industries by expanding the network of railways (Chapter 5). In the realm of political participation, another area long subject to authoritarian state control, settlers serving on city and provincial councils joined hands with other community leaders to campaign for the right to vote in Japan's national elections, going beyond their demand for greater local autonomy in Korea (Chapter 6).

In pursuing each of these projects, the brokers of empire also deepened their engagement with Koreans, as allies as well as adversaries. Whether as scholar-journalists seeking to indoctrinate Korean minds or as businessmen lobbying for industry, settler leaders confronted the growing thrust of local nationalism, which forced them to modify their strategies along the way. Moreover, whether in aiding the colonial state or countering its autocratic tendencies, the settlers often aligned themselves with Korean elites, turning each domain of activity into an exercise in bourgeois collaboration. For settlers, their alliance with powerful Koreans provided a means to further their local dominance and influence over colonial politics. For Korean elites, by contrast, working with the Japanese offered opportunities to elevate their social standing and realize other aspirations denied to those who operated outside the colonial system. As Chapters 5 and 6 make clear, new economic interests and political visions generated through their interactions not only brought settlers and Korean elites into temporary or more long-lasting alliances against the state. They could also set the two groups of allies fundamentally apart—bringing in the state as arbiter as much as a common point of access to power—and even allow the influence of nationalists to penetrate and fragment their bourgeois unity. Rather than mere "collaboration," then, each locus of settlers' joint activity with Koreans became a dynamic arena of contestation, negotiation, and accommodation. Relations always remained asymmetrical, but in each changing historical context that asymmetry took on a new form.

What appeared to be fragile relations among settlers, Korean elites, and the colonial state by the end of the 1920s were significantly reshaped by Japan's seizure of Manchuria in 1931. Japan's ensuing drive for military expansion, from the 1930s to the end of war in 1945, sets the context for Part III, which traces how the brokers of empire morphed into organs of the state, as their activities and imagination expanded beyond the peninsula's borders. As Chapter 7 shows, Japanese military actions in Manchuria and the Chinese continent significantly enlarged the spatial circuits of settlers' economic activity, while rendering Korean migrants as key agents of territorial colonization. In response to the call by Governor-General Ugaki Kazushige (1931–1936) to prepare the nation for "emergency," old-time settlers also worked alongside a new generation of middle-class leaders to help the state launch a series of "moral suasion" campaigns targeting youth, women, and Koreans at large. Through this mechanism of social management, the brokers of empire acquired greater authority yet became further subsumed in the state's ruling structure, a paradoxical dynamic I highlight in explaining their increasingly official character.

This corporatist structure of governance was transmuted into an apparatus of total war following the outbreak of the Sino-Japanese War in 1937. Chapter 8 examines this process by focusing on the role of settlers as grassroots agents of the campaign for *naisen ittai* instigated by Governor-General Minami Jirō (1936–1942). I explore the pivotal yet ambivalent collaboration by local settlers to the wartime regime in carrying out two interrelated projects: building a structure of mass mobilization in Korea (one that emerged, in many ways, ahead of the metropole), and accelerating the assimilation of Koreans through a series of imperialization (*kōminka*) policies (from the extension of military service to the notorious name-changing campaign). These measures, which extended some salient features of metropolitan citizenship to the colony, aimed at exploiting its labor and resources more fully for war, but they also reflected and inspired new Korean demands for equality with the Japanese. Their demands, in turn, forced settlers to come face to face with their own liminality, not only in legal or political terms but culturally and racially as well. Ethnic divisions widened over the question of nationhood beneath a clarion call for wartime unity, allowing the central contradiction of Japan's multiethnic empire to surface at the height of settlers' collaboration with Koreans.

What ultimately emerges from these sites of local encounter is a picture of colonial power more complicated and decentralized than a view from the state provides. The effort to capture these sites has led my research beyond the public and state documents stored at key archives in Japan and Korea, into private materials and memories. I use official reports, surveys, and papers of the Government-General, not only to analyze colonial policy-making, but also to look beneath the "imperial mind" for various local players in the management of Korean economy, the suppression of nationalist activities, and the promotion of assimilation policy. I supplement these sources by incorporating transcribed interviews of former colonial bureaucrats, and oral and written testimonies obtained from former Japanese residents of Korea. To trace the diverse lives and aspirations of settlers, I have also read memoirs, biographies, gazetteers, magazine articles, and other local Japanese publications on Korea. The core of this study explores interactions among local elites as they are documented in Japanese- and Korean-language newspapers and magazines, company histories, chambers of commerce reports, proceedings of local council meetings, and secret local police reports and other classified materials that chronicle previously unknown details and activities of "pro-Japanese" organizations.

A study of settlers ultimately brings us back to the fundamental question of what colonialism *is*, forcing us to think ever more deeply of power as a practice rather than an attribute. Rarely was colonialism a simple exercise of coercion. Nor was it simply diffused through culture or disembodied as discourse. Colonialism is at once an economic, political, cultural, and discursive phenomenon; we cannot adequately explain it without understanding its multifaceted character.[65] By tracing the activities of settlers across a variety of domains, this book proposes a more dynamic and multidimensional analysis of empire that takes account of political economy as well as culture, the coercive structures of colonialism as well as the hegemonic effects of modernity. Moreover, this study offers an understanding of colonialism as a process mediated by ordinary people and their experiences, desires, and quotidian practices—what we might call "brokered colonialism." Settlers, in short, serve as a particularly useful prism through which to refract the complex and contingent inner workings of colonial power, yielding an anatomy of colonialism on the ground.

The significance of settlers is not limited to the colonial context: it also projects back to the metropole. The question of Japan as a modern nation-state, as Alexis Dudden and others have shown, was posed starkly in the context of Japan's colonization of Korea.[66] This colonial project was driven by the anxieties and aspirations of a country faced with a dual task of becoming a modern nation-state and an empire. Settlers in Korea were a mirror of this duality writ large: the self-confidence of

---

65. Since the end of the Cold War and the corresponding decline of the Marxist paradigm and an explosion of new (especially postcolonial) approaches, works on colonialism have focused analysis on the culture and discourse of empire rather than the politics and economics of imperialism. In Japan, a similar trend has given rise to a rough division between a group of younger scholars concerned with the culture and social history of empire (*teikokushi*), and a traditional camp of scholars focusing on the economic and empirical analysis of imperialism (*teikoku shugishi*). See Komagome 2000, 224–31. I heed the call made by several historians (R. Roberts 1996, 1–38; Cooper and Stoler 1997, 1–37; Yanagisawa and Okabe 2001, 12–13) who have cautioned against such a division.

66. Dudden 2005. Through the case of Taiwan's colonization, Robert Eskildsen (2002) similarly points out how nation- and empire-building were simultaneous rather than sequential processes in Meiji Japan.

a rapidly modernizing nation as epitomized by enterprising youth who yearned for success, and the anxiety of a nascent empire struggling to attain the status of a first-class nation.[67] Their actions and thoughts reveal how tensions produced by Japan's modernizing changes spilled over into the colonial periphery, and how that process transformed ordinary and hard-pressed Japanese into cruel oppressors overseas. The history and legacy of settlers indeed bespeak the need to reconceptualize the space in which Japan modernized itself.

67. Oka 1982, 212.

# PART I

# *Emergence*

# ONE

## *The World of Settlers*

The brokers of empire had multiple beginnings. They emerged from a ragtag group of Japanese men and women who made their way to Korea at their own expense, well before the Meiji state imprinted its political presence. The process by which these overseas migrants joined the creation of their nation's empire was as diverse as their origins, pushed by a complex set of forces including commerce, war, education, land seizure, and political maneuver. Each of these facets of colonization, we will see, brought a variety of middling actors—petty merchants and traders, young educators and journalists, political adventurers and carpetbaggers—who, in their sheer number and diversity, made lasting changes to the Korean land and its people. And through each act, increasingly understood as a fulfillment of patriotic duty, they became self-conscious participants in the construction of empire.

To situate the history of commoners (*shomin*) more firmly in Japan's imperial trajectory helps us understand not only the empire's origins and agents, but the mutually constitutive processes of how empire transformed ordinary Japanese and how individual Japanese guided the course of empire. Early settlers in Korea were mostly struggling civilians who sought refuge from the devastating effects of the modernizing reforms wrought by the Meiji government. Yet whether "pushed" by the revolutionary changes at home or "pulled" by the allure of opportunities abroad, overseas settlers had one thing in common: more often leading than following the flag, they laid the basis of Japan's East Asian empire.

Charting how subalterns of a modernizing nation became agents of foreign domination reveals simultaneously how they became "Japanese" on the colonial periphery. A close look at the cultural world of settlers in turn-of-the-century Korea illustrates how migrants of diverse provenance came to forge a distinct community with a growing awareness as members of the "Japanese nation" (*kokumin*)—a category, as some scholars have observed, "not in full existence at the end of the 1880s."[1] Through investments by the state and the actions of private citizens, Korea was transformed into a space coextensive with the modernizing metropole, where settlers fashioned their own imagined communities around the new notion of Japaneseness.[2]

## *Migrants as Trailblazers*

When Korea was formally annexed in 1910, Meiji Japan had effectively been intervening in its diplomatic and domestic affairs for over three decades. Convinced that the best defense against the Western powers was to join their imperialist club, Japan emulated their practice of gunboat diplomacy by foisting its own version of "unequal treaties" on Korea in 1876, shortly after dispatching an armed expedition to colonize Taiwan, Japan's first mimetic attempt at civilizing faraway "savages."[3] A treaty concluded at gunpoint in Kanghwa forced Korea not only to open trade, but to cede its sovereign rights by granting Japanese nationals extraterritoriality and immunity to tariffs. Thereafter, migrants and settlers in fin-de-siècle Korea mediated Japan's passage from *imperialism* (the projection of political and military power over Korea) to *colonialism* (territorial domination of the peninsula).

With the exception of a few years when Hawai'i and the United States became a magnet for Japanese seasonal workers, in the late nineteenth and early twentieth centuries Korea was the most popular overseas destination.[4] According to a travel guide published around the turn of the century, "It costs a mere 15 yen to get to Korea's first trading port of Pusan, and with costs of travel to the United States, one can

1. For instance, see Kyu Hyun Kim 2007, 10.

2. Anderson 1983; Stoler 1989, 137.

3. Eskildsen 2002, 388–418.

4. The exceptions were 1893, 1899, and 1900, when the Japanese migrated in greater numbers to Hawai'i and to the United States (Kimura 2001a, 169).

use cheap Korean labor at will and manage a business on one's own."[5] Lured by such promises of quick money and easy success (*ikkaku senkin*), thousands of Japanese men and women began crossing the Tsushima Strait, seeing Korea as an ideal outlet for hopes and ambitions unfulfilled at home.

The earliest to blaze the trail were lower-class Japanese—a mixed bag of sojourners, petty merchants, laborers, carpenters, artisans, impoverished farmers, maids, prostitutes, and *rōnin* (adventure-seekers). In their socioeconomic background, these migrants were strikingly reminiscent of the "poor whites" (*petits blancs*) who first arrived in Algeria, Morocco, India, or the East Indies.[6] Most initially hailed from the southwestern prefectures situated in close proximity to Korea (Nagasaki, Fukuoka, Yamaguchi, and Hiroshima), although over time emigrants came increasingly from the rest of the archipelago, spreading the pattern of chain migration as far north as Hokkaido.[7] For those living in Kyushu or western Honshu, it was as easy to travel to Pusan or Seoul as to a mainland metropolis like Tokyo or Osaka. Such a spatial conception made for anecdotes like that of one fisherman in Amakusa, who evidently addressed his letters to "Nagasaki prefecture, Pusan port," assuming that Pusan was an island extension of a prefecture in Kyushu.[8]

Early emigrants had little thought of putting down roots in Korean soil. Few migrated under state auspices, and fewer, if any, would have linked their activity with national purpose. The poorest among them had lost their properties and fled their homes in search of a better life abroad. Some farmers came to Korea to supplement their income as day laborers or sojourners during the agricultural off-season. These déclassé and impoverished migrants were joined by aspiring youths who, following the footsteps of overseas pioneers, pursued grander dreams of *risshin shusse* ("rising in the world"). Mixed among them were a not-insignificant number of *shizoku* (former samurai)—including popular rights activists, as well as those from Satsuma who had followed Saigō Takamori (1828–1877), "the last samurai," and turned their energies abroad after losing

5. Quoted in Satogami 1996, 285.

6. Gregory Henderson (1973, 263–65) notes many parallels between Japanese immigrants in Korea and the *pieds noirs* in North Africa.

7. Duus 1995, 314–16.

8. Hattori 1931, 33.

a last-ditch battle against the new men of Meiji. And troops of prostitutes, recruited from poor rural families, accompanied these soldiers of empire to support their otherwise lone ventures abroad, just as they sustained blue- and white-collar male workers at home.[9] Far from a homogeneous lot, these early migrants were, each in their own way, builders of Japan's nascent empire.

Quite contrary to their inflated hopes for upward mobility, the lives of early settlers and sojourners were often as hard as those they had left behind. Many failed and returned home, while those who stayed eked out their living by switching from one odd job to another as opportunity beckoned, and lived no less poorly than Korean farmers. The Japanese settlement at the foot of Namsan (South Mountain) in southern Seoul was "a nest of beggars,"[10] recalled Hiroe Sawajirō, one of the leading settler merchants in the city. The lowly demeanor of Japanese migrants also invited the contempt of Korean elites. Faithful followers of Neo-Confucianism, they often juxtaposed the image of Japanese as "vulgar" and "dwarf barbarians" to that of Chinese as "a beacon of civilization,"[11] a dichotomy that was slow to fade.

Although the Tokyo government regarded migrants as key to enhancing national strength, officials grew increasingly concerned that those of plebian descent threatened to undo the image of a civilizing nation that Japan was assiduously cultivating to achieve parity with the West.[12] "At the time of the opening of the Wŏnsan port in 1880," recalled a trader named Wada Tsuneichi, "the Ministry of Foreign Affairs required local Japanese merchants to live in two-storied Western-style buildings, and required men to wear Western dress while prohibiting them to disembark a ship in kimono."[13] No wonder that Kobayashi Genroku of Chōjiya, the Western clothier, found no trouble expanding

9. Kajimura 1992, 201; Song Yŏn-ok 2002, 69. For an insightful analysis of the gender dynamics of the settler community and the Japanese perception of (single) women as overseas pioneers, see Brooks 2005.

10. A stenographic record of the first retrospective roundtable talk (*kaiko zadankai*) on the early Seoul Chamber of Commerce (14 March 1940), in *KSKN* 1941, 3:29.

11. Duus 1995, 256.

12. For Korean newspaper descriptions of lower-class emigrants, see Schmid 2002, 97–98.

13. Wada 1927, 11. On the consular police efforts' to regulate Japanese dress in Seoul and Pusan, see Yi Chong-min 2004, 329–34.

his clientele immediately after arrival. To avoid tarnishing the national image in the eyes of foreigners, furthermore, the government in the 1880s issued regulations to stem the flow of "the unpropertied and vagabonds" and unlicensed prostitutes into the treaty ports.[14] The Japanese consulate also made punishable by law such "uncivilized" conduct as public nudity, which echoed a host of "misdemeanor laws" issued by the Meiji government in the 1870s.[15] To an insular nation looking for international approval, empire-building was a highly self-conscious endeavor, undertaken within a panoptic view of the West.[16]

## *Merchants as the Vanguard of Imperialism*

Conspicuously absent from these early migrants were religious workers. Whereas missionaries were among the first Europeans to set foot in Africa and Asia, they were, as one Japanese settler bemoaned in 1911, "the last ones to come" to the peninsula.[17] And when they did come, they were far fewer and less successful than the raft of Western missionaries already active there.[18] In response to the rise of State Shinto at home, to be sure, Japanese Buddhists, while reinventing their faith as a world religion, had earlier launched a few overseas initiatives spearheaded by the Higashi Honganji (Eastern Temple of the Original Vow). Following the opening of Pusan, Buddhists of various sects crossed the Korea Strait, in the hope not only of spreading Japanese culture but of reviving the status of their religion that had been eclipsed during the Chosŏn dynasty. But though they forged a dynamic alliance with local monks,[19] their sermons seldom reached the ordinary Korean people; instead, they became primarily stewards of the settler community,[20] and

14. Kimura 1989, 25.

15. Keijō-fu 1936, 591, 622.

16. It was to this end that Meiji Japan carefully adopted the terms of international law to legitimize its annexation of Korea in 1910 (Dudden 2005, 4).

17. Aoyagi 1911, 153. For the case of European missionaries, see Daughton 2006.

18. The Japanese Congregational Church, which operated a short-lived mission under the aegis of the Government-General in the 1910s, had dispatched a few members to investigate Korea's Christian communities around the time of the Russo-Japanese War, but no significant activity was seen before annexation (Kawase 2001).

19. Hwansoo Kim 2007.

20. Ōtaniha Honganji Chōsen Kaikyō Kantokubu 1927, 174.

above all operated as servants of empire by supporting Japan's military operations and later assimilation policies of the colonial government.[21]

Among the early emigrants, merchants played a pivotal role in laying the basis for Japan's colonization of Korea. Writing around the turn of the twentieth century, when Britain in the course of the European "scramble for Africa" brought a quarter of the globe under its control, economic theorists of imperialism saw industrial growth as a precondition for a nation's ability to expand overseas, a process driven by "finance capital" or "monopoly capital."[22] The order was reversed in the case of Japan, where imperialism abroad antedated industrial growth at home. That Japanese capitalism was still in its infancy meant that big capital played a relatively small role in the early phase of empire-building in Korea. To be sure, the business community stood firm behind the national policy of expansion from the start. At the behest of the Meiji oligarchs, politically influential businessmen—notably Ōkura Kihachirō (1837–1928) and Shibusawa Eiichi (1840–1931)—played a key role in jumpstarting Japan's trading operations and land investment in Korea.[23] A host of *zaibatsu* conglomerates were also granted monopolistic rights for railway construction, mining, and the like, and private shipping firms received subsidies for developing long-distance shipping lines on the peninsula.[24] Yet few capitalists were willing to stake their money on the politically uncertain future of Korea, and most were, at

21. In the years leading to the annexation, Japanese Buddhists of both the Sōtō sect (Hur 1999; Hwansoo Kim 2007) and the Shin sect (Hishiki 1993) sought to bring Korean Buddhists under their influence by building an extensive network of temples, efforts that came under increased state regulation. For most of the colonial period, however, it appears that Japanese religious workers captured Korean souls less by faith than by education and philanthropy, through which they promoted Japan's assimilation policy (Auerback 2007).

22. Wright 1976.

23. Beginning with the creation of a branch of Japan's First National Bank (Dai-Ichi Bank) in 1878, Shibusawa, a protégé of Foreign Minister Inoue Kaoru (1836–1915), became involved in Korean land investment, and set up the Chōsen Development Company in 1904 to acquire land under cultivation through low-interest loans and facilitate the introduction of Japanese farming techniques (Duus 1995, 386).

24. The Meiji government offered protection and financial assistance to big corporations and banks such as the Dai-Ichi Bank, and gave special rights to the Ōkura-gumi for railway construction; mining rights to the Furukawa, Asano, and Shibusawa *zaibatsu*; and a monopoly on the ginseng trade to the Mitsui combine (Kimura 1989, 19–20).

any rate, drawn to China. Save for a few tycoons like Shibusawa, Japan in the end produced no colonial pioneers like Cecil Rhodes in southern Africa or George Goldie on the Niger river, who combined patriotic service with a quest for personal wealth abroad to undertake conquest on behalf of their home government.

Without the full benefits of the industrial revolution or surplus capital to invest offshore, a modernizing Japan penetrated into Korea with a rather different sort of economic vanguard: hordes of small and midsize merchants. Seeing them as an important "beachhead" for continental expansion vis-à-vis Qing China and Tsarist Russia, the Meiji government provided emigrants to Korea with a variety of protection and support—measures that were not extended to Japanese migrants working on sugarcane plantations and factories in Hawai'i or on railways, mines, and farms in North America. For one thing, the government facilitated Japanese migration by exempting travelers to China and Korea from strict departure inspections and removing the requirement for passports altogether in 1904. It also helped build the Japanese settlement in each treaty port, where migrants incurred tough competition from Chinese and Western traders. In Wŏnsan, for instance, official support ran the gamut from financially helping migrants set up shop to constructing a hall to display Japanese products. To further ensure that their countrymen could safely pursue business, the Japanese government stationed police officers and even sent a battleship to be moored in full public view, in addition to providing funds for increasing ports of call for mail steamers and liners.[25]

Early emigrants played an indirect role in Japan's metamorphosis from an agrarian nation into an exporter of manufactured goods by transforming Korea into a stable market and a supplier of raw materials for the industrializing metropole. Most typically they sold sundry goods manufactured in Japan or imported from the West at small retail stores, catering to a limited market with Koreans as their main customers. "Japanese merchants before 1904 struggled very hard," recalled one ceramics merchant in Seoul, noting how "we took meticulous care in studying Korean tastes and preferences to manufacture lacquerware

---

25. Kimura 1989, 21, 25.

and hardware."[26] Settlers shipped home gold[27] and a range of farm commodities such as rice and soybeans, which Koreans traded, often at an unfavorable exchange rate, for a full line of imports from Japan (including cotton goods, hardware, kerosene, dyestuffs, salt, and farming tools).[28] Settlers in the ensuing decades continued to operate largely to sustain this two-way movement of goods and produce shuttling between metropole and colony.[29]

Most aggressively expanding their business turf in this period were Japanese cotton and rice traders. Cotton manufacturers availed themselves of the rapidly growing domestic production of textiles that led Japan's industrial "takeoff" to meet the rising Korean demand for foreign goods in the early 1890s. Without state support, they formed export cartels and employed other aggressive commercial tactics to dominate the Korean cotton textile market, so effectively that they rendered Japan's political presence almost superfluous.[30] More dependent on the state yet no less astute were Japanese rice traders. During the Russo-Japanese War and in its aftermath, when Korea fell under protectorate rule, Japanese rice dealers took advantage of the freedom of travel to penetrate rapidly into interior markets by making advance payments to farmers, often via Korean merchants (*kaekchu* and *yŏgak*), to claim their produce at harvest time. In Kunsan, which became the largest entrepôt for the Korean rice trade, local Japanese merchants even began to supplant the role of Korean middlemen and deal directly with farmers in the interior by extending credit for purchasing seed and tools and by dispatching their own agents.[31]

But the realities of other migrants were often far less impressive. Many hard-pressed settlers looked for the easiest ways out of poverty by engaging in practices that bordered on fraud. These ranged from tricking

---

26. Fuchigami Teisuke, "Furuki omoidebanashi," in Fujimura 1927b, 33.

27. It furnished the basis for creating a yen-based gold-exchange standard into which Korea was integrated (Metzler 2005, 30–33, 52–55).

28. In the 1870s and 1880s, Japanese traders engaged almost entirely in the sales of Western manufactured goods first imported to Japan and resold to Korea, and then from the mid-1890s on, imported a growing number of domestic manufactures, especially cotton goods (Duus 1984, 152).

29. Chōsen Sōtokufu Shomu Chōsaka 1924, 76.

30. Duus 1995, 285, 287.

31. Ibid., 276–77.

Koreans into buying shoddy goods and overcharging them for imported Japanese items, to more wide-scale operations such as illicit ginseng trade and the forging of counterfeit Korean coins.[32] The local authorities responded by issuing warnings and security regulations, but they often purposely fell short. Because migrants and settlers were seen as critical to national expansion, the Japanese government tended to restrain only the most egregious of their activities and otherwise overlooked their early excesses by taking only half-hearted measures of control.[33]

Settlers, for their part, pursued increasingly aggressive commercial tactics, with or without state support. In doing so, many took advantage of Japanese immunity from tariffs acquired by the 1876 treaty. Yamaguchi Tahee (1865–1934), a native of Kagoshima who came to Korea penniless at age 20 in 1884, became one of Seoul's most powerful merchants by wielding his extraterritoriality quite literally as a weapon. When his merchandise (ox hides) bound for Inch'ŏn was seized at the Namdaemun city gate by Korean military guards because he failed to pay the required taxes levied on all commodities leaving Seoul at the time, Yamaguchi appealed to the Japanese consul for assistance, but the consul refused to heed his request for negotiation with the Korean authorities. Determined to "take the law into his own hands" and "punish" the "Korean robbers" "in accordance with the treaty provisions," the implacable Yamaguchi rushed back to the gate with a "Japanese sword," and frightened the Korean guards into giving him what he wanted—a moment of "heroic bravery" he later proudly recounted to his biographer.[34]

Such arrogance and avarice at times escalated into diplomatic conflict, as settlers openly flouted the treaty restrictions on their trade and residence. In response to bans on rice exports the Korean government periodically imposed as a way to deal with grain shortages, for example, Japanese merchants and traders frantically prodded Tokyo via a local consul to negotiate indemnities for the losses they incurred.[35] In 1889,

---

32. Nikkan Tsūshō Kyōkai 1983 [1895], 19. For example, see the case of Urao Bunzō in Muramatsu 1972.

33. For the case of an armed group of itinerant peddlers called the Keirin Shōgyōdan, see [Gaimu Daijin Kanbō] Bunshoka 1898, 1193–97.

34. Kitagawa Yoshiaki 1934, 25–27.

35. The revision of the terms of the Kanghwa treaty in 1883 allowed the Korean government to embargo the export of rice, barley, and soybeans with one month's notice

when such grain embargoes were ordered in Hwanghae and Hamgyŏng provinces, settlers in Wŏnsan and other cities urged the local diplomat to pressure the Korean government into suspending its ban. They even dispatched representatives to Tokyo and appealed to popular parties that were beginning to shift to more hard-line diplomacy. Ultimately, the settler lobbyists succeeded in moving the Japanese government to force Korea to lift the embargoes and dismiss the local officials responsible, as well as extracting indemnities of 110,000 yen.[36] Incidents like this where the state took its cue from its vociferous subjects vividly underscore the role of settlers as subimperialists—or as David Fieldhouse famously phrased it, the way "the metropolitan dog" was constantly "wagged by its colonial tail."[37] By the early 1890s, owing not least to these migrants and their relentless pursuit of profit, the Japanese came to dominate Korea's foreign trade—with over 90 percent of Korean exports going to Japan and more than half of Korean imports coming from Japan—as well as the carrying trade at the Korean ports, where over 70 percent of merchant ships bore the mark of the rising sun.[38]

## *Battling Chinese Imperialism*

On more than a few occasions, profit-seeking settlers demonstrated they could also be patriotic citizens by coming together in moments of crisis. No events brought them closer than the Sino-Japanese War and the Russo-Japanese War—and the series of political intrigues surrounding the outbreak of each war that punctuated the final decades of Chosŏn Korea.

If Meiji Japan mobilized migrants for its continental drive against Qing China and Tsarist Russia, settlers for their part demanded that the state rid Korea of these rival powers so that they could better pursue their profit. Chinese merchants, backed by their increasingly assertive home government, presented the largest obstacle of all. In response to

---

to the Japanese consular authorities. However, local Korean officials were forced to impose ad hoc embargoes without following the proper procedures, as Japanese traders increasingly penetrated into the interior and imposed pressures on the local food supply.

36. Yoshino 1978, 101–31.

37. D. K. Fieldhouse, "Imperialism and the Periphery," in Wright 1976, 186.

38. Eckert et al. 1990, 215.

the pressures of Western gunboat diplomacy, the Qing Empire in the 1880s tightened its suzerainty over Korea by refashioning itself from a ceremonial authority into a Western-style imperialist. Deploying the sinews of a nineteenth-century empire—from gunboats to treaties and international law—the Qing government controlled Korea's foreign policy and intervened in domestic reforms through its powerful local representative, Yuan Shikai (1859–1916).[39] A bilateral agreement concluded with Japan in 1885 further brought Korea under Chinese sway for the next decade.[40]

Local Japanese merchants incurred the brunt of this new Chinese "imperialism," evidently on a daily basis. One of them bitterly recounted their sheer helplessness in the face of absolute Chinese commercial dominance, underpinned by the power of Yuan Shikai: "The morning market at Namdaemun would be totally dominated by Chinese. Even when a Japanese merchant managed to find an open spot, a Chinese would come over later and knock him over, claiming it as his territory."[41] Out of desperation, Seoul's Japanese residents often appealed to force. They petitioned both the local consul and Foreign Minister Mutsu Munemitsu (1844–1897), pleading with them to increase the number of consular police officers or to send in more Japanese troops to combat "Chinese and Korean oppression."[42]

In the decade following the 1885 treaty, the Meiji leaders came to desire a military solution to remove Chinese influence from the peninsula once and for all. When a major peasant rebellion—the Tonghak Uprising—broke out in the spring of 1894, therefore, the Japanese government followed the Chinese in rushing some 8,000 troops to the peninsula under the pretext of protecting local Japanese residents from the insurgents, and demanded parity with China in their control over Korea's internal affairs. When rebuffed by the Chinese, the Japanese diplomats launched a coup d'etat against the Korean government in cooperation with local settlers and continental *rōnin* (such as Okamoto

39. Kim Key-Hiuk 1980, Chapter 8. For a more comprehensive discussion of Qing "imperialism," see Larsen 2008.

40. Deuchler 1977, 223–25.

41. For a stenographic record of the first retrospective roundtable talk (*kaiko zadankai*) on the early Seoul Chamber of Commerce (14 March 1940), see *KSKN* 1941, 3:26.

42. *KSKN* 1941, 1:30–33; Kawabata 1910, 31–32.

Ryūnosuke [1852–1912], who served as an advisor to the Korean court), with the goal of ousting the conservative pro-Chinese Min faction. After carrying the reluctant Taewŏn'gun (1821–1898)—father of King Kojong (1852–1919) and a disgruntled old regent who had been dislodged from power in 1873—into the royal palace, they forced the Korean government to sign a "treaty" to expel the Chinese troops with Japanese forces in 1894.[43]

Upon hearing the rumor that the Tonghaks were going to attack the Japanese settlement in Seoul, the aforementioned merchant Yamaguchi Tahee and other settlers in Seoul petitioned Foreign Minister Mutsu to station more police officers for their protection. Meanwhile, the consul Sugimura Fukashi coordinated with local residents and Imperial Navy and Army officers to prepare for emergency with "90 rifles."[44] When the Qing troops landed at the port of Asan, settlers in Seoul urged Mutsu to dispatch "several thousand of your best soldiers" to Korea, to oust the "tyranny" of Chinese and allow "Japanese residents to live in eternal peace and to project the power of our nation overseas."[45] Seeing the empire's fate as coinciding with their own, local Japanese residents in Inch'ŏn prepared special facilities to accommodate the encamped troops, while in Wŏnsan they built new garrison barracks. And settlers everywhere aided the military operations, supplying food and shelter, serving as interpreters, and volunteering their labor for miscellaneous tasks.[46] One war correspondent later recalled with excitement how the Japanese troops in one battle at P'yŏngyang crushed the Chinese "in just five hours," clearing a path for their country's first large-scale military victory overseas.[47] And this victory, as many settlers saw, owed in no small part to their patriotic acts of service, which were replayed in the Russo-Japanese War a decade later.

If the war transformed settlers into patriotic citizens, it also turned some of them into rich men overnight. Each battle brought lucrative opportunities to Japanese merchants and camp followers alike, and the

---

43. Pak Chong-gŭn 1982, 58–62, 85–89; Kitagawa Kichisaburō, "Nyūkyō tōjitsu no konwaku," in Fujimura 1927b, 53–56; Okamoto Ryūnosuke 1912, 265–71.

44. Keijō-fu 1934, 561.

45. Keijō Kyoryūmindan Yakusho 1912, 66–68; Keijō-fu 1934, 562.

46. Kimura 1989, 74; Keijō-fu 1934, 714; Fujimura 1927b, 25, 46.

47. Kikuchi 1936, 271.

wartime boom allowed rice and cotton traders to penetrate the interior market still further. Japan's victory over the Qing, above all, broke the impasse for struggling emigrants. Since it removed the power of Chinese merchants, retail merchants found themselves better positioned to take advantage of the novelty of Japanese and Western manufactures in catering to Koreans. In the interwar period and beyond many gleefully amassed profits that more than redeemed their earlier losses,[48] in a more secure environment provided by the Japanese government, including stable currency, uniform weights and measures, and credit and banking facilities.[49] According to Kimura Kenji's study, by the time of the Russo-Japanese War, whereas it took on average a decade or two to set up a business in metropolitan Japan, it took only about eight years in Korea—allowing the quickest learners to become self-employed within a year or two after arrival.[50] Although "self-made men" such as Yamaguchi Tahee claimed to have built their wealth on nothing but hard work and astute marketing strategies, settlers owed the state far more than they were apt to acknowledge.

### *Political Collaboration among "Men on the Spot"*

Between the two wars, some settlers were drawn into dramatic political intrigues at the Korean court. After the opening of the country in 1876, the Korean government had plunged into several decades of complex and shifting power struggles over the pace and strategies of reform.[51] This conflict within leadership was further complicated by the intervention of concession-seeking powers including Japan, whose policy of supporting Korea's reforms had remained inconsistent since the 1880s. Japan's naval victory over China, indeed, removed but one of many obstacles in what would be a halting process of expanding its grip on the peninsula. No sooner had they expelled Chinese influence from the Korean court than the victorious Japanese found their leverage diminish after the Triple Intervention by Russia, Germany, and France, followed by King Kojong's flight to the Russian Legation. The Japanese

48. *Chōsen oyobi Manshū*, April 1910, 83–85.
49. Duus 1984, 155.
50. Kimura 2002, 5.
51. Deuchler 1977; Eckert et al. 1990, Chapter 13.

continued to struggle to find stable Korean allies in the government, as the Korean court "used barbarians against barbarians" to keep all foreign powers at bay.[52] As they doled out railroad concessions to American and French businessmen, the Korean leaders looked especially to the Russians to fend off Japanese pressure.

Local Japanese officials and settlers once again joined hands to reverse the political tide. In one of the most extraordinary instances of collaboration among these "men on the spot"—and one of the most egregious acts of violence in the history of modern colonialism—settlers worked with the legation officers in Seoul in a plot to assassinate Queen Min (1851–1895), the perceived head of the anti-Japanese (and pro-Russian) faction in the Korean court. Queen Min was seen to be standing in the way of Japanese control over Korea's reforms—known as the "Kabo reforms," which began with the Japanese seizure of the Kyŏngbok Palace in 1894 and lasted for sixteen months until 1896. As she threatened to overthrow the cabinet of Kim Hong-jip (1842–1896) recently installed under Japanese sponsorship, Miura Gorō (1847–1926), the new Japanese minister to Korea, masterminded a scheme to assassinate the queen, with the full backing of the Taewŏn'gun, the archenemy of the Min faction.[53]

According to one of its participants, Kikuchi Kenjō (1870–1953), then a correspondent for *Kokumin shinbun* run by Tokutomi Sohō (1863–1957), the coup was an exemplary collaboration of officials (*kan*) and civilians (*min*), involving a total of some 120 Japanese in Seoul. Never before or after this event, he wrote, were the two so united as Japanese "nationals" (*kokumin*) in "carrying out international fidelity and contributing to their neighbor by means of national pure-heartedness."[54] When the coup was finally carried out in early October by Korean *hullyŏndae* troops and the legation's military attaché and police officers, they were backed by "a flying column of 40-odd volunteers,"[55] as Kikuchi described in his letter to Tokutomi. They included ultranationalists

52. Duus 1995, 131.

53. The Japanese cooperated with the reformist officials to co-opt the Taewŏn'gun in ousting the pro-Chinese Min oligarchy from government and launching the Kabo reforms under his nominal leadership (Eckert et al. 1990, 223–24).

54. Kikuchi 1931, 1:79, 82.

55. Kikuchi to Tokutomi (October 1895): 222.

like Okamoto Ryūnosuke, Japanese employees of the Korean government, and a variety of local settlers, from merchants to educators and journalists. Most prominent among the latter were the editorial staff of the *Kanjō shinpō*, a bilingual (Korean and Japanese) newspaper founded by a patriotic political party in Kumamoto prefecture and financially supported by the Ministry of Foreign Affairs.[56] In this collaborative undertaking, as surviving records chronicle in detail, the Japanese legation guard and the Korean troops escorted the Taewŏn'gun, Japanese policemen "scaled the wall to open the gate" to the Kyŏngbok Palace, and Japanese civilian toughs with drawn swords joined the troops in storming inside—actions that culminated in the slaughter of the queen, her ladies-in-waiting, and the minister of the royal household.[57] During the coup, Kikuchi himself served as "a guard at the rear gate" of the Unhyŏn'gung, the Taewŏn'gun's palace, and "contributed to the best of [his] limited ability to pulling the Taewŏn'gun out" of his palace when the coup commenced.[58] And at the Taewŏn'gun's behest, Kikuchi personally delivered reports on developments during the ensuing mayhem, including an eyewitness report on the bloodstained murder scene in the queen's bedchamber.[59]

Having provoked Korean ire, Miura and 47 other Japanese privy to the plot were deported to Japan after a highly public trial, followed by an elaborate farewell banquet thrown by local settlers who praised them as "national heroes." Anxious to ward off international censure, the government in Tokyo summoned them to stand trial in Japan. Although they were imprisoned upon arrival in Hiroshima, they were eventually acquitted for lack of evidence.[60] Out of desire to regain control over the Korean court, the Meiji leaders, in effect, sanctioned the reckless action

---

56. Sasa 1977, 21–22, 29. Its office in Seoul became "a den of *rōnin* and *sōshi*" where Kikuchi would find his new home (*Chōsen kōron*, July 1933, 123).

57. Kokuryūkai 1966, 511–47; Pak Chong-gŭn 1982, 255–303. For more details on the coup, see Kikuchi 1936, 303–13; Duus 1995, 108–12.

58. Kikuchi to Tokutomi (October 1895): 222.

59. Kikuchi 1940 [1937], 417–18; Kikuchi 1936, 272–310. This experience furnished rare material for a number of books on Korean history that Kikuchi later authored, including a biography of the Taewŏn'gun that was translated into Korean (Kikuchi 1910a and 1910b).

60. Some members of the residents' association demanded that the central government rescind the expulsion order altogether (Kokuryūkai 1966, 537).

of their countrymen by turning a blind eye to it. Given the political stalemate at the time, Miura and his supporters may have carried out their scheme with the full knowledge that they could intervene with impunity, anticipating a diplomacy of *fait accompli* that would become a pattern in Japan's military drive on the continent.

This incident and its aftermath signaled the emergence of some of the most influential brokers of empire. Although the president of the *Kanjō shinpō*, Adachi Kenzō (1864–1948), stayed in Japan to enter parliamentary politics, later becoming Minister of Communications, most of the journalists and other *rōnin* returned to Korea to resume their careers, becoming the key voices of the Japanese resident community. But Kikuchi's career took a more unusual turn. Since he first arrived in Korea in 1894, on a special mission from the Ministry of Foreign Affairs to report on the clash between the Chinese and Japanese troops, Kikuchi, under circumstances largely unknown, came to be involved in the internal affairs of the Korean court, winning the personal favor of the Taewŏn'gun. After returning to Korea from Hiroshima, Kikuchi not only became president of the *Kanjō shinpō*, by then the most authoritative Japanese-run paper, but appointed himself a role that would grant him further leverage over the court: to help Korea counter the threat of Russia.

By his own account, Kikuchi was "the first one to learn about Russia's demand for a leasehold over Masan," a city located in the southernmost part of the peninsula. He furnished this critical information to the Japanese minister in Seoul, Hayashi Gonsuke (1860–1939), who then relayed it to Tokyo—an act of national importance that later "earned [Hayashi] the honor of baron," according to Kikuchi.[61] Around this time, too, Kikuchi evidently caught the attention of King Kojong by reporting daily on the savagery of Russian soldiers in North China and Manchuria in the *Kanjō shinpō*, stoking Korean antipathy.[62] In addition to keeping the Korean Minister of Foreign Affairs, Pak Che-sun (1858–1916), abreast of developments along the northern border, in 1901 Kikuchi presented to Kojong his idea of a Japanese-Korean defense alliance, an agreement to support each other in the case of an imminent Russian invasion of

61. Kikuchi 1931, 2:43.

62. Aoyagi 1926a, 876; Kikuchi 1931, 2:431.

the peninsula. This proposal won full support of Prince Konoe Atsumaro (1863–1904), who visited Seoul around that time as head of the Tōa Dōbunkai (East Asia Common Culture Society, for which Kikuchi doubled his duties in Korea). It also allowed Kikuchi to "get [even] closer to the Korean court and obtain a ticket to ride the train of court diplomacy," "an opportunity I celebrated to serve my homeland."[63]

Kojong subsequently made a remarkable move. For starting discussions with the Japanese government concerning the defense alliance, the king appointed Kikuchi along with Ku Wan-hŭi as imperial envoys to deliver his order to Cho Pyŏng-sik, the new Korean minister in Japan (chosen by Foreign Minister Pak evidently based on Kikuchi's suggestion). Not only was it unprecedented for a Korean king to appoint a Japanese journalist to act as his personal envoy, it was considered equally outrageous by the legation authorities for Kikuchi to bypass Minister Hayashi. Indeed, Kikuchi's operations remained so obscure that Hayashi was reportedly "completely taken aback" by the news of his mission to the metropole.[64] Bearing the king's confidential letter concerning the alliance and the expulsion of political exiles, according to Konoe Atsumaro's diary, Kikuchi moved stealthily between Foreign Minister Aoki Shūzō of the second Yamagata cabinet and the Korean minister Cho Pyŏng-sik.[65] By this time, he was effectively acting as a diplomatic go-between who negotiated with Tokyo leaders on behalf of the Korean government.

Although the sudden dissolution of the Yamagata cabinet nullified the ongoing discussions on the alliance, Kikuchi's influence outlasted his proposal. While launching a few newspapers and magazines of his own, Kikuchi continued to maintain close ties to the Korean royal household as "a Japanese supervisor" during the protectorate period. By the time of annexation he had gained an unshakable status as an authority on Korean affairs, with leverage extending into the inner circles of the Korean court that "became the envy of fellow *rōnin* settlers."[66] The role of settlers like Kikuchi may be somewhat exaggerated by their biographers

63. Kikuchi 1931, 2:44. Unfortunately, the exact details of his proposal remain unknown.

64. Aoyagi, 1926a, 890–91.

65. Quoted in Sakurai 1998, 409.

66. Fujimura 1927b, 232.

(and themselves), and details of their political maneuvers unfortunately remain skeletal. Nonetheless, traces of their influence, visible everywhere in existing accounts, reveal how the realm of formal diplomacy frequently melted at its edges into the unruly world of adventurers, visionaries, chauvinists, and political gadflies. And they hint at the extent of influence some settlers may have projected over the Korean court, beyond the pale of the local representatives of Tokyo. Paying tribute to their influence, the settler journalist Aoyagi Tsunatarō later declared to fellow Japanese, "We must definitely not forget the contribution of behind-the-scenes activities of journalist Kikuchi Chōfū [his pen name] who steered the course of the Japanese annexation of Korea."[67]

## *Lobbying for Railroads*

Political actions and visions of "men on the spot" like Kikuchi begin to illustrate how local settlers, in pushing the frontier of Japanese expansion, often guided rather than trailed the imperialistic designs of their government. The same dynamic drove the expansion of Korea's railway grid. As Japanese leaders by this time agreed, construction of railroads held the key to gaining a more permanent foothold on the peninsula. Army men such as Yamagata Aritomo (1838–1922) envisioned a line stretching from Pusan through Seoul to the Manchurian border as "a great thoroughfare across the Asian continent" where Japan could emerge as a dominant political and military power.[68] Local settlers embraced this argument with more pressing zeal. The Japanese control of railways, which sustained the flow of goods and migrants between metropole and colony, would ensure not only the stability of settlers' trading activities, but the security and growth of their communities far into the future.

But even after a victory over China, the path to a global status remained uncertain. In the wake of the Triple Intervention, Western rivals gained important railway construction rights during a momentary lapse of Japanese influence at the Korean court. While local representatives of the Tokyo government labored hard to recover the promised concessions, in the spring of 1896 Seoul's leading Japanese merchants rose

67. Aoyagi 1926a, 898.
68. Quoted in Duus 1984, 139.

in protest against the Korean court's recent decision to grant construction rights for two major lines to American and French interests.[69] The merchants called especially for securing the right to build the Seoul–Pusan line as Japan's "urgent necessity," a resolution echoed by local settlers in Inch'ŏn, Pusan, and Wŏnsan.

When Vice-Foreign Minister Komura Jutarō (1855–1911) opposed the settlers' plan to lobby in Japan out of fear that such an action "might endanger national politics," Yamaguchi Tahee, by then a leading settler merchant in Seoul, decided to go to Tokyo alone. Having visited Fukuzawa Yukichi (1835–1901), whose support was not forthcoming, he called on the general chief of staff of the Imperial Japanese Army, who was so impressed by Yamaguchi's enthusiasm that he immediately summoned Major General Terauchi Masatake (1852–1919; later to become the last Resident-General and first Governor-General of Korea) to assist Yamaguchi and introduce him to other powerful individuals.[70]

Yamaguchi, Wada Tsuneichi, and other settler leaders subsequently linked up with a group of metropolitan capitalists and concessionaires led by Ōmiwa Chōbee (1835–1908). Together they pressed the reluctant Tokyo government to seize the right to build the Seoul–Pusan line while keeping out Western competitors. Prime Minister Itō Hirobumi (1841–1909) and other like-minded leaders were initially reluctant to negotiate with the Korean court, given the difficulty of attracting investors in a risky overseas venture and out of desire to avoid antagonizing Western powers, especially Russia. As the mass media and business interests began to rally behind the railway promoters, however, Itō agreed to back their movement if the lobbyists recruited at least 100 supporters. In July, having gathered more than the required number, in addition to the critical backing of the anti-Russian Yamagata faction in the government, the lobbyists obtained state approval to proceed with the creation of the Seoul–Pusan Railway Company.[71] When the French also made their move toward the Seoul–Pusan line, Yamaguchi returned at once to Seoul, and used his "private money" to "buy off several officials," including Foreign Minister Yi Wan-yong (1858–1926), to ensure that

---

69. For the background and details on this development, see Duus 1995, 138–57. Here I will focus on the role and involvement of Japanese settlers in Korea.

70. Kitagawa Yoshiaki 1934, 34–35, 56–57.

71. Takahashi 1993, 271; Nakai 1915, 13–15.

these rights were properly transferred into the Japanese hands. After a few more twists and turns, the right to construct the railway was finally secured in September 1898, and under more direct government involvement the line was completed in January 1905.[72]

By the eve of the Russo-Japanese War, the Japanese had come to control all of Korea's key railway lines, including the Seoul–Pusan line, the Seoul–Inch'ŏn line, and the Seoul–Ŭiju and Masanp'o military lines that formed Korea's longitudinal trunk rail line.[73] All were completed under the supervision of contractors and engineers from the metropole who would dominate the construction of other physical infrastructures around the peninsula. Each line reflected not only the military and diplomatic designs of the Meiji government, but also the strong imprint of settler influence. A humble merchant like Yamaguchi, his fellow settler Shin Tatsuma later reminisced with awe, had such foresight to link railway-building to the future of Japan-Korea relations as to "cast a net of spies deep into the interior of the Korean government to keep watch on the developments." Yamaguchi was not only ahead of his time, Shin asserted, but his selfless "contribution to the state" went beyond "the usual work of a merchant guided by the abacus" and exemplified a heroic act of "a patriot" (*kokushi*) or "a loyalist" (*shishi*).[74] Although such vainglorious rhetoric, characteristic of settler biographies, masked the profit motive of colonial merchants, their lobbying activities also underscored an increasingly worrisome tendency to act as agents of expansion in their own right—and to see themselves as "true builders of empire," nameless national heroes who stood on a par with the great men of Meiji. In launching what was essentially a grassroots effort to wrest railway concessions from the Korean court, indeed, settlers battled not only Western rivals on the concession hunting ground, but the cautious orientation of their own government. In conjunction with metropolitan allies and the press, they managed to persuade leaders like Itō and Komura to embrace a more aggressive policy of economic expansion into Korea by the turn of the century.[75]

72. Kitagawa Yoshiaki 1934, 58–60; Duus 1995, 141–45.
73. Takahashi 1995, 58–60.
74. Shin Tatsuma, quoted in Kitagawa Yoshiaki 1934, 147–48.
75. Duus 1984, 140.

## *Japan's "Civilizing Mission"*

Along with soldiers, journalists, and merchants, another lesser-known group of Japanese—teachers—came to Korea with the mission to spread the "beacon of civilization" on the benighted frontier. Japanese educators and language teachers began to trickle into Korea in the wake of the Sino-Japanese War and came in droves during the Russo-Japanese War, partly to meet an increased demand for interpreters to accompany the Japanese troops encamped on the peninsula. An emerging Japanese-language "boom" led to the rapid growth of language schools, spearheaded by the private initiatives of the Dai-Nihon Kaigai Kyōikukai (Greater Japan Overseas Education Association), the Tōa Dōbunkai, and the Buddhist Higashi Honganji.[76] These institutions brought to Korea many teachers of a strong patriot (*kokushi*) character, determined to inculcate Korean youth with Japanese culture, manners, and "pro-Japanese" ideology, often with the tacit goal to counter the competing influence of Western missionaries.

One of these teachers was Ayukai Fusanoshin (1864–1946). After studying Korean at Tokyo Foreign Languages School, Ayukai settled in Seoul and established an academy called Itsubi Gijuku in the spring of 1895. He was joined by his best friend, Yosano Tekkan (1873–1935), later the husband of the poet Yosano Akiko (1878–1942). The Itsubi Gijuku offered classes in Japanese language and primary school education with an aim to "transplant Japanese culture," being allegedly the first school to teach Japanese songs and literature to Korean pupils to that end.[77] Restless and fiercely patriotic like many men of their generation, both Ayukai and Yosano also participated in the plot to assassinate Queen Min, for the pressing reason that the anti-Japanese Min faction threatened to requisition their academy. Although their involvement in the coup led to the closure of the school within less than a year of its creation and Yosano's eventual return to Japan, Ayukai made Korea his permanent home. While establishing his career as a scholar and avid collector of Korean antiques, Ayukai, like Kikuchi, cultivated personal

---

76. See Inaba 1997. Korean elites also established many private schools, including Japanese-language schools, in this period.

77. Inaba 1999, 253–54, 257; Inoue Manabu 1969, 57. The school had over 700 students enrolled in its main school and five branch schools in Seoul.

relations with the Taewŏn'gun and Korean officials,[78] and continued to dabble in diplomacy, for instance, "on an island facing the port of Mokp'o [where he] bought lands contiguous to the area the Russians laid their eyes on."[79]

Among the few Japanese Buddhists who crossed the ocean were Okumura Enshin (1843–1913), a chief priest of Higashi Honganji, and his sister Ioko (1845–1907). Seeking to relive the legacy of their ancestor—one of the earliest Buddhist missionaries to set foot in Korea in the late sixteenth century—the Okumura siblings in 1898 settled in the remote village of Kwangju in South Chŏlla.[80] Encircled by "hostile natives" and with nothing but "a swordsman and a Buddhist rosary" to protect them (as their biography narrates), the Okumuras set out to create a "Japan village"—or "a paradise village" as they called it—by first building a vocational school, a project financially supported by Prince Konoe Atsumaro. Ioko's daily open-air sermons initially met with deep suspicion by the Korean locals, who, stirred by rumors that the school was a military outpost in disguise, greeted the newcomers with stones. Undeterred, the Okumuras, joined by supporters from home, continued to teach local farmers agricultural skills and silkworm rearing techniques as well as the Japanese language, convinced that they would "ultimately become our comrades," evidently anticipating Japan's annexation of Korea.[81]

Whereas the Okumuras' venture in Kwangju—and Japanese missionary activities in general—ultimately fizzled out,[82] more successful was Fuchizawa Yoshie (1850–1936), a prominent Japanese educator and

78. Ayukai 1942, 3; Imamura Raen 1942, 315. Ayukai became especially close to Kim Yun-sik (1903–1950), who had served on the short-lived Kim Hong-jip cabinet and shared his passion for scholarship. Meanwhile, the unremitting Yosano planned another abortive coup when King Kojong fled to the Russian legation in the wake of Queen Min's murder. Upon hearing a rumor that the king would move into a nearby palace, Yosano schemed with a local Japanese shopkeeper to mobilize his Japanese employees in setting fire to the palace and kidnapping the king and sending him back to the Japanese legation (Hino 1981, 215).

79. Ayukai 1942, 3.

80. The Okumuras' ancestor went to Pusan in 1585 to open a temple for propagating Japanese Buddhism (Inaba 1999, 266; Aikoku Fujinkai 1908, 149–50).

81. Inaba 1999, 161–63, 270.

82. Aikoku Fujinkai 1908, 146, 154.

later a leading member of the Aikoku Fujinkai (Patriotic Women's Association) founded by Okumura Ioko in 1901. Inspired by Fukuzawa Yukichi's best-seller *Seiyō jijō* (Conditions in the West, 1870), Fuchizawa at age 31 crossed to the United States as a housemaid for the family of an American engineer, and later studied the English language on her own in San Francisco. After returning home, Fuchizawa enrolled at Dōshisha Women's School in Kyoto and subsequently taught at various girls' schools, later opening her own academy in Tokyo. In 1905, her passion for education took Fuchizawa to the Korean peninsula, where she embarked on more ambitious ventures. For the purpose of educating upper-class Korean women, Fuchizawa cooperated with Yi Chŏngsuk (1858–1935), and with Kikuchi Kenjō's mediation received support from the Korean royal household to establish the Myŏngsin Women's School, a forerunner of Korean female education, and a dormitory for students from the provinces where she also lived for the next twenty-odd years.[83] Education, she believed, would not only liberate Korean women shackled by the social conventions of patriarchal society, but it would also contribute to national strength, a message that she strove to propagate among Korean parents and the general public.[84] Her foremost task was to socialize aristocratic women by bringing them literally out of their homes into the public, for which she deployed measures that were considered rather radical at the time, such as introducing male teachers into the classroom. More generally, she explained in an interview later, Fuchizawa aimed to reform Korea's "old corrupt customs" by promoting an overall Japanization of the Korean lifestyle in the areas of housing, cooking, and marriage.[85] Fuchizawa devoted the rest of her life to educating Korean women and training Korean teachers, many of whom imbibed her message to play an active role in female suasion and social management in the late colonial period.

Although some of these grassroots ventures launched by Japanese civilians proved more ephemeral than others, on the whole they did

83. The school was renamed the Sungmyŏng Women's Higher Ordinary School in 1911 (Nakamura Shiryō 1926, 299). The student enrollment increased from five in 1905 to over 300 in 1914, and to about 550 by the mid-1930s (*Chōsen kōron*, September 1914, 69; Morikawa 1935, 930).

84. Song Yŏn-ok 2002, 78.

85. *Chōsen kōron*, September 1914, 68–69; *Chōsen oyobi Manshū*, April 1914, 190–91.

more than complement Japan's expansive military ambitions. While soldiers battled the nation's foes to remove the final obstacles to Japanese dominance, teachers who came in growing numbers planted seeds of Japanese culture on Korean soil to ensure their country's lasting influence. Rallying behind an empire with few missionaries who could aid its effort to win over the Korean masses, these educators and language schools laid the foundations for a more rigorous regime of conversion—assimilation through Japanese colonial education—before the state authority fully assumed the role of training and dispatching teachers from late 1905 onward.[86]

## *A Failed Malthusian Dream*

Japan's war against Russia—fought with the same patriotic support from local settlers as the previous war against China, but now with the clear intent to establish direct political control over Korea and a foothold in Manchuria—removed the last imperialist rival from the peninsula (and East Asia).[87] The subsequent establishment of protectorate rule in 1905 brought the largest migration wave, with the year 1906 adding a phenomenal 40,000 people, and increasing the Japanese population in Korea to nearly 100,000 by the end of 1907.[88] These developments reaffirmed the vision of Korea as a colony of settlement (*ijū shokuminchi*), first articulated in the cabinet's decision in mid-1904 to transform the peninsula into a protectorate. In the Malthusian vision of Japanese leaders, Korea was to be "an immigration colony for our excess population," who would "engage in agriculture" to maintain Korea as a supplier of foodstuffs and raw materials and Japan as an exporter of manufactured goods.[89] The idea of Korea as an outlet for anticipated population pressure at home, along with its image as a sparsely populated fertile land, gained a wide range of adherents, from a Korea lobby in the Diet to colonial theorists like Tōgō Minoru and Takekoshi Yosaburō, many of

86. Japanese teachers in Korea became "government officials" in January 1908. After the annexation of Korea and the establishment of government-run schools, private Japanese-language schools lost their raison d'être and most of them disappeared (Inaba 1999, 286).

87. Duus 1995, 182–87.

88. Chōsen Sōtokufu Shomu Chōsaka 1924, 4.

89. Quoted in Duus 1984, 141.

whom had in mind the model of Hokkaido, Japan's first successful case of mass colonization.[90] A focus on Korea, moreover, was promoted by the rise of racial animosity toward Japanese immigrants in the Americas and especially in Hawai'i. In 1909, Foreign Minister Komura Jutarō issued a call for "concentrating [emigration] in Manchuria and Korea" (*Man-Kan shūchūron*).[91]

For the purpose of diverting emigrants from the Americas to the Korean peninsula, the Finance Ministry, in cooperation with business leaders like Shibusawa Eiichi, established a quasi-public corporation, the Tōyō Takushoku Kabushiki Kaisha (Oriental Development Company; hereafter ODC) in 1908.[92] The ODC inherited the vision of the earlier so-called Nagamori plan, devised by a former official of the Ministries of Justice and Finance, as a cunning method to bring most uncultivated land (to be designated as "wasteland") on the peninsula under Japanese management, within the framework of Korean government ownership but outside of treaty restrictions. Like the British colonizing efforts in Ireland, the plan essentially envisioned the use of agricultural settlers from home to open and develop Korean land. Nagamori's proposal met an enthusiastic response from local Japanese residents, who echoed him in touting its potential benefits to the Korean agrarian economy. But the plan failed due to overwhelming Korean public resistance, demonstrated for months on the streets of Seoul.[93]

The ODC's founders, like Nagamori before them, hoped the company would export a band of "experienced and skilled" self-cultivating farmers to jump-start mass agrarian colonization of the peninsula.[94] But their Malthusian dreams soon ran aground. For one thing, Japanese

---

90. Peattie 1984b, 89; Lynn 2005, 28–29. A Korea lobby in support of this view was represented by the Chōsen Kyōkai (Korea Association), formed in March 1902 by an eclectic group of Konoe Atsumaro's aides such as Ogawa Heikichi (1869–1942), entrepreneurs like Shibusawa Eiichi, scholars, and other individuals with connections to Korea, including a former settler leader, Nakai Kitarō. The Chōsen Kyōkai was disbanded in March 1905 and merged into the Tōa Dōbunkai (Chŏng Ae-yŏng 1999, 54, 59–62).

91. Kimura 2001a, 173–74.

92. For more information on the formation and operation of the ODC in Korea and Asia, see Kawai Kazuo et al. 2000; Kurose 2003; and Lynn 2005.

93. Duus 1995, 368–75.

94. Gragert 1994, 54–55, 59–64.

farmers showed only a modicum of interest. Handsome government subsidies and guarantees on returns still did not suffice in overcoming the costs and risks farmers foresaw in settling abroad, particularly at a time of relative rural prosperity in Japan. Like the capitalists, most farmers preferred to stay on home soil. The ODC's plan to settle between 10,000 and 30,000 farm families per year (or a total of 2 million over a 10-year period) turned out to be as unrealistic as their original estimates of land available for Japanese cultivation. Even after the annual target was scaled down to 1,500 households, who were given money to move, land to farm, and long-term low-interest loans to ensure productivity, the number of applicants remained dismally small.[95]

Following the failure of the ODC venture, the mass settlement of Japanese nationals dropped off the list of state priorities, becoming a perennial source of settler discontent.[96] Apparent decline in official enthusiasm for colonization underscored the betrayal of an agrarian vision by emigrants themselves, who continued to seek quick cash rather than land to farm. Farmers would remain a tiny minority, making up never more than 10 percent of the increasingly white-collar settler population, and dipping below 5 percent by 1940.[97] But these percentages also attest to the comparatively modest scale of Japanese land seizure. Around the time of annexation, 170,000 Japanese settlers held no more than 3 to 4 percent of Korea's arable land, usually of lesser quality than that owned by Korean landlords.[98] Twenty years later, half a million settlers owned less than 10 percent of Korean land.[99] As one study has shown, even during the peak period of emigration and land transfers, Korea's arable

95. Duus 1995, 307–8; Moskowitz 1974, 97–98; Lynn 2005, 33.

96. Having failed in its attempts to increase applicants, the ODC suspended the program of farm colonization in 1927 (Lynn 2005, 32).

97. See Table 4. The vision of settling farmers en masse, as well as the idea of using them as a human buffer on the frontline of imperial expansion, would only materialize in Manchuria, where the Tokyo government overcame similar difficulties in settling Japanese to lay a stronger claim on the territory by making it a central priority of national policy in the 1930s (Matsusaka 2001, 173–84; L. Young 1998, 46, 311–12).

98. This figure is for December 1912 (Gragert 1994, 73). According to Peter Duus, by 1910 Japanese landowners came to possess a little less than 3 percent of the cultivated land in Korea "concentrating in the fertile riverine plains of North Chŏlla, South Chŏlla, and South Kyŏngsang, or the northwestern coastal plain in the hinterland of P'yŏngyang and Chinnamp'o" (1995, 395, 377).

99. Elkins and Pedersen 2005, 12.

land changed hands without significantly disrupting the existing patterns of landholding and small-scale agricultural production.[100] In this respect, Japanese imperialism was quite different from that of the European powers, who claimed wide swaths of land for their own farmers,[101] or transformed their colonies into plantation economies.[102] In Korea, by contrast, the density of the indigenous farming population compelled most Japanese to turn to commerce or trade, an experience that paralleled that of Indians in East Africa.[103] Meanwhile, the few Japanese who settled to farm—predominantly tenant farmers who worked for Korean and Japanese landlords—struggled to compete with the Korean farmers' lower wage level and failed to perform very well.[104]

Nonetheless, the Japanese steadily increased their land holdings, a process that accelerated with the arrival of speculators. They typically acquired land by lending money to cash-hungry Koreans with their farmland as collateral. Many engaged in usury targeting poor farmers: dishonest lenders would hide from their debtors until the due date for repayment of a loan had passed as a way of claiming their land pledged as security.[105] As their communities grew rapidly after the Russo-Japanese War, moreover, local settlers began prodding their government to pressure Korea to give Japanese the right to buy, sell, or permanently lease privately owned land outside the treaty limit.[106] Pressures from the settlers and Tokyo eventually compelled the Korean government to permit foreigners to hold land in the interior and to obtain leases to develop un-reclaimed land owned by the government. The Agricultural and Residential Land Certification Law enacted by the Residency-General in Oc-

100. Gragert 1994, 109–10.

101. Elkins and Pedersen 2005, 8–10; Stora 2001, 6–7; Elkins 2005, 12.

102. Fage and Oliver 1986, Chapter 2, 85. The Japanese, however, built plantations in Southeast Asia and Micronesia (Peattie 1988b, Chapter 6).

103. Kennedy 1987, 96–97.

104. Gragert 1994, 60, 62.

105. Yi Yŏng-mi 2005, 65, 84.

106. When Yi Yong-ik, a former leader of the Kabo reforms and governor of North Kyŏngsang province, outlawed land sales to Japanese, the local Japanese press in Taegu ran numerous articles bashing him and inciting local Japanese resistance (Kawai Asao 1931, 145–46; Yi Hae-ch'ang 1971, 293–94).

tober 1906 legalized foreign ownership,[107] and the ODC lent money to private individuals to finance land purchases. Because land was so cheap, the entire cross-section of settlers joined metropolitan investors in the land grab. From shopkeepers and moneylenders to police officers, schoolteachers, and Buddhist priests, settlers became absentee landlords who owned and rented out small plots of land in the countryside to supplement their regular income.[108]

The pace of land acquisition accelerated in the colonial period. With official support and the completion of a land survey that facilitated investments, Japanese land developers and individuals gained greater control over agricultural production, making technological improvements that reduced the need for farm labor. With ownership concentrated in fewer hands, especially Japanese absentee landlords who exported most of their produce to the home market, uprooted Korean farmers were compelled to migrate northward and across the border into southern Manchuria in search of land and work—a pattern that continued to the end of colonial rule.[109]

## *The Growth of Settler Communities*

Conditions in early Japanese settlements were not dissimilar to "those of the native American frontier"—a metaphor settlers themselves used to liken their struggle to that of pioneers in the New World, who had constantly to defend themselves against the unfriendly natives.[110] By the Russo-Japanese War, migrants flooded into treaty ports and spread through the countryside, taking "land, food, and farm animals from an increasingly outraged Korean populace."[111] While collectively engaged in acts of plunder, one former settler recounted later, Japanese displayed

107. Gragert 1994, 62, 69. Later, the Civil Code of 1912 allowed the Japanese to own and transfer all land legally.

108. Toyoda 1963, 12–13.

109. Gragert 1994, 111–12; Lynn 2005, 36. The gap between Korean and Japanese landholdings, in both rural and urban areas, widened over time, with the Japanese on average owning triple or quadruple the amount owned by Koreans by the mid-1920s (*Chosŏn ilbo*, 7 April 1924).

110. For instance, see *Chōsen* (Chōsen Zasshisha), February 1911, 8.

111. Peattie 1988a, 261.

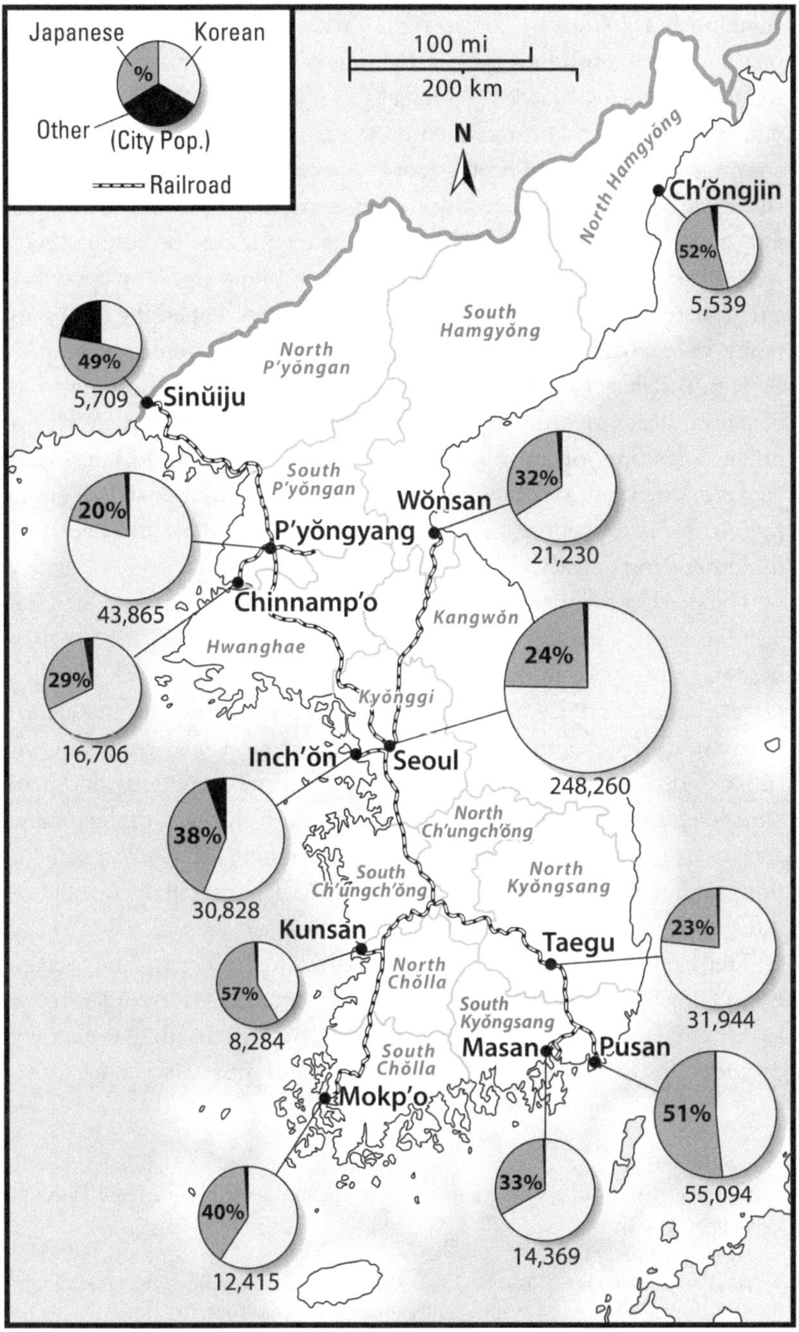


Map 2 Distribution of Japanese Population in Korea, 1914

anything but a spirit of cooperation, "with merchants competing with one another, gangsters [*yakuza*] fighting over their turf, and gamblers frequently causing brawls."[112] Out of this chaos, nonetheless, emerged a new spatial order that came to embody a colonial hierarchy. As Japanese continued to settle around the newly opened ports—often near a consulate, under the protective flag of the rising sun—frontier towns grew into cities like Pusan and Inch'ŏn, and as restrictions on interior travel were lifted, satellite cities like Taejŏn also sprang up. The growth of cities, paired with an expanding grid of railways, reshaped the local geography by eclipsing the status of older interior cities, and pushing the Korean dwellers to the outskirts and hinterlands.[113] By the time of annexation, steady streams of Japanese migrants came to dominate Korea's urban landscape, occupying the heart of cities such as Pusan, Masan, Mokp'o, Inch'ŏn, and Sinŭiju, where they formed almost half of the population and "kept the Korean masses at bay simply by sheer force of number and density."[114]

The world of settlers that emerged in these cities and along new railway lines was culturally distinct but by no means homogeneous. Japanese migrants were so diverse that to speak of them in terms of a single category would not be useful. Hailing from throughout the archipelago, Japanese in Korea constituted a cultural hodgepodge of emigrants who spoke in diverse regional dialects, followed different customs, and maintained sentimental ties to their places of origin through prefectural associations (*kenjinkai*) or native place associations (*dōkokujinkai*), institutions unique to "new territories" (*shinkaichi*) that "exert[ed] considerable influence" over settler politics.[115]

Tremendous diversity in class, social status, income, and occupation characterized each local Japanese community. If colonialism was largely driven by a bourgeois ethos in the late nineteenth and twentieth centuries,[116] the process of overseas settlement most assuredly was not.

---

112. Toyoda 1963, 16.

113. Delissen 2000, 139. For a tour of the Japanese settlements around Korea, see Duus 1995, 325–34.

114. Duus 1995, 334.

115. *Chōsen kōron*, June 1935, 68. On the *kenjinkai* of settlers from the Hokuriku prefectures (Fukui, Ishikawa, Toyama, and Niigata), see Ogino 1927, 251–72.

116. Cooper and Stoler 1997, 2–4.

Table 1: Growth of Japanese Population in Korea, 1880–1944

| | 1880 | 1890 | 1900 | 1910 | 1920 | 1930 | 1940 | 1944 |
|---|---|---|---|---|---|---|---|---|
| Male | 550 | 4,564 | 8,768 | 92,751 | 185,560 | 260,391 | 356,226 | 345,561 |
| Female | 285 | 2,681 | 7,061 | 78,792 | 161,059 | 241,476 | 333,564 | 567,022 |
| TOTAL | 835 | 7,245 | 15,829 | 171,543 | 347,850 | 501,867 | 689,790 | 912,583 |

SOURCES: Tange 1943, 3–4 (for 1880–1940); Chōsen Sōtokufu, *Jinkō chōsa kekka hōkoku* 1944, 1 (for 1944).

Table 2: Growth of Japanese Population in Cities, 1890–1940

| City | 1890 | 1900 | 1910 | 1920 | 1930 | 1940 |
|---|---|---|---|---|---|---|
| Pusan | 4,344 | 5,758 | 24,936 | 33,085 | 44,273 | 54,266 |
| Wŏnsan | 680 | 1,578 | 4,636 | 7,134 | 9,334 | 12,923 |
| Seoul | 609 | 2,115 | 38,397 | 65,617 | 97,758 | 150,627 |
| Inch'ŏn | 1,612 | 4,208 | 11,126 | 11,281 | 11,238 | 18,088 |
| Mokp'o | | 894 | 3,612 | 5,273 | 8,003 | 8,018 |
| Chinnamp'o | | 339 | 4,199 | 4,793 | 5,894 | 6,879 |
| Kunsan | | 488 | 3,737 | 5,659 | 8,781 | 9,901 |
| Masan | | 252 | 7,081 | 4,172 | 5,559 | 5,643 |
| P'yŏngyang | | 159 | 6,917 | 16,289 | 18,157 | 27,635 |
| Taegu | | | 6,492 | 11,942 | 29,633 | 19,506 |
| Sinŭiju | | | 2,742 | 3,824 | 7,907 | 9,431 |
| Kaesŏng | | | (1,470) | (1,212) | 1,390 | 1,858 |
| Ch'ŏngjin | | | (2,182) | 4,114 | 8,355 | 27,805 |
| Hamhŭng | | | (1,383) | (3,097) | 7,096 | 10,929 |
| Taejŏng | | | | (4,164) | (7,262) | 9,550 |
| Chŏnju | | | (1,541) | (2,804) | (6,484) | 6,338 |
| Kwangju | | | (1,326) | (2,825) | (8,160) | 8,293 |
| % URBAN | 100.0 | 99.8 | 66.4 | 52.5 | 56.8 | 56.2 |

SOURCES: Naikaku Tōkeikyoku, ed., *Nihon teikoku tōkei nenkan 1890, 1900*; Kankoku Tōkanfu 1909; and Chōsen Sōtokufu, *Chōsen Sōtokufu tōkei nenpō* 1911–1944.
NOTE: Figures in parentheses indicate the number of Japanese residents in a district (*gun*).

Although the British, from aristocrats down to the working classes, established residence across the empire,[117] the Japanese in Korea, like the

117. British civil administrators and military officers were generally drawn from the middle class (Gann 1984, 521), but the social composition of local settlers in Africa was quite diverse. Southern Rhodesia attracted British mostly of lower-class origins,

French in Algeria, stood out in fully replicating the metropolitan social hierarchy (including its lowest strata) in a single territory. Geographical proximity and the ease of travel ensured that this remained a permanent characteristic of Japanese colonists on the peninsula. One Korean-language paper observed in 1924 that the Japanese pattern of seizing "ancestral lands of several thousand years" in Korea was rivaled by the English in Ireland, but that in their range of settlers, the Japanese were matched by no one: "Not only landlords and merchants, but everyone from railway and postal clerks to, outrageously, rickshaw haulers, deliverymen, servants, and even tenant farmers board a ship from Japan." "Consequently," the paper lamented, "Koreans lose not merely the only land they own, but nearly all of their jobs."[118]

From the beginning, the Japanese in Korea remained highly mobile. Early emigrants tended to seek quick money, without much thought of settling down. As Japanese political control over Korea stabilized after 1905, however, a growing number of emigrants came over with their families, as indicated by a gender ratio that became more equal over time (see Table 1).[119] The proportion of females in the settler population stayed high, with their rate of growth outpacing that of males from the mid-1920s. This demographic trend distinguished Korea as a relatively more "settled" territory than Taiwan, Karafuto, or the South Sea islands,[120] not to mention European overseas colonies where single men vastly outnumbered women among migrants from the metropole.[121]

---

for instance, and Kenya was socially and politically dominated by aristocratic farmers (Kennedy 1987, 92–94), though poor Europeans who failed to make ends meet in South Africa continued to migrate and settle there (Elkins 2005, 10, 15). As for Portuguese settlers in Mozambique and Angola, before their central government strengthened its commitment to Africa in the 1950s, they remained a humble class of poor farmers, planters, traders, and political exiles, with a small but growing number of soldiers and civil servants (Penvenne 2005, 83–84; A. Roberts 1986, 501–31).

118. *Tonga ilbo*, 24 February 1924.

119. In the 1880s and 1890s, women constituted about 30 to 40 percent of the Japanese population, but this figure rose to 45 percent in the 1900s (due largely to the growing number of geisha and waitresses) and remained at this level through the 1920s (Tange 1943, 3–4).

120. "Chōsen ni okeru naichijin seikatsu no kōsatsu," *Ryokujin* 3 (September 1935): 76–77.

121. Prochaska 1990, 20.

Table 3: Occupations of Japanese Residents in Korea, End of 1907

| Occupation | Number of employed | Number of family members | Total | % |
|---|---|---|---|---|
| Agriculture | 1,298 | 2,251 | 3,549 | 4 |
| Fishing | 1,218 | 1,353 | 2,571 | 3 |
| Manufacturing | 4,070 | 6,677 | 10,747 | 11 |
| Commerce | 12,571 | 22,407 | 34,978 | 36 |
| Officials | | | | |
| Government officials | 3,940 | 6,052 | 9,992 | 10 |
| Public officials | 221 | 442 | 663 | |
| Laborers | 4,405 | 5,476 | 9,881 | 10 |
| Geisha, waitresses | 2,562 | 113 | 2,675 | 3 |
| Professionals | | | | 2 |
| Doctors | 206 | 461 | 667 | |
| Midwives | 80 | 83 | 163 | |
| Teachers | 252 | 270 | 522 | |
| Journalists | 119 | 233 | 352 | |
| Lawyers/prosecutors | 25 | 45 | 70 | |
| Buddhist monks/missionaries | 86 | 84 | 170 | |
| Shinto priests | 10 | 27 | 37 | |
| Miscellaneous | 7,264 | 10,487 | 17,751 | 18 |
| Unemployed | 423 | 2,791 | 3,214 | 3 |
| TOTAL | 38,749 | 59,252 | 98,001 | 100 |

SOURCES: Tōkanfu 1909, 46–47.

As the resident Japanese community stabilized, it became increasingly middle-class in composition. Beneath a transient group of elite bureaucrats and company managers developed a substantial number of more permanent settlers who represented a hybrid of "old" and "new" middle classes. In the early colonial period, the "old middle class" of retail merchants, wholesalers, and petty manufacturers made up the largest social category of Japanese residents. They supplied goods and services to a growing "new middle class" of corporate employees, professionals, technicians, and engineers, in addition to administrative clerks and officials who staffed the expanding bureaucratic apparatus of Japanese rule.[122]

122. Although this reflected the pattern of social stratification in the metropole, the pace of growth of the white-collar population was faster in overseas settlements than

Table 4: Occupations of Japanese Residents in Korea, 1910–1940

| | 1910 | 1920 | 1925 | 1930 | 1935 | 1940 |
|---|---|---|---|---|---|---|
| Agriculture, forestry, livestock farming | (20,623) | 39,894 | 39,030 | 42,093 | 37,321 | 32,980 |
| Fishing, salt manufacturing | | 10,921 | 12,802 | 12,603 | 10,473 | 9,935 |
| Manufacturing | 26,811 | 59,895 | 66,864 | 72,434 | 80,606 | 144,937 |
| Commerce, transportation | 67,625 | 117,289 | 133,273 | 147,438 | 175,118 | 191,247 |
| Officials, professionals | 41,269 | 102,022 | 140,925 | 176,795 | 235,964 | 258,260 |
| Other occupations | 44,475 | 12,928 | 21,362 | 31,892 | 22,914 | 28,615 |
| Unemployed, unknown | 9,886 | 4,901 | 10,484 | 18,612 | 21,032 | 23,816 |
| TOTAL | 210,689 | 347,850 | 424,740 | 501,867 | 583,428 | 689,790 |

SOURCE: Chōsen Sōtokufu, *Chōsen Sōtokufu tōkei nenpō* 1911–1940.
NOTES: Figure in parentheses for 1910 combines agriculture, forestry, and fishing. Classifications are slightly different for the year 1940: the category "Manufacturing" combines figures for mining (22,273) and manufacturing (122,664); "Commerce, transportation" combines figures for commerce (147,346) and transportation (43,901).

From the beginning of Japanese migration in the 1880s, local settlers more or less managed their own daily affairs. In treaty ports like Pusan where the Japanese population mushroomed in no time, they set up chambers of commerce to oversee their daily economic activities,[123] before the system of local autonomy (*chihō jichi*) was fully implemented in metropolitan cities, towns, and villages in 1888.[124] These chambers of

on the home islands. By the 1930s, as indicated by their higher tax payment and lower rate of unemployment, settlers on average enjoyed better living standards than metropolitan residents, and had acquired a solidly middle-class character ("Chōsen ni okeru naichijin seikatsu no kōsatsu," *Ryokujin* 3 [September 1935]: 77–80).

123. They were established first in Pusan (1876) and subsequently in other treaty ports—Wŏnsan (1881), Inch'ŏn (1885), Seoul (1887), and Mokp'o (1890)—and after the Russo-Japanese War in the cities of Chinnamp'o, Kunsan, Masan, Taegu, and Ch'ŏnjin (Chōsen Sōtokufu, *Saikin Chōsen jijō yōran* 1912, 2:319–20).

124. Kang Jae-ho 2001, 143. We should note, however, that Japan had created a system of prefectural assemblies in 1878, and well before this local notables had set up voluntary political associations all over Japan (Kyu Hyun Kim 2007, Chapter 5).

commerce promoted mutual aid, mediated conflicts,[125] and regulated dubious commercial practices among the emigrants to prevent a loss of trust from Korean customers. They also petitioned the authorities repeatedly to remove all tariffs on Korean imports and to build better port and harbor facilities, more telegraph and shipping services, and new roads and railways.[126]

For dealing with public affairs beyond commerce, settlers by the late 1880s were also permitted by local consuls to elect their own headmen and convene residents' assemblies.[127] These steps culminated in the creation of residents' associations (*kyoryūmindan*) in eleven cities in early 1905. Although the residents' associations were placed under the authority of the Residency-General and each association under the vigilant supervision of his local representative, they allowed local setters to exercise a wide range of self-governing responsibilities. Empowered with an ability to issue bonds and levy taxes and fees on local Japanese, residents' associations granted settlers a stable and sufficient flow of funds for building and managing public utilities in their communities.[128] From water supply to schools, Shinto shrines, and medical facilities, they took on the same tasks that were financially borne by local governments in Japan.[129]

The maintenance of settler health was deemed particularly important for expanding Japanese influence on the peninsula and for preventing the spread of epidemics to the homeland. To this end, residents' associations offered smallpox vaccination, created hygiene associations, invited

---

125. This was, as one guidebook noted, where the greatest Japanese commercial weakness lay, in contrast to the solidarity of Chinese merchants (Arakawa 1906, 180–81).

126. Representatives of regional chambers also convened a joint forum every year to discuss strategies of promoting settler interests vis-à-vis Korean merchants, "bandits," and even newcomers from the metropole. See the proposals discussed at the seventh and eighth general assemblies of the Japanese Chambers of Commerce in Korea in Keijō Kyoryūmindan Yakusho 1912, 334–36.

127. Kimura 1993, 29, 36.

128. Tōkanfu 1907, furoku, 12–13. During protectorate rule, settlers in the eleven cities of Seoul, Inch'ŏn, Pusan, Kunsan, Chinnamp'o, P'yŏngyang, Masan, Wŏnsan, Mokp'o, Taegu, and Sinŭiju, each of which had one thousand or more Japanese residents, managed their communities through residents' associations. Others clustered in smaller numbers in another dozen cities or large towns along the new trunk railroad lines, and formed Japanese clubs (*Nihonjinkai*) to conduct a similar range of activities.

129. Gluck 1985, 37.

doctors, and quarantined cholera patients. They also administered physical examinations of geisha and prostitutes for syphilis, measures considered critical for sustaining the virility of empire-builders.[130] Of no lesser concern to the settler leaders was to keep up the appearance of fellow migrants. "Despite the status of our country as an advanced nation," they bemoaned, Japanese often bared their bodies in broad daylight and hawked their merchandise by shamelessly walking the streets in shorts with a hand towel wrapped around their head, looking "inferior to Koreans." To regulate such "disgraceful behavior and unbearably barbaric appearance," in 1904 residents' representatives of Mokp'o, Inch'ŏn, and Seoul petitioned Japanese consuls around Korea, urging them to keep newcomers under surveillance and commensurate with their nation's claim to a civilized status.[131]

## *The Making of Seoul as a Settler City*

Nowhere did the Japanese more deeply inscribe their influence than in Seoul, the traditional capital of the Chosŏn dynasty. Renamed Keijō under Japanese rule, Seoul was a center of both consumption and administration, dominated by bureaucrats, officials, and company employees. After 1910, the city expanded with its merger with the port town of Yongsan (Ryūzan)—the headquarters of the Chōsen Army and a nucleus of railway transportation—and supplanted Pusan as home to the largest number of Japanese residents (Table 2). Transforming the royal capital of Korea into the city of Keijō replicated the emerging imperial order on a variety of levels. As a number of studies have recently shown, that order manifested itself in how railways and electric tramlines were laid, streets were aligned and named, neighborhoods were zoned and boundaries delimited, public utilities were distributed, buildings were designed and located, and social relations were mapped on all of these physical layouts.[132] The governing logic behind colonial

---

130. Keijō Kyoryūmindan Yakusho 1912, 339; Kimura 1989, 73. For an analysis of Japanese preoccupation with sanitation that informed the construction of early colonial Seoul, see Henry 2005.

131. Keijō Kyoryūmindan Yakusho 1912, 134.

132. For a detailed analysis of this process of transformation, see Chŏn 2001; Yŏm 2004; Henry 2008. For a sample of the most recent Korean works on the urban his-

urban design was to impose order, by drawing on the authority gained from the *appearance* of rationality,[133] and above all to impress upon local inhabitants the power of colonial rule by supplanting icons of Korean royalty with new architectural symbols of Japanese supremacy.[134]

Although most of these projects were undertaken by the colonial state, local settlers had already embarked on their own space- and boundary-making before 1910. The Korean government initially confined Japanese residents to a tiny area at the foot of the Namsan peak dubbed "muddy town" (*deiken* or *chinkōkai*), an area of relative neglect that had been inhabited by impoverished *yangban* elites and Chinese merchants in the Chosŏn period. Within a few decades, Japanese settlers and state investments transformed this strip of land into a mini-Tokyo that they christened Honmachi. In building the basis for this "Japantown," settlers to a considerable extent acted independently from the local authorities, a process vividly chronicled in a memoir by Nakai Kitarō (1864–1924), a newspaper man who headed the Keijō Kyoryūmindan (Seoul Residents' Association) in its early years. In planning Honmachi, Nakai apparently envisioned replacing existing Korean dwellings with two-storied brick buildings for Japanese residents to rent "just as the Meiji state had done along the streets of the Ginza." As a first step, he mobilized sixteen fire fighters to uproot a Korean shed and simply "abandon it to the nearby street."[135] To create an additional source of revenue for the residents' association, especially for defraying the much-needed costs of settler children's education and public hygiene projects, Nakai also proposed the construction of pleasure quarters (*yūkaku*).[136] Another former resident recounted how the Japanese made Seoul their own by inscribing their culture and forebears in the nomenclature of the land they settled. They renamed Korean towns and streets with Japanese words such as "the rising sun," names of Japanese military officers stationed there,

---

tory of Seoul, see "Colonial Modernity and the Making of Modern Korean Cities," a special issue of *Korea Journal*.

133. See Mitchell 1988.

134. For a detailed study on this process, see Kim Paeg-yŏng 2003, 76–102.

135. Nakai 1915, 113.

136. Akahagi Yosaburō, "Yūkakugai nijūgonenshi," *Chōsen kōron*, October 1935, 47.

and toponyms inspired by the famous cherry blossoms in Yoshino (Nara prefecture).[137]

Settlers pushed ahead with these steps in blithe disregard for official caution. The Japanese legation and the consulate, anxious to avert diplomatic trouble, initially opposed the idea of renaming roads without negotiating with the Korean government; they also prohibited the creation of brothels, out of concern that it would blemish their national reputation.[138] Flouting such official orders, Nakai and other settler leaders in Seoul resorted to directly petitioning the Ministry of Foreign Affairs in Tokyo, "even demanding that the consul be replaced." After aggressive lobbying, they ultimately persuaded the authorities in 1904 to approve a licensed pleasure quarter, laying the basis for what became the city's red-light district, Shinmachi (also known as "Iromachi").[139] Settlers and local officials may have shared a vision of transforming Korea in the image of their homeland, but the politics governing the construction of colonial space often set their interests in conflict, exposing the fragility of authority the state exerted over its subjects.[140]

By the time of annexation, a dual structure characteristic of a "settler colonial city" had emerged in Seoul.[141] The city was roughly divided along an east-west axis, with the street of Chongno becoming a symbolic border that separated the Japanese Namch'on (South Village) from the Korean Pukch'on (North Village). The majority of Koreans lived to the north of Ch'ŏnggyech'ŏn, along the southern foot of Pugaksan, gradually moving outward to suburbs like Ch'ŏngniangni, Wangsimni, and

---

137. Soga Tsutomu, "Ōhi jiken no tenmatsu," in Fujimura 1927b, 66–67.

138. Ibid., 65, 206–7. But while regulating illegal prostitution, from the 1880s the Japanese government permitted the management of brothels (*kashizashiki*) under the name of "restaurants" (*ryōriten*) and the operation of legal prostitutes under the names of entertainers (*geigi*) or waitresses (*shakufu*) in Japanese settlements (Song Yŏn-ok 1993, 54).

139. Imamura Tomo, "Nijūnen mae no Chōsen," in Fujimura 1927b, 207.

140. Henry 2006 and 2008. The colonial state's respatialization of city space through what Todd Henry calls "officially-sanctioned, social" (*kōkyō*) projects instigated a decades-long process of contestation with local inhabitants, including Japanese settlers who wished to reorder the city around their settlements centered on Honmachi. This involved a fascinating competition between settler-built Keijō Shrine and the state-built Chōsen Shrine in the 1920s (2006, 372–99).

141. David Prochaska offers a useful typology of a "settler colonial city" (1990, 22–25). This dual structure was also observed in other cities, including Pusan, Taegu, and Mokp'o. See "Colonial Modernity and the Making of Modern Korean Cities," 5–132.

Map'o. Japanese settlers, by contrast, concentrated in land that sprawled from the slope of Namsan to Yongsan and stretched southward beyond Ch'ŏnggyech'ŏn.[142]

A rough dichotomy between the two "villages," which more or less remained in place to the end of colonial rule,[143] was etched in the local terrain by a variety of markers: street names,[144] architectural styles, the distribution of modern amenities, and everyday cultural practices (of which more later). These boundaries became immediately perceptible to a visitor crossing Ch'ŏnggyech'ŏn and entering Honmachi. Its narrow streets that stretched five blocks (*chōme*) were fronted with a jumble of family-based retail stores, selling the entire range of Japanese goods, from kimono and books to confectionary, and imported Western items. With its alleys of thatched-roof tile houses standing behind the store-fronts, Honmachi evoked a familiar downtown neighborhood in Tokyo. Japanese residents came to dub the area "Keijō's Ginza" after Tokyo's high-class shopping district, and not least for its real estate value, which fetched several hundred yen per *tsubo* (about 3.3 square meters) by the mid-1920s.[145] Around Honmachi also unfolded a modernizing and cosmopolitan landscape that boasted mastery of the latest techniques of urban design, crisscrossed by wide thoroughfares, and flecked with banks, companies, hotels, a post office, a chamber of commerce, and other multistory Western-style buildings of brick and stone.[146] The

---

142. Keijō-fu 1941, vol. 3: 658. For a detailed comparison of the socio-economic conditions of the two "villages," see Son 1996, 355–98.

143. This is a general conclusion reached by the existing studies on the history of colonial Seoul, which are primarily based on the use of population data and statistics compiled by the Government-General's "national strength surveys" (*kokusei chōsa*). For a detailed study that traces the changing patterns of residence for Japanese and Koreans in Seoul from the late 1920s to 1942, see Sŏ 2000.

144. Even after the old district system was abolished and new uniform administrative boundaries were imposed in 1914, separate names of *chō* (K. *chŏng*) and *dō* (K. *tong*) continued to be used to distinguish Japanese and Korean neighborhoods (Keijō-fu 1936, 2:536). For a full list of Japanese *chō* and their etymology, see ibid., 536–40.

145. Fujii Kamewaka 1926, 71.

146. Many illustrated guidebooks appeared to showcase Seoul as an emblem of Japanese modernity, built by colonial architects and planners who had mastered Western aesthetics and techniques of urban design (which in turn were often exported back to the metropole). One such guidebook takes the readers on a visual tour through the

Fig. 1 Honmachi in Seoul, circa 1930

brightness of Honmachi, teeming with entrepreneurial vigor and well-lit by gas and electric street lights, one gazetteer observed, contrasted starkly with the darkness of the Korean town marked by the lack of creativity, organization, and hygiene.[147] The new spatial order also manifested itself in an uneven distribution of modern amenities—electricity, tap water, gas, and sewers, each regarded as "a barometer of civilization"—which spread more quickly in Japanese settlements than in the suburban and rural peripheries inhabited by Koreans.[148]

---

city by providing an annotated picture of the façade of each landmark—such as the Seoul Chamber of Commerce, Seoul Station, the Chōsen Hotel, and the Mitsukoshi Department Store—so that they could marvel at its architectural beauty and savor the "pride of our Chōsen," just as visitors would physically stand in front of the building (Fujii Kamewaka 1926; Koshizawa Akira, quoted in Sand 2005, 217).

147. Oka Ryōsuke 1915, 278–80.

148. For a comparison of Japanese and Korean use of "cultural facilities," including schools, postal and telegraph service, water supply, gas, and electricity, see *Chōsen oyobi Manshū*, October 1915, 9. In 1921, 87 percent of Japanese households throughout the peninsula had electricity, as opposed to only 20 percent of Korean households (*Chōsen oyobi Manshū*, May 1927, 46–47).

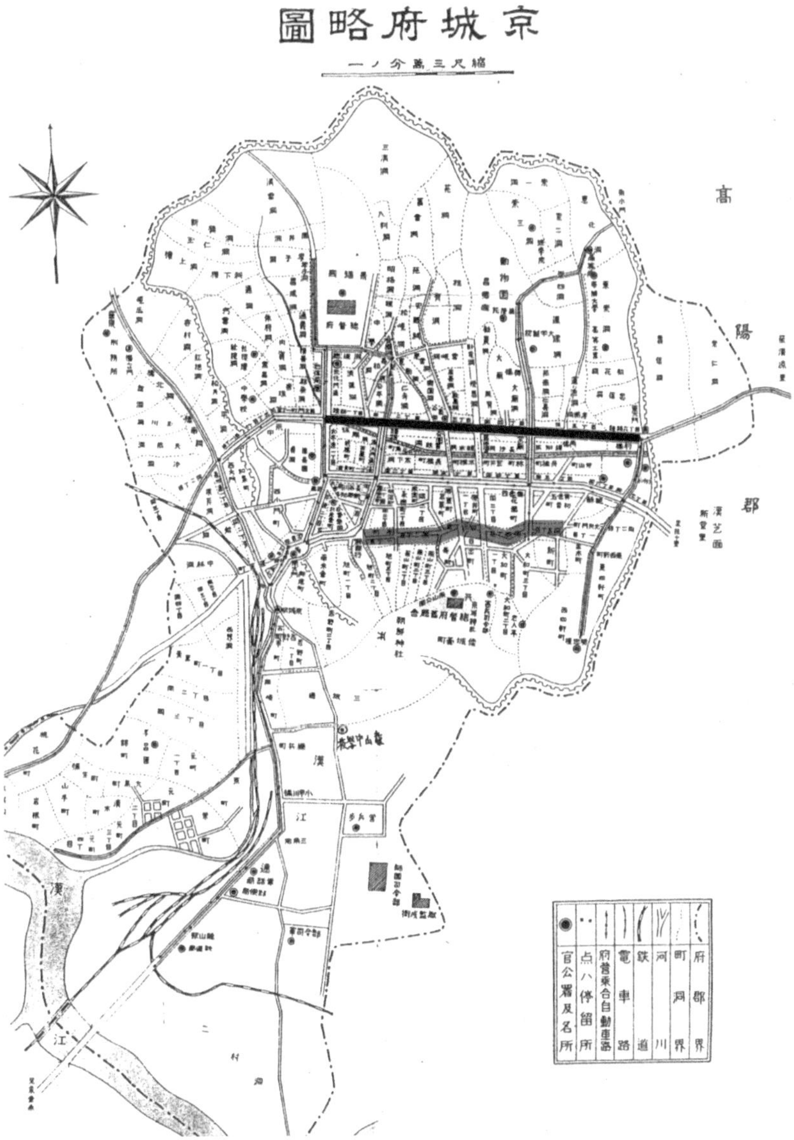


Map 3 Seoul, circa 1930.
Solid black bar denotes Chongno street; shaded gray area denotes Honmachi.

This spatial-cum-temporal imbalance, created by colonial architects and urban planners, persisted even as roads, streetlights, and multistoried structures spread north of the Chongno thoroughfare in the 1930s. By then, the Japanese settlement bore only a slight resemblance to the muddy "nest of beggars" it had been. At once quintessentially Japanese and highly cosmopolitan, the colonial city of Keijō afforded emigrants access to both the comforting sight of their culture and the dazzling spectacle of modernity. As Honmachi acquired further glitter and glamour in its architectural splendor and the bewildering array of consumer goods it offered, as the iconoclastic Yi Sang (1910–1937) described in his autobiographical novel in 1936, crossing into the southern half of the city for Koreans could become a moment of alienated experience, for it captivated them as much as reminding them of their own "pre-modernity."[149]

## *Everyday Life and Culture of Settlers*

In this colonial space, where a dichotomy of progress and backwardness mapped onto ethnic hierarchy, "the Japanese and Koreans were living 'together' as if 'water and oil,'" observed Watanabe Manabu during his visit to Seoul in the late colonial period.[150] Rather than a melting pot, what visitors like Watanabe saw were Japanese cultural enclaves floating in a sea of Koreans—not unlike the "islands of white" the British settlers fashioned on the Highlands of Kenya and Southern Rhodesia.[151] Like overseas migrants elsewhere, Japanese settlers tried to replicate their home environment in Korea by transplanting metropolitan customs and institutions, an effort most fully undertaken in cities.[152] In order to maintain their national identity, rendered fragile by distance from home and the effects of overseas living, they sought to maintain a strictly Japanese lifestyle in terms of diet, shelter, dress, and language.[153] In this cultural enclave, the rhythms and cycles of daily life revolved around the Japanese national calendar. Settler families followed Japanese traditional customs and rituals through the seasons—the Boys' Festival and the Girls'

---

149. Kawamura 2000, 107. See also Sin Myŏng-jik 2003, Chapter 1.

150. Watanabe and Umeda 1980, Preface.

151. Kennedy 1987. But Southern Rhodesia lagged behind Kenya in the development of white highlands, most of which was based on land speculation.

152. Prochaska 1990, 22.

153. The use of standard Japanese (then being institutionalized as a mother tongue on the home islands) proved instrumental in transforming members of the multi-dialect expatriate community into a community of national subjects coextensive with the metropole (Sakai, de Bary, and Iyotani 2005, 17–31).

Festival in the spring, and *obon* (a Buddhist commemoration of the dead) in the summer, for instance. They also observed Japanese national holidays such as Kigensetsu (National Founding Day, 11 February) and Tenchōsetsu (Emperor's Birthday, 3 November), which celebrated the emperor in his new dual guise as a modern sovereign and an emblem of Japan's timeless tradition.[154]

If "clubs" were symbols and citadels of white power in European colonies,[155] the social life of Japanese settlers in Korea revolved around shopping and leisure, pleasure quarters, and Shinto shrines—ubiquitous features of overseas Japanese settlements across Asia.[156] For most settlers, especially women, a local Japanese commercial complex (*shōtengai*) became their central universe where they purchased all daily necessities and tableware imported from the metropole (which, reflective of the demographic dominance of Kansai natives in the colony, exuded the "gaudy and rich" flavors of Osaka).[157] As the settler community became more white collar in character to project its image as a classless society, conspicuous consumption became a mark of colonial living. Overseas allowance (*zaikin kahō*), which amounted to 50 to 60 percent of a regular salary,[158] allowed corporate employees and public servants to relish a life of luxury, as demonstrated by the flamboyant lifestyle of their wives, whose favorite pastime was shopping at Mitsukoshi and local drapers in Honmachi.[159] For other migrants, too, life in the colony generally appeared to be easier than at home. Daily necessities were often lower-priced than in the metropole,[160] and Japanese of all classes consumed great amounts of alcohol and cigarettes, both relatively inexpensive items due to their lower taxes in Korea.[161] Wide wage differentials cre-

---

154. They are part of what Takashi Fujitani calls "mnemonic sites" that Meiji leaders painstakingly devised to make emperor part of the everyday practice of the people (1996, especially Chapter 3).

155. Kennedy 1987, 179–86; Sinha 2001; Elkins 2005, 11.

156. Hashiya 2004, 81.

157. Zenkoku Shinbun Tōkyō Rengōsha 1912, 123–24.

158. Aoyagi 1916, 246.

159. Every time the Patriotic Women's Association run by these elite women held a general assembly in Seoul, it was said, all luxury items at Mitsukoshi would be sold out (*Chōsen kōron*, March 1914, 80).

160. *Chōsen* (Chōsen Zasshisha), October 1910, 7.

161. *Chōsen* (Chōsen Zasshisha), July 1911, 83.

ated by the colonial labor market, moreover, allowed settlers to hire Koreans for a variety of menial jobs around the house: babysitters to raise their children, maids or *omoni* (literally, "mother"; an older domestic helper) to assist in household chores, and farmhands to tend their fields. This freed time for leisure, such as trips to hot springs and weekend excursions to a beach in Masan, an amusement park in Pusan, or the famous zoo within Ch'anggyŏng Palace in Seoul.[162] Although settler society in reality remained highly stratified,[163] upper-class Japanese and those of more modest means occupied the same cultural universe, bound by a common privilege of belonging to the dominant ethnic group.

Local settlers also created their own entertainment complex. In Pusan, Ōike Chūsuke (1856–1930) and other leaders raised money and invited architects from Osaka to build several theaters, which featured Japanese plays, from *sōshi* (patriot) dramas and the *naniwabushi* storytelling to *nō* plays and *jōruri* puppet shows, that transported the audience back to their cultural roots.[164] Movies also became a popular form of mass entertainment by the 1910s, with Seoul's four movie theaters showing both Japanese and imported Western films accompanied by silent-film narrators (*benshi*).[165] In rural areas, where settlers lived more modestly, local Japanese families regularly socialized with one another over traditional games such as *go*, *shōgi*, *hanafuda*, cards, and mahjong, or more cultured hobbies such as *haiku*, *tanka*, calligraphy, flower arrangement, and tea. These social get-togethers, as recalled by a former teacher who lived in a remote village of South Chŏlla province, offered rural settlers solace and a momentary escape from "the loneliness of living as an ethnic minority amid a sea of Koreans."[166]

While wives shopped on the streets of Honmachi, their husbands just as frequently went pleasure-seeking in Shinmachi, the city's famous red light district, where they enjoyed Japanese geisha who offered them

---

162. Kimura 1996, 55.

163. For a detailed discussion of the internal diversity of settlers, see Cohen 2006, Chapter 2.

164. See Kagaya 2001. One of the theaters constructed was the Pusan-za, a three-storied theater built in 1907, which boasted a 1,540-seat capacity unrivaled in Korea and Manchuria at the time (*Chōsen no jitsugyō*, August 1907, 47–48).

165. *Mankan no jitsugyō* 96; *Chōsen oyobi Manshū*, February 1916, 122–24; and January 1922, 118–20.

166. Iwasaki 1966, 187.

food, drinks, dance, and often sex. Such pleasure quarters were completed in Pusan in 1900, Inch'ŏn in 1902, and Seoul in 1905.[167] Until the 1920s, Japanese prostitutes outnumbered Koreans in the trade, catering to both Japanese and Korean men, but Japanese men also actively sought out Korean women as sexual partners and female companions.[168] Bureaucrats and business elites patronized high-class Korean entertainers or *kisaeng*, who soon became a fixture in Japanese dinner parties at the local restaurant Kagetsu,[169] whereas Japanese shop clerks apparently frequented low-class Korean prostitutes called *kalbo*.[170]

Shinto shrines, as spiritual guardians of national identity, were also ubiquitous icons of Japanese colonial culture. Like brothels, these sprang up quickly across the peninsula.[171] Early emigrants to Korea actively campaigned for creating in their cities a branch of Ise Shrine, where the sun goddess Amaterasu was enshrined, as a means of "solidifying the [Japanese] motivation for permanent settlement."[172] It was to this end

---

167. Hashiya 2004, 98. For the history of the development of pleasure quarters in Seoul, see "Keijō karyūkai ryakushi," *Chōsen oyobi Manshū*, November 1921, 117–21.

168. Prostitutes, entertainers, and waitresses made up the majority of early female emigrants (Table 3; Kankoku Tōkanfu 1909, 56), with the category of "entertainers" constituting a high proportion of lower-class Japanese residents well into the 1930s (Song Yŏn-ok 2002, 70–74). Around 1887 the local consulate authorities in Seoul apparently tried to forbid Japanese prostitution with Korean men, but the ban was later removed (*Chōsen* [Chōsen Zasshisha], May 1908, 27). In fact, as Barbara Brooks notes, Japanese women were encouraged to marry Korean men as part of assimilation policy (2005, 307–8). Meanwhile, Japanese settlers in the 1890s began inviting Korean prostitutes and entertainers into their communities especially in Inch'ŏn and in Pusan, where local brothel owners hired many of them by taking advantage of their cheap labor (Song Yŏn-ok 1993, 59–60).

169. Imamura Tomo 1927, 209–10. One former head waitress of Kagetsu recollected: "After the Former Resident-General Itō came to Korea, [our business] became so hectic with parties one after the other" (*Keijō shinpō*, 3 February 1912). Japanese patronage of *kisaeng* continued through the end of the colonial period. Interview with Kudō Masumi (former employee of the colonial police affairs bureau), 26 February 2002; Kudō 1983, 128–129, 130.

170. *Chōsen oyobi Manshū*, March 1914, 76.

171. Out of their own pockets, Japanese residents invited carpenters from home to build Buddhist temples (which reflected the religious orientation of the majority of settlers) as well as shrines and managed them on their own until 1915 when they were brought under unified official administration (Keijō-fu 1941, 3:421–22). For studies on Japanese colonial shrines, see Suga 2004; Aoi 2005; and Henry 2006.

172. Kimura 1996, 52; Aoi 2005, 148, 153.

that Nanzan Shrine (renamed Keijō Shrine in 1912) was built by local settlers in Seoul as a miniature of Ise Shrine, where they could daily affirm their emotive connection to their homeland and their blood ties to their imperial ancestors.[173] Around the colonial shrines soon evolved a web of patriotic rituals, which mirrored the metropolitan practices of national remembrance that emerged during the Russo-Japanese War.[174] Local shrines were used to conduct memorial services for the war dead, celebrate victories, and hold festivals in honor of the nation's mythical founder, Emperor Jinmu, all of which provided occasions for unifying the sentiment of emigrants of diverse origins with collective *banzai* salutes to the emperor.[175] Through this empire-wide nexus of national communion, emperor ideology spread to overseas peripheries—or, to borrow the words of Carol Gluck, became naturalized as "a common language"—almost as quickly as it diffused to villages on the home islands.[176] In 1907, when the Japanese Crown Prince [later Taishō Emperor] visited Seoul accompanied by a group of "military heroes," a patriotic crowd of local settlers (including children), flush with euphoria about Japan's recent victory over Russia, greeted the imperial entourage "in tears."[177] And five years later when the prince ascended to the throne, Japanese-owned businesses "from eating houses to public baths" shut their doors to celebrate the joyous occasion.[178]

Invented tradition begot further inventions. To the public commemorations imported from Japan, settlers added their own rituals to celebrate their identity as overseas pioneers. Every October in Seoul, for instance, local Japanese residents organized a "Keijō Shrine Autumn Festival," whose splendor recalled the famous Hakata Festival and regional festivities of southwestern Japan from which the majority of emigrants came. On this gala occasion, a portable shrine (*mikoshi*) was

---

173. Aoi 2005, 39.

174. Seraphim 2006, 14.

175. The Jinmu Emperor's Festival was held on 3 April every year since the protectorate period (*Chōsen oyobi Manshū*, April 1915, 7). For an example of a commemorative festival to honor the war dead (*shōkonsai*) held in 1906 in Seoul, see *Chōsen no Jitsugyō*, December 1906, 41–42.

176. Gluck 1985.

177. Toyoda 1963, 23.

178. Keijō-fu 1941, 3:251, 253.

Figs. 2a–b Keijō Shrine Autumn Festival (*top*) and Keijō Shrine (*bottom*)
SOURCE: Fujita 1978, 5, 10.

carried from Namsan through the area of Yongsan Train Station and back to Namsan, so that Korean residents—whether they liked it or not—were made to see the procession.[179] A route was later extended to Chongno, where the settlers made a brief stop for a further display of their culture.[180] During the festivity, a string of decorated carts furnished by local merchants moved through the streets of Honmachi, lined by exhilarated Japanese residents and curious Korean onlookers. The procession did not merely have the effect of uniting the spectators around the moving image of "an epitome of Japan," as one former settler recalled.[181] It also embodied gender and colonial hierarchies: the masculine grandeur of the portable shrine was balanced with the feminine elegance of Japanese geisha enrobed in ceremonial dress, and from 1915 on with Korean *kisaeng* who joined the parade in "everyday clothes" to mark their lower status.[182] Through such ostentatious displays, settlers constructed and affirmed their "Japaneseness," and demonstrated their presence as the dominant class in the colony.

Yet the world of settlers was not completely sealed from the Koreans who surrounded them. Their daily life, in fact, teemed with cross-cultural encounters not typically seen in European colonial cities. Most colonists in Algiers, Calcutta, and Nairobi, while living surrounded by native servants, isolated themselves in hill stations, white towns, and other protective cocoons of bourgeois culture.[183] In and outside of Seoul, by contrast, Japanese tended to settle and intrude into the local habitat in ways that not only displaced Korean dwellers but implanted themselves in their midst.[184] For this reason, many contemporary observers char-

179. *Chōsen kōron*, November 1913, 58; Sawai 1996, 72–73.

180. Henry 2006, 139.

181. Interview with Hamada Inosaburō, Tokyo, 13 February 2002.

182. Henry 2006, 131–32.

183. Hashiya 2004, 69–80; Osterhammel 2005, 88.

184. In the case of Seoul, after annexation Japanese migrants steadily pushed into Korean residential areas where they had earlier encountered resistance (Chŏn 2001, 168). By 1919, almost every town had some Japanese residents, generating occasional border disputes especially during World War I, when inflation and surging land prices created a serious housing shortage (*Chōsen oyobi Manshū*, October 1911, 51; Keijō-fu 1941, 3:658). The "northern advance" of Japanese settlers picked up pace in the 1920s and accelerated in the 1930s, as new government buildings and company housing complexes were constructed in the northern half of the city (Yŏm 2004, 205–6; Son 1996, 383–84). The urbanization and administrative expansion of Seoul in the mid-1930s further promoted

acterized Korea as a "mixed-residence" (*zakkyo teki*) colony,[185] where the extent of social segregation (which was "determined more by ethnic and racial factors than by class" in European colonial cities[186]) appeared to be less stark. To be sure, colonial life was rife with discrimination: whether on buses, where the Japanese often forced Koreans to give up their seats, or in Japanese shops, where Koreans regardless of class were treated to verbal abuse and often not welcome.[187] But unlike the settler colonies in Africa, where the indigenous population was barred from buses, taxis, clubs, and other public facilities, such spaces were not ethnically segregated in Korea.[188] Nor were disruptive "economic and social contacts" between settlers and native inhabitants regulated by local officials or policed by law.[189] To the contrary, Japanese authorities quite consciously promoted the diffusion and sharing of sanitation facilities, parks, theaters, and even Shinto shrines[190] as part of assimilation policy—or in the words of one local official in Seoul, as a means of spreading the concept of hygiene, an awareness of "communal living," and habits of "hard work and thrift" among the city's Korean residents.[191]

---

the growth of more mixed neighborhoods, especially in the southern part of the city, introducing finer differentiations within the overall dual structure of the city (Sŏ 2000, 245–59).

185. *Chōsen oyobi Manshū*, September 1915, 58; and June 1915, 68. One observer characterized Korea as an "inter-stage colony" to describe the Japanese pattern of penetrating into local Korean habitat (*Chōsen* [Chōsen Zasshisha], May 1911, 48).

186. According to Prochaska, "Classes do form but within the overall racial structure, much as residential segregation by class occurs, especially in the Western community, but within an overarching framework of ethnic and racial segregation" (1990, 20).

187. Such bus incidents are described in Iwasaki 1966, 56. Korean visitors to Japan often drew a contrast between the "kind Japanese" in the metropole and the discriminatory settlers in Korea. For instance, see *Chōsen* (Chōsen Zasshisha), September 1911, 23; and *Yomiuri shinbun*, 29 September 1920.

188. Elkins and Pedersen 2005, 12.

189. Berman and Lonsdale 1992, 121.

190. In 1915, the colonial state entrusted the daily management of shrines to local notables by designating them as shrine representatives (*ujiko sōdai*), in Japanese-dominated *chō* as well as Korean-dominated *dō*, though Koreans were not fully integrated into the shrine management system until 1926 (Aoi 2005, 244–46). For the deeply ambivalent efforts of Korean elite parish leaders to negotiate their terms of inclusion into the settler-led Keijō Shrine festival of 1931, see Henry 2006, 429–32.

191. Shiokawa Ichitarō, "Chōsenjin ni taisuru goraku kikan no setsubi to kairyō o hakare," *Chōsen oyobi Manshū*, May 1911, 16–18; and Henry 2005.

Even Honmachi, a quintessential Japanese town, over time became a contact zone between the two worlds of settlers and Koreans, a shared site of cosmopolitan modernity frequented by residents across differences in class, age, gender, and ethnicity.[192]

This meant that settler communities, and their daily practices, became a crucial medium through which Japanese cultural hegemony took root, modifying Korean tastes, habits, and lifestyles in countless subtle ways. In Seoul, this process spread unevenly along the north-south divide of Chongno, and to a large extent followed the pattern of class stratification in Korean society. Many local *yangban* elites, for instance, patronized Japanese specialty stores and boutiques in Honmachi, purchasing the most "expensive items that even the Japanese could not afford," from suits and shoes to silk handkerchiefs, observed grocer Shin Tatsuma, and "loved newfangled goods more than the Japanese did."[193] Local elite patronage of Japanese shops attested to the existence of a distinctive social pyramid in Korea where wealth and ethnicity were not always perfectly aligned: the colonial "middle class" was dominated by settlers, but the uppermost strata of society were invariably dominated by Korean elites of landed wealth, whose income was unmatched even by the highest ranking bureaucrats, including the Governor-General.[194] Yet consumption of Japanese culture was not limited to the elite. Ordinary Korean residents adopted a wide range of Japanese products and habits, from tea drinking to the use of sugar and soy sauce in cooking, and

---

192. For a fascinating discussion of the diverse Korean experience of the streets of colonial Seoul, see Oh 2008, 83, 92–101.

193. *Chōsen* (Chōsen Zasshisha), April 1910, 83–85. "The most extravagant among the Koreans" was apparently Song Pyŏng-jun, leader of the Ilchinhoe (Chapter 2), whose pattern of purchasing cigarettes, wine, and brandy was comparable to that of the former Resident-General, Itō Hirobumi (*Chōsen oyobi Manshū*, June 1915, 69). The haircut decree issued by the Kabo-reform cabinet in 1895 also boosted the sales of Western clothes, hats, and other accessories sold by local Japanese merchants (Moon 2010, 183).

194. *Chōsen oyobi Manshū*, May 1936, 78; and July 1936, 112–13. This pattern persisted to the end of colonial rule, as corroborated by my interviews with former settlers, who invariably ruminated about how Korean *yangban* families looked down upon Japanese "upstarts" and lived a life of luxury unimaginable to even the richest settlers in the city. An informal roundtable meeting with graduates of the Nanzan Primary School, Tokyo, 21 July 2003.

acquired a taste for Japanese *sake* and sweets.[195] Other reported changes in Korean lifestyle, induced by settlers, included the wearing of colored clothing in place of traditional white dress (*hanbok*), the greater use of soaps for doing laundry,[196] and the practice of midwifery.[197] The use of public baths (*sentō*) also spread to Koreans of all classes. According to one Japanese owner of a public bath in Ch'unch'ŏn, Korean customers he described as "modern" (*haikara*) came every evening and "liked to keep themselves clean more than the Japanese did"—though many public-bath owners also prohibited Korean entry, or created separate tubs for Korean customers.[198]

Colonial encounter was by no means reducible to simple acculturation. Though governed by the context of unequal exchange, contact between Japanese and Koreans was always a two-way dynamic. In what some anthropologists have called "interculturation," the colonizer and the colonized adopted each other's customs, habits, and values, transforming each other's culture, if unevenly and unconsciously, in the process.[199] Japanese settlers, of necessity and on occasion by choice, incorporated Korean customs and acquired new sensibilities through this unplanned process. Most migrants of humble roots, for instance, moved directly into existing Korean homes, rather than build new Japanese- or Western-style houses, and tended to "rent one corner of a native's house with fellow migrants, or share one home with two or three other families."[200] Environmental constraints also made it difficult for settlers to maintain a strictly Japanese lifestyle on Korean soil. The harsh continental winter, for instance, obliged settlers to install a Korean *ondol* (heated floor) at least in one room, a lifestyle that often became

---

195. They also bought mosquito nets, towels, beer, and wine if they were inexpensive, as well as petrol, matches, lamps, cotton and cotton yarn, hardware, and tobacco sold at rural markets (Kimura 1996, 58). On the increasing Korean consumption of Japanese *sake* (*seishu*), see *Chōsen* (Chōsen Zasshisha), April 1910, 85, and July 1911, 78; *CKZ* 126 (June 1926): 9.

196. *CKZ* 153 (September 1928): 11.

197. Yoo 2008, 180.

198. *Chōsen oyobi Manshū*, April 1915, 60; *Chōsen* (Chōsen Zasshisha), August 1911, 87. For the case of bath houses in Chinju, see *Chōsen no jitsugyō*, March 1907, 36.

199. Munasinghe 2006, 555. Anthropologists also use "transculturation" to refer to the development of creole cultures (see Pratt 1992).

200. Zenkoku Shinbun Tōkyō Rengōsha 1912, 124–26.

an addiction "hard to abandon once you have lived in Korea." [201] Some Japanese women wore the Korean *ch'ima* (skirt), especially in the summer, which was considered superior to kimono in terms of comfort and labor efficiency.[202] Korean food remained largely a curiosity in their own kitchens, but Japanese ventured into Chongno to sample the fare at high-class Korean restaurants like Myŏngwŏlgwan, and some developed a taste for local staples like *kimchi* and *koch'ujang* (which Japanese housewives often learned how to make from their housemaids).[203] Many Japanese residents also patronized Korean ginseng products, which boasted a strong sales network that extended to the metropole.[204]

Contact with Koreans transformed settlers in other ways, beyond material aspects of their daily life. Many Japanese reflected, for instance, that they learned to speak more clearly and directly through their long-term business dealings with Korean merchants or daily conversations with their Korean employees—a behavioral change also noted by settlers who grew up in Korea in the 1930s.[205] Korean adherence to Confucian tradition reminded some Japanese of what they might have lost in their furious pursuit of modernity, such as ancestor worship and respect for the elderly.[206] Occasionally the local press alerted readers to the existence of a few Japanese who had gone "native" in the backwaters of Korea, where they immersed themselves so thoroughly in local society that they fell out of the settlers' cultural universe.

The process of interculturation became complex as the settler community became internally more differentiated over time. The high-class life of corporate or bureaucratic employees and their families, sur-

---

201. Zenkoku Shinbun Tōkyō Rengōsha 1912, 125; informant questionnaire survey (see Appendix 2).

202. *Chōsen oyobi Manshū*, January 1926, 48–49; interview with Hozumi Shigetoshi, Tokyo, 2 February 2002.

203. *Keijō nippō*, 11 May 1911; roundtable discussion with members of the Chūō Nikkan Kyōkai, 2 February 2002; informant questionnaire survey. Many settler families, according to my informants who grew up in Seoul in the 1930s and 1940s, went to Korean markets to buy fresh vegetables and fruit, and ate at food stalls in Tongdaemon Market on weekends (interview with a former female resident of Seoul, 12 July 2001; interview with son of a former restaurant owner in Seoul, 14 January 2002).

204. *CKZ* 153 (September 1928): 10.

205. Kimura 1996, 57; informant questionnaire survey.

206. Informant questionnaire survey.

rounded by maids and isolated in gated communities, contrasted sharply with that of the more numerous small and midsized retailers and factory owners who lived in more mixed areas—a contrast that more or less mirrored a division between the "new comers" (*shinraishu*) and the "old timers" (*zairaishu*) that emerged by the early 1920s.[207] At the same time, the boundaries of the Japanese and Korean communities, whether in cities or in the country, continued to blur at both ends of the social spectrum, where a few struggling migrants dwelled amid Korean laborers and upper-class Japanese fraternized with *yangban* elites.[208] The overall trend in Japanese-Korean relations across the colonial period seemed to be one of more contact rather than less, in contrast to another heavily settled colony of French Algeria where, David Prochaska has noted, "the gap between Algerian colonized and European colonizers was widening rather than narrowing in virtually every sphere of colonial life."[209]

## *Fears of Contact*

As the two communities began to intertwine closely, fear of contact emerged as a powerful emotion among settlers. The Japanese transplanted to the peninsula might, they worried, degenerate by acquiring the habits and character of the natives, and pose a threat to Japanese identity and to the social cohesion of the settler community. Such concerns were raised on the pages of local Japanese papers and magazines around the time of annexation, and heightened in the course of the 1910s. One such magazine, *Chōsen oyobi Manshū*, constantly alerted its readers to the danger, warning them against becoming "Koreanized," or "*yobo*-ized" in the derogatory parlance of the day. Similar to the

---

207. Minobe Shunkichi's remark recorded in Chōsen Sōtokufu, *Sangyō Chōsa Iinkai giji sokkiroku* 1922, 231. The degree of settlers' contact with Koreans and incorporation of local customs varied immensely according to class, region, occupation, gender, and length of stay (informant questionnaire survey).

208. This sense of diversity and heterogeneity of settler culture is also conveyed by a series of *senryū* (comic poetic genre) studied by Helen Lee (2008b).

209. In the city of Bône, where the Europeans outnumbered the Algerians two to one, in all aspects of daily life including residence, occupation, and the use of modern amenities, "the French and Algerians were at least as segregated from each other at the time of the last French census in 1954, before the Algerian war, as in 1911" (Prochaska 1990, 155, 164).

way the Europeans spoke of "colonial neurasthenia" in the tropics,[210] "Koreanization" was explained as a physical as well as psychological affliction, which not only affected one's outward appearance and behavior ("wearing *hanbok*" and "smoking long pipes") but one's mentality and mores (becoming "dispirited," "feckless," "negligent and lax").[211] By the end of the 1910s, the magazine reported, its debilitating effects were allegedly widespread and contagious, particularly among those who dwelled in "small settlements or mixed settlements with Koreans."[212] And just as the Europeans in colonial Africa devised an array of idiosyncratic strategies to protect their cultural identity from the "black peril" and the tropical sun,[213] Japanese in Korea pondered how to combat the harmful effects of contact. As one quick remedy, merchant Kugimoto Tōjirō (1868–1933) proposed "traveling to the mother country about three times a year to refresh one's eyes and ears."[214] Many Japanese parents also warned their children not to play with Koreans, even in the late colonial period when ethnic unity was systematically promoted as official policy.[215]

As the official exhortations on Japanese residents to assist the empire's task to enlighten—and, after 1910, to "assimilate"—Koreans increased, concern about Koreanization deepened. So did their dilemma about standing at the forefront of colonial encounter, but also having to keep their national identity from withering through exposure. This issue was addressed by local educator Ayukai Fusanoshin, founder of the short-lived Itsubi Gijuku, shortly after the colonial government declared assimilation as official policy. "To assimilate Koreans requires [us] first to naturalize [*shizenka*] with Korea to a certain extent," Ayukai admitted, for "so long as there is a separation" between Japanese and Koreans "as if water and oil," "true assimilation would be hopeless." But "rather than assimilate Koreans," he argued, the Japanese must first "think about how to unite and overcome [Korean] nature." For Ayukai,

210. Stoler 2002, 66–67; Kennedy 1987, Chapter 6.

211. *Chōsen oyobi Manshū*, October 1912, 1–4; February 1916, 1; and January 1917, 60–68.

212. *Chōsen oyobi Manshū*, April 1918, 2–8.

213. For the case of the British in Kenya, see Kennedy 1987, Chapters 6 and 7.

214. *Chōsen oyobi Manshū*, January 1917, 61.

215. Morita Kiyoshige, response to questionnaire, 12 May 2002.

assimilation was a matter of conquering nature before nurturing natives. The ability of Korean nature to mold Japanese—as historically demonstrated by the fate of migrants to the peninsula, especially during "the time of building the Japanese government of Mimana"—might prevail over the Japanese project of assimilating Koreans. If left to itself for months and years, he wrote, the power of Korean nature would transform settlers in all aspects, from lifestyle and habits, to character, mental dispositions, even possibly ideological orientation. As Japanese dwellings became "*ondol*-style," for instance, their "temperament [would] become gloomy, negligent, and self-indulgent." Likewise, as their diet came to "favor extremely spicy [food]," the settlers would become "unbalanced and acquire a temperament of running from one extreme to the other." "While it may not immediately affect their loyalty and patriotism," Ayukai prophesied, the process of acculturation would "surely give rise to a unique label of '*naichijin* in Korea,'"[216] a category of people who were neither fully Japanese nor Korean.

What worried Ayukai, and other concerned observers, was not so much the prospect of settlers going completely "native" as of their falling into that hazy, intermediate realm *between* colonizer and colonized.[217] Thus, Ōmura Tomonojō (1871–?) of the Seoul Chamber of Commerce considered most worrisome "those Japanese who lack self-awareness [as leaders and developers of Koreans] and pick up Koreans' evil customs,"[218] such as sloth, extravagance, wastefulness, and fortune-seeking. All of these traits came to be associated with simply being a colonial resident. When the Home Ministry in 1908 issued the Boshin Rescript (also known as the "diligence and frugality" rescript), some local leaders responded to the occasion with a call for rectifying these unflattering characteristics of Japanese in Korea,[219] while Japanese resident papers enjoined their countrymen to maintain "self-awareness" as "members of a superior civilized nation," alerting them to the "duty to develop Korea and enlighten Koreans."[220]

---

216. Ayukai 1913, 146–47.
217. I owe this insight to Buettner 2000, 292.
218. *Chōsen oyobi Manshū*, January 1917, 63.
219. *Chōsen* (Chōsen Zasshisha), November 1908, 26–28.
220. *Chōsen* (Chōsen Zasshisha), May 1908, 27–28.

Settlers' concerns about falling into this in-between space found their most urgent tone in regard to the issue of their children's education—a concern that lasted into the 1930s and 1940s, as Nicole Cohen has shown.[221] Local Japanese parents and educators worried that their children would grow up in Korea without knowing their homeland or fully comprehending emperor ideology, including the symbolic significance of Yasukuni Shrine and the meaning of Shinto worship.[222] As early as 1908, observers sounded the alarm about the lack of patriotism among young settlers, who, evidently seeing conscription as a nuisance rather than a mark of privilege as Japanese citizens, submitted a petition to the Japanese government demanding that the exemption clause be extended to residents of Korea.[223] None of these issues was limited to overseas settlers; indeed, reverence for the imperial house and the mythology behind it took almost as long to take root among metropolitan youth, and draft evasion was also widespread in Japan before the 1890s.[224] Nonetheless, the challenge of inculcating young Japanese seemed more daunting on the peninsula, where they had to overcome not only the obstacle of distance from home but the countervailing force of "Koreanization."

Ultimately, however, settlers' fear about Koreanization reveals less the social reality of migrants than the fragility of "Japaneseness" they sought to maintain in their interstitial existence. In spite of the colonizers' efforts to maintain identity and mold that of the colonized, everyday encounters made contact a more complex process than acculturation. Whether living prodigally in cities or more humbly in the country, settlers were transformed in ways that placed them always somewhere between *naichi* and Korea, fully anchoring them in neither place. The discourse on Koreanization was, in this sense, a mirror of settlers' inner anxieties about being a numerical minority, being under an authoritarian regime, and being of lower origins. Such anxieties shaped their liminality and deepened under the Governor-General's rule.

---

221. Cohen 2006, Chapter 3.

222. Yasuda 1927, 224–25.

223. *Chōsen* (Chōsen zasshisha), November 1908, 104; Kimura 1996, 45.

224. Gluck 1985, 264; Gordon 2003, 137.

## *Conclusion*

In the trajectory of early Japanese expansion into the peninsula, the colonial state and the settlers were co-builders of empire. From the ousting of Chinese overlordship to the establishment of protectorate rule following Japan's victory over Russia in 1905, ordinary Japanese through a wide variety of roles bolstered their nation's struggle to claim a place in the world. To be sure, Korea meant different things to different people. To merchants and sojourners, Korea was a place to make quick and easy money. To aspiring youth, Korea represented a chance to rise in the world. To educators, Korea offered an opportunity to inject the civilizing influence of Japanese culture. And to journalists and continental *rōnin*, Korea became a theater of revolution as large as their political ambition. Yet local settlers also rallied behind their country in times of crisis, and some sought a more direct part in defining Japan's imperial policy. Although their personal ambitions and national interests were often only loosely connected, settlers provided a source of momentum for Japan's colonization and helped forge their nation in the process. As also demonstrated by the everyday life and cultural practices of overseas settlers, it was the diversity of modernizing Japanese, rather than the coherent force of a modernized Japan, that propelled the construction of empire in Korea.

From these early communities of migrants and settlers emerged those I call the "brokers of empire"—influential long-time Japanese residents who came to constitute the ranks of the local elite. They represented areas as varied as petty commerce, foreign trade, construction, banking, journalism, and education. Most of the key brokers of empire emerged from Japan's early entanglements with Korea: merchants like Yamaguchi Tahee who led the railway lobbying movement, journalists like Kikuchi Kenjō who buttressed imperialism through print and political maneuver, teachers like Ayukai Fusanoshin who launched their pedagogical mission abroad, and (as we will see in the next chapter) political fixers like Ōgaki Takeo who joined Korean reformers in shaping the future of East Asia. Diverse as they were, the brokers of empire also constituted a collective identity. Fired by individual ambitions and an equally intense sense of commitment to the nation, they shared a history of struggle and a sense of pride as the earliest Japanese to settle and succeed on the peninsula.

Most of the brokers of empire were based in Seoul, though their influence extended beyond the capital to become a veritable "who's who" in Korea. The nucleus of the local Japanese leadership was provided by those born between the 1860s and 1880s, the first three decades of Meiji, who arrived in Korea in their teens and twenties and spent most of their adult life on the peninsula. They may be subdivided into three groups (see Appendix 1).[225]

The Japanese who came to Korea before the Sino-Japanese War represented the earliest "pioneers," and their careers displayed the most spectacular pattern of success. They came to Korea with little or no capital, survived tough competition from Chinese, and amassed a certain measure of wealth or influence by the time of the Russo-Japanese War. Prime examples were Seoul's powerful merchants, Yamaguchi Tahee, Wada Tsuneichi, and Nakamura Saizō—Korea's "elder statesmen" (*genrō*), as they came to be called—who were known to have built everything from roads and railways to schools, hospitals, banks, and the rest of the "Japantown."[226] Their influence also extended to the metropole. Yamaguchi in particular, as a fellow settler reminisced later, served as "a guiding light" not only for local Japanese residents but for "metropolitan policy and decision makers regarding diplomacy toward Korea."[227]

More Japanese arrived to settle in the interwar period, between 1894 and the eve of the Russo-Japanese War in 1904. This group of settlers represented a wider range of occupations—merchants, entrepreneurs, engineers, building contractors, journalists, and other professionals—and tended to be more educated and less dependent on kinship or native place ties than the first group. Taking advantage of a commercially less risky environment after the Chinese departure, many settler merchants obtained wealth and status very early in their careers. And more skilled

225. Drawing on available biographical dictionaries published in the colonial period, Appendix 1 lists 112 civilians based in Seoul who led the local Japanese community from 1905 through the late 1930s and beyond. Excepting colonial officials and members of the garrison/army, local Japanese leaders generally fall into the following main categories, though in many cases they overlap: (1) merchants and entrepreneurs; (2) building contractors and engineers; (3) bank/company executives; (4) free professionals (journalists, lawyers, educators) and *rōnin.*

226. *Chōsen oyobi Manshū*, April 1927, 126.

227. Fujimura Tokuichi in Kitagawa Yoshiaki 1934, 201.

and semi-skilled labor arrived to work on infrastructural projects and new railways that began to crisscross the peninsula.

This pattern of migration was reinforced by those who arrived between the Russo-Japanese War and the annexation of 1910. They constituted a more numerous, more diverse, and overall more gentrified group. In contrast to the earlier emigrants who invariably began from humble origins, this group usually enjoyed more stable careers as corporate employees, professionals, and other salaried white-collar workers. Some were former bureaucrats, local government officials, or army officers who turned to enterprise upon retirement. Many settlers in this group had made early forays into the Diet or local politics before coming to Korea, and some former popular rights activists, as we will see later, became involved in the Korean self-strengthening movement. Some late Meiji youth dealt with their sense of psychological malaise by turning inward,[228] while others embraced change by looking outward—many to the Korean peninsula, where they became avatars of the new capitalism or apostles of the culture of protest that emerged in the wake of the Russo-Japanese War.[229] The brokers of empire, in short, were solidly products of the Meiji era.

The emergence of brokers of empire signified the transformation of subaltern migrants into subimperialists, a trajectory that mirrored the rapid rise of Japan on the global stage. Settlers made a point of highlighting this linkage. Although marginalized in official records, ordinary emigrants became subjects of a slew of "success stories" that echoed the stories of "self-made men," a staple of Meiji biography that captivated the metropolitan reading public.[230] By the time of annexation in 1910, hagiographies of rich settler businessmen charting their rise from rags to riches, and offering their coveted advice on "secrets of success,"[231] filled the columns of local Japanese papers and magazines. Settlers also wrote their own autobiographies. They reveled in chronicling the trials and tribulations of their earlier life as rugged pioneers—whether battling their way out of poverty or building a city from scratch—and in collect-

---

228. See Pyle 1969.

229. Oka Yoshitake 1982, 197–98.

230. See Kinmonth 1981, 164–65.

231. A typical example is Yamaguchi Tahee, "Shōten keiei no hiketsu," *Chōsen kōron*, June 1914, 71–74.

ing their reminiscences as "valuable living documents" for posterity.[232] For some exceptional figures, biographies were not quite enough. Local settlers honored these "founding fathers" by erecting bronze statues, another element imported from Japan, to mark their illustrious place in history.[233] Those who were canonized in both print and stone included Kashii Gentarō and Ōike Chūsuke of Pusan, Yamaguchi Tahee of Seoul, and Nishizaki Tsurukichi of Chinnamp'o.[234]

The colonial state also awarded pioneering settlers with due recognition, albeit more slowly than the Japanese resident press demanded. Throughout the colonial period a variety of influential settlers were feted as "civilian men of merit" at imperial and commemorative ceremonies.[235] Kikuchi Kenjō, who partook in the assassination of Queen Min and supported the Ilchinhoe (see Chapter 2), received from the colonial government a medal of merit for his "contribution to the annexation of Korea." For their roles in developing industry and philanthropy, merchant Kobayashi Genroku and a few others earned the blue medal of merit bestowed by the emperor,[236] and entrepreneurs like Kashii Gentarō and Tomita Gisaku attained still higher honors and titles that were rare even among top-class businessmen in Japan.[237]

For settlers, writing biographies, building statues, and garnering honors were all symbolic acts of writing themselves into the national folklore as pioneering builders of Korea and patriotic citizens of Japan. Each of these commemorative sites was invested with "alternative meaning and memories"[238] that foregrounded nameless heroes who constructed nation and empire—and challenged the narrative centered on achievements of the state. And yet, settlers were careful to stress links between their personal travails and triumphs and those of their nation's leaders,

---

232. Fujimura 1927b, 3. A group of settlers who had lived in Korea for more than twenty years, for instance, formed a social club called the Chōsen Futamukashi Kai, and published *Kyoryūmin no mukashi monogatari* (Past Tales of Settlers, 1927), a self-edited collection of individual reminiscences about their struggles on the peninsula.

233. Fujitani 1996, 123–24.

234. Takahara 1935; Tanaka Ichinosuke 1936, 56–57; *Chōsen oyobi Manshū*, September 1928, 75.

235. For instance, see *Chōsen oyobi Manshū*, November 1928, 84; and Morikawa 1935.

236. Abe Kaoru 1937, 59–60.

237. *Chōsen oyobi Manshū*, December 1928, 62.

238. Fujitani 1996, 231.

to insist on the autobiography of settlers as the story of empire. What became a typical refrain in settler writings, as a result, was not the collaboration of the abacus and the sword so much as the singular feat of settlers in bearing them both. According to one such narrative:

> Everywhere a commercial flag went up before the national flag, merchants went ahead of officials, and *rōnin* went ahead of soldiers. Each merchant and each *rōnin*, vested with . . . a mission to rule and develop Korea, penetrates deep into the Korean interior and into various islands, and carrying an abacus on the right and a sword on the left, or shouldering a rifle and a portrait of Japan's emperor, or clutching sugar in their fists, enters into Korean hamlets where no Japanese has ever gone.[239]

This narrative, if enshrined as part of Japan's colonial mythology, seldom matched the settlers' realities, and the gap between them widened over time. As a new class of bureaucrats, military officers, and corporate executives arrived on the peninsula, local settlers began to harbor a kind of "inferiority complex" and fear of being treated as déclassé "sojourners" (*dekaseginin*),[240] although they never ceased to lay claim to a status as true "pioneers" who "came to Korea before the Japanese flag."[241] In their road from struggle to success, the brokers of empire developed a complex *colon* mentality that would deepen with the consolidation of Japan's control over Korea, and stay with them to the end of colonial rule.

---

239. *Chōsen* (Chōsen Zasshisha), May 1908, 25.

240. Shin Mi-sen 1995, 59.

241. Kojō Kandō, "Shinshisei ni taishite," *Chōsen* (Chōsen Sōtokufu), October 1921, 66–69; Hattori 1931, 32–33.

# TWO

## *Settlers and the State: Uneasy Partners*

Before he departed for Seoul in 1905, Ōgaki Takeo (1862–1929), a journalist from Ishikawa prefecture, bid farewell to his readers in a local newspaper, recording his determination to "permanently settle" on the Korean peninsula. "Rather than end my life as nobody in Japan," Ōgaki explained with contrived modesty, "I could serve a millionth part of my obligation to the nation and fulfill my duty as a citizen [*kokumin*] by educating Koreans . . . and assisting the empire's Korean policy."[1] By helping to reform Korea, Ōgaki hoped, he could reinvent his own life. In many ways, he was a typical emigrant who, in flight from the limits of his circumstances, sought opportunities abroad, and once settled there refused to "go back to being a mediocre man."[2] But Ōgaki also turned out to be no ordinary colonist—he would indeed become one of the most influential brokers of empire—and not nearly as humble as he portrayed himself.

After the "conquest of Korea" (Seikanron) debates that divided the Meiji oligarchy in 1871–72, Korea became the yardstick with which the nation's leadership measured its political success at home.[3] Domestic triumphs—such as the suppression of the popular rights movement and

1. Quoted in Ikegawa 1986, 79.
2. Memmi 1965, 61.
3. Dudden 2005, 49–50.

the taming of the samurai—no less than overseas victories strengthened the Meiji leaders' resolve to rule Korea. But Japanese abroad were far from an obedient herd. While developing their own cultural world, overseas settlers emerged as a voice in imperial politics during the formative phase of Japanese dominance over Korea, from 1905 to 1919. The Japanese state tightened its hold on the peninsula after driving away the Russians, but what followed was a period of fragile stability at best. Vociferous settlers and local officials cooperated in planting on Korean soil the flag of the rising sun, but not without sowing seeds of conflict. And they grew farther apart as the peninsula came more fully under Japanese control.

Behind their uneasy partnership loomed a number of issues that pitted settler interests against state policies. At the core of their tension was a cognitive gap: where settlers saw themselves as partners in governance, the state treated them as interlopers. Politically ambitious journalists like Ōgaki, and adventurers from home, sought a role in transforming Korea, each according to his own interests. Neither merchants nor bureaucrats, these migrants operated on the ground to engage in political intervention, a form of activity that became a permanent occupation of the brokers of empire.

The settlers' struggle for inclusion in the imperial project became entangled with the quest for citizenship. As the period of political activism gave way to the onset of the Governor-General's rule after 1910, settlers' autonomy came under threat from state autocracy. The ensuing conflict harked back to the agitation for freedom and popular rights (*jiyūminken undō*) in Meiji Japan, and paralleled a renewed fervor for democracy in the era of Taishō. A related and equally fractious issue was the "native policy"—vaguely packaged as a mission to civilize and assimilate Koreans. The Japanese, in short, brought to Korea not only a shared mission to civilize but also the divisive politics of the *kan* (officials) and the *min* (people).

These tensions, which remained endemic for decades, underscore the difficulty in separating empire-building from nation-building, the history of colonial Korea from the history of modern Japan. Colonialism, as recent scholarship has shown, was central to the making of modern citizenship. The concepts of rights, nation, and identity that gained global currency around the turn of the century were debated in imperial metropoles, where colonial subjects were discussed as "potential citizens" and settlers were expected to "set an example for the colonized" by maintaining respectability and demonstrating model subjecthood.[4] Metropolitan debates, at the same time, translated into contentious politics on the periphery, where local settlers proved to be more clamorous than the state could control. While touting assimilation, the settlers strove to negotiate their ambivalent status—being politically and legally suspended between colony and metropole—by deploying the rhetoric of popular rights and the power of the press to confront two faces of the state, on the peninsula and at home. It was the precarious synergy between the people's desire to participate and the state's desire to mobilize its subjects without losing control that drove Japan's construction of nation and empire. The brokers of empire plied their trade in the interstices of this process, where state and society, no less than the two worlds of Japanese and Koreans, collided and intertwined.

## *Settlers' Attack on Itō's Policy of "Self-Rule"*

In 1905, in the wake of the war against Tsarist Russia, the victorious (though financially pressed) Meiji state established a protectorate over Korea under Resident-General Itō Hirobumi. Occupying a position directly under the Korean emperor, Itō implemented a kind of indirect rule by placing Japanese advisors in all key sections of the Korean government—police affairs, defense, finance, and economy—and by usurping the functions of local authorities.[5] Another treaty signed two years later gave Japan complete control over Korea's diplomatic affairs, signaling its de facto annexation of the peninsula.[6]

Japan's first prime minister and the foremost statesman of the Meiji era, Itō brought to Korea a goal his government had steadfastly pursued for its own countrymen: to civilize.[7] In the name of "nurturing Korean self-rule" under Japanese protection, Itō followed twin policy

---

4. See Evans et al. 2003; Keller 2007, 5; S. Roberts 2010, 20–31.

5. As the former police official Matsui Shigeru recollected later, these steps had been taken months prior to the start of protectorate rule (Matsui 1952, 238–40).

6. Moriyama 1992, 140. On the question of the legality of the annexation, see Unno 1995 and Dudden 2005.

7. On the centrality of the notion of "civilization" to Japan's legal and "legislating mission" in Korea to make its empire legitimate in the court of world opinion, see Dudden 2005.

objectives—to guide Korea's modernizing reform and build the country as a reliable political ally—while being careful not to provoke other powers. The professed aim of his administration was to accelerate reforms already underway (that had been launched in fits and starts by Korean reformist officials) in the areas of land registration, taxation, industrial development, hygiene, education, and civil engineering, while adding new programs such as legal and judicial reforms, agricultural stations, and the creation of a uniform currency.[8] But under the pretext of bolstering Korean sovereignty, the Japanese pursued a thinly disguised imperialistic agenda. The protectorate government vastly increased its military and political power by dissolving the Korean army and forcing Kojong to abdicate the throne as emperor in 1907, after he had secretly dispatched a delegation to the Hague Peace Conference to protest the protectorate treaty. These measures sparked a wave of Korean resistance, culminating in the rise of "righteous armies" (*ŭibyŏng*) organized by the disaffected Confucian literati and joined by soldiers of the disbanded army.

Yet Japan's "civilizing mission" in Korea was not always matched by fixity of purpose. The process of guiding Korean reform, as Peter Duus has shown, was fraught with constant and bitter argument that cast the government against the opposition, hawks against moderates, and on occasion capitalists against military leaders. All this was further complicated by ultranationalists who pursued expansive agendas of their own.[9] During his tenure as the Resident-General, Itō constantly faced criticism from his political rivals in the Diet, and struggled to block interference from the military and the Foreign Ministry who argued for a strong-arm policy toward the Asian continent. But the harshest attack on Itō came from local Japanese settlers, whose number climbed to almost 100,000 a few years following the Russo-Japanese War. One bone of settler contention was Itō's announced plan to abolish extraterritoriality in Korea. This was part of his policy of nurturing "self-rule"

---

8. Duus 1995, 220. The creation of a new currency system based on the yen and a central bank, the Dai-Ichi (later Chōsen) Bank, through which to leverage the gold standard and extend loans to China, were particularly crucial steps in Japan's effort to establish the financial center of its East Asian empire on the Korean peninsula (Metzler 2005, 52–55, 66).

9. Duus 1995, 29 and Part 1.

and reflected his desire for Japan to "set an example for other nations to follow."[10] Apart from his vision of installing a system of "self-rule based on Japanese-Korean cooperation" (*Nikkan kyōdō no jichi*), Itō's intention behind the abolition of extraterritoriality was to remove legal constraints on Japanese landownership and allow his countrymen to expand their economic activities outside of the treaty ports. Nonetheless, settlers feared that such a measure would threaten their community by increasing state control over their private assets—which as of June 1906 stood at almost 20 million yen, an amount roughly equivalent to the Korean government's budget for the fiscal year 1909—and more specifically by ending their immunity from property taxes levied by the Korean government.[11] What they considered shabby official treatment of migrants was another source of settler discontent. "No sooner had Resident-General Itō arrived in Korea than he began to speak of Japanese residents as vagrants and vagabonds," complained one local journalist, noting how Itō began to restrict their local autonomy by issuing the Hoan Kisoku (Security Regulations) in 1906, which were applied exclusively to settlers to prevent fraud in business and employment, illegal usury, and rampant debt collection.[12]

Mounting frustration with the protectorate government culminated in settlers' sustained press campaign against Itō. In April 1908, at a political rally that drew an audience of 500 people, local Japanese journalists one after another ascended the podium, claiming that "the development of Korea depends on the power of us *kokumin* [citizens]" and fulminating against tightened press control as "contradicting the freedom of speech guaranteed by the constitution."[13] To critique and render advice to bureaucrats was the "right" and the "duty" of "settlers" (*kyoryūmin*), argued Tokanō Shigeo of the *Daikan nippō*. A self-proclaimed "representative of the Yamato race [*minzoku*]," Tokanō dismissed "those who flatter and blindly obey the authorities [as] not worthy of being settlers." Given the incompetence of protectorate officials, Minegishi Shigetarō, editor of the *Keijō shinpō*, claimed hyperbolically that "only

10. Asano 2008, 170.

11. Asano and Matsuda 2004, 152*n*6; Asano 2008, 172.

12. *Chōsen* (Chōsen Zasshisha), March 1908, 29; Asano 2008, 173.

13. The following quotations of journalists come from a police report, Keihi no. 1515-1 (23 April 1908), reprinted in *T'onggambu munsŏ* 1998, 1:127–31.

newspaper reporters can render advice, and to muzzle them would be tantamount to killing them." Another correspondent vowed to fight the official "suppression" even to the point of risking "an expulsion order from Korea."

In what became a typical settler tirade, the journalists also bitterly complained that the protectorate "authorities are compassionate toward the Korean people and cold toward [Japanese] compatriots." Tachibana Kōkitsu of the *Chōsen taimusu* asserted Itō's "policy of accommodation is fundamentally flawed," even "futile," for "the Korean people have materially and spiritually fallen so low." Since the Koreans did not appreciate Japan's tutelage, as evidenced by increasing guerrilla resistance, critics of Itō argued that Japan should take a more firm imperialistic posture toward obstinate natives. While shifting its focus to "transplanting many Japanese to Korea," they prodded, "the Residency-General should respect the rights of his own countrymen, protect their profits, and promote the expansion of their power."[14] Such a claim conceptually pushed the vision of Korea from a site of migration to a settler colony where the welfare of natives was rendered superfluous to the interests of metropolitan nationals.

Throughout the protectorate period, perhaps the most relentless and vituperative attack on Itō was carried out by Minegishi Shigetarō. From the very first issue of the *Keijō shinpō* in November 1907, Minegishi engaged in incendiary rhetoric, lambasting Itō's policy of governing Koreans as "weak-kneed" like "Lord Cromer's policy in Egypt," and urging him to go beyond protectorate rule—in effect arguing for annexation before the home government did. Feeling ignored, in subsequent issues he went so far as to argue that Itō was "unfit to be Resident-General" (10 April 1908) and declared his "policy of accommodation" (*kaijū seisaku*) a complete failure, expressing his preference for "the military-style strategy" (*budanteki shudan*) deployed by European empires everywhere (4 June 1908).[15]

More than a polemic, Minegishi's opposition to Itō reflected larger political divisions at home. Existing records suggest that Minegishi had personal connections to Katsura Tarō (1848–1913), prime minister of

14. *Chōsen* (Chōsen Zasshisha), September 1908, 2–3.
15. *Keijō shinpō*, 10 April 1908; and 4 June 1908.

Japan in 1901–1906 and 1908–1911, who alternated the post with Itō's protégé, Saionji Kinmochi (1849–1940). A self-proclaimed member of the conservative "Katsura faction," Minegishi was apparently seen as its "secret emissary" toward the end of Itō's tenure in Korea, as the faction vied for control over the government with the ruling party Seiyūkai headed by Saionji. During his visit to Tokyo in late 1909, Minegishi met with Katsura to discuss a range of issues concerning Japan's colonial affairs, from the management of Manchurian and Korean railways to the current status of Korean political organizations. Using the occasion, Minegishi also pointed out numerous "flaws" of the ODC, which reportedly stirred journalist Shibukawa Genji and novelist Natsume Sōseki, both prominent opinion-makers in Japan, to investigate the matter.[16] In spite of Itō's efforts to contain domestic debates and divisions within national borders, these conflicts made their way into Korea via the Japanese resident press, which sided with his critics.

Activities of journalists like Minegishi also map the extensive social network through which the brokers of empire operated and advanced their interests by borrowing, and frequently manipulating, the growing power of the press. Perhaps at no other time in prewar Japan did the press play a more influential role in shaping national politics. Men of letters who operated in fin-de-siècle Korea were products of the great age of *yoron* (public opinion) led by newspapers, which started as political organs in Meiji Japan, as they did in Britain earlier. As these organs developed into mass dailies, those who managed them soon entered politics or remained well connected to the small and tight apex of ruling elites that grew out of their old political circles.[17] Journalists, in short, were very powerful. And their influence, along with their politics, extended to the empire. The protectorate government issued its own bulletin, the *Keijō nippō*, to publicize its policies and win over articulate segments of the Korean public; settlers used the new authority of the press to present a collective voice to outsiders, including Koreans and their own government. Papers like the *Keijō shinpō* and political speeches by journalists, moreover, had the effect of enhancing jingoism within the settler com-

16. Keihi no. 3257-1 (15 October 1909), and Keihi no. 3225-1 (14 October 1909), in *T'onggambu munsŏ* 1998, 10:391–94.

17. On the political power of the press in the Meiji period, see Huffman 1997; and Kyu Hyun Kim 2007, 86–98.

munity. They fanned a vitriolic response among their readers, for instance, when some Korean students in Sinŭiju destroyed the Japanese flag distributed to them for greeting the Korean emperor on his progress through the northern provinces. In addition to condemning the act as "an insult to the Japanese empire," the journalists used the incident as another occasion for chiding the Residency-General's leniency toward Koreans.[18] And the journalists' posture appears to have struck a chord with local settlers, from merchants to schoolchildren, who apparently expressed joy rather than regret upon hearing the news of Itō's resignation that year, viewing it as a long-awaited end to his "Korea-centered policy."[19]

## *Japanese Advisors in the Patriotic Enlightenment Movement*

Although the protectorate government found itself having to contend with two forces of opposition—Korean resistance and settler public opinion—it would be misleading to think that Itō's critics opposed the idea of reform. To the contrary, many individuals and groups sought a part in the process, in greater numbers than the state was willing to accommodate. While the Korean bureaucrats worked with Itō's government, students, scholars, journalists, entrepreneurs, former officials, and other elites outside the ruling circles launched programs and formed organizations to cultivate Korea's national strength, providing the momentum for what came to be known as the Aeguk Kyemong Undong (Patriotic Enlightenment Movement).[20]

Some politically ambitious Japanese came to Korea to add themselves to this constellation. They became advisors and supporters of a variety of local organizations, a trend noted with lament by the *Taehan Maeil sinbo* (Korea Daily News), a main vehicle of nationalist dissent.[21] Among the largest such organizations that worked closely with the Japanese were the Ilchinhoe (Advancement Society), the Taehan Chaganghoe (Great Korea Self-Strengthening Association; later Taehan Hyŏphoe), and the

18. Kenki no. 466 (1 March 1909), in *T'onggambu munsŏ* 1998, 6:49–51.

19. *Jiji hyōron* article reprinted in Kŭm 1999, 3:150–51; Kōhishū no. 3214-1, in *T'onggambu munsŏ* 1998, 10:354–55.

20. For comprehensive studies on the Patriotic Enlightenment Movement, see Pak Ch'an-sŭng 1992; and Kim Chŏk-pong 1994.

21. *Taehan Maeil sinbo*, 20 March 1907.

Sŏbuk Hakhoe (Northwest Educational Association).[22] Like other self-strengthening organizations, they shared a broad goal of protecting Korean "sovereignty," but the Ilchinhoe, founded by Yi Yong-gu (1868–1912) in 1904 and led by Song Pyŏng-jun (1857–1925), distinguished itself by its non-elite approach to achieving this goal and in its mass membership.[23] The Ilchinhoe was a "populist organization" with a strong anti-monarchical agenda of attacking "tyrannical government" and demanding "popular sovereignty," according to the historian Yumi Moon, but it also exhibited a pro-Japanese character in pursuing a Pan-Asianist vision of reform.[24] The organization found its original goals and public legitimacy increasingly compromised as it fell under the supervision of Uchida Ryōhei (1874–1937) and Tōyama Mitsuru (1855–1944), leaders of Japan's largest patriotic society, the Kokuryūkai (Black Dragon or Amur River Society), whose members had fanned out to the Asian mainland to link up with Chinese and Korean reformers around the time of the Sino-Japanese War.[25]

In addition to these swashbuckling nationalists from Kyushu whose involvement in the Ilchinhoe is well known, Japanese settlers also aided the Ilchinhoe or its rival organizations. This local story remains more obscure. Many of these Japanese advisors, like Uchida, had been politically active before coming to the peninsula, as young supporters of the popular rights movement in the 1870s and 1880s. Others had made forays into parliamentary politics in its aftermath, as in the case of Sase Kumatetsu of the Ilchinhoe and Takahashi Shōnosuke of the Sŏbuk Hakhoe, who briefly served in the Lower House of the Diet. To understand their motivations for intervening in Korean reforms, it is important to recall that popular rights advocates had shown themselves to be

---

22. According to Pak Ch'an-sŭng (1992), the Korean "self-strengthening movement" does not include the Ilchinhoe, but the Japanese protectorate authorities tended to categorize it as part of it.

23. By 1910, its membership had reached a little over 140,000, most of whom were followers of the Tonghak religion (Gaimushō 1960 [1908], 854–55). The Ilchinhoe leaders claimed their organization had nearly one million members at its peak, though more realistic estimates would place the figure somewhere between 120,000 and 140,000 (Hayashi Yūsuke 1999, 46–48).

24. Moon 2010. Also see Chandra 1974.

25. See Kyō 1988.

among the most ardent proponents of expansionism in Meiji Japan.[26] Tokutomi Sohō, a former activist who took a conservative turn like many of his contemporaries, by 1895 was speaking of a Japanese mission "to extend the blessings of political organization throughout the rest of East Asia and the South Pacific, just as the Romans had once done for Europe and the Mediterranean."[27]

Among these unofficial propagandists for imperialism, no one more actively embraced the vision of transferring the institutional achievements of Meiji to Korea than Ōgaki Takeo, the seasoned journalist from Ishikawa introduced at the beginning of this chapter. Ōgaki rallied behind the Ilchinhoe's biggest rival, the Taehan Chaganghoe, formed in 1906 by a group of former bureaucrats in Seoul.[28] They pursued a gradualist approach to recovering Korean sovereignty through education and economic development, while countering the "excessively pro-Japanese" activity of the Ilchinhoe.[29] A self-proclaimed Meiji loyalist (*shishi*), Ōgaki studied under Fukuzawa Yukichi and devoted his adolescence to the popular rights movement. He also became involved in a short-lived campaign, waged in the early 1890s by foreign-policy hardliners, to criticize the Itō cabinet for allowing foreigners to operate beyond treaty restrictions, under the slogan of "banning mixed residence in the interior." Ōgaki continued to prod the government to take a hawkish stance, while building his career as a journalist in Nara, Kaga, and Tokyo.[30]

Ōgaki's trajectory represented the ruthless mind of his generation, who viewed liberalism and imperialism as perfectly compatible projects. To Ōgaki (and other advisors), entering Korea, as he did in his 40s, was synonymous with entering a stage of world-historical significance, a

26. Kajimura 1992, 127–29; Siniawer 2008, 53.

27. Quoted in Pyle 1969, 181.

28. Gaimushō 1960 [1908], 854–55. The Taehan Chaganghoe was initially chaired by Yun Ch'iho and soon placed under the stewardship of Chang Chi-yŏn and Yun Hyojŏng. For the founding prospectus, membership, and aims of the organization restructured as Taehan Hyŏphoe, see Taehan Hyŏphoe 1907, and Kankoku Chūsatsu Kenpeitai Shireibu 1910. For studies on the Taehan Hyŏphoe, see Yi Hyŏn-jong 1970; and Kim Hang-gu 1999.

29. Ōgaki became an advisor to the Taehan Chaganghoe shortly after he arrived in Seoul in 1906. For a detailed study of his involvement in the Taehan Hyŏphoe, see Ikegawa 1985, 525–67; and Ikegawa 1986, 65–84.

30. Ikegawa 1986, 67–70.

threshold of revolution as epochal as the beginning of the Meiji. Though bitterly critical of the Ilchinhoe's activity that "merely fanned anti-Japanese sentiment" (and of the "lowly and base" peasants and day laborers who made up its rank and file),[31] Ōgaki was no less committed than Uchida and other chauvinists to promoting the goal of a Pan-Asian alliance, and placing the course of Korean reform under Japanese tutelage. Just as the boundary between journalism and political adventure remained blurry in this era, Ōgaki's thoughts and activities reveal just how fluid the distinction remained between an aggressive call for expanding Japanese hegemony in Asia—what one historian has termed "Greater Asianism"—and a horizontal vision of East Asian solidarity.[32]

Echoing contemporary Pan-Asian thinkers, most notably Tarui Tōkichi (1850–1922) who inspired the Ilchinhoe leaders,[33] Ōgaki argued for "an alliance of three nations" (*sangoku dōmei*)—Japan, Korea, and China—to combat the threat of Western invasion, while stressing the need for Korea to cultivate its strength with Japanese support. Ōgaki's thesis, which first appeared in the *Hwangsŏng sinmun* in February 1906, held considerable appeal to the Korean intelligentsia, many of whom overcame their initial ambivalence to accept his argument.[34] Unlike Tarui, however, the alliance Ōgaki envisaged from the beginning was predicated on the superiority of Japan as an undisputed "leader of the East" (*Tōyō no meishu*).[35] Nor did he question the legitimacy of protectorate rule. The implicit guarantee of Korean sovereignty in his argument masked a pragmatic premise: "if it becomes evident that [Korea] cannot maintain itself as a sound independent nation, we have no choice but to occupy its territory from the perspective of the empire's security."[36] At the slightest hint of a failure to fulfill his vision, Ōgaki's political stance, like that of many of his contemporaries, could glide from "assistance" to outright domination.[37]

---

31. Ōgaki 1927, 111.

32. Hatsuse 1980, 20–23. A similar distinction is adopted in Saaler and Koschmann 2007.

33. For Tarui's thesis on an "Eastern federation," see Tarui 1975 [1893].

34. Ikegawa 1985, 539; Pak Ch'an-sŭng 1992, 57.

35. *Hwangsŏng sinmun*, 26 February 1906.

36. Quoted in Ikegawa 1986, 79.

37. Tarui himself changed his stance by the time of annexation (Hatada 1969, 58–59).

Ōgaki sought especially to influence "the educated and anti-Japanese Confucian literati and *yangban*" and transform them into trustworthy allies, an effort that mirrored Itō's political agenda.[38] Ōgaki's main strategy was to highlight Confucian civilization as a common point of reference between Japan and Korea. In his thesis, "Ch'ŏngnyŏn ipji p'yŏn" (On the Self-Striving of Youth) published in Korea in 1908, for instance, Ōgaki sought to buttress the position of progressive elements in the local gentry by defending Confucianism against its detractors who single-mindedly advocated Westernization. And he chided Korean scholars for failing to better apply the wisdom of their Confucian masters, while noting the centrality of Confucian ideals in the Imperial Rescript on Education, an emblem of Japan's neo-traditional approach to modernization. Such a move initially won over influential Koreans like Pak Ŭn-sik (1859–1925) and Kim Yun-sik, who had been groping for ways to move their country forward without discarding its Confucian heritage.[39] Ōgaki also conveyed particular admiration for the ability of Anglo-American nations to combine modernity and tradition, to "protect ancestral customs and institutions, while eradicating their ills to improve them gradually." Styling himself as a Meiji enlightenment thinker, Ōgaki preached to the Korean leaders that "great nations" were made by "people who advanced not by means of revolution [*hyŏngmyŏng*] but by means of reform [*kaehyŏk*]."[40]

Although Ōgaki managed to garner considerable respect from the Korean intelligentsia, their relationship was not always amicable. Tensions flared in 1907 when the Taehan Chaganghoe endorsed the nationwide campaign to repay debts Korea had incurred to Japan as a measure to recover sovereignty, and also objected to Japanese pressure on Kojong to abdicate following the revelation of the "Hague Incident." The organization was consequently ordered by the Residency-General to dissolve, though its members quickly regrouped themselves as the Taehan Hyŏphoe.[41] Nonetheless, these tensions did not escalate into open conflict, as the Korean leaders remained, for the most part, as optimistic about their nation's ability to recover independence as about the even-

38. Ōgaki to Kurachi (12 January 1911).
39. Han 2005, 171.
40. Ōgaki 1906, 1–5.
41. Ikegawa 1985, 556–58.

tual Japanese departure promised in the protectorate treaty.[42] Ōgaki's efforts at persuasion also appear to have paid off. By 1909, the general orientation of the Taehan Hyŏphoe had shifted from an "anti-Japanese" to an accommodationist stance toward protectorate rule, as personally affirmed by its leader Kim Ka-jin (1846–1922). While "we absolutely cannot agree with the merger of Japan and Korea [*Nikkan gappō*] and annexation [*gappei*] as proposed by the Ilchinhoe," Kim explained to a local reporter, "there is not a single person [in our organization] who harbors anti-Japanese thought."[43] Although the interviewer considered the truthfulness of Kim's claim suspect, Chŏng Un-bok (1870–1920) seconded his colleague, describing the Taehan Hyŏphoe as "neither intractable resistors" nor a slavish "Japan faction" (*Nihon-tō*) like the Ilchinhoe.[44]

If the Korean reformers walked a fine line between resistance and collaboration vis-à-vis the protectorate government, so did their Japanese supporters. Fostering Pan-Asianism and dampening anti-Japanese sentiment may have helped the goals of the Residency-General, but Ōgaki and other Japanese advisors pursued another agenda that frequently unnerved the authorities: to develop their organizations into political parties.[45]

Biographical sketches of these Japanese advisors as former popular rights advocates suggest that many of them found in Korea, as Pan-Asianists like Miyazaki Tōten did in China, an outlet for their frustrated dreams of popular democracy, and a new political theater where the foot soldiers of Meiji might reclaim their revolution.[46] Ōgaki specifically entertained the idea of introducing a two-party system to Korea, and developing the Taehan Chaganghoe into one mass political party, time

---

42. Pak Ch'an-sŭng 1992, 59.

43. *Chōsen* (Chōsen Zasshisha), April 1910, 14.

44. Chŏng Un-bok 1908, 20. Taking such a moderate stance could make one susceptible to new accusations of "playing both sides of the fence as pro-Japanese and as anti-Japanese," for which Chŏng himself was criticized by his political rivals (*Chōsen* [Chōsen Zasshisha], April 1910, 13).

45. Ikegawa 1996, 120–21.

46. It was in this vein that some popular rights activists like Ōi Kentarō (1843–1922) had schemed to export their vision of a democratic revolution to Korea (known as "Osaka Incident") and import it back into Japan to redeem their failed political reforms (Kajimura 1992, 131).

and again prodding its leaders in this direction.[47] Equally important for nurturing "nationalist thought" (*kokkateki shisō*) was to create a system of local autonomy, he stressed, explaining in detail how it worked in Japan through a welter of articles in the local press and in the organization's bulletin.[48]

In the spring of 1907, speaking at a political rally organized by the Taehan Chaganghoe, timed to coincide with another rally held by the Ilchinhoe, Ōgaki told his Korean audience how the two organizations were already operating like modern political parties. "Korea's two large political parties stand face to face, . . . and each entrusts the judgment of its ability to public discussion [*kongnon*]. This so-called battle of men of virtue [*kunja*] is naturally an inherent characteristic of public parties [*kongdang*]." Moreover, "For Korea's parties [*tangp'a*] to publicly present their political views and investigate the state's [*kukka*] interests and people's merits and demerits is truly a blessing for high and low, and [one that] advances the level of civilization." With this lesson in mind, Ōgaki exhorted the assembled members, "devote [yourselves] to expanding the party's strength," until the organization became a true "spokesman for the entire nation."[49]

If Ōgaki's vision resonated with that of the Taehan Hyŏphoe leaders, who were equally keen on organizing their influence into a political party,[50] it increasingly became a point of contention with the protectorate authorities. From the beginning, Itō took a pragmatic approach to dealing with civilian interlocutors like Ōgaki and the Korean reformers operating outside the government. He permitted their activities as long

---

47. Pak Ch'an-sŭng 1992, 65. For the Ilchinhoe's own perception as a political party, see Moon 2010, Chapter 4.

48. See *Taehan Chaganghoe wŏlbo* 4 (25 October 1906), 5 (25 November 1906), 6 (25 December 1906), 8 (25 February 1907), 10 (25 April 1907), 11 (25 May 1907), and 12 (25 June 1907).

49. Ōgaki Takeo [Taewŏn Changbu], "Ponhoe ŭi changnae," *Taehan Chaganghoe wŏlbo* 11 (25 May 1907), 7–8, 12.

50. Sase 1927, 69. According to historian Pak Ch'an-sŭng (1992, 47), the newly formed Taehan Hyŏphoe was effectively functioning as a political party that collected dues from its members and held rallies and national conventions to work out a platform. One Korean leader of another organization likened the Taehan Hyŏphoe to the Seiyūkai in Japan ("Nikkan gappōron ni taisuru Kanjin no gendō," Otsuhi no. 2711 [7 December 1909]).

as they remained "lawful," but he was just as ready to clamp down on their activities anytime they threatened to derail his reform program. Most Japanese advisors initially operated with the full knowledge of Itō, who welcomed their support in advancing Korean reform and minimizeing dissent. It was in this vein that in 1906, for instance, Itō appointed Uchida to the Resident-General's staff, in the hope of using the Ilchinhoe to co-opt pro-Japanese officials and bring the Korean cabinet under Japanese control. As the protectorate government consolidated its hold over Korea after 1907, however, Itō began to check the excesses of enthusiasts like Uchida whose self-aggrandizing behavior seemed merely to stoke public antipathy. He also withdrew support from the Ilchinhoe (while reviving the power of traditional elites), whose populist strategies, as expressed in tax resistance movements, ran afoul of the Japanese desire for stability and control.[51] Itō took a similar approach to Ōgaki. He supported Ōgaki's early endeavors, periodically asking for information and advice, but when Ōgaki and his comrades sought to organize a political party as a way of reviving the disbanded Taehan Chaganghoe, Itō balked.[52] He hobbled Ōgaki's attempt to support the newly formed Taehan Hyŏphoe by prohibiting its leaders from creating an office to recruit new members. If permitted, the Korean reformers might make common cause with veteran ideologues of parliamentarianism who had risen in opposition to the Meiji leadership, which was far from what Itō wanted in a time of social unrest.[53]

The decades of confronting politically aroused masses at home help to explain Itō's attitudes toward Ōgaki. To be sure, Itō was not inherently opposed to the idea of parties. In fact, he was the first prime minister to recognize their value, ultimately founding the conservative Rikken Seiyūkai in 1900. But this strategy of alliance with parties came after more than a decade of confronting raucous agitation for mass democracy and violence at the polls in the first Diet elections of the early 1890s—an experience that hardened into bureaucratic suspicion of parties and the efforts to achieve the "denaturing of politics."[54] The protectorate authorities, indeed, began to worry that emigrants and *rōnin*,

51. Moon 2010, Chapter 5.
52. Ōgaki 1911; Kankoku Chūsatsu Kenpeitai Shireibu 1910.
53. Ikegawa 1996, 119–21.
54. Gluck 1985, 49–60.

who had earlier spread images of lowly Japanese injurious to national prestige, might now spread more unsettling ideas of political participation in Korea.

## *Settlers' Call for Annexation*

As Itō grew increasingly wary of local reformers, the Japanese advisors and supporters themselves were divided over the pace of Korean reform. Their differences became manifest in the wake of Itō's resignation as Resident-General in June 1909, which came two years after a costly and ruthless counterinsurgency campaign had left the provinces still rife with anti-Japanese hostility. Itō's departure, which signaled an admission of the failure of his gradualist policy, opened the way for his critics in the Katsura government to move in and prepare the country for full annexation—what Itō had considered as a last resort.[55] Abandoning the idea of a horizontal alliance of the East Asian nations that Meiji leaders had never fully embraced anyway, Japan shifted its focus from reform to realpolitik.

Yet what unfolded in the months leading up to annexation was shaped less by the Tokyo metropole than by a set of competing agents on the ground. At the center were journalists and political fixers like Ōgaki and Uchida. As the gradualist policy appeared to reach a dead end, leaders of the Ilchinhoe, the Taehan Hyŏphoe, and the Sŏbuk Hakhoe, in negotiations brokered by Ōgaki, briefly pondered ways of bridging their differences to regain control over the government.[56] But when the prospect of alliance soon broke down, the Ilchinhoe leaders went ahead with their own plan: to bring about the immediate Japanese political absorption of Korea.[57] An opportune moment arrived in October 1909, when Itō was assassinated in Harbin by a Korean nationalist, An Chung-gŭn.[58] Uchida quickly mobilized the Ilchinhoe to submit a memorial to Sunjong (1874–1926), son and successor of Kojong, and petitions to Yi Wan-yong (now prime minister) and new Resident-General Sone

55. Duus 1995, 230, 234–37.
56. Hatano 1993, 74; Pak Ch'an-sŭng 1992, 52–53.
57. Kuzuu 1930, 510–11.
58. Keijō Kenpeibuntai 1910, 31.

Arasuke (1849–1910), asking for the abdication of the monarch and a "political merger" (*seigappō*) of Korea and Japan.[59]

Shocked and outraged by the Ilchinhoe's move, the city of Seoul exploded in protest. Leaders of the Taehan Hyŏphoe and the Sŏbuk Hakhoe organized a mass rally to condemn the Ilchinhoe's "rash" and "premature" demand for annexation,[60] and the vernacular press helped spread the public outcry beyond the capital to the provinces. Meanwhile, the reactions of Japanese settlers, as one police report noted, "appeared to be unanimously hostile."[61] The most vocal were again the journalists in Seoul, including the likes of Minegishi Shigetarō. Save for a few sympathizers,[62] they collectively assailed Uchida for his self-aggrandizing actions, and promptly wired their protest to Tokyo. Unlike the majority of Koreans, the settlers were not fundamentally opposed to the idea of annexation. Quite the contrary, according to a statement issued by the journalists on 21 December, what infuriated them were the Ilchinhoe's use of an evasive term, "political merger" (*seigappō*),[63] and its "crafty and abominable" conduct engineered by Uchida, who dared to "carry out such a grave incident without consulting us."[64] Not only did the settlers feel sidelined by the ultranationalists, they also felt the chauvinists did not go far enough in calling for a full takeover of Korea.

59. Hatano 1993, 82.

60. But the two organizations did not essentially object to the idea of a merger, as Ōgaki explained to the leaders in Tokyo (Ōgaki, "Kankoku kokujō ippan," appended to Otsuhi no. 2891 [28 December 1909]).

61. Keihi no. 4249-1 (10 December 1909), in *T'onggambu munsŏ* 1998, 8:95.

62. Some settlers welcomed the Ilchinhoe's campaign as breaking the stalemate. See Kyokuhōsei, "Gappō mondai," *Chōsen* (Chōsen Zasshisha), January 1910, 6. According to police reports, Uchida also tried to bribe a few journalists, including Minegishi, and appealed to settler leaders such as Ikeda Chōjirō for their support in mobilizing the settler public opinion behind the movement for the merger (Kimitsu tōhatsu no. 2095 [18 December 1909]; "Kan-Nichi gappō mondai ni taisuru sōgō hōkoku no ken," besshi 4; Keiki no. 2489 [17 December 1909], "Zai Keijō Nihon kyoryūmin no shinbunsha baishū mata gappō undō no ken," in *T'onggambu munsŏ* 1998, 8:157–58).

63. According to Yumi Moon (2010, 225–26), in calling for a political union the Ilchinhoe leaders appear to have had in mind Germany and Austria-Hungary as models, but they remained ambiguous on the question of Korea's autonomy in internal government.

64. Keihi no. 4141-1 (6 December 1909), in *T'onggambu munsŏ* 1998, 8:56; Kenki no. 2394 (9 December 1909), in ibid., 85; *Yomiuri shinbun*, 26 December 1909.

The personal conflict between the two Japanese advisors, Uchida and Ōgaki, seems to have discomfited the local authorities. One army commander anxiously reported to War Minister Terauchi Masatake that Yi Wan-yong and other Korean leaders were "sneering [at them] behind their backs" and might be scheming to exploit Japanese discord to their own advantage.[65] In order to resolve the differences between Uchida and Ōgaki and mitigate public outrage, fellow journalist Kikuchi Kenjō intervened.[66] Kikuchi managed to have Uchida admit his rashness in making the Ilchinhoe submit a petition "in disregard of Korean people's sentiment" and agree to entrust Ōgaki with the task of "salvaging the Isshinkai [Ilchinhoe]."[67] Ōgaki, for his part, agreed to finesse the Taehan Hyŏphoe's position by making its leaders clarify their stance that the merger was "premature" rather than that they were "absolutely opposed" to the idea.[68] Meanwhile, the Katsura cabinet dispatched its own investigation to settle the tension between the journalists and the Ilchinhoe. When this effort proved futile, the Japanese government ordered the Ilchinhoe to suspend the annexation campaign. Faced with the virulent public reaction, Resident-General Sone, too, decided he had no choice but to order Uchida and Ōgaki to leave the peninsula as "a last strategy to restore harmony in the Korean political world."[69] But the annexation campaign ultimately carried the day. By this time, Uchida and fellow ultranationalists were securing an agreement from Tokyo that

---

65. Hatano 1993, 77, 81.

66. Kimitsu tōhatsu no. 2087 (8 December 1909), in *T'onggambu munsŏ* 1998, 8:70–71, 72–73.

67. From Resident-General Sone to Prime Minister Katsura, Kimitsu tōhatsu no. 2087 (8 December 1909), besshi 1 hōkokusho (Kenki no. 2365), besshi 5 hōkokusho (Kenki no. 2380), in *T'onggambu munsŏ* 1998, 8:70–71, 72–73.

68. From Superintendent-General of Police Wakabayashi Raizō to Resident-General Sone Arasuke, Keihi no. 4417-1 (20 December 1909), in *T'onggambu munsŏ* 1998, 8:166. When the Korean leaders of the Taehan Hyŏphoe held an assembly to discuss submitting a statement of opposition to the merger, to request the government to punish the Ilchinhoe leaders, Yi Yong-gu and Song Pyŏng-jun, Ōgaki accused them of holding a meeting without consulting his opinion as an advisor and managed to make them retract their proposal by arguing such a rash action would only harm Japan-Korea relations and threatening to leave the organization (Keiki no. 2530 [21 December 1909], in *T'onggambu munsŏ* 1998, 8:172).

69. Hatano 1993, 77, 81; Kenki no. 2535 (21 December 1909) and Keihi no. 4513-1 (22 December 1909), in *T'onggambu munsŏ* 1998, 8:173–74.

it would take the initiative toward annexation with no Korean intervention in the matter.[70] Ōgaki himself appears to have concluded that annexation provided a way to "fundamentally resolve" the situation and planned to persuade the Japanese government to move ahead.[71] Yi Wanyong signed the annexation treaty on 22 August 1910.

Claiming to bring stability to the crisis-prone peninsula, Japan proved to be the most destabilizing of all powers that transformed Korea around the turn of the century. Yet this image of a wild-card imperialist emerges not so much out of the actions and visions of Itō's protectorate government as those of political fixers like Ōgaki and journalists like Minegishi. Like their ultranationalist rivals, these men operated beyond the pale of official control. Neither innocent bystanders nor mere irritants on the stage of imperialist politics, local settlers, through the interpenetrated realms of politics and press, rarely stayed out of what on the surface appeared to be a confrontation between the Japanese state and Korean nationalists. The picture that emerges from the settlers' call for outright annexation, indeed, is one of a reluctant empire being goaded by its chauvinistic citizens who wished to take up the task themselves. Though their impact was indirect, their impulse as subimperialists fully embedded settlers in a political gyroscope through which a set of contending forces propelled Japan toward territorial conquest of Korea. Settlers' incendiary attack on Itō's "self-rule" policy, and their jingoistic call for a takeover, steadily eliminated alternatives to direct political control by snarling the already convoluted relationships among the Japanese protectorate, the Korean cabinet, and political reformers, exacerbating tension between hardliners and gradualists in both Tokyo and Seoul, and sharpening divisions within the Korean self-strengthening movement. The journalists' run-in with ultranationalists in this sense was the straw that broke the camel's back. Not only did the settlers' reaction highlight the failure of the Residency-General to build a stable framework of rule, it gave the Japanese hardliners, inside and outside the cabinet, a final pretext to push for full colonization of the peninsula.

---

70. Hatano 1993, 75, 82.
71. Kenki no. 2591 (25 December 1909), in *T'onggambu munsŏ* 1998, 8:184–85.

## *Assimilation Policy*

Despite the turmoil in the months leading up to the annexation, when it finally occurred, local settlers unanimously welcomed their government's decision. Korea's sovereignty was formally ceded to Japan by the annexation treaty, which declared all inhabitants "subjects of the monarch or imperial subjects" (*shinmin*). This congratulatory mood, however, soon turned sour. Indeed, tension between the colonial state and Japanese settlers reached its height after 1910, when Terauchi Masatake assumed the mantle of leadership as the first Governor-General of Korea. Although he largely inherited the administrative machinery of protectorate government perched on the Korean court, the new colonial ruler was a state unto himself. Responsible only to the emperor and given broad legislative powers, Governor-General Terauchi ruled through a deluge of ordinances he personally issued, while relying on an extensive network of armed police (*kenpeitai*) and security forces. His style of governance not only earned the unflattering label of "military rule" (*budan seiji*), but also brought detrimental consequences for settler agency and citizenship, as we will see.[72]

If "military rule" misleadingly implies exclusive reliance on coercion, it appropriately captures the rigor with which the new colonial governor sought to transform his territory. Korea was rapidly reshaped into a site of extraction through a nationwide cadastral survey and a series of "state works"—"the visible, material embodiments of [state] authority and 'civilizing' modernity,"[73] such as railways, roads, harbors, port facilities, and irrigation projects. Although the survey served to entrench the powers of the *yangban* elite and secure their support for the colonial regime,[74] the Government-General shifted the balance of power drastically in its own favor by making all local groups, including the once-powerful landed aristocracy, subject to its authority. More centralized and intrusive than the Chosŏn government it had displaced (as well as

72. For details on the appointment of the Governor-General of Korea, the scope of his power, and his relationship with Tokyo (in comparison with that of colonial Taiwan), see E. Chen 1970; Okamoto Makiko 2008.

73. Goswami 2004, 46.

74. Gragert 1994, 71–72.

most contemporary European empires),[75] the Japanese colonial state reached deeper into daily lives of local residents through a vast network of policemen, who oversaw day-to-day administration of Korea from tax collection and the maintenance of order, to the supervision of education and hygiene.[76] The Japanese authorities also launched vigorous measures of social engineering by building colonial schools, while absorbing or abolishing Korean private academies, and by issuing a panoply of laws and regulations to eradicate "backward" customs and suppress the entire range of Korean public life.[77]

Many of these colonial practices represented "an overspill" of Meiji reform programs underwritten by the spirit of disciplinary enlightenment,[78] which became part of the rationale behind the Japanese colonial policy of *dōka* (assimilation). In his "Proclamation of Annexation," Governor-General Terauchi explained the implementation of *dōka* as follows: "It is the natural and inevitable course of things that the two peoples [of Korea and Japan] whose countries are in close proximity with each other, whose interests are identical and who are bound together with brotherly feelings, should amalgamate and form one body."[79]

Designed to legitimate Japanese rule as a corollary of cultural and ethnic affinities, *dōka* became Japan's cardinal principle of governing Korea and other territories in the empire. Distinct from the French republican ideal of assimilation,[80] the concept of *dōka* developed from a theoretical ensemble consisting of the Confucian-derived notions of *dōbun dōshu* (same script, same race) and *isshi dōjin* (impartiality and equal favor), the national mythology of an emperor-centered family state, and the notion of Japanese as a mixed nation that had historically assimilated various Asian peoples.[81] Central to the justification of assimilation policy

---

75. On the relative weakness of the Chosŏn state, see Palais 1975; on European empires, see Gann 1984, 509, 515.

76. C. Chen 1984, 224–25. Koreans constituted about 60 percent of the overall policing force (Yamada 2000, 138).

77. C. Lee 1999, 39.

78. This concept of "overspill" is drawn from Gann 1984, 518.

79. Government-General of Chosen 1912, 242.

80. On the French notion of assimilation and ideology of citizenship, and the struggle for rights among a group of French-educated African elites (*évolués*), see Conklin 1997, 151–73.

81. Peattie 1984b, 96–98.

were the theories of Japan as a mixed nation (*kongō minzoku*) and shared ancestry of Japanese and Koreans (*Nissen dōsoron*),[82] which developed out of the work of the country's first generation of historians, anthropologists, archaeologists, and linguists in the course of their search for "the origins of the Japanese."[83] In defining "the Japanese" in relation to colonial subjects and minority groups in the empire, these scholars also introduced and familiarized the Western-derived concepts of *minzoku* (a culturally and nationally defined notion of ethnic group or ethnos) and *jinshu* (a biologically defined notion of race) along with their fluid and interchangeable usage.[84]

Before annexation, however, the extent to which the idea of affinity was accepted by local settlers in Korea is far from clear; it was rarely mentioned in the Japanese resident press before 1910.[85] Along with the notion of affinity existed the idea of Japanese purity and homogeneity, which was promoted by *kokutai* (national polity) theorists who highlighted the institution of emperor, maintained through an unbroken line of successors, in conceptualizing the Japanese as a unique nation bound by consanguineous descent (*ketsuzoku*).[86] Most settlers appear to have favored this latter concept when they began to discuss the viability of assimilation as policy. Around the time of annexation, two interrelated issues of *dōka*—the "assimilability" of Koreans and the Japanese ability to assimilate—became the subject of considerable debate in the Japanese resident press. When solicited opinions on questions like "Whether or not Koreans should be educated" and "the Korean ability to assimilate," many settlers initially conveyed pessimism. One of them, Ayukai Fusanoshin, who chose the life of a scholarly recluse after years of political activism (see Chapter 1), apparently saw "no hope" in educating Ko-

---

82. For a detailed explanation of these theories, see Oguma 2002.

83. Pai 1999, 366–67; S. Tanaka 1993, especially 164–67, 244–48.

84. On the conflation of race, ethnicity, and nation in prewar Japanese discourse, see Weiner 1995, 442.

85. Satogami 1996, 293.

86. This was a view propounded by *kokutai* theorists, such as Inoue Tetsujirō and Hozumi Yatsuka (Oguma 2002, Chapter 3). But Oguma perceptively points out that these two apparently conflicting notions of "the Japanese" were in fact coterminous. The theory on "shared ancestry" was both a subspecies of "the mixed nation theory" and the idea of Japan as a homogeneous nation calibrated to an enlarged spatial scale of its East Asian empire (ibid., 64).

reans, having failed in such a venture himself, and completely shunned the idea of common racial origins.[87] Settler discourse also contained an increasingly sharp and gendered dichotomy of "backward" Koreans and "civilized" Japanese, as expressed in the words of another settler who predicted that educating "effeminate" Koreans would be almost as difficult as "nurturing women and children."[88]

If the idea of common racial heritage remained contested, however, equally uncertain in this period was an equation between civilization and Japanization. As Song Pyŏng-jun of the recently disbanded Ilchinhoe told a local Japanese reporter, Koreans, as faithful custodians of Confucian tradition, tended to view Japanese people, culture, and literature as rather "shallow" and "flimsy."[89] While such perceptions took decades to fade, civilization and Japanization also remained separate affairs in the eyes of some Japanese. "Assimilating to Japan is more difficult than assimilating to modern civilization" for Koreans, observed one settler in 1915, admitting "they tend to consider it more honorable and enjoyable to study Western customs and manners."[90] If British colonists derided Westernized Africans as savages trying to imitate civilization against their true nature,[91] the Japanese rulers, in their mimetic attempt to civilize the "natives" in Korea, encountered cultural contempt that inconveniently echoed their own backwardness vis-à-vis the West.

Nevertheless, the annexation and the formal declaration of assimilation policy soon rendered skeptics a minority. As colonial publications began to peddle the idea of common origins, which had by then become all but a scholarly consensus in Japan, the question regarding *dōka* changed from *whether* to *how*.[92] The official stance on assimilation policy became almost unshakable. As chief of the educational bureau, Sekiya Teisaburō (1875–1950), explained, "those of us who work for the government have no choice but to believe that assimilation is possible and

87. *Chōsen* (Chōsen Zasshisha), June 1908, 7.

88. *Chōsen* (Chōsen Zasshisha), July 1908, 8.

89. *Chōsen* (Chōsen Zasshisha), October 1911, 43–44; *Chōsen jijō kimitsu tsūshin*, no. 1 (December 1924): 23.

90. *Chōsen oyobi Manshū*, October 1915, 9.

91. Kennedy 1987, 163.

92. In the mind of Japanese administrators, it appears that the question of assimilation as a viable colonial policy ceased to be a moot point after 1895, when Taiwan was colonized (Caprio 2009, 71–73, 81).

proceed with all aspects of [colonial] management under this principle."[93] Most local settlers, too, came to share with officials a broad consensus on *dōka* as policy ideal—and naïve optimism about its future success. Even as *dōka* was enshrined as policy, however, few colonial officials were certain about what it precisely meant. For the education bureau chief, assimilation referred to "a policy to guide Koreans toward a new civilization and make them loyal and good Japanese imperial subjects [*Nihon teikokumin*]," with "the diffusion of Japanese language" being its foremost goal. Singling out "indolence" as "the greatest weakness of Koreans," Vice Governor-General Yamagata Isaburō (1858–1927) stressed a long-term administrative goal of "transforming [them] into an industrious and hard-working people."[94]

The nebulousness of the term invited a stream of interlocutors from the settler community, who offered a variety of definitions of *dōka*—cultural, spiritual, economic, judicial, environmental—to delineate the policy contours of this amorphous process. Like colonial officials, many of them rendered the overall aim of *dōka* in terms of exporting Japan's modernizing reforms. This was to be done gradually according to Korea's evolving "cultural level" (*mindo*), with an aim to rectify what they considered the problematic aspects of Korean ethnic character. To eradicate traditional elite scorn toward moneymaking and cultivate industrial thought, for instance, was a step toward "relieving Korean daily hardship."[95] Local Japanese teachers also appear to have considered character improvement a priority in their pedagogy. They spoke of remedying Korean "lack of hygiene," "unscrupulousness," and "insolence,"[96] echoing the early Meiji official discourse on "foolish commoners" (*gumin*) at home.

More radical calls for *dōka* emerged from some local journalists, to whom assimilation was ultimately a matter of spiritual conquest. According to Shakuo Shunjō, it meant a fusion between "Koreanness" (*Chōsensei*) and "Japanese spirit" (*Nihon damashii*) "to the extent that 10 million new subjects would swear their life and death with us Japanese in the presence of the emperor." This, he argued, required the eradication

93. *Chōsen* (Chōsen Zasshisha), November 1911, 2–5.

94. Ibid., 2–3.

95. This is an opinion of Kikuchi Kenjō (*Mankan no jitsugyō*, August 1910, 19–22).

96. *Chōsen* (Chōsen Zasshisha), November 1911, 6–7.

of all things Korean—language, customs, character, sentiments—"to the point where it becomes difficult to distinguish between 'us' and 'them.'"[97] This task, wrote another like-minded journalist, Aoyagi Tsunatarō (1877–1932), rested on the shoulders of young Japanese settlers. By leading the effort to spiritually assimilate Koreans, local Japanese youth, "devoid of patriotism and steeped in rampant individualism," could be spiritually revived in turn. Combining his vision of *dōka* with a call for making Japan a "world empire" (*sekai teikoku*) second to none, Aoyagi called on "250,000 young [Japanese] men in Korea" to muster their "Yamato spirit" for undertaking "Greater Japanism" (*Dai Nihonshugi*) in accordance with the words of the sun goddess Amaterasu to "pacify" and "govern" countries "in all four corners under heaven."[98]

For most of the colonial period, the policy of *dōka* remained less a fixed set of practices than a vaguely defined administrative credo. While settlers continued to debate and refine its meaning, assimilation as official policy remained an amorphous mélange of processes with ill-defined criteria for evaluating its progress.[99] Still, we may tease out from the early colonial discourse and practices several distinct processes implied by the policy of *dōka*: namely, civilization (*bunmeika*), Japanization (*Nihonka* or *Nihonjinka*), imperialization (*shinminka*), and nationalization (*kokuminka*).[100] These processes may be seen as going at once with different degrees of emphasis—and as later chapters will show, periodically reshuffled to suit the prevailing needs of Korean governance, though not necessarily along the lines desired by Japanese settlers.

---

97. Ibid., 10–13.

98. Aoyagi 1916, 11–18, 27–29.

99. Mark Caprio (2009) makes a crucially important point that Japanese assimilation policy in Korea, especially in the area of education, drew on the repository of knowledge accrued from elsewhere in the empire, including Okinawa, Hokkaido, and Taiwan. In seeking to evaluate the success of Japanese rulers—the main concern of his book—however, Caprio assumes the coherence of assimilation as a colonial project and an official consensus on its meaning, which, in my view, remained more contested and ambiguous than his analysis suggests.

100. I am grateful to Andre Schmid for parceling out these processes from my earlier manuscript.

## *Conflicting Visions of Expansion*

In the course of debating how best to assimilate Koreans, settlers soon found their own lives being yoked to the Governor-General's rule. For justifying the policy of *dōka*, Terauchi adopted a slogan of *isshi dōjin* (impartiality and equal favor), a concept derived from Confucian thought. When interviewed by a local journalist in late 1913, Terauchi restated his policy "to make no distinction between natives and countrymen [*hongokujin*]."[101] This proved to be no mere rhetoric. Terauchi placed both Koreans and settlers under his uniform authority in areas spanning public speech, press, political activity, commerce, land ownership, and overseas migration.[102] This broad oversight differed radically from most European colonies, where settlers and native inhabitants were administered separately.[103]

The professed Japanese policy of *isshi dōjin*, to be sure, was fraught with contradictions. By virtue of the annexation treaty, Koreans along with settlers were deemed Japanese nationals and "subjects of the emperor."[104] Yet in each area of governance, the Government-General made finer differentiations between Korean and Japanese subjects by following the "separate but equal principle," which was implicitly underwritten by the colonial legal system.[105] Most criminal laws, for in-

---

101. *Chōsen oyobi Manshū*, December 1913, 5.

102. On the police regulations of public life of Korea's residents including Japanese settlers, see Yi Chong-min 2004, 340–42.

103. In the case of Kenya, for instance, local officials, faced with the virulent settler population, had already abandoned hopes for racial "interpenetration" and in the early 1910s opted for "an increasing administrative segregation between white and black" (Berman and Lonsdale 1992, 94). The case of French Algeria was more complex (see Introduction, n. 37).

104. C. Chen 1984, 245–46.

105. Highly pluralistic and complex, this system was operated broadly by three kinds of laws: the Governor-General's ordinances, which formed the bulk of overseas (*gaichi*) laws; metropole-enacted laws that were extended to the colony by means of "imperial command" (*chokurei*); and laws specifically enacted for institution in the colony with the assent of the imperial assembly. These laws were further divided into laws based on the principle of the person or nationality (*zokujin-hō*) and laws based on the principle of residence (*zokuchi-hō*), which determined the applicability of citizenship rights and duties to Koreans, settlers, or both. For more details (including efforts to unify colonial and metropolitan laws concerning marriage and crime punishment through the Common Law of 1918), see Asano and Matsuda 2004, 112–13.

stance, were administered independently for settlers and for Koreans, the notorious example being the "Flogging Ordinance" whose exclusive application to Koreans was justified on the basis of their "low *mindo*."[106] The same was true of early education ordinances, which allowed Japanese primary schools to enjoy metropolitan-level education while limiting Korean "ordinary schools" to vocational training and Japanese language lessons.[107] More fundamentally, a set of metropolitan laws that defined Japanese citizenship on the basis of one's membership in a family (*ie*)—namely, laws concerning family registration (Minseki hō),[108] the civil code (Minpō), and conscription—were extended only to overseas settlers.[109]

Under this system that separated nationality from citizenship, Japanese and Koreans remained by no means equal before the law, but settlers still faced constraints unique to their overseas status. In some areas of civil and criminal affairs, for instance, Japanese and Korean residents were made subject to the same laws concerning political crimes and punishment (1919) and peace preservation (1925).[110] Above all, with the abolition of extraterritoriality, settlers lost their right to vote in national elections, which was determined by the principle of residence (*jūsho shugi*). Because suffrage in Japan had no legal restrictions based on race or ethnicity, this created a peculiar juridical situation where Korean (and Taiwanese) residents in Japan who met residence and tax qualifications acquired the right to vote, whereas Japanese overseas settlers were disenfranchised.[111] This Japanese practice departed

---

106. C. Lee 1999, 34.

107. Kim Puja 2005, 70.

108. Family registration (*koseki*) was a key mechanism for delimiting the boundaries of citizenship: it defined one's eligibility for conscription and overseas allowance (*zaikin kahō*) as well as matters related to relatives and inheritance. This system was partially extended to Koreans by enacting a separate family registration law (Asano and Matsuda 2004, 127, 131).

109. For details on the application of different types of laws to Koreans, see Chōsen Sōtokufu 1922, 485–86, 489; Yi Yŏng-mi 2005, 119, 204.

110. Asano and Matsuda 2004, 137.

111. Ibid., 131. Although settlers could still run for office from their places of family registry in Japan, this provision to grant voting rights on the basis of residence appears to have reflected an official concern to mollify indigenous elites. The authorities wished to allow a few qualified individuals from the colony to participate in metropolitan politics, rather than deny such an opportunity altogether and breed anti-Japanese sentiment

from that of Europeans in Africa, where metropolitan nationals carried full citizenship wherever they settled, constituting a whites-only "civil society" in the "heart of darkness."[112]

Japanese residents in Korea, by contrast, found themselves in juridical limbo.[113] By their own lights, overseas settlers were every bit as Japanese as metropolitan residents. But in the realm of law, they remained on an ambiguous frontier in what Tessa Morris-Suzuki has aptly characterized as "the many concentric circles of colonial citizenship," which radiated from "Japan proper" (governed fully by the Meiji Constitution and metropolitan laws) to overseas peripheries (subject to the Governor-General's rule).[114] Within the system of colonial citizenship in Korea, operated largely at the discretion of the Governor-General, settler ambivalence and bitterness seemed to magnify particularly in light of the official effort to win over Korean elites, who were powerful candidates for assimilation and contenders for citizen status. Just as British colonial officers often identified Indian princes and African chiefs as their social

---

(Oguma 1998, 195–200). That race or ethnicity did not become a major issue to lawmakers should not surprise us, considering that less than 5 percent of the metropolitan Japanese population could vote before 1925.

112. Stora 2001, 6; Ruedy 2005, 74–76, 80, 86–87. According to Mahmood Mamdani, civil society was all but a preserve of white settlers in colonial Africa (1996, 19). We might add, however, that they enjoyed full citizenship only where a separate judicial infrastructure was created to support their status. In the British Empire, the official practices regarding political rights of settlers and natives varied enormously among colonies. Whereas all Aborigines in Australia and natives in South Africa were denied the vote, for instance, the Maoris and whites in New Zealand had similar political rights, but settlers in these new democracies had become fully enfranchised by 1910. See Evans et al. 2003.

113. According to the prewar concept of *kokumin* (people, nation)—whereas *shinmin* (imperial subjects) was the term used in the Meiji Constitution to refer to the Japanese people (Doak 2007, 148–49)—Japanese in the metropole, too, were neither completely rights-bearing citizens nor oppressed subjects (one historian has glossed them as "citizen-subjects" [Kyu Hyun Kim 2007]). But under the Governor-General's rule, overseas settlers occupied a more ambivalent position, where they were more citizens than subjects vis-à-vis Koreans, but less citizens than subjects vis-à-vis metropolitan residents.

114. Morris-Suzuki 1998, 168. In Meiji Japan, as Daniel Botsman (2005) has argued, membership in the modern nation for its new subjects was defined by more equal protection under the law. In colonial Korea, where the Governor-General became all but the law, settlers felt excluded from the liberating effects of the law and participation in modern citizenship.

equals, Japanese authorities recognized Korea's *yangban* elites as natural rulers and ideal collaborators. And just as native elites garnered more respect and attention than poor white settlers, so influential Koreans imparted a greater sense of affinity and value to Government-General officials than low-class Japanese migrants.[115] Anxious to palliate the hostility of Korean leaders, the colonial state showered former government officials and Confucian scholars with honors and aristocratic titles, granted them seats in the Chūsūin (K. Chungch'uwŏn; hereafter, Central Council), and awarded pensions to compensate for their loss of political power.

Such conciliatory gestures toward Koreans made settlers feel both uncomfortable and ignored. Speaking on their behalf, Makiyama Kōzō (1882–1961), editor of the local Japanese magazine *Chōsen kōron*, demanded the state grant proper recognition to Japanese residents as well. "Our countrymen in Korea not only fulfilled their duties as imperial subjects during the Sino-Japanese and the Russo-Japanese Wars," he claimed, "[they] also built schools, roads, hospitals, and temples without asking for official assistance and founded the basis for the expansion of Japanese settlements around the country." For their selfless sacrifice and contribution to the empire, he argued, they "must be honored as civilians who rendered distinguished service to the development of Korea."[116]

Settlers' demands for recognition were almost always paired with accusations of official favoritism toward the "natives," a tendency also seen among European settlers in Africa.[117] An article entitled "The Defects of the Governor-General's Rule: The Abandoned Japanese" summed up such abject sentiment.[118] In one of the most commonly cited examples of official neglect, the author complained that whereas the colonial state financed Korean education, Japanese settlers had to bear the cost of their children's schooling on their own. Yet the settlers, "supposed paragons and leaders for the Koreans," must remain content with shabby school buildings, which paled in comparison to the newly built facilities for Korean pupils. Contrary to the general assumption, the author noted, many Japanese migrants were "economically feeble" and

115. Cannadine 2002, 125.
116. *Chōsen kōron*, December 1913, 6–7.
117. For instance, see *Chōsen oyobi Manshū*, April 1914, 88–103.
118. *Chōsen oyobi Manshū*, March 1913, 7–9.

in need of official protection, especially in rural areas where power relations between Japanese and Koreans were often "reversed." In one such village, he even claimed to have witnessed a Japanese child receiving leftover food from a Korean resident, a moment that stirred the author to ask, "how can we even talk about assimilating the Koreans, when we Japanese beg for Korean sympathy and invite their contempt?" The Japanese resident press teemed with such invidious comparisons that overplayed settler misery while conveniently ignoring the plight of Koreans.

In the area of economic management, the settlers' call for protection ran directly counter to Terauchi's policy. Nowhere did this tension become more evident than in the instructions Terauchi issued in 1913 on "the protection of small farmers,"[119] an occupational category that represented the majority of Koreans. Seeing the dominance of "big landlords" and the lack of "social pillars" (*chūken*) as main factors that "hampered the growth of industry and general social progress," Terauchi stressed the urgent need to protect and promote "owner-cultivators" (*jisaku nōmin*) in Korea. But there were worrisome trends of land speculation and rampant land sales, caused by Japanese migrants who had recently begun to flock to the peninsula in droves. Terauchi particularly dreaded the arrival of "speculators" who threatened not only to "undermine steady agricultural management" but to destroy the fabric of Korean society by enticing "many middling and small Korean farmers . . . to sell off their ancestral fields." In order to protect native farmers and keep them on the land, Terauchi called on the provincial governors to "make every effort to forestall these trends" of Japanese land seizure.

Terauchi's instructions illustrate a larger challenge for the colonial state, shared by administrators in French Algeria and British Kenya, to balance the contradictory needs of legitimacy and control: to act "as arbiter in the clash of settler and native interests" while aiding the economic activities of their countrymen.[120] Worried about the evils of speculation and land seizure, Terauchi opted to act as a patron for Ko-

119. His instructions appeared in *Keijō nippō*, 25 August 1913 (the original issue is not extant), and are cited in full in Aoyagi 1913. They closely echo the Government-General's survey report on tenant farmers compiled a year before (Chōsen Sōtokufu Torishirabekyoku 1912, 465–69, 474, 523–25, 535).

120. Lustick 1985, 65; Berman and Lonsdale 1992, 88–89, 95, 119, 193.

rean farmers by regulating the activities of metropolitan capitalists, large or small, just as did the British administrators of Kenya in its formative years as the East Africa Protectorate. Japanese migration, if left uncontrolled, would subject Koreans to increased tenancy and poverty, hindering the growth of landowning cultivators who should form the backbone of the rural economy. Such concerns, which echoed contemporary anxieties about the adverse effects of capitalism on the Japanese countryside, partly informed Terauchi's decision to issue the Kaisharei (Company Law), which required an official license to start a business in Korea (discussed further in Chapter 5). The colonial authorities, moreover, continued to regulate the entry of Japanese and monitor their activities after arrival, placing under police surveillance a wide array of settlers: from "rascals and vagabonds" to journalists, businessmen, corporate executives, and religious workers.[121]

While putting on an impassive face of neutrality, Terauchi made no effort to hide his contempt for settlers. In an interview with a local journalist in 1915, he complained that Japanese residents had the worst record in tax payment and still harbored dreams of "striking it rich" (*ikkaku senkin*), many living only by their wits. Even men of means displayed "arrogance" and had "no aspirations to assimilate and enlighten" the Koreans, "busying themselves [instead] with petty conflicts over honor and profit."[122] At the root of bureaucratic scorn for migrants was the state's tendency, frequently chided by the local press, of "placing officials above the people" (*kanson minpi*) and seeing the latter as no more than "foolish commoners" (*gumin*). From the perspective of the ruling elite, Japan was still a nation of peasants who had no business in the affairs of national, let alone colonial, politics.

Local journalist Aoyagi Tsunatarō identified in such official attitudes an unbridgeable chasm between settlers and the state—or what he construed as a portentous "clash [of visions] between emigration policy and development policy." In his lengthy and emotionally charged response to Terauchi's instructions on small farmers, Aoyagi claimed that "our government's policy to promote emigration" through the ODC and "Your Excellency's policy" were "fundamentally irreconcilable." He

121. Yamamoto 1984, 125, quoted in Yi Sŭng-yŏp 2008.
122. *Chōsen oyobi Manshū*, May 1915, 5–7.

continued: "When big capitalists come to engage in land management, Your Excellency talks of the evil of land seizure, and when small capitalists come to buy land, Your Excellency suppresses them as speculators."[123] This "peculiar phenomenon" of the colony contradicting the imperial policy of Tokyo had a detrimental impact on settlers' morale, he argued. The Japanese community was afflicted with "dangerous social problems" that began to mirror the situation in the metropole, with "petty capitalists and the unpropertied busily looking for work on the streets like stray dogs," and some in dire straits "living day by day on leftovers from Koreans." Nor, at the same time, did Terauchi's policy of "assimilationism" (*dōka shugi*)—to "cosset [*aibu*] the Korean people and try to immerse them rapidly in civilization the same way as the countrymen at home"—help to foster ethnic harmony. To the contrary, he averred, it only presaged "the rise of a terrible evil of ethnic conflict in the future."[124]

More in sync with the trend of the industrial world was emigration accompanied by land seizure and increased tenancy, which Aoyagi defended as a necessary evil for "humankind's progress and development." Even should dispossession occur, he reassured Terauchi, Koreans would quickly rebuild their lives by bringing barren lands under cultivation, a task he considered more "appropriate to entrust to native inhabitants" than to Japanese migrants. And in defense of land colonization, Aoyagi put forth a new economic equation that would bridge a perceived gap between emigration and development: that "the growth of Japanese settlers and land sales means the cultivation of [more] uncultivated lands" on the peninsula.[125] In settler visions of colonization, the law of arithmetic clearly ran counter to the state's logic of control.

## *In Defense of Settler Autonomy*

The growing tension between state and settlers over assimilation policy reflected more than a semantic gap. It signaled the beginning of local settlers' protracted struggle for citizenship. Seeds of conflict had already been sown during protectorate rule, especially in 1908, when the Meiji

---

123. Aoyagi 1913, 331–36.
124. Ibid., 329, 336–37.
125. Ibid., 329, 333–34.

government empowered the Resident-General to appoint the chief of each residents' association and allowed public officials to run for posts in those associations. These acts were seen by local settlers as an affront.[126] A more decisive blow came when Terauchi announced his intent to end settlers' self-government (*jichi*) by dismantling the system of residents' associations altogether and absorbing their functions into the Government-General.[127] Predictably, the news of dissolution provoked howls of protest from around the peninsula. In 1912, lobbyists were dispatched to Tokyo to plead with the home government, and local residents' associations sent a battery of petitions to the Governor-General, the prime minister, key ministers, and chairmen of both houses of the Diet.[128] Settler leaders mounted ferocious opposition to the prospect of being treated on the same level as the Koreans, claiming "an irreducible gap" in their "levels of culture" (*mindo*). "Our countrymen in Korea today are already neither mere emigrants nor sojourners [*dekaseginin*]," the settlers asserted, imploring the state not to undermine their spirit as "pioneers of continental development."[129]

Settlers enhanced this argument with grander historical claims. "If the system of self-government for settlers [*kyoryūmin*] were discontinued," one petition argued, "it would blemish our constitutional history with a retrogression to bureaucratic rule" and "hinder the path of our empire vested with a special role to protect peace and happiness in East Asia."[130] Writing at a time when elected Diet members showed themselves to be too feisty to ignore, and placing their struggle firmly within the Taishō culture of political dissent, the settlers claimed that the democratic foundation they had laid would crumble under the weight of the "bureaucratic authoritarianism" the Governor-General threatened to revive on Korean soil. Their claim was not entirely baseless; the oldest residents' assemblies, as we have seen, began to operate in Korea before the metropolitan system of local government went fully into effect in the 1890s.[131] What the settlers wanted was thus not only to preserve their

126. Kimura 1989, 78–79; *Chōsen* (Chōsen Zasshisha), September 1908, 4, 7–12.
127. Duus 1995, 362–63.
128. Keijō-fu 1936, 896.
129. Zaisen Mindan Giin Rengōkai 1912, 43–44.
130. Tanaka Hanshirō et al. 1913, 39–40.
131. Kang Jae-ho 2001, 143.

associations, but to create "a system of self-rule [*jichi*] superior to the current system" by following Japan's now more advanced model.[132] In defending 30 years of self-government, the settler leaders desired to inscribe themselves in Japan's history as the earliest apostles of their nation's democracy—indeed, to claim their status as overseas builders and practitioners of a constitutional system at home.

But these protests came to naught. With the revision of foreign treaties and the termination of overseas settlements (*kyoryūchi*) in 1911, the system of settler self-government lost its rationale, and despite the clamor of dissent, the residents' associations were abolished in 1914. Settlers did not quietly submit to the Governor-General's order, however. That same year, they launched a campaign to protest "taxation without representation."[133] And as far as they could push the bounds of censorship, settler leaders continued to oppose stringent press control and demand greater political freedom for their community. Through petitions, personal protestations, and whatever limited means they had at their disposal, local settlers continually fulminated against Terauchi's rule as an empire that failed to make good on the constitutional spirit of Meiji.

It was no coincidence that these settler campaigns came at the height of so-called imperial democracy in Japan, "the era of the political crowd" inaugurated by the Hibiya Riots of 1905, when a vibrant culture of dissent emerged to challenge the oligarchs' monopoly on power.[134] While continuing to borrow the Meiji rhetoric of popular rights, the language used in the settlers' petitions also echoed the parades, rallies, and demonstrations that rose in the aftermath of the 1889 promulgation of the constitution and the Diet battles of the 1890s. Only under a political system that respected the popular will and a constitutional right to participate in politics, the settlers argued, could Japan continue to prosper. Some settlers became indirect participants in metropolitan politics. Local journalists, for instance, supported the Seiyūkai-led Goken Undō (Movement to Protect Constitutional Government) of late 1912 to early 1913, rallying behind its goal to combat the dominance of the Satsuma-Chōshū clique, whose influence extended to Korea through the appoint-

---

132. Zaisen Mindan Giin Rengōkai 1912, 44.
133. *Chōsen oyobi Manshū*, February 1914, 2–8.
134. Gordon 1991.

ment of army men, most notably Terauchi as the Governor-General and Akashi Motojirō (1864–1919) as the dual head of the *kenpeitai* and the police bureau.[135]

No journalist was more eager to link the metropolitan ferment for democracy to the settlers' quest for citizenship than Shakuo Shunjō (1875–?). Born in Okayama prefecture in the midst of the popular rights movement, Shakuo crossed to Korea in 1900 after graduating from Tōyō University. Having worked as a schoolteacher in Pusan and other cities, he moved to Seoul in 1907 to relaunch his career as a journalist. Shakuo landed a job as the chief editor of a magazine run by Kikuchi Kenjō, which he inherited in 1908 and transformed into what became his trademark magazine, *Chōsen* (later renamed *Chōsen oyobi Manshū*).[136] Although he did not have a party affiliation, Shakuo worshipped Inukai Tsuyoshi (1855–1932),[137] a prominent politician from his native Okayama and a leading opponent of the Satsuma-Chōshū government.

From the start, Shakuo's magazine became the platform of radical settler politics.[138] Having launched a searing tirade against Itō's policy, Shakuo after 1910 championed a new political cause: freeing the colony from Terauchi's tyranny. At a time when most journalists were "singing the praises of the Governor-General," Shakuo served as a lone voice of dissent, indefatigably committed to "guiding and disciplining colonial rule," as he described his vaunted crusade. And his jeremiads against Terauchi's paternalism toward Koreans, like his earlier protests against Itō's policy of self-rule, found an eager audience among local settlers who were denied a voice in colonial politics. The magazine survived the demise of many other papers at the hands of the colonial police in the 1910s, and for many years hung on by its teeth, giving Shakuo a distinctive sense of pride and status in the colonial publishing industry.

---

135. *Chōsen oyobi Manshū*, February 1913, 1–3; Mabuchi 1987, 70–71.

136. Nakamura Shiryō 1926, 424–25; Yi Hae-ch'ang 1971, 291. Shakuo's last name is unusual, but it is read as such, as the name is listed under "shi" in the index of every colonial biographical dictionary where he is listed (see for instance, Kawabata 1913, 28; Nakamura 1926, 17).

137. Kim Kyu-hwan 1959, 227*n*66.

138. For a study of Shakuo's editorials and the role of his magazine as a political voice of the Japanese expatriate community in Korea, see Brooks 2005.

In each editorial (unless deleted by the censors), Shakuo railed against official suppression of the liberal values dear to Meiji Japan in language rarely found in the contemporary metropolitan press. Korea was no more than "a paradise of *kenpei* and patrolmen," and Terauchi's rule an epitome of "Machiavellian bureaucratic absolutism" that "enslaved" his own countrymen. Shakuo styled his cause as advancing "the great trend of the world," while depicting the Governor-General's rule as pulling the settlers back into the feudal age. An ideological triad of emperor, empire, and democracy framed his attacks on Terauchi. "To incorporate the public opinion of us Japanese settlers [*naichijin*] into governance," Shakuo claimed, was mandated by the very "words of the Meiji Emperor" as enshrined in the Charter Oath, which stipulated that "affairs of the state must be decided by public discussion [*kōron*]."[139] "To ignore the spirit of the constitution by excessively issuing laws and regulations to constrain people's freedom," therefore, "is neither our empire's true aim nor our emperor's ethos." Shakuo charged the colonial governor with an intolerable "violation of popular rights," and concluded with an emphatic plea: "Instead of making a Chōsen for one Governor-General and the bureaucrats, I cry out loud for making a Chōsen for the people [*kokumin*]."[140]

By "people," Shakuo clearly meant rights-bearing citizens, a class in which he considered only settlers were civilized enough to fit. By contrast, Koreans—"whose levels of character, intellect, and civilization remain extremely base"—were no more than "Japanese in training" (*Nihonjin minaraisei*).[141] Except for a few occasions when he made a gesture toward including Koreans into "the people" as a strategy to demand broader political freedom on the peninsula,[142] Shakuo categorically insisted: "Koreans today are *Japanese imperial subjects* [*Nihon shinmin*] just as we are, but they are [still] not *Japanese* [*Nihonjin*]. . . . Until they become completely Japanized in intellect, character, customs, and language a century from now, Koreans will remain Koreans."[143]

139. *Chōsen oyobi Manshū*, April 1914, 6–7.
140. *Chōsen oyobi Manshū*, November 1915, 6–7.
141. Ibid., 7.
142. *Chōsen oyobi Manshū*, April 1914, 6–7.
143. *Chōsen oyobi Manshū*, July 1912, 2. Emphasis mine.

To draw a distinction between "Japanese imperial subjects" (a statist and constitutional definition of the people) and "the Japanese" (a national and ethnic term used by the Nationality Act of 1899) meant to demarcate the boundaries of citizenship in a novel way.[144] The settlers, that is, separated "subjects" from "citizens" where such divisions officially and legally did not exist. Whereas the metropolitan government arguably recognized only "subjects" before 1945, Japanese settlers like Shakuo extended to Koreans only the strictly constitutional definition of Japanese as "subjects of the emperor," while demanding an extra-constitutional status of "citizens" exclusively for themselves. Their liminality compelled them to insist on such rigorous taxonomy.

## *Assimilation Anxiety*

Settlers often responded to the ambiguity of their political status in Korea with calls for outright separation, echoing their cousins in colonial Taiwan.[145] Instead of *isshi dōjin*, they urged the state to follow the more common colonial practice where natives and settlers were ruled separately. In a July 1912 article, for instance, Shakuo proposed following the crude model of Cecil Rhodes, the famed British pioneer in southern Africa, who allegedly "argued for granting freedom to the Anglo-Saxons and meting out suppression to deal with the natives."[146] "Currently Koreans do not have the same family registration, their education is separate, and they have no duty of military service," he pointed out in another article, interpreting this as the surest sign that the Tokyo government was "treating [Koreans] separately from Japanese [*Nihonjin*] in terms of their fundamental conditions as *kokumin*."[147] He defended such discrimination as "perfectly natural" and only "politically fair" to the

144. Doak 2007, 148–49. The Meiji Constitution did not define who a Japanese national was, nor did it mention *kokumin* or *minzoku*. It referred to the Japanese people as merely "subjects of the monarch or imperial subjects" (*shinmin*). See note 113 of this chapter.

145. On the 1914 "assimilation movement," launched in Taiwan by Itagaki Taisuke and his liberal followers to extend the Meiji constitutional rights to local inhabitants, and Japanese settlers' opposition to it, see Lamley 1970–71.

146. *Chōsen* (Chōsen Zasshisha), July 1912, 2–3.

147. *Chōsen oyobi Manshū*, July 1914, 6.

culturally more advanced settlers, who deserved "a certain degree of freedom guaranteed by the constitution."[148]

What was "politically fair" to settlers was measured by the degree of constitutional progress at home. "The Japanese who possess a high level of civilization and have breathed [the air of] freedom" all but devolved from citizens to colonized subjects "once they land on Korean soil," Shakuo complained to Terauchi in an interview in late 1913.[149] And he likened the settlers' struggle for citizenship under the Governor-General's rule to that of American pioneers in the New World, who had fought in defense of democracy and freedom against the imperial metropole.[150] It was, indeed, in the early colonies of settlement like North America that the contradiction between domestic and overseas practice led settlers to wage a movement that culminated in the founding of new democracies. The same contradiction, as the political scientist David Abernethy has noted, became particularly glaring in newer settler colonies such as Kenya and Algeria: their parent societies of Britain and France built and operated sophisticated political systems on the principles of liberty and equality, while administering overseas territories on the contrary principles of subjugation and racial segregation.[151]

In the case of colonial Korea, much as local settlers protested these contradictions between metropole and colony, they resolutely defended discrimination against natives as the key to successful rule. Shakuo, in one article, urged the Japanese colonial officials to consider British India, French Algeria, and German Alsace-Lorraine as models. What particularly impressed him about these colonies was that "While they may be willing to respect the rights of natives and promote their happiness, none of them sacrifices the rights of metropolitan nationals [*hongokujin*] for the sake of natives."[152] Without following their most oppressive measures, he argued, the Government-General should emulate the way they deftly combined paternalistic native policies with the administrative practices of segregation. That Shakuo, who advanced a radical vision of assimilation, made an equally radical call for separation should not surprise us.

148. Ibid.; *Chōsen oyobi Manshū*, November 1915, 6–7.

149. *Chōsen oyobi Manshū*, December 1913, 5.

150. *Chōsen* (Chōsen Zasshisha), February 1911, 8.

151. Abernethy 2000, 328; see also Oguma 1998, 205–6.

152. *Chōsen oyobi Manshū*, July 1914, 3–4.

For such a complete fusion to take place required "several decades or even centuries," he predicted, arguing that the Japanese in the interim should follow the norm set by European colonizers.

This duality toward assimilation goes a long way toward explaining settlers' ambivalence about Terauchi's "military rule." Although eager to pounce on any aspect of the Governor-General's rule that menaced settler interests, Shakuo fully backed Terauchi's repressive policies toward Koreans—the reason why his magazine survived the stringent press control in the 1910s. Even in the midst of a typical diatribe against military rule, Shakuo argued that "Koreans should be happy with the Governor-General" for "annually injecting over 10 million yen into Korea to develop its governance, industry, and people's welfare." Rather than constitutional rule like that of the metropole, Shakuo averred, "the Governor-General's rule is the best [form of government] for Koreans today."[153] In short, settlers could be either the most vociferous critics of the Governor-General's rule or its most ardent defenders, or in Shakuo's case, both at the same time.

Underlying the settlers' desire for separate and unequal treatment was the lingering fear of "Koreanization." Anxiety about reverse assimilation in Korea intensified in the course of the 1910s, when the colonial regime enforced rigorous Japanization policies. Whereas some had attributed the cause of Koreanization to the force of nature or environment (see Chapter 1), settlers now claimed it was man-made: specifically, Terauchi's military rule was to blame. Merchant Kugimoto Tōjirō wondered if the Governor-General's policy of assimilation "might not be *yobo*-izing Japanese rather than Japanizing Koreans." A lawyer in Seoul explicitly charged Terauchi's policy with stifling competition, ambition, and the spirit of enterprise among settlers. Noting the rising trend of "fraud and deceit," he worried that "[they] have now ossified into Japanese stripped of Yamato *damashii* [spirit]." Another settler apparently "fretted day and night" that the Japanese, whom he considered "the most nationalistic of all the world's peoples," were "completely forgetting [their duty] to transform Koreans into the Yamato *minzoku*,"

153. *Chōsen oyobi Manshū*, July 1912, 2–4.

instead being assimilated by Koreans who embodied the contrary ideal of "individualism."[154]

To be sure, some settlers believed "Koreanization" was not such a bad thing. "To actively cooperate and harmonize with them, [and] to Japanize them," argued Ōmura Tomonojō of the Seoul Chamber of Commerce, "naturally requires us to be willingly transformed by them," defining Koreanization as "a duty of our countrymen [*bokokujin*] toward the newly incorporated *kokumin*." A few other settler leaders concurred that assimilation should be a mutually transformative process, advocating Koreanization of Japanese as an effective method of assimilating Koreans.[155]

In the final diagnosis, however, voices of paranoia tended to prevail among settlers, underscoring the depth of their colonial neurosis. The task of assimilation, if not undertaken with caution, could bring serious consequences; far worse than a failure to assimilate Koreans would be to be assimilated by them. Maintaining sufficient distance from Koreans, culturally as well as politically, thus became critical for maintaining settler power. The settlers' demand for constitutional rights as "superior" and "culturally advanced people" was necessarily predicated upon the denial of these same rights to Koreans as "inferior" and "less cultured people"; given their ambiguous citizenship status, the expansion of settler prerogatives required insisting on this gap. If assimilation was seen by the state as an antidote to Korean "backwardness," keeping them in their backwardness was, for settlers, a prophylactic against their own political downfall.

Assimilation anxiety was by no means unique to settlers; it also existed on the part of Government-General officials. Consider the 1911 law to prohibit Koreans from adopting "names that are easily confused with Japanese" (*naichijin ni magirawashii seimei*), a measure taken out of concern for preserving the colonial hierarchy.[156] Nonetheless, while the state and settlers shared fear about Koreans "passing" as Japanese, in day-to-day governance colonial officials made few distinctions between

---

154. *Chōsen oyobi Manshū*, January 1917, 60–68.
155. Ibid., 63.
156. Mizuno 2008, 28–30.

Korean and Japanese residents.[157] Both were effectively treated as imperial subjects who fell unequivocally under the Governor-General's control.

Terauchi's departure in 1916 did little to ameliorate settlers' relations with the colonial government. When his successor Hasegawa Yoshimichi (1850–1924) arrived in October 1917, one of the foremost settler demands for the new governor—as articulated by Ōmura—was to "remove the barrier that was built between the civilians and the Governor-General" and to "listen to the voices of the people."[158] Settlers were soon disappointed. Hasegawa more or less carried on Terauchi's policies of control and order, paying no more attention than his predecessor had done to the settlers' demand for "popular rights." As Hasegawa told Shakuo in an interview in late 1916, "Because you people were born in the Meiji era, you talk freely of popular rights and freedom, but we were born in the late Tokugawa era and are quite accustomed to autocratic rule [*assei seiji*]." At a time when Korea was undergoing a phase similar to "the period of transition from the Tokugawa to the early Meiji era," he argued, it was "too early to talk about" rights and freedom, whose impact on Koreans, "glib talkers" as they were, would be simply "dangerous."[159]

As this generational gap continued to divide settlers from colonial mandarins, their relationship rapidly eroded in the late 1910s. And as the colonial state seemed to invest its energy almost entirely in appeasing Koreans, settler fear and loathing of Koreans increased, finding expression in physical abuses and verbal insults. Where the state touted ethnic affinity and bureaucratic impartiality, many settlers continued to shun any practice that might breach the ethnic barriers they constructed around their identity as "the Japanese."[160]

---

157. The dynamic of "passing" was also observed among Okinawans (Christy 1993, 617).

158. *Chōsen oyobi Manshū*, January 1917, 63.

159. Shakuo 1930, 16.

160. A case in point was a resolution passed by the Seoul Residents' Association and submitted to the mayor, asserting that "mixed education of Japanese and Koreans must be absolutely forbidden" (*Chōsen kōron*, August 1914, 85).

## *Conclusion*

If settlers and state formed a partnership in building empire, they also became its contradictory foundations. By the time of annexation, what Peter Duus has called a relationship of "the abacus and the sword" had evolved from one of mutual dependence to one of mutual suspicion. Local settlers continued to expect and depend on the state's political protection and military support, but they also demanded freedom from its control. The colonial state, for its part, made control its first order of business. In the midst of efforts to suppress local resistance, none of the new administrators—all of whom had recently witnessed the streets of Tokyo being taken over by angry crowds—believed that the kind of mass politics or constitutional rights the settlers demanded were suitable for export.

At root was the difference between the state's self-understanding as the supreme landlord of Korea and the settlers' self-image as pioneering builders of the peninsula. This tension, to be sure, did not hinder official-civilian cooperation in furthering Japan's domination of Korea, but it also did not disappear. A central insight that emerges from this period of imperial consolidation—from protectorate rule after 1905 to the first decade of military rule from 1910 to 1919—is that settlers became a political entity, not only through their encounter with Koreans but through their increasingly conflict-ridden relationship with the colonial state. And the settlers' dogged campaign to protect their autonomy, and the aftermath of its defeat, set the stage for more conflict to come. To conflate settlers and state as fellow "colonizers" is to miss the messy nature of this partnership that drove the construction of empire.

The hardening of the boundaries of *kan* and *min* in turn threatened to blur the distinctions between Japanese and Koreans. The making of a colonial society inspired debates about what it meant to be Japanese and civilized, when the two categories meshed but uncomfortably, and about how far the boundaries of the nation could be stretched to accommodate the peoples of new overseas possessions. Who belonged to the nation, and who ought to decide and participate in the affairs of the nation, were essentially questions about citizenship—debated throughout the world at the time—that were neither settled by the Meiji leaders nor discussed solely among metropolitan Japanese. In their politically ambivalent status, settlers confronted these questions daily through encounters with Koreans as well as disagreements with officials, and they arrived at significantly different conclusions. Precisely because settlers felt excluded from the constitutional system, the early Meiji debate on Japanese national identity, framed around the question of whether the nation resided in the state or the people,[161] lingered in the colony, whose political situation was now seen to be a few decades behind that of the metropole. If this debate, at one level, found a resolution in the passage of the constitution at home, it manifested itself in a deepening antagonism between the colonial state and settlers in fin-de-siècle Korea. This came at a time when local Korean scholars and reformers also began using the neologism of *minjok* to rethink the nation and its relationship to a state that fell increasingly under foreign control.[162] The subtle and implicit tension between state nationalism (*kokka shugi*) and ethnic nationalism (*minzoku shugi*) that historian Kevin Doak has identified in metropolitan political discourse arguably came into sharper relief in Korea, an overseas periphery where the political and legal boundaries of citizenship were only imperfectly extended to Japanese nationals. Here the colonial state and settlers developed conflicting visions of the Japanese nation: one envisioning a political community of imperial subjects institutionally defined by the Meiji government; the other an ethnically and culturally distinct community of Japanese bound by shared customs, mores, and blood lineage. The inclusion of Koreans into the empire had the effect of widening this chasm between a state logic that maintained the authority of the Government-General and a settler logic that insisted on the privileged and separate status of the Japanese *minzoku*.[163] Overseas settlers, no less than metropolitan residents, were indeed part of an ongoing debate over the meaning of Japanese identity and nationhood.

Within the first decade of the Governor-General's rule, legal and political marginality came to define what it meant to be a settler in Korea. And yet, settlers' opposition to the state, if anything, served to strengthen rather than fray their ties to Japan, underscoring the success, not the failure, of bureaucratic-led efforts to forge a coherent nation.[164]

---

161. Doak 2007, 221.

162. Schmid 2002, 174–75.

163. Oguma 1998, 207.

164. I draw on a similar point made by Andrew Gordon on the domestic political opposition in Japan (1991, 55).

The culture of dissent that traversed Japan and Korea was marked by a strong sense of identification with the emperor-centered nation-state, as the language of settlers' petitions and press campaigns made plain. Contestation with the state heightened their sense of entitlement to inclusion in national and colonial affairs as overseas pioneers, and their larger sense of identity as "the Japanese" (a process that mirrored the experience of Japan's rural peripheries, whose regional identities were similarly shaped through resistance and accommodation to the center).[165] Anti-bureaucratic yet pro-imperial, settlers in Korea were not nearly as raucous and violent as the agitated crowds on the streets of Tokyo, yet their demand for inclusion was just as pressing.

The settlers' incomplete and at best partial incorporation into colonial governance was a major factor underlying their emergence as brokers of empire. In the course of the Governor-General's rule, while the majority of settlers remained excluded from participation in colonial politics, a group of aspiring individuals—the likes of Kikuchi, Ōgaki, and Shakuo—found various channels to fight their way in. Operating in liminal spaces at the interstices of the Governor-General's rule, they took up a variety of roles: spokesmen for settler interests, collaborators with the colonial government, intermediaries between Japanese and Korean communities, and representatives of "Chōsen" vis-à-vis the metropole. But their fluid and multifarious identities, which began to emerge in the maelstrom of late Chosŏn politics, did not fully congeal until the new crisis of empire in March 1919 thrust them, once again, into positions of influence.

165. Lewis 2000, 12–14.

# PART II

## *In Action*

# THREE

## *Building an Empire of Harmony*

On 1 March 1919, a group of Korean nationalist leaders convened at a restaurant in Seoul to read the Declaration of Independence, a ceremony replicated by their regional delegates throughout the country. Shortly thereafter, Korean residents spilled onto the streets to demonstrate against Japanese rule, a cry of freedom that spread to the rest of the population like wild fire. Triggered by a combination of catalytic factors—notably Emperor Kojong's death and his funeral slated for early March 1919, and President Woodrow Wilson's Declaration of Fourteen Points the previous year—the movement drew in over a million men and women of all ages and from all walks of life, marking "the most massive demonstration of nationalism in the modern history of Korea."[1]

What had started as peaceful demonstrations turned into violent confrontations in many places where the colonial police and gendarmes reacted with brute force. In addition to assaults on officials and administrative buildings, some isolated attacks took place against local Japanese residents. One gendarmerie report bordered on hysteria:

> Japanese settlers in certain districts of Kyŏnggi and North Ch'ungch'ŏng provinces had to leave their farms, homes, and shops and evacuate to emergency assembly points to escape danger. Many gendarme substations were abandoned as indefensible. Japanese settlers hastily formed self-defense units led by army reservists and firemen to defend themselves until gendarmes or soldiers arrived

1. "The March First Movement," in Lee 1996, 430.

with help. The units set up night patrols and guards. . . . Japanese in Seoul were restricted to their homes after dark. In the Suwŏn area, where Japanese civilians had been threatened and police killed, the settlers vowed to kill fifty Koreans for each Japanese slain.[2]

Even allowing for exaggeration and distortion in the official reports, that the movement terrorized Japanese residents was beyond doubt. For a couple of months, a barrage of petitions streamed into the Governor-General's office from terrified Japanese residents pleading for "the continuation of a garrison" or "the permanent stationing of troops" in their vulnerable settlements scattered around the peninsula.[3] The number of Japanese emigrants also registered a precipitous fall in 1920.[4]

The March First Movement shook the young empire to its core. For the Japanese rulers who had mistaken Korean silence for submission, the movement exposed their complacency to devastating effect. Tokyo responded to the crisis by appointing a new Governor-General: Saitō Makoto (1858–1936), who promptly announced his intention to inaugurate an era of "cultural rule" (*bunka seiji*). More than a mere policy change instigated in the metropole, Saitō's cultural rule reflected a profound and potentially durable ideological shift in Korean colonial strategy.

Faced with the surge of nationalist sentiment, the colonial administration retooled its policy of assimilation by defining the goal in terms of *naisen yūwa* (harmony between Japanese and Koreans). Under this policy ideal, the crude call for Japanization receded into the background, as the authorities emphasized their commitment to granting Koreans more opportunities in education, enterprise, politics, and other realms of public life (what we may collectively call colonial citizenship) without forcing them to renounce Korean national identity.[5] This experiment of carrying

---

2. Quoted in Baldwin 1979, 145.

3. *SMB* 12:635–81. For the activities of settlers' armed self-defense corps, see Yi Sŭng-yŏp 2005, 120–29.

4. The number of emigrants fell by 1,231 in 1920, though the pace picked up the following year (*Chōsen Sōtokufu tōkei nenpō* 1921).

5. Building on my discussion in the previous chapter, I will use the term "colonial citizenship" to refer to a limited form of membership in Japan's national community, where one's basic duties and rights as citizen-subjects (*kokumin*) were defined in accordance with laws issued by the multiple centers of power: the emperor, the metropolitan government, and, most importantly, the Governor-General, who issued his own ordinances and determined the extent of application of metropolitan laws to the colony. For

on *dōka* under the guise of ethnic coexistence signaled a novel challenge for the Japanese rulers in the 1920s. In the aftermath of World War I, which witnessed the dissolution of old empires and the rise of new nation-states worldwide, the Japanese had to engage Korean nationalism not only as a local movement, but as part of a broader, global discourse on autonomy. And in undertaking this experiment, they were increasingly forced to ponder to what extent the empire should accommodate heterogeneity among its subjects, when its ostensible goal was to promote their homogeneity.

Japan's challenge of balancing the imperative of the nation-state (to maintain the unity of the dominant ethnic group) and the imperative of colonialism (to recognize diverse ethnic constituencies) mirrored a new dilemma faced by the brokers of empire. Since annexation, as we have seen, local settlers had been nursing grudges against the Governor-General's professed policy of administrative neutrality (*isshi dōjin*); few believed their livelihoods depended on good relations with Koreans. Yet in the face of changing political currents after 1919, they could ill afford to remain indifferent to the official call for ethnic coexistence. The anxiety of the new government to reach out to the Korean population and the desire of settler leaders to protect their vested stakes in the empire meshed a complex geometry of collaboration. As the colonial state launched a peninsula-wide propaganda drive, spreading the message of unity—long anathema to settlers—ironically came to the fore of their activity. Some long-time settlers worked for Saitō's administration as advisors, informants, and ideologues, assisting its effort to win over influential Koreans to his new policy of cultural rule. Others joined hands with Korean elites to develop industry and education, promote social work, and combat radicalism, dressing each project not only in the rhetoric of self-strengthening but in broader terms of Pan-Asian unity. The brokers of empire, in short, became close allies of the new colonial government.

In assisting the state efforts to rebuild the empire on the ideal of ethnic harmony, the brokers of empire began frequently to traverse two kinds of boundaries: those that separated settlers from the state, and

---

a similar discussion of "imperial citizenship" as a means of obtaining political rights within the framework of the British Empire in India, see Banerjee 2010.

those dividing settlers from Koreans. By offering themselves as Janus-faced intermediaries between the state and Korean society, and by carrying on their erstwhile quest for political influence into the era of cultural rule, these men labored to ensure their inclusion in the new colonial enterprise. Their partnership with the regime, in turn, expanded the very scope of Korean governance into areas hitherto unexplored by the authorities—although not without injecting new tensions and contradictions into the fraught project of *dōka*.

## *Saitō's Cultural Rule*

Although the Korean call for independence was ultimately unable to move the court of world opinion, it did succeed in compelling a swift response from the Japanese government under new Prime Minister Hara Takashi (1856–1921). Hara assumed office at a turning point in Japan's national politics, when the declining influence of the *genrō* and the military gave way to the increasing power of the Diet and the political parties. A long-standing advocate of civilian rule in the colonies, Hara promptly declared his intent to carry out a thorough overhaul of the colonial administration in Korea.

Hara's response to the March 1919 debacle was not to lessen but to redouble efforts at assimilation. Rather than looking to the British system of colonial self-rule, his model was that of Algeria under France or Alsace-Lorraine under Germany: that is, a contiguous settler colony annexed to the national domain. Hara called for binding the colony ever more closely to a modernized Japan under the policy of *naichi enchō* (extending the mainland), just as he had successfully pushed for a similar assimilation policy for Taiwan in the 1890s. Assimilation (*dōka*) for him meant to make the colonized "members of the Japanese nation" (*kokumin*), which referred not so much to the transplanting of culture as to the political, legal, economic, and educational integration of the colony into the metropole. Through such a process, he hoped, Koreans would naturally come to assimilate to the Japanese way of life just as the Okinawans had.[6] Hara had in mind an empire where Koreans were

6. Oguma 1998, 85–86, 244–46. Colonial and metropolitan leaders, including Hara, feared the specter of Korea turning into the Ireland of the Japanese empire—a reference to its demise as an imperial state.

Fig. 3 Governor-General Saitō Makoto
SOURCE: Fujita 1978, 21.

"allowed" to remain ethnically and culturally Korean, at least for now, while the authorities worked toward the full administrative integration of Korea with Japan through the application of metropolitan laws and institutions wherever feasible, including the gradual extension of political rights in the future.[7]

Although his vision of civilian rule in Korea was thwarted by the military, and his assassination in 1921 led to a sudden halt in the more ambitious programs of reform, Hara's ideal of *naichi enchō* found expression in the new cultural rule of Governor-General Saitō Makoto. Cultural rule in many ways embraced a goal more ambitious than that of its predecessor: to create an empire where persuasion prevailed over force as a central governing strategy.[8] Deploying a new trope of *naisen yūwa*, the Saitō administration sought to finesse assimilation policy into a more acceptable form of rule by modifying its method and rhetoric to focus

---

7. Hara 1950, 292–94.
8. Gi-Wook Shin and Michael Robinson (1999, 5–18) have characterized this strategy of cultural rule in terms of "colonial hegemony."

less on acculturation than on accommodation, less on Japanization than on mutual advancement of the two peoples. These subtle adjustments—gestures to broaden the parameters of colonial citizenship, underpinned by a tacit recognition of ethnic diversity among those citizens—crystallized into an extensive range of reforms designed to "promote greater economic prosperity and political expression of the Korean people." Saitō rescinded the Company Law that had choked off local enterprise, and removed some barriers to Korean employment in the lower and middle tiers of colonial bureaucracy. He also permitted the publication of independent Korean vernacular papers and relaxed bans on the freedom of assembly and the formation of organizations, which spurred moderate degrees of nationalist activity.[9] In order to foster respect for Korean traditional customs and culture, moreover, the Governor-General encouraged his officials to learn the Korean language as well as local customs, history, art, and archaeology.[10]

A professed departure from military rule by no means rendered the use of force obsolete, however. While stripping the empire of its most visible signs of oppression—the gendarmeries and the wearing of swords among officials and teachers, for instance—Saitō kept the structures of coercion intact by placing two of Japan's best army divisions on the northern peninsula, enlarging the police force, and refining the system of censorship control. This duality also characterized Saitō's policy toward Korean nationalists. A new relaxed political atmosphere lured Korean exchange students in Japan, as well as political exiles in the United States and China, back to the peninsula, ushering an upsurge in Korean political and cultural activity. Saitō's policy toward those who remained on the peninsula was to repress radicals harshly while countenancing moderate nationalist activities. More sophisticated and effective than outright repression, this time-honored strategy of "divide and rule" aimed to weaken and ultimately destroy Korean nationalism by fostering internal divisions and co-opting disaffected leaders into collaborating with the colonial regime.[11]

---

9. Chōsen Sōtokufu, *Chōsen ni okeru shinshisei* 1921, 35–94.

10. Brudnoy 1970, 177.

11. For a detailed analysis of ideological divisions within the nationalist movement, see M. Robinson 1988.

As it sought to break the nationalist coalition, the colonial government cemented its own ties with a variety of Korean elites, an effort that had been narrowly focused on landlords and former bureaucrats before 1919. The March First demonstrations, as colonial officials discovered to their dismay, drew in many educated and "progressive" Korean leaders whom they had regarded as "pro-Japanese." The Saitō administration thus labored hard to corral aristocrats, officials, landlords, entrepreneurs, and other powerful individuals into the ruling structure by firming up whatever tenuous ties the colonial state had already forged with them.

Anxiety to secure elite support underlay Saitō's widely publicized effort to "solicit public opinion" (*min'i chōtatsu*) on affairs of Korean governance. As a first such gesture, in September 1919 he summoned to Seoul local Korean and Japanese leaders from every province to sound out their views on administrative reform and to solicit their support in propagating cultural rule.[12] He also resuscitated the Central Council, composed of Korean aristocratic and bureaucratic elites, as an advisory body to the Government-General.[13] Departing from precedent, furthermore, the colonial government incorporated civilians as informal advisors by creating a variety of joint official-civilian committees and deliberative councils. Prominent individuals such as settler tycoons Tomita Gisaku (1858–1930) and Aruga Mitsutoyo (1873–1949) and Korean entrepreneurs Han Sang-nyong (1880–1949) and Cho Chin-t'ae (1853–1933) were appointed to these committees along with officials to discuss policies in such key areas as education, finance, and industry.[14]

Journalist Kikuchi Kenjō archly described this phenomenon as "a fad in committees" spawned by Saitō's "total mobilization" of local elites,[15] but this fad, it turned out, became a permanent structure of colonial government. Saitō's nominal commitment to *min'i chōtatsu* ensured that influential civilians remained involved in policy formulation

---

12. Chōsen Sōtokufu, *Chōsen ni okeru shinshisei* 1921, 47.

13. *Chōsen* (Chōsen Sōtokufu), April 1921, 240–41.

14. *Chōsen Sōtokufu shisei nenpō* 1921, 14, 149–55; *Chōsen* (Chōsen Sōtokufu), February 1921, 4–5; Yūhō Kyōkai 1984, 52–53. For more on the involvement of civilians in economic policy-making, see Chapter 5.

15. Kikuchi 1925, 270.

Fig. 4 Research Committee on Education
SOURCE: Ōzorasha 2008, 10. Used by permission.

to a certain extent throughout the 1920s. As a result, a new and lasting relationship of interdependence developed among state, settlers, and Korean elites vis-à-vis the Korean nationalist movement.

### *Settlers' Response*

For their part, local settlers pondered long and hard before they breathed life into this new apparatus of collaboration. The watershed event of 1919 rattled all segments of the Japanese resident population—not only journalists but merchants, entrepreneurs, educators, and religious leaders, who convened meeting after meeting to make sense of the rupture and deliberate on its repercussions for their community. Local Japanese papers and magazines ran myriad articles that chronicled the uncertainty felt by settlers, who disagreed widely over the causes and culprits of March First, blaming Terauchi, "recalcitrant Koreans" (*futei Senjin*), Christians, the Korean people, or whomever they chose.[16]

Meanwhile, an altogether different assessment emerged from the police reports streaming into the Government-General's headquarters. One of the proximate causes for the March First Movement, they sug-

16. For instance, see *Chōsen oyobi Manshū*, December 1919, 143–50.

gested, lay in none other than the Japanese community.[17] According to one classified official survey that gleaned a cross-section of Korean voices, Japanese residents—from loan sharks and farmers sponsored by the ODC to low-ranking officials and policemen—habitually insulted Koreans by calling out to them in crude language such as *omae* (you), *oi* (yo), *kora* (hey), and *yobo*.[18] "The Japanese who use these derogatory words were doubtless the true cause of the independence incident," averred one Korean youth, explaining the March First demonstrations as "an explosion of trivial [anti-Japanese] sentiment" that had accumulated through daily encounters with settler abuse, verbal or physical.[19] This view was privately echoed in the diary of Yun Ch'i-ho (1865–1945), an influential Christian leader whose moderate political stance made him an ideal collaborator for the regime. Though Yun himself was deeply ambivalent about Japanese rule, on settlers he minced no words [original in English]: "The greatest hindrance to the promotion of friendly relations between the two races is the arrogance, aggressiveness and avarice of the Japanese residents in Korea."[20] The message was loud and clear: settlers spread nothing but hatred for the Japanese.

Abe Mitsuie (1862–1936), former president of the *Keijō nippō*, therefore had good reason to list "local Japanese residents" along with "Korean youths" and "foreign missionaries" as the "three greatest barriers" to Japanese colonial rule, and to urge the Governor-General to devise appropriate measures to keep the troublemakers in check.[21] Settlers had a propensity "to outflank the authorities and take the law into their own hands," wrote the pro-government *Keijō nippō*.[22] The Japanese in Korea might have lacked the political resources and avarice of white settlers in Africa, but their sheer numbers (over 350,000), paired with their proverbial ambivalence about *dōka*, could still have had a corrosive effect on cultural rule. The Saitō government had to take particular care in

17. Chōsen Sōtoku Kanbō, Shomubu Chōsaka 1924, 22.

18. The Korean word *yobo* (which means "dear" and is usually used to refer to one's spouse) was corrupted into a derogatory term by the Japanese to refer to a Korean person during the colonial period.

19. Chōsen Sōtoku Kanbō, Shomubu Chōsaka 1925, 43–44.

20. Taehan Min'guk Mun'gyobu Kuksa P'yŏnch'an Wiwŏnhoe 1987, 8:144–45 (entry for 1 October 1920).

21. Abe Mitsuie 1919.

22. *Keijō nippō*, 25 March 1919.

balancing concessions to the Korean elite and to local settlers lest the latter become a liability rather than an asset to the regime.

Settlers' reaction to Saitō's cultural rule was predictably mixed. His liberalization measures were welcome, but they also prompted anxiety over how he would govern the Korean population. This ambivalence was palpable when some 120 leading Japanese businessmen gathered secretly at the Seoul Chamber of Commerce in late 1920. For three days they groped for strategies to cope with anti-Japanese sentiment still smoldering among Koreans, worried that "years of business in Korea might be destroyed from their foundations," as Maruyama Tsurukichi (1883–1956), head of the police bureau who attended the meeting, later evaluated the mood.[23] Although the settlers vowed to assist one another in protecting their ongoing ventures, tellingly, almost half the participants renounced their faith in assimilation policy. Where the colonial government sought a remedy in greater commitment to ethnic reconciliation, some settlers called for the return of military-style rule, asking for expansion of the army divisions and revival of the *kenpeitai* police. In addition to luring more migrants and capital from the metropole, they proposed settling military colonists (*tondenhei*), as though their community was threatened with extinction, arguing it was a matter of "being assimilated by the Koreans or retreating to the mainland."[24] And throughout the conference, settlers complained acidly about Saitō's "Korean-centered" reforms to pacify the *yangban* elites while ignoring the voices of his own countrymen.

Yet in the aftermath of the March First Movement, when worries about nationalism ruled the day, settler leaders also realized that they had no choice but to accept the new political reality that placed their empire on the defensive. In order to secure and expand their vested interests amid the increasingly volatile Korean populace, the settlers understood, albeit with reluctance, that in the long run it was for their benefit to move in step with Saitō's cultural rule. Such an admission was reflected in a tentative conclusion reached by the businessmen. At the end of the three-day meeting, they pledged to support the new Governor-General by setting for themselves five objectives that echoed his

23. *Chōsen* (Chōsen Sōtokufu), July 1923, 19.

24. Zensen Naichijin Jitsugyōka Yūshi Konwakai 1920, 30, 129, 161. For the overall negative official response to these settler demands, see Yi Sŭng-yŏp 2005, 136–37.

policy concerns: "elevating the character of settlers," promoting "Korean thought guidance," carrying out "social work, philanthropy, relief, and juvenile reform," and fostering metropolitan understanding of "Korea's true state of affairs."[25]

More than window dressing, these objectives heralded important changes in the settlers' modus operandi.[26] Just as the colonial state sought to refashion itself as an enlightened ruler in the wake of 1919, the brokers of empire, bent on protecting their interests and status as they had ever been, recognized the need to reconfigure the place of their community in the shifting political constellation of empire. For the first time, Koreans became a significant factor in settler politics. Whereas settlers had earlier spoken almost solely from a sense of entitlement, in the face of mounting nationalism they began increasingly to justify their power and privilege in terms of what they perceived to be shared values and goals of Koreans and Japanese, be it in the sphere of industry, culture, or education. In other words, the settlers had to change not only their strategies of pursuing interests, but the very terms of defining them, to move away from their reactionary politics and instead seek middle ground. For many settlers their endorsement of official policy translated into only tempered enthusiasm for *naisen yūwa*; others, however, jumped on its bandwagon, valiantly taking up the role of guiding the new administration under Saitō. Multiple roles lay in store for these settlers who, seeking to rebuild their lost cachet, gradually became self-appointed intermediaries of cultural rule.

## *Settlers as Advisors and Informants*

From the start, the promotion of *naisen yūwa* unfolded as a collaborative undertaking. Having put down the March First "uprising," the Saitō administration solicited the aid of local elites in launching an elaborate propaganda campaign to make the public fully understand the benefits of cultural rule. For this purpose he not only dispatched his officials to the provinces and mobilized members of the Central Council, but enlisted the support of aristocrats, entrepreneurs, elders, notables, and

25. Zensen Naichijin Jitsugyōka Yūshi Konwakai 1920, 14–15, 183.

26. As we will see below, these objectives would become the central focus of the settler-led campaign to promote *naisen yūwa* through the Dōminkai.

other men of influence. In turn, Saitō always made himself available for civilian critics, who wished to inform him of better ruling strategies or simply to bring their requests to the doorstep of the Government-General. As his personal memoranda indicate, Saitō regularly met with Korean businessmen such as Kim Sŏng-su (1891–1955) and nationalist leaders such as Yi Kwang-su (1892–1950), in addition to a host of influential settlers. By the end of his term of office, Saitō's dossier had also accumulated about 6,000 private letters and confidential missives from 300-odd figures—Japanese, Korean, Chinese, and American—and a wide assortment of petitions from regional, occupational, and religious organizations.[27] Unlike his predecessor who remained rather impervious to voices on the ground, Saitō made dialogue the keystone of his policy.

From this motley group, Saitō called upon several individuals with a journalistic background, who professed to know Korean customs, language, and mentalities better than the new colonial officials, to aid him in dealing with local nationalism. Among his most prized advisors was Abe Mitsuie. Cultivating close ties to Korean aristocrats, Abe also worked hard to win over Yi Kwang-su and fellow nationalists who, disillusioned by exile politics, returned more and more often to Korea after 1919. Even after he moved back to Japan, Abe continued his effort, with Saitō's discretionary fund, to co-opt moderate nationalists as well as Korean exchange students through scholarship grants.[28] Another informal advisor to Saitō who shuttled between Tokyo and Seoul was Hosoi Hajime (1886–1934), a journalist and a former supporter of the Ilchinhoe. An amateur scholar and a key figure behind the Japanese domination of "Korean studies" (see Chapter 4), Hosoi with Saitō's support founded the Jiyū Tōkyūsha (Freedom Investigation Company) in Tokyo, through which he published a series of translations of Korean statecraft manuals and historical literature for the purpose of "analyzing Korean ethnic characteristics."[29] Drawing on examples culled from these

27. Kang Tong-jin 1979, 457.

28. Abe Mitsuie to Saitō (29 May 1922), (23 June 1922), (16 July 1922), (23 April 1923), (2 May 1923).

29. The translated texts included Chŏng Yag-yong's *Mongmin Simsŏ* and the *Chŏng Kam nok*. Vice Governor-General Mizuno Rentarō (1868–1949) enthusiastically endorsed the translation of *Mongmin Simsŏ* as "the best guide for studying Korean mentalities" and

texts, Hosoi gave lectures, sent letters to officials, and wrote numerous articles and monographs, all of which converged on a static portrait of Korea as "an example of corrupt rule unknown in the history of humankind"[30]—what he construed as testament to the Korean inability to govern themselves.

In addition to Abe and Hosoi, who were based in the Tokyo metropole, settlers who had made Korea home also came to Saitō's aid. Some of these men are already familiar to us. Ōgaki Takeo (Chapter 2), for instance, wrote letters offering his diagnosis of the recent "disturbance" to the new Governor-General, and with influential Koreans such as Han Sang-nyong toured the provinces as civilian agents of a peninsula-wide "campaign to spread understanding of government policies" (*shisei shūchi undō*).[31] Ōgaki's journalist colleague Kikuchi Kenjō personally worked for Saitō by surveying rural conditions and reporting on Korean political activities within the peninsula and across the northern border into Manchuria. Like the other advisors, Kikuchi corresponded with Saitō on a regular basis, meeting him on average more than ten times a month between 1922 and 1924, and for information gathering duties received a handsome monthly reward of 300 yen.[32] In January 1923, moreover, Kikuchi went on a week-long circuit lecture along the Honam Line, preaching the need for "restructuring Korean culture" and stressing the importance of "self-strengthening" (*jitsuryoku yōsei*)—making more than passing allusions to the central ideological tenets of Korean nationalism.[33]

Whereas Kikuchi and other advisors to Saitō conducted their jobs on an ad hoc basis, some settlers became part of the formal apparatus of colonial government. This was the case with members of the Jōhō Iinkai

---

understanding the extent of Korea's "corrupt rule in the past" (*Chōsen* [Chōsen Sōtokufu], September 1921, 52, 54–77).

30. Hosoi to Saitō (17 September 1923): 642–48.

31. Ōgaki 1919; *Chōsen* (Chōsen Sōtokufu), May 1921, 125–31.

32. *Keijō shinbun*, 20 February 1932; Kikuchi to Saitō (5 December 1920); Kang Tong-jin 1979, 53, n. 25. Three hundred yen was a hefty sum at the time when the monthly salary of the president of *Keijō nippō* was about 500 yen and that of the president of *Tonga ilbo* only 150 yen (Cho Sŏng-gu 1998, 248, n. 43).

33. Kikuchi to Saitō (2 February 1923). Saitō himself made his own rounds between 1919 and 1927, a total of 35 trips (Kang Tong-jin 1979, 25).

(Information Committee), created in 1920.[34] Headed by Vice Governor-General Mizuno Rentarō, the committee was composed of 22 high-ranking bureaucrats and several "learned civilian experts," who included, at various times, journalists Ōgaki Takeo, Hagitani Kazuo, and Yamagata Isoo, local scholar Ayukai Fusanoshin, and Christian educator Niwa Seijirō (1865–1957). All were influential settlers, whose connections to key Korean groups made them nearly as valuable as native collaborators. Both Ōgaki and Ayukai, through their earlier involvement in the Korean reforms, carried considerable clout in the Korean political circle. Niwa and Yamagata arrived in Korea slightly later but developed close ties to Korean Christian leaders, becoming trusted "personal friends" of Yun Ch'i-ho.[35] For Yamagata—who ran a pro-government English-language newspaper, the *Seoul Press*—his job on the committee was part of an ongoing and evidently successful effort through the paper "to explain our Government-General's rule to foreign residents in Korea, especially missionaries, and make them cater to our government's grand policy."[36]

The Information Committee conducted a mix of duties where propaganda shaded into intelligence work, and where officers, like Saitō's advisors, combined the search for allies with a mission to civilize.[37] Performing a role comparable to that of "native informants," the committee officers gathered and translated a mass of data and documents and wrote reports that were "classified, processed, and analyzed into knowledge *of* or *about*" Korea.[38] Through films, lectures, bilingual pamphlets, and photo albums (some with English captions), they disseminated that knowledge to achieve four specific aims: introduce Korea's internal affairs to Japan and foreign countries; introduce metropolitan affairs to Koreans; spread "the truth of colonial administration"; and propagate

---

34. The creation of the Information Committee was most likely based on an idea hatched in a proposal (submitted by Assistant Secretary of the Army, Yamanashi Hanzō to Saitō just before his departure for Korea) to create a "secret propaganda organ" of the Government-General. Yamanashi to Saitō 1919, 151, 157; *Chōsen* (Chōsen Sōtokufu), January 1921, 148–49.

35. Taehan Min'guk Mun'gyobu Kuksa P'yŏnch'an Wiwŏnhoe 1987, 8:234 (entry for 6 April 1921).

36. Yamagata 1916, 195, 199–200.

37. In some ways, their operation resembled that of British intelligence officers in what Priya Satia (2008) calls a "covert empire" in the Middle East.

38. For the case of British India, see Cohn 1996, 51.

the colonial policy widely.[39] The Jōhō Gakari (Information Section) to which the committee belonged also made an annual tour of metropolitan cities and held lectures and film screenings to furnish "evidence of Korean progress in industry, education, and transportation," targeting local politicians and potential investors.[40] In a more creative attempt to "introduce the situation of *naichi* to the people of Korea," the Information Committee held an empire-wide contest soliciting "songs of *naichi*" from the Japanese living at home and abroad (including Taiwan, Manchuria, and Shanghai) and made the winner among the 160 entries "a teaching material to be used in Korean schools."[41]

Surviving records suggest that members of the Information Committee spent the bulk of their time collecting and analyzing data on the Korean independence movements in and outside of the peninsula, especially in the United States. In what appear to be confidential publications for official eyes only, they carefully monitored English-language media coverage of Korean affairs and scrutinized their critiques of the Governor-General's rule.[42] Paired with the Saitō government's own effort to exploit the mainstream Western media to publicize its rule,[43] these activities show how the international gaze, following the debacle of military rule, bore heavily on the new administrators in Korea.

Saitō's advisors and civilian officers on the Information Committee were essentially a community of old-time settlers, buoyed to positions of influence by their personal ties to powerful Koreans. What emerged from their alliance with the colonial state was a new governing strategy, in which official and civilian agents worked in tandem to undertake covert operations in social control, surveillance, and propaganda—areas in which most settlers had hitherto no business (for they themselves had been targets). Although information on their mostly clandestine activity remains spotty, the deployment of grassroots allies was extensive enough to come to public attention. One Korean publisher upbraided the Government-General for squandering its limited budget on police affairs and funneling most of it into a discretionary fund to reward its

39. *Chōsen Sōtokufu kanpō* 1920, 231; Kang Tong-jin 1979, 19.

40. For instance, see *Chōsen* (Chōsen Sōtokufu), June 1923, 129–30.

41. *Chōsen* (Chōsen Sōtokufu), August 1922, 167.

42. See Chōsen Jōhō Iinkai 1921a, 1921b, and 1921c.

43. See Saitō 1920, 167–69.

"spies" at the expense of Korean industry and education.[44] Far from winning the people's hearts, the colonial propaganda campaign appears to have alienated Korean sentiment by investing more energy in remunerating its own agents.

## *Nurturing Pro-Japanese Collaborators*

The operations of some settlers working for Saitō's government extended far beyond deskwork. The Japanese effort to deal with the challenge of nationalism evolved into a more intense search for local allies and collaborators, with an aim to infiltrate every rung of Korean society including "nobles, *yangban* aristocrats, Confucian scholars, the wealthy, entrepreneurs, educators, and religious leaders."[45] Already in the mid-1910s, the colonial government had created the Taishō Shinbokukai, a fraternal organization of colonial bureaucrats and Korean elites under the supervision of Ōgaki Takeo, who met "far more Koreans than Japanese everyday."[46] In order to bring other social groups within the state's reach, the authorities also cooperated with influential Koreans like Song Pyŏng-jun, former head of the disbanded Ilchinhoe, to engineer a variety of pro-government organizations in the first half of the 1920s (see Table 5).[47]

Although most of these organizations were presided over by "pro-Japanese" Koreans at the state's behest,[48] their actual operation was often entrusted to long-term settlers. Two men of letters who had etched their mark in the annals of late Chosŏn politics, Kikuchi Kenjō and Ōgaki Takeo,[49] left traces of their influence in the sparingly chronicled Japanese attempt to co-opt three traditionally important social groups:

---

44. Chōsen Sōtoku Kanbō, Shomubu Chōsaka 1925, 13.

45. Yamanashi to Saitō 1919.

46. Ōgaki in *Chōsen* (Chōsen Sōtokufu), September 1921, 109.

47. For details of these Korean-run organizations, see Kang Tong-jin 1979, 229–59. My discussion of pro-government organizations in this chapter is much indebted to Kang's seminal work on Saitō's cultural rule, though I also question his claim that they were simply "top-down" creations of the colonial government.

48. The activities of the Kungmin Hyŏphoe will be discussed in more detail in Chapter 6.

49. See Chapters 1 and 2.

Table 5: Main Pro-Government Organizations, 1915–1925

| Name | Date formed | President | Aim |
|---|---|---|---|
| Taishō Shinbokukai 大正親睦会 | Nov. 1916 | Min Yŏng-gi | fraternal interaction among Japanese and Korean capitalists and bureaucrats |
| Taedong Samunhoe 大東斯文会 | Nov. 1919 | Ŏ Yun-jŏk | conciliation and co-optation of Confucian scholars |
| Kungmin Hyŏphoe 国民協会 | Jan. 1920 | Min Wŏn-sik | promotion of *naichi enchō* policy and attainment of suffrage |
| Yudo Chinhŭnghoe 儒道振興会 | Jan. 1920 | Kim Yŏng-han | promotion of Confucianism and revival of *hyanggyo* (county school) |
| Chosŏn Sojagin Sangjohoe 朝鮮小作人相助会 | Aug. 1920 | Song Pyŏng-jun | prevention of tenant disputes in cooperation with landlords |
| Taedong Tongjihoe 大東同志会 | Oct. 1921 | Sŏnu Sun | "co-prosperity and co-existence" of Japanese and Koreans in S. P'yŏngan |
| Dōkōkai (Korean branch) 同光会朝鮮支部 | Feb. 1922 | Yi Hŭi-gan | petitioning the Diet to bring Korea under direct rule of the emperor |
| Sōaikai (Korean branch) 相愛会朝鮮支部 | Apr. 1924 | Yi Ki-dong | suppression of labor and nationalist movements; ethnic harmony |
| Dōminkai 同民会 | Apr. 1924 | Hōjō Tokiyuki | promotion of assimilation ideology, industry, and social education |
| Kōshi Club 甲子倶楽部 | Aug. 1924 | Ōgaki Takeo | attainment of suffrage based on *naichi enchō* policy; promotion of industry |

SOURCES: Chōsen Sōtokufu Keimukyoku, *Chōsen Chian jōkyō* 1922; Chōsen Sōtokufu Keimukyoku Hoanka 1927 [1984]; and Kang Tong-jin 1979, 230–56.

NOTES: The Dōkōkai and the Sōaikai (Sōaikai Sōhonbu Bunkabu 1923) were metropolitan-based organizations that had Korean branches. But the Dōkōkai, formed by Uchida Ryōhei and other leaders of the Kokuryūkai, with its Korean branch run by a few stragglers from the disbanded Ilchinhoe, was ordered to dissolve within a year of its formation, after submitting an erratic petition to the Diet, demanding the abolition of the Government-General for placing Korea directly under the emperor-centered system (Dōkōkai Honbu 1922). On the Sōaikai's role in managing and policing Korean workers in Japan, see Kawashima 2009, Chapter 5.

Confucian elites, shamans, and a corporation of peddlers. Efforts to transform these rather disparate segments of the local population into allies of the regime, as the pioneering study by Kang Tong-jin suggests, derived from technologies of Chosŏn statecraft. Rather than suppress their activities as remnants of Korean tradition, the colonial authorities sought to refashion them into agents of the state and its modernizing reform by retaining their "useful" functions—emphasis on morality, maintenance of hierarchy, obedience to authority—while eradicating "superstitious" aspects of their activity.[50] A few documents survive to suggest how key brokers of empire were involved.

To woo the Confucian literati, a group that was both influential and vehemently anti-Japanese, Ōgaki supervised the Taedong Samunhoe (Great Eastern Way Society) in Seoul, and Kikuchi oversaw the Yudo Chinhŭnghoe (Society for the Promotion of the Confucian Way) based in North Kyŏngsang province. In addition to propagating cultural rule by going on lecture tours, members of the two organizations renounced participation in nationalistic activities, devoting themselves to "nurturing morality," "upholding law and order," and "setting a model for the general populace."[51] They were expected to revive Confucian values by teaching in provincial academies (*hyanggyo*), publishing bulletins, and lecturing local villagers on thrift and the elimination of "evil customs."[52] In return for their services, Saitō rewarded key members by appointing them to the Central Council. By deploying the Korean gentry as both instrument of civilizing reform and vessel of Confucian ethics, the Japanese rulers hoped to claim for themselves a dual role as modernizer and custodian of Korean tradition.

In addition to the Confucian literati, Korean shamans (K. *mudang*; J. *fugeki*) also came under Ōgaki's charge after the government received a complaint about another Japanese who had apparently tried to bring shamans under his control.[53] The petition in question (dated August

50. This strategy resembled, and in some ways presaged, how the Japanese rulers in Manchukuo would utilize local redemptive societies (Duara 2003, 115).

51. "Kak to sijŏng sŏnjŏn kangyŏn" in *Yudo* (Yudo Chinhŭnghoe), 2 (n.d.), 115; Kang Tong-jin 1979, 238.

52. *Maeil sinbo*, 29 January 1920; and 9 December 1921.

53. As much an object of ethnographic curiosity as a target of official "surveillance," Korean shamans drew the attention of many Japanese, from local scholars such as Ayukai

1923) was submitted to Saitō by three Koreans who identified themselves as founders of the Keijin Kyōfūkai (Society for Respecting the Divine and Correcting Customs).[54] Since antiquity, the petitioners explained, Korean shamans who "prayed for happiness and exorcised evil spirits from a person upon request" enjoyed "countless believers ranging from high-ranking royal officials at the top to commoners at the bottom." The Japanese policy since annexation was to suppress such "superstitious" and "evil customs of the Korean people," though it did little to stem the flow of visitors to shamans. Seeing this as a business opportunity, one Komine Gensaku (who went by his Korean name, Kim Jaehyŏn), in 1919, contrived to create a licensing agency, allegedly with the police bureau's approval, to register shamans and to dispatch them upon request to "spy on recalcitrant Koreans." Komine exacted from shamans onerous membership and miscellaneous fees, and meted out harsh punishments when they defaulted on their payments or filed grievances with the police. No longer able to overlook his tyranny, the Korean authors of the petition had "pleaded with the police bureau to bring the shamans under its direct control by creating an organization to be headed by Mr. Ōgaki." He at once agreed to undertake this responsibility.[55] As a way of monitoring and regulating their activities, shamans were then herded into the Keijin Fugeki Kumiai (Guild of Pious Shamans). Operating as the Keijin Kyōfūkai, the organization aimed to "eliminate people's superstition and advance material civilization" by regulating the "evil shamanic customs of deluding society" and gradually attenuating their influence in Korean village life.[56] Even after the society came into being, however, Komine's abuse persisted; he continued to hold separate meetings with shamans and "extort money from them." Such an act to re-

Fusanoshin, to Government-General employees such as Murayama Chijun (1891–1968) who emphasized the link between shamanism and Shinto to substantiate the theory of shared ancestry (Sakurai Yoshiyuki 1964, 285–86; Sakano 2005, Chapter 5). Rather than dismiss shamanism as a form of superstition, Murayama recognized its function to integrate society. Ironically, his studies were used by Korean nationalists such as Ch'oe Nam-son to establish the cultural autonomy and identity of the Korean *minjok* (Sakano 2005, 310–20).

54. "Chinjōsho" in *SMB* 16:625–46. Throughout the petition, its authors' obeisance to the emperor and the Governor-General suggests their pro-Japanese orientation.

55. Ibid., 626–36.

56. Ibid., 625.

plenish his own pocket "merely perpetuated the evil custom of shamanism," the petitioners charged, urging the authorities to stop his misdeeds as a way of showing Koreans proof of "cultural policy and *isshi dōjin*."[57]

Although few details about their activities remain, Japanese efforts to control both the Confucian literati and shamans appear to have proven wholly ineffective. Korean villagers continued to visit shamans as before, and the two Confucian organizations attracted only marginal and undesirable elements; prominent literati, on the other hand, boycotted participation by "secluding themselves in the mountains," according to Hosoi's report to Saitō.[58] Chronic financial trouble, coupled with competition between the two Confucian organizations, also hastened their decline.[59]

More willing to cooperate with the authorities were itinerant "pack and back" peddlers known as *pobusang*. In the Chosŏn dynasty, these peddlers operated through a state-sanctioned network of guild-type cooperatives set up in every province and city. They owed exceptional loyalty to the throne, and until the final years of the dynasty assisted the Korean court in gathering intelligence and countering such anti-governmental activities as the Tonghak Uprising.[60] Hosoi Hajime, advisor to Saitō, was among the first to recognize their utility for the new colonial regime. Hosoi recommended using Korean peddlers as "messengers" in times of state emergency and as "spies" in tracking down dissidents to aid the police in suppressing nationalist movements.[61] Accordingly in 1920, the colonial government created a peddlers' organization called the Shōmu Kenkyūkai (Commercial Affairs Research Association), with its headquarters in Seoul. In addition to pledging to "become good citizens," members were required to carry a card that on its back printed rules prohibiting political debates and assemblies, and their conduct was monitored through a finely graded system of rewards

57. Ibid., 637–43. Kang Tong-jin (1979), who examined the same petition, writes that Komine was actually working for Ōgaki as his "minion" (54, n. 29) but this assumption is not supported by this document or any other evidence.

58. Quoted in Kang Tong-jin 1979, 239.

59. These two problems were reported to Saitō within a few months of the formation of Yudo Chinhŭnghoe by its leaders, asking for relief (Kim Yŏng-han, "Chōsen Judō Shinkōkai keika jōkyō hōkokusho," in *SMB* 9:162–63).

60. For more information on *pobusang*, see "Fuhōshō no raireki," in *SMB* 8:929–32.

61. Hosoi to Saitō (13 April 1920): 530–35; Kang Tong-jin 1979, 241.

and punishments.[62] The Sangmusa (Commercial Affairs Company) was created two years later to further unify a dozen or so existing peddlers' guilds under the leadership of Yi Chi-yong and several former members of the Ilchinhoe.[63] As early as that November, some peddlers demonstrated their potency in quelling an anti-Japanese demonstration of Christians joined by some 300 Korean school pupils and radical youth in Seoul.[64] The peddlers were also highly prized by the colonial police bureau for their "remarkable achievements" in collecting intelligence and suppressing "bandits."[65]

When Kikuchi Kenjō, who had been controlling the organization behind the scenes, replaced Yi Chi-yong as its president in 1927, he refashioned the peddlers' activity in ways that could more fully service the empire. In addition to obtaining a permit for selling medicine, ostensibly to provide better welfare to the peddlers' families, Kikuchi created a labor department within the company for the purpose of assisting large-scale Japanese economic ventures around Korea. Drawing on their traditional duty to transport procurements to distant regions, peddlers were dispatched to help "the construction of hydroelectricity in South Hamgyŏng province and the irrigation works in the coastal regions of North Chŏlla province," in addition to "averting labor disputes" at various workplaces.[66] Appropriating their time-tested functions of loyalty to the state and patriotic labor, Kikuchi invested the peddlers with yet another role by reconfiguring them as grassroots agents of colonial capital.

This patchwork of pro-Japanese organizations that emerged in the wake of 1919 was, in essence, a map of a new strategy of accommodation, drawn and redrawn by official as well as civilian architects. The activities of men like Ōgaki and Kikuchi provide a glimpse of how, in this period of improvisation, "collaboration" functioned on the ground. A look into the Japanese effort to rule through the social fabric of Ko-

62. In forming this association, the colonial government cooperated with a former Ilchinhoe member, Kim Kwang-hŭi ("Shōmu Kenkyūkai kisoku," in *SMB* 8:681–714).

63. For details of the Sangmusa's activities, see "Shōmusha gaisetsu," in *SMB* 8:721–31.

64. Ibid., 722.

65. Kang Tong-jin 1979, 242.

66. "Shōmusha gaisetsu," *SMB* 8:731.

rea reveals its rough informal lining: a haphazard blend of initiatives launched by settler leaders (and Korean elites) in conjunction with the colonial police bureau. Their efforts to secure allies, combat radicals, and co-opt nationalists—bankrolled by the governor's discretionary funds—entailed many failed experiments. The operation of these local agents and organs remained at best makeshift. Hurriedly devised and installed, few would last the entire duration of Saitō's regime.

In the proliferating web of organizations that rose and fell in support of Saitō's cultural rule, the most fundamental problem facing them all was a conspicuous lack of mass support. Their membership was limited and their leadership often flaccid. From their inception most organizations came under fierce attack by the vernacular press, and all faced an uphill battle against the surging activity of Korean nationalists. This decade witnessed the rise of nationalists, socialists, and communists, who instilled a new life in Korean anticolonial struggle on the peninsula and abroad. Whereas radicals and communists chose strategies of confrontation (going underground or joining an exile group in Shanghai), moderates of bourgeois orientation—those Michael Robinson has called "cultural nationalists"—launched a host of projects in the early 1920s to promote Korean self-awareness, literacy, and industry.[67] Wide-ranging in scope and character, the activities of cultural nationalists were guided by a belief in the pragmatic need to cultivate Korean national strength for the eventual goal of independence, a gradualist strategy redolent of the Patriotic Enlightenment Movement in the late nineteenth century.

In this period of Korean cultural effervescence, Japanese-Korean relations hit a new low after the Great Kantō Earthquake struck Tokyo in the fall of 1923. About a week following the calamity, the news that hundreds of Korean residents had been massacred by panic-stricken Japanese filled the headlines of vernacular newspapers, stirring public outrage. By then the announced reforms of cultural rule had been slowly put in place, but the massacre did not augur well for the future of the Japanese presence on the peninsula. To the most pessimistic observers, it delivered an ill omen of backsliding to the hardline policies of the

67. Cultural nationalists were a growing and diverse class of educated and progressive Koreans, many of whom had studied in Japan. Their major activities included the Movement to Establish a National University and the Korean Production Movement. For more details on the cultural nationalist movement, see M. Robinson 1988, 92–100.

March First era, or even a "premonition of the inevitable abandonment of Korea."[68] Hosoi Hajime's top-secret memorandum to Saitō, later circulated among his officials, paraded unsettling examples of the Korean mass boycott, abetted by the press, of Japanese goods, Japanese education, and tax payments around the country. Fear of Korean retribution prompted settler vigilante groups to hastily form in the provinces, a scene eerily similar to the spring of 1919.[69]

Renewed anti-Japanese hostility further weakened pro-Japanese organizations that were already weighed down by accusations of national betrayal. Determined to "stamp out the current, short-sighted trend of communism or independence," Korean leaders of these floundering organizations coalesced in March 1924 to form the Kakp'a Yuji Yŏnmaeng (League of All Parties of Local Notables). They offered themselves as the last bastion against radicals, but to no avail.[70] The league's activity, including an incident of violence against their nationalist opponents,[71] added fresh fuel to public animosity. Compounded by internal strife, the organization became moribund after 1925.

## *Assimilation Campaign: The Dōminkai*

As the Korean-run organizations teetered under nationalist pressure, settler elites rose to the challenge of mending ethnic relations by launching a countermeasure. To salvage what was left of the increasingly hollow talk of *naisen yūwa*, they joined hands with the colonial state and its trusted Korean allies in the spring of 1924 to form an ideological organization, fittingly christened the Dōminkai (Association of One People). Like many other organizations, the Dōminkai operated under the auspices of the police bureau, but from its inception it was a unique body of collaborators: a joint Japanese-Korean creation (the largest of its kind) formed in the 1920s with Saitō's personal blessing, specifically for promoting cultural rule.[72] A close look at the activities of the Dōminkai,

---

68. Hosoi to Saitō (17 September 1923): 566.

69. Chōsen Sōtokufu Keimukyoku 1930c, 133.

70. Chōsen Sōtokufu Keimukyoku 1923; *Chōsen jijō kimitsu tsūshin* 2 (February 1925): 14–15.

71. *Tonga ilbo*, 10–11 April 1924.

72. The discussion of the Dōminkai in this chapter is based on Uchida 2003, 173–201.

whose web of support extended to the metropole, illustrates the new role and influence of bourgeois settlers as allies of official policy, especially their pivotal part in countering Korean nationalism. As self-proclaimed practitioners of *naisen yūwa*, moreover, they translated the colonial rhetoric into a set of concrete projects, allowing us to probe the local dynamics as well as limits of the Japanese attempt to fashion an empire of harmony.

The formation of the Dōminkai was directly inspired by a Japanese patriotic society in Tokyo called the Kōminkai (Imperial Subjects' Association), headed by Hōjō Tokiyuki (1858–1929), the former president of Gakushūin University.[73] Hōjō's son-in-law was none other than the colonial police chief, Maruyama Tsurukichi, the mastermind behind the operation of many pro-Japanese organizations. After a visit to Seoul by the Kōminkai leaders on their lecture tour in early 1923, Saitō relayed to Maruyama his wish to create a similar organization in Korea. Maruyama entrusted this task to Nakamura Kentarō (1883–?), a long-time settler with rare proficiency in Korean, by appointing him as a part-time employee (*shokutaku*) of the police bureau. Nakamura had come to Korea in 1899 as a language exchange student from Kumamoto; his teacher was the Pan-Asianist Sasa Masayuki (1862–1928), brother of a famed nationalist, Sasa Tomofusa (1854–1906), and a participant in the assassination of Queen Min. Fluent in Korean by the time of annexation, Nakamura had cut his teeth on journalism by working for the *Keijō nippō* and *Maeil sinbo* in the 1910s before being entrusted with the task of organizing the Dōminkai. Nakamura thereafter functioned as a central liaison between the Dōminkai and the Government-General.[74]

The Dōminkai's formation and membership both demonstrate how critically important personal contacts were to the operation of brokers of empire like Nakamura. Urged by Saitō, who apparently opined that "[you] cannot just operate on a small scale in Korea for fully carrying out *naisen yūwa*,"[75] Nakamura headed to Tokyo with two other representatives chosen at an organizational meeting: Satō Torajirō (1864–1928), a settler entrepreneur and former Diet member, and Sin Sŏng-nin

---

73. *Dōmin* 1 (June 1924): 80.
74. Nakamura Kentarō 1969, 9–18, 85–93.
75. Ibid., 83.

Fig. 5 Dōminkai leaders: Sin Sŏng-nin (*top*), Nakamura Kentarō (*left*), and Satō Torajirō (*right*). SOURCE: Dōminkai 1926.

(1865–?), a Central Council member and Kungmin Hyŏphoe executive who was close to Saitō.[76] By the end of their three-month trip, they managed to obtain over a hundred pledges of support and 30,000 yen in private donations to found the Dōminkai. These funds came from a variety of individuals,[77] including former colonial bureaucrats and famous figures with long-term ties to Korea such as Tokutomi Sohō and Shibusawa Eiichi.[78] Satō also used his extensive social network as a former Diet member to marshal support from such high-profile political leaders as Inukai Tsuyoshi and Katō Takaaki (1860–1926), and ultranationalists Tōyama Mitsuru and Uchida Ryōhei, his former *rōnin* comrades.

---

76. Sin Sŏng-nin served as a colonial bureaucrat since 1911 and became the governor of Kangwŏn province in 1921. From 1923 to the 1930s, Sin served on the Central Council, while also working as the governor of South Ch'ungch'ŏng province between 1927 and 1929 (Morikawa 1935, 33).

77. Nakamura Kentarō 1969, 83–89; *Dōmin* 1 (June 1924): 11–12, 80–81.

78. Shibusawa financially supported many other organizations including the Daitō Dōshikai and the Sōaikai (Shibusawa Seien Kinen Zaidan Ryūmonsha 1960, 31:745–67).

By the time the Dōminkai formally came into being on 15 April 1924, the organizers had gathered an equally impressive cast of members featuring a veritable "who's who" of Korea. Hōjō Tokiyuki, the organization's first president, was backed by two vice presidents: a Korean baron, Yi Chae-gŭk, and the Japanese head of the Seoul Railway Bureau, Andō Matasaburō. A host of "advisors" included prominent individuals with aristocratic titles, and a wide assortment of Korean elites—public officials, entrepreneurs, landlords, company executives, members of the Central Council, and leaders of pro-Japanese organizations—filled the board of directors.[79] The Dōminkai's rank and file, split almost equally between Japanese and Koreans, embodied the ideal of *naisen yūwa*, reflecting the organizers' desire to reconstitute ethnic relations by promoting class as a new basis of unity.[80]

In its goals, strategies, and activities, the Dōminkai was the very epitome of Saitō's cultural rule. According to its prospectus, the group professed to wage an ideological battle on two fronts: against ethnic friction and radical thought in Korea, and against Western imperial encroachments in East Asia. A panacea for both problems, in the Social Darwinistic terms of the prospectus, was to "cement the bond and mutual support" between Japanese and Koreans in order to ensure their racial survival and common prosperity. With this in mind, the Dōminkai upheld three objectives as general guidelines for its activities: "the complete realization of *naisen yūwa*" to counter Western global dominance and discrimination against the Asian *minzoku*; "thought guidance" (*shisō zendō*) to eradicate socialist ideas and independence advocacy; and the promotion of industry, labor, and discipline to eliminate the "habits of aimless behavior and indolence."[81] By recasting assimilation as a joint Japanese-Korean project to combat the imperial West, in other words, the Dōminkai aimed to ensure Korea's sound capitalistic development

79. Most Korean executives of the Dōminkai served simultaneously on the executive boards of such organizations as the Kungmin Hyŏphoe, the Yudo Chinhŭnghoe, and the Taishō Shinbokukai.

80. The creation of the Dōminkai may be seen as a long-awaited response to the official desire expressed in the wake of the March First Movement to create an influential organization based on "cooperation between Japanese and Korean capitalists" (Yamanashi to Saitō 1919, 155–56).

81. *Dōmin* 1 (June 1924): 80–81; "Dōminkai sōritsu shushi," *SMB* 12:279–89.

while averting its unsettling side effects of class conflict and social disorder.

First and foremost, the Dōminkai's mission was to spread the gospel of ethnic harmony. Specifically it sought to provide a new ideology—what its founders collectively referred to as "the spirit of *dōmin*"—and a space in which to promote the joint Japanese-Korean construction of capitalist Korea. According to one of the founders, Takashima Heizaburō of Tōyō University, the term *dōmin* had a dual meaning. At the broadest level, it meant to "make no superior-inferior distinctions between Japanese and Koreans" and to treat both groups as "citizens of the same nation" (*onaji kokumin*) as well as "subjects of the imperial state" (*teikoku no shinmin*). It also meant "for the people bound by a common will to come together and cooperate in building one respectable state [*rippa na kokka*]."[82] This definition of *dōmin*, which straddled the citizen-subject dichotomy left vague in the Japanese notion of nation (Chapter 2), captured a changing perception of Korea as a colonial polity. Emblematic of what Prasenjit Duara has called the "East Asian Modern,"[83] the ideology of *dōmin* functioned to translate modern political ideals of autonomy and citizens' rights in global currency after World War I, and fuse them with the "traditional" Japanese notion of imperial subjecthood, an emphasis of Meiji statecraft thinking and *isshi dōjin* policy in the 1910s. In part a Japanese response to the "Wilsonian moment"[84] or the rise of anti-imperialist nationalism, this awkward synthesis reflected a new, if belated, awareness among the colonial rulers of the political need (now rendered as a global norm) to recognize the existence of multiple ethnic groups under their jurisdiction. At the logical end of this understanding stood the idea of a multiethnic state (*kongō minzoku kokka*) with nominal equality of all members, a vision that prefigured Manchukuo.[85] This idea was hinted, if not enunciated, in the activities of the Dōminkai that buried the project of assimilation in its rhetoric of harmony.

82. Takashima Heizaburō, "Dōminkai no konpon seishin," *Dōmin* 1 (June 1924): 26.

83. For the internal workings of the "East Asian Modern" in Manchukuo, see Duara 2003, 2–3, 62–63.

84. Manela 2007.

85. Duara 2003. This heterogeneous vision of Korea was also entertained by Government-General officials. See, for instance, Hirai 1924, 4–5.

Using its growing network of regional branches, the Dōminkai sought to diffuse "the spirit of *dōmin*" in "every corner of Korea" by incessantly holding lectures, film screenings, study groups, and "Japanese-Korean informal discussion forums" to promote a dialogue between the two communities.[86] Nakamura, who spoke on many of these occasions, "almost always lectured in Korean," because the use of Japanese had not spread to Koreans in their 40s and 50s.[87] And at a time when "only anti-Japanese articles sustained a newspaper business in Korea," the Dōminkai labored hard to prove that "assimilation is making strides" around the country.[88] Every month the association distributed 5,000 copies of its bulletin, *Dōmin*, which periodically furnished "evidence of ethnic harmony" by featuring various "laudable anecdotes" (*bidan*) between Japanese and Korean residents, and tallying up statistics on intermarriage (while inviting even non-members to report their unions to receive Dōminkai's special blessing, an act that foreshadowed the wartime state policy).

The Dōminkai explicitly linked its activity to a broader racial struggle unfolding beyond the peninsula's borders. The Immigration Act of 1924, which barred entry of Japanese and other Asian immigrants into the United States, took effect on 1 July of that year. The Dōminkai declared this day "a memorial day of insult to the colored races (*yūshoku jinshu*)," and through posters and postcards distributed in the thousands called on "Japanese and Koreans to cooperate as superior beings of the world."[89] A focus on Pan-Asian unity signaled a continuity with the old agenda of imperial loyalists like Uchida Ryōhei, but it also absorbed the new ideological currents that began to alter the face of Japanese empire. First, the passage of anti-immigration legislation in the United States encouraged Japan to see itself as a victim rather than a perpetrator of imperialism.[90] Second, the global rise of anticolonial nationalism presented an opportunity to revive the idea of an Eastern alliance against Western dominance as a racial struggle of "oppressed nations." Juxtaposing Asian egalitarianism with Anglo-American expansionism, the

---

86. *Dōmin* 7 (December 1924): 8.
87. Nakamura Kentarō 1969, 89–90.
88. *Dōmin* 5 (October 1924): 11; and 1 (April 1924): 17.
89. *Dōmin* 7 (December 1924): 5.
90. Duara 2003, 78.

Dōminkai leaders not only hoped to strengthen Japanese-Korean relations by countering the subversive ideas of ethnic solidarity and class struggle. They also sought to reconstitute the "Orient" (*Tōyō*) by reorienting the axis of conflict along the West-East divide—indeed, to turn it into a clash of civilizations.

The Pan-Asianist call was supplemented by an equally urgent, and certainly no less arduous, task to convert local settlers to the message of ethnic coexistence. Where the authorities spoke of paternalistic obligations to their charges, the Dōminkai leaders worried, local settlers behaved as if they owed nothing to Koreans. The Dōminkai circulated tens of thousands of handbills in cities around Korea, calling on Japanese residents to refrain from using the derogatory word *yobo* as a pronoun for Koreans.[91] They also posted announcements in the bulletin *Dōmin* urging a "Japanese awakening toward Korea." One such notice printed in 1926 exhorted all Japanese residents to "make sure to be good settlers," "elevate each other's awareness of coexistence and co-prosperity with the 20 million [Korean] compatriots [*dōhō*]," "reform metropolitan misunderstanding about Korea," and "guide and awaken government authorities, learned individuals, and politicians toward improving national policy."[92] The Dōminkai urged every humble resident to shoulder the burden of empire by mending ethnic relations from the ground up, in effect appointing each settler a broker of empire.

Korean members of the Dōminkai occasionally joined the chorus in exhorting settlers, including their own colleagues, to rectify their behavior. One regular contributor to the bulletin, Ch'oe Chŏng-ho, complained that "the Japanese always talk of *naisen yūwa* by goading Koreans to work harder, while flaunting their privileges and arrogance." Such "a discriminatory sense of superiority," he argued, was rooted in erroneous assumptions the Japanese held about Korea's place in their country's history, such as "seeing Korea as the cause of the Satsuma Rebellion [of 1877]" and "misunderstanding Japan's annexation of Korea as a quid pro quo for the sacrifices made during the Sino-Japanese and Russo-Japanese Wars."[93] *Naisen yūwa* could only begin, Ch'oe sug-

---

91. *Dōmin* 4 (September 1924): 17; and 7 (December 1924): 8.
92. *Dōmin* 19 (February 1926): 14.
93. *Dōmin* 7 (December 1924): 22–23; and 15 (September 1925): 24–26.

gested, by re-educating the misguided colonists about their nation's recent path to modernity.

Korean nationalism was a principal target of the Dōminkai's campaign. In order to undermine the Korean demand for independence, the Dōminkai sought, as Abe Mitsuie had earlier suggested to Saitō, to "link up with the [Korean] argument for self-strengthening" and to "promote education and industry as two main objectives."[94] Its activities were framed to coincide with the goal of moderate nationalists to promote Korea's capitalistic development while combating socialism, and their priority of creating a middle-class leadership over building a mass base. By co-opting these bourgeois agendas, the settler leaders hoped, Japanese hegemony might slowly take root amidst the bitter divisions that were fast emerging within the nationalist movement.

In order to accommodate the growing Korean demands for welfare, education, and economy, the Dōminkai offered a variety of programs figured in terms of "social work" (*shakai jigyō*). Using philanthropy as insurance against radicalism was by then an old strategy in Japan,[95] but it found a new application in the management of colonial Korea: to dampen nationalism. In the name of *naisen yūwa*, the Seoul headquarters provided a variety of services such as "private counseling to economically hard-pressed individuals," and "the offering of condolences to the bereaved families of its members in times of misfortune." Regional branches undertook more laborious projects. The Kongju branch managed "a relief house for impoverished orphans," while the Kanggyŏng branch engaged local children in manufacturing ropes and straw sacks, in order to help farmers and laborers generate extra income and "relieve their hardship."[96]

The Taegu branch went a step further by encouraging local Korean landlords and entrepreneurs to form an agricultural inspection team. The group toured some "prominent and progressive model farms and irrigation facilities" owned by Japanese in North Chŏlla province, where they observed first-hand "how ideally *naisen yūwa* is being carried out" by local landlords and tenants.[97] In cooperation with the Government-

94. Abe Mitsuie to Saitō (6 September 1921).

95. Gluck 1985, 91.

96. *Dōmin* 54 (March 1929): 5; and 75 (December 1930): 3.

97. *Dōmin* 15 (September 1925): 29; and 16 (October–November 1925): 50–56.

General and several agricultural associations, the Dōminkai headquarters also organized an annual workshop on sericulture, then considered the most promising sideline for local farmers. During the first such workshop held in October 1925, some 300 Korean and Japanese silkworm raisers from all thirteen provinces attended lectures offered by technical experts, watched films, and toured leading silk mills and experiment stations in Seoul. The Dōminkai's initiative was much welcomed by the authorities especially at a time of budgetary restraint, when the Government-General had to place its own "Fifteen-Year Plan for Sericulture" on the back burner.[98]

Of all its programs, the Dōminkai poured the most money and effort into promoting education. To bring more youths into its orbit of activity and stem their trend of radicalization, the Dōminkai launched various initiatives to soak up the increasing Korean zeal for education, which outpaced official school construction.[99] In 1926 the Dōminkai began offering "mail-order lectures" covering the curricula of the upper primary school and middle school years. With the assistance of provincial governors and educational associations, the Dōminkai distributed these textbooks at low cost to Korean children in rural areas who could not attend school due to work or economic reasons.[100] Assuming that the number of sales roughly corresponded to the number of subscribers, the Dōminkai managed to reach quite a large number of students, totaling over 10,000.[101] Children and adolescents might study together under the tutelage of the local young men's association, and some even conducted graduation ceremonies.[102]

---

98. *Dōmin* 17 (December 1925): 51–55.

99. Furukawa 1993, 51, 54–55.

100. *Dōmin* 23 (July 1926): 50. According to its Korean-language advertisement, the Dōminkai's textbooks were "the only self-study lecture transcripts available in Korea."

101. Unfortunately, there is no data on the number of subscribers and their regional distribution. Available records indicate that the Dōminkai sold 3,138 copies of its primary school textbook and 6,070 copies of its middle school textbook in 1928. In the early 1930s, the annual sale of its middle school textbook hovered around 5,000, and that of its primary school textbook increased to about 7,000 copies. *Dōmin* 54 (March 1929): 7–8; *Dōminkai kaihō* (February–May, 1933): 19–20, and (May 1933–February 1934): 17.

102. For the example of one village in Kyŏngsŏng district of North Hamgyŏng province, see *Dōmin* 54 (March 1929), fuhen: 1.

Fig. 6. Advertisement for the Dōmin "Mail-Order Lectures."
SOURCE: *Dōmin* 71 (August 1930): 8.

With the aid of district governors and local chambers of commerce, the Dōminkai also sought out and rewarded "hidden persons of virtue" who contributed to the promotion of education and industry in their communities. Most were locally influential Koreans, such as *sŏdang* (private elementary school) teachers, exemplary farmers engaged in "local reforms and industrial development," and dedicated members of school councils and ward chiefs who advanced "mass social education." For their contributions to the state and society, the Dōminkai bestowed upon them "letters of appreciation" and publicized their exemplary deeds in its monthly bulletin.[103] By highlighting the unity between Korean national interests and Japanese colonial projects, the Dōminkai aimed to subsume the entire stratum of local leaders under its movement as grassroots practitioners of *naisen yūwa*.

These pedagogical endeavors extended to nurturing pro-Japanese collaborators, an activity that mirrored and complemented the state's ongoing effort. Starting in the summer of 1925, the Dōminkai held an annual leadership training program called the "Dōmin Summer University." This ten-day crash course was designed to train "prospective local leaders," handpicked by the governor in each province, in "social enlightenment, thought guidance, and the promotion of industry" while

103. *Dōmin* 5 (October 1924): 9.

Fig. 7 Class of the First Dōmin Summer University, August 1925
SOURCE: *Dōmin* 14 (July and August 1925): inside cover.

infusing them with "the spirit of *dōmin*." The university, in short, was an incubator for ideologues of *naisen yūwa*. The first session held in Seoul hosted a total of 90 participants—60 Koreans and 30 Japanese—who came from all provinces, with the majority from Kyŏnggi. The largest group of participants was ordinary school teachers,[104] followed by members of local councils serving at various administrative levels, and leaders of youth organizations. Their occupational breakdown reveals the organizers' desire particularly to co-opt young Koreans staffing the lower levels of government, or "technocratic collaborators" (*tekuno-kurāto-gata kyōryokusha*), as the historian Namiki Masato calls them,[105] whose numbers grew steadily in response to the expansion of colonial bureaucracy in the 1920s. Efforts to indoctrinate this new generation of Korean office holders, who most likely regarded their jobs as avenues to social advancement rather than acts of imperial service, were deemed critical to the success of the *yūwa* campaign.

The Dōmin summer workshop was held almost every year through the late 1930s. The theme and curriculum of each session were carefully tailored to the Government-General's policies, with most lectures de-

104. "Ordinary schools" (*futsū gakkō*) referred to officially created primary school facilities for Korean pupils.

105. Namiki 1993, 40–45.

livered by high-ranking colonial bureaucrats who spoke on their own areas of expertise. In 1926, when the campaign to increase Korean rice production resumed, the program focused on training local leaders in the development of agriculture. In 1930, in the midst of the Kwangju student demonstrations, lecturers outlined and critiqued various "scholarly arguments on contemporary ideological trends" to a class that included local Japanese and Korean students in Seoul.[106] In some years bureaucrats were joined by prominent scholars of empire-wide fame, whose authority the Dōminkai borrowed to enhance its own ideological claims. Kuroita Katsumi (1874–1946), a conservative historian of early Japan from Tokyo Imperial University, clarified the meaning of our "national polity" (*kokutai*) and the origins of imperial Japan; Ōkawa Shūmei (1886–1957), a renowned Pan-Asianist, informed students of the current conditions in Manchuria and expounded on the importance of "blending multiple insights from Western and Eastern, old and new philosophers to generate one's own insight." These lectures were made available to its members and the wider reading public in the form of booklets, a project the Dōminkai launched in 1929 out of fear about further "deterioration of thought."[107]

After the ten-day workshop, all participants received a certificate of completion and a commemorative badge at a graduation ceremony attended by high-ranking colonial officials. Vice Governor-General Shimooka Chūji (1870–1925) congratulated the class of 1925 by sending them off with the exhortation that "Japan and Korea must not only harmonize [among themselves], but unite all the colored races against the white races," and urging them to make use of the "treasure" they had acquired during the workshop "to guide and enlighten the Korean people."[108] Representing its participants, Ch'oe Sang-ok, a provincial government employee from Hamhŭng, responded with a pledge: "When we go back to our home provinces . . . we will work toward a more thorough diffusion of the spirit of *dōmin*, fulfill our duty as members of the national society [*kokka shakai*], promote greater affinity, philan-

106. *Dōmin* 23 (July 1926): 44–45; and 71 (August 1930): 6.
107. "Dōmin sōsho no hakkan ni tsuite," in Kudō Takeki 1929, inside cover.
108. *Dōmin* 14 (July–August 1925): 1–4.

thropy, and coexistence of [our] brethren, and mutually contribute to the unity of the Asian races."[109]

The Dōminkai's activities represented official-civilian cooperation at its finest. To what extent its sermon on *naisen yūwa* captured new souls or the already converted is hard to tell from the existing sources, but the Dōminkai experienced significant growth in its size and status. Along with prominent Japanese-run Buddhist organizations like the Wakō Kyōen and the Kōjō Kaikan that targeted Koreans for philanthropic work,[110] the Dōminkai within a few years of its creation gained official recognition as one of the leading "moral cultivation centers" in Seoul.[111] By 1930, it had a network of branches (run by members of provincial councils) in Taegu, Pusan, Kongju, and Kanggyŏng, and its membership, totaling about 3,000, extended to Japan and Manchuria. As the brainchild of cultural rule, the Dōminkai overall functioned like a fringe organization of the Government-General. Its wide-ranging agenda—to counter nationalists, awaken settlers, promote industry and education, and nurture pro-Japanese collaborators—essentially distilled the key projects of Saitō's regime. As Nakamura put it, the Dōminkai and the colonial government operated as "two sides of the same coin."[112] No metaphor more aptly captured the modus operandi of the brokers of empire, who had moved from the margin to the center of action.

## *Grassroots Agents of* Naisen Yūwa

Outside of the organized activities of the Dōminkai, individual settlers unfurled their own efforts to promote *naisen yūwa*. Self-driven and often iconoclastic, they ranged from simple philanthropy, such as distributing sacks of rice to the city's poor,[113] to more elaborate ventures, such as offering vocational training to the underprivileged and sending Korean

109. Ibid., 37.

110. The two institutions were supported by many Seoul-based settler leaders (Wakō Kyōen 1927, 79–81; Ōtaniha Honganji Chōsen Kaikyō Kantokubu 1927, 174–84). Both had an ambivalent relationship with the colonial government, promoting the official policy of assimilation on the one hand and abiding by more purely philanthropic thinking on the other (Yun Chŏng-uk 1996, 160–61, 166–68).

111. Keijō-fu 1927, 48–50.

112. Nakamura Kentarō 1969, 91.

113. Sin Yŏng-hong 1984, 87–88.

monks to Japanese universities.[114] Tracing these initiatives brings our focus further down to the grassroots level. They demonstrate how ideas and strategies of rule emanated not only from policy-makers, but also from the interface of local Japanese and Korean communities, where diverse brokers of empire pursued their own idealistic (or chimerical) visions of multiethnic Korea.

Spreading ethnic unity became a central vocation of some devoted ideologues like Sugi Ichirobei (1870–?), who had already carved out a niche in the business of promoting *naisen yuwa* by the time he became the Dōminkai's secretary in 1924. A former *kenpeitai* officer and a supporter of the Ilchinhoe, Sugi was a classic *rōnin* type, who, while bouncing from one job to another, and after a flirtation with politics, made Pan-Asianism a lifetime mission.[115] This mission began shortly following annexation, when Sugi cooperated with Korean aristocrats like Cho Chung-ŭng and local settlers in Seoul to launch the Senshinkai (Washing Minds Society), allegedly "the precursor to *naisen yūwa* organizations" on the peninsula. In response to the March First Movement, Sugi created another organization, the Tōa Kyōshōkai (East Asian Coprosperity Society), and traveled through the provinces, touting assimilation through speeches and exchanging opinions with local Korean youths. He dissolved the society to devote himself entirely to the Dōminkai in 1924, overseeing its management until it became incorporated the following year. Once he placed the Dōminkai in orbit, Sugi joined hands with some *kenpeitai* commanders, for the purpose of "spiritual enhancement" (*seishin sakkō*), to create the Chōsen Nogi Society, named after the Russo-Japanese War hero (and Sugi's former commander) General Nogi Maresuke (1849–1912). To honor its namesake, the society built a "magnificent shrine" on top of Namsan in Seoul.[116] In the 1930s, Sugi was actively involved in Seoul's community and educational affairs, especially in the management of the Risshō Academy, which offered boarding and education to about 300 impoverished Korean children—

114. Chōjiya Shōten 1936, n.p.

115. Sugi's biographical information comes from Keijō Shinbunsha 1936, 32–33; Fujimura 1931, 49–56; Keijō-fu Shakaika 1934, 123.

116. *Kyōshō no michi* 1 (September 1923): 7–8.

a career that earned him wide public recognition and helped him get elected to the Seoul City Assembly.[117]

Among the local settlers, perhaps no merchant was more committed to the cause of assimilation than Kobayashi Genroku, the aforementioned owner of Chōjiya. Kobayashi was known not only for his feat of transforming a clothier into a department store within a single generation; as a devout Buddhist, he was even more famous for living a life of charity. Among his extensive list of social service included helping the Salvation Army maintain its childcare center (a financial commitment he began when he temporarily sheltered a crowd of famished Korean orphans in 1918) and assisting another philanthropic organization, the Kōjō Kaikan, where he ran a sheltered work program for Korean youth.[118] Kobayashi's commitment to "Korean welfare" also translated into his store management. Unlike many settler retailers, he hired a large number of Koreans—even placing a Korean head clerk in the department of heavy silk brocades—and provided them with boarding facilities, a company cemetery, and vocational training.[119] And every morning Kobayashi assembled his employees to preach "the Buddhist Commercial Way," enjoining them particularly to "value Korean customers who have patronized our store since its foundation."[120]

In order to "accelerate assimilation of Japanese and Koreans" on a spiritual level, in 1925 Kobayashi founded the Chōsen Bukkyōdan (Korean Buddhist Association) with Yi Wŏn-sŏk, a Korean Buddhist monk from Wŏnsan, and Nakamura Kentarō of the Dōminkai.[121] Kobayashi personally contributed over 10,000 yen every year to support its activities, which included organizing missionary tours, film screenings, and lectures; promoting respect for the elderly; providing medication for the sick and the impoverished; and distributing free copies of the monthly magazine *Chōsen Bukkyō* to "enlighten and guide the minds of Koreans." The association's most ambitious project was to train a number of Korean monks and send them to Buddhist universities

---

117. Dai-Keijō Kōshokusha Meikan Kankōkai Hensankakari 1936, 32–33.

118. "Kyūseigun Ikuji Hōmu no oitachi," and "Kōjō Kaikan sōritsu," in Chōjiya Shōten 1936; Morikawa 1935, 933–34.

119. Chōsen Sōtokufu Gakumukyoku Shakaika 1933, 110.

120. "Shinkō," in Chōjiya Shōten 1936.

121. Nakamura Kentarō 1969, 95–96, 172–73.

in Japan,[122] with an implicit goal to counter the dominant influence of Christian missionaries.[123]

For Kobayashi, the boundary between business and charity was often blurred, and his devotion to *naisen yūwa* was matched by few settlers. However, his life of good works included a calculated appeal to Koreans. On the political balance sheet of post-1919 Korea, the benefit of touting harmony was probably higher than the cost of remaining silent, especially for a business like Chōjiya where fully half of the factory hands and one-third of the customers were Korean. Kobayashi, in other words, had a high commercial stake in the *yūwa* campaign. Herein lay the logic of settler capitalism. Cultural rule allowed settlers to don a mask of bourgeois beneficence while continuing to exploit cheap Korean labor (and reap political dividends).[124] By promoting industry and education, moreover, even if efforts to assimilate Koreans should fail, settler retailers might still capture their growing purchasing power.[125] For merchant capitalists like Kobayashi, it seems, *naisen yūwa* was ultimately business as usual.

Some grassroots ideologues of assimilation, instead of targeting Koreans, focused their energy on enlightening their own countrymen, whose ignorance and indifference created a challenge of a different order. Watanabe Benzō, a former district official in North Kyŏngsang province who managed the Taegu branch of the Dōminkai, devoted his life after retirement to "clarifying Korea's conditions" by going on lecture tours around Japan.[126] But a more pressing task remained on the peninsula: to convert intractable settlers to the message of ethnic coexistence. This was undertaken with evangelical resolve by Hayashi

---

122. Kobayashi Genroku 1926.

123. "Chosŏn'go," *Kaebyŏk*, July 1924, 18–19. But this particular venture seems to have failed utterly. As one local magazine reported in late 1930, after a decade of activity the Chōsen Bukkyōdan had dispatched a mere "20 or 30 Korean monks" to the metropole—and half of them had come back to Korea "awakened to radical nationalist sentiment" (*Chōsen oyobi Manshū*, December 1930, 5).

124. Interview with grandson of Kobayashi Genroku, Chiba, Japan, 16 December 2001.

125. One annual industrial chronicle published in 1943 reported that 60 percent of Chōjiya's clientele was Korean by that time, also noting the "rapid advance in the peninsular people's purchasing power" (Ogura 1943, 145).

126. Yi Jin-ho et al. 1934, 11, 15.

Shōzō, who managed an orchard in the vicinity of Pusan after crossing to Korea at the age of 26. Outraged at the abusive conduct of Japanese usurers in Korea, in March 1923 Hayashi launched a moral crusade he christened the Feet-Washing Movement—a name inspired by his deep Christian faith—in order to revive their dignity as "the Yamato *minzoku*" and instill in them the ideal of assimilating with Koreans.[127] Perturbed by the news of the Korean massacre following the Great Kantō Earthquake, Hayashi distributed copies of his manifesto and posted leaflets at train stations in cities where Japanese concentrated. With support from Maruyama Tsurukichi, he also traveled from province to province, delivering speeches, warning settlers against exploiting Koreans, and enjoining them to "love and save the Koreans" instead.[128] This message evidently reached the ears of Yoshino Sakuzō (1878–1933), who sent Hayashi a postcard endorsing his movement from Tokyo.[129]

His sympathy for the plight of Korean farmers, which led to a criticism of the official agricultural policy,[130] may have distinguished Hayashi from other ideologues, but his movement in the end served no less to buttress Japan's political designs on Korea. Hayashi was a Christian nationalist who desired to rectify Japanese rule without questioning its foundation, convinced as he was that "the purpose of Japan's annexation of Korea is the coexistence and coprosperity" of the two peoples.[131] That a stream of visitors to Hayashi's farm included members of the Kokuryūkai and Manchurian *rōnin* also reveals his connections with more aggressive proponents of Japanese expansionism.[132] In fact, Hayashi's movement drew support from Koreans and Japanese of all persuasions, from right-wing Pan-Asianists to the most outspoken critics of the Governor-General's rule, attesting to its wide appeal across the political spectrum. Though far from achieving a hegemonic status, *naisen yūwa*, with its vision of Korea as a multiethnic polity, appears to have

---

127. Hayashi Shōzō 1964, 278.

128. Ibid., 278, 303–16.

129. Ibid., 281.

130. *Chōsen Jitsugyō Kurabu kaihō*, December 1930, 17–22.

131. So blind was Hayashi to his complicity that he was taken aback when his critique of the Government-General passed the censor and won third place in an essay contest held by the *Keijō Nichinichi shinbun* (Hayashi Shōzō 1964, 306).

132. Ibid., 318.

taken root among a contending array of ideological formulations—including nationalism, socialism, and communism—that drove the rapidly shifting political landscape of Korea.

## *Limits of the* Yūwa *Campaign*

If Hayashi was largely unaware of his complicity with imperialism, the Dōminkai, for its part, was quite unabashed about the presence of radical chauvinists in its leadership. Shared antisocialism brought settler leaders into alliance with metropolitan patriotic societies, including the Kōminkai and the Dai-Nihon Kokusuikai (Greater Japan National Essence Association).[133] Whereas the Kōminkai was relatively obscure, the Kokusuikai was large enough to extend its activities to the empire.[134] Its Korean branch quickly gained notoriety as a kind of mafia (*bōryokudan*), its members occasionally stunning the public with shows of violence.[135] One such incident occurred in the summer of 1925, when a member disrupted an assembly of Korean socialists by "brandishing a short sword" in the middle of a speech by Nakanishi Inosuke (1887–1958), a comrade invited from the metropole.[136]

If Korean and Japanese socialists were able to demonstrate their doctrine—how easily "class consciousness" could override "the power of ethnic unity," as the *Tonga ilbo* reported on the assembly—their bourgeois opponents struggled harder to follow their manifesto on ethnic harmony. Their connection to the Kokusuikai did not help, as the Dōminkai leaders learned to their chagrin not long after the above incident. In April 1926, two Dōminkai executives, Takayama Takayuki and Satō Torajirō were leaving Ch'angdŏk Palace after making a condolence call for the death of the last Korean emperor, Sunjong, when they were mistaken for high-ranking colonial officials and stabbed by a Korean

---

133. The latter was a patriotic society founded in 1919 and controlled by the ruling Seiyūkai party. For a detailed study of the Kokusuikai and the culture of political violence in Japan more generally, see Siniawer 2008.

134. As of January 1923, the Kokusuikai's Korean branch was chaired by Watanabe Sadaichirō, a building contractor who headed the Seoul Chamber of Commerce, and its vice-chair was Makiyama Kōzō, a Diet member and owner of the *Chōsen shinbun*. Both were executive members of the Dōminkai.

135. "Sinŏ taesajŏn (4)," *Pyŏlgŏn'gon* 30 (1 July 1930): 51.

136. Keijō Honmachi Keisatsu Shochō (18 August 1925); *Tonga ilbo*, 1 January 1926.

mourner outside the palace gate.[137] Takayama also happened to be a member of the Kokusuikai. On hearing of the attack, his fellow Kokusuikai members, "clad in judo wear" and armed with "clubs," rushed to the scene of the crime and broke into the palace to rescue their comrades.[138]

What followed was a series of unforeseen consequences that quickly spiraled into disaster. Forceful entry into a sacred royal compound provoked an immediate Korean public outcry.[139] This, in turn, exacerbated official anxiety that Korean mass "wailing" during the king's funeral might "spark a riot." But the subsequent tightening of police control over the mourning crowd only increased Korean animosity, "fundamentally causing a fissure in [ethnic] harmony." Apart from creating a public relations disaster, the Kokusuikai's outrage also appears to have emboldened the Korean communists to stage anti-Japanese riots during the king's funeral a month later—the so-called June Tenth Movement.[140]

Rare as incidents like this may have been, they served to expose the central structural weakness of the *yūwa* campaign: its fragile base of public support. To be sure, the Dōminkai's initiatives, such as the textbook production and agricultural workshops, managed to absorb some of the Korean fervor for education and industry, enticing not a few allies from the upper crust of the local population. Their success partially owed to the timing; there was no more opportune moment to bridge the worlds of Japanese and Koreans than when the nationalists were internally divided.[141] Nonetheless, while internecine strife may have plagued the nationalist movement, it did not mute the Korean attack on the *yūwa* campaign. And while modest state subsidies and corporate largesse sustained the activities of Dōminkai and other pro-government groups, they ultimately won few devoted participants from the settler

137. *Dōmin* 24 (August 1926): 35–38; Chōsen Sōtokufu Keimukyoku Toshoka 1989 [1926], 247–330.

138. Keijō Honmachi Keisatsu Shochō (5 May 1926).

139. Keijō Shōro Keisatsu Shochō (5 May 1926).

140. Chōsen Sōtokufu Keimukyoku Toshoka 1989 [1926], 313.

141. The radicals' charges of accommodation beleaguered the cultural nationalist movement, especially following the appearance of Yi Kwang-su's five-part editorial in *Tonga ilbo* in early 1924 ("Minjokchŏk Kyŏngnyun," 2–6 January), a sequel to his earlier controversial thesis on Korean national reconstruction ("Minjok Kaejoron," *Kaebyŏk*, May 1922).

community, much less from the Korean public.[142] The welter of assimilation drives even inspired parody, as when a Korean member of the Dōminkai wryly pointed to the emergence of "harmony traders" who, through a subversive kind of alchemy, turned assimilation into a profit-making opportunity.[143]

Even those favorably disposed to Saitō's cultural rule responded to the *yūwa* campaign coolly. In the name of ethnic harmony, Yun Ch'i-ho noted in his diary, the campaign pursued a goal of Japanization:

> The pro-Japanese elements among the Koreans are making unusual efforts for the realization of their ideals—viz.: The Japanization of the Korean people. 國民[協]會 [Kungmin Hyŏphoe] and 同民會 [Dōminkai] are two organizations now actively engaged in the job. They are making speeches distributing papers advocating 日鮮融和 [*Nissen yūwa*] etc. All no use. As long as the Japanese policy in Korea justifies our belief that it is Korea and not Koreans that Japan wants—so long it will be impossible to make the Koreans feel reconciled to the Japanese domination. These subsidized activities of the pro-Japanese elements will only make the anti-Japanese feeling grow stronger.[144]

In touting *yūwa*, in Yun's view, what the Japanese wanted was "Korea without Koreans," just as the French *colons* wanted Algeria without Muslims (and Jews).[145] Yun's observation was not far off the mark. As a 1933 *kenpeitai* report made plain, exhortations of harmony had scant effect on local settlers—including geisha, housewives, and even primary school students—who continued to stamp racist traits on their daily encounter with Koreans.[146]

Yun's sentiment was, in fact, shared by many Korean members of the Dōminkai. One Korean executive, Song Tal-byŏng, complained that

---

142. Some observed that all too many unqualified individuals parroted *yūwa*, generating an "overproduction of social work," while a derogatory term, "a trumpet" (*nap'al*), circulated widely among Koreans to refer to a Japanese who "blared out *naisen yūwa* without any foresight or knowledge about the Korean people" (*Dōmin* 18 [January 1926]: 27–30; *Chōsen jijō kimitsu tsūshin*, no. 1 [December 1924]: 24).

143. Pang Tae-yŏng in *Chōsen oyobi Manshū*, April 1927, 133–34.

144. The passage is in English, mixed with Chinese characters (Taehan Min'guk Mun'gyobu Kuksa P'yŏnch'an Wiwŏnhoe 1987, 8:457–58 [entry for 3 May 1924]).

145. Prochaska 1990, 6. Even after obtaining French citizenship, the Jewish Europeans continued to confront anti-Semitic politics in municipal governance (S. Roberts 2010).

146. Chōsen Kenpeitai Shireibu 1933.

his Japanese colleagues had a tendency to "forget about Koreans" and "always give priority to fellow Japanese when electing [someone] or allocating something at joint meetings."[147] "The Japanese constantly harp on *naisen yūwa* and urge Koreans to promote harmony," another member bewailed, "while flaunting special privileges and a sense of superiority."[148] Even as the two groups of local elites joined hands in reconstituting ethnic relations around a shared vision of capitalist Korea, few Korean allies failed to recognize the old Japanese agenda of dominance beneath the veneer of ethnic unity, which wore off very quickly in their interactions with settlers.

Within a few years of the *yūwa* campaign, indeed, it became clear that the greatest obstacles to unity were none other than its Japanese preachers who, in thrall to prejudice, failed to embrace their own rhetoric. Repeated Korean complaints, which held settlers responsible for the sorry state of ethnic relations, attested to their inability to reconcile an old sense of entitlement with the new imperative of sharing power with Korean elites. For the pursuit of *naisen yūwa* struck at the heart of their socially privileged yet politically uncertain status in the colony. That settlers remained at best ambivalent allies of Saitō's policy of accommodation bespoke the tensions of their liminal position—tensions that would only grow more acute in the course of the 1920s.

## *Conclusion*

Japan's colonial project of assimilation never looked more vulnerable than in the wake of the March First Movement. Although the empire continued to depend on force in ruling Korea, the need for legitimacy and for local collaboration was dire in the post-1919 order. To carry on, colonial officials knew, would require accommodation with Koreans—a realization gradually, if grudgingly, shared by settler leaders. Even as the ultimate goal of assimilation remained fundamentally intact, the rhetoric of *naisen yūwa* provided a new ideological framework for guiding Korean participation in Japanese colonial citizenship. The same strategy would be deployed elsewhere in due time. As some scholars have suggested, in reconciling the needs of colonial governance with the demands

---

147. Song Tal-byŏng in *Dōmin* 12 (May 1925): 37.
148. *Dōmin* 7 (December 1924): 22–23.

of a multiethnic citizenry, as well as the contradictions between an imperialist power structure and an anticolonial rhetoric, Saitō's cultural rule provided a template for the "multinational state" of Manchukuo.[149]

Cultural rule, in this sense, signaled a new stage in the evolution of a political relationship between state and settlers. The boundaries separating *kan* and *min*, strategically kept porous by Saitō's policy of *min'i chōtatsu*, created more opportunities for settlers to intervene in affairs of Korean governance. In the aftermath of the March First Movement, widespread accusations that settlers were a threat to Japanese rule had prompted many to reassess their position and fall in line with the official policy of Korean accommodation. By the mid-1920s, Saitō knew where to look for allies, and settlers knew where to look for influence. Many felt they had transitioned from outsiders seeking a voice in the governing process to insiders assisting colonial bureaucrats.

Settler leaders who answered Saitō's call for *naisen yūwa* formed a crucial informal sphere of influence through which the empire was refashioned from above as well as from below. A diverse assortment of individuals came to operate in the shadow of colonial bureaucracy, in an autonomous or semiofficial capacity. Much of the grassroots effort at winning the hearts of the Korean population took place in this informal sphere. Selective incorporation of influential civilians into policymaking, moreover, served to institutionalize this informal sphere of local governance. The activities of the Dōminkai in particular demonstrate how, in practices often assumed to be the work of bureaucrats, settler leaders effectively coauthored strategies of rule. The brokers of empire played a critical role in reconfiguring *dōka* as ethnic harmony, and colonial Korea as a multiethnic polity—a central trope as the fledgling empire sought to solve its crisis by adopting the global discourse on autonomy.

Finally, the activities of the brokers of empire in this period illustrate how long-term settlers attained a degree of influence unusual for civilians, on the merits of their firsthand knowledge of Korea. For old

149. It was in Korea, as Prasenjit Duara suggests, that the Japanese first experimented with the technique of ruling a multiethnic body (Duara 2003, 77–78). In a similar vein, Oguma Eiji points out that the Japanese rulers like Hara Takashi had in mind Okinawa as a model for Korean governance in tolerating cultural differences of the colonized (1998, 245–46).

Korea hands like Ōgaki and Kikuchi, Saitō's cultural rule enlarged the space in which they could exercise further influence. While operating in the covert realm of propaganda and surveillance, these men of letters also assisted the empire through the public medium of print, where they combined their pursuit of influence with their search for common ground with Korean nationalists. It is to this domain of discursive interchange that we will now turn.

# FOUR

# *The Discourse on Korea and Koreans*

In reviewing a book on Korean history by a Japanese author in 1924, Kim Yun-sik, a former bureaucrat and scholar of local repute, offered a perceptive critique of empire. Noting the unrivaled eagerness of Japanese "to understand Korean psychology as part of their continental management," Kim observed, "If Western imperialism turned missionaries into its tools [*tesaki*], Japan used scholars as its principal tools" of domination.[1] Kim's analogy captures another crucial mechanism of power: discourse in the service of empire,[2] through which the brokers of empire shored up the colonial state and its claim to legitimacy, against mounting Korean defiance. The March First Movement of 1919 not only compelled the Japanese to rebuild the institutional scaffolding for governing Korea, but also called into question its epistemological foundations. Since annexation, the question of how best to assimilate Koreans inspired spirited debates among settlers, as we have seen. The Korean desire to assimilate, however, was simply presupposed, as were their docility and lack of political awareness. Once proven wrong by the mass Korean demonstrations for independence, the brokers of empire, through countless articles, pamphlets, and monographs, strove to

---

1. Kim Yun-sik's comments on Hosoi 1924, quoted in Takasaki 1982a, 112.

2. But, to slightly correct his analogy, this mechanism also sustained modern European colonial regimes, as Edward Said and others have shown. See Said 1978; Spurr 1993; Richards 1996.

capture the "Korean mind," which to many Japanese seemed suddenly inscrutable.

The main agents of this discourse were again journalists like Kikuchi Kenjō and Hosoi Hajime (the very author of the book that inspired Kim's pithy commentary), who doubled as experts on Korea and advisors to Governor-General Saitō Makoto. These men of letters produced cultural representations that they hoped would make Korea legible to the colonial authorities and provide a veritable manual for governance. Such efforts drove the growth of "Korean studies" (*Chōsen kenkyū*), a body of knowledge tailored to the colonial project. This archive began to develop even before the onset of cultural rule, contrary to what most existing studies suggest. It congealed under the auspices of "military rule," out of efforts to answer the most essential of all questions facing the Japanese: how to govern the Korean *minzoku*. While the colonial state surveyed Korea's land and population, the brokers of empire searched for clues by combing through its ancient manuscripts, political treatises, and historical novels, with little regard for Koreans' own efforts to make sense of the peninsula's rich literary tradition. Along with the vast military and police apparatus, therefore, the Saitō administration inherited from its predecessors a keen awareness that knowledge was power.

To fully understand the role of settlers in shaping the production of knowledge about Korea—and advancing their own interests in the process—we need to look at how Korean studies emerged in the 1910s and evolved in dialogue with Korean nationalism in the 1920s. More than a repository of information, as scholars have noted, the colonial archive registers subtle shifts in the anxiety of those who govern.[3] A look into the Japanese colonial archive, built for the purpose of dissecting the Korean mind, allows us to enter the shifting imperial mind of its architects, a task already begun by Hyung Il Pai and other scholars.[4] Behind the theories and caricatures of Koreans that constituted the en-

---

3. Stoler 2002b, 100; Dirks 2002, 54.

4. What we often regard as the "official archive" of the colonial state was built upon the work of a diverse assortment of civilian scholars and private collectors of indigenous knowledge from the metropole. See Pai 1999, 353–82; S. Tanaka 1995; Shimizu 1999, 115–71; Walraven 1999; Brandt 2007; and Atkins 2010, Chapter 2. A further look into this archive reveals that some of its architects and agents were leading opinion-makers of the local Japanese community.

during heart of Korean studies in this era extends a trajectory of "epistemic worries" as well as failed visions for ruling the peninsula. The looming specter of Korean nationalism is indelibly etched in its pages.

## *The Emergence of the Colonial Archive*

Ironically, settler collaboration with the state in producing knowledge about Koreans began with the end of what they retrospectively referred to as the "golden era of journalism." During protectorate rule, the industry had been surprisingly unregulated. Although local journalists at the time complained much about press censorship, what they experienced after 1910 was on another scale altogether. No sooner had the new Governor-General assumed the mantle of rulership than he declared himself the sole spokesman for Korea by moving swiftly to silence all voices of dissent. The vernacular press that had championed the Patriotic Enlightenment Movement became the first and foremost target. Save for a handful of literary and youth magazines that kept alive the spirit of vernacular print culture, all major Korean-language papers disappeared while the *Taehan Maeil sinbo*, renamed the *Maeil sinbo*, was transformed into the propaganda arm of the colonial regime.[5] Within a few years of the new Governor-General's rule, the once vibrant Korean voices had become barely audible. Thus began what Japanese colonial journalists and postcolonial Korean historians, writing decades apart, would dub a "dark period" (J. *ankokuki*; K. *amhŭkki*) in Korean history.[6]

The situation was no more sanguine for the Japanese resident press. Though they incurred far less stringent measures of state control, Japanese papers, both local and imported, were not spared the brunt of censorship. Journalists raised much hue and cry against Terauchi Masatake,[7] but their activities soon floundered under the apparently successful official policy of buying up local papers or suspending their publication altogether. By the mid-1910s, harsh press control had driven much critical journalism out of business. Gone were the feisty journalists like Minegishi Shigetarō of the *Keijō shinpō* ("Korea's only civilian independent newspaper that dared to style itself as an enemy of the Governor-

5. M. Robinson 1984, 320.

6. Epilogue by Shakuo Kyokuhō in Aoyagi 1916; Eckert et al. 1990, 260.

7. *Chōsen* (Chōsen Zasshisha), May 1911, 2–3.

General's rule"[8]), who simply left for a democratizing Japan after their publications were suppressed by the uncompromising police bureau chief Akashi Motojirō.[9] Most who stayed on the peninsula gave in to official pressure, becoming colonial propagandists in all but name.[10] None of the journalists, to be sure, supported the new regime without deep misgivings; as described in Chapter 2, settlers raised clamorous voices against the state in defense of their autonomy. But on the policy of suppressing Korean public life and dissent, they generally kept quiet.[11]

While critical journalism waned, one cultural industry flourished in this period: research on Korea and Koreans. The inquiry into Korean ethnicity became the specialized pursuit of a group of journalists and scholars based in Seoul, who, in cooperation with their colleagues in Japan, founded the Chōsen Kenkyūkai (Korea Research Association; hereafter KRA) a few years prior to annexation in 1908. At its inception, the KRA was an eclectic mix of nearly two dozen individuals: local journalists (including Kikuchi Kenjō, Shakuo Shunjō, Aoyagi Tsunatarō, and Hosoi Hajime); two professors of literature at Tokyo Imperial University, Hagino Yoshiyuki and Mikami Sanji, and a lecturer at Waseda University, Yoshida Tōgo; local educators and school administrators such as Ayukai Fusanoshin and Takahashi Tōru; colonial educational bureaucrats with doctoral degrees such as Oda Shōgo and Akiyama Masanosuke, and Shidehara Taira, a Japanese advisor to the Korean Ministry of Education during the protectorate period; and leading metropolitan journalists and critics, Yamaji Aizan and Fukumoto Nichinan.[12]

Soon after annexation, this scholarly organization, while retaining its diverse membership, fell into the hands of settler intelligentsia, and under the charismatic leadership of Aoyagi Tsunatarō, who transformed it into something of a support organ for the colonial regime. A native

---

8. Quoted in Shibazaki 1983, 70.

9. *Maeil sinbo*, 29 March 1912; Shakuo 1930, 12.

10. *Chōsen oyobi Manshū*, October 1915, 78, 80–81.

11. Following annexation, Ōgaki Takeo made what appeared to be a leap of faith in his attitudes toward the state. While fellow journalists bridled at the flurry of repressive laws issued by Terauchi, Ōgaki openly defended his policy of control as indispensable for preventing "Korean ideological confusion" and ensuring the stability of Japanese rule ("Sōtoku seiji o hinan suru ronja no gokai o tadasu," in Aoyagi 1916, 260–63).

12. U Kai Zai 2001, 184.

Fig. 8 Aoyagi Tsunatarō (Nanmei) in his study
SOURCE: Aoyagi 1916. Used by permission of HathiTrust Digital Library, University of Michigan.

of Saga prefecture, Aoyagi had come to Korea in 1901 as a young correspondent for the *Ōsaka Mainichi shinbun*. Like his colleague Kikuchi Kenjō, Aoyagi's life represented a fascinating blend of politics and scholarship. After heading the post offices in Naju and Qingdao, in 1905 he worked for the Ministry of Finance in the Korean government, under the Japanese advisor Megata Tanetarō (1853–1926). Between 1908 and 1910, Aoyagi, like Kikuchi, served as a part-time employee for the Korean royal household in charge of collecting and editing historical documents on the Chosŏn dynasty, a job that launched him on his lifetime career. By the time of his death in 1932, Aoyagi had become one of the most prolific colonial writers in Korea. In addition to managing a weekly newspaper, the *Keijō shinbun*, he authored over a dozen monographs on Korean history, several critiques of the Governor-General's rule, and a variety of guidebooks.[13]

13. Aoyagi 1935, preface; and Nakamura Shiryō 1926, 348–49.

Fig. 9 Chōsen Kenkyūkai (Korea Research Association)
SOURCE: Aoyagi 1916. Used by permission of HathiTrust Digital Library, University of Michigan.

According to its founding prospectus, the KRA aimed to bring under its microscope everything about Korea—"people and literature" as well as "manners, customs, systems, traditions, and rituals"—for the ostensible purpose of aiding Korean "guidance and enlightenment."[14] In adopting such a totalizing approach, the KRA saw itself filling a role that no other group had yet taken up. Its main objective, as one founding member explained, was "to discover living materials from old Korea and furnish them for the management of our new Korea," a task best accomplished by translating and publishing Korea's antiquarian books (*kosho*).[15] Important lessons for governing Koreans, the settler pundits believed, abounded in the peninsula's vast trove of literature that chronicled its kingdom's rise and fall, from ancient times to the end of the Chosŏn dynasty. "If one wishes to understand a country's conditions and customs," Hosoi Hajime explained, "there is nothing of more vital impor-

---

14. "Shuisho," in Makiyama 1911, back cover.

15. This member also cited the example of the British effort to rule India by "pouring money and energy into research" (Ōmura 1911, preface).

tance than to appreciate that country's unique literature." For "literature not only reveals the spirit of the age, but it has controlled and influenced the character and sentiment of the people [*kokumin*] across all time periods."[16] In search of a usable past, then, the KRA members aimed to unearth the enduring kernel of "Koreanness" from the *longue durée* of the peninsula's recorded history.

Availing themselves of access to rare archives and technology to print their findings—both of which had fallen increasingly into Japanese hands since the protectorate period—the KRA under Aoyagi engaged in the laborious task of collecting, reprinting, editing, and publishing a corpus of extant historical documents, novels, antique manuscripts, and other statecraft literature produced since the Three Kingdoms period (57 BCE–668 CE). In the seven years between 1911 and 1918, the KRA issued a total of 65,000 publications that included works by individual members in more than 40 genres,[17] in addition to disseminating their research findings through lectures, workshops, exhibitions, and articles in a local magazine run by member Shakuo Shunjō.[18]

Through the KRA's voluminous and wide-ranging publications ran one consistent principle that guided their editors. Rather than assess the literary value or character of each work, Aoyagi explained, they concerned themselves with identifying and investigating "solely political and social issues from the standpoint of historical problems."[19] And in analyzing Korea's historical relations with Japan, the KRA members pur-

---

16. Hosoi 1911, 1.

17. Aoyagi 1916, preface; Aoyagi 1911–1918.

18. "Chōsen Kenkyūkai kari kitei" (dated November 1908), *Chōsen* (Chōsen Zasshisha), December 1908, 91–92. These projects were supported by a combination of membership fees, state subsidies, and private donations. Shakuo Shunjō launched his own publishing venture by creating the Chōsen Kosho Kankōkai (Society for the Publication of Korean Antique Books) in October 1909, hoping both to facilitate research on Korea and to make rare historical books available to the wider public (*Chōsen* [Chōsen Zasshisha], September 1909, 8–9, and November 1911, 14). Between 1909 and 1916, the Society published the *Chōsen gunsho taikei* (A Compendium of Various Korean Writings), a work of 80 volumes in which ancient texts written in literary Chinese were translated and annotated in Japanese. This became the largest publication on Korean historical documents in the colonial period (Kokushi Daijiten Henshū Iinkai 1988, 608). This enormous undertaking was bankrolled by a host of high-ranking colonial officials and influential local Japanese and Korean elites, including Kim Yun-sik and Yu Kil-chun.

19. Preface to Kin 1914.

sued two rather paradoxical aims: clarifying their affinities and parsing their differences.

"The great mission of our scholarly community," Aoyagi declared in the preface to one of his books, "is to clarify the historical facts of Japan-Korea relations and to achieve a spiritual fusion of the two peoples [*minzoku*]."[20] Their goal to "clarify" presumed the unity of Japanese and Koreans, treating "facts" of their ties as parts of a narrative ready to be excavated from the existing body of knowledge. The notion of shared ancestry was the premise upon which many KRA members, like colonial officials, justified annexation and assimilation policies as "natural" if unprecedented in Korean history. "There is almost no impugning the fact that Korea and Japan are peoples [*minzoku*] of the same script and same race [*dōbun dōshu*]," member Yamaji Aizan wrote in 1913.[21] Aoyagi opened his monograph, *Chōsen yonsen nenshi* (Four Thousand Years of Korean History, 1917), with a similar claim: Japanese and Koreans had once been "brothers of one family bound by the same racial roots [*dōshu dōkon ikka*]," just as Tan'gun, Korea's mythical founder, had belonged to "the same race" (*dōshuzoku*) as Japan's divine imperial ancestors, parting from them as if by "a family feud."[22]

The arguments of the KRA writers were nothing original. Absorbing the theory of shared ancestry advanced by metropolitan scholars like Kita Sadakichi (1871–1939) and Kanazawa Shōzaburō (1872–1967), they built as well on understandings of Japan's historical contact with Korea and China as expounded by practitioners of *Tōyōshi*, or "Eastern History." Both schools of thought spread to Korea during the protectorate period.[23] The brokers of empire through the KRA, in other words, became part of a larger imperial project, spearheaded by historians, ethnographers, and anthropologists operating at the forefront of Japan's expansion in Korea, Taiwan, Manchuria, and the Chinese continent.

Aoyagi's thesis on Korean history contained all the basic tenets of the mixed nation theory, which had become received wisdom among

20. Aoyagi 1917, preface.
21. Yamaji Aizan, "Nissen dōzoku no shiteki sashō," in Aoyagi 1913, 81.
22. Aoyagi 1917, 4–6.
23. Oguma 2002, 86.

Japanese historians and linguists by this time.[24] This theory drew heavily on the analysis of Japan's foundation myths recorded in ancient chronicles, namely the *Kojiki* and the *Nihon shoki.* In the age of gods, Aoyagi wrote, Japan's divine ancestors ruled Korea or migrated to the peninsula to become Korea's gods, with Susano-o (younger brother of the sun goddess Amaterasu) reigning over ancient Silla.[25] During the time of the early emperors, Japan again controlled Korea by territorially integrating it into its domain, as epitomized by Empress Jingū's "conquest of Silla" in the third century.[26] This point was elaborated by a fellow member, Hagino Yoshiyuki, who asserted, "the sphere of influence of the imperial nation [*teikoku*] following the conquest extended over almost the entire peninsula."[27] In the mid-sixth century, the Yamato court established on the southern peninsula a colonial outpost called Mimana, prompting a wave of Japanese migration and settlement.[28]

In advancing these claims to "clarify the historical fact of the same race and same roots," the KRA members pursued another important agenda: to correct "mistakes and fabrications" that abounded in the dynastic historiography on Korea. These were attributed to "Chinese politicians and scholars [who] have modified and falsified Korea's history and geography since the era of Tang and Sung."[29] Their strategy to counter Chinese domination of Korea's historiography was to rhetorically reclaim its national geography. Aoyagi, for instance, argued that Manchuria used to be "an old territory of Koguryŏ," echoing an assertion made earlier by Kikuchi Kenjō in the *Keijō shinpō* that evidently pleased the ears of King Kojong.[30] Although this narrative strategy mirrored the efforts of contemporary Korean historians to rewrite their own country's past—to create "self-knowledge" by "de-centering the Middle Kingdom" as Andre Schmid has explained[31]—the settler writers

---

24. The notable exception was Shiratori Kurakichi, a practitioner of *Tōyōshi*, who was the only leading Japanese scholar of his time to explicitly reject the theory of common ancestry (ibid., 238–39).

25. Aoyagi 1917, 203–8.

26. "In one sense Japanese constructed the Kingdom of Silla" (Aoyagi 1924, 1025).

27. Hagino Yoshiyuki, "Heianchō jidai to hantō no shūzoku," in Aoyagi 1913, 97.

28. The foundation of Mimana is discussed in detail in Aoyagi 1924, 39–44, 1023–25.

29. Aoyagi 1917, preface.

30. Aoyagi 1926, 876.

31. Schmid 2002, Chapter 2.

de-Sinified Korean history only to Japanize it. For them, to extricate the Korean past from the fetters of its Sinocentric legacy meant to recenter it around the national mythology of imperial Japan. Hence, just as "Japan's annexation of Korea is a political restoration of Japan-Korea [*Nikkan*]," they rendered Korean history as "a history of being part of the great Japanese empire."[32] For the KRA leaders, rewriting the peninsula's history symbolized a retrospective act of assimilating Korea into Japan's imperial genealogy of knowledge.

Parallel to clarifying the affinity between the two peoples, however, an abiding concern of the KRA was to explain how and why Koreans had "fallen from history." Despite their shared beginnings, the settlers wondered, how did Koreans lag so far behind as to become such a different *minzoku* from the contemporary Japanese? In virtually every issue of his magazine, Shakuo Shunjō derided a constellation of purported Korean characteristics—"indolence," "toadyism," "craftiness," "effeminacy," "sloth," "lack of hygiene"—as the inveterate "ethnicity" (*minzokusei*) that modernizing Japanese came to rectify.[33] Some members of the KRA such as Ayukai Fusanoshin and Hosoi Hajime argued against their colleagues in claiming that Koreans were essentially made up of different and inferior racial stock.[34] Having emphasized difference by inventing Koreans as alien and other, settler journalists unsurprisingly took pains to convince themselves of affinity before instilling the idea in the minds of their readers. After 1910, whether they believed Koreans descended from the same racial origin or considered them a foreign race only recently integrated into the emperor's realm, the KRA members agreed on the need, first and foremost, to study their ethnicity before asking whether or not assimilation would succeed.[35]

Settler pundits plumbed the vast array of Korean literature for a causal link between the peninsula's past and its current political woes. In doing so they lent a historical dimension to the explanations—biological, social, environmental, cultural—being advanced by Japanese scholars and amateurs alike at the time to explain "Korean stagnation" (*Chōsen*

---

32. Aoyagi 1917, preface.

33. Shakuo 1914, 94–95. For more examples of Japanese ethnographic discourse on Koreans, see Duus 1995, Chapter 11; and Henry 2005.

34. Hosoi 1911, 34.

35. Ayukai 1913, 137; Hosoi 1911, 16.

*teitairon*).[36] In its most typical formulation, this quasi-scholarly theory opened with a well-worn myth on the common origins of Japanese and Koreans and ended with a story of great divergence.

Aoyagi was a master storyteller of this view. In his *Chōsen tōchiron* (On the Administration of Korea, 1923), Aoyagi drastically abridged 2,000 years of recorded Korean history into a monotonous tale of foreign subjugation, political corruption, and moral decay. The intermixing of Japanese and Koreans in ancient times gave way to a Darwinian struggle for survival, with the Koreans falling off the imperial family tree while the Japanese marched off to greatness. Korean history was effeminized as devoid of any "masculine excitement" and juxtaposed against Japan's history of "loyal, brave, heroic and chivalrous activities." Aoyagi asserted: "Korea had never been independent in the past," because "it possessed only a nation [*minzoku*] and no state [*kokka*]."[37] By the time of annexation, Koreans had become a stateless people with an innate disposition to depend on foreign powers (*sadae*), an unfortunate orphan in need of a new paternalistic ruler.

The annexation by imperial Japan was a divine intervention in this tale of decline. Aoyagi explained the assimilation of Koreans, indeed of all alien races, as "a mission" of the Japanese state since its foundation, as ordained by the words of the sun goddess Amaterasu. Moreover, he described assimilation as a project passed on from one conqueror to another throughout Korean history, highlighting the failure of the Chinese dynasties in particular. Only the Japanese, their blood kin, were fit for the task, he seems to claim. Evoking the concept of primordial brotherhood, Aoyagi concluded that Japan had a unique mandate to govern and restore Korea to the path of civilization, long sabotaged by foreign conquerors and by its own rulers.[38]

Aoyagi's narrative illustrates the key internal workings of the colonial archive, which, as Nicholas Dirks has noted, "produced ethnographic subjects, not political ones." Aoyagi's thesis, published at the height of Korean nationalism in the early 1920s, aimed to achieve this effect by denying the historical existence of a state on the peninsula and recognizing only the presence of an ethnic group. The accumulation of eth-

36. See Duus 1995, 419–20; Hatada 1975, 42–47.

37. Aoyagi 1923, 58, 64, 229.

38. Aoyagi 1923, 106, 118–19, 120, 128.

nographic knowledge thereby worked to "proclaim the colonial subject as lacking both in political capacities and in historical understanding,"[39] critical faculties that the Japanese claimed only they could furnish.

Of all the possible causes of Korean decline, the KRA members isolated factionalism as the most decisive variable. In their translations and analyses of such works as *Sassi namjŏnggi* (Record of Lady Sa's Journey to the South), a piece of historical fiction authored by Kim Man-jung in the late seventeenth century, factionalism became a dominant leitmotif of Korean dynastic history. By editorial sleight of hand, this history often became no more than a catalogue of political turmoil that shook the Korean court, peaking in the fierce struggles between Westerners (*Sŏin*) and Southerners (*Namin*) during the reign of Sukchong (1674–1720). The effect of this narrative technique was to "satirize" the Korean past as a string of court dramas and highlight a recurring pattern of chaos, offering yet more "evidence" of Korean incapacity for unity.[40]

Monographs published by individual members echoed this narrative arc. In a detailed biography of Korean political leaders he published on the eve of annexation, Hosoi also ventured a diagnosis of Korea's "ills," concluding that "the history of Korea's rise and fall is all about factional conflict." He faulted a long genealogy of the peninsula's ruling elite for letting their country languish while dissipating themselves in endless squabbles, but he singled out King Kojong as the one who bore the greatest blame. "It is His Majesty who lived a life of intrigue and was destroyed by intrigue," Hosoi asserted, noting how his feuding aides remained mired in a power struggle with those of his successor Sunjong, even after Kojong's abdication in 1907.[41] Kikuchi Kenjō painted a similar picture for the more recent past. In his biography of the Taewŏn'gun, published in the year of annexation, Kikuchi portrayed the last decades of the Chosŏn dynasty as riven by a personal contest between the Taewŏn'gun and Queen Min, depicting the former more favorably as "a hero." In his view, the leadership of the Taewŏn'gun represented a real missed opportunity for Korea. By sloughing off the country's traditional *sadae* diplomacy, Kikuchi wrote, the Taewŏn'gun sought to carry out "a grand task of national reconstruction" to regain Korean autonomy, but

39. Dirks 2002, 60–61.

40. U Kai Zai 2001, 200–201.

41. Hosoi 1910, 8-9; Moriyama 1997, 479. See also Hosoi 1911, 17.

his effort was derailed by internal troubles and external challenges, only to be exacerbated by Queen Min who was a notch above her rival in political skills.[42]

None of these claims was unique to settler writers, but some authors distinguished their narrative from official accounts by writing themselves directly into it. In his personal reminiscences on the last years of the Chosŏn dynasty, for instance, Kikuchi turned his solitary venture into the imperial court into the heroic story of a diplomatic go-between who moved both the Korean king and the Japanese government from below.[43] Other settler chronicles on late Chosŏn politics were likewise conflated with their authors' biographies, generating a record of "men-on-the-spot" diplomacy that put humble migrants at the forefront of Japan's national struggle.[44] While supporting the official master narrative, settlers claimed their own place in the sun as anonymous protagonists of an unfolding imperial saga on the peninsula.

In tracing the passage from sameness to difference, these settler writers performed a precarious act of embracing both, defining the Koreans as kin as well as foreign to the Japanese. Keeping the two peoples purposefully undifferentiated, or stressing "ambivalent sameness rather than radical difference,"[45] was also a way for settlers to grapple with their own liminality. In justifying their dominance in the colony, the brokers of empire sought to create a conceptual order that allowed them to at once stress affinity and "deny coevalness" between Koreans and Japanese.[46] Combining the transcendental notion of shared origins with the

42. Kikuchi 1910a; Sakurai 1998, 76, 78, 112.

43. Kikuchi 1931, 1: Chapter 2.

44. A slippage between fact and fiction also characterized many "first-hand" accounts of political adventure written by members of the Kokuryūkai (1966) who glorified the patriotic exploits of their forebears such as Uchida Ryōhei and Tōyama Mitsuru.

45. This is Leo Ching's reading of Oguma Eiji's characterization of Japanese colonial discourse on assimilation (2001, 197). In the words of David Askew, Japanese anthropology was concerned with "an examination not of the Other but of Self and Near-self" (2003, 140).

46. The "denial of coevalness" is a central point of Johannes Fabian's criticism of anthropology for creating ethnographic descriptions that placed the Other suspended in time (see Fabian 1983, especially Chapter 2). E. Taylor Atkins also adopts this notion in his recent analysis of Japanese ethnographers in Korea, but insightfully adds that theirs combined a nostalgic longing for the communal past and an intense self-reflection on Japan's own path to modernity induced by the West (2010, 91–93).

temporal concept of cultural level (*mindo*), settler pundits structured the Japanese relationship to Koreans in which race (*dōshu*, or common origin) sanctioned homogenization, while culture and history (*mindo*) sanctioned differentiation.[47] This fluid conjunction in identity,[48] where difference became a function of temporality, allowed not only settlers to claim perquisites of the ruling class even in their interstitial status, but colonial officials to flexibly alternate between the principles of equality and separation in governing Koreans, while deferring *dōka* as a long-run goal of Japanese rule. Assimilation and discrimination, in effect, became virtually synonymous in colonial discourse.

The quasi-scholarly activity of settlers also took on the more ambitious political project of countering Korean nationalism. "The true objective of our ongoing efforts to edit and publish Korean history," Aoyagi would reflect in 1925, was "to imprint in the heads of [Korean] youth an image of a stupid and ugly homeland, and impel them to discard their thought of recovering it."[49] The real audience the KRA had in mind, indeed, was not Japanese but Koreans, who would take lessons from their nation's decline "in order not to repeat [such] history."[50] Through reconstructions of history, the brokers of empire aimed to restructure Korean national consciousness. In so doing, they also hoped to answer Korean critics, such as historian Pak Ŭn-sik and Pak Yŏng-hyo (1861–1939), who declared assimilation "impossible," given that the Korean people possessed an "ineffaceable ethnic consciousness [*minzoku ishiki*]" nurtured through 4,000 years of history.[51] By his own account, Aoyagi personally advised Terauchi and the secretary of the Central Council, Kokubun Shōtarō, on the use of history in colonial

47. I derive this point from Hyung Il Pai's study (2000, 35–42), which has shown how ethnographic, archaeological, and historical studies on Korea stressed the *racial* affinity between Japanese and Koreans, and maintained their difference in terms of *cultural* progress (made only under the debilitating influence and dependence on China) according to the unilinear notion of social evolution.

48. Race, ethnicity, and culture conveniently blurred in the Japanese concept of *minzoku* (Weiner 1995, 442).

49. Aoyagi 1925 (reprinted as Aoyagi 1926b), 146–47.

50. Ibid., 240.

51. Aoyagi 1923, 129–31; Han Kee-hyung 2005, 172. These were motivations behind the translation of some member publications into Korean language, including Aoyagi's *Yijo obaengnyŏnsa* (1915) and *Chosŏn sach'ŏnnyŏnsa* (1917).

education. Rather than prevent Koreans from studying their history entirely, as Terauchi was wont to do, Aoyagi argued that colonial educators must teach "correct history": that is, one of "factionalism, secret strife, intrigues, exploitation, and hideous revolutions" that unmistakably demonstrated the lack of Korean capacity for independence.[52] The most effective way of assimilating Koreans, he suggested, was to rectify "their erroneous assumption that their country possessed a glorious past"—a notion being actively fostered by contemporary Korean scholars at the time—and instead persuade them that their nation was unworthy of remembrance. The goal was nothing less than engineering collective amnesia.

The discourse on Korea and Koreans mediated by the KRA spread far from the site of production, gaining an audience beyond the narrow circle of the colonial intelligentsia. By the mid-1910s, its 500-odd members not only embraced a wide range of local elites and officials (including a handful of Korean provincial administrators), but extended to readers in Japan, Manchuria, and Taiwan.[53] Government-General officials were among the most avid KRA readers. Even Terauchi, who relied heavily on coercion, was not unaware of the role of pedagogy. The KRA publications often carried the imprimatur of the Governor-General and prominent metropolitan political leaders who wrote their introductions, endorsing them as a valuable guide for Korean governance.[54] In addition to sponsoring these civilian publications, the Government-General conducted its own project of compiling records of the reigns of Kojong and Sunjong, transmitting its version of history to Korean readers through the *Maeil sinbo*.[55] Terauchi's administration evidently did not ignore Aoyagi's advice that "it is reckless to rule Korea without paying attention to history."[56]

---

52. Aoyagi 1925, 146.

53. See the list of KRA members at the end of Aoyagi 1916.

54. For instance, see ibid., preface.

55. Kokushi Daijiten Henshū Iinkai 1988, 604; Schmid 2002, 159. It also promoted archaeological research and the study of Korea's traditional customs and folklore, assigning these tasks to the Central Council and enlisting local scholars such as Ayukai Fusanoshin (Pai 1994, 22). On the role of Japanese ethnologists commissioned by the colonial government, notably Imamura Tomo (1870–1943) and Murayama Chijun, see Walraven 1999, 223–26; and Atkins 2010, 66–74.

56. Aoyagi 1923, 8–9; 1926, 146.

If this overlapping and merging of settler and state discursive practices was essential to the functioning of the colonial archive, it was what accorded the brokers of empire a voice in the production of colonial knowledge.[57] The birth of the KRA also coincided with the rapid institutional growth of anthropology, which in Japan as elsewhere developed along the frontier of imperial expansion in the late nineteenth and early twentieth centuries. The KRA members characteristically operated on the ill-defined boundary separating scholars from amateurs, scientific from quasi-scientific methods, and myths from history that marked this embryonic discipline.[58] While calling themselves experts on Korea, settlers remained a community of amateurs in historical scholarship who nonetheless had considerable resources and state support at their disposal. Hosoi and Aoyagi, for instance, were quite candid in acknowledging the amateur nature of the research from which their "expert" knowledge was drawn. And yet, in spirited defense of their amateurism, the settlers insisted that their works—"guided by unrivaled passion"—were by no means insipid.[59] Their professed expertise on Korea carried within it a claim to a role in colonial governance otherwise denied to civilians.

The discursive intervention of settlers into colonial politics illustrates, more importantly, how their version of Korean history became established as orthodoxy. The web of contacts that settlers formed with local officials and metropolitan men of letters—a key modus operandi of brokers of empire—became an important conduit through which knowledge about Korea circulated across the empire.[60] This circuit of knowledge also systematically fostered the interconnectedness of texts, as agents recycled the same "historical evidence" and extensively quoted

---

57. There is also reason to believe that settlers' writings shaped the official narrative on Korean history. Hosoi's biography of Korean political elites, as one scholar has noted for instance, most likely became the basis for the 1925 publication of the Governor-General's own biographical dictionary of 80 Korean aristocrats (Moriyama 1997, 479).

58. Shimizu 1999, 117–18, 136–37; Walraven 1999, 239; Oguma 2002, 53–54. For recent studies on the growth of colonial anthropology in the Japanese empire, see Nakao 2000; 2004; and Sakano 2005.

59. Aoyagi 1917, preface; Hosoi 1911, 17–18.

60. Numerous travelogues and guidebooks, for instance, were based on interviews with local Japanese residents and their already voluminous writings on Korea (Duus 1995, 401).

from one another.[61] Any utterance about Koreans made by one pundit affirmed and reinforced the claims of another.[62] Empress Jingū's conquest of Korea's Three Kingdoms, the existence of the Japanese colony of Mimana, and *sadae* thought all became staples of what the Japanese came to teach as historical "facts."[63] And all were peddled by KRA writers—and elaborated by officially employed historians like Inaba Iwakichi (1876–1945)—as "proof of the superiority of the Yamato *minzoku*" over Koreans "even in ancient times."[64]

One cannot help being struck by the monologic nature of settler studies on Korea, which carried little or no imprint of consultation with professional Korean historians.[65] Before the onset of protectorate rule, scholars such as Ch'oe Nam-sŏn (1890–1957) and Sin Ch'ae-ho (1880–1936) had already begun to investigate their nation's history and folklore, unencumbered with biases in the official *sadae* historiography of the Koryŏ and Yi dynasties. As Andre Schmid has shown, however, the two parallel, and seemingly diametrically opposed, projects of Koreans and Japanese in fact exhibited many areas of overlap.[66] Both Korean and

---

61. Kikuchi Kenjō's *Kankoku heigōshi* (A History of Korean Annexation) was one such canonical text. Nakamura Kentarō, a former Korean-language exchange student, recounted how he and his cohort also read Kikuchi's *Chōsen hantō* (Korean Peninsula), which was packed with "extremely useful" information on Korean history, geography, and social affairs (Nakamura Kentarō 1969, 14).

62. This interconnectedness of texts is key to the productive and reciprocal relationship between knowledge and power (Said 1978, 36).

63. Isoda 1999, 197–98. Informed by this orthodoxy, some metropolitan politicians apparently came to consider knowledge of Korean history an important measure of bureaucratic skills. At the fortieth Imperial Assembly in 1918, a Diet member named Takagi Masutarō argued that Susano-o must be enshrined along with Amaterasu and Emperor Meiji at the planned Chōsen Shrine. When Vice Governor-General Yamagata Isaburō replied in the negative, reasoning that Susano-o's influence over Korea was still subject to debate, Takagi retorted that to deny such an "obvious fact" in history would "threaten the very foundation of Japan," shouting "you are not worthy of being a Vice-Governor General!" (*Chōsen Kōron*, June 1918, 50–52).

64. Inaba Kunzan, "Hibun ni yorite risshō serareta Jingū kōgō no shiraki seibatsu," in Shakuo 1931, 383–86.

65. This was in contrast to the case of Japanese official and academic ethnographers who relied on Korean informants and assistants (Walraven 1999, 230; Atkins 2010, 93).

66. In his analysis of Korean scholars, Schmid has shown how they sought to find an alternative and autonomous space outside of the colonial framework of knowledge,

Japanese writers, for instance, incorporated new Social Darwinist ideas into their histories, speaking in the common language of racial science, albeit to deliver radically different messages: one to restore the glory of the Korean people and the other to demonstrate their foreordained decline. Korean writers also borrowed modern, scientific techniques of history writing from the Japanese, whose authority they frequently evoked to substantiate their scholarly claims. Some of the Korean and Japanese narrative strategies of representation, as a result, closely resembled each other. Thus, Korean scholars, too, insisted on a "linear history" that enshrined the nation (*minjok*) as the resilient and unchanging core, as resolutely as its Japanese reconstruction stressed the intractable Korean ethnicity. More substantially, they converged on some critical assessments of history, such as the perception of the *yangban* as a metaphor of Korean disunity and corruption, and an emphasis on *sadae* thought (*sadae juŭi*) as an embedded trait of Korean political culture, with the effect of establishing a degree of complicity between nationalist and colonial projects.[67] Each of these discursive constructions was ultimately a joint Japanese-Korean creation, driven by a shared desire to explain Korea's contemporary ailments.

Yet settlers could and did turn their findings against the Korean effort to rescue their nation from history, with a bold claim that there was nothing worth saving. Shakuo, for example, found the "discoveries" from his archival digs "disappointing" and hastily concluded that "Korea has no great art, no great literature, no great people, no great thought, and therefore no great history."[68] Needless to say, this conclusion reaffirmed his conviction that Koreans should "forget Korean history" and "abandon the Korean language and customs" "to become more purely Japanese."[69] Hosoi went further to deny Korean autonomy from their nation's provenance. Dismissing both the Tan'gun myth (as unworthy of scholarly inquiry) and its rival Confucian myth of Kija (as "fabricated by Korea's Confucian elements out of their *sadae* thought toward the continent"), Hosoi declared that "Korea ceased to exist just

---

but how hard it was for them to escape the hegemonic embrace of Japanese discourse (Schmid 2002, especially Chapter 2).

67. Ibid., 110–13.

68. *Chōsen oyobi Manshū*, February 1916, 1.

69. *Chōsen* (Chōsen Zasshisha), November 1911, 12–13.

as it emerged as a nation."[70] In retelling the peninsula's past, the Japanese colonial scholars denied Koreans not only the historical basis for sovereignty, but their very historicity. Indeed, the raison d'être of the colonial archive was its very refusal to evolve: its insistence on being the sole and unchanging recorder of the authentic past, an embodiment of "state monumentality" against the flow of time.[71] As far as the settler writers were concerned, Korean history was no more than an allegory of national demise. Although their narrative strategy had a resemblance to what Edward Said has termed "Orientalism," the Japanese "Koreanists," in insisting on assimilation as solution, departed from their European contemporaries in one fundamental way: in addition to creating a fixed and unchanging past for "the Other," they also insisted on its future erasure.

### *Cultural Imperialism versus Cultural Nationalism*

The outbreak of the March First Movement in 1919 shook this closed circuit of knowledge, unsettling the Japanese conceit that their archive was as reliable as their empire was durable. Attuned to the image of Korean backwardness, Japanese officials had utterly underestimated the people's capacity for mass action, a failure for which their own discourse was to blame. In the wake of 1919, to be sure, the ideological scaffolding of colonial discourse did not entirely collapse. Not a few settlers dismissed the March First Movement as an intrigue staged by a cabal of dissidents—the opportunistic "horseplay" of a few radical activists, in the words of Hagitani Kazuo of the *Chōsen shinbun*—or at most a reflection of the "crowd psychology" of the ignorant masses, as Ōgaki Takeo wrote in a letter to Saitō Makoto.[72] Ethnic stereotypes also died hard, as did representations of Korean history as an inevitable march toward stagnation and decline. Hosoi Hajime warned new colonial officials to beware of the inherently "double-hearted" character of Koreans, flip-flopping between treachery and subservience toward their ruler across all time periods.[73] As Korean nationalism continued to grow and diver-

70. Hosoi 1911, 34.
71. The colonial archive "resisted the onset of modern history" (Dirks 2002, 61).
72. *Chōsen oyobi Manshū*, December 1919, 143–50; Ōgaki 1919, 119.
73. Hosoi 1924b, 56, 63.

sify after 1919, indeed, "treachery" appeared to take the place of "backwardness" as a favored theme of Japanese writings, which soon transformed the label "recalcitrant Koreans" (*futei Senjin*) into a synecdoche, a category imagined to apply to the entire Korean population.

A look beneath the seemingly stable edifice, however, reveals some important shifts that began to take place in the colonial archive. Changes were especially visible on its edges, where the brokers of empire confronted the "recalcitrant" realities of the Korean *minzoku*. Since Governor-General Saitō permitted Koreans to publish their own papers, the settler pundits could no longer content themselves with consulting elite opinion, nor could they ignore the Korean voices of dissent that began to permeate the colonial publishing industry. The effect of these developments was to gradually transform a Japanese monologue on Korea into a complex, if uneven, dialogue with Koreans who articulated their own visions of nation and critiques of empire.

First of all, the relaxation of press control, which allowed Koreans to publish their own papers and many Japanese journalists to return to their original profession,[74] opened a volley of Korean attacks and settler countermoves around the policies of the Government-General. As an intellectual vanguard of nationalism, three vernacular dailies—the *Tonga ilbo*, the *Chosŏn ilbo*, and the *Sidae ilbo*—in particular risked seizure, deletion, and suspension of publication in unraveling the exploitative and discriminatory aspects of colonial policy. Yet all three managed to get their views across to the reading public in some ingenious ways: exploiting the loopholes and ambiguities in the system of censorship or Japanese unfamiliarity with Korean language, and rushing to get copies printed and distributed with the aid of high-speed presses.[75] Many settler journalists, in response, hurriedly came to Saitō's defense. Their writings were not reluctant to complain about the Governor-General's rule, but they defended the colonial authority just as staunchly as they promoted settler interests vis-à-vis Koreans. Miyakawa Gorōsaburō of the *Heijō shinbun*, with remarkable candor, declared his paper's mission as "the

74. The number of Japanese papers nearly doubled within a year of Saitō's arrival (Kye 1979, 246, 249–50, 538–39). By the end of the 1920s, Japanese were running 31 newspapers, 11 magazines, and 8 news agencies (*tsūshin*), far outnumbering the 6 newspapers and 5 magazines run by Koreans (Chōsen Sōtokufu Keimukyoku 1930b, 3–14).

75. M. Robinson 1984, 332–35.

propaganda of colonial policy,"[76] and Yamafuku Noboru, who worked for Ōgaki Takeo's *Keijō tsūshin*, "poured all his energy" into "advocating the colonial government."[77] Anxious to guide the untutored bureaucrats, Aoyagi Tsunatarō started a new paper, *Keijō shinbun*, with his colleague Shakuo. He also set up his own propaganda bureau to promote Korean assimilation, seeing officially sponsored lecture tours to Japan or film screenings on Korea—what made up the bulk of Saitō's propaganda campaign—as "utterly useless" and a waste of money.[78]

At the same time, settler pundits faced new obstacles in reproducing their well-worn discourse on Korea, as they found themselves increasingly forced to contend with counter-narratives constructed by Korean writers. For instance, when Hosoi Hajime's book on the Taewŏn'gun, written with the explicit aim to educate the public about "how and why Korea has perished [*horobiru*]," started serialization in the *Ōsaka Asashi shinbun* from June 1926, an outraged Yi Kwang-su responded by accusing Hosoi of "an unfounded slander, if not complete ignorance about Korean ethnicity."[79] Hosoi's colleague in the KRA, Oda Shōgo (1871–?), for his part, complained about a history book his "Korean friend" had recently authored. The book evidently omitted any mention of the spread of Japan's sway over the southern peninsula in the Three Kingdoms period, while stressing "how a Confucian scholar from Paekche introduced Confucianism to Japan and its culture became greatly enlightened as a result." Chiding his unidentified friend for exclusively relying on the *Samguk sagi* (History of the Three Kingdoms), Oda vainly urged Korean scholars to consult the *Nihon shoki*, which he deemed a more authoritative source to "supplement missing facts,"[80] while conveniently ignoring omissions in his own reconstructed version of Korean history.

The vernacular press not only advanced its own theories on Koreans to counter colonial stereotypes, but also presented bitter caricatures of settlers that became stock images of Japanese in Korea. Korean papers brimmed with contempt for settler landlords and nouveau riche who accumulated wealth on the backs of debt-ridden peasants. In fact, they

---

76. Quoted in Kang Tong-jin 1979, 32.
77. Morikawa 1935, 1172–73.
78. Aoyagi 1926, 87–90.
79. Quoted in Takasaki 1982a, 113.
80. Oda Shōgo, "Chōsenshi taikan (1)," *Dōmin* 19 (February 1926): 19–20.

rendered Japanese of all classes as nothing but sources of Korean misery;[81] in one of the more arresting metaphors, they were described as "venomous snakes" who "sucked the lifeblood of Koreans."[82] Their ire was especially directed at farm migrants sponsored by the ODC who, although numerically small, became the foremost symbol of Japanese oppression. The Korean press charged this quasi-official company with depriving the people of their land, harvest, and very livelihood.[83] A group of Korean farmers and workers in Kimje went so far as to pass a resolution calling for "an end to the system of [Japanese] emigration,"[84] a plea echoed by editors of the *Tonga ilbo* who demanded that the ODC "dissolve itself or the government abolish it" on behalf of "all 20 million Koreans."[85]

To these Korean diatribes, Japanese writers often presented a hackneyed response, recasting migrants as missionaries of modernity and claiming that Korea, left to its own devices, would have remained in stasis. In defense of the ODC farmers in the villages of South and North Kyŏngsang, for instance, one local official claimed that they spread industry, progress, technology, and local reform as well as values of thrift and savings, labor, hygiene, punctuality, even ethnic harmony.[86] Settler journalists echoed the official reports. "Rather than abetting nationalistic fever," the editor of *Chōsen oyobi Manshū* asserted, Korean publishers should "devote themselves to improving the [Korean] personality and character, reforming their life customs, promoting wealth, and self-strengthening [*jitsuryoku no yōsei*]."[87] Like official propagandists, the brokers of empire used the rhetoric of *naisen yūwa* for strategic effect, rendering Japanese exploitation into development, settler dominance into paternalism, and Korean assimilation into a matter of ethnic harmony.

---

81. See, for instance, *Tonga ilbo*, 21 May 1922; 13 May 1924; and 13 December 1927.

82. *Sidae ilbo*, 5 September 1924.

83. In one egregious example cited by the *Chosŏn ilbo*, the ODC reportedly "evacuated" Japanese migrants from a flood-damaged village in Chaeryŏng, and dragged "Korean tenant farmers" from outside to settle the village (30 April 1924). *Kaebyŏk* (1 March 1925, 59–68) also portrayed the ODC as "venomous" and "an evil devil" that took away Korean land and threatened Korean livelihood.

84. *Chosŏn ilbo*, 21 May 1924.

85. *Tonga ilbo*, 4 November 1924.

86. *Chōsen* (Chōsen Sōtokufu), November 1921, 91–95.

87. *Chōsen oyobi Manshū*, May 1930, 10.

For settler journalists, the greatest threat to their fading dominance in the publishing industry was the *Tonga ilbo*, placed in the able hands of young and brilliant minds like Song Chin-u (1890–1945). Claiming an unmatched readership of 37,000 by the end of the decade,[88] the paper's popularity, it seemed, could be countered only with the aid of official censors, whose grip on the *Tonga ilbo* apparently tightened as the *Keijō nippō* expanded in the same period.[89] As a surging variety of Korean magazines, booklets, and novels began to flood the colonial publishing market, settler journalists demanded more stringent censorship control, remarkably chiding the colonial police for their "laxity." Such reactionary attitudes drove a further wedge between the Japanese and Korean communities. The *Tonga ilbo* bewailed the Japanese resident press for making settlers "so hostile" as to "boycott assimilation" and "cling to their special privileges." Settler journalists not only chastised Saitō's cultural rule for "making Koreans grow arrogant," the paper complained, they also "long for the revival of Terauchi-style military rule for oppressing Koreans—the very rule that they themselves once suffered from and cursed day and night."[90]

## *Listening to Voices of the Colonized*

Behind the daily exchange of rhetorical barbs, however, a dawning recognition of the strength of local nationalism gradually compelled the brokers of empire to alter their mode of engagement with Korea. As neither censorship nor verbal assault seemed to daunt the vernacular press, it became clear to the Japanese that simply chastising "the recalcitrant Koreans" or harping on their backwardness would no longer suffice. Like the *Maeil sinbo*, for instance, local Japanese publishers made more conscious efforts to reach out to the Korean reading public by evoking the goal of "self-strengthening."[91] While some papers posted more articles written by Korean authors, others—including regional papers such as the *Seisen nippō* (Chinnamp'o) and the *Gunsan nippō* (Kun-

88. Kye Hun-mo 1979, 538–39.

89. Kim Kyu-hwan 1959, 192.

90. *Tonga ilbo*, 1 August 1920.

91. This effort was already launched by the *Maeil sinbo*, the sole Korean-language paper in circulation in the 1910s that presented competition to the vernacular dailies in the 1920s. See Yi Hŭi-jŏng 2008.

san)—changed their sales tactics by mixing Japanese and Korean scripts to enhance their appeal among different demographics.[92]

Most notably, Japanese settlers who had seldom treated Korean public opinion in their writings began, as one of them put it, to read "studies on Korea by Koreans" and "listen to the voices of Koreans as the colonized." An organization that made this its founding mission was the publisher of the *Chōsen shisō tsūshin* (Korean Thought News). Begun in 1926 under the editorship of Itō Usaburō (pen name: Itō Kandō),[93] the magazine was an outgrowth of a study group formed a few years earlier by local Japanese journalists and correspondents of metropolitan dailies, with the intent to translate and study select articles from the Korean-language press.[94] Spawned by a new anxiety to heed the voices of the colonized, the *Chōsen shisō tsūshin* took a systematic approach to probing the ideological underpinnings of their nationalist thought. It featured monthly translations of vernacular publications, whose authors ranged from editors and correspondents of leading dailies and magazines such as the *Sinmin* (New People) and the *Kaebyŏk* (Creation), to schoolteachers, religious leaders, and executive members of "pro-Japanese" organizations such as the Kungmin Hyŏphoe. We may glimpse the Japanese efforts to tap these Korean voices in a collection of translated essays entitled *Chosen oyobi Chōsen minzoku* (Korea and the Korean People), issued by the publisher of *Chōsen shisō tsūshin* on its first anniversary in 1927.[95] Among the translated "studies on Korea by Koreans" was Ch'oe Nam-sŏn's famous thesis on Tan'gun and Korea as "the font of Eastern Culture," an effort to speak back to the colonizer and to re-

92. Kang Tong-jin 1979, 31. By the end of the 1920s, there were ten Japanese-run papers that published in both languages (Kye Hun-mo 1979, 537).

93. *Maeil sinbo*, 28 April 1926.

94. *Tonga ilbo*, 9 July 1920. The previous year, Itō had also founded the Chōsengo Kenkyūkai (Korean Language Study Association) with Yi Wan-ŭng, with the aim to "teach Korean language to Japanese and foster their harmonious interaction with Koreans, while giving them an opportunity to observe the psychological conditions of Koreans" (ibid.).

95. Both the final publication and the handwritten original draft survive (on microfilm at the Yūhō Bunko, Tōyō Bunka Kenkyūjo, Gakushūin University, Tokyo), offering a rare opportunity also to see how press censorship might have affected settlers' efforts to analyze the Korean mind.

cover national pride.[96] A more direct assault on the colonial archive was launched by an essay entitled "Global Trends and the Korean Future" written by the president of the *Tonga ilbo*, Song Chin-u.[97] The opening paragraph set the tone for Song's thesis by flatly rejecting colonial assimilation policy, declaring "We are Koreans [who] cannot stand up or live for a moment without Korea." Placing the *minjok* (nation) above divisive politics, Song claimed "the concept of Korea among Koreans" had survived and transcended the vicissitudes of history, adding, "Koreans have always absolutely resisted the long-term intervention or rule by a foreign country." Song's notion of the transcendental *minjok*,[98] in effect, invalidated all the common claims Japanese made about Korean history as one of toadyism, foreign subjugation, and incapacity for self-rule.[99]

Diverse in focus and level of criticism, these Korean writings sent a clear collective message that was not lost in translation: a *minjok* could exist and endure outside of the framework of the nation-state.[100] This message upturned Aoyagi's assertion underlying his denial of Korean autonomy that Korea historically had "no state but only a nation." Eagerness to heed, as much as to monitor, the discourse on Korea by Koreans was widely shared by a cross-section of Japanese who joined the magazine's membership, including current and former colonial officials, metropolitan leaders, fellow journalists, and even advisors to Saitō like Abe Mitsuie, who evidently relied on the journal "all the time."[101] Yet the fact that this book was heavily censored for publication reveals, ironically, that the colonial state could also interfere with settlers' efforts to dissect the Korean mind. The police authorities appear to have considered these Korean materials too perilous to appear even in transla-

---

96. Janelli 1986, especially 31–34; Atkins 2010, 93–95.

97. Song's article was the longest in the volume but was deleted from the final publication.

98. This notion echoed the historian Sin Ch'ae-ho's view of states as no more than ephemeral embodiments of the more fundamental spirit of the *minjok* (Schmid 1997, 32).

99. Song Chin-u 1927, n.p.

100. Nation-states, however, were the only political entities recognized by "international law," as Koreans had discovered to their dismay in 1910. See Dudden 2005, Chapter 1.

101. *Chūō Chōsen Kyōkai kaihō*, August 1928, 88–89. Leaders of the Central Korea Association (Chapter 5) were also regular readers.

tion, especially when Japanese socialists could look up their ideological cousins across the Korea Strait.[102] Some Japanese residents in Korea evidently agreed. One reader of the *Chōsen kōron* wrote in a letter to the editor how "amazed" he was to see a local Japanese paper "brazenly" translate and post a *Tonga ilbo* article on the recent police suppression of Korean students' movement. Such an act, he fumed, was tantamount to paying tribute to the nationalists and degenerating into "a tool of the *Tonga ilbo*."[103] Apparently a mere act of translation could bridge the conflicting terrains of imperial knowledge production and political subversion.[104]

The brokers of empire thought otherwise. Local Japanese media occasionally carried their own translations of Korean articles, appending detailed analysis and commentaries for their readers. Among the most eager settler publishers was Ishimori Hisaya (1891–?) of the *Chōsen kōron*, by then the largest Japanese magazine in Korea. In its March 1925 issue, Ishimori offered a point-by-point evaluation of a critique of the Governor-General's rule that had recently appeared in the *Kaebyŏk*.[105] His commentary began by almost entirely agreeing with the *Kaebyŏk*'s denunciation of Terauchi's military rule—its treatment of Koreans as "slaves," the evils of "military dictatorship" (*gunbatsu seiji*), the failure of the *kenpei* system, and the flogging ordinance—noting "these were also our [Japanese in Korea] reasons for opposing Terauchi's rule," and restating his "absolute opposition to the entry of remnants of the clique government [*hanbatsu seiji*] into the colony."[106] But Ishimori and the *Kaebyŏk* diverged considerably over the assessment of Saitō's cultural rule.

102. Abe Mitsuie (12 July 1925).

103. "Dokusha no koe," *Chōsen kōron*, August 1920, 150.

104. For a brief period between June 1926 and the fall of 1927, a group of local Japanese and Korean Esperantists published the *Chōsen jiron*, whose sympathetic coverage of Korean social and political movements and opposition to the imposition of Japanese language on the local population distinguished it from other Japanese-language papers. With an aim to remedy the ignorance of local settlers about Korean affairs, the paper featured a host of translated Korean publications, and proposed that the Korean language should be taught as a mandatory subject for settler children. As its short life span suggests, the magazine most likely fell victim to colonial censorship for its leftist bent. See *Chōsen jihō*, 1926–27; Takayanagi 1997.

105. "Chosŏn chŏngch'i ŭi kwagŏ hyŏnjae," *Kaebyŏk*, March 1925, 33–40.

106. Ishimori Hisaya, "Onmon ni arawaretaru bunka seiji no hihan o hyōsu," *Chōsen kōron*, March 1925, 3–4.

Ishimori particularly took issue with the *Kaebyŏk*'s claim that "the contents of the General [Saitō]'s cultural rule and Terauchi's military rule are not as different as they appear to be," when considering the flaws in the current system of local government, the lack of official promotion of Korean education, and the increased number of Japanese police officers relative to Koreans, in addition to stringent press control. Ishimori acknowledged some imperfections, such as the poor choice of individuals appointed to local councils and the insufficient educational system, but he still insisted it would be "grossly misleading" to equate Saitō's rule with Terauchi's. "While we completely concur with the observations on Terauchi's rule in the magazine *Kaebyŏk*," Ishimori concluded, "we find it difficult to express unqualified approval for its observations on Saitō's rule."[107]

In addition to translating Korean critiques of Japanese rule, on occasion the *Chōsen kōron* posted letters from Korean readers. Their comments almost always endorsed Ishimori's editorial views, but also added their general grievances against Japanese. One devoted Korean reader, for instance, praised the magazine for issuing a statement of apology for the massacre of Koreans during the Great Kantō Earthquake, an act that apparently "moved [him] to tears." Yet he also bitterly complained about the Japanese habit of saying that "Koreans cannot be helped" (*shikataga nai* or *shōganai*)."[108] Writing in support of Ishimori's editorial of August 1927 that chided Japanese neglect of Korean poverty, another Korean reader in North Hamgyŏng province bewailed, "Koreans cannot live on," due not least to the "blind, profit-seeking" entrepreneurs and migrants from the metropole.[109]

Efforts of local journalists like Ishimori to incorporate Korean voices and to establish common points of reference reflected a new anxiety, not only to counter Korean critics but also to bring them into dialogue with the wider Japanese community. Like the *Chōsen shisō tsūshin*, local Japanese papers and magazines served as the primary medium through which members of the dominant class stayed in touch with the colo-

---

107. Ibid., 6–8.
108. *Chōsen kōron*, April 1926, 71.
109. *Chōsen kōron*, September 1927, 69–71.

nized.[110] Translation may have fallen far short of direct conversation, but it opened a window into the other side of the colonial divide and created a channel between the two separate linguistic worlds. Henceforth, even as they continued to live in a largely monolingual environment, settlers were in one way or another forced to connect to the world of Koreans, and to make sense of the shifting political reality and its impact on their community "dialogically."[111]

On the few occasions when Japanese and Korean publishers did engage in direct interchange, they staged theoretical debates on issues including the very question of nationalism. One such debate occurred in 1926, remarkably between the pro-government *Keijō nippō* and the Korean dailies. The debate was opened by the *Chosŏn ilbo*'s editorial of 14 June on the relationship between "class consciousness and national consciousness." The paper made a conceptual distinction between national consciousness (*minjok ŭisik*) and state consciousness (*kukka ŭisik*) by highlighting the former as "particularly vigorous among the oppressed peoples,"[112] an oblique reference to Korea. "The current global trend is mutual cooperation" between the working class movement and the independence movement of "weak and small nations," the editorial added in a socialist vein. A few days later, the *Keijō nippō* made a rare gesture of responding directly to the Korean editorial. "The strengthening of a universal common consciousness of the proletariat ought to entail the weakening of statist thought [*kokkateki kannen*] and nationalist instinct [*minzokuteki honnō*]," argued the *Keijō nippō*, showing reluctance to frame Japan's relationship to Korea as a battle between the capitalist and the proletariat. To those who would "talk about a united front with socialists," the paper professed that the current economic condition of Koreans "does not hinge on whether or not one *minzoku* constitutes a state." "There are more multiethnic states [*kongō minzoku kokka*] than ethnically

110. Korean publishers, in turn, translated and posted excerpts from the Japanese press coverage of Korean nationalist and social movements; indeed, Japanese and Korean writers were mutually engaged in monitoring each other's discourse. For instance, see "Ilbon saram i pon Chosŏn ŭi minjok undong kwa sahoe undong," *Kaebyŏk*, May 1923, 27–28.

111. I draw on Mikhail Bakhtin's insight that there is always space for intersubjectivity in everyday life encounters and communications (1981, 259–422).

112. *Chosŏn ilbo*, 14 June 1926.

homogeneous states [*tan'itsu minzoku kokka*] in the world," it claimed, as if to suggest that Japan's Chōsen represented a global norm. "To think that economic difficulty can be eliminated once the state becomes independent is a nationalistic superstition," the editor concluded, just as the idea of Korean autonomy was "an ideological delusion."[113]

The Korean editors welcomed the challenge from the *Keijō nippō*, giving credit to its willingness to "directly discuss the Korean independence movement" rather than dismiss the subject altogether.[114] The *Chosŏn ilbo* admitted that national consciousness could potentially conflict with class consciousness, and also acknowledged the existence of many multiethnic states. But the paper still maintained that nationalists and socialists in Korea could unite in an anti-imperial struggle, declaring "The Korean people, who possess 5,000 years of national history and 23 million masses, can lead an independent national life." The *Tonga ilbo*, too, wrote a rebuttal to the *Keijō nippō*, in a somewhat sharper tone.[115] Pushing the *Chosŏn ilbo*'s argument further, the editorial insisted, "so long as the capitalistic economic principle forms the basis of rule over weak and small nations," one could not separate class from national consciousness; their theoretical difference ultimately dissolved into insignificance when applied to the "actual movement."

The idiom of the above exchange reveals as much as its content. First of all, that the *Tonga ilbo* (which had always prioritized ethnic unity over class interest)[116] should join the *Chosŏn ilbo* in emphasizing a merger of class and national struggles reflected a larger conversation between moderates and radicals in the nationalist movement about forging a new basis for mass action.[117] Both Korean papers seemed keen to invite the Japanese into their dialogue on the nation. The *Keijō nippō* reciprocated this enthusiasm by demonstrating a new willingness to engage Koreans as interlocutors rather than mere objects of control. To answer its Korean critics by deploying the same concepts of nation, state, and class—categories that became salient worldwide in the aftermath of World War I—meant to move beyond the narrow parameters of colonial discourse

113. *Keijō nippō*, 17 June 1926.
114. *Chosŏn ilbo*, 19 June 1926.
115. *Tonga ilbo*, 19 June 1926.
116. See *Tonga ilbo*, 1 April 1923.
117. This resulted in the joint creation of the Sin'ganhoe in early 1927.

and engage on a new global terrain, where both parties could validate their ideological positions and scrutinize each other's claims.

Each such engagement, one may surmise, led to greater understanding on each side of how to justify one's position in the other's ideological terms. Such understanding drove the constant Japanese evocation of the Korean ideology of "self-strengthening" to legitimize their colonial pursuits; conversely, it also accounted for the Korean appropriation of cultural rule and its rhetoric of *naisen yūwa* to demand ethnic parity. These rhetorical strategies, seen throughout the 1920s and beyond, reflected how settlers and Koreans of various ideological stripes began to advance their agendas in terms of what they perceived to be shared values and interests. In short, Japanese and Koreans, each in their own way, and for their own purposes, began to seek an ideological middle ground.[118]

## *Changing Assessments of Korean Nationalism*

The Japanese search for a middle ground translated into a new assessment of Korean nationalism. In the wake of 1919, we have seen, many settler pundits attributed the independence demonstrations to a handful of instigators towing the ignorant masses. Yet even the most bigoted ideologues of *dōka* were forced to concede that the tidal wave of nationalist activities that ensued in the 1920s was a sign of something bigger. Rather than a radical nationalist fringe or a remnant of *sadae* mentality, Korean nationalism was given a new reading as part of a global struggle of colonized nations against imperialism. Hosoi, for instance, even as he continued to preach the inevitability of Korean historical decline, saw in the minds of contemporary Korean youth a pastiche of modern revolutionary ideas, from Irish nationalism to communism, Leninism,

118. My understanding and use of the concept of a "middle ground" in this chapter is inspired by the work of Richard White (1991). Through his detailed study of interactions between British and Native Americans in colonial America, White defines a "middle ground" as "the place in-between" (x), where European colonists and native Indians engaged one another through strategic efforts to understand and use "the terms of the other's discourse," and were mutually transformed as a result of such encounter. Although by "middle ground" White is referring to a specific historical space of European-Indian interactions in the Upper Country of French Canada, the "middle ground" as process, I believe, has broader insights to offer for analyzing cross-cultural encounter in general, including the present case of colonial Korea.

and even Gandhi's *satyagraha* (passive resistance). These ideas coursed through transnational circuits with the aid of modern-day communications, which, he admitted, "make it difficult to erect national borders to [the diffusion of] thought."[119] "Japan is now sleeping with a bomb," he warned Saitō in the wake of the Great Kantō Earthquake; like young Turks elsewhere, Koreans harbored "a violent revolution" as the latest model for the overthrow of the empire.[120] The Korean nationalist movement, Hosoi concluded, was a local variant of the larger, global discourse on anti-imperialism.

As colonial ideologues were increasingly preoccupied with such scenarios of revolt, even Aoyagi Tsunatarō, head of the KRA and peerless defender of assimilation, began to show signs of vacillation. In his 1923 treatise on the Governor-General's rule, written at the height of Korean nationalism, Aoyagi called for a policy of "aggressive assimilation" (*sekkyokuteki dōka*) to be enforced in two specific ways. First, seeing government-run schools as having failed in their goal of making loyal imperial subjects, he argued for "eradicating Korean language and making Koreans use Japanese, while educating them in a Japanese style by fundamentally revising textbooks." This would be paired with the task of "settling many [more] Japanese *minzoku* in Korea, in order to exert the power of ethnic fusion."[121]

Beneath the façade of confidence in assimilation policy, however, Aoyagi also began to temper his vision. In another bulky thesis on Korean rule published in 1925, Aoyagi repeated his proposal for aggressive assimilation, but expounded at greater length on the obstacles that lay ahead. Tellingly, his treatise began by noting the collapse of the Roman empire, an example commonly cited by metropolitan thinkers such as Hozumi Yatsuka who rejected the idea of Japan as a mixed nation.[122] The downfall of Rome, Aoyagi explained, resulted from its "extreme assimilation policy toward alien *minzoku*, annexed regardless of their cul-

---

119. Hosoi to Saitō (17 September 1923): 614. Even the Japanese metropole "exhibited a medley of ideologies from around the world," Hosoi observed, proposing a Pan-Asianist solution of creating "one large alliance of colored races embracing the world's small and weak nations" under Japanese leadership (615, 663).

120. Ibid., 576.

121. Aoyagi 1923, 128, 131–40.

122. Oguma 2002, 42–46.

tural level and ethnic character." Its "active promotion of intermarriage" especially led to "the decline of the superior blood of Romans" and "the adulteration of their warrior-like purity." Aoyagi saw in ancient Rome the future fate of imperial Japan—unless, that is, it corrected its course to achieve "true assimilation" by "preparing the two peoples to become one [*yūgō*] in thought and daily life" and "transplanting more Japanese settlers from the metropole."[123] Calling for ethnic fusion while sounding caution about adulteration, Aoyagi's thesis conveyed an ambivalence that undercut its viability.

Another difficulty of assimilating Koreans, he noted, lay in the fact that state nationalism (*kokka shugi*) and ethnic nationalism (*minzoku shugi*), central ideological pillars of modern political thought, came increasingly into conflict on the peninsula. To illustrate this point, Aoyagi asked his readers to imagine themselves, for a moment, in Korean shoes: "Gentlemen of Japan, suppose our island nation was annexed by America and was placed under its educational policy. . . . Would you gentlemen be able to discard the Japanese mind, break with the national destiny called Japan?" "You could never do it," he swore, "down to the very last person." "If so, isn't it the same situation for the Korean people?" he mused. "I find it impossible to think that the Korean people's traditional psychology can be eliminated by Japan's educational policy" to foster identification with the emperor-centered state. When ethnic nation (*minzoku*) seemed to trump all forms of identity "in the present world condition," Aoyagi was uncertain that Japan's state ideology of *kokutai* would ever be able to transcend its national borders to supplant the concept of *minzoku*, much less develop into a universal ideal of "humanism."[124]

Underlying Aoyagi's doubt was a poignant perception that the failure of the current assimilation policy stemmed from Japan's persistent lack of national power. Seeing Japan as still "a second- or third-class inferior country" lagging behind the West, Aoyagi implicitly concurred with his "close Korean friends" that unless Japan defeated the United States, the Japanese effort to capture Korean minds might forever be doomed. For someone who had spoken of Japan as "a world empire" only a few

---

123. Aoyagi 1925, 3–5, 66–74.

124. Ibid., 142–45, 159.

years earlier, this was a radical reassessment. "Unless the Government-General of Korea does something to stem the current trend of thought," he warned, "the Korean people's spirit of defiance against Japanese is certain to explode with extraordinary power, exhibiting ten-fold or a hundred-fold more strength than the recent independence uprising."[125]

Intended as a guide to colonial governance, Aoyagi's treatise was also a confession of the settlers' internal dilemma. While touting ethnic harmony, settler pundits silently began to recalibrate their stance on Korean nationalism, which, in turn, compelled them to look inward at their own fragile foundation. Increasingly frustrated by Saitō's cultural rule, whose efforts at accommodation were clearly inadequate to mute Korean dissent, settlers began to modify their perception of Korea and Koreans as they were transforming before their own eyes.

But if the brokers of empire became unsure of their ability to counter nationalism, their Korean opponents, meanwhile, grew no less uncertain about maintaining their organizational unity. Faced with tightening press control and a renewed police crackdown on radicals, Korean nationalists in the late 1920s were forced to temper their confrontational edge.[126] The resulting moderation within *both* the colonial and nationalist projects created the conditions for the emergence of a new middle ground.

One sign of accommodation was seen in the most unlikely of places: the relationship between Shakuo Shunjō of the *Chōsen oyobi Manshū* and Song Chin-u of the *Tonga ilbo*, long archenemies in the colonial press. At the Governor-General's New Year's Party in February 1928, these two journalists unexpectedly entered into a one-to-one conversation on colonial politics after both of them had walked out of a film screening on *naisen yūwa*, finding it "too contrived" and distasteful. During the course of their exchange, Shakuo and Song discovered they had more in common than they had previously acknowledged. Song frankly confided his moderate political stance, conceding that independence was an unrealistic goal "buried deep down in our hearts." His greater concerns were "the liberation of Korean speech" and the eradication of ethnic

125. Ibid., 82, 86, 146. But Aoyagi offered no solution other than teaching "correct history" to convince Koreans of the futility of recovering sovereignty.

126. This also accounted for the growing rifts within the leadership over the Sin'ganhoe (M. Robinson 1982–83).

discrimination in bureaucratic and corporate appointments. These demands, that is, for the expansion of Korean rights and opportunities within the colonial system, seemed entirely reasonable to Shakuo. Other points of agreement emerged. Both men desired the state to relax its harsh controls on the vernacular press while keeping vigilant watch over radical talk of independence or communist revolution. They concurred, too, that Koreans needed to "improve their character and intellect," while Japanese must remedy their sordid behavior. When Shakuo asked Song why he was being unusually "moderate" that night, Song responded candidly, "When it comes to practical issues, we cannot help but be moderate." Shakuo was convinced that this was Song's true standpoint, hidden behind the mask of a "fanatical nationalist," and careful to differentiate Song from Sin Sŏk-ku of the *Chosŏn ilbo*, who still "curses Japan and calls Japanese a sworn enemy every time he opens his mouth."[127]

These rare personal exchanges enacted in the margins of the colonial archive—along with records of joint action among Japanese and Korean journalists to protest official censorship—suggest that some rapport did develop between the two sides even as they continued to take each other to task.[128] The conversation between Shakuo and Song, moreover, provides a glimpse not only into how Korean nationalists experienced Japanese rule, but how Japanese settlers understood Korean nationalism as well. Shakuo's characterization of Song's public persona as a "fanatical nationalist," for instance, attests to how the Japanese tended to lump moderates and radicals together as implacable foes of colonial rule. More importantly, his revelation about Song's "unusually moderate" political stance shows how personal contact could make a settler like Shakuo a profound student of the Korean dilemma. Vulnerable to radical accusations of accommodation with the regime, as Michael Robinson has pointed out, Korean cultural nationalists had to "continuously construct and tighten national unity in the face of multiple narratives or competing

127. *Chōsen oyobi Manshū*, February 1928, 35. In another episode that reveals even greater intimacy between Song and Japanese journalists, Shakuo described Song as "a true *Chōsen shishi* [Korean patriot]" who would "struggle to the very end" for his people, while displaying "surprisingly little of the craftiness characteristic of Koreans" (ibid., April 1928, 61–63).

128. For instance, see *Maeil sinbo*, 9 and 15 October 1925.

interpretations of what constitutes the nation."[129] Shakuo's observations on Song suggest a sympathetic, if fleeting, recognition of this dilemma. That Shakuo and Song each seemed willing to back down from their initial uncompromising stance, furthermore, reflected a broader shift in the attitudes of both cultural nationalists and imperialists. Increasingly aware of the limits of their own ideological positions, both began to grope for a middle ground.

On the part of Korean nationalists, this search for a middle ground reflected a pragmatic compromise.[130] While efforts to forge a united Korean front quickly faltered, the tightening censorship control began to take a financial and psychological toll, fragmenting the ability and resolve of vernacular papers to maintain a position of outspoken defiance.[131] Faced with fewer choices, they steadily jettisoned the idea of political battle for business security. But the middle ground was just as eagerly sought by their Japanese adversaries, who were undergoing a crisis of their own. As they began to plumb the depth and complexity of Korean resistance, settler pundits muted their earlier zeal for assimilation and began a serious reappraisal of their colonial project. Even a fervent imperialist like Shakuo admitted that the Japanese were fighting a losing battle against the Korean press,[132] and gradually toned down his call for cultural conquest. Others expressed frustration with an unreformed administration in thrall to its own rhetoric of assimilation. Hosoi Hajime, who was equally unsparing in his denigration of Koreans, nonetheless urged the colonial government as early as 1923 to abandon the policy of *naichi enchō*, and its "fundamentally flawed" assumption that the Korean people could be transformed into Japanese simply "by administrative orders." Echoing Korean critics, Hosoi even argued for abolishing the ODC, "an instrument of exploitation" based on "mimicry of white men's colonial policy" in British India.[133]

---

129. M. Robinson 1993, 167.

130. This is a key observation in the analysis by Andre Schmid (2002) of Korean publishers such as the *Hwangsŏng sinmun* in the protectorate period. Building on his point, I argue that what had largely been a compromise on the part of Korean publishers became a mutual process of creation between Japanese and Koreans after 1919.

131. M. Robinson 1984, 338–39. Seizures and deletions of articles reached their peak between 1927 and 1930.

132. Shakuo 1931, 58.

133. Hosoi to Saitō (17 September 1923): 580, 653.

Aoyagi's pessimism ran deeper. The self-doubt that had occasionally crept into his writings turned into a crisis of faith in assimilation by the end of the 1920s. His perception of Korean history changed to the point of contradicting the theoretical premise underlying all his earlier writings. The difficulty of assimilating Koreans was attributed after 1928 to the "completely separate blood lines [*kettō*]" Japanese and Koreans had developed over the course of centuries. Aoyagi now downplayed the "incorporation of Korean blood into our Yamato *minzoku*" in ancient times as "minimal," and emphasized the existence of two separate ethnic spirits (*minzoku seishin*): "Chōsen *damashii*" and "Yamato *damashii*."[134] "Korea possesses 2,000 years of history, a large *minzoku* of 20 million, genetic ethnic thought, old customs, and an authoritative ethnic language," he wrote, prophesying that "Chōsen *damashii* will begin to counter Yamato *damashii* as new education expands [their] ethnic thought [*minzoku shisō*]." Hitherto convinced of the power of history to transform Koreans, Aoyagi instead found history gradually being transformed by them.

Along with its past, Korea's future also began to look different. In predicting an impending conflict between the two ethnic spirits, Aoyagi now expressed "great sympathy" toward the idea of Korean self-rule—the very argument he had dismissed in his *Chōsen tōchiron*. "Today we see the entire [Korean] people longing for the recovery of their homeland," he wrote, declaring, "I might in ten or fifteen years venture to clearly and candidly advocate the argument for self-rule," instead of supporting "fruitless assimilation policies."[135] No statement was more explicit in disavowing his radical stance on *dōka*. In forecasting a complete reversal of his position, Aoyagi came close to accepting the very conclusion of Pak Yŏng-hyo that he had categorically rejected earlier: the impossibility of assimilating an ethnically and culturally distinct Korean people.

In the closing years of the 1920s, an ironic convergence propelled settler and Korean journalists toward the middle ground. Japanese ideologues of assimilation began to equivocate, just as Korean nationalists began to lose their organizational vim. It was this confluence of pessimism that forced cultural imperialists and cultural nationalists to seek a

---

134. Aoyagi [Kusamura Gakuto, pseud.], "Soejima haku no jichiron no konpon o kōsatsushi dōka seisaku no kenkyū o tenshōsu (3)," *Keijō shinbun*, 3 June 1928.

135. Aoyagi [Kusamura Gakuto, pseud.], "Soejima haku no jichiron no konpon o kōsatsushi dōka seisaku no kenkyū o tenshōsu (4)," *Keijō shinbun*, 10 June 1928.

new accommodation across their deep divisions.[136] Although this development occurred almost by default, my point is that both sides came to believe that compromise was necessary to pursue their disparate political agendas. Precisely in this vein, Ishimori of the *Chōsen kōron* argued that spontaneous dialogue, rather than tired narratives on shared ancestry and *naisen yūwa*, was far more effective in fostering "a spiritual union with the Korean people."[137] Instead of foisting the threadbare rhetoric of unity on a divided society, encouraging debates would more surely push Japanese and Koreans into each other's arms.

## *Conclusion*

After Korea fell under Japanese rule, local settlers strove to understand the world on the other side of the colonial divide, but almost solely on their own terms. The Japanese simply assimilated Koreans into their conceptual universe, rendering them as backward, divided, and incapable of developing on their own. Koreans, too, viewed the Japanese monolithically, seeing them as no more than lowly migrants or rapacious colonists. Yet even as these stereotypes persisted and spread beyond the site of contact, the nature and context of their discursive interchanges became internally more complicated.

The surge of Korean nationalism after 1919 spelled the end of the Japanese colonial monologue. The settler pundits increasingly came to recognize that the premises on which the Japanese built their theories about Koreans were not as unshakable as they had previously assumed. As the vernacular press launched new and sustained assaults on the colonial archive and challenged its power to define the parameters of discourse, the Japanese monologue was modified through conversation and debate with Korean interlocutors. And as the settlers began to probe the ideological sources of dissent—anxious efforts to make sense of what happened in 1919 and what would happen in the post-1919 world—they discovered that Korean ethnicity could neither reliably fit

---

136. Scholars such as Pak Ch'an-sŭng (1992) and Kim Tong-myŏng (1997) have noted a similar convergence between the colonial state becoming more cognizant of the limits of its assimilation policy and the moderate Korean Right who sought a compromise with colonial authority by downgrading their goal from independence to self-rule. For more discussion of this dynamic, see Chapter 6.

137. *Chōsen kōron*, August 1925, 9.

in existing categories nor readily be explained by history as they knew it. Instead, the pundits were forced to acknowledge that their Korean counterparts were progressive, politically keen, and in touch with global trends. More direct interchanges like the debate between the *Keijō nippō* and two vernacular dailies showed that through a cross-fertilization of ideas, Japanese and Koreans could also establish a mutually constructive dialogue about nationhood.

To be sure, settlers and officials alike never ceased to apply their understanding of the Korean past to the assessment of current political situations. Nor did they abandon efforts to modify Koreans' understanding of their history. As late as 1930, a *Chosŏn ilbo* editorial complained that local settlers spoke of Korea only to "malign, ridicule, and disdain," holding the so-called Japanese experts on Korea accountable.[138] But even as the Japanese tried to keep Koreans in a cultural and temporal limbo, dynamic political realities continually intruded to upset the deceptive coherence of their narrative, calling into question the veracity of their assumptions. Settlers' reassessments of nationalism, prompted by an increasingly vocal and awakened Korean populace, conveyed epistemic uncertainties that continued to haunt the colonial project of *dōka*. Local architects of colonial knowledge like Aoyagi even began to participate in *dōka*'s destruction as the decade drew to a close. Rather than substituting for the panoptic gaze of the Governor-General, the colonial archive became a locus for anxieties about empire, a record of moments of uncertainty when imperial agents began to question their own knowledge, or when official categories no longer seemed to describe realities on the ground.[139]

By the end of the decade, increased interchanges, paired with crises in their respective projects, spurred both settlers and Koreans to seek a bridge across their ideological gulf. The Japanese, of course, were not prepared to forfeit the right to govern the context of such interchange. Their search for a middle ground also did not fundamentally change their ideological positions as nationalists and imperialists; after all, Song did not abandon the struggle for his nation, nor did Shakuo completely back down from his advocacy of assimilation. But their in-

---

138. *Chosŏn ilbo*, 2 February 1930.

139. Stoler 2008.

teraction resulted in considerable adjustment of their worldview. It was in mutual encounter that settlers confronted the deep dilemmas of assimilation policy, and that Korean nationalists faced the greatest challenge of unity. Both anxieties increasingly eddied around the colonial archive.

Print was but one of many domains where a middle ground emerged, not only between colonists and nationalists, but also between settlers and Korean elites, where the two parties learned the ideological terms and premises of each other's position. On the one hand, settlers sought such a middle ground to rally the empire through crisis; on the other, they could also transform this arena into a field of joint action against state authority. Such collaborations with Koreans occurred most often in the realms of economy and politics, where local settlers, too, felt the coercive power of the colonial government. When the state chose to manifest its "strong" as opposed to "weak" modality of control, to borrow the phrase of Bruce Berman,[140] settler leaders responded just as flexibly. Positioned ambivalently at the margins of the ruling class, local settlers could align themselves with Koreans vis-à-vis Tokyo even as they stood behind their government vis-à-vis Korean nationalists. The next two chapters will explore this other side of the Janus-faced brokers of empire.

---

140. Berman 1990, 424–25.

# FIVE

## *Industrializing the Peninsula*

In October 1934, a group of settlers in Seoul gathered to honor the city's oldest Japanese merchant "pioneer," Yamaguchi Tahee. From his humble beginnings in the ox-hide trade, they extolled, Yamaguchi built the Japanese community from scratch, lobbied hard for railroads, and laid the basis for an entire infrastructure—"trade, finance, gas, electricity, transportation, banks"—all by deftly combining "samurai spirit and merchant talent." To celebrate his life and enshrine his achievements, which earned him the nickname "Keijō's Shibusawa" (a reference to the foremost business tycoon in Japan), fellow settlers launched two commemorative projects. They edited a biography to chronicle Yamaguchi's half-century struggle on the peninsula as "a valuable chapter in living history," and they made a bronze bust of him to be unveiled on his 70th birthday at Nanzan Park in the heart of Korea's oldest Japanese neighborhood. The peninsula was dotted with such self-congratulatory monuments to early settlers' contributions to their nation and empire, made at a time "when Japan, consumed with internal politics, had no attention to spare elsewhere."[1]

Yamaguchi and the merchants, traders, engineers, and contractors who followed in his footsteps carried with them a distinct sense of pride as "self-made men," even as their success continued to depend on the military and political sinews of empire. Long beyond their years of struggle, they claimed the status that became virtually a synonym for the bro-

1. Kitagawa Yoshiaki 1934, 3–4.

kers of empire: pioneers of Korean development. Agents of the state, by contrast, had ostensibly trailed the robust initiatives of civilians. But the trajectory of settlers' economic activities after annexation, like that of their press counterparts, reveals a more humble picture than the one painted by their biographers. After 1905, chances of "striking it rich" steadily diminished as wartime demand for supplies and construction works disappeared. Moreover, the new colonial government tightened control over the Korean economy, appointing itself as the central orchestrator of development—just as it declared itself the sole voice of Korea, putting many journalists out of business. The capitalist activities of most settlers, as a result, remained modest in scale and their voice in affairs of commerce and industry limited by the Governor-General, the ultimate colonial censor. Even leading Japanese and Korean businessmen, allied to the regime through ties of patronage, were largely excluded from the policy-making loop.

This situation began to change after 1919. Governor-General Saitō Makoto solicited the aid of local elites, not only in propagating cultural rule, but in formulating new industrial policy, starting with the Sangyō Chōsa Iinkai (Industrial Commission) of 1921. The brokers of empire seized this window of opportunity to further expand their leverage with the hope of revitalizing their fading roles as builders of the peninsula. The inclusion of settler leaders into economic governance institutionalized the dynamic of official-civilian cooperation, even as it complicated their partnership with the state and Korean elites. In addition to the contest between colonial and indigenous capital, a central, if overlooked, tension surfaced in this era between the Government-General as an agent of metropolitan authority and settlers as local economic actors. Although the colonial state aimed to keep Korea an agrarian economy to meet Japan's expanding food needs, ambitious calls for industrializing the peninsula emerged from the local business community—well before it became full-fledged official policy in the 1930s. The brokers of empire stood at the forefront of what unfolded as a peninsula-wide campaign to promote Korean industries (*sangyō kaihatsu*), for which the expansion of railways was critical. And yet, when the production of Korean rice was threatened by Japanese import controls, they devoted equal energy to protecting its privileged status in the metropolitan market in the name of Korea's industrial progress. Operating in the crosscurrents of financial retrenchment at home and economic nationalism on the peninsula, settler leaders set out to build a broad alliance with Korean elites to present a local voice of capital vis-à-vis the state in Tokyo—a front that nonetheless thinly masked, rather than bridged, the conflicting visions and interests of the various parties involved.

## *Uneasy Partners in the Colonial Enterprise*

In many ways, the economic transformation of Korea after 1910 was a familiar colonial story, but the experience of settlers provided a different twist. The Korean economy was reshaped by the colonial state, first and foremost, to serve the needs of the industrializing metropole: to provide a market for its manufactured goods, and to supply raw materials and foodstuffs for a growing population.[2] The Government-General instigated a rigorous program to expand Korea's crop production, especially of rice, while limiting the growth of non-agricultural industries and curtailing entrepreneurial freedom to ensure "sound economic development." Central to maintaining state control over the economy was the infamous Company Law. Issued in 1911, this law aimed to regulate "inappropriate business plans" by requiring all firms to obtain official permission before starting a business or opening a branch in Korea.[3] As the licensing system was designed primarily to weed out petty Korean capital, Japanese settlers managed to carve out their niche in urban commerce and trade, making forays into the area of manufacturing during the wartime boom in the late 1910s.[4] But the capital contribution of settlers to the colonial economy was miniscule as compared to the state's share (which consistently stood at about 60 percent);[5] the industrial output by local Japanese-run factories, according to a 1924 official survey, "still remained at a primitive level."[6]

---

2. Ho 1984, 347.

3. *Keijō shinpō*, 21 January 1911. For a study on the Company Law, see Kobayashi Hideo et al. 1994. Consequently only about 170 companies operated in Korea in the first half of the 1910s (Kaneko Fumio 1986, table 3, 180; *Keijō nippō*, 27 March 1917).

4. Kaneko Fumio 1986, 181.

5. Government investment spending accounted for the bulk of Korea's capital formation, and most of it drew on metropolitan capital supplies (Mizoguchi and Umemura 1988, 71).

6. Chōsen Sōtokufu Shomu Chōsaka 1924, 114–17.

The fetters of state control over the Korean economy began to loosen after 1919, as the new Government-General under Saitō wrestled with twin administrative imperatives. On the one hand, it had to make sure that Korea, like Taiwan, continued to fuel the engine of Japan's industrializing economy. On the other hand, to prevent further unrest from below, the state had to grant opportunities for local development beyond primary commodity production, a task further complicated by Korea's financial dependence on the metropole.[7] As a way to meet these conflicting needs, the Saitō administration declared a new economic policy to foster "cooperative capitalist development" between Japan and Korea. Maintaining its focus on agriculture, the colonial state permitted manufacturing and commodity processing to the extent that they would complement, not compete with, Japan's domestic industries.[8] Moreover, the authorities repealed the much-despised Company Law. These measures served not only to stimulate Korea's industrial activity, but also to bring aspiring businessmen into class-based cooperation with the colonial regime.[9]

Saitō's policy to promote *naisen yūwa* in the economic realm built on a pattern of bourgeois cooperation that had emerged during the protectorate period, when local Japanese merchants began to cultivate ties to Korea's landed and business elites. In their early years, the Japanese-run chambers of commerce, controlled by metropolitan capital, tended to operate as tools of imperial domination, and their Korean counterparts as organs of resistance.[10] But this relationship gradually changed from enmity to amity, as both organizations joined hands to tackle pre-

---

7. For a similar challenge of meeting the contradictory demands of accumulation and legitimation in colonial Africa, see Berman 1990, 151. Although the principle of fiscal self-sufficiency was observed, it was never realized in the vast territory of Korea, whose costs of governance, security, and modernizing projects ran far higher than anywhere in Japan's colonial empire (Mizoguchi and Umemura 1988, 74–75; Mizoguchi and Yamamoto 1984, 404–11).

8. Eckert 1991, 57.

9. Saitō Makoto, "Sangyō kaihatsu wa Chōsen kokka no kyūmu ni zokusu," *Chōsen* (Chōsen Sōtokufu), October 1922, 5. This, as we saw in Chapter 3, was a primary motivation behind the creation of the Dōminkai, which enrolled Korea's nascent bourgeoisie in its membership.

10. Yi Chae-hang 1984, 58–71; Kim Tong-sun 1979, 119, 121.

vailing economic issues of the day.[11] The two groups of businessmen, moreover, came to see their growing ties as useful for furthering the interests of their respective communities: settlers for penetrating more effectively into the local marketing network, and Koreans for accessing capital, technical know-how, and business opportunities. It was in this spirit that local businessmen moved at the encouragement of the colonial governor to merge the Japanese and Korean chambers of commerce in 1915.[12] And some businessmen, with varying degrees of success, launched a number of joint ventures that served as laboratories for multiethnic cooperation rarely seen in Europe's settler colonies.[13] In the case of British South and East Africa, a small rural indigenous bourgeoisie developed through contact with settlers,[14] but white colonists generally took refuge in exclusion of educated and urban-based natives, preferring instead to work with tribal "chiefs" of their own invention.[15] In Korea whose industrial transformation outstripped that of European "empires on the cheap,"[16] a number of entrepreneurs in this period also began to develop what would become long-lasting ties to the authorities. They did so by serving on semi-official banks and corporations such

---

11. One such issue was the "Nickel Coin Depression." *KSKN* 1941, 1:131.

12. The newly joint chambers, predictably, were dominated by settler capital (ibid., 138–44, and reminiscences of Song Pyŏng-jun and Ye Chong-sŏk in ibid., 134–35; Chōsen Sōtokufu, *Chōsen Sōtokufu shisei nenpō* 1915, 244–46).

13. The number of joint ventures rose, albeit modestly, from 16 in 1911 to 29 in 1915 (Chōsen Sōtokufu, *Chōsen Sōtokufu tōkei nenpō* 1911 and 1915). One of the few successful ventures was the Kyōekisha (Mutual Profit Company), founded in 1914 by Nishihara Kamezō, Pak Sŭng-jik, and other cotton traders in Seoul (Nakamura Shiryō 1925, 238–39).

14. Austin 1996, 179–80.

15. A. Roberts 1986, 33–35; Berman and Lonsdale 1992, 89–91, 197. Throughout colonial Africa, from Portuguese Angola to the Belgian Congo, the European administrators relied on indigenous elites as necessary intermediaries between the state and the subject population, but with strong ambivalence about allowing them opportunities beyond their auxiliary role in local administration (C. Young 1994, 227–28). The French in West Africa, for instance, pursued a policy of boosting the status of chiefs but undermined that of elites by making it hard to obtain French citizenship (*évolué*), which required renunciation of one's personal status in Muslim law (ibid., 34–35). In Portuguese Africa, those who acquired the status of "assimilated citizens" (*assimilados*) were to a certain extent nurtured by the colonial government, but unwelcomed and undercut by local settlers (A. Roberts 1986, 497–48; Penvenne 2005, 91).

16. Cooper 2005, 157.

as the ODC, which undertook the state's economic projects by proxy. Their executive boards were filled with prominent Japanese and Korean businessmen—top-class capitalists such as Cho Chin-t'ae and Han Sang-nyong became fixtures—who came to represent the corporate aristocracy of colonial Korea.[17]

While helping the state implement its policies, from the enforcement of business taxes to more grandiose projects like the Korea Exposition of 1915,[18] these capitalists used local chambers of commerce to steadily enlarge the boundaries of activity beyond their semi-official role.[19] Through peninsula-wide conventions and joint forums held with their Manchurian counterparts,[20] local businessmen not only discussed strategies to promote further economic integration of Korea and Japan (such as abolishing tariffs and expanding transportation), but time and again prodded the state to unshackle what they regarded as a realm of laissez-faire capitalism by abolishing the Company Law.[21] These industrial visions began to crack through the surface of state dominance in the

---

17. Cho Chin-t'ae was the president of the Chōsen Commercial Bank. After his early bureaucratic career, Cho entered the entrepreneurial world and chaired the Korean-run Seoul Chamber of Commerce in 1905. He also served as the president of the Hansŏng Warehouse Company and served on the executive boards of many banks and corporations including the ODC. Cho served as the Korean vice head of the Seoul Chamber of Commerce from 1915 to 1925 (Nakamura Shiryō 1926, 94). Han Sang-nyong was the founder and a senior managing director of the Hansŏng Bank. He was also the maternal nephew of Yi Wan-yong, the prime minister in the protectorate period. Having studied English and graduated from Seijō Gakkō in Japan, Han founded the Hansŏng Bank in 1903 and became its president in 1924. Like Cho Chin-t'ae, Han became an executive member of the ODC at the time of its creation. Han founded and served on the executive boards of other corporations, such as the Chōsen Life Insurance Company and the Chōsen Trust Company, and launched many joint ventures with Japanese capitalists. Han also served as the executive member of the Seoul Chamber of Commerce from 1915 to 1925, and as the Korean vice head from 1925 to 1928 (Nakamura Shiryō 1926, 154–55). For a detailed biographical account of Han, see Han Ik-kyo 1941; for more details of Han's entrepreneurial activities, see Kim Myŏng-su 2000.

18. For studies on colonial expositions, see Kal 2005; Henry 2006, Chapters 3 and 7; and Oh 2008, Chapter 1.

19. The 1915 merger of the Japanese and Korean chambers led to the loss of their right to petition and advise the authorities on matters of commerce and industry, though local merchants would soon retrieve that right in a somewhat scaled-back form (Kimura Kenji 1989, 100).

20. Mansen Shōgyō Kaigisho Rengōkai 1918, 74–81.

21. Kimura Kenji 1997, 55–58.

1920s as the scope of civilian participation in economic governance broadened under Saitō.

The businessmen's partnership with the new colonial government formally began with the Industrial Commission of 1921. Inaugurated by Saitō "to realize common economic interests between Japan and Korea" through "harmonious cooperation of entrepreneurs from both countries,"[22] the commission represented a milestone in colonial governance: for the first time, businessmen were invited to join high-echelon bureaucrats in formal economic policy-making.[23] The resulting commission was an imperial assembly of "big men," a total of 48 officials and civilians, who shaped the colonial enterprise on the peninsula and from the Japanese metropole.[24]

Those with the greatest stake in the commission were the 28 representatives from Korea, consisting of 8 colonial bureaucrats, 10 settler businessmen, and 10 Korean businessmen.[25] The Korean delegates included aristocrats (such as Yi Wan-yong and Song Pyŏng-jun), bank and company executives (such as Cho Chin-t'ae and Han Sang-nyong) who represented the Korean financial community, and big provincial landlords who invested their growing wealth in finance and industry. The settler participants represented a similarly prominent circle of the Japanese business community: heads of banks and large corporations, agricultural entrepreneurs, and capitalists involved in everything from stock farming to marine products and steel manufacturing. Most powerful by far was Tomita Gisaku, a mining parvenu (*kōzan narikin*) whose unrivaled fortune made in Chinnamp'o earned him nicknames like "Korea's Shibusawa" (a status he shared with Yamaguchi Tahee) and "ci-

22. Chōsen Sōtokufu, *Chōsen Sōtokufu shisei nenpō* 1921, 191.

23. Eckert 1991, 104. Carter Eckert briefly mentions the 1921 commission (and instead focuses his analysis on the second and third conferences in the 1930s), but I analyze in greater detail its proceedings and their significance.

24. The participants from Japan included four bureaucrats (from the cabinet legislation bureau, and the Ministries of Finance, Agriculture and Commerce, and Colonization), several scholars, and a dozen corporate executives representing such companies as the ODC, the South Manchurian Railway, the Dai-Ichi Bank, and *zaibatsu* interests Mitsui and Mitsubishi.

25. For a complete list of participants, see Chōsen Sōtokufu, *Sangyō Chōsa Iinkai kaigiroku* 1921, 17–20.

vilian Governor-General" (*minkan sōtoku*).[26] Fujii Kantarō (1876–?), Korea's "irrigation king" (*suiri-ō*), built his wealth by instigating land reclamation projects in Kunsan and other provinces.[27] Hailing from Pusan was Kashii Gentarō (1867–?), who became a "king of marine products" after obtaining, through Resident-General Itō's mediation, the right to manage the best fisheries owned by the Korean royal household.[28] In extracting the riches of Korea, these colonial tycoons together transformed the peninsula into an atlas of personal success.

For a period of six days, the commission split into three subcommittees to discuss and amend specific areas of industrial policy outlined in the official draft. They then reconvened on the last day to scrutinize each other's proposals, before submitting them to the Governor-General. Not a single aspect of colonial economy was left untouched. The foremost priority, the businessmen agreed, was expanding agricultural production to meet the empire's food needs. The completion of railways and other physical infrastructures was also deemed critical for developing Korea's budding industries—sericulture, lumber, marine products, raw materials processing, and mining—as was the development of power sources and the even more "urgent need to secure the necessary capital" for realizing these objectives.[29]

Given its impressive lineup of participants, the commission in the end added very few substantial changes to the official draft, which was approved more or less in its original form.[30] But the gathering did expose serious disagreements among the businessmen as well as fundamental tensions underlying their partnership with the state. In demanding an official pledge of commitment to the various projects outlined in the draft, for instance, settler businessmen made requests that well surpassed the scope of industrialization envisioned by the authorities. Fujii Kantarō complained that the colonial government after the March First Move-

26. For a biography of Tomita, see Tomita 1936.

27. Nakamura Shiryō 1926, 304–5.

28. Tanaka Ichinosuke 1936, Fuzan-hen, 56–57. Kashii was also a former *sōshi* from the patriotic society, Gen'yōsha, who had studied under Katsu Kaishū.

29. Chōsen Sōtokufu, *Sangyō Chōsa Iinkai kaigiroku* 1921, 29–35. Top economic bureaucrats such as industrial bureau chief Nishimura Yasukichi and finance bureau chief Kōchiyama Rakuzō sat in on each subcommittee to respond to queries and to clarify various parts of the draft.

30. See Chōsen Sōtokufu, *Sangyō Chōsa Iinkai giji sokkiroku* 1922, furoku, 101–200.

ment devoted its resources to the maintenance of security, while "expenses related to industries [*sangyō*] since annexation have amounted to only about 1 percent of the Government-General's revenue."[31] Echoing his sentiment, Kada Naoji (1877–?) and his subcommittee members proposed extending Korean railways "to 3,500 total miles in the next ten years," but finance officials responded by noting the "extreme difficulty of securing a budget."[32] And when one metropolitan bureaucrat spoke in favor of modest and gradual promotion of industries "suitable to Koreans," Matsuyama Tsunejirō, owner of an irrigation company, strongly demurred, urging the injection of more state support and metropolitan capital into Korea to nurture local enterprise "even to the point of doing away with its [principle of] fiscal self-sufficiency."[33]

If the official response to these settler demands was mostly lukewarm, an even deeper gulf of opinion emerged between the Korean and Japanese delegates. It is significant to note that a few days prior to the commission, Korean organizations had held their own industrial conventions and submitted an array of petitions to the authorities. Their proposals, echoed by the vernacular press, were taken up as their own by the Korean delegates throughout the commission.[34] The most compelling set of demands came from the Yuminhoe, an organization of Korean capitalists in Seoul led by Pak Yŏng-hyo. Their petition demanded that the ODC "end its program of settling Japanese farmers" and called for "immediate protection of [Korean] tenant farmers" languishing under oppressive landlords.[35] Moreover, they urged the creation of a special bank with a reserve of 20 million yen and an agricultural firm with capital of 1 billion yen, both to be "managed entirely by Korean executives."[36] Collectively the petitions expressed Korean elites' desire to regain a measure of control and ownership over their own economy—an act the colonial police bureau chief Maruyama later hy-

31. Chōsen Sōtokufu, *Sangyō Chōsa Iinkai giji sokkiroku* 1922, 218.
32. Ibid., 177–78.
33. Ibid., 162–63, 166.
34. Ibid., 140, 162, 246–48.
35. Ibid., 247.
36. Ibid., 247–49. See also *Tonga ilbo*, 14 and 20 September 1921.

perbolically interpreted as "a revolt against the importation of Japanese capital."[37]

Maruyama was hasty in seeing these requests as part of a united nationalist movement "to get rid of Japan in all areas" from education to industry,[38] but the behavior of Korean delegates in some ways supported his impression. Throughout the commission, the Korean entrepreneurs, some relying on an interpreter, spoke almost entirely in the idiom of national (*minjok*) interests. The president of the Taegu Bank, for instance, demanded that the state give preferential subsidies and protection to Korean-run industries for at least a decade until they had caught up with the Japanese.[39] The former head of the pro-Japanese Ilchinhoe, Song Pyŏng-jun, repeatedly alerted fellow participants to "the current plight of Korean tenant farmers," urging rural relief and pleading with them not to "disappoint the 80 percent of the Korean population"[40]—a request reiterated by Pak Yŏng-gŭn, a landlord in North Chŏlla, who observed that "the difficulty of living has caused the people's minds to steadily deteriorate."[41] One after another, the Korean delegates argued for a more "Korean-centered" (*Chōsenjin hon'i*) industrial policy, claiming to speak on behalf of "the Korean people."[42]

Rather than reject colonial rule, these Korean elites demanded a fair share of the empire's growing economic pie. Han Sang-nyong, perhaps the most powerful and respected native entrepreneur, candidly stated, "Koreans do not welcome Japanese efforts to promote joint Japanese-Korean ventures because profits are not apportioned equally." Lament-

---

37. Maruyama Tsurukichi, "Chōsen no chian," *Chōsen* (Chōsen Sōtokufu), July 1923, 24.

38. Ibid., 25.

39. Chōsen Sōtokufu, *Sangyō Chōsa Iinkai giji sokkiroku* 1922, 55, 142–43. Hyŏn Kibong, who owned several companies in South Chŏlla province, specifically requested the state to bolster "Korean cottage industries such as textiles" that were currently under threat from the influx of Japanese capital.

40. Ibid., 239–41.

41. Ibid., 212.

42. That the Korean capitalists strategically phrased their demands in terms of national (*minjok*) interests signals a political gesture aimed not solely at the Japanese but also at their own people. By emphasizing the primacy of "happiness of the general majority" rather than "the profit of a minority propertied class," the Korean elite delegates appear to have sought legitimacy and influence over their own national community that increasingly shunned them as agents of colonial capital.

ing such "disregard for coexistence and coprosperity [*kyōson kyōei*]," Han entreated the Japanese participants to "distribute profit equally to the Koreans, even allocate honor and status to Korea sufficiently."[43] Han's remarks, echoed by his colleagues throughout the 1920s, took aim at settler capitalists like Fujii Kantarō, who would habitually enjoin Koreans to "tolerate small disadvantages for the sake of larger interests" and insist on delayed gratification in order to build a more solid foundation for Korea's future.[44] To be sure, many local elites accepted the colonizer's argument that Koreans, given their "low level of wealth and knowledge,"[45] must depend on Japanese assistance. But they simultaneously demanded a means to uplift themselves (that their Japanese partners were wont to withhold) by turning the promised package of colonial modernity into a potent "claim-making device."[46] The Korean businessmen, in other words, operated within the hegemonic framework of Japanese rule without accepting the premise of settler dominance, and appropriated the colonial trope of ethnic harmony to demand proper returns from their cooperation with official policy.[47]

The reactions of most settler delegates to these Korean requests were predictably hostile.[48] Where the Koreans demanded the state limit the entry of Japanese migrants and capital, the settlers insisted Korea could not develop without them. And where the Korean delegates called for

---

43. Ibid., 160, 245.

44. Fujii Kantarō, "Sangyō Chōsa Iinkai ni taisuru kansō," *Chōsen* (Chōsen Sōtokufu), October 1922, 65–66.

45. Chōsen Sōtokufu, *Sangyō Chōsa Iinkai giji sokkiroku* 1922, 159.

46. Cooper 2005, 146–47.

47. Here we may speak of "bourgeois nationalism"—or a bourgeois variant of a multifaceted nationalism led by moderates and radicals—as historian Yun Hae-dong (2003, Chapter 3) has done by using the case of Sin Ch'ae-ho, as a way to move beyond the framework of "ethnic nationalism" and to rethink the identity and strategy of *minjok* bourgeoisie. Working alongside the Japanese, the Korean elites, indeed, constantly invoked the nation, spoke on behalf of the nation, and justified their activity in terms of the nation (see also a memoir of Pak Hŭng-sik in "Pak Hŭng-sik" 1981; and Chapter 6). These political gestures cast doubt on the familiar view of collaboration that denies the agency of its participants or assumes the precedence of class over nation. Class and nation, instead, remained closely entwined in the Korean bourgeois partnership with settlers.

48. The problem of translation partly contributed to the lack of settler response (Chōsen Sōtokufu, *Sangyō Chōsa Iinkai giji sokkiroku* 1922, 139–40).

protecting native farmers and cottage industries, the settlers pushed for railways to expand their own communities.[49] In response to the Yuminhoe's demand for companies run by "Koreans only," Fujii Kantarō pleaded with the Korean delegates to "stop insisting on the priority of the Korean people" for the sake of *naisen yūwa*. And he resolutely defended the role of Japanese emigrants as conduits to material progress who "cultivated barren land," created "beautiful rice paddies," and introduced the latest farming technologies to Korea,[50] a tacit reference to his ongoing venture to create "a model Japanese village" on his farm near Kunsan.[51] Kugimoto Tōjirō, a leading merchant in Seoul, likewise argued that settlers spread modernity by example. "Whether fishermen or farmers, Japanese as teachers in action [*jitsubutsu kyōju*] have always helped Koreans raise their productivity," he claimed, urging the expansion of railroads as the best method of implanting more such "teachers" in undeveloped parts of the peninsula.[52]

The idea of "Korean centeredness" appears to have fallen on deaf ears among settler delegates; instead, as the *Tonga ilbo* snidely observed, the Industrial Commission ended up establishing a "Japanese-centered policy."[53] But Korean voices were not entirely discounted. Aware of the problems of the countryside and anxious to secure the goodwill of Korean elites, official participants and some local entrepreneurs like Kada Naoji showed willingness to heed the Korean demands, which were echoed in various parts of the final proposal. While stressing food production, for instance, the proposal emphasized the need to devise measures to "improve customs regarding tenancy and protect small farmers," a clause included after the relevant subcommittee "thoroughly studied the petitions and proposals" submitted by Korean organizations.[54] Other Korean opinions, such as Han Sang-nyong's suggestion to expand industrial supervision and vocational facilities, were directly incorpo-

---

49. Ibid., 144–45, 171, 217.

50. Ibid., 250.

51. Fujii Kantarō 1922, 7. His program was seen as "a grave threat" to local Korean villagers (*Tonga ilbo*, 28 January 1929).

52. Chōsen Sōtokufu, *Sangyō Chōsa Iinkai giji sokkiroku* 1922, 147, 171–72.

53. *Tonga ilbo*, 23 September 1921.

54. Chōsen Sōtokufu, *Sangyō Chōsa Iinkai giji sokkiroku* 1922, 184.

rated,[55] as was the Korean demand for "the protection and promotion of small manufacturers."[56]

The Industrial Commission thus set a pattern of uneasy partnership between Korean and Japanese businessmen, and their ambivalent relationship with the state for the rest of the decade. The vernacular press often criticized the cozy relations among local elites as emblems of colonial capitalism, but as the proceedings at the Industrial Commission showed, what drew the settler and Korean businessmen to each other was more complicated than it seemed.[57] Despite their shared commitment to capitalistic development, conflicting industrial visions and tensions over equity persisted, if seldom surfaced, in their entente.[58] So while the chambers of commerce remained under settler control, the Korean capitalists created their own institutional outlets, most notably the Korea Business Club,[59] for addressing general economic issues as

---

55. Ibid., 186.

56. In response to the Yuminhoe's request, the finance bureau chief Kōchiyama even gave an explicit verbal promise to create "another Korean-centered bank" akin to the Chōsen Industrial Bank (ibid., 205). Governor-General Saitō would also later offer industrial subsidies and other measures of support to promising Korean-run firms such as the Kyŏngsŏng Spinning Company (Eckert 1991, 81–84).

57. This was particularly true with the case of young and upwardly mobile merchants and entrepreneurs (below the status of top-class capitalists like Han Sang-nyong), whose goal was often simply to climb the social ladder by seizing limited opportunities available in the colony (Im Tae-sik 1997, 117).

58. For more Korean business elites' views on industry, see the special issue on industrial development in *Chōsen* (Chōsen Sōtokufu), October 1922. Beneath the façade of submission, moreover, the activities of Korean capitalists bore traces of nationalist politics. For instance, Korean members of the Pusan Chamber of Commerce reportedly fell into the following categories: 1) the "anti-Japanese type," such as Ch'oe Chun and An Hŭi-je of the Paeksan Trading Company, who used enterprise and the chamber as a strategy of anti-Japanese struggle and devoted themselves to collecting funds for independence movements; 2) "those who approved of Japanese rule" such as Ŏ Tae-sŏng and Chŏng Tae-sŏng to take an active part in the development of Korea; 3) the "pro-Japanese type" who overtly cooperated with the regime and as a result became frequent targets of Korean nationalist attacks; and 4) "those who sought to get ahead in the world and protect themselves" by seeking a seat on the chamber's executive board (Yang Chŏng-mo 1982, 253–54).

59. The Korea Business Club (Chōsen Jitsugyō Kurabu) was a fraternal organization formed in 1920 by Korean bank and corporate executives (with a few Japanese advisors), which, as its chairman Han Sang-nyong proudly explained, represented "the sole exception to the general rule that Japanese mainly initiate projects and Koreans [merely]

well as concerns unique to Koreans, from rural poverty to the lack of educational opportunities.[60] As both Japanese and Korean businessmen would soon discover, however, the prospect of *any* industrial project in Korea, whether irrigation works or railways, ultimately turned on factors that lay beyond even the Governor-General's control, for these powers resided squarely with Tokyo.

## *Lobbying for Korean Industry*

To ensure that the various projects discussed at the Industrial Commission did not remain a mere sketch, the brokers of empire and their Korean colleagues began pressing the authorities to implement them as swiftly and thoroughly as possible. This effort coalesced into an intense lobbying campaign that extended to Tokyo. In February 1922, the Chōsen Shōgyō Kaigisho Rengōkai (Korean Federation of Chambers of Commerce; hereafter Korean Federation) put forth "Four Great Points for Korean Industrial Development."[61] The "Four Points" called for the expansion of Korean rice production, the completion of Korea's railway systems, the removal of import tariffs, and the improvement of port facilities for developing marine products industry. These goals, as the businessmen proposed, would be achieved by applying part of a metropolitan government surplus of 200 million yen generated by the naval disarmament agreement Japan recently signed in Washington, DC.[62]

If the "Four Points" were tailored to the official economic programs already underway, they were also closely harnessed to key areas of settler interests—rice markets, irrigation works, railways, and marine products—each backed by its own powerful lobby. The "Four Points," in other words, reflected the effort of settlers to mold official industrial

---

follow" (Han Ik-kyo 1941, 380). In the 1930s, the club began enrolling more Japanese members, who appeared on its executive board (*Chōsen Jitsugyō Kurabu*, January 1936, 58). According to available records on its activities in the 1930s, the club promoted conversation on Korean industry among local businessmen and colonial officials by holding monthly meetings, lectures, and roundtable forums on issues such as industrial rationalization, Korean manufacturing, and Manchurian trade.

60. For instance, see *Chōsen Jitsugyō Kurabu kaihō*, March 1930, 12–13, 25–27.

61. The Korean Federation was an umbrella organization for all chambers of commerce, headed by the Japanese chair of the Seoul Chamber.

62. *KSKN* 1941, 1:179–83.

policy by narrowing its focus to coincide with their own business interests. Such motivation clearly underlay their first lobbying trip to Tokyo. Armed with the "Four Points," the league's three Japanese representatives—Shiki Shintarō of Seoul, Kashii Gentarō of Pusan, and Fukushima Sōhei of P'yŏngyang—lobbied the prime minister and leading members of both houses of the Diet for a one-month period between 23 February and 23 March 1922. In asking for greater financial commitment to Korean industrial development, the lobbyists, first of all, alerted the metropolitan leaders to the halting expansion of settler strength in the colony. "The Japanese population in Korea has barely increased since annexation," they complained, whereas Koreans were vigorously expanding across the northern border where "nearly 3 million have already settled in Manchuria and Siberia."[63] Korean development required luring more Japanese capital and migrants, a task they felt the authorities had utterly neglected since the turn of the century.

In presenting the "Four Points," the lobbyists pointed out the "slow construction of railways that even pales in comparison to Taiwan," not to speak of the "utter neglect of Korea's marine products enterprise" despite its promise of quick return on investment. "No place was more ideal than Korea for increasing rice production as a solution to the empire's food problem," the lobbyists also argued, while urging the immediate abolition of import tariffs they considered as "a grave matter" of the Government-General's "prestige" (*ishin*). "So long as Korea is not a colony but an extension of the mainland [*naichi enchō*]," they concluded, "Korea should be given equal consideration whenever there is a plan to develop industries in the metropole [*naichi*]." Appropriating the spatial logic of *naichi enchō*, the settler lobbyists demanded that Korea be industrialized as an organic extension of Japan, with a budget commensurate with its geographical size, which was "almost equivalent to the main island of the archipelago [Honshu]."[64]

Having received no concrete official response to their petition, the three lobbyists made another trip to Tokyo in late September, timed to coincide with the period of budget talks. This time, they specifically requested an annual government investment of 100 million yen for the

63. *KSKN* 1941, 1:183–84; *KSKN* 1941, 2:29.
64. *KSKN* 1941, 1:184.

first ten-year period of their industrial campaign. Such a commitment, they claimed, would promote both settler prosperity and Korean welfare, "goals of Japanese rule since annexation." The lobbyists reiterated the need to expand settlers' numbers and economic power, but with the new rationale that this was the best method of assimilating Koreans. "To realize true *naisen yūwa* and fully carry out cultural rule requires the promotion of mixed residence and intermarriage between the two peoples," the settlers argued. Such a task would require "settling [a number equivalent to] at least 10 percent of the [current] Korean population, that is, between 1.5 or 1.6 million and 2 million Japanese."[65] Worried about the growing climate of financial retrenchment, the settlers pleaded with Tokyo to sustain its business subsidies for Korea. To do otherwise, they warned, "would immediately oppress the livelihood of the [Korean] people, and would be certain to destabilize their minds and give rise to dissidents."[66] Defining the promotion of Korean industries as the "grand cultural mission of the empire," as well as a matter of its security and native welfare, the lobbyists asserted that the interests of metropole and colony alike could be served by industrializing the peninsula.

Among the "Four Points," the abolition of tariffs and the expansion of rice production were implemented rather swiftly after Saitō's arrival as top economic agendas for the new administration. All tariffs except those on liquor and textiles were abolished by 1923.[67] In 1920 the colonial government also launched the Campaign to Increase Korean Rice Production, specifically to meet a food shortage that had recently triggered a series of rice riots in Japan.[68] Although the campaign floundered for financial and other reasons within a few years, it was relaunched in 1926,[69] and some settler participants in the Industrial Commission became directly involved in its operation.[70] More expensive and slower to

65. *KSKN* 1941, 1:190; *KSKN* 1941, 2:30.

66. *KSKN* 1941, 1:191.

67. Kimura Kenji 1997, 59.

68. It was a 30-year plan to reclaim 800,000 *chōbu* of agricultural land. Using the first fifteen years, the campaign aimed to bring about half this land under cultivation to yield 9 million *koku* of rice, half of which would be exported to the metropole (Kawai Kazuo 1986, 102–5).

69. Ibid., 111–13.

70. They included Fujii Kantarō, who presided over the Chōsen Land Reclamation Co. (Nakamura Shiryō 1931, 370) and Aruga Mitsutoyo of the Chōsen Industrial Bank.

commence was railway construction, the central focus of the industrial lobbying campaign in the mid-1920s.

There was no better way to promote the growth of industries, argued the settler leaders, than to expand Korea's railway grid, part of which some old-time members of the chambers of commerce had had a direct hand in laying. Since the late nineteenth century, owing not least to the lobbying effort of local Japanese merchants like Yamaguchi Tahee, the network of railways had steadily grown to connect major cities and ports around Korea, operating about 1,500 miles of track by 1924, or about one-sixth of the metropolitan lines.[71] From the perspective of the colonial state, the railways were built for the purpose of transforming Korea into an agricultural colony, maintaining internal security, and developing a military and economic artery to the Chinese continent.[72] For the majority of settlers, however, railways were more than tools of governance; their entire economic life was tied to the lines, and their communities and culture of retail grew along the tracks. But the brokers of empire envisioned for Korean railways an industrial horizon extending beyond their role of transporting manufactured goods from, and farm produce back, home. The railway building plan that they now put forward was one that would make Korea not simply an agrarian appendage to Japan, but a robust extension of the industrializing metropole.

Their contrasting perceptions of railways here should not obscure the fact that both the colonial state and settlers fundamentally agreed on their importance to Korea's industrial development. Rather, the crux of the issue lay in the allocation of limited colonial funds. Even as settlers and like-minded officials conceptually broke away from the classical colonial division of labor, the Korean economy remained fettered to metropolitan coffers. Large-scale industrial projects required massive capital outlays and state support, and securing ample subsidies was a

---

Fujii is said to have "drafted the plan [for the campaign] and moved Vice Governor-General Shimooka" behind the scenes (Ishimori n.d., 70). Through the bank, Aruga reportedly raised the bulk of the needed private capital funds. The rice campaign was one of many economic programs (including mining) over which Aruga exerted influence as a "civilian Governor-General, as if Korean development was his personal project," according to a former chief of the Bureau of Agriculture and Forestry (Aruga san no jiseki to omoide Hensankai 1953, 141–44, 158–59).

71. *Chōsen* (Chōsen Sōtokufu), October 1923, 67; and May 1924, 86–87.

72. Ko Sŏng-bong 2006, 47–50.

critical step to this end.[73] In no area did this ring more true than in railway construction, according to Kugimoto Tōjirō, a settler entrepreneur involved in the management of Korean Railways (Chōsen Tetsudō). "The paucity of capital in Korea" made it "next to impossible to set up and run a large enterprise on one's own," he observed. The railroad business was too risky to attract private capital, making state support indispensable.[74]

The brokers of empire launched a vigorous lobbying effort in Tokyo. They called for building at least 150 miles every year, as the Japanese businessmen had urged at the Industrial Commission, emphasizing "the first ten years" in the 30-year official railway plan as the most critical period of expansion.[75] But the railway lobbyists faced an unexpected setback when the Great Kantō Earthquake hit eastern Japan in September 1923. Massive expenses required for the reconstruction of the imperial capital threatened to postpone, reduce, or cancel outright the promised official subsidies for Korea's industrial projects—fears that were soon confirmed.

The industrial campaign could have easily floundered without the new leadership of Watanabe Sadaichirō (1872–?). A building contractor who also chaired the Korean branch of the Kokusuikai, Watanabe succeeded Kugimoto Tōjirō to become head of the Seoul Chamber of Commerce in August 1924. He would serve in his post through the spring of 1931. Following his first, brief stay in Korea to oversee the construction of the Seoul–Ŭiju line in 1904, Watanabe had permanently returned to the peninsula in the early 1910s to manage land reclamation projects in Hwanghae province. In 1918 he set up an irrigation company, Kōkaisha, with fellow contractor Matsuyama Tsunejirō and took over its entire operation in early 1926 when Matsuyama resigned its presidency to join the imperial Diet.[76]

Later nicknamed "One-Eyed Dragon," a dual reference to his partial loss of vision and his dogmatic personality, Watanabe led the industrial

73. Mizoguchi and Umemura 1988, 71–73.

74. Kugimoto Tōjirō, "Chōsen tetsudōkai ni taisuru shiken," *Chōsen* (Chōsen Sōtokufu), October 1923, 74.

75. *Chōsen* (Chōsen Sōtokufu), October 1923, 67.

76. Nakamura Shiryō 1926, 133–34.

Fig. 10 Watanabe Sadaichirō
SOURCE: Fujita 1978, 24.

campaign with the force of his charisma, and with the critical backing of fellow contractors in the construction and civil engineering sector.[77] Though outnumbered by merchants in each chamber, Japanese building contractors exerted disproportionate influence in this period, overseeing the entire range of Korea's public works from irrigation to roads, bridges, harbors, and railways.[78] Leading voices in the industrial campaign were powerful long-term settlers such as Narimatsu Midori, Arai Hatsutarō, and Tagawa Tsunejirō, who, like Watanabe, first came to Korea around the turn of the century to work on the hard-won Seoul–Pusan line and other military railways as engineers, supervisors, and suppliers. Many had also made early forays into the Diet or local politics before permanently settling on the peninsula.[79] Having helped build Korea's initial industrial infrastructure, these men now called for enlarging it further—indeed, beyond what the authorities thought was financially viable.

77. Their lobbying platform was the Chōsen Doboku Kenchiku Kyōkai (Korea Civil Engineering and Construction Association), formed in 1918, with net assets of nearly 70,000 yen by the end of 1920 (Sasaki Taihei 1930, 345–47).

78. Matsuo 2002, 13–15.

79. See Appendix 1 for references on their biographical information.

For Watanabe, and the secretary of the Seoul Chamber Ōmura Tomonojō who accompanied him, a trip to Tokyo became almost an annual or a semiannual affair.[80] Watanabe also worked closely with Shimooka Chūji, who served a brief but influential tenure as Vice Governor-General from July 1924 to late 1925. Embracing a vision of Korean "industrialism" (*sangyō daiichi shugi*), Shimooka became the most valuable official ally for the settler leaders, and an important liaison with the metropolitan government. Crucial, too, was the support of influential Koreans, such as entrepreneurs Cho Chin-t'ae and Wŏn Tŏk-sang (1883–?) and the seasoned bureaucrat Yi Jin-ho (1867–1943), who joined in lobbying the metropolitan leaders in Tokyo.[81]

Together with these powerful allies, the brokers of empire traversed Seoul and Tokyo, negotiating with the state authorities on both sides of the Korea Strait to ensure a steady and uninterrupted flow of capital into the peninsula. In addition to petitioning the Government-General, the lobbyists pleaded directly with Prime Minister Katō Takaaki who headed the recently formed three-party coalition cabinet, and key bureaucrats like Finance Minister Hamaguchi Osachi (1870–1931), asking them not to cut back on state subsidies and industrial funds earmarked for Korea. They also appealed to business leaders, former colonial officials, and other influential individuals, a total of over a hundred contacts.[82] Meanwhile, the Korean Federation negotiated with the three financial institutions that channeled metropolitan capital into Korea—the Chōsen Bank, the Chōsen Industrial Bank, and the ODC—asking them to lower the lending limits, expand the range of collateral, and not suspend loans to ongoing local projects or real estate developments.[83]

The settlers' call for industries, to be sure, was not entirely at odds with the opinion of some economic bureaucrats. Like Vice Governor-General Shimooka, the industrial bureau chief Nishimura Yasukichi (1865–1942), for instance, argued that Korea should pursue the principle

80. Their trip was funded by donations from fellow contractors, supplemented by a few sympathetic colonial bureaucrats and Korean capitalist elites (*KSKN* 1941, 3:42).

81. *KSKN* 1941, 1:196, 198.

82. *CKZ* 104 (August 1924): 5; *KSKN* 1941, 1:192. For the details of their lobbying movement, see *CKZ* 103 (July 1924): 1–6; 104 (August 1924): 1–5; and 128 (August 1926): 58–64.

83. *KSKN* 1941, 1:193.

of "parallel development of agriculture and manufacturing" (*nōkō heishin*).[84] But the extent to which Government-General officials could pursue such a vision was ultimately constrained by their status as local representatives of Tokyo. Their foremost duty was to ensure Korea's subordinate role within the framework of *naichi enchō*, that is, to meet Japan's need for foodstuffs and provide a market for domestic manufactures. To violate this colonial division of labor was considered "out of the question," when Japan's own industries had not yet matured enough to expand fully into the area of overseas investment, and when the sentiment among domestic manufacturers overwhelmingly militated against the idea of competitive industry in the colony.[85] "Should one broach the development of manufacturing in Korea at any meeting or at the cabinet in Japan," Shimooka explained, "it would instantly provoke strong opposition."[86]

The lobbyists from Korea, indeed, struggled to persuade metropolitan leaders, who were less inclined to heed the argument for colonial industry, especially when the national treasury was feeling the pinch. Under the Seoul Chamber's leadership Korea's business leaders and regional delegates repeated their demands in subsequent trips to Tokyo, while asking the Government-General to curtail their expenditures to make funds available for local industries.[87] Their efforts did not yield immediate results, however, and some of the already approved subsidies were postponed and public loans canceled.[88] A sense of desperation was palpable. In the words of one settler lobbyist, Shiki Shintarō, "If the home government continues to give the cold shoulder to Korea's development, we settlers who struggled hard for years on this peninsula will have no choice but to roll up our flag and repatriate [to the mainland]."[89]

---

84. *Chōsen oyobi Manshū*, September 1921, 38–39; *Chōsen* (Chōsen Sōtokufu), October 1922, 15.

85. Kawakita 1995, 172, 184; Kaneko Fumio 1986, 196–97; Duus 1984, 159.

86. *KSKN* 1941, 3:87.

87. The lobbyists included vice chair Cho Chin-t'ae and secretary Ōmura Tomonojō, as well as representatives of a "citizens' rally" (*shimin taikai*), Wŏn Tŏk-sang and Ōmura Momozō.

88. *CKZ* 106 (October 1924); *KSKN* 1941, 1:196–98; *Chōsen oyobi Manshū*, November 1925, 80.

89. *KSKN* 1941, 1:195.

The lobbyists suffered other serious obstacles along the way. The sudden death in 1925 of Shimooka, the crucial prop of the industrial campaign, struck a blow to their effort to secure official commitment to infrastructural projects including railroads.[90] The Zenkoku Shōgyō Kaigisho Rengōkai (National Federation of Chambers of Commerce) in Japan, meanwhile, proved less than supportive. When delegates from the Korean Federation submitted their proposal for Korean railroads, with the hope that this would be adopted as a national agenda, metropolitan business leaders responded by dismissing it as a "regional problem,"[91] underscoring their perception of Korea as no more than an agrarian periphery.

The lobbyists also ran into criticism from their own business community. Voices of dissent emerged from the "commerce faction" in the Seoul Chamber led by Kugimoto Tōjirō, Watanabe's predecessor. Although the merchants were by no means opposed to railways, they complained that Watanabe and his "industry faction" tended to use the chamber for "a political campaign," even for the purpose of self-aggrandizement.[92] In response to similar media accusations of meddling in state policy concerns at the expense of more immediate issues affecting local merchants, a frustrated Watanabe insisted, "The Four Main Points are identical to [Japan's] national policy." He defended his lobbying activity as readiness to ignore "Seoul's parochial interests" for the sake of broader Korean development, and justified his commitment to railways as nothing other than a selfless act of patriotism—in his own words, "what someone who loves Keijō and loves Korea naturally should do."[93]

The prospects for the industrial campaign gradually improved, owing not only to the resilience of the lobbyists, but also to some new developments in the colonial political economy. In April 1925, the management of Korean Railways, which since 1917 had been entrusted to the South Manchurian Railway Company (SMRC), was returned to Korea. The new railway bureau chief, Ōmura Takuichi (1872–1946), soon began

90. *Chōsen kōron*, December 1925, 16–24.

91. *KSKN* 1941, 1:199.

92. *KSKN* 1941, 1:251–52; *KSKN* 1941, 3:46, 76, 92–95; *Chōsen kōron*, October 1924, 34–36.

93. Watanabe Sadaichirō, "Kaigisho no jigyō ni tsuite," *CKZ* 121 (January 1926): 2.

working on a comprehensive plan to expand the existing network for the twin purposes of resource development and national defense.[94] Moreover, the railway lobbyists received the pivotal support of the Chūō Chōsen Kyōkai (Central Korea Association), established in Tokyo in January 1926.[95] Chaired by Sakatani Yoshirō (1863–1941), a seasoned politician committed to Japan's diplomatic affairs, and composed of former colonial bureaucrats, entrepreneurs such as Shibusawa Eiichi, and Diet members such as Makiyama Kōzō, the Central Korea Association provided a crucial institutional pipeline to the metropolitan political circles and social networks through which the lobbyists from Korea could generate support for their campaign. Abe Mitsuie, one of the directors and also Saitō's advisor, served as a key liaison between the association and the Government-General, and a familiar cadre of pioneering settlers managed its branch in Seoul.[96] As indicated by its exclusively Japanese membership, the association doubled as a mouthpiece for settler interests and a "Korea Lobby" in the metropole, offering a central medium for the brokers of empire to bring their voices to bear on policymakers and potential investors in Tokyo. In all their subsequent trips to the metropole, indeed, the Central Korea Association became a must-stop through which every lobbyist from Korea passed to obtain personal introductions to the movers and shakers of imperial politics.[97]

These developments finally moved members of the Teikoku Tetsudō Kyōkai (Imperial Railway Association) in Tokyo to conduct a serious investigation of Korean railroads. Based on their findings, they submitted a petition to the Diet bearing most of the lobbyists' demands in March 1926.[98] This gave further momentum to the railway campaign, culminating in the creation of the Chōsen Tetsudōmō Sokusei Kiseikai

---

94. *KSKN* 1941, 1:197. This plan was later submitted to the Diet by Governor-General Saitō, after personally visiting the prime minister to win Tokyo's support in August 1926 (*Asahi shinbun*, 16 August 1926; and 30 January 1927).

95. For more information on the background and the role of the Central Korea Association, see Yi Hyŏng-sik 2007 and Lynn 2008.

96. The branch was managed by Watanabe Sadaichirō, Aruga Mitsutoyo, and Kōchiyama Rakuzō, with an executive board staffed by merchants and entrepreneurs such as Fujii Kantarō, Tomita Gisaku, and Kobayashi Genroku, and journalists such as Shakuo Shunjō and Ōgaki Takeo.

97. *Chūō Chōsen Kyōkai kaihō* 1 (August 1926): 13.

98. Teikoku Tetsudō Kyōkai 1926; Senkōkai 1986, 76.

(Association for the Rapid Construction of Korean Railroads) in July. With Shibusawa Eiichi as its chairman, the association brought together settler and Korean bourgeois elites, colonial bureaucrats, and a host of influential metropolitan supporters including members of the Central Korea Association, cementing an empire-wide platform of cooperation in pressing for a railway bill in Tokyo.[99]

By strategically placing their headquarters in Tokyo and staging their last petitioning drive during the budgetary reformulation in late 1926, the lobbyists finally managed to see a proposed railroad bill through both Houses of the Diet in March 1927.[100] The bill resulted in the formulation of the "Twelve-Year Plan on Korean Railroads," which aimed to double the existing railway lines, especially toward Korea's northern border with Manchuria.[101] This set in motion a process of expanding Korea's railway grid that, though waylaid by new obstacles in the ensuing years, would eventually surpass that of British India, forming "the most developed rail system in Asia outside of Japan" by 1945.[102]

The lobbying movement for industries and railways illustrates the dynamic of settler colonialism at its best. As in the ideological and discursive realms of their activity (discussed in Chapters 3 and 4), working through informal or semi-official channels of communication remained the brokers' central modus operandi. In shuttling between the Government-General and their business communities, between Tokyo and Seoul, the settler leaders drew some key bureaucrats (such as Shimooka and members of the "Korea Lobby" in the Diet) as well as Korean elites into their network of allies, through which they actively pursued their industrial vision. Even in the case of settlers in Kenya, their influence over policy formulation in the key areas of land, labor, taxation, and public expenditure did not obviate the need for similar "behind-the-scenes" tactics in their attempt to "pressure local authorities" and mold policy in their best interests.[103] The need for such informal conduits of

---

99. *KSKN* 1941, 1:203–4; *CKZ* 131 (November 1926): 1–5; Senkōkai 1986, 77; Yi Hyŏng-sik 2007, 114.

100. *CKZ* 136 (April 1927): 49–52.

101. Ōhira 1927; *KSKN* 1941, 1:205–8.

102. Cumings 1984, 487.

103. Berman 1990, 137, 140; Elkins 2005, 12.

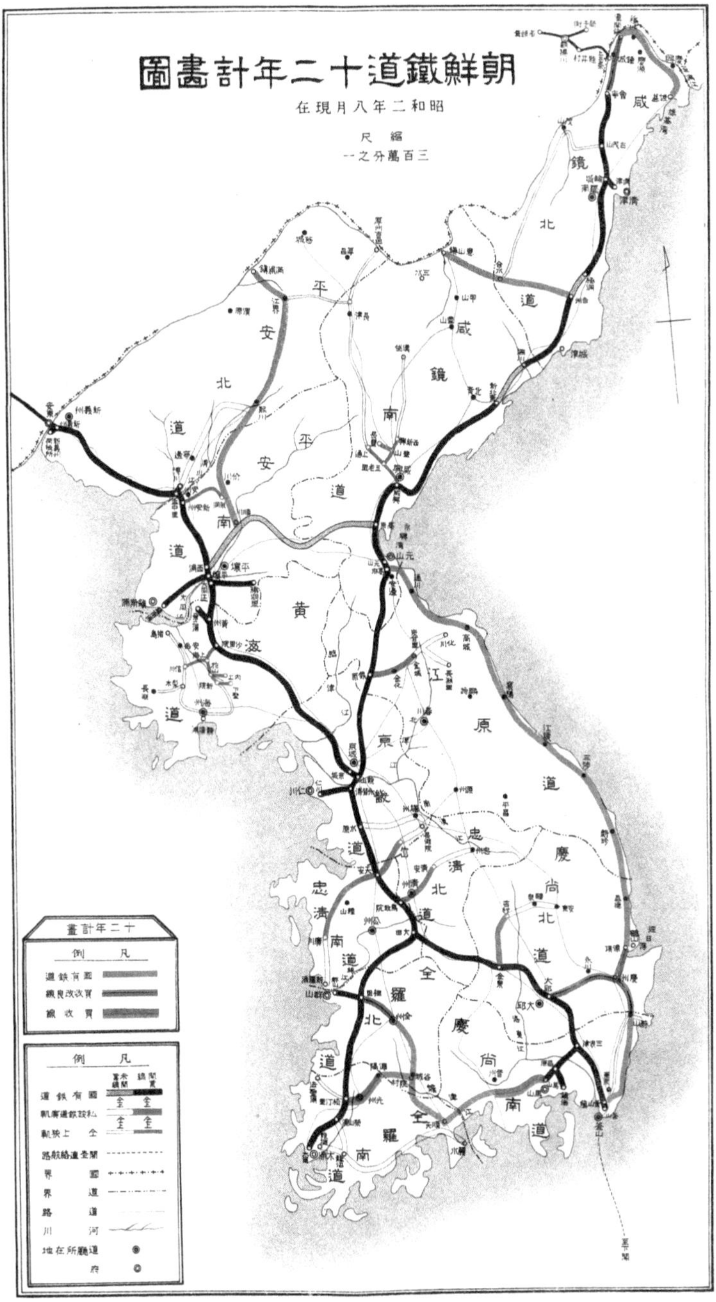


Map 4 "Twelve-Year Plan on Korean Railroads," August 1927

influence was even more acute for Japanese settlers, who had neither fiscal autonomy nor formal representation in the administration of the colony. "In the absence of a system of self-government [*jichi*]," as Jinnai Mokichi (1873–?; later head of the Seoul Chamber) explained, "nothing could be achieved at the time unless the chamber became the driving force, so it always operated politically."[104] Yet their lack of attachment to any government bureau could also work to the settlers' advantage, for it allowed them to pursue their own interests while helping the state meet its policy goals, even when they were not perfectly aligned. As intermediaries between the state and its local subjects, the brokers of empire could avail themselves of their relative flexibility to lobby beyond the metropolitan agenda that tended to bind colonial officials, a situation the settlers fully exploited in pressing for Korean industries.

## *Local Economic Nationalism*

By the last quarter of the 1920s, Korea's industry lobbyists had seen the rice campaign reimplemented, a railway bill approved, the majority of tariffs eliminated, and more and better port facilities being constructed along the southern coast of the peninsula. Having thus more or less achieved their initial "Four Points" goals, the settler leaders launched another campaign, the "Six Great Points," ranging from afforestation and flood control to the development of manufacturing, mining, and marine industries.[105] The settlers now urged the colonial state to embark on a comprehensive policy of industrialization (*kōgyōka*),[106] and alerted capitalists and potential investors "around the world" to the "inexhaustible deposits" of iron ore, coal, gold, and silica on the peninsula.[107]

The Korean public reception, meanwhile, remained chilly from the beginning of the industrial campaign. Where the settlers urged more industries in the name of Korean progress, the *Tonga ilbo* noted an ironic truth: "the more industry increases, the more Koreans suffer,"[108] as

---

104. *KSKN* 1941, 3:44.

105. Chōsen Shōgyō Kaigisho Rengōkai 1927; *KSKN* 1941, 1:208–12.

106. The promotion of manufacturing industries was as an area that, leading industrialists who assembled at a convention in 1927 claimed, "the government has all but ignored" (*Keijō nippō*, 5 May 1927).

107. *Ōsaka Asahi shinbun*, 27 March 1926.

108. *Tonga ilbo*, 10 August 1924.

farmers were increasingly forced to subsist on imported Manchurian millet instead of their own harvest. The *Chosŏn ilbo* echoed its rival's lament: Koreans "are daily deprived of industrial rights" as they eked out a living "under the exploitation of a legion of foreigners, from large banks and corporations to small loan sharks, and as our farmlands, dwellings, and forests flow ceaselessly into their hands."[109] "We want neither the campaign to increase rice nor industrial development," one Korean reader of the *Chōsen kōron* flatly declared in a letter to the editor. Whether irrigation works, mining, or agriculture, "they satisfy nothing other than the interests and greed of Japanese entrepreneurs" and only "exacerbate the daily hardship of Koreans."[110]

Korean nationalists sought to galvanize such sentiments into action by launching their own campaigns. Emblematic was the Chosŏn Mulsan Changnyŏ Undong (Korean Production Movement), founded in late 1922 by Cho Man-sik (1882–1950?) and Yi Kwang-su and joined by such prominent nationalist businessmen as Kim Sŏng-su. Embodying the global currents of economic nationalism that swept through countries like India and China after World War I, this movement aimed at promoting Korea's economic self-sufficiency and nurturing the growth of a native bourgeoisie.[111] Through a network of regional branches, it called on the people to "buy and use products made by Koreans" and to "manufacture and supply goods on one's own," leading to some boycotts of Japanese goods during its peak in 1923.[112]

After the initial enthusiasm and success in its first few years, the Korean Production Movement began to falter under official suppression and criticism from the left wing. But the Japanese took the movement seriously. The police bureau chief Maruyama saw lurking "behind this seemingly beautiful label of promoting local products"[113] a subversive

---

109. *Chosŏn ilbo*, 23 May 1924.

110. *Chōsen kōron*, September 1927, 69–71. For a similar article that fans a sense of Korean fear about the Japanese domination of industries in Hwanghae province, see *Kaebyŏk*, June 1925, 82–86.

111. For a detailed study of the Korean Production Movement, see Pak Ch'an-sŭng 2007, 117–31; Yun Hae-dong 1992; and Pang 2002, 47–108.

112. The movement's "statement of purpose," quoted in Pak Ch'an-sŭng 2007, 123; Chōsen Sōtokufu Keimukyoku, *Chian jōkyō* 1930, 39–40.

113. Maruyama Tsurukichi, "Chōsen no chian," *Chōsen* (Chōsen Sōtokufu), July 1923, 24–25.

call for "boycotting Japanese currency" (although Korean leaders claimed the contrary).[114] Settler leaders also suspected that the production movement was driven by a "spirit of no compromise."[115] Such lingering fear of local dissent appears to have motivated the settlers to align their industrial campaign not only with the official policy of accommodation (by joining hands with Korean capitalists), but also with the very source of their anxiety: the Korean nationalist call for self-sufficiency.

Particularly useful in this respect was the rhetoric of promoting "Korea-made products," which conveniently blurred the distinctions between settler industrial activities and the Korean nationalist movement. For instance, the Chōsen Bussan Kyōkai (Association for Korean Products), founded by Tomita Gisaku in 1924, promoted the sale of Korea-made goods in Osaka and other Japanese cities by holding "Korean fairs," which principally benefited settler traders, though they were couched in the general interests of the Korean economy.[116] The following year Shimooka also issued instructions to regional governors to "prioritize the use of Korea-made products." Bearing more than a faint echo of the nationalist ideology of self-strengthening, his call was enthusiastically adopted by local Japanese businessmen and entrepreneurs as an opportunity to develop more manufacturing industries on the peninsula.[117]

Beneath the seeming parallels between the Korean Production Movement and the Japanese promotion of Korea-made products, however, there were fundamental differences. As the *Tonga ilbo* reminded its readers, the production movement called upon Koreans to manufacture daily necessities by "their own hands," while "rejecting the use of not only imported goods but everything not produced by Koreans in Korea."[118] The Japanese promotion of Korea-made products, by contrast, "extends beyond consumption within Korea to production for export," and "rejects imports from foreign countries as well as Japan," purely out of a selfish desire among settlers to "increase their jobs" or to "lower their cost of living." As the paper noted, "Whereas the former has a

114. Pak Ch'an-sŭng 2007, 129.
115. Hosoi to Saitō (17 September 1923): 581–83.
116. *CKZ* (November 1924): 50–52; *Chōsen kōron*, July 1925, 114; Tomita 1936, 381–87.
117. *CKZ* 115 (July 1925): 49–50; *CKZ* 51 (July 1928): 5.
118. *Tonga ilbo*, 30 June 1927.

nationalistic hue of promoting self-sufficiency, the latter actively promotes Korea-made products by treating Korea in a regional sense." By supplanting "nation" with "region" as the basis for their industrial movement, in other words, the Japanese strategically made their colonial pursuits look like nationalist projects.[119]

All the same, the convergence of Japanese and Korean calls for industry cannot be dismissed as a mere rhetorical effect created by cunning imperialists. Settlers' demand for industries was fundamentally driven by concerns that were seldom shared either by Tokyo leaders or by high-ranking colonial bureaucrats, who resided in Korea only temporarily. In criticizing the authorities for hewing so closely to the classic vision of Korea as an agrarian colony, the settlers understood that their own businesses were by no means immune to the effects of official policy to prioritize agriculture over manufacturing. Insofar as all economic activities in the colony were structurally bound to Japan's needs, it was possible for settlers and Koreans to identify some common ground, and even find each other useful allies in the struggles over policies that catered to the metropole at the expense of local interests.[120]

Throughout the 1920s, indeed, efforts to develop Korea's industries often brought settler and national capital into such alliance vis-à-vis the colonial state. Local chambers of commerce, though dominated by

---

119. This move was scorned by the Korean nationalists who chafed at the colonizers for appropriating the very cause they had initially suppressed (Chōsen Sōtokufu Keimukyoku, *Chian jōkyō* 1930, 40). Although the vernacular press was equally critical of Korean capitalists for joining the Japanese in their industrial campaign, it is hard to miss how the overall message of the Korean Production Movement resonated with a call for "Korean-centered" industrial policy made by these capitalists at the 1921 Industrial Commission. In their mutual emphasis on Korean self-strengthening, and in their struggle to expand "national" (*minjokchŏk*) rights within the colonial system while gradually weaning their economy away from Japanese control, the two groups almost echoed each other. Moderate nationalists—mostly "landlord-entrepreneurs" from the rice-growing region in the Chŏlla provinces—were arguably as capitalistic as "pro-Japanese" elites were nationalistic, a point that becomes particularly apparent when compared to the strategy of radicals and communists who ruled out all options of compromise. Precisely for this reason, as Michael Robinson has pointed out, moderate nationalists, who embraced capitalism as ardently as did their elite adversaries, had to walk a tightrope between cooperation and contestation, without falling into overt collaboration with the Japanese (1988, 104).

120. For instance, see McNamara 1996, Chapter 7; Uchida 2008.

settlers, played an especially critical role by lobbying the authorities on behalf of small- and mid-sized Japanese as well as Korean merchants and manufacturers, addressing such shared concerns as easier access to low-interest loans.[121] From mid-decade, moreover, the chambers dispatched trade missions, composed of Korean and Japanese merchants, to Manchuria, China, Taiwan, and different parts of Japan in search of prospective markets for Korean exports.

Common interests in developing industries could even generate a kind of local "economic nationalism" uniting settlers, Koreans, and colonial officials in a temporary alliance against the metropole.[122] We see this, for instance, in the peninsula-wide campaign to protect Korean rice (*Senmai yōgo undō*).[123] The movement was launched in the summer of 1932 to oppose the Japanese government's decision to curb Korean rice production, an action prompted by domestic farmers' protest against the influx of cheap colonial rice. A steady stream of colonial grain, disgorged into metropolitan circulation by the rice campaign, imposed pressures on prices and contributed to a long-term depression of Japanese agriculture in the 1920s, provoking a riptide of protest from local farmers and rice merchants that lasted through the late 1930s.[124]

Behind their protest loomed the menacing influence of colonial rice merchants, the primary beneficiaries of the Korean rice campaign.[125] Their influence began to spread to the metropole after export merchants cooperated with the Government-General in late 1923 to establish the Senmai Kyōkai (Korean Rice Association), a colonial trade lobby for marketing Korean rice in Japan.[126] Tightened rice inspection procedures

---

121. It was precisely for this purpose, for instance, that the Keijō Shōkō Kumiai Rengōkai (Seoul League of Commerce and Industry Associations) was established in 1920. *KSKN* 1941, 1:158.

122. In using the term "economic nationalism," I expand on the usage in Berman 1990, which is limited to an alliance between the colonial state and settlers against the metropole (178).

123. For a detailed study of the settlers' role in this campaign, see Ki Yu-jŏng 2009.

124. For example, see *Kōbe shinbun*, 10 July 1936; *Tōkyō Asahi shinbun*, 15 August 1936; *Keijō nippō*, 28 August 1936; and *Ōsaka Asahi shinbun*, 1 October 1936.

125. Since the pre-annexation period, Japanese rice exporters in Korea had steadily expanded control not only over marketing and distribution, but over each stage of production after harvest: drying, preparing, and polishing (Yi Hyeong-nang 1996, 213).

126. *Tonga ilbo*, 9 December 1923; Aruga san no jiseki to omoide Hensankai 1953, 163.

reduced the export of unrefined Korean rice to Japan, which hurt the metropolitan rice millers but worked to the advantage of the colonial rice millers and exporters of refined rice in Korea.[127] The latter group came to wield enormous leverage to the point of moving Japan's largest grain market in Osaka as refined Korean white rice rapidly increased its market share, gradually pushing domestically refined rice out of competition. Indeed, the lucrative rice trade mediated by settler merchants deepened the pattern of Korea's monoculture economy and metropolitan dependence on colonial rice, which penetrated aggressively into the "kitchens of consumers in large and small cities throughout Japan."[128]

Not surprisingly, these settler rice merchants and traders formed the backbone of opposition to Tokyo's decision to restrict the importation of colonial rice. Pusan's rice merchants initiated the protest,[129] which quickly fanned out to other provinces to become a peninsula-wide movement, drawing in grain dealers, exchanges, and landlords, down to rice-growing farmers. Powerful Japanese rice merchants and landlords, such as Matsui Fusajirō, Saitō Hisatarō, and Tada Eikichi, led the opposition through the Senmai Yōgo Kiseikai (Society for the Protection of Korean Rice). The Society was formed with the full backing of the colonial government, and with an express aim to mobilize "a purely civilian [*jun minkan*] movement" that would "support and urge a political solution by the Government-General" from below.[130] While colonial bureaucrats negotiated directly with Tokyo, the Society's leaders wired their protest to the metropolitan government, arguing that to regulate colonial rice production would "destroy our budding industries in Korea from their foundation." And Korean and Japanese lobbyists together flocked to Tokyo and upbraided the government for flip-flopping in its treatment of Korea, playing up the sacrifice Korea had made in serving the economic needs of the metropole.[131] Meanwhile, regional "assemblies

---

127. Yi Hyeong-nang 1996, 217; *Fuzan nippō*, 27 July 1933.

128. *Chōsen kōron*, May 1939, 24–25, 28.

129. *Fuzan nippō*, 22 July 1932.

130. *Keijō nippō*, 15 July 1932; *Chōsen shinbun*, 15 July 1932.

131. *CKZ* 199 (July 1932): 95–96; *KG* (November 1932): 39–41. Aruga Mitsutoyo, who presided over the Korean Rice Association, played an instrumental role as an in-

for the protection of Korean rice" emerged all over the peninsula. Local chambers of commerce and provincial assemblies also launched their own petition drives to rally the public behind the defense of "our Korean rice," "our lifeline."

True, the movement to protect Korean rice, like the industrial campaign, was centered on the interests of big landlords and merchant capitalists. Tenant farmers not only bore the primary burden of the rice campaign,[132] but were now threatened with the loss of their livelihood.[133] Nonetheless, since rice production intersected the Korean economy at all levels, its prospect of decline forged a space for some common ground to develop among Korean producers, Japanese merchants, and landlords of both communities. Just as the Korean farmers saw the rice campaign as a matter of survival, settlers considered such shared concerns critical to pursuing their trading interests, given the lack of political wherewithal to influence metropolitan policy.[134] Despite their divergent stakes, therefore, Koreans and Japanese across the board seemed strategically united in defense of Korean rice. Speaking on behalf of local farmers, the vernacular papers warned darkly that proposed control would destroy the Korean economy "built on rice."[135] Even the *Keijō nippō*, a pro-government paper, deployed unusually blistering language, charging Tokyo with "egoism" for treating Korea as "a mere object of exploitation."[136]

As protests roiled the peninsula, the unbending Japanese government in September 1933 resolved to partially suspend the colonial rice production programs in Korea and Taiwan.[137] The Society responded by dispatching a group of Japanese and Korean "crusaders for the protection of Korean rice," including Mitsui Eichō, Matsui Fusajirō, Han Sang-nyong, and Chang Hŏn-sik, who were later joined by Arai Hatsu-

---

termediary between Korea's organizations and the metropole (Aruga san no jiseki to omoide Hensankai 1953, 159, 161–62).

132. Matsumoto 1991, 107–16; *Samch'ŏlli*, July 1931, 6–8.

133. *Tonga ilbo*, 11 September 1933, evening edition.

134. They lacked a kind of leverage that settlers in Algeria enjoyed, through their seats in the French Chamber, to protect their viticulture from domestic competitors (Ruedy 2005, 87, 116).

135. *Chosŏn ilbo*, 16 September 1933.

136. *Keijō nippō*, 19 July 1932.

137. *Heijō Mainichi shinbun*, 9 September 1933.

tarō and Saitō Hisatarō.[138] At times ignoring the Government-General's counsel of discretion, the Society and its member organizations "rained heavy fire onto the metropole in chorus" by wiring a battery of protest that amounted to some 6,000 petitions in March 1934.[139] Ultimately, the collusion of pressures from Japanese farmers and resolute opposition from Korea resulted in a compromised form of rice control and a half-hearted campaign to ramp up Korean rice production,[140] measures that would do little to undermine the continued popularity of Korean rice among metropolitan consumers.

The campaign to protect Korean rice was one of several examples of "local economic nationalism," where a diverse array of interests and social groups momentarily cast aside their differences to present a united front vis-à-vis "outsiders," including the metropole and Manchuria.[141] Operating in the interstitial spaces between state and society, and between metropole and colony, the brokers of empire often placed themselves at the center of these movements, while enhancing their claim as defenders of local Korean interests.[142] Through a battery of petitions and the "Korea lobby" in Tokyo, these self-appointed spokesmen of Korea in each case managed to make a modest impact on policy-makers, all in spite of the Japanese government's propensity to erect what the historian Komagome Takeshi has called a "breakwater" (*bōhatei*) against such colonial incursions.[143]

---

138. *Keijō nippō*, 6 February 1934.

139. *Keijō nippō*, 6 March 1934.

140. *KG* 219 (March 1934): 121–22. From 1932, the colonial government focused its energy on the Rural Revitalization Campaign, which aimed to promote rural self-sufficiency (see Chapter 7).

141. Another example of "local economic nationalism" was a Korea-wide lobbying campaign in 1929 to attract the SMRC's new steel mill to Sinŭiju as opposed to Ansan in Manchuria.

142. This was especially the case for Watanabe Sadaichirō, who came to "single-handedly undertake all of [Korea's] petitions and requests for the central government" and establish his status as Korea's "civilian representative," at least in the eyes of Tokyo (*Keijō nippō*, 14–15 August 1930).

143. Komagome 1996, 217.

## *Conclusion*

If the Japanese were more invested than European rulers in developing their colonies, any such development in Korea, as elsewhere, was governed by the needs and dictates of the imperial metropole. The primary responsibility of the Government-General was to ensure that agrarian Korea fuel the engine of a rapidly industrializing Japan. Local Japanese merchants and capitalists helped to keep Korea in this role by reducing its primary producers to dependency, often miring them in a cycle of debt and poverty. But the evolution of the economic relationship between colony and metropole was more complicated than has often been assumed. When the colonial government after 1919 permitted limited industrialization of Korea and invited local businessmen to participate in policy formulation, settler leaders demanded more than a token measure of inclusion. By this time the brokers of empire had clearly evolved from agents of metropolitan capital into local actors with their own vested stakes and interests in the colonial periphery. This status brought them into alliance with Koreans, especially those of the upper strata who—out of common capitalistic interests, but also for their own purpose of national strengthening—joined the settlers in lobbying for Korean industry.

This chorus of voices, which grew ever louder in prodding the state to industrialize the peninsula, should alert us to the danger of overestimating colonial authority. Paying attention to these voices allows us to understand, for instance, how the colonial state modernized Korea despite its own deep ambivalence about developing local industries (and in the face of resistance from Tokyo). Changes, moreover, did not always emanate from above. The settler-led industrial campaign, and its Korean nationalist counterpart, especially complicates the familiar view that colonial industrialization did not begin until the 1930s and that it was primarily driven by wartime state demands.[144] Rather, Korean industrialization was a long-term and internally contested process, driven by a constant negotiation between the colonial and metropolitan au-

144. A few scholars who have challenged this view include Kaneko Fumio (1993) and Kim Nang-nyŏn (2003).

thorities and local economic actors, in which the role of settler businessmen as brokers remained crucial.[145]

The lobbying for railways and rice served to lay bare the growing contradiction in Korea's status as at once an agricultural appendage to the metropolitan economy and a heavily settled colony with autonomous demands for industry. This tension, on the one hand, pitted bourgeois elites, bureaucratic allies, and at times broader segments of Korean society, against Tokyo. On the other hand, it allowed the settlers to evoke and appropriate the Korean goal of self-sufficiency as the surest means of protecting their business interests in the colony. Around the vision of industrial Korea, and across the dichotomy of colonial and national capital, grew new, if tenuous, linkages between settlers and Koreans, capitalists and nationalists, and diverse interest groups operating on the basis of ethnicity, class, and occupation.

The settlers' industrial campaign also demonstrated further advantages of operating in an informal sphere. The brokers of empire continued to work through a web of personal contacts and patronage they established with officialdom, but without subjecting themselves to the policy concerns that bound colonial bureaucrats to the needs of the metropole. By lobbying personally, moreover, the settlers established their own direct channels of communication with metropolitan leaders, while the colonial state maintained an official outlook of conformity to Tokyo. Allowing businessmen to lobby for Korean rice, industry, and railways meant that colonial bureaucrats like Nishimura Yasukichi could entrust to private parties an agenda that they supported but could not publicly pursue. Here was another illustration of how local settlers availed themselves of their liminality, to turn a source of their weakness into one of strength.

Settler leaders acted as allies of their government no more than they were partners of the Korean bourgeois elites, whose behavior exhibited similar pragmatism. When working together through local chambers of commerce or nationwide industrial campaigns, Korean capitalists gen-

145. The role of local capitalists becomes all the more relevant when considering the limited involvement of private metropolitan capital until the 1930s. Among the major *zaibatsu* interests, only Mitsubishi had since the late 1910s claimed a significant share of the corporate investment in Korea (Mizoguchi and Umemura 1988, 74–75; Peattie 1984a, 33).

erally followed the Japanese lead. Perhaps more at home in the company of colonizers than with their own countrymen, as Carter Eckert has pointed out, many Korean businessmen, especially those educated in Tokyo, accepted "the language, manners, and even many of the goals of the Japanese."[146] As historians have observed elsewhere in the colonial world, indeed, class often became a more powerful ideology of encounter than race or ethnicity.[147]

Yet at the same time, as settler leaders found time and again through their face-to-face engagements with Korean elites, class could go only so far in the age of anticolonial nationalism. At the Industrial Commission and other venues (including the bulletins of their business club), Korean capitalists, even as they stood accused of collaboration, claimed to represent their nation almost as resolutely as did their nationalist critics. And even as they were forced to act on the linguistic terrain of Japanese, they developed their own language of resistance, advocating "Korean-centeredness" at almost every occasion. If such voices of dissent remained submerged under their shared pursuit of capitalism, they came to the fore in municipal and provincial politics—another key realm in which the brokers of empire sought influence over colonial governance, in alliance as well as competition with the Korean bourgeoisie.

---

146. Eckert 1991, 230.
147. Cannadine 2002.

# SIX

## *In Search of a Political Voice*

After the onset of the Governor-General's rule, settlers and Korean elites became collaborators separated by a common ambition: to rise in a world of limited access to power, wealth, and influence.[1] Behind their outlook of submission was a tacit pact with the colonial regime. Korean elites agreed not to meddle in politics in exchange for the opportunity to take part in the benefits of capitalistic modernity. Settlers, for their part, accepted their role as junior partners to the state as a means of expanding their economic interests and ensuring their local dominance. Neither of these social compacts held for long after 1919.

As opportunities for political participation increased under Saitō's cultural rule, the brokers of empire sought a greater voice in colonial governance. However, they also faced new problems, of which the most pressing was how to maintain their dominance without inflaming Korean hostility and undermining official policy. Their usual strategy was to join hands with native bourgeois elites—a course of action rare for European residents in Africa, but quite logical for Japanese set-

1. The term "collaboration" is used most commonly to refer to a traitorous act of working for a foreign power. As I explained in Introduction (note 31), I use the term more loosely and broadly to refer to a political engagement between the colonial state and its local subjects. The latter includes settlers, who formed another group of local collaborators to the colonial state, an important point raised by Ronald Robinson (1972), but often missed by scholars of the Japanese empire.

tlers, given their political weakness relative to the colonial government.[2] Alienated from Korean society as a dependent class of "collaborators," as Abe Mitsuie observed, Korean elites were ipso facto inclined to form partnerships with their settler counterparts around shared capitalistic interests and political stakes in the colonial enterprise.[3] This dictum, for the most part, worked as Abe predicted. Not only did settler leaders and Korean elites work together to assist officials in developing the local economy or countering the threat of nationalism, as we saw in the preceding chapters; they also aligned themselves on occasion against the authoritarian structure of the colonial state.

Under the Governor-General's rule, Japanese settlers and Korean elites worked toward expanding their political rights in a kind of parallel universe. At times the settlers' efforts to overcome their marginal status in the empire, which oscillated between assimilation and autonomy vis-à-vis the metropole, intersected with the Korean struggle for equality to forge a powerful alliance against the colonial state's monopoly of power. Mutual frustration with local administration, for instance, led them to create their own space of political action outside of parastatal institutions, launching a movement for local autonomy that expanded into a joint campaign for suffrage in the metropole. As they straddled the shifting borders of colonial politics, the brokers of empire and their Korean allies steadily pushed the boundaries of their activism beyond the Governor-General's authoritarian rule.

This political alliance, however, was always an uneasy symbiosis riddled with tensions. In agitating together for political concessions, the Japanese and Korean elites found that the specific grievances of their respective communities were quite divergent. And they soon began to imagine different political futures for the peninsula, with Koreans advocating self-rule and settlers insisting on full integration of Korea into the metropole (a stance the settlers, nonetheless, often contradicted in

2. Faced with the rapid growth of nationalist activities after 1919, Japanese settlers in Korea had to eschew a kind of segregationist politics pursued stridently by the European colonists in Africa. Especially in French Senegal, German Southwest and East Africa, and British Southern Rhodesia and Kenya, settlers had significant legislative powers and control of local representative institutions, from which educated Africans were largely, if not completely, excluded (A. Roberts 1986, 34–35).

3. Abe Mitsuie to Saitō (11 November 1929).

their defense of Korea's autonomy from Tokyo). What unfolded as a result was a complex matrix of cooperation and conflict between the brokers of empire and their Korean allies, whose joint quest for citizenship simultaneously embroiled them in a protracted rivalry for local dominance, where the state became an object as well as an arbiter of contestation.

## *Limits of Settler Political Power*

During the first decade of Japanese rule, the Government-General largely succeeded in keeping colonial policy beyond the reach of public criticism. Outside of the fringe of collaborators who worked for various levels of colonial bureaucracy, the political life of Koreans, along with the vernacular press, all but vanished from view—that is, until they erupted with cries of freedom in March 1919. Meanwhile, by ending local Japanese self-rule, the regime also produced a permanently bitter and disenfranchised class of settlers, who had meant to be pioneers but were left as struggling emigrants with little or no say in government affairs. The political meekness of Japanese settlers in Korea becomes particularly telling when compared to the status of colonists elsewhere. By this time, European residents in the British and French colonies of settlement, who had transplanted metropolitan institutions of democracy to constitute a "civil society" separate from the native majority, had gained a significant measure of local representation or were well on their way to self-government.[4] No such developments ever occurred in colonial Korea. Rather than recognize settlers' "legitimate interest" in the formulation of public policy, and debate *to what extent* political power should be delegated to them, as the local administrators in these European colonies did, the issue for the Government-General of Korea was whether or not it should be granted to them at all.[5] And the answer was resoundingly negative: the colonial governor told his subjects to steer clear of politics altogether. Although Saitō, and to a lesser extent his predecessors in the 1910s, valued the ostensible expertise of long-time settlers as we have seen, the authorities allowed them no formal institu-

4. Evans et al. 2003, 8; Ruedy 2005, 86–87. In Algeria, self-rule was limited to municipal governments, as it was in the Four Communes of Senegal.

5. Berman 1990, 137.

tional channels such as legislative councils through which they could leverage official policy. Two considerations dictated this decision: the regime's desire to centralize all authority in the Government-General, and the imperative of forestalling Korean demands for self-rule.

The first Governor-General, Terauchi Masatake, set the tone by abolishing the system of residents' associations in 1914, leaving only matters of education in settlers' hands.[6] In their place, a system of multiethnic city councils (*fukyōgikai*) was installed in twelve cities (J. *fu*; K. *pu*), new municipal administrative units created that year. For local Japanese residents who had managed their communities for decades before Terauchi's arrival, city councils were far from sufficient alternatives. The main duty of each council as prescribed by the state was to discuss selected matters related to municipal governance—the enactment, revision, and abolition of municipal ordinances; the creation of an estimated budget; and the issuance of municipal bonds—all at the behest of the mayor who chaired each council.[7] Since its authority was merely advisory, it is doubtful the council proceedings had any significant impact on municipal administrators. Typically filled with handpicked Japanese and Korean elites, who were mostly capitalists and landlords favorably disposed to Japanese rule, the city councils were designed less to aid the mayor and his staff than to appease local men of influence by allowing them a role on the margins of colonial politics.[8] Although many incumbent members of the residents' associations were appointed to the new city councils, such measures of accommodation did little to endear the colonial state to settler leaders who grudgingly split their seats with Korean elites.

Bereft of meaningful institutions for local representation, the brokers of empire deployed a variety of informal methods to transmit their voices to the authorities. In addition to utilizing the press and the chambers of commerce, settler leaders sent letters and petitions, made personal visits to the Governor-General, and used informal social pressures, hoping to cultivate face-to-face contact with officials, obtain their pa-

6. For more information on school boards for Japanese and Koreans, see Kang Jae-ho 2001, 227–28, 239.

7. Kang Jae-ho 2001, 151–53. Later the Government-General instituted a similar but much more restricted system of *myŏn* (town) government in October 1917 (ibid., 168–70).

8. [Chōsen Sōtokufu], "Senkyo seido no enkaku," 1929; Kim Tong-myŏng 2006, 64.

tronage, and potentially sway their opinions.[9] These overtures were reciprocated to some extent by Government-General officials, who were anxious to secure local collaboration with their policies. Even Terauchi, who had nothing but scorn for settlers, invited businessmen, journalists, and other influential civilians to the Government-General headquarters for annual dinners, end-of-year parties, and other informal gatherings. The invitees included his most vocal critics such as the journalist Shakuo Shunjō, known within the official circle as "a nuisance" who reveled in "maligning bureaucrats."[10] Shakuo later reminisced how he looked forward to these occasions: "because [the authorities] did not permit us to attack Terauchi or criticize the Governor-General's rule in newspapers and magazines, every time I was invited I would not miss this golden opportunity to candidly reel off my pent-up complaints."[11]

Opportunities for such interchange increased dramatically after 1919, becoming a signature policy of Governor-General Saitō.[12] While patronage continued to supply the basis for settler-state relations, Saitō moved cautiously to broaden the scope of local political participation in the 1920s. Making good on his intention to enlist "public opinion," and to woo local elites into his program of cultural rule, Saitō allowed the election of city councilors (hitherto appointed by the provincial governor), extended their terms of office to three years, and increased the number of seats. He also created similar elected advisory councils in "designated towns" (J. *men*; K. *myŏn*) where the proportion of Japanese residents was relatively high. Moreover, he installed advisory councils at provincial and other town levels where no such institutions had previously existed.[13] According to the recollection of Tominaga Fumikazu,

9. Similar strategies were deployed by the British settlers in Kenya (Berman 1990, 139). Needless to say, such opportunities were denied to the majority of the local population in Korea.

10. *Chōsen oyobi Manshū*, February 1916, 18–23.

11. *Chōsen oyobi Manshū*, January 1936, 6.

12. The police bureau chief and Vice Governor-General Mizuno Rentarō, the principal architect of cultural rule, also religiously attended meetings of local businessmen and journalists, not only to explain official policies but to sound out their critics. According to Shakuo Shunjō, "Korea in reality was entrusted to the discretion and skill of Mr. Mizuno" and the Vice Governor-General wielded "greater authority than Governor-General Saitō" (Shakuo 1930, 397, 433).

13. Chōsen Sōtokufu Naimukyoku 1922, 39–48.

a former bureaucrat in charge of local government affairs, the colonial authorities took these steps with a great degree of uncertainty, in the atmosphere of "extreme unrest" and "growing rebelliousness" observed among Koreans in the wake of the March First Movement.[14] These local political reforms, in other words, represented something of a bold social experiment for the new colonial regime.

After years of being denied a meaningful voice in politics, many local Japanese and Korean elites welcomed the opportunity to participate, but this experiment turned out to be a very disappointing one, indeed. The city councils, deemed most important to colonial governance,[15] continued to be filled with prominent Japanese settlers and a few upper-class and ideologically moderate Koreans. Many of the city council members already held or would soon hold other executive posts in the entire array of community institutions, from chambers of commerce and school boards, to Shinto parish organizations.[16] While the nexus of local institutions expanded, they remained more or less in the hands of the same cadre of well-heeled civilians. The ostensibly "popular" elections, moreover, were held only in cities and select towns with heavy concentrations of Japanese. Given a much higher proportion of eligible voters, settlers had a definite numerical advantage over Koreans in municipal elections; as late as the mid-1920s, only about 1.5 percent of the Korean population were eligible to vote. The colonial authorities were fully aware that by restricting voting rights to males of 25 years or older who paid more than 5 yen in annual municipal tax, a Japanese majority would be guaranteed in each of the twelve city councils.[17] In such a context, we may surmise, the interests of local settlers were prioritized over those of the more numerous Korean residents in the discussion of municipal affairs.[18] The need to place interpreters for some Korean delegates also

14. Remarks of Tominaga Fumikazu, transcribed in Gakushūin Daigaku Tōyō Bunka Kenkyūjo 2002, 241.

15. [Chōsen Sōtokufu], "Senkyo seido," 1929.

16. For a roster of the Seoul City Council members, see *Chōsen oyobi Manshū*, November 1920, 56.

17. [Chōsen Sōtokufu], "Senkyo seido," 1929; Gakushūin Daigaku Tōyō Bunka Kenkyūjo 2002, 252–54.

18. The tendency of settlers to "deliberate and decide among themselves without consulting Koreans" was one of the very reasons cited by Chŏn Sŏng-uk to run for the Seoul City Council in 1920 (Ki 2007, 10). The domination of Japanese settlers was particularly

appears to have given the Japanese delegates a natural linguistic advantage in debates and limited the scope of Korean participation from the floor.

Yet against these odds, the elected Korean representatives still managed to prevent settlers from turning these councils completely into instruments of their own interests. A comparison with colonial Africa again helps to illustrate this point. In the civil communes where European residents concentrated in Algeria, for instance, after 1884 a small number of propertied Muslim males and office holders could elect the Muslim members of the municipal councils, initially limited to a quarter and later raised to a third of the representation. European settlers, who enjoyed the exclusive right to elect mayors, dominated these councils, which "collected and disposed of tax revenues extracted overwhelmingly from the native majorities." In addition, they allocated their own budget through the *Délégations financières*, also placed under European control.[19] In the case of city councils in Korea, the relative representation of settlers and native inhabitants, and the electoral body, were similarly skewed in the former's favor, but the ratio became less unequal over time. Consider the results for the first three elections of 1920, 1923, and 1926. Although Japanese dominated seats in all twelve city councils, more Koreans than Japanese voted in each of the two large cities of Seoul and P'yŏngyang.[20] In the first elections of 1920, Koreans claimed fully a quarter of the 446 elected or appointed posts on town, city, and provincial councils. That year in Seoul, 19 Japanese and 11 Koreans won seats in the city council, but three years later Koreans and Japanese split the 30 seats equally, and the number of qualified voters almost doubled from 4,773 (J. 2,147 and K. 2,626) to 9,297 (J. 4,356 and K. 4,941).[21] In provincial councils, moreover, it was the Koreans who enjoyed a numerical advantage. Though they were not popularly elected, the principle of proportional representation allowed Koreans to occupy more than half the seats on all provincial councils for the entire colonial period.[22]

---

pronounced in the membership and the administration of the Pusan City Council in the 1920s. See Hong Sun-gwŏn 2006a.

19. Ruedy 2005, 86–87, 111.

20. [Chōsen Sōtokufu], "Senkyo seido," 1929.

21. Ibid.; *Chōsen oyobi Manshū*, November, 56.

22. Kasuya 1992, 141.

These statistics suggest that a politically active and expanding body of Koreans existed alongside the vociferous settlers, and that even a few honorary and advisory seats on the local advisory councils were worth competing for if the alternative might be total exclusion. Competition for seats, indeed, intensified over the course of the decade—a trend one local magazine interpreted as "a sign of increasing Korean self-awareness and their rising sentiment of competing against, even overwhelming, the Japanese."[23] Throughout the 1920s, close to 80 percent of eligible Koreans and 85 percent of eligible Japanese settlers voted, indicating that Saitō's reforms created sustained interest in local politics, at least in the upper crust of colonial society.[24]

But a more prohibitive factor militated against settlers' effort to bring local councils fully under their control: that they were ultimately superseded by state authority. This was the case even for city councils in which settlers were expected to exert the greatest amount of influence. In the early 1920s, indeed, no sooner had the newly elected members of city councils begun their tenure than they found themselves shackled by various built-in constraints on their power.[25] They were allowed to have discussions with the mayor and ask him questions regarding affairs of municipal governance such as the budget and municipal bylaws, but their decisions were not binding. Their supposed "autonomy" was also curtailed by a web of restrictions and easily overridden by the legislative power of the mayor who presided over each council.[26] Elections, in short, did little to expand civilian leverage over municipal governance. Such limitations, combined with the infrequency of assemblies, made it next to impossible for settlers to mold local politics in their interests.

If the elected representatives of city councils felt excluded from local governance, the appointed members of provincial councils fared far

---

23. *Chōsen oyobi Manshū*, November 1923, 80; and December 1923, 55.

24. Enthusiasm for politics was also evinced by the rising number of bribes and voter fraud, which compelled the police to issue regulations to monitor electoral campaigns (*Chōsen oyobi Manshū*, April 1931, 82).

25. Kojō Kandō, "Shinshisei ni taishite," *Chōsen* (Chōsen Sōtokufu), October 1921, 66–69.

26. Kasuya 1992, 133–34; Gakushūin Daigaku Tōyō Bunka Kenkyūjo 2002, 253.

Fig. 11 Scene of a provincial council (North Kyŏngsang province)
SOURCE: Ōzorasha 2008, 40. Used by permission of Ōzorasha.

worse. Still aggrieved at the dissolution of residents' associations he had once led in Seoul, Kojō Kandō (1858–1934) complained that the Kyŏggi Provincial Council he recently attended "felt like a floor for reporting on the conditions of the province to some information bureau" rather than a forum for the authorities to consult civilian opinions.[27] Although many Korean delegates welcomed the new system, some echoed Kojō's complaint that their powers were token. So Byŏng-cho of the North Kyŏngsang Provincial Council alerted the authorities to Korea's "long history" of political debate, and Kang Tong-ŭi of the North Ch'ŏlla Provincial Council called for a more complete system of "local self-government" (*chihō jichi*).[28] Watanabe Toyohiko, a colonial bureaucrat in charge of local government affairs, responded with the usual platitudes: "To demand a complete system of local autonomy where the people had hitherto no experience or training in self-rule . . . would be to ignore the order of things." Much progress, he insisted, had been made in the

27. Kojō Kandō, "Shinshisei ni taishite," *Chōsen* (Chōsen Sōtokufu), October 1921, 69.

28. So Byŏng-cho, "Shōsōron wa nakarazu," and Kang Tong-ŭi, "Kanzen naru chihō jichi no jitsugen o nozomu," in *Chōsen* (Chōsen Sōtokufu), October 1921, 222, 248–49.

system of local government—so much so that it was "almost equivalent to [a system of] legislative councils."[29]

### *Lobbying for Greater Local Autonomy*

Feeling increasingly frustrated with the limits on their power, Japanese settlers and Korean elites began to align themselves against the authoritarian power of the colonial state. In forging such an alliance, they took their discontent to another level: they began to demand not only greater local autonomy in Korea, but also a voice in imperial politics in Tokyo. The first to raise their voice were members of the Seoul City Council, where some key brokers of empire ensconced themselves. They had already begun holding their own "tea forum" (*sawakai*) before each council was convened to discuss matters on municipal governance—itself a gesture of defiance to the mayor. The newly elected members in 1923 carried on this tradition of meeting informally among themselves and began to call for greater political freedom, in the wake of a run-in with the mayor over a local stock-raising company at the 1924 city council. Feeling snubbed by a mayor who could run roughshod over the council as he saw fit, the civilian representatives concluded that as long as they remained an advisory body, it would be impossible to bring the "popular will" to bear on the "despotic" municipal government.[30] Their frustration led them to contemplate the creation of a peninsula-wide forum where civilian leaders could freely exchange opinions on matters related to Korea as a whole, outside the strictures of local bureaucracy.

This vision culminated in the first ever attempt to assemble civilian leaders from all twelve cities in Seoul in June 1924.[31] The meeting brought together over 100 delegates, mainly businessmen, who served on city councils, chambers of commerce, and school boards in their cities. Because civilians who served on these community institutions were referred to as "public officials" (*kōshokusha*), their meeting was christened the Zen-Sen Kōshokusha Taikai (All-Korea Public Officials' Convention; hereafter Public Officials' Convention), held every year

---

29. Watanabe Toyohiko, "Jisshi no ato ni kaerimite," in ibid., 133–34.
30. *Tonga ilbo*, 6 April 1924; Keijō Honmachi Keisatsu Shochō (29 May 1924).
31. Keishō Hokudō Keisatsubu [Pak Chung-yang] 1934, 53.

until 1930.[32] The Public Officials' Convention functioned as a rare forum where civilian elites discussed a combustible mix of issues bearing on colonial governance, from Korean education and industry to local autonomy, and voted on a series of proposals to be submitted to the authorities as a collective voice of "the people." But beyond a shared desire to assert a democratic check on the colonial government, no consensus existed on the ultimate goal of the convention, even among its Japanese founders. Some treated the convention as a training ground for self-rule in the spirit of "a Korean assembly," and others saw it "as a strategy to make the mainland recognize Korea's power," with an eye toward sending their spokesmen to the Imperial Diet in Tokyo.[33] This difference of opinion, as we will see, reflected an increasingly divisive debate on the political fate of Korea that would engulf the wider reading public.

Among the topics on the agenda, of utmost concern to the settler leaders was the extension of metropolitan suffrage to residents of Korea. As we saw in Chapter 2, settlers, by virtue of their overseas residence, automatically lost their right to vote (*senkyoken*) in national elections for the imperial assembly. That right was based on residence (*zokuchi hō*) rather than ethnicity (*zokujin hō*) in Japan, where until 1925 the franchise remained a privilege conferred on men of property. Because their family registers (*koseki*) were located in Japan, however, settlers could still run for office (*hisenkyoken*) from their place of registry, a right governed by household registration not by residence. And some ambitious settlers did run from their home prefectures, seeking a direct route into the metropolitan assembly as an indirect way to participate in colonial politics. One of the few who proved successful was Makiyama Kōzō, a newspaper tycoon who pocketed enormous wealth from Korea's tungsten mines during World War I. While serving on the Seoul Residents' Association just prior to its dissolution, Makiyama launched the magazine *Chōsen kōron* in 1913; he later took over the management of a daily, the *Chōsen shinbun*, in 1920. Makiyama ran from his home island of Iki in Nagasaki as a candidate from the Seiyūkai, the ruling conservative party in Japan. After he was first elected to the House of Representatives in

32. Yi Sŭng-yŏp 2003, 109.

33. Keijō Honmachi Keisatsu Shochō (29 May 1924): 769–71.

1917, Makiyama won six consecutive elections, in the course of which he also switched his party affiliation to the rival Minseitō. His career continued to blossom into the 1930s, when he was appointed parliamentary secretary (*seimu jikan*) under Prime Minister Saitō Makoto.[34]

Another Diet member who entered the world of party politics after amassing some wealth in Korea was Matsuyama Tsunejirō (1884–1961). A native of Wakayama and a Christian convert, Matsuyama arrived in Korea as a seasoned engineer in 1915. Along with the contractor Watanabe Sadaichirō (mentioned in Chapter 5), he founded an irrigation and electricity works company in Hwanghae province in 1918. While continuing his business ventures in Korea, Matsuyama ran for the Diet as a Seiyūkai candidate from Hyōgo prefecture in 1920, defeating his Kenseikai opponent to be elected to the House of Representatives for the first time. From 1924 onward, Matsuyama ran from his home prefecture of Wakayama and served 20-odd years in the Diet until his retirement in 1946.[35] Watanabe himself contemplated running, and a few other settlers gave it a try, but most were not successful.[36] Without the wealth and stature of Makiyama, the difficulty of getting elected while living abroad is not hard to imagine.

The presence of a few settler spokesmen like Makiyama and other "Korea hands" in the metropolitan assembly, usually former settlers or business owners in Korea,[37] made a difference, just as it most certainly did for the European settlers in Kenya[38] and for the *colons* in Algeria.[39] The "Korea hands" in the Diet ensured, first of all, that settler welfare and general affairs of the peninsula were not overlooked by metropolitan political leaders. In addition to providing a valuable internal channel

---

34. Chōsen Shinbunsha 1935, 431–32.

35. Nakamura Shiryō 1926, 285.

36. *Chōsen kōron*, February 1928, 2.15–2.17.

37. They included Yamamichi Jōichi (Minseitō), Adachi Kenzō (Minseitō), and Nakano Seigō (Kenseikai/Minseitō) and former colonial bureaucrats such as Takeuchi Tomojirō (Seiyūkai). *Chōsen kōron*, February 1928, 2.15–2.17. Also see *Chōsen kōron*, September 1925, 89–92, for a list of Diet members who used to work in Korea.

38. Their "fathers, brothers, and uncles" along with their most prominent leader, Lord Delamere, sat in the House of Lords in the British parliament (Elkins 2005, 11).

39. Settler deputies often prevailed over metropolitan politicians and successfully blocked reform concessions to the natives in parliamentary sessions focused on the Algeria question (Ruedy 2005, 111).

through which settler leaders could generate support for their cause, Makiyama and other assemblymen sympathetic to overseas affairs gave voice to these settlers' concerns in debates on the Diet floor. At the fortieth imperial assembly in 1918, for instance, Makiyama and his colleagues confronted Vice Governor-General Yamagata Isaburō by upbraiding the colonial government for "ignoring the people's local conditions" and "relying solely on extremely misleading reports made by low-ranking provincial officials to establish policies." Makiyama grilled another colonial official regarding his recent appointment of Korean executives for the Chōsen Industrial Bank. Noting how Koreans dominated the executive boards of other colonial agricultural and industrial banks, he compelled the official to pledge to "appoint as many Japanese in the future as possible."[40] By way of such provocative questioning, the "Korea hands" used the metropolitan assembly to directly address settler concerns and to critique official policies in a host of areas, from the "incomplete railway" construction to "Korean exchange students and spies" in Japan.

Given the low likelihood of success in running from overseas, however, a more pragmatic way for settlers to influence imperial politics was to send their own representatives to the Diet—hence their demand for extending the metropolitan legislature to the peninsula. Japanese settlers, who dominated the first Public Officials' Convention, pushed this issue to the center of discussion. Some serious disagreements emerged among the Japanese delegates, but most of them endorsed the idea of extending suffrage to Korea unambiguously. Watanabe Sadaichirō and Ōmura Momozō, both organizers of the convention, saw suffrage as the key to promoting Korea's industrial development, the central ongoing agenda of the Seoul Chamber of Commerce. Suffrage in their view would provide a means of increasing Korea's bargaining power with Tokyo and securing funds needed for its industrial projects, especially railway construction. Establishing connections to metropolitan political parties, they hoped, would solve Korea's chronic financial shortage, but the failure to gain suffrage would oblige Korea to "continue to play the role of beggar to the central government."[41]

40. *Chōsen kōron*, July 1918, 43–46.
41. Keijō Honmachi Keisatsu Shochō (15 June 1924): 662–63, and (16 June 1924).

The settlers' call for suffrage also embodied a longer-standing desire to regain their local autonomy, denied by Terauchi a decade earlier. Speaking on behalf of the pioneers, Takahashi Shōnosuke, who had once headed the abolished residents' association in Seoul, bitterly recalled how Terauchi forcibly ended settler self-government as part of his design to bring Korea under his control and to make Korea financially independent from Japan. Terauchi's insistence on fiscal self-sufficiency, Takahashi contended, had lessened the metropolitan commitment to Korea, ironically forcing its residents to travel all the way to Tokyo to lobby for subsidies every year. Takahashi thus urged public officials, in conjunction with pressing for suffrage, to bolster the industrial campaign led by the chambers of commerce, in order to ensure a continuous flow of metropolitan capital into the peninsula.[42]

For Takahashi and other brokers of empire, then, their demand for autonomy lay "not in its creation but in its recovery."[43] It was in this vein that the likeminded Japanese public officials and residents of Seoul, joined by their Korean associates, founded the Kōshi Club two months after the first Public Officials' Convention. The Kōshi Club was created as the convention's "standing lobby" to press for suffrage in Tokyo. Although it had the appearance of a joint Japanese-Korean organization, the Kōshi Club at its core was a cadre of old-time settlers dominated by the "party of twenty" (*nijūnen-tō*), who had lived in Korea for at least two decades. (Their ranks included Ōgaki Takeo, known by then as one of the most influential settler "elders" [*chōrō*] in Seoul.) Apart from sharing seats on various local councils, the club's other Japanese leaders and their Korean colleagues also served on the executive board of the Dōminkai (see Chapter 3).[44] The overlap in their personnel attests to the intimate ideological link between the two organizations, emblems

---

42. Keijō Honmachi Keisatsu Shochō (15 June 1924): 665–67.

43. Fujimura 1927a, 31.

44. Chōsen Sōtokufu Keimukyoku Hoanka 1927, pt. 5, 6, 8; Keishō Hokudō Keisatsubu 1934, 54. The Japanese executives included Ōmura Momozō (1872–?), Takahashi Shōnosuke (1864–?), Narimatsu Midori (1880–?), Koezuka Shōta (1866–?), and Terao Mōzaburō (1870–?); the Korean executives included Cho Pyŏng-sang (1891–?), Sin Ŭnghŭi (1859–1928), and Chŏn Sŏng-uk (1877–?). In late 1926, the club had 40 Japanese and 12 Korean members. The membership increased to 64 a year later.

of ethnic harmony that respectively embraced the colonial ideal of *naisen yūwa* and the political principle of *naichi enchō*.

Although the Kōshi Club's political orientation was avowedly moderate, the colonial police watched its activities with "utmost caution."[45] The club's leaders began by volunteering as something of an outside policy consultant. Viewing the management of Korea as a "common responsibility of officials and civilians," the Kōshi Club tendered various unsolicited "proposals" and "advice" to the colonial authorities; in August 1924, for instance, it offered up to the Vice Governor-General a list of proposals for streamlining the bureaucracy and restructuring its finances.[46] Later that year, the Kōshi Club submitted a more explicit request: to revise the current electoral laws so as to allow some residents of Korea to vote in the Diet elections.[47]

Echoing the delegates at the first Public Officials' Convention, the Kōshi Club's petition reflected the hope of local elites that suffrage would empower them to negotiate metropolitan subsidies and loans for Korea's industrial projects, without having to rely on colonial bureaucrats.[48] It was no coincidence that Watanabe Sadaichirō became head of the Seoul Chamber (and the Korean Federation of Chambers of Commerce) the summer when the Kōshi Club came into being. From the outset, the leaders of the Kōshi Club and the Korea Federation carefully coordinated their petition movements for industry and for suffrage. Given the worrisome social instability on the peninsula, the brokers of empire had to deploy subtle strategies to advance their economic privilege and political influence. This was particularly so in the aftermath of the Great Kantō Earthquake, which not only curtailed the promised official subsidies for Korea's infrastructure projects but rekindled Korean antipathy toward Japanese. Such concerns prompted Matsuyama Tsunejirō to circulate a pamphlet among fellow Diet members a few months later, proposing the extension of suffrage to Korea as "the only

45. Keishō Hokudō Keisatsubu 1934, 53.

46. Keijō Chihō Hōin Kenjisei, Kakibara Takurō (16 September 1924): 111. The petition was based on the "Shingensho" passed on 19 August. See Keijō Honmachi Keisatsu Shochō (19 August 1924).

47. Chōsen Sōtokufu Keimukyoku Hoanka 1927, pt. 5, 6; Keijō Honmachi Keisatsu Shochō (15 November 1924): 491–93.

48. Keijō Honmachi Keisatsu Shochō (29 May 1924).

accommodative [*kyōchōteki*] solution" to the rise of anti-Japanese hostility stoked by the post-quake tragedy, which "Korea's independence faction exploited to their advantage."[49] The settler leaders thus had all the more reason to cloak their recovery of lost subsidies and lost "rights" to self-government in terms of a broad "demand of the people,"[50] though such a fiction fooled no outside Korean observer.[51]

In early 1925, the year that universal male suffrage went into effect in Japan, the Kōshi Club leaders launched a vigorous petition drive in Tokyo. Their demands were two-fold: 1) "the revision of the Law of the House of Peers to grant the same rights enjoyed by Japanese aristocrats to the Korean aristocracy" and "to open up a way for residents of Korea to be appointed to the House of Peers by imperial decree"; and 2) the extension of the Election Law of the House of Representatives to Seoul, Pusan, Taegu, and P'yŏngyang, and the enactment of laws concerning the qualifications for voting and the eligibility for election "suitable to Korea's condition." These items constituted the core of the Kōshi Club's petition,[52] which was signed by Ōgaki Takeo and 56 other representatives and formally submitted by Matsuyama Tsunejirō to the Diet in February 1927—a time when the Kenseikai, which championed expanded suffrage, held control of the cabinet. Guided by a sense of urgency and opportunity, the Kōshi Club's petition represented an effort to present colonial suffrage as a solution to the new crisis on the periphery and place the issue on the metropolitan agenda precisely when the boundaries of participation were being broadened at home. Like industry, it suggested, suffrage would not only advance Japan's national and colonial interests, but would also fulfill the shared desire of settlers and Koreans.

In lobbying for suffrage, the Kōshi Club cooperated with a group of Korean elites who, a few years ahead of settlers, launched their own campaign through the Kungmin Hyŏphoe (People's Association). This flagship organization was run by a small circle of "pro-Japanese" Ko-

---

49. Matsuyama 1924.

50. Watanabe Sadaichirō, "Kaigisho no jigyō ni tsuite," *CKZ* 121 (January 1926): 1–8.

51. In response to the passage of a suffrage proposal at the Public Officials' Convention, the *Tonga ilbo* argued that "this is not a demand of us ordinary people, but one merely 'disguised as a voluntary demand'" (18 June 1924).

52. Ōgaki et al. 1927; Chōsen Sōtokufu Keimukyoku Hoanka 1927, pt. 5, pp. 6–7.

reans: bureaucrats, aristocrats, entrepreneurs, and members of the Central Council who had moved in lockstep with the Japanese since annexation.[53] Under the banner of "New Japanism," coined by its first president Min Wŏn-sik (1887–1921),[54] the Kungmin Hyŏphoe called for full implementation of *naichi enchō*, first and foremost by extending metropolitan suffrage to Korea. As early as February 1921, Min Wŏn-sik had personally traveled to Tokyo to ask Diet members to support Korean suffrage. He did so at a heavy price; Min was assassinated by a nationalistic youth only a year after the group's birth.[55] Min's petition was adopted by the House of Representatives but never acted upon, with the government reasoning that it was "premature" to extend suffrage to Korea.[56] Almost every year, the Kungmin Hyŏphoe leaders submitted more or less the same petition, which was introduced and sponsored by Seiyūkai members like Matsuyama Tsunejirō and Makiyama Kōzō, the "Korea hands" who advocated the policy of *naichi enchō*.[57]

Although the parallel campaigns for suffrage led by settlers and Korean elites ultimately merged into one movement in the 1930s,[58] some differences still existed between the two. Whereas the settlers saw the granting of suffrage to Koreans as a useful strategy of accommodation, the Korean leaders considered it a fundamental matter of obtaining full recognition as Japanese citizens (*kokumin*). The current government had failed to live up to the ideal of *isshi dōjin* (administrative neutrality), the Kungmin Hyŏphoe leaders complained, lamenting that "while born as equal children of the emperor, the Korean people alone are banned from national politics as if remnants of a ruined country." Their petition assumed a tone of urgency in 1925, when universal male suffrage in Japan was about to go into effect. "To meet the ardent desire of

53. The organization at one point embraced over 10,000 members, though it also became one of the most reviled collaborators in the Korean public (Asano and Matsuda 2004, 368). For more details on the Kungmin Hyŏphoe's activities in the 1920s, see Kokumin Kyōkai [Kungmin Hyŏphoe] Sendenbu 1931.

54. Min Wŏn-sik 1919, 123–25. Min retired from his post as the county magistrate (*kunsu*) of Koyang county in order to devote himself to the "New Japan movement" under Maruyama's direction (Maruyama 1955, 66–67).

55. *Tonga ilbo*, 21 February 1921; and 2 March 1921.

56. *Ōsaka Asahi shinbun*, 27 March 1929.

57. Keishō Hokudo Keisatsubu 1934, 52–53.

58. Asano and Matsuda 2004, 400–401.

the Korean populace on this occasion would be most appropriate," lest continued inequity exacerbate the "mounting discontent of the 20 million people and the unmitigated confusion of thought."[59] In calling for *naichi enchō*, the Korean leaders essentially championed a vision of assimilation close to that of Hara Takashi—the gradual extension of political and other citizenship rights to the colony—but demanded these rights immediately, claiming that the Korean people were more than ready to participate in national politics as self-conscious "members of the state [*kokka*]." The Kungmin Hyŏphoe thus prodded the Japanese government to take its policy of *naichi enchō* to its logical conclusion, going well beyond the Kōshi Club leaders (who envisioned only controlled elections in four cities without specifying the electorate).[60]

The Kungmin Hyŏphoe's pretensions to represent the voices of the people in the language of *naichi enchō* drew fire from the vernacular press. When the organization submitted its petition to the Japanese government for the third time in 1924, the *Tonga ilbo* accused its members of committing a "crime" against their own *minjok*, driven by "an illusion that continually obstructs our nation's effort to unite."[61] But the goals of these "pro-Japanese" elites and their nationalist detractors were not as far apart as the vernacular press made them out to be. Even as they collided viciously over strategy, as the historian Matsuda Toshihiko has pointed out, both sought "national rights" within the colonial system rather than the right to secede from it, out of shared conviction that the fundamental priority was self-strengthening. "In order to nurture the practical ability to compete with advanced countries in the future," the Kungmin Hyŏphoe argued, "the most urgent task [for Korea] is to promote education, nurture intellectual power, encourage industry, and advance wealth." Suffrage was only part of this larger call for Korean self-strengthening, which echoed the approach of moderate nationalists.[62] As

59. Quoted in Abe Kaoru 1925, 97–98, 101.

60. Kim Tong-myŏng 2006, 128–36, 415–17; *Ōsaka Asahi shinbun*, 21 February 1929.

61. *Tonga ilbo*, 28 June 1924.

62. Quoted in Asano and Matsuda 2004, 379–80. In articulating their opposition to socialism and communism, Matsuda further notes, the Kungmin Hyŏphoe balanced its embrace of modernism (*kindai shijōshugi*) with a Confucian emphasis on "old morality" (such as order and restraint)—a neo-traditional approach to modernity strongly reminiscent of the nationalist Right.

with the case of the promotion of Korean industry, the Korean suffrage campaign is notable not so much for its obvious overlap with the settler counterpart as its less often acknowledged links with the nationalist opponents. Indeed, collaborators and resistors "could mobilize the same arguments for national self-strengthening to construct opposing ideologies,"[63] as the historian Timothy Brook has similarly observed in the context of occupied China. For the same reason, one might add, their confrontation was driven by mutual weakness: both parties claimed to speak for a nation they could not fully represent.

This link became apparent enough to bother some settler conservatives, making collaborators and resistors blur in their eyes. Aoyagi Tsunatarō could not have better expressed their anxiety. "Since the [March First] uprising, some Korean intellectuals have recently grown imprudent due to the generosity of the imperial government and the paternalism of the Government-General, demanding suffrage, demanding self-rule, demanding internal self-government, and eagerly claiming rights as *kokumin*." To these vociferous Koreans he enjoined, "Before claiming rights, you must first cultivate character and economic power to reach the level [where you could] partake in military service, and nurture the concept of national duty toward the empire."[64] Regardless of class or ideological orientation, he argued, Koreans had yet to earn the status of citizens by completing their "unfinished" tasks of self-strengthening and imperial subjecthood.[65]

## *Between Suffrage and Self-Rule*

Although Aoyagi endorsed the Kōshi Club's petition, Japanese settlers were by no means united on the issue of suffrage. Outside of a circle of public officials, the most enthusiastic advocates of suffrage were found among journalists such as Abe Kaoru, who came to Korea at the height of democratic ferment in Japan in the late 1910s. Rather than immediately extend suffrage to all of Korea as the Kungmin Hyŏphoe de-

63. Brook 2000, 162.

64. Aoyagi 1923, 216–20.

65. The KRA, led by Aoyagi, expressed support for the Kōshi Club's petition on the basis of the policy of *naichi enchō* (Chōsen Kenkyūkai 1932, 44, 48–49). But, as we saw in Chapter 4, Aoyagi would later change his position on the issue of Korean political participation.

manded, Abe argued that the election law to the lower house should be first extended to cities where Koreans had "frequent contact with Japanese." But Abe called, first of all, for appointing to the House of Peers only Korean elites like "Yi Wan-yong and the deceased Song Pyŏng-jun [who] are of a totally different caliber from the senile Japanese in the Kizokuin [Peerage] or the Sūmitsuin [Privy Council]." Sending such Korean delegates would not only "serve as a kind of stimulant to the sleepy Peerage" and revitalize the dormant half of the Diet; it would prevent further radicalization of Korean thought. Echoing the pamphlet circulated by Matsuyama Tsunejirō—and the broader rationale behind the 1925 passage of universal male suffrage in Japan—Abe argued that "it would be most safe" to allow Koreans to "openly battle their subversive [*futei*] views on the assembly floor" rather than foment clandestine dissent.[66]

Other settlers did not endorse the Kōshi Club as wholeheartedly as Abe did. Immediate resistance to the club's suffrage campaign, in fact, came from fellow Japanese at the Public Officials' Convention. While supportive of the idea of suffrage, not a few delegates, especially those from the cities left out of its petition, were acerbic about what they considered as the club's Seoul-centered parochialism. Some younger public officials in Seoul also did not support the campaign without demur, insisting on a broader extension of suffrage to Korea beyond the four cities.[67] The club's petition invited criticism from local Japanese opinion-makers as well. Even that long-time advocate of settler autonomy, Shakuo Shunjō, ridiculed the Kōshi Club as "a gathering of the senile" who entertained "a faint hope to embellish their last years with seats in the Imperial Diet." He correctly predicted that their demand for suffrage would not be taken seriously by Tokyo, for it "does not represent the general opinion of residents in Korea."[68]

The mixed reactions to the Kōshi Club's petition attested to the wide spectrum of Japanese opinions on suffrage, which began to appear in

66. Abe Kaoru 1925, 102–4.
67. Keijo Honmachi Keisatsu Shochō (11 June 1924): 629–33.
68. *Chosen oyobi Manshū*, March 1927, 8.

local magazine forums after settlers lost their right to self-rule.[69] Hattori Toyokichi, a member of the Seoul City Council, envisioned the eventual political absorption of Korea into Japan by abolishing the Government-General and treating Korea just like the metropolitan prefectures. Motoki Fusakichi of the Taegu City Council, by contrast, advocated greater political autonomy for Korea by empowering the Governor-General with authority "above the level of the Prime Minister" and creating "a special assembly" to install an independent legislature in Korea. A more egalitarian view was advanced by the head of the Wŏnsan Chamber of Commerce, Motooka Uichirō, who called for an elected multiethnic assembly composed of one house for Koreans and another for Japanese settlers,[70] something akin to the Algerian assembly, with separate electoral colleges for French and non-French voters.[71] There was even a proposal for merging Taiwan and Korea into a unified colonial assembly.[72] Unlike the Kōshi Club leaders, many settlers were willing to consider possibilities other than an overseas extension of the metropolitan legislature, even the idea of Korean self-rule. This was "a huge stride" from Terauchi's times, as former Governor-General bureaucrat Hozumi Shinrokurō (1889–1970) later reflected, a sign that "the Japanese during Mr. Saitō's era gradually began to understand Korean nationalistic consciousness."[73]

In the course of the 1920s, settlers' opinions on suffrage gradually crystallized into two camps. While many, like the Kōshi Club leaders, argued for sending Korea's representatives to the imperial assembly on the basis of *naichi enchō*, others argued for the creation of a separate Korean assembly, whether out of concern to avoid sending colonial rebels into the Diet, or out of respect for the political maturity and cultural unique-

69. Local discourse on suffrage occasionally consulted foreign examples such as French Algeria and Britain's relationship to Ireland. For instance, see Akiyama Masanosuke, "Chōsen to kenpō," *Chōsen oyobi Manshū*, January 1916, 33–35.

70. *Chōsen kōron*, September 1925, 56–58.

71. Instituted amid settler suspicion in 1919, the Algerian assembly "created, in effect, a kind of intermediate native citizenship" (Ruedy 2005, 112).

72. Abe Kaoru 1931, 67.

73. Interview with Hozumi Shinrokurō in Yūhō Kyōkai 1986, 37.

ness of Korea.[74] These two contrasting settler positions—assimilation versus autonomy—mirrored a similar division among Koreans between advocates of *naichi enchō* (represented by the Kungmin Hyŏphoe) and advocates of self-rule (entertained by moderate nationalists).[75] More fundamentally, it stemmed from settlers' own ambivalent political standing in the empire. A paradoxical tendency to tighten and loosen their tie with the metropole was similarly observed among the early *colons* in French Algeria,[76] but it also bespoke a unique and enduring dilemma facing Japanese settlers: how to win metropolitan citizenship rights without losing local advantage in the colony.

Interestingly, these two clashing visions of Korea's political future were rooted in discrepant understandings of Japan's historical relations with the peninsula. Advocates of Korean self-rule generally emphasized Korea's distinct history, language, and customs, often contrasting the success of the British system of self-rule with the failure of the French assimilation policy in their colonies.[77] Conversely, their critics stressed the long centuries of contact between Japan and Korea, often evoking the theory of *dōgen dōshu* (same origin, same race). One of them, Ōgaki Takeo cited the alleged Japanese colony of Mimana as a point of such contact. The "naturalization" of a prince of Silla and other Korean royal visitors to Japan during the reign of Emperor Seimu was the earliest instance of assimilation, he asserted, speculating that "probably half of the current 60 million [Japanese] are Korean descendents."[78] Among the more contemporary examples they cited, their perennial favorite was Scotland. "I would like Korea to learn not from Ireland but from Scotland," Satō Torajirō of the Dōminkai told his audience in 1926. Transposing a cache of images onto local inhabitants of the two British possessions, he contrasted the Irish—"unhappy people locked in constant quarrels" and "full of dangerous individuals"—to the "diligent,"

74. For instance, see the debate among Seoul's journalists in *Chōsen oyobi Manshū*, November 1925, 9–11, and responses to a questionnaire conducted by the *Chōsen oyobi Manshū*, published in its January 1927 issue.

75. Kim Tong-myŏng (2006) differentiates these two Korean political movements in terms of "assimilationist collaboration" and "separatist collaboration" vis-à-vis the colonial government, respectively.

76. Lustick 1985, 8–9; Ruedy 2005, 86; S. Roberts 2010, Chapters 1 and 2.

77. *Chōsen oyobi Manshū*, April 1923, 25.

78. Quoted in Abe Kaoru 1929, 119–20.

"self-reliant," and "productive" Scots—a first-hand insight Satō supposedly gained from his business dealings with Scottish entrepreneurs. "*Naichi* and Korea should be inseparable as one family like England and Scotland," he concluded, with the hope that Korea would some day "produce its own William Gladstone to guide the Japanese empire."[79]

Settler discourse became more starkly divided in the wake of one incident that rattled the colonial intelligentsia. In November 1925, Soejima Michimasa (1871–1948), the president of the *Keijō nippō*, published an article in support of Korean self-rule. Partially inspired by Lord Thomas Macaulay's work on colonial India, Soejima openly endorsed the idea of implementing a system of local autonomy ("home rule") in Korea.[80] He was not alone in advocating this idea, to be sure. Colonial theorists and critics of assimilation policy such as Yanaihara Tadao (1893–1961), and metropolitan politicians such as Shimada Saburō and Ōkawa Takichirō, similarly argued for the swift enforcement of self-rule in Korea and in Taiwan.[81] Nonetheless, for the president of a pro-government paper to publicly argue for Korean self-rule—an idea diametrically at odds with official doctrine—was quite unheard of.

Many members of the Korean intelligentsia welcomed Soejima's argument, but most settler leaders were less than enthusiastic. In fact, Soejima's article raised a furor among Japanese journalists in Seoul, many of whom turned out to be die-hard advocates of *naichi enchō*. Its appearance in what they considered a mouthpiece of the Government-General also led them to question the official stance on the cardinal administrative principle of *dōka*. Their festering suspicions compelled the colonial government to issue a public statement affirming its ongoing commitment to assimilation as policy, but it did not calm the journalists. Even after Governor-General Saitō told the journalists that Soejima's argument did not represent the viewpoint of his administration, a barrage of press attacks on the *Keijō nippō* ensued.[82] Leading the pack to Saitō's door was Ōgaki Takeo. In a critique of Korean rule he

---

79. "Shokan," in Dōminkai 1927, 10–15.

80. Soejima Michimasa, "Chōsen tōchi no konpongi," *Keijō nippō*, 26–28 November 1925, editorial.

81. Abe Kaoru 1925, 106–11. Prime Minister Katō Takaaki reportedly considered Korean suffrage "a matter of time."

82. Cho Sŏng-gu 1998, 148–50, 173.

later authored, Ōgaki chided advocates of self-rule for unknowingly advancing the cause of "recalcitrant Koreans [who] call for independence"; to treat Japanese and Koreans as separate *minzoku* and argue that Koreans should be allowed to govern themselves was, he opined, tantamount to "giving the pretext" for rejecting Japanese rule. To adopt self-rule as policy "must be absolutely avoided by an empire that had a bitter experience during protectorate rule," he added, harking back to the period of his earlier involvement, and subsequent disappointment, with the Korean reform efforts (see Chapter 2).[83]

Ōgaki's long-time colleague Shakuo Shunjō also presented a searing critique of Korean self-rule, drawing on deeper sources of settler anxiety. Shakuo worried about the settlers' status plummeting due to the simple law of demographics. Had the Koreans succeeded in implementing self-rule, he speculated, it would have brought something far worse than the Governor-General's authoritarian rule: "Koreans would bring their hatred of Japanese to bear on every aspect of politics by restricting their migration and settlement in Korea, suppressing their enterprise, and letting them all fall into depression."[84] If the state consigned settlers to a subaltern status, Korean self-rule, he prophesied, betokened nothing less than the settlers' total downfall.

In response to these critics of self-rule, a handful of settlers rushed to the defense of Soejima. Machida Kōsaku (Tenmin) of the *Minshū jiron*, a long-time advocate of self-rule for Japan's overseas territories, went so far as to argue that "*naichi enchō* is impossible to realize." And he reassured those who regarded self-rule as no different than independence by noting how Australia and Canada "still maintained their mother-child relationship" with England, which controlled their national defense. At the same time, Machida used these same examples to point out the "weakness" of the *dōgen dōshu* premise underlying the argument for assimilation, claiming that few ethnic groups (*minzoku*) bound by shared roots actually formed unified nation-states in the contemporary world.[85]

83. Ōgaki's article is summarized in Abe Kaoru 1929, 116–21.

84. *Chōsen oyobi Manshū*, January 1926, 2–9; and April 1930, 5.

85. Machida Tenmin, "Jichi hantai ronja ni ichigen su," reprinted in Abe Kaoru 1929, 122–23, 128, 130–33. Before Soejima's controversial article appeared in the *Keijō nippō*, Machida had called for "the creation of a Korean assembly based on the model of English colonies."

But the majority of settler public opinion shunned the idea of Korean self-rule. And as no amount of official reassurance could allay their doubts, the journalists' feud eventually pressured Soejima to resign his post as president of the *Keijō nippō*.

Soejima's departure may have signaled for many settlers the triumph of an argument for *naichi enchō*, but the idea of Korean self-rule increasingly gained currency among Koreans, from members of the intelligentsia like Yun Ch'iho (who found the example of Ireland "intensely interesting" to study),[86] to bourgeois nationalists and even some socialists.[87] The idea was taken up most seriously by a group of moderate nationalists in the mid-1920s, when Kim Sŏng-su, Song Chin-u, Cho Man-sik, and Ch'oe Rin (1878–?) planned the creation of the Yŏnjŏng-hoe, an institutional forum through which to launch a self-rule movement in Korea.[88] In its struggle to balance control and concession, the Government-General seems to have deliberately encouraged their movement. It was with this intent that Abe Mitsuie, Saitō's trusted advisor, from around mid-1925 approached these prominent nationalists, hoping to establish common ground between their movement and the colonial regime.[89] Abe's overtures, in the end, were to no avail. It appears that only Ch'oe Rin expressed serious interest in working with Abe, and the radicals' charges of collaboration at any rate forced the moderates to shelve the idea of a self-rule movement no sooner than they had begun to plan its launch.[90] Nonetheless, it is noteworthy that self-rule was even contemplated by the colonial authorities as one way to negotiate with nationalists and potentially win them over to the regime. This approach ran counter to the increasingly dichotomized settler view that suffrage promised—and self-rule threatened—Japanese dominance over Koreans.

---

86. Taehan Min'guk Mun'gyobu Kuksa P'yŏnch'an Wiwŏnhoe 1987, 8:10–11 (entry for 20 January 1920).

87. Keikidō Keisatsubu 1929, 290–303.

88. Keikidō Keisatsubu 1928, 76–77; Keikidō Keisatsubu 1931, 290–91; Keishō Hokudō Keisatsubu 1934, 45–46.

89. Pak Ch'an-sŭng 2007, 140–44. For more details of this movement, see Kim Tong-myŏng 2006, 299–315.

90. Cho Sŏng-gu 1998, 164–68.

## *Combat at Close Quarters*

The idea of self-rule, it turned out, gradually spread to the very Korean allies with whom the brokers of empire were agitating for suffrage. As part of a larger argument for Korean empowerment within the framework of colonial citizenship, it was added to a growing list of elite political demands including better Korean education,[91] a greater role for the Central Council, and more protection of Korean tenant farmers. Needless to say, these issues were of lesser concern to settler leaders. New fissures, as a result, emerged within the political alliance of elites in the last half of the 1920s. At the annual Public Officials' Convention and at local councils, Korean representatives pressed their agendas with sufficient intensity to interfere with the settlers' own quest for citizenship and local supremacy. And despite their control over these forums, the brokers of empire found that they could not rest assured of their dominance, for the Koreans began to turn the situation around.

The watershed came at the third Public Officials' Convention of May 1926, where, according to one police report, "the settlers' political demands were relatively slighted and [the convention] was appropriated by the Koreans instead."[92] Their "rebellion" began when a Korean delegate from P'yŏngyang, Pak Sang-hŭi, made an emergency motion by bringing forth his deleted proposal in defiance of the screening committee, which met prior to the convention to select agenda items from a pool of proposals submitted by regional public officials. He demanded the convention take up his proposal that members of the Central Council, an advisory organ composed of Korean aristocrats and former bureaucrats, should be elected by members of provincial councils instead of appointed by the colonial government.[93] In response to the Korean delegate's motion, however, a Japanese member of the screening committee and a Kōshi Club executive, Ōmura Momozō, retorted by denigrating the Central Council as "a useless relic" from Terauchi's era, of "no interest to our daily lives, whether it was popularly elected or officially

91. The use of Korean as a language of instruction and the employment of Korean principals and teachers in ordinary schools became particularly sore points of ethnic friction among the public officials (Yi Sŭng-yŏp 2003, 105–6).

92. Chōsen Sōtokufu Keimukyoku 1930c, 200–201.

93. Keijō Honmachi Keisatsu Shochō (12 May 1926): 183.

appointed."[94] Pak roared at him in anger and the convention turned into an imbroglio. Ōmura's dismissal incited another Korean delegate from P'yŏngyang, Kang Pyŏng-ok, who happened to be a member of the Central Council himself, to deliver a long sermon on the council's "mission" and its indispensable role for Japanese rule in Korea. Having "made the whole audience listen with dutiful attention," Kang introduced yet another emergency motion, this time to propose the inclusion of members of the provincial councils who had thus far been excluded from the Public Officials' Convention. This motion had nationalistic overtones, for the majority of provincial councilors were Korean, and the Koreans believed their exclusion from the convention was intentional on the part of the Japanese. Kang's motion was passed on the spot.[95]

When the fourth Public Officials' Convention was convened, a new gulf of opinion also emerged between Japanese and Korean advocates of suffrage. When one Japanese delegate argued that Koreans must first "become assimilated to Japanese" as a precondition for obtaining suffrage, Cho Pyŏng-sang and other Korean delegates insisted that the process was quite the reverse, explaining suffrage as a means of assimilating Koreans.[96] Upending the hoary Japanese refrain of duties over rights, the Korean elites demanded representation before assimilation.

These episodes were but a few among many instances of internal discord between Japanese and Korean public officials, which ultimately boiled down to the question of citizenship. Remarkably, some of the most dramatic quarrels occurred in the provincial councils, known for the docility of their appointed members. In January 1928, when the South Chŏlla Provincial Council was in session, for instance, one Japanese delegate named Yamano managed to offend his Korean colleagues by making a series of gaffes at every dinner, comparing Korean school pupils to prisoners acquiring technical skills, and dismissing the idea of building schools for Koreans as almost a futile endeavor given their "low economic level." The Korean delegates called Yamano's words "an insult to the Korean people," and one after another demanded a formal apology on the assembly floor. When Yamano obliged, this time fellow Japanese delegates rose in protest, accusing the Korean delegates

94. Ibid., 184–85.
95. Ibid., 194–95; *Keijō nippō*, 13 May 1926.
96. *Tonga ilbo*, 6 June 1927.

of violating the rules by speaking on issues outside of the council's formal agenda. They also turned angrily on the Korean governor, Sŏk Chin-hyŏng (1877–1946), for taking the side of the Korean delegates and forcing Yamano to apologize—an incident one local Japanese paper called "a memorial day of shame unforgettable to the 500,000 Japanese settler compatriots in Korea [*zaisen naichijin dōhō*]." As the resident press joined in attacking the governor, the "scene of carnage" on the assembly floor spilled over into the public, generating "an emotional problem between Japanese and Korean residents."[97]

New boldness was also observed among members of the Central Council, who met once a year at the Governor-General's behest to respond to his queries and discuss matters in secrecy. Indeed, Kang Pyŏng-ok's speech and his motion at the 1926 convention was only a facet of a broader shift in their political behavior, as demonstrated unequivocally to the new Governor-General Yamanashi Hanzō (1864–1944) who replaced Saitō briefly from late 1927 to 1929. Ahead of their annual meeting in January 1928, "the Central Council members, hitherto as subservient as kittens, flipped their conventional attitude,"[98] as a local journalist reported, and submitted to Yamanashi a petition bearing a host of demands, such as "placing a Korean *san'yokan* [councilor] in each bureau of the Government-General," "expanding the Central Council," "appointing Korean executives in special banks and corporations," and "instituting a tenancy system to prevent the outflow of farmers overseas." When the session opened, the Korean members added further requests including "the implementation of universal education and conscription," "the eradication of discrimination between Japanese and Koreans," and "the permanent appointment of a Korean to the post of governor in North P'yŏngyang province."[99] "Alarmed at the boldness" of the Central Council members (who "band as they please to make demands incommensurate with their status"), and even

97. Details on this incident are recorded in "Zenra Nandō hyōgikaiin naisenjin atsureki no tenmatsu," 381–419. For another serious confrontation between Korean provincial council members and the governor in South Kyŏngsang over the issue of Korean education, which compelled the Tokyo government to dispatch an investigation commission, see Son Chŏng-mok 1992, 227–30.

98. Abe Kaoru 1932, 170.

99. *Keijō nippō*, 15 January 1928; 12 January 1928, evening edition.

more at "Governor-General Yamanashi's generosity in patiently hearing them out," the *Keijō nippō* under a new Japanese president launched a vicious diatribe against the Korean members, dismissing almost every item of their petition as "inappropriate, even erratic," and disparaging their demand for military service as "a monkey's imitation" (*saru no monomane*).[100] The Korean members counterattacked, chiding the paper for inveighing against "the only organ that incorporates the popular will" and for hindering the goal of *naisen yūwa*.[101] Yamanashi evidently concurred. He summoned the *Keijō nippō* president and admonished him for "stirring up a controversy among Koreans" by "using disrespectful language," not to speak of leaking out the content of what was supposed to be a confidential meeting. The paper took full responsibility by issuing a statement of apology.[102]

Given the traditionally subservient character of Korea's political elites, these gestures, paired with the state's response as an arbiter who did not necessarily adjudicate on the part of settlers, were nothing short of remarkable. Rather than mere stooges of Japanese rule, the Korean elites could as well be its harshest critics, exposing the utter lack of settler awareness of Korean issues, and a loosening Japanese grip on the peninsula. In the closing years of the decade, the Public Officials' Convention increasingly morphed from a platform of political collaboration into a theater of contestation, as more radical and disturbing proposals were submitted to the screening committee from the Korean side of the aisle. The Korean public officials in Ch'ŏngjin, for instance, introduced such proposals as "the appointment of a Korean Vice Governor-General," "the protection of participants in the March First Movement," and "the establishment of a Korean legislative assembly." The settler leaders dismissed these proposals as "wild fantasies," but alarmed officers in the police bureau apparently took them seriously for "frankly displaying the psychological state of Koreans."[103]

By the close of the decade, nothing seemed to be able to hold back this tide of rebellion waged by a phalanx of feisty Korean delegates

100. *Keijō nippō*, 15 and 18 January 1928.

101. *Chōsen kōron*, February 1928, 2–8. This bickering was apparently abetted by the *Chōsen shinbun* (*Chōsen oyobi Manshū*, February 1928, 80).

102. *Keijō nippō*, 28 January 1928.

103. Chōsen Sōtokufu Keimukyoku 1930a: pt. 5, p. 3.

against the settler old guard. By 1929, what had once been dismissed as a delusion—the creation of a Korean legislature—was accepted as a formal agenda for discussion at the sixth Public Officials' Convention. The issue was brought forward by a Korean delegate from the school council in Taegu, Son Ch'i-ŭn. Much to the dismay of the Kōshi Club leaders, Son explicitly rejected the extension of metropolitan suffrage to Korea and its underlying premise of *naichi enchō*. Only a Korean legislature separate from the Imperial Diet, he insisted, would solve the prevailing problem of educated Koreans, who had become "high-class idlers" (*kōtō yūmin*) bereft of "any voice in laws concerning their own lives and property."

Japanese settler delegates opposed Son's proposal, claiming "there is no discrimination between *naichi* and *gaichi*" under the current policy. Ikeda Chōjirō, a veteran member of the Seoul City Council and a Kōshi Club executive, added, "Japanese too are suffering from economic depression." These comments raised Korean eyebrows. Ikeda's colleague in the city council, Han Man-hŭi, rushed to the defense of Son's proposal, giving the Japanese delegates a reality check. "Korea's current situation would become evident if you read Korean newspapers," said Han in a provocative tone.[104] Although "an atmosphere of conflict" between Korean and Japanese delegates compelled Son to retract his proposal in the end, such confrontation did not deter him from submitting the same proposal at the next convention held in P'yŏngyang in 1930—where after much debate it was finally passed as a resolution by the majority.[105]

What explained this "unprecedented phenomenon"? The increasing skill and assertiveness of the Korean delegates to "carry through their demands at a stretch by winning a majority"[106] attested, first of all, to the new political subjectivity of Korean elites, which was a product of their direct and deepening exchange with settler interlocutors. If the Public Officials' Convention provided another avenue through which settler leaders sought to influence colonial politics, it also brought Japanese and Korean "allies" toe to toe, allowing the latter to air their pressing concerns or long-standing grievances and negotiate their demands directly

---

104. *Keijō nippō*, 6 October 1929, evening edition; 8 October 1929.
105. *Keijo nippo*, 27–29 April 1930.
106. Chōsen Sōtokufu Keimukyoku 1930a, 56–57.

with the colonizer,[107] to wage what the historian Namiki Masato has aptly called "combat at close quarters" (*sekkinsen*).[108] As the Korean elites began to feel their concerns were at odds with those of their settler colleagues, they found themselves increasingly drawn into the shifting currents of nationalism. While the public officials absorbed the new thinking emerging from the moderates' search for self-rule, the radicals also expanded their influence by forming the first Korean Communist Party in 1925, and backing a surge of peasant and labor movements. In late 1927 the Kōshi Club leaders petitioned the authorities to be especially "vigilant" about the activity of the Sin'ganhoe, a united front of radicals and moderates,[109] and urged tighter control over the vernacular press.[110] As the assimilation campaign staggered under the nationalist assault, an acute sense of crisis also prompted the Kōshi Club, the Kungmin Hyŏphoe, the Dōminkai, and other "pro-Japanese political organizations" to close ranks in their ideological battle, while prodding the state to tighten counterinsurgency measures.[111]

---

107. The closer to the Japanese, the longer the litany of Korean grievances, according to one report from South Kyŏngsang province. Whereas ordinary Koreans of lower classes were generally "indifferent," even "amicable," toward Japanese, "those of the middle class and above constantly harbor deep hostility in their minds and utter anti-Japanese remarks behind their back." In particular, "the so-called local notables and men of influence such as members of the town [*myŏn*] councils tend to avoid interacting with Japanese," an attitude "pronounced among those who are fluent in Japanese, well-informed of the metropolitan conditions, and highly educated, especially those who have studied in Japan or used to work for government office" (Chōsen Sōtoku Kanbō, Shomubu Chōsaka 1924, 34).

108. Namiki 1993, 40. More broadly, Kim Tong-myŏng (2006) has conceptualized the dynamic of negotiation between the Government-General and the elite Korean leaders who launched political movements for suffrage and subsequently for self-rule in terms of "bargaining"—though this concept somewhat misleadingly implies that power relations between the two were equal.

109. The rise of the Sin'ganhoe signaled a potentially powerful resurgence of mass-based Korean nationalism, and in its brief existence posed a threat to Japanese settlers and their Korean allies. By 1930, the Sin'ganhoe had a network of 386 branches, which fell to the control of radicals and communists, and 76,939 members from youth groups, labor and peasant organizations, and scholarly associations (Scalapino and Lee 1972, 112).

110. Chōsen Sōtokufu Keimukyoku Hoanka 1927, pt. 5, p. 7; Chōsen Sōtokufu Keimukyoku 1930c, 237–38. Some agitated members of the Kōshi Club evidently proposed the formation of a secret organization akin to *bōryokudan* (organized crime group) "to punish [nationalists] by brute force."

111. *Chungoe ilbo*, 28 November 1927; Chōsen Sōtokufu Keimukyoku 1930c, 240.

The thrust of nationalism appears to have weighed even more heavily on the Korean public officials who staffed the lower rung of colonial bureaucracy, where the line between day-to-day administrative duties and more ideologically charged acts of "collaboration" blurred in the eyes of the public. In their increasingly untenable ideological position, many of these men at the close of the 1920s seemed quite eager to forsake the idea of assimilation in favor of self-rule. And they pressed for "Korean-centered" demands that, as the police noted, had the effect of "turning the convention to their advantage" and confounding the original design of Japanese organizers.[112] By the time the proposal for a Korean legislative assembly formally appeared on the discussion table in 1929, the Korean delegates were speaking openly of "independence thought" and explaining their stance in terms of "ethnic character" (*minzokusei*). The delegate from Taegu, for his part, defended his call for a Korean assembly by citing the words of a renowned theorist, Yamamoto Miono (1874–1941), who had recently argued for replacing Japan's policy of *naichi enchō* with that of national self-determination in its overseas possessions.[113] This kind of behavior by Korean delegates was a far cry from the earlier media portrayal of their convention as a gathering of pro-Japanese collaborators no different from the Ilchinhoe, who blatantly ignored "the popular will" and slavishly accepted *naichi enchō* at "Japanese instigation."[114]

So infectious was the idea of Korean self-rule that it appeared to spread even to the well-known "pro-Japanese" elites, as settler political watchdogs did not fail to notice. Kikuchi Kenjō, for instance, expressed consternation to Saitō about those Koreans who "scheme to obtain suffrage and limited local self-government." Even the activities of "pro-Japanese" elites in the Kungmin Hyŏphoe and the Dōminkai, in his view, had "come to resemble a nationalist movement."[115] One secret official report drafted around 1930 similarly held the allegiance of most trusted Koreans in doubt. Han Sang-nyong was quoted by the author

---

112. Keishō Hokudō Keisatsubu 1934, 53.

113. *Keijō nippō*, 8 October 1929. Yamamoto's comments come from the first roundtable conference on colonial affairs organized by the Ministry of Colonial Affairs in September 1929 (*Yomiuri shinbun*, 10 September 1929).

114. *Tonga ilbo*, 18 June 1924.

115. Kikuchi Kenjō to Saitō (September 1929).

as uttering openly anti-Japanese remarks at one dinner, proof enough to suggest that he had converted from assimilation to self-rule.[116] And the report implied his case was not isolated. The Japanese resident press also fueled suspicion of a growing number of "collaborators" consorting with nationalists and waiting to withdraw their support from a failed colonial project.[117] Nothing, of course, explicitly linked these pro-Japanese elites to nationalists trying to undermine the empire, but the Japanese were wont to throw them into the same lot. By the close of the decade, it appeared, Japanese officials and settlers alike came to believe they should beware of Koreans, be they nationalist or erstwhile "pro-Japanese"; the distinctions had become meaningless.[118]

Though increasingly fractious, local elite debates on Korea's political future had a significant collective impact on the colonial authorities. In early 1927, Saitō had his officials draft "an opinion on suffrage and local self-government by the residents of Korea"—right around the time the Kōshi Club launched its suffrage campaign in Tokyo and the proposal for a "Korean assembly" appeared at the Public Officials' Convention. Saitō's "opinion" envisioned the implementation of a complete system of self-rule by turning the local advisory councils into legislative organs, followed by the extension of limited suffrage to Korea.[119] Setting aside

---

116. "Kan Sō Ryū [Han Sang-nyong] no gendō ni kansuru ken."

117. For instance, see *Keijō shinbun*, 30 March 1930.

118. Settlers' insistence on assimilation had calcified into the most bigoted opinion, with their suspicion spreading even to colonial officials and metropolitan allies. Their sense of paranoia was not lost on the executives of the Central Korea Association who visited Seoul in June 1928. Because of the association's close ties to the Government-General, one of them recounted later, the executives were greeted by intense suspicion from the Dōminkai leaders, who "reprimanded" them for harboring sympathy with the idea of Korean self-rule—an accusation that took them by complete surprise (*Chūō Chōsen Kyōkai kaihō* 11 [September 1928]: 45). Although the association's leaders were not united on this issue, it did create a special committee to investigate the question of Korean suffrage by appointing scholars including Izumi Tetsu and Yamamoto Miono (Yi Hyŏng-sik 2007, 119–20).

119. Two handwritten documents entitled "Chōsen ni okeru sansei ni kansuru seido no hōsaku" (one has no date and another is dated 2 December 1929), a handwritten draft entitled "Chōsen ni okeru sanseiken seido no hōsaku" (n.d.), and a typed document entitled "Chōsen ni okeru sansei ni kansuru seido no hōsaku" (n.d.). Saitō asked Nakamura Toranosuke, a chief secretary of the archives and documents section of the colonial government, to draft the opinion in early 1927. Saitō made further revisions in this "opinion" in 1929 (Kang Tong-jin 1979, 365–88; Kim Tong-myŏng 2006, 439–54).

the policy of *naichi enchō*, furthermore, Saitō apparently discussed with his officials the pros and cons of creating a "Korean local assembly."[120] A confluence of factors—the tenacity of nationalism, the new assertion of public officials, and the growing limits of cultural rule that these developments exposed—compelled the Governor-General at least to contemplate the extension of suffrage to Korea, and even the possibility of a Korean assembly, as the decade drew to a close.[121]

Although neither suffrage nor self-rule materialized on Saitō's watch, a second round of local government reforms effectively empowered the existing local councils with legislative authority, a process completed by his successor in the early 1930s.[122] Around the same time, the Kōshi Club also joined former colonial bureaucrats and organizations like the Dōminkai in supporting the candidacy of a few individuals from Korea—Pak Yŏng-hyo, an aristocrat; Pak Ch'un-gŭm (1891–1973), head of the Sōaikai; and Aruga Mitsutoyo of the Chōsen Industrial Bank—who were successfully appointed or elected to the Imperial Diet in 1932.[123]

---

120. See the typed document entitled "Chōsen ni okeru sansei ni kansuru seido no hōsaku" (n.d.), 10–20; Yūhō Kyōkai 1986, 38. But should the Government-General take the idea of self-rule seriously, Abe Mitsuie also warned Saitō, it would "provoke very strong objections" from Japanese settlers, who would be certain to complicate, even impede the process of local political reform (Abe Mitsuie to Saitō, 11 November 1929).

121. The sudden dissolution of the Wakatsuki Reijirō cabinet and the new Tanaka Giichi cabinet that "did not have any room to discuss" the issue of Korean suffrage prevented Saitō from formally submitting his "opinion" to the metropolitan government (Kang Jae-ho 2001, 201). Several scholars (Kang Tong-jin 1979; Pak Ch'an-sŭng 1992; Kim Tong-myŏng 2006) have variously explained how the Government-General, increasingly aware of its own limits, shifted its policy orientation from assimilation to the idea of Korean self-rule (as a "bargaining point" or as a compromise with the nationalists) in the late 1920s. Matsuda Toshihiko (2004), by contrast, is skeptical of their assertion that the Government-General decisively leaned toward self-rule. Official attention ultimately did not extend beyond the level of discourse to become an actual policy for implementation, and the metropolitan government and the Government-General outwardly continued to maintain a stance of opposition, reasoning suffrage was "premature" in light of Koreans' "low *mindo.*"

122. City assemblies (J. *fukai*; K. *puhoe*) and town assemblies (J. *yūkai*; K. *ŭmhoe*) came into operation in 1931, and provincial assemblies (J. *dōkai*; K. *tonghoe*) in 1933 (Gakushūin Daigaku Tōyō Bunka Kenkyūjo 2002, 248*n*16).

123. Pak Yŏng-hyo was appointed to the House of Peers and Pak Ch'un-gŭm and Aruga elected to the House of Representatives in 1932, the year when Saitō Makoto became prime minister (*Dōminkai kaihō* [1 December 1932–15 February 1933]: 4–5; *Chōsen kōron*, July 1939, 4). The elected Pak Ch'un-gŭm, in return, aided the flagging suffrage

These outcomes were due not least to the decade-long campaign for political rights launched by settlers in alliance with Korean elites—and their vibrant debates that marked the last years of the 1920s.

## *In Defense of Korea's Autonomy from the Metropole*

While they sought to expand their voice to Tokyo, the brokers of empire and their Korean colleagues also aligned themselves against metropolitan incursion into colonial politics. In April 1929, the Japanese government proclaimed its intention to create a cabinet-level Ministry of Colonization (Takushokushō) to bring the colonial governments in five overseas territories including Korea under its uniform control. The idea had already emerged around 1920, and a Bureau of Colonial Affairs (Takushokukyoku) had been set up as an auxiliary organ to the cabinet in late 1925.[124] But it was the Seiyūkai cabinet under Prime Minister Tanaka Giichi (1864–1929) that hammered out a specific plan to create a central organ vested with full authority to manage the administrative affairs of all overseas possessions, while simultaneously making a revision in the organic regulations (*kansei*) of the Governor-General of Korea. The announced plan to create a colonial ministry implied a significant decline in the governor's status for he would have to give up his relative autonomy from the metropole.[125] Taking a cue from Saitō, who objected to the plan at the Privy Council on the grounds of *naichi enchō*,[126] the brokers of empire and their Korean allies in "pro-Japanese" organizations responded by presenting a united front of opposition to Tokyo—although, as in the case of their joint suffrage campaign, internal divisions and contradictions remained only slightly beneath the surface.

---

movement of the Kungmin Hyŏphoe by sponsoring their petition to the Diet every year. For studies on Pak Ch'un-gŭm, see Matsuda 1995; Bayliss 2008.

124. Yamazaki 1943, 23.

125. Since 1919, the Governor-General of Korea had been required to "address the emperor and receive imperial sanction through the office of the prime minister," but the Tanaka plan would oblige him, along with other colonial governors, to do so "through the Ministry of Colonization." On how the issue affected the evolution of party cabinets, see Katō 1998 and Okamoto 2000.

126. *Keijō nippō*, 14 April 1929.

The first to rise in defense of Korea's "autonomy," interestingly, were the Korean leaders of the Dōminkai, an organization devoted to the cause of assimilation. In short order, Vice-President Pak Yŏng-ch'ŏl (1879–1939) and thirteen other Korean executives resigned from the Dōminkai in protest. The Tanaka plan "to render Korea a colony," they argued, "transgressed the Meiji Emperor's Imperial Rescript on Annexation and the Taishō Emperor's Imperial Rescript on *isshi dōjin*" and "violated the spirit of consanguinity [*dōmin*]" that the Dōminkai championed.[127] Stirred by this action, one pro-government organization after another wired its protest to Tokyo, with the same line of reasoning that the Tanaka plan "infringes on the policy of *naichi enchō*."[128] The Kungmin Hyŏphoe even went so far as to threaten to dissolve itself, playing the martyr. "For more than a decade," the Korean leaders argued, "our Kungmin Hyŏphoe has endured persecution and oppression of all kinds to devote itself solely to *naisen yūwa*," but the creation of the Colonial Ministry would force their struggle to "end in vain" and render their existence "meaningless."[129]

Settler leaders, however, felt their Korean allies were committing an ironic blunder. For the Korean members to take a separate course of action from their Japanese colleagues "deterred their very aim of *dōmin*," argued the Kōshi Club leaders, chiding the Dōminkai for allowing its executives to resign in the first place.[130] The Kōshi Club scrambled through the next few days to avert a feared erosion of unity by calling on the breakaway members of the Dōminkai and other "imperialist organizations" that "rendered distinguished service to the state" (namely, the Kungmin Hyŏphoe, the Taishō Shinbokukai, and the Kyōiku Kyōseikai) to form a joint platform.[131] This led to the birth of the Taku-

127. *Chōsen kōron*, June 1929, 2.8; *Maeil sinbo*, 20 April 1929. The mass resignation of the Korean leaders caught their settler colleagues by surprise, momentarily throwing them "into panic," but they promptly followed up by declaring "absolute opposition" to the plan and dispatching a resolution to that effect to Prime Minister Tanaka and the president of the Privy Council (*Asahi shinbun*, 18 April 1929; *Chōsen kōron*, May 1929, 38–39).

128. *Keijō nippō*, 21 April 1929.

129. *Asahi shinbun*, 19 April 1929; *Chōsen kōron*, June 1929, 2.8.

130. *Keijō nippō*, 19 April 1929, evening edition; 21 April 1929.

131. *Keijō Nippō*, 21 April 1929, evening edition; Keijō Honmachi Keisatsu Shochō (April 23, 1929).

shokushō Kansei Hantai Dōmeikai (Alliance for Opposition to the Organic Regulations on the Colonial Ministry; hereafter, the Alliance).

Under the watchful eyes of the police, the Japanese and Korean leaders of the Alliance held a meeting where they passed a collective resolution to "absolutely oppose" the Tanaka plan. The next day they telegraphed this message to the prime minister, the president of the Privy Council, chairmen of both houses of the Diet, heads of the two leading parties, and several other influential figures in Japan.[132] The Alliance also dispatched three Korean delegates to Tokyo, where they appealed for support to Sakatani Yoshirō and members of the Central Korea Association and used their introduction to visit key ministers and politicians as well as major newspaper agencies. Their petition, distributed in several thousand copies, enunciated the Alliance's objection to treating Korea "on the same level as Taiwan and the South Sea islands," while portraying Japan as an anticolonial empire whose policy of *naichi enchō* must be categorically distinguished from the "oppressive practices of Western imperialists."[133]

Although their protest did not prevent the Tokyo government from creating the Colonial Ministry, with Saitō's opposition and Sakatani's mediation the Alliance was able to have some impact on the final outcome. Together with the Privy Council, the lobbyists managed to pressure the central government to change the "Ministry of Colonization" to the "Ministry of Colonial Affairs" (Takumushō) and to create "a special Korean section" within the ministry to distinguish the status of Korea from that of other colonies. Moreover, when the regulations for the Ministry of Colonial Affairs were formally issued on 10 June 1929, Prime Minister Tanaka issued a statement that acknowledged the people in Korea as "imperial subjects" equal to the Japanese in the mainland (*naichi*), pledging that the new ministry would "not treat Korea as a colony."[134] When the Tanaka cabinet fell in July and Saitō was reappointed as Governor-General of Korea, he negotiated with Hamaguchi

---

132. Keijō Honmachi Keisatsu Shochō (25 April 1929): 321–23.

133. Takushokushō Chōsen Jogai Dōmei 1929.

134. *Keijō nippō*, 21 April 1929, evening edition; 21 May 1929; and 11 June 1929.

Osachi to have the proposed revision in the status of the Governor-General rescinded as well.[135]

The Alliance thus succeeded in partially defending Korea's autonomy from the metropole, but not without exposing serious contradictions in their argument for *naichi enchō*: members of the Alliance insisted on the Governor-General's autonomy from Tokyo while battling his authoritarian rule in the colony, and they resisted Korea's integration into a metropolitan ministry while stressing the principle of political amalgamation into Japan.[136] The *Asahi shinbun* was quick to pinpoint this incongruence. "Rather than [continue] its special treatment under the Governor-General's rule," the paper argued, a more progressive step in the direction of *naichi enchō* would be to "have the Colonial Minister represent Korea directly at a cabinet meeting." Yet the Alliance rejected this option, the editor wrote in bemusement, opposing the very plan that would theoretically advance its professed objective of *naichi enchō*.[137] Leaders of the Alliance nonetheless seemed unfazed by the inconsistency of their own position. By their lights, the Tanaka plan fell short of true *naichi enchō*, which "would be realized only when Korea became directly subordinate to the Home Ministry, not to the Ministry of Colonial Affairs."[138] They envisioned only full political integration of Korea into the metropole; otherwise, they would reject any partial measures and insist on the maintenance of the status quo.

How to interpret such a Janus-faced response? Both Japanese settlers and Korean elites appear to have had their own reasons for fearing the loss of Korea's relative independence while insisting on the imperial fiction of Korea as "annexed" not "colonized"—two theoretically irreconcilable positions that respectively endorsed Korea's autonomy from

135. *Ōsaka Mainichi shinbun*, 25 May 1929, Korea edition. However, because the issue of metropolitan control over the Governor-General of Korea was ambiguously handled, it later developed into a major political debate in the metropole (Okamoto 1998, 7–11).

136. A similar issue regarding the governor's autonomy surfaced in Manchuria since 1905, though the context in which this debate took place—notably the rivalry between the Army and the Foreign Ministry for control over jurisdiction—was very different from the case of Korea (Matsusaka 2001, 88–90).

137. *Asahi shinbun*, 23 April 1929; *Keijō nippō*, 19 April 1929, evening edition.

138. The Kungmin Hyŏphoe similarly desired "an eventual transfer of Korea into the jurisdiction of each ministry in the metropole" and the dissolution of the Government-General (*Ōsaka Mainichi shinbun*, 25 May 1929, Korea edition).

and its amalgamation into Japan. As for settlers, their response was utterly typical of their ambivalence toward the metropole, rooted in their liminal status as at once agents and subalterns of empire. In opposing the demotion of the Governor-General, settler leaders most likely wished to avoid metropolitan meddling in their pursuit of economic advantage and local dominance; yet they simultaneously desired continued state patronage and military protection in the event of Korean unrest. As also demonstrated by their discourse on suffrage, the settlers' oscillation between assimilation and autonomy vis-à-vis the metropole reflected their shifting political calculus regarding how best to maintain and expand their interests in the colony.

The Korean elites' opposition to the Tanaka plan stemmed more fundamentally from their status as the colonized. As one of them later explained to his Japanese colleagues, "the Koreans object to becoming a colonial people, while the Japanese merely take pity [on their situation]."[139] Another Korean executive, when prompted by settlers to explain his motives for having left the Dōminkai, cited Japanese discrimination against Koreans as one of the main reasons.[140] To be sure, outside observers could barely conceal their scorn for these Korean elites and the rationale they used to oppose the Tanaka plan. As Yun Ch'iho fumed, "Fools! What difference does it make whether Korea is under a Colonial Office or a Government-General?"[141] But Japanese settler leaders interpreted their colleagues' action as a worrisome lack of allegiance to the empire. The renegade Koreans who resigned the Dōminkai en masse, as the Kōshi Club leaders saw it, were driven by "machinations arising from the self-centered egoism of Cho Pyŏng-sang and his ilk," who, desperate for influence, forged an "impure relationship" with the vice-president of the Dominkai, Pak Yŏng-ch'ŏl, a political boss of the Korean community. In the settlers' eyes, nothing more clearly attested to the "hidden ambitions" of these Koreans than their decision to leave the Dōminkai while remaining in the Kōshi Club, in order to carry on their quest for suffrage in conjunction with the Kungmin Hyŏphoe to which many of them also belonged. Some Kōshi Club

139. Keijō Honmachi Keisatsu Shochō (23 April 1929): 318.

140. *Ōsaka Asahi shinbun*, 21 April 1929.

141. Taehan Min'guk Mun'gyobu Kuksa P'yŏnch'an Wiwŏnhoe 1987, 9:211 (entry for 24 April 1929).

leaders apparently acknowledged they had nothing essentially in common with their Korean colleagues, blurting out that they were "merely forced to work together out of concern for *naisen yūwa*."[142]

The growing tendency among Korean elites to bypass their Japanese colleagues and lobby the state directly was also noted by Kikuchi Kenjō,[143] who addressed an unspoken yet widespread settler concern that Koreans might someday leapfrog into a position of dominance. The brokers of empire certainly found alliance with Korean elites instrumental in their quest for political rights after 1919, but they never ceased to worry that their long-time allies might in fact be wily adversaries. By the late 1920s, such settler ambivalence came to the surface, signaling the limits of the anticolonial empire of harmony they claimed to champion.

## *Conclusion*

At the start of Saitō's cultural rule, the lines of political cleavage in colonial Korea had appeared clear enough. People seemed more or less to fall into one of the two categories: those working for the regime became collaborators, and those working against it became resistors. But the lines that separated them were far from fixed and static, as the local alignments of power continually shifted in the course of the 1920s. For settler leaders and Korean elites, to be sure, the parameters of their political activity were ultimately defined and delimited by the Governor-General's rule, the common denominator for their pursuit of interests. Yet the fact that all but politically moderate Koreans were repressed by the police or driven into exile meant that some of the most important struggles for power in Korea took place within, not against, the colonial state structure. And because political power was centralized in the state, most of these struggles took place at the local, not national, level. The vantage point from which to understand the nature and the dynamic of contestation lay, indeed, at the heart of the colonial system, where local Japanese and Korean elites engaged the state and each another, as allies as well as adversaries.[144]

---

142. Keijō Honmachi Keisatsu Shochō (26 April 1929).

143. Kikuchi Kenjō to Saitō (September 1929).

144. Their relationship is comparable to the one between "the white settler bourgeoisie and African petit-bourgeoisie" in Kenya, who "were called into being by the colo-

As they worked to shore up the empire, neither settler leaders nor Korean elites remained subservient collaborators to the colonial regime. In the post-1919 order, the colonial state's ability to impose its arbitrary will on the local population was checked by the new political ferment from below: not only from the moderate and radical wings of the nationalist movement, but also from an expanding body of civilians who made forays into the arena of local governance. City and provincial councils, originally designed as a safety valve for popular discontent, quickly became hotbeds of political dissent, where their elite participants began to question the authoritarian nature of the colonial state they serviced. The formation of the Public Officials' Convention and the ensuing campaign for local autonomy and suffrage—initiatives launched by settler old hands—were as much a testament to the failure of the colonial regime to sequester its subjects from politics as they were legacies of the pre-annexation period, when emergent settler leaders and continental *rōnin* learned to bypass official channels to pursue their own political visions. The activities of organizations like the Kōshi Club in particular reveal the extent to which the brokers of empire could shape the local contours of imperial politics. If they never succeeded in mobilizing the public or reorienting official policy to make it serve their interests, these men at least influenced the tenor of governance by making alliances with Korean elites and forming an important lobby, not only in colonial politics but in the metropole—leverage they sought to extend still further by obtaining suffrage.

From the beginning, however, the political alliance of elites sat on a shaky foundation. Alliance, after all, worked only insofar as it served the interests of all parties involved, and settlers and Korean elites increasingly saw their interests as distinct. The Public Officials' Convention was one testing ground of their political collaboration. Shared desire for a greater voice in colonial politics led the two groups to instrumentally unite against the state authority, but they faced still greater challenges of maintaining their unity. The convention witnessed a portentous clash of political visions, where the Japanese delegates concerned with local supremacy and the Korean delegates intent on claiming parity became

---

nial state" and had "an intensely ambivalent relationship of opportunity/dependence and constraint/conflict with the colonial state" (Berman and Lonsdale 1992, 195).

adversaries rather than allies in their struggle for citizenship. By the end of the decade, even Korean capitalists like Han Sang-nyong, who had seldom traded in the currency of resistance, began to dissent from the official line by abandoning their support for *naichi enchō*. Although the colonial architects of collaboration designed its structure to isolate bourgeois elites from the rest of society, nationalist politics gradually undermined the tenuous consensus on suffrage and politicized even the most trusted Korean allies, pulling many out of their old ideological categories.

Conflicts among local elites at times drew the state in as an anxious ruler faced with the growing problem of disunity. While maintaining its policy of assimilation, the Saitō administration even began to contemplate the prospect, however distant, of Korean self-rule. In the late 1920s, faced with the unrelenting growth of nationalism, an existential crisis of the empire once again opened the way for a serious reappraisal of the reigning approach to governance. In this fluid context, the settlers' stance on assimilation was less ideologically coherent than it appeared. Holding fast to their position on *naichi enchō*, settler leaders seem to have continually teetered between assimilation and autonomy, and their legal and political ambivalence as "the Japanese" assured that the pendulum would continue swinging.

By the end of the 1920s, the old political map of opposition between resistors and collaborators was being redrawn significantly. The state's increasing reliance on coercion to suppress local dissent betrayed the failure of Saitō's policy of accommodation, and police reports presented a picture of gathering threats to the colonial project of assimilation, in which long-term collaborators were implicated. In a flurry of paranoid speculation, settler leaders began to question whether their Korean associates (and even the colonial state they aided) were bona fide allies, a fact that their behavior failed to authenticate. How did the brokers of empire cope with their growing sense of estrangement from their Korean allies and the colonial government? The Japanese seizure of Manchuria in September 1931 was a timely intervention in this respect. Just as it provided a remedy to the festering social and economic troubles in the metropole, Manchuria could potentially prevent the delicate social fabric of Korea from being further torn apart—an opportunity the brokers of empire seized with determination in the 1930s.

# PART III

## *Organs of the State*

# SEVEN

## *The Manchurian Impact*

After the Russo-Japanese War, no international event galvanized Japanese national sentiment more than the Kwantung Army's seizure of Manchuria in September 1931. Appearing to solve Japan's foreign and domestic crises in one stroke, the officers' action was greeted with mass euphoria on the home islands, and sent a wave of excitement across Japanese overseas communities in Asia. Buoyed by the news, Japanese emigrants decorated their houses and storefronts with flags of the rising sun, and proudly paraded through the cities' thoroughfares with victory lanterns. In all corners of the empire, this moment of jubilation over the acquisition of Manchuria became a ritual of national remembrance, to be observed on the anniversary of the incident every September.[1]

Among the first to respond in Korea were the civilian men of influence in Seoul. Under the call of the Kōshi Club, the city's entire spectrum of Japanese and Korean leaders took to the streets in early October to "rouse public opinion" for the "defense of our interests in Manchuria." A plane flew over Seoul dispersing 10,000 propaganda handbills, and the local elites, following a morning prayer at Chōsen Shrine, rode around the city in dozens of automobiles, calling on pedestrians and onlookers to join in Japan's imperial cause: "Fellow countrymen, wake up for the state! Defending the national interests is our duty. Citizens,

---

1. For an analysis of the cultural impact of the colonization of Manchuria in Japan, see L. Young 1998.

rise up for the home country! Let's solve the Manchurian problem in this one stroke."[2]

Elite enthusiasm did not immediately translate into mass public support, however. Ordinary passersby just "stared" at the jingoistic parade, and a mere 1,500 Koreans among the 10,000 spectators who gathered at a rally were moved by the impassioned calls "to unite the nation as one body." Japanese-language papers published exuberant accounts of the imperial army's advances, but the Korean press coverage remained subdued, even detached, in tone. The people's attitudes toward the Manchurian Incident "steadily cooled down as days passed by," a police report noted, while Korean nationalists and socialists "sneered at . . . the bourgeoisie" for having failed to attract the "general proletarian masses."[3] In what had become a common gesture of disapproval, the majority of Koreans responded by simply ignoring the spectacle.

If Korea did not erupt into spontaneous outbursts of euphoria, the impact of Manchuria nonetheless reverberated through the plethora of linkages to the continent that soon developed across the northern border. The birth of the dependent state of Manchukuo in 1932 made empire once again the focal point of Japanese national life, reconfirming, in turn, Korea's significance as a strategic and economic passage to the Asian mainland.[4] The activity of settlers, too, steadily extended along this imperial frontier, transforming them effectively into brokers of Japan's new continental empire.

Standing behind their nation's bid for global supremacy, a diverse cast of settlers pursued a variety of local agendas. One such task was to rally the seemingly indifferent Korean public, a challenge taken up by journalists and propagandists. They portrayed the colonization of Manchuria as a joint Japanese-Korean venture, hoping for the beneficial side effect of mending fragile ethnic relations on the peninsula. Merchants and traders, meanwhile, strove with equal zeal to capture a share

---

2. Keikidō to Keijō Chihō Hōin Kenjisei (3 October 1931).

3. Keikidō to Keijō Chihō Hōin Kenjisei (2 October 1931).

4. The centrality of Korea to Japan's continental expansion was symbolized by the exchange of two key leaders between the colony and the metropole: when the military took over the control of the Tokyo government and inaugurated a new "national unity cabinet" with Saitō Makoto as the prime minister, Army Minister Ugaki Kazushige succeeded Saitō as the Governor-General of Korea in 1931.

of the Manchurian market for Korean products, a step ahead of colonial officials and metropolitan entrepreneurs.

Although their scope of activity and influence expanded beyond the Korean peninsula, the brokers of empire at the same time fell steadily into the arms of the colonial state. With further military conflict on the horizon, in the early 1930s newly appointed Governor-General Ugaki Kazushige (1868–1956) embarked on preparing Korea's residents for continental emergency. In cooperation with civilian leaders and organizations, the colonial authorities, in the name of moral suasion (*kyōka*), unfurled an avalanche of campaigns—to promote "national spirit," improve daily life, guide youth, enlighten women, and cultivate religious devotion—through which state power permeated people's everyday life. The settler leaders began to operate within this loose yet increasingly institutionalized nexus of moral suasion, alongside a new generation of middle-class Japanese and Koreans, including women, educators, and religious workers, who were empowered by the state to manage local communities on its behalf. Local initiatives for directing the moral suasion, like the *yūwa* campaign of the 1920s, became diffused through a network of civilian volunteers that steadily reached beyond the small cadre of settler pioneers and "pro-Japanese" Korean elites.

In mediating the new political and economic ties between Korea and Manchuria, the brokers of empire, who had been operating behind the scenes and in the shadow of official policy, began to morph into agents of the colonial state. In the process, the sphere of settlers' activity and influence grew ever larger, as they managed society in alliance with an equally expanding bureaucracy. To trace the changing modus operandi of settlers in the 1930s sheds further light on the dynamic of interpenetration between state and society, at work in the metropole as well as on the peninsula, that drove the construction of Japan's continental empire.[5]

---

5. This dynamic drove the construction of Japan's "total empire" centered on Manchuria, as Louise Young has shown, where the "socially interventionist state," in its effort to mobilize the masses, simultaneously allowed a variety of civic groups to penetrate the official ruling structure (1998, 398).

## *Manufacturing Manchurian Fever*

Following the October rally, settler leaders and their Korean counterparts continued for months to trumpet the narrative of national defense and martyrdom through speeches, forums, and "patriotic prayer meetings" held at local Shinto shrines. The war relief (*imon*) drive spread rapidly around Korea on a gendered division of labor: while members of the Patriotic Women's Association and local women's groups collected donations and relief goods for the Kwantung Army, male leaders formed national defense associations and paid visits to the imperial guards serving at the Korean-Manchurian border.[6] And with shouts of *banzai*, the media reported, settlers, alongside Koreans of all ages and classes, rushed to the local train station to send off conscripted Japanese soldiers en route to Manchuria.[7]

But these patriotic gestures remained sporadic and largely limited to local officials, elites, and pupils who were mobilized by their teachers. To foster and sustain broader Korean support for the Manchurian cause required a more rigorous strategy. While echoing the metropolitan papers in portraying Japan as a victim of Chinese oppression, the Japanese colonial press and official propagandists added a distinctly Korean cast: they painted the Korean migrants in Manchuria, especially in the border region of Kando (Ch. Jiandao), as the biggest martyrs of all. Located north of Paektusan and just across the Korean-Manchurian border separated by the Yalu and Tumen rivers, Kando had historically been a disputed territory with uncertain boundaries where Koreans formed the majority of the local population.[8] In 1909, just prior to the annexation of Korea, Japan had concluded a treaty with the Qing government that recognized Kando as Chinese territory in exchange for the Japanese right to build railroads in Manchuria. The Japanese migration and colonization of Korea continued to drive impoverished farmers out of their land and across the border into the Kando area. By the time of the Manchurian Incident, the Korean population in Manchuria had reached

---

6. Chōsen Sōtokufu, *Shisei nijūgonenshi* 1935, 940.

7. See *Keijō nippō*, 2–3 February 1933; *Tonga ilbo*, 1, 4, and 8 February 1933.

8. The main causes of early Korean emigration to Manchuria included oppressive taxation, a search for uncultivated land, and flight from rebellion in the latter years of the Chosŏn dynasty (Schmid 2002, 38).

630,000, about 400,000 of whom lived in Kando, alongside 116,000 Chinese and 2,000 Japanese.[9]

In addition to witnessing frequent skirmishes between Korean settlers and local Chinese officials and residents, Kando became a bastion of resistance activity, luring exiled political groups and guerrilla forces from Korea and mainland China. In May 1930 the Korean and Chinese communists launched a mass anti-Japanese uprising, torching and destroying the consulate and other public facilities in the area, while browbeating local residents to support their cause,[10] much to the horror of Japanese settlers in northern Korea whose number began to increase considerably since the late 1920s. But apart from reinforcing border defense and adding garrisons in Manchuria—partly in response to a battery of petitions from the Dōminkai, the Kōshi Club, and others that addressed these settler concerns while urging the "protection of brethren in Kando"[11]—neither the metropolitan government nor the Government-General could do much else to remedy the situation. Since Kando was legally Chinese territory, affairs in the region had to be handled diplomatically by the Ministry of Foreign Affairs and its 400 policemen who supported the Japanese consulate stationed there.[12] Unsurprisingly these complexities led many to view Kando as "a cancer for Manchurian policy as well as for Japanese rule in Korea."[13]

A cluster of incidents around the turn of the decade transformed this cancer into the crux of Japan's continental strategy. The protection of Korean settlers in Kando became a rallying cry, as a chorus of Korean papers and magazines alerted their readers to intensified Chinese efforts to "expel" Koreans from Manchuria by threatening their life and prop-

---

9. *Chōsen kōron*, December 1930, 17, 40–44.

10. Scalapino and Lee 1972, 156–59; Suh 1967, 232–33, 259–60; Esselstrom 2009, 99–104.

11. *Dōmin* 75 (December 1930): 6; Dōminkai, "Seimeisho" (9 November 1931).

12. Interview with Hozumi Shinrokurō (chief of the Foreign Affairs Section) in *Chōsen oyobi Manshū*, November 1930, 36. The local Japanese army and police often overstepped the boundaries of their jurisdiction to prosecute radical Korean nationalists operating in the region (Hyun Ok Park 2000, 211). On the jurisdictional ambiguity of Kando and the evolution of the consular police in response to the Korean resistance activity, see Esselstrom 2009, 50–53, 72–78. On the protection of local Japanese nationals in China, see Brook 2000, Chapter 3.

13. *Chōsen kōron*, November 1930, 5.

erty.[14] Japanese publishers, in a calculated move to stir the public, joined the vernacular press in cataloging endless details of "grave injuries inflicted by the Chinese" on Korean settlers, calling them "our brethren" (*dōhō*). Through such media portrayal, the Koreans in Manchuria by the eve of the invasion came to symbolize all the principal assets of the Japanese empire: railways, commerce, and a leasehold on the Kwantung Peninsula exacted at heavy cost in the Russo-Japanese War.[15] In the months prior to the takeover, another incident allowed colonial propagandists to successfully play up Manchuria as a locus of a united struggle of Japanese and Koreans against Chinese oppression. In July 1931, in the town of Wanbaoshan (J. Manpōsan) located on the outskirts of Changchun, local Chinese residents and officials destroyed an irrigation conduit that was being built by Korean migrant farmers, provoking an open clash between the two communities. Japanese publishers and local groups exaggerated the incident as a problem of "great urgency for the fate of our compatriots in Manchuria," while the colonial authorities abetted anti-Chinese sentiment through media propaganda.[16] The campaign proved effective. Korean riots and assaults on Chinese residents broke out throughout the peninsula, including the looting of Chinatowns by the mobs in P'yŏngyang, Inch'ŏn, and other cities that left 127 dead and hundreds more injured.[17]

The Wanbaoshan incident was used by the Japanese as a convenient pretext for justifying the Kwantung Army's invasion of Manchuria—a moment, as one settler journalist put it, when "the empire bravely stood up for the protection of life and property of one million Korean brethren in Manchuria."[18] In reporting on the threats and violence they incurred from Chinese "bandits" and soldiers in the wake of the takeover, the colonial press continued to deploy what had by then become

---

14. From around the mid-1920s, the Korean media began reporting on the condition of Koreans in Manchuria and calling for their relief. Shortly following the Manchurian takeover, as the *Tonga ilbo* reported, "even the squatters [*t'omangmin*] demonstrate their love for their kinsmen" by donating clothes, a phenomenon observed around the peninsula (29 October 1931). For a discussion forum on the issue of Koreans in Manchuria, see *Samch'ŏlli*, September 1933, 47–51.

15. *Chōsen kōron*, December 1930, 18–37; *Chōsen oyobi Manshū*, October 1931, 5.

16. *Maeil sinbo*, 5 July 1931, evening edition; 2 September 1931.

17. *Maeil sinbo*, 5–8 July 1931; *Chōsen oyobi Manshū*, July 1931, 12.

18. *Chōsen kōron*, December 1931, 2–3.

a stock narrative of "protecting our brethren in Manchuria" to rally the Korean public.[19]

The image of Koreans in Kando surrounded by Chinese bullies was further bolstered by an irredentist claim that they were the original settlers and rulers of Manchuria. When the Kwantung Army commander Mutō Nobuyoshi (1868–1933) visited Seoul on the eve of the birth of Manchukuo, Cho Pyŏng-sang and other Korean businessmen entreated him to protect "one million Korean brethren" they dubbed "pioneers of Manchuria."[20] This image of pioneers, internalized by the Korean settlers themselves,[21] implicitly reprised a diasporic vision of Korean racial expansion across the northern border, which had captured the imaginations of native scholars like Sin Ch'ae-ho and Japanese scholars of "Mansenshi" (Manchuria-Korea history) around the turn of the century. Although their political purposes were divergent, both groups of scholars stressed the "inseparability of Manchuria and Korea." They argued that the territorial bounds of the ancient kingdom of Koguryŏ had encompassed Manchuria, rendering the Korean emigration to Kando as a process of "returning to the ancestral homelands."[22] In the 1920s and 1930s, Japan's continental ambition and Korea's age-old search for the nation once again converged on Manchuria. Where writers like Sin Ch'ae-ho had pinned their hopes for the resurgence of their *minjok* on "the northern lands" occupied by Korea's ancient dynasties, the Japanese writers appropriated the ethnic vigor of the Korean "brethren" to promote the continental expansion of their own *minzoku*.

Kikuchi Kenjō was among the earliest Japanese to manipulate the irredentist idea of a "lost" Korean Manchuria as a strategy to win over Korean political leaders.[23] Echoing Sin Ch'ae-ho's account and metro-

---

19. For instance, see *Chōsen shinbun*, 17–19 September 1931; 1–2 March 1934. For a survey on the extent of "damage on the brethren in Manchuria" following the Japanese invasion, see *Tonga ilbo*, 8 December 1931.

20. *Chōsen Jitsugyō Kurabu*, September 1932, 2–5.

21. For instance, representatives of the Korean settlers of Kando, on their visit to Seoul in late 1933, invited fellow Koreans to join them in the construction of "a second home" (Kim Nae-bŏm, "Manshū zaijū dōhō shisatsudan o mukaete," *Chōsen Jitsugyō Kurabu*, January 1934, 49).

22. Schmid 2002, 224–36; Hatada 1969, 183.

23. Kikuchi had argued that Kando was originally Korea's territory and that during the Koguryŏ period Korea held the land east of the Liao river. The idea of recovering

politan Japanese scholarship, Kikuchi's narrative traced the historical movements of Korean ethnic ancestors—especially the Puyŏ *minjok* or "the most heroic *minzoku* among the Mongolian races"—who emerged in the Changbaek Mountain region and spread their "civilizing influence" over the lands south of the Tumen and Yalu rivers. He hoped to see the Japanese retrace the footsteps of these Korean "pioneers of Manchuria,"[24] especially eying the highland located between the upstream Amur river and South Hamgyŏng province "as an expansive route for the Yamato *minzoku*." "We must definitely cultivate this region" to advance into the Jilin area, he argued, by first settling Koreans who were "second to none in the production of agricultural commodeties." Their population would spread from Kando into northern Manchuria, he predicted, reaching "as many as 5 million in the next 50 years." By then "the Korean *minzoku* would be recognized as a great world *minzoku*" who had pioneered "the construction of a great free colonial nation [*jiyū shokuminkoku*] in the Songhua river basin."[25]

In envisioning Koreans as agents of Manchurian colonization, settler writers at the same time evoked their own vaunted past as overseas pioneers. Whether as a solution to the problem of surplus population or as a human buffer against threats from China and Russia, what was expected of the Korean "brethren" in Manchuria closely echoed the role of early Japanese migrants to the peninsula. Such an association led Abe Kaoru of the *Minshū jihō* to view the birth of Manchukuo as a perfect moment to officially honor Japanese civilian "pioneers" in Korea, as well as Taiwan, Karafuto, Okinawa, and other "new frontiers," as a means to "stimulate more overseas ventures."[26] Others used the occasion to remind the authorities that the Japanese project of settling the peninsula

---

these territories as suggested by Kikuchi "greatly stimulated King Kojong's ambition" (Aoyagi 1926, 876; Kikuchi 1931, 2:431).

24. Kikuchi 1925, 34–35; Chōfū Sanjin, "Tairiku ni utsutta Chōsenjin," *Keijō nippō*, 4 September 1935. For a discussion of the metropolitan Japanese scholarship on the Puyŏ *minjok*, see Pai 2000, Chapter 2, and Byington 2003, 13. For a Korean view on the mixed ethnic origins and superiority of the Korean *minjok* in relation to the "Manchurian races," see Kim Myŏng-sik, "Chosŏn minjok kiwŏn ŭi munhwajŏk koch'al," *Samch'ŏlli*, February 1935, 52–58.

25. Kikuchi 1922, 10–11; Kikuchi 1925, 39.

26. Tairiku Kenkyūsha 1934, 523–28.

was far from complete. Concerned that "our developing territory of Korea recently tends to be neglected by our citizens" who had shifted their attention to Manchuria, Shakuo Shunjō argued for redirecting the colonizing drive in such a way that "Japanese migrants first fully spread in Korea" while "Koreans spearhead the emigration to Manchuria."[27] In the changing topography of empire that threatened to deepen their marginality in Korea, the settler leaders were determined as ever to claim a part in the continental project, where Japan's imperial aspirations were transposed onto the diasporic imaginations of Koreans.

Behind the portrayal of Koreans as martyrs and pioneers lay an implicit hope to use Manchuria as a diversion from interethnic tension that continually beset the peninsula. In spite of Saitō's policy of accommodation, Korea at the tail end of the 1920s was a long way from ethnic harmony, as unmistakably shown by the Kwangju Student Demonstrations of 1929–1931. A convenient solution to this lamentable state of affairs seemed to lie outside of the conflict-ridden peninsula, in the healing power of the Manchurian opportunity. Colonial bourgeois elites were especially keen to cast the exploitation of Manchurian resources as a joint Japanese-Korean project: one that, as a Korean observer optimistically predicted, would not only bring material benefits but generate "a favorable impact on the promotion of *naisen yuwa*."[28]

Some settlers found in the birth of Manchukuo a reaffirmation of their long-standing Pan-Asian ideals, and hoped this diversionary tactic of social imperialism might be deployed to eliminate radical dissent in Korea once and for all. One such member of the Dōminkai, Fujii Kantarō, saw Manchuria as an outlet for land-hungry farmers as well as radical-prone youth, proposing in this vein that "Korean migrants to Manchuria should be mostly limited to graduates of ordinary schools and agricultural schools."[29] Other Japanese observers advanced a more utopian vision of fashioning a new political community, much like the "East Asian League (*Tōa kyōdōtai*)" that informed the construction of Manchukuo. Tomikasu Hajime urged the Japanese to rid themselves

---

27. *Chōsen oyobi Manshū*, October 1933, 2–4.

28. Kin Ken Chū [Kim Kŏn-jung], "Manmō ni okeru Senjin hakugai," *Chōsen kōron*, June 1928, 40–41.

29. Fujii Kantarō, "Manshū oyobi Chōsen imin no taisaku," *Chōsen kōron*, August 1932, 60.

of a "sense of superiority" and the Koreans of their "nationalist consciousness" in order to create "one new great Asian race who were neither Japanese *minzoku* nor Korean *minzoku.*" "To realize this ideal," that is, to build higher unity on the basis of liminality, "hinges on our second generation," he argued, proposing mixed education as one of the crucial steps in "starting with a clean slate."[30]

For many settler businessmen, however, the prospect of ethnic harmony was merely a gloss over tangible profit, which Korean migrants promised to secure by clearing the path for Japanese expansion. Jinnai Mokichi of the Seoul Chamber of Commerce and Industry, a long-time settler advocate of Korean migration to Manchuria, urged the completion of the Jilin–Hoeryŏng line, with a vision of economically penetrating from northern Korea into the Manchurian interior[31] (where 600,000 Korean "farmer brethren" had reportedly begun "opening every land no matter how remote"[32]). As a solution to Japan's problems of food supply and overpopulation, Fujii Kantarō had an even more ambitious colonization plan in store. Priding himself on his experience of developing "Asia's best irrigation system in Korea," Fujii called for injecting 3 billion yen to reclaim 60 million *chōbu* of Manchurian land—equivalent to the total cultivated acreage in Japan—using Korean surplus labor to "make neighboring Manchukuo an inalienable part of our Great Japanese Empire."[33]

These industrial proposals effectively rendered Korean settlers in Manchuria as agents of Japan's cascading colonizing drive, or what Hyun Ok Park has called "territorial osmosis," from the peninsula onto the Asian mainland, a vision shared by colonial officials since the 1920s.[34] The Government-General for its part saw Manchuria as all but a panacea

30. Tomikasu Hajime, "Minzoku shinri yori mitaru naisen yūwa mondai," *Chōsen kōron*, October 1932, 31–32. In the Kando region, since the 1920s a variety of Pan-Asianist groups apparently operated in conjunction with "disaffected Korean elites" to "create their own utopian, anti-Western polity called the Koryo (Gaoli) nation" (Duara 2003, 98–99).

31. *Chōsen oyobi Manshū*, May 1932, 85.

32. *Chōsen shinbun*, 11 July 1934.

33. *Gunsan nippō*, 19 and 21 June 1935.

34. Hyun Ok Park 2000, 193–214. On the Japanese use of Korean migrants for continental expansion through the pro-Japanese organization Hominkai, see Kim Chuyong 2004.

to Korea's social and economic troubles, just as the Tokyo leaders did to their own country's woes. It offered a ready outlet for surplus farm labor produced by the acute food shortages following harvest (*shunkyū*) that annually hit Korea's southern provinces. Exporting these tenant farmers would, in turn, help "alleviate population pressures and tenancy disputes" while "reducing Korean migration to the metropole to lessen Japan's social problems." Skillful Korean rice growers in Manchuria could also feed the growing population of settlers and soldiers stationed on the continent.[35] While the metropolitan government promoted the mass migration of Japanese farmers, therefore, the Government-General of Korea and the ODC coordinated with the authorities in Manchuria to settle as many Koreans as needed for large-scale land reclamation, railway construction, and other infrastructural projects, offering prospective immigrants reduced train fare, land grants, and "preferential treatment" over Chinese residents.[36]

The Japanese authorities provided more opportunities to the educated, heeding requests from Korean elites like Han Man-hŭi who entreated the commander of the Kwantung Army "to hire many Koreans in bureaucracy as well as in finance and enterprise."[37] In the 1930s, a growing number of Korean school graduates found employment in the Manchurian police force, the Manchurian National Army,[38] the SMRC, and the lower tiers of the colonial bureaucracy, where they effectively joined the ranks of Japanese rulers in Manchukuo.[39] To engage in such acts of "surrogate imperialism," as Carter Eckert has noted, gave Koreans an opportunity to transfer the kind of oppression they had been suffering under the Japanese onto the Chinese.[40]

There was bitter irony in the Japanese touting the protection of Korean settlers, whose status was effectively inverted from victims to agents

---

35. Ugaki 1935, 30, 32.

36. Eckert 1991, 163. In 1936, the Korea-Manchuria Colonization Company was established for the purpose of overseeing the settlement of Koreans in Manchuria.

37. *Chōsen Jitsugyō Kurabu*, April 1932, 3–4; September 1932, 5.

38. From 1936 on, the Manchurian National Army recruited Korean graduates of higher ordinary schools as cadet or officer candidates (*kanbu kōhosei*) and trained them for two years (*Keijō nippō*, 25 July 1935).

39. For activities of these Koreans in Manchuria, see *Samch'ŏlli*, May 1937, 12; June 1940, 13; and October 1940, 67–68, 140–43.

40. Eckert 1991, 169–71.

of empire by the very colonists who had driven them out of their homeland. And yet, more than a fig leaf drawn over the fragile multiethnic polity, the rhetoric of mutual expansion of the two peoples began to speak of a growing reality across the northern border.[41] Owing not least to the Manchurian enthusiasts who sought to divert public attention to the frontier of new opportunity and to the shared outrage in Kando, social imperialism gradually went to work in Korea to unite a divided society around a collective pursuit of the continental empire.[42]

## *Korean Quest for Citizenship and Settler Response*

Seizing such opportunities in Manchuria, Korean elites in this period pressed their claim to citizenship with renewed rigor. The metropolitan government and the local consular police generally discouraged Koreans in Manchuria from naturalizing as Chinese citizens in order to keep them "Japanese,"[43] though their rhetoric of inclusion was often superficial if not deceptive.[44] The Korean elites, however, were more determined than ever to hold the Japanese to their rhetoric, both in the new state of Manchukuo and on their home soil. In the wake of the takeover, Han

41. This rhetoric had an undeniable appeal to young nationalists, as the media reported. Following the Wanbaoshan incident, the number of thought crimes dropped dramatically in P'yŏngyang, and in North Kyŏngsan province, the old bastion of communism, many radicals evidently "converted to Asianism" with astonishing speed (*Heijō Mainichi shinbun*, 6 November 1932; *Fuzan nippō*, 27 February 1934). The birth of Manchukuo, followed by Japan's withdrawal from the League of Nations in 1933, accelerated this trend of conversion (*tenkō*) by impressing upon young Koreans Japan's resolve toward the Western powers and the futility of a struggle for independence (see Hong Jong-uk 2004).

42. For the case of metropolitan Japan, see L. Young 1998, Chapters 7–9.

43. Hyun Ok Park 2000, 205–9. But, as Park notes, there was no consensus among the Japanese authorities on this issue, with some arguing that naturalization of Koreans as Chinese might facilitate land acquisition and protect Koreans from Chinese discrimination. On the issue of the Korean citizenship status in Manchuria, see Brooks 1998, 25–44; Sin Kyu-sŏp 2000, 93–121; and Tanaka Ryūichi 2007, Chapter 7. On the efforts of Koreans in Manchuria to tackle their problem in the early 1930s, see Ch'oe Byŏng-do 2006. On the collaboration of Koreans in Manchukuo (Harbin) with the Japanese, see Tanaka Ryūichi 2007, Chapter 8.

44. Barbara Brooks (1998) has shown through her analysis of the Japanese contemporary media and diplomatic discourse on the Korean "brethren" that the Japanese government conveniently classified ethnic Koreans in Manchuria as Japanese "citizens," only insofar as it suited their imperialistic goals on the continent.

Sang-nyong had made a sanguine prognosis: "The resolution of the current state of affairs in Manchuria" would not only "protect the empire's rights and interests," but "allow Koreans to enjoy the benefits of an equal distribution of interests. . . . In short, *naisen yūwa* would result in a complete unity of interests [between Japanese and Koreans]."[45] Manchuria and its vast horizon of possibilities promised the Korean capitalists not only business opportunities, which they were no less eager than settlers to exploit,[46] but a chance, at last, to achieve parity with the Japanese. It was with such a hope that the Central Council members prodded the Manchurian authorities to recruit more Koreans in enterprise,[47] and Korean delegates in local assemblies pressed the Government-General to promote "coeducation of Japanese and Koreans"[48] or to open a path to Korean military service.[49] Cho Pyŏng-sang, an officer of the Kōshi Club, averred that complete elimination of ethnic discrimination offered the only solution to the persistent lack of Korean allegiance to the empire. "So long as Korea is treated as a slave [*reizokubutsu*] to Japan, a spiritual union of Korean popular minds will forever remain difficult," Cho asserted in front of his Japanese colleagues, calling for "eradicating all distinctions between Koreans and imperial Japan's subjects [*shinmin*], such as through the extension of suffrage."[50]

The strategy of appropriating the rhetoric of assimilation to demand citizenship spread even to radicals and socialists. As young Korean nationalists began to enter the realm of formal politics, the police noted, local city and provincial assemblies further shed their traditional subservience to demand greater ethnic equality, from the expansion of Korean education to the elimination of the practice of granting Japanese nationals an "overseas allowance" (*kahō*), the most hated symbol of institutional discrimination against Koreans.[51] When organized agitation became nearly impossible after 1931, Korea's social movements report-

45. Kan Sō Ryū [Han Sang-nyong], "Dai 71-kai reikai sekijō ni okeru aisatsu," *Chōsen Jitsugyō Kurabu*, January 1932, 5.

46. For instance, see Han Sang-nyong's comments in *Chōsen Jitsugyō Kurabu*, April 1932, 37–39.

47. *Chōsen Jitsugyō Kurabu*, April 1932, 3–4.

48. *Keijō nippō*, 9 March 1934.

49. Chōsen Sōtokufu Keimukyoku 1938, 48–50.

50. *Chōsen kōron*, October 1932, 128–30.

51. Chōsen Sōtokufu Keimukyoku 1938, 36–45.

edly switched from confrontational tactics to "legal efforts to bring local assemblies within their sphere of influence and to politically train the populace for the future." Nationalists, in other words, began to move into the very institutions they had hitherto boycotted, with the effect of radicalizing the Korean delegates who now "willingly lodge political attacks on local administrators" or "form cliques as if following the example of metropolitan political parties."[52]

These developments, already evident in the late 1920s (see Chapter 6), were welcomed by some settlers, but caused unease among many others. Even the Korean press began to request specific civic rights such as greater freedom of assembly and publication,[53] noted Ishimori Hisaya of the *Chōsen kōron*, celebrating these gestures as expressions of their "ardent desire to claim liberty as constitutional citizens [*rikken kokumin*]"—what Pak Ch'un-gŭm had also recently demanded on the floor of the metropolitan assembly.[54] With respect to their attitudes toward the empire, Ishimori averred, the Koreans had narrowed their courses of political action to two: "assimilation or independence," with "absolutely no interest in such ideas as self-rule" except "as a temporary expedient to independence."[55] In late 1935, Shakuo Shunjō similarly predicted that "the Koreans who pave the path to assimilation and the Koreans who pave the way to non-assimilation will proceed in parallel in the future."[56] But he was decidedly more hesitant about the prospect of enfranchising Koreans. Although he endorsed the idea of implementing an army volunteer system in Korea or sending a few handpicked Koreans into the imperial assembly "as an experimental measure," Shakuo urged caution, alerting his readers to "the severity of Korean nationalistic sentiments" that lurked under "the veneer of peace."[57] As for the majority of Japa-

---

52. Ibid., 35.

53. For instance, see *Tonga ilbo*, 10 September 1931.

54. Ishimori Hisaya, "Chōsen tōchi seisaku no taiyō," *Chōsen kōron*, July 1932, 13.

55. Ibid., 11–13.

56. Shakuo Shunjō, "Kongo no Chōsen ni okeru shisei to jūyō mondai," *Chōsen oyobi Manshū*, December 1935, 6.

57. Ibid., 5–6; *Chōsen oyobi Manshū*, October 1935, 5. Shakuo's observation was not far-fetched, as vernacular publishers continued to submit manuscripts that betrayed what the colonial censors worried was "a nationalistic bias." In one famous example, at the occasion of the victory of two Korean marathon runners at the Berlin Olympics in

nese settlers, they made no effort to hide their displeasure at the prospect of Korean peasants turning into Japanese countrymen: they tended to "oppose coeducation of Japanese and Koreans in primary school," one local reporter told Ugaki, simply because they "do not want to be treated the same as Koreans."[58]

Speaking to such settlers' sentiment, a corollary of their liminal status in the empire, the journalist Kikuchi Kenjō, as we have seen, had already signaled concern about the Korean trend to claim rights in his letter to Saitō Makoto at the close of the 1920s. Now, in the aftermath of the Manchurian Incident, he saw Korean leaders beginning to harbor the even more worrisome idea of an Asian ethnic league (*minzoku renmei*). Each participating nation in the league was to be treated "independently" (*dokuritsuteki*), based on the principle of "egalitarian treatment." When this concept was applied to a state in which multiple *minzoku* coexist and a certain *minzoku* enjoys "discriminatory privileges" over another *minzoku*, he added, "it has a proclivity to foster a trend of separation from and resistance to the state."[59] The ideological roots of this theory lay in Pan-Asian discourses that had emerged in the late nineteenth century, especially the Sŏbuk Hakhoe leader Chŏng Un-bok's call for a "Japan-Korea league" (*Nikkan renpō ron*) and the Ilchinhoe leader Yi Yong-gu's argument for a "Japan-Korea merger (*Nikkan gappō ron*)," which he identified as precursors to the argument for an Asian league of independent *minzoku*. Dismissing both as examples of "Small Asianism," and seeing the recent brand of Asianism as no more than window dressing for Korean nationalism, Kikuchi charged, "To conceal a nationalistic movement under the rubric of Asianism and try to change even a bit the attitude of Great Japan facing the world is a tremendously bad idea." He even caviled at the Kungmin Hyŏphoe's ongoing campaign for suffrage as an example of "Smaller Japanism" that fell short of overcoming ethnic nationalism, questioning its pro-Japanese cre-

---

1936, their photo was posted in the *Tonga ilbo* with the Japanese flag on their uniform deliberately erased (Chōsen Sōtokufu Keimukyoku Toshoka 1938, 62).

58. *Chōsen oyobi Manshū*, November 1933, 10.

59. Chōfū Sanjin, "Kindai Chōsen ni arawareta Ajiashugi no kentō," *Chōsen kōron*, April 1934, 32. This theory inspired the formation of new political groups among Korean advocates of *naisen ittai* (see Chapter 8).

dentials.[60] Ultimately he urged "both the Japanese and Korean *minzoku* [to] stand on the principle of one ethnic nation [*ichizoku shugi*],"[61] shunning the heterogeneous vision of Korea as a community of two distinct *minzoku* that had informed cultural rule. Even as many contemporary observers pronounced Korean nationalism dead by the mid-1930s,[62] settler opinion-makers like Shakuo and Kikuchi remained vigilant, urging fellow Japanese to stay on guard against the resilient spirit of the Korean *minjok*.

### *Capturing the Manchurian Market*

Touting Manchuria as a joint Korean-Japanese venture, settler businessmen sought new trade opportunities in the region before anyone else got there. A few years prior to the Government-General's first "fact-finding mission" to Manchuria, leaders of regional chambers of commerce had already made several trips to the Kando area to evaluate its value as an export market.[63] Driven by anxiety to "seize the golden opportunity" for Korean farm and marine products, and to promote "Korea's manufactured goods for future export to Manchuria," these local initiatives coalesced in the formation of the Chōsen Bōeki Kyōkai (Korea Trade Association; hereafter KTA) in February 1933.[64] Chaired by Katō Keizaburō (1873–1939) (president of Chōsen Bank), the KTA was operated by many familiar brokers of empire based in Seoul.[65] Its rank and file were also dominated by Japanese.[66] For the first five years of its exis-

---

60. Chōfū Sanjin, "Kindai Chōsen ni arawareta shisō shiron (6)," *Keijō nippō*, 27 February 1935. The Kungmin Hyŏphoe's petition was again adopted (*saitaku*) by the Diet in February 1933, though the Ministry of Colonial Affairs responded that "to implement it as a specific policy is premature" (*Chōsen shinbun*, 18 February 1933).

61. *Chōsen kōron*, April 1934, 33.

62. *Chōsen kōron*, October 1935, 28.

63. *CKZ* 153 (September 1928): 31–44; *KG* 199 (July 1932): 20–27; *KG* 208 (April 1933): 1–19.

64. On the formation of the KTA, see Chōsen Bōeki Kyōkai 1943, 183.

65. Until 1938 all but one director were Japanese settlers: merchants and company owners engaged in the trade of marine products, rice and agricultural commodities, and industrial goods; and executives of regional chamber of commerce and industry. The only Korean director was Pak Sŭng-ŏk, a prominent Korean sock manufacturer in P'yŏngyang (Chōsen Bōeki Kyōkai 1937, 104–5).

66. KTA membership increased from 133 in 1933 to 238 in 1937 (Chōsen Bōeki Kyōkai 1938, 101). As of June 1936, settlers constituted close to 90 percent of individual

tence, up until after the outbreak of the Sino-Japanese War when Koreans began to enter the area of foreign trade in greater numbers,[67] the KTA functioned as all but an instrument of settler economic interests for penetrating the new market of Manchukuo.

The significance of the settler-run KTA lay in its pioneering efforts to cultivate the Manchurian trade when it was still low on the list of official priorities.[68] Because Korea's trade with Manchuria was miniscule and "unrecognized" when the KTA began its operation, recounted a founding member Watanabe Sadaichirō, the association could only secure an official subsidy of 20,000 yen or a fifth of what it originally requested.[69] The early activities of the KTA focused on removing various obstacles to trade, which the settler businessmen regarded as "the tenacious legacies of anti-Japanese policies of the Manchurian warlords, Zhang Xueliang and Zhang Zuolin."[70] No sooner had they founded the KTA than the settlers began urging the SMRC to lower the freight rate on the Andong–Mukden line and stop "unfairly discriminating against Korean exports." With equal persistence, the KTA leaders petitioned the Manchukuo government, asking it to reduce the "exorbitant" and "irrational" tariffs imposed on the entire range of Korean products, from rubber shoes and socks to sugar, fish, medicine, and bamboo ware.[71] The authorities in Korea and Manchukuo responded to their demands gradually and selectively by improving cargo transportation and revising

---

members, who overwhelmingly came from Kyŏnggi and South Kyŏngsang provinces (Kimura 2005, 75).

67. Kimura 2005, 80. But some Korean firms such as the Kyŏngsŏng Spinning and Weaving Company (Kyŏngbang) in the early 1930s began to extend its sales network to Manchukuo. See Eckert 1991.

68. Nonetheless, local Japanese and Korean businessmen enthusiastically supported Ugaki and his commitment to industrializing Korea as a continental supply base. His "industry-first policy" continued to emphasize rice and cotton production in the south, while inviting metropolitan *zaibatsu* capital (notably Noguchi Shitagau [1873–1944] of Chōsen Nitrogenous Fertilizer Company) to develop heavy and chemical industries in northern Korea. For studies on the industrialization of Korea with a focus on the 1930s, see Nakamura and An 1993; Hori 1995; Sŏn 1998; and Soon-Won Park 1999. On the growth of competitive industries between Korea and Manchuria, see Pang 2004, 75–76.

69. Chōsen Bōeki Kyōkai 1943, 183.

70. *Chōsen kōron*, September 1934, 11.

71. *Seisen nippō*, 26 September 1934; *Fuzan nippō*, 11 October 1936; *Keijō nippō*, 20 October 1934.

tariff rates a few times. But in some areas tariff walls, along with freight rates, remained high, "preventing the blood circulation" within the yen bloc, as a KTA director complained in 1937.[72]

Finding new consumers and trading partners in Manchuria was a grassroots effort from the outset. The KTA strategically set up branches in such key cities as Mukden (Fengtian), Andong, Xinjing (Changchun), Harbin, and Dalian, where merchants and traders from Korea held spot sales and sampling booths at department stores and local trade fairs, "with an aim to export as many [Korean products] as Japan was exporting to Manchuria."[73] Individual merchants struggled even harder. As Yoshida Masakazu, vice chair of the Chōsen Suisankai (Korea Marine Products Association), reminisced later, he took boxes of Korean fish with him and peddled them daily on the streets of Mukden and Xinjing. Intent on making "every individual [in Manchuria] eat one yen worth of fish," Yoshida went around each city, showing pictures of Korea's coastal fishing grounds and fish processing centers in the guise of "a film narrator" (*katsuben*). At the end of each pictorial "show," he distributed to each person in the crowd a bag of dried fish and salted fish as a souvenir, hoping that they would soon be on the dinner table of every Manchurian family.[74]

Thanks to increased support from the Government-General, the KTA and its expanding repertoire of services began to obviate such marketing trouble. With new official subsidies and resources, the KTA staff conducted voluminous research on Manchurian commerce, creating a separate research organ for this purpose in 1936. As Manchuria's retailers and wholesalers came to rely on the KTA's extensive network of business contacts and invest "considerable trust" in its activity,[75] the association also offered to mediate the trade of Korean products, which quadrupled from 50 transactions in 1933 to about 200 in 1936.[76] More-

72. *Chōsen Jitsugyō Kurabu*, June 1937, 90, 108–9.

73. *Ōsaka Mainichi shinbun*, 1 September 1935, Korea edition; Chōsen Bōeki Kyōkai 1943, 284.

74. Chōsen Bōeki Kyōkai 1943, 295.

75. *Chōsen suisan jihō*, 15 March 1938. For example, rice millers in Korea relied on the KTA's contact with wholesalers in Manchuria to mass export Korean rice (*Seisen nippō*, 24 June 1938).

76. Kimura 2005, 78.

over, the KTA helped put Korea's businessmen in touch with Manchukuo officials, SMRC representatives, and Japanese expatriate businessmen based in Manchuria through the dozen roundtable discussions, joint trade forums, and product exhibitions it organized every year. Not unlike the Manchurian railways its members used to transport their products, the KTA's network increasingly functioned as an economic artery through which settler capital, goods, and influence flowed into the heart of Manchukuo.

Following the outbreak of the second Sino-Japanese War in 1937, the KTA continued to spearhead Korea's trade expansion by forging its own web of exchange with the continent, extending its tentacles to key cities in North China including Tianjin, Beijing, Qingdao, and Shanghai.[77] The association now opened its membership to a larger number of Korean entrepreneurs such as Pak Hŭng-sik (1903–1994) of Hwasin Department Store who began to make forays into overseas trade.[78] By this time, moreover, prominent local businessmen including Kada Naoji and Han Sang-nyong came to be fully integrated in high-level policy discussions on Japan's emerging yen-bloc trade. At the industrial research committees of 1936 and 1938 (sequels to the Industrial Commission of 1921),[79] these men joined bureaucrats in affirming Korea's role as an "advance military supply base" to the continent, while arguing against the direct extension of Japan's industry control laws to the peninsula.[80] Their discussion extended to national defense concerns as well as the

---

77. Kimura 2005, Chapter 3; Song Kyu-jin 2001, Chapter 4.

78. Pak joined the KTA and its executive board in 1938. For details on Pak's entry into overseas trade, see Hwasin Sasimnyŏnsa P'yŏnch'an Wiwŏnhoe 1966, 94, 222–23. Other Korean businessmen followed suit in growing numbers, which reflected the rapid expansion of indigenous enterprises in wartime (Kim In-ho 2000, 68–73).

79. The second Industrial Research Committee was planned by Ugaki, partly in response to the local businessmen's demand to reassess Korea's industrial policy, and convened by the new Governor-General Minami Jirō in October 1936 (*Fuzan nippō*, 7 August 1935; *Heijō Mainichi shinbun*, 30 August 1936).

80. *Keijō nippō*, 22 October 1936; *KG* 250 (November 1936): 16–17, 33–44. Their opposition reflected their fear that the state promotion of strategic industries and its control over production (from the allocation of raw materials to the distribution of finished products) would hamper the ongoing process of Korea's industrialization (see also note 85). Precisely for this reason, rather than welcome the metropolitan demand for munitions industries after 1937, the businessmen in Korea worried about the adverse effects of wartime government controls (Nada 2003).

wartime policy of transforming Koreans into full-fledged imperial subjects through Shinto rites, the emperor cult, and Japanese language, all geared toward consolidating the "Japan-Manchuria-China bloc."[81] Korean rule was sustained by such "an unparalleled unity of opinion among the colonial government, the Chōsen Army, and civilian leaders," one Chōsen Army official observed in the late 1930s, a dynamic hardly seen north of the Yalu river among the Japanese builders of Manchukuo.[82]

The wide-ranging activities of the KTA and the growing leverage of its leaders demonstrate how settler businessmen served as crucial conduits for Japanese capital to flow into Manchuria, albeit on the sidelines rather than the center court of continental expansion occupied by metropolitan migrants and the army. Melding their pursuit of private gain with patriotic service to the empire, with little initial assistance from the state, these brokers of empire helped to lay the basis for a yen bloc that mediated a growing volume of commercial exchange between Korea and Manchuria.[83] By prodding the authorities to remove the existing obstacles to trade, and helping Korea's producers meet new consumer demand in Manchukuo, the KTA indirectly helped to create a captive market for Korea's manufactured goods—a catalyst for its "industrial takeoff." As a consequence, Korea's economic relationship to Japan was becoming "less colonial" in character by 1937.[84] Whereas the peninsula had merely channeled metropolitan goods to the continent as a conduit for Japan's transit trade, it now exported its own manufactured goods to Manchuria and other foreign markets, and imported raw materials, machinery, and daily life goods from the metropole. The vision of in-

81. *Keijō nippō*, 7 September 1938; *Chōsen oyobi Manshū*, October 1938, 5–6. For more on the active Korean participation in these committees, see Eckert 1991, 104–5.

82. Ihara Junjirō's comments at the Japan-Manchurian Business Council's roundtable meeting held in Seoul in June 1938 (*Manshū Nichinichi shinbun*, 4–8 June 1938).

83. Korea's exports to Manchuria (which became its largest trading partner) in the first half of the 1930s expanded especially in the areas of lumber, cotton goods, sugar, and marine products (Kimura 2005, 78–79); from 1935 on, a wider array of manufactured goods included flour, cement, rubber shoes, ceramics, enamelware, light bulbs, canned seafood, and beer (Chōsen Bōeki Kyōkai 1943, 83, 88).

84. *Chōsen Jitsugyō Kurabu*, May 1937, 42. This was also demonstrated by the rise of large-scale enterprises founded purely on Korea-based capital after 1937, which signaled the peninsula's decreasing dependence on metropolitan capital and technology (Chōtori Kabushiki Kenkyūkai 1939, 21–22).

dustrial Korea for which the settler leaders had lobbied hard in the 1920s came to resonate and overlap with the Governor-General's policy, indeed to the point of causing friction with Tokyo.[85]

## *Preparing the Masses for War: The Moral Suasion Campaign*

While pushing the frontier of their economic activity on the continent, the brokers of empire became further subsumed under the state apparatus of social control on the peninsula. This seemingly paradoxical process occurred not entirely against their will or at the expense of their influence. In preparation for an impending armed conflict with the Chinese and Western powers, the colonial government recalibrated its goal to mobilize all residents, "whether official or civilian, Japanese or Korean, as one united body," as Ugaki put it, for "developing [Korea's] resources in the current time of emergency."[86] Supporting Japan's continental drive required not only raising Korea's industrial productivity, he believed, but enlisting the active spiritual participation of the entire population. On the eve of the Manchurian takeover, a time when the empire demanded a new level of unity, the central policy concern was to accelerate Korea's economic transformation while ensuring social order. With the countryside reeling from the effects of depression, and cities equally rife with the strain of urbanization and "ideological confusion" (a situation not unlike that of the metropole), a movement for moral suasion (*kyōka*) emerged to refashion the colonial body politic.[87] This also galvanized the brokers of empire into action, albeit less as autonomous actors than as subordinate agents of the colonial government.

---

85. To create a favorable environment for investing in Korea's industries, from mining to iron and steel, Ugaki lured capitalists from the metropole through protective tariffs and business subsidies, while avoiding the application of the Jūyō Sangyō Tōsei Hō (Major Industries Control Law, 1931) and other factory laws that inhibited entrepreneurial freedom at home. These measures were pursued at odds with Tokyo, which grew increasingly anxious to extend its control laws to overseas territories, in order to protect domestic industries and producers from trade competition (Pang 2004, 79–80, 85–86).

86. Chōsen Sōtokufu, *Shisei nijūgonenshi* 1935, 668.

87. The translation of *kyōka* as "moral suasion" follows Sheldon Garon (1997). For an analysis of moral suasion campaigns in metropolitan Japan, see Garon 1997, Chapters 1–4.

Drawing on the well-established metropolitan formula of state paternalism,[88] Ugaki during his five-year tenure between 1931 and 1936 poured astonishing energy and money into thought guidance, promotion of labor, vocational training, physical training, adult education, and poverty relief. Ugaki enlarged the bureaucratic functions of the state in all these areas by adding a new budget for social moral suasion projects (*shakai kyōka jigyō*), and by consolidating the administration of religion, moral suasion, and social work into a single "social section" (*shakai-ka*) in the colonial education bureau, as well as in each provincial government.[89]

Though Ugaki placed the bureaucracy in charge of orchestrating social reform, he did not intend this to be the work of the state alone. In the first half of the 1930s, local administrators co-opted and empowered a variety of civilian groups and individuals to manage their communities in order to meet the new goals of empire—a strategy that Gi-Wook Shin and Do-Hyun Han have called "colonial corporatism."[90] In adopting this corporatist strategy the Ugaki administration both built on the colonial practices of the previous decades,[91] and borrowed from the metropolitan precedent of nurturing social "mainstays" (*chūken jinbutsu*) in a small but growing middle stratum of the population. In Seoul and a few other cities, for example, members of this emerging middle

---

88. Ugaki especially harked back to the late Meiji period when the Japanese government began to reach deep into rural communities through a network of Shinto shrines, youth and women's groups, and other hamlet organizations, and "diligent and thrift campaigns" that later crystallized into the "Everyday Life Reform movement" (ibid., 79–81; see also Pyle 1973).

89. Chōsen Sōtokufu, *Shisei sanjūnenshi* 1940, 386, 392; Chōsen Sōtokufu, *Chōsen shisei ni kansuru yukoku* 1937, 855–56.

90. According to Shin and Han (1999), corporatism "encourages the formation of a limited number of officially recognized groups that interact with the state in clearly defined and regulated ways." A corporatist strategy in the colonial context aims to "license or create new, semiofficial, semivoluntary, intermediary associations for colonial control and mobilization" (72–77).

91. In addition to continuing the *yūwa* campaign to promote assimilation through social work (see Chapter 3), the moral suasion movement involved a parallel effort to promote sanitation and hygiene. Launched and led by the police in the 1910s, this colonial project increasingly passed into the hands of local elites in the 1920s and 30s, according to Todd Henry, when a "localized regime of sanitary surveillance" emerged through a network of neighborhood sanitation cooperatives (2006, 547–56).

class were designated as district commissioners (*hōmen iin*) to visit the homes of the poor and provide welfare services.[92] Many of them simultaneously served on community councils (J. *chōkai/dōkai*; K. *chŏnghoe/tonghoe*) created at the neighborhood level of municipal governance. Headed by established settlers and well-heeled Koreans,[93] community councils functioned as grassroots organs of moral suasion by clarifying and reinforcing the link between the daily life of local residents and the new military objectives of empire.[94] Furthermore, local civic, educational, and philanthropic institutions, many of which were run by more or less the same group of bourgeois elites, were organized into regional federations and integrated into the empire-wide network of "moral suasion groups" centered in Tokyo.[95]

Through this growing apparatus of moral suasion, local officials worked in tandem with a nexus of civilian volunteers and organizations, in which the brokers of empire were further embedded as "deputies of the state."[96] In performing this role, long-time settler and Korean bourgeois allies were joined by the emerging urban middle class of schoolteachers, journalists, religious leaders, and members of women's and youth groups. Settler power, in other words, began to penetrate the state's ruling structure, while state power began to envelop key institutions through which settlers advanced their interests, in cooperation or competition with Korean elites. This dynamic of interpenetration took shape through an increasingly routinized pattern of cooperation between state and society in launching a variety of moral suasion campaigns, from planning to implementation on the ground.

---

92. Sin Yŏng-hong 1984, 195, 344–45, 384–87, 389–93. For the operation of this system in Japan, see Garon 1997, 52–58.

93. Community councils were created in 1933 by enlarging the system of community heads (*chō* or *dō sōdai*) first installed in the early 1910s. For a roster of community heads, see Dai-Keijō Kōshokusha Meikan Kankōkai Hensankakari 1936.

94. *Keijō ihō* 145 (October 1933): 4, 47. Community councils were required to convene a monthly moral suasion assembly (*kyōka jōkai*). *Keijō ihō* 147 (November 1933): 39. In Seoul, which was divided into five "moral suasion" wards (*kyōka-ku*)—East, West, South, North, and Yongsan—over 200 moral suasion commissioners (*kyōka iin*) were selected to run moral suasion committees (*kyōka iinkai*), set up in their respective wards, in cooperation with a local police chief (Sin Yŏng-hong 1984, 197).

95. Sin Yŏng-hong 1984, 165.

96. Their role was akin to that of middle-class reformers in interwar Japan (Garon 1997, 144).

The rough contours of these campaigns emerged from the first Korea-wide symposium on social work (*shakai jigyō*) held in Seoul in November 1930. For the purpose of discussing "facilities that need to be swiftly implemented for social and moral education in Korea," the symposium assembled some two hundred individuals and "experts" on social work. They included provincial and municipal administrators, district commissioners, religious workers, school principals, youth group leaders, social reformers, journalists, entrepreneurs, and leaders of *yūwa* and pro-government organizations (many of whom have already been discussed in earlier chapters).[97] Particularly eager to offer advice and wisdom on the matters of moral suasion were Korean and Japanese leaders of the Dōminkai (see Chapter 3). Drawing on his "ten years of research and experience," Chŏn Sŏng-uk, for instance, explained the utility of the traditional institution of the "village compact" (*hyangyak*) for fostering "coexistence and coprosperity," and his colleague, Sin Sŏng-nin, proposed mixed education of Japanese and Korean pupils as an effective method of "thought guidance."[98] Many Dōminkai leaders, such as Nakamura Kentarō, Maeda Noboru, and Yamato Yojirō, also became part of a task force formed by 32 symposium participants to further deliberate on the issue.[99] Echoing their metropolitan counterparts, the committee emphasized the foremost goal of "thoroughly realizing the aim of the Kokumin Seishin Sakkō Shōsho [Imperial Rescript on the Promotion of the National Spirit]," promulgated by the Japanese government in the wake of the Great Kantō Earthquake, by "nurtur[ing] the concept of revering gods [*kami*] and worshipping ancestors as well as religious devotion [*shinkōshin*]." For the rural areas, they stressed the need to "expand the facilities for village improvement" and "train leaders [*chūken jinbutsu*] for moral suasion." More specific measures were proposed for guiding youth, from the creation of athletic facilities and "sound and stable" youth groups, to the publication of "wholesome

97. The civilian participants included Nakamura Kentarō and Kobayashi Genroku—ideologues of *naisen yūwa* who promoted Buddhism as a spiritual link between the Japanese and Korean communities—and journalists like Aoyagi Tsunatarō and Shakuo Shunjō who had since annexation devoted their writing to the issue of assimilation (*Chōsen* [Chōsen Sōtokufu], December 1930, 94–95).

98. *Chōsen shakai jigyō* 8, no. 12 (December 1930): 15–17, 19–20, 31.

99. Ibid., 53.

reading" and the prevention of underage drinking and smoking, areas in which mothers and housewives were expected to play a central role.[100]

Ideas discussed at the symposium gradually crystallized into a series of "moral suasion" events to be launched in the next few years. The Ugaki administration turned, first of all, to the rural areas where the majority of Koreans lived in poverty. Seeking to harness rural residents directly to the official goals of expanding production and ensuring social stability, the colonial government launched the Rural Revitalization Campaign,[101] in parallel to its metropolitan counterpart, in November 1932.[102] Its ostensible aim was to rehabilitate Korea's agrarian economy, torn by landlord-tenant disputes and hardship, by "cultivating the national spirit and self-reliance" (*kokumin seishin sakkō, jiriki kōsei*), which was considered as pivotal as raising material productivity.[103] In addition to drafting and implementing a detailed revitalization plan to ensure better farm management for each household, the authorities facilitated the formation of agricultural cooperatives, and revived traditional village institutions for mutual aid and self-sufficiency.[104] As a long-term measure to prevent class conflict, they especially promoted the growth of a new leadership of young semi-tenants and owner-cultivators to supplant landlords as the mainstay of rural society.[105]

As rural revitalization commenced in the country, however, "cities," Ugaki rued, "tend to lag far behind farm and fishing villages in promoting the national spirit and self-reliance."[106] The promotion of "the national spirit" in cities proceeded in a more ad hoc manner, through officially sponsored events such as occasional lectures delivered by po-

---

100. One of the participants, Shakuo Shunjō, also turned his attention to settlers, urging "Buddhist monks, clergymen, and scholars" in particular to band together for the task of morally rehabilitating their fellow countrymen "steeped in the pursuit of money, power, business, and pleasure" (Shakuo Tōhō, "Chōsen no kyōka jigyō," *Chōsen oyobi Manshū*, December 1930, 4–5).

101. For more details on the campaign, see Matsumoto 1998, 161–205; Shin and Han 1999; and a transcribed interview with Yahiro Ikuo, who was in charge of the campaign, in Yūhō Kyōkai 1984, especially 7–41.

102. See K. Smith 2001, Chapter 6.

103. "Minshin sakkō shisetsu yōkō," in Kōtō Hōin Kenjikyoku Shisōbu 1932.

104. Shin and Han 1999, 81–83.

105. Ugaki 1935, 127–28; Chōsen Sōtokufu, *Shisei sanjūnenshi* 1940, 304–5.

106. Ugaki 1935, 132–34.

lice and municipal officials and assemblies convened by community councils. But out of these efforts emerged one annual campaign, first launched peninsula-wide on the tenth anniversary of the promulgation of the Imperial Rescript on the Promotion of the National Spirit in November 1933. The National Spirit Promotion Week, a practice transplanted from the metropole, had the express aim of propagating "the national spirit of fortitude" to prepare the nation for "total spiritual mobilization." The idea was to mobilize people before the advent of war, assuming that "a state of emergency" was the ordinary state of affairs.

In Seoul, where an infrastructure for moral suasion developed faster than other cities, the usual array of local groups and community leaders were called upon to lead the week's events on the ground. Civilian ideologues of assimilation, such as Cho Pyŏng-sang of the Dōminkai and Tsuda Sakae of the Ryokki Renmei (of which more later), delivered lectures on enduring hardship and "our country's mission" to local residents, while goading them to engage in specific activities planned for each day of the week. On the first day, designated for "worshipping at shrines," residents and school children accompanied by teachers visited Chōsen Shrine and Keijō Shrine carrying "National Spirit Promotion Week flags." On the second day, community councils and other civic groups, in observance of Confucian tradition, held "meetings to show respect to the elderly" (*keirōkai*). For "daily life improvement," a theme for the third day, the campaign promoted rising early, punctuality, hygiene, and thrift.

While such slogans echoed the metropolitan campaign, the spiritual mobilizers also added prescriptions specifically targeting Korean residents—such as "wearing colored clothing" instead of traditional white dress, and cutting expenses on funerals, marriages, and other costly traditional ceremonies—each of which would develop into a campaign of its own. For the rest of the week, local residents were exhorted to practice abstinence from alcohol and smoking to train themselves in "enduring hardship and shortage"; save and donate money to national defense funds; foster "civic morality" by keeping public facilities clean, preventing fire, and paying taxes properly; and promote health through "citizens' health exercises" (*kokumin hoken taisō*) and recreational activities. Each household was also encouraged to hoist a Japanese rising-sun flag, and on the last day of the week "make a bow toward the Japanese Imperial Palace" and "express gratitude toward one's ancestors."[107]

The first National Spiritual Promotion Week garnered little enthusiasm from the public. Despite massive and costly propaganda efforts, only about 10 percent of the city's population visited local shrines, and the impact of the campaign on lower-class residents proved particularly disappointing. Lectures held at ten separate venues, which often amounted to vague and moralistic hectoring from above, attracted a mere 1,760 listeners. No less apathetic were bank and corporate executives; some bureaucratic offices apparently had no knowledge of the campaign.[108] Nonetheless, the National Spiritual Promotion Week, to be repeated every year, provided a preview of programs that would later be implemented with greater militancy—Shinto worship, personal discipline, war support, "life on the home front," physical training, and the promotion of emperor ideology—all of which had a bearing on the state's long-range policy to Japanize Koreans. And brokers of empire like the Dōminkai played a central role in these campaigns, making the connection between social work and assimilation ever more transparent in the context of preparing the masses for war.

## *Daily Life Improvement and Female Suasion*

The most "colonial" aspect of Korea's moral suasion campaign was its unapologetic effort to eradicate "Koreanness" in people's daily life. In the name of "life improvement" (*seikatsu kaizen*),[109] another slogan imported from the metropole, the colonial state and its local agents aimed to regulate the daily lives, habits, and thoughts of the Korean people, with a new goal of making assimilation a matter of self-discipline.[110] Emblematic of this effort were the Girei Junsoku (Regulations on Ritu-

107. *Chōsen shakai jigyō* 11, no. 11 (November 1933): 59–61.

108. *Chōsen shakai jigyō* 12, no. 1 (January 1934): 67, 70, 75–77, 79.

109. The "life improvement" movement first emerged in the 1920s, drawing a wide array of Korean social, religious, and political organizations (including Sin'ganhoe). It picked up pace in the early 1930s, only to be co-opted by the Government-General (Inoue Kazue 2006).

110. Some scholars have adopted Michel Foucault's concept of "disciplinary power" to explain this goal of Japanese assimilation policies. See Kim and Chŏng 1997; Yun Hae-dong 2003, Chapter 1.

als), issued by Ugaki in 1934 to "rationalize" what were considered superfluous and costly Korean marriages, funerals, and festivals, while preserving their "solemnity" and "spirituality."[111] Although these regulations echoed the moral injunctions directed at peasants in Japan,[112] some colonial programs enforced in the 1930s, most notably the promotion of colored clothing (*irofuku shōrei*), had no known metropolitan counterpart.

Wedding the colonial logic of assimilation to the bourgeois values of hard work and discipline, the authorities encouraged Koreans to wear colored dress by using the following rationale. Traditional Korean white dress (*hanbok*) needed to be washed regularly, which demanded "inordinate time and female labor." But constant washing led the fabric to deteriorate quickly, causing an "enormous economic loss."[113] Wearing white dress, moreover, discouraged people from working hard because they "fear staining and damaging" their clothes, thereby "lowering [labor] efficiency."[114] The campaign for colored clothing was designed to break this vicious life cycle of "sloth" and "inefficiency." The creation of a well-disciplined labor force required fundamental reform of the ethnic character of Koreans by instilling in them bourgeois values of thrift, diligence, and industry—and all of this could be accomplished, so went the official rationale, by a single effort to clothe them in color.[115]

The promotion of colored clothing spread through the countryside as well as in cities, as a collaborative effort of local officials and bourgeois proselytizers. In order to "make them experience how economical it is [to wear colored clothing],"[116] in September 1933 Seoul's municipal

---

111. The new regulations simplified wedding ceremonies and reduced betrothal gifts from the family of the groom to the family of the bride. They made mourning dress less ornamental and shortened the period of mourning, and abolished the custom of "formal wailing" for condolences. Ancestor worship was limited to two generations instead of four as stipulated by convention, and the number of seasonal festivals was drastically reduced as well (*Chōsen shakai jigyō* 12, no. 12 [December 1934]: 9–17).

112. See K. Smith 2001, 319–29.

113. According to the calculation of the social section of the colonial education bureau in 1933, for a Korean family of five, wearing colored clothes would save them 15 yen 40 sen and 680 hours of time annually (cited in Kong 2006, 148).

114. Keijō-fu Shakaika 1934, 87.

115. This rationale had already spread among Korean intellectuals, since the Korean government in 1903, and under Japanese protectorate rule in 1906, had first issued bans on white clothes in winter (Kong 2006, 142–47; Lynn 2004, 79–80).

116. *Chōsen shakai jigyō* 11, no. 11 (November 1933): 18.

government enlisted district commissioners to distribute instructional pamphlets and organize free workshops where Korean residents could dye their clothes on the spot; in four *hōmen* districts some 2,400 residents attended these workshops and dyed 7,735 pieces of clothing.[117] The Dōminkai and the Kungmin Hyŏphoe as well as settler philanthropic institutions also lent a hand.[118] Most active on the ground were members of the Dōminkai, who offered free workshops for dyeing fabrics from 22 to 25 May 1935. During the four-day event held all day from 10 AM to 6 PM in Sŏbinggo and Noryangjin, 750 residents dyed a total of 5,340 pieces of clothing, an outcome the organizers evaluated as "a great success."[119]

Local Japanese tailors did not miss this opportunity to expand their Korean clientele. Particularly enterprising was Chōjiya, the department store owned by Kobayashi Genroku, who not coincidentally was also a member of the Dōminkai. According to its company history, the promotion of colored dress had been Chōjiya's motto since the Meiji period; indeed, it began a business of dyeing Korean dress within a year of opening shop in 1904.[120] In order to "speed up the unification of people's dress," Kobayashi later designated 12 November as the "Memorial Day of Western Dress," commemorating the Meiji Emperor's declaration of Western dress as the official attire for the Japanese Imperial Household. Harking back to the emperor's sartorial instructions to ordinary citizens shortly afterwards, Kobayashi sought to extend this imperial decree to the Korean "brethren," to assimilate them in the new garb of Japanese modernity.[121]

The peninsula-wide effort to promote colored dress offered the Korean public a tangible example of the colonial project's transformative power, but its results betrayed wide regional disparities.[122] As early as

---

117. Chōsen Sotokufu Gakumukyoku Shakaika 1933, 122–23; Keijō-fu Shakaika 1934, 88.

118. *Keijō ihō* 144 (September 1933): 43–44; Chōsen Sotokufu Gakumukyoku Shakaika 1933, 122–23.

119. *Keijō ihō* 165 (June 1935): 43.

120. See Chōjiya's advertisement in *Hwangsŏng sinmun*, 24 October 1905.

121. Chōjiya Shōten 1936.

122. For the case of North Kyŏngsang province, see *Chōsen minpō*, 15 January 1932; and *Chōsen shinbun*, 10 June 1933. For the case of North Ch'ungch'ŏng province, see *Chōsen shinbun*, 24 January 1932. The South P'yŏngyang provincial government selected "model

September 1933, the Korean governor of North Kyŏngsang province, well known for his devotion to the cause, proudly reported that while progress was slow in local cities, 80 to 90 percent of rural residents had already switched to colored clothing.[123] According to a survey conducted by the Kyŏnggi provincial government in February 1934, nearly all local children (96 percent) and most adults (87 percent) had shed their old wardrobe. But Seoul, where the campaign originated and a draconian "ban on white dress" (*hakui hatto*) was imposed on government employees,[124] was among the lowest achievers, with only 63 percent of adults wearing colored dress.[125] In the end, ceaseless propaganda, lectures, and workshops appear to have had little long-term impact on the majority of Koreans.[126] In some areas the campaign turned into outright compulsion, as local officials, anxious to produce good results, would "occupy the central place in the market and spray Indian ink on every passerby in white dress."[127]

The promotion of colored clothing evolved as part of a larger effort to involve women in daily life improvement. "Housewives hold wide-ranging responsibilities outside of the home," the secretary of the Chōsen Shakai Jigyō Kyōkai (Korea Social Work Association) Hanada Kinnosuke had already noted in 1926, especially "in moral suasion matters

---

villages" and provided close guidance in "expelling white dress" to demonstrate their effectiveness to the rest of the province (*Ōsaka Asahi shinbun*, 2 August 1933, Korea edition; *Seisen nippō*, 3 August 1933).

123. *Chōsen shinbun*, 26 September 1933.

124. *Keijō nippō*, 31 October 1933.

125. *Fuzan nippō*, 27 June 1934 A similar result was reported in an on-site survey conducted that month by municipal officials who stood for an hour in the five busiest Korean districts in the city (*Keijō ihō* 151 [April 1934]: 65–66). These statistics were not enumerated by ethnicity, suggesting that the actual percentage of Koreans wearing colored clothing was even lower.

126. Even in the 1940s, the white *hanbok* was prevalent in many rural areas of Korea (Lynn 2004, 82). There were some reported cases of Korean resistance to the coercive ban on white dress (Kong 2006, 156–59). One case of police compulsion in Hwanghae province led to a tragic suicide by a local Korean scholar (*Ōsaka Mainichi shinbun*, 7 December 1934, Korea edition).

127. *Seisen nippō*, 15 January 1934; Takenaka Kiyoshi, personal correspondence, 7 January 2003; testimony of Yang Sŏng-dŏk in H. Kang 2001, 100. In the Kilchu district, wearing white dress became all but a crime: the local authorities prohibited Koreans garbed in white from entering official and public buildings (*Hokusen Nichinichi shinbun*, 1 December 1934).

of youth education, thought guidance, daily life improvement, and the cultivation of civic morals."[128] Such recognition was given greater official attention in the 1930s, when increased focus on the management of everyday life inspired debates on the role of women as custodians of bourgeois values and public morality. Local Japanese women themselves had long embraced this role, at least since the time of the Russo-Japanese War. Through the Patriotic Women's Association, female settlers—especially wives of bureaucrats and corporate elites—actively participated in public life by organizing war support activities and engaging in local charity. No less adept than their metropolitan counterparts in highlighting the special aptitude of women, they periodically held roundtable discussions on marriage, family, and other topics of daily life, and cooperated with the authorities to organize an Infants Protection Week every May to elevate women's knowledge about childcare.[129]

Of greater concern to the regime, however, was to bring more Korean women into the public domain of activity. Local Japanese educators like Fuchizawa Yoshie had made this their personal mission since the time of annexation (see Chapter 1). They continued to spearhead this effort in the 1930s by retooling the ideology of the "good wife, wise mother" (*ryōsai kenbo*) to make the home a central locus of social reform. Speaking at a women's forum in 1936, for instance, Tsuda Setsuko (1902–1972) of the Ryokki Renmei preached that "a 'good wife, wise mother' from now on must become a woman who bears a responsibility toward society" by "actively working in the public realm [*shakaiteki ni hataraku*],"[130] offering herself as a prime example.

This message was echoed by moral suasion (and largely male) leaders as their campaign's mantra. Declaring that "the revitalization of the economy must start from the kitchen," in September 1933 Seoul's municipal

128. Hanada Kinnosuke, "Shakai jigyō no jūshinten," *Chōsen oyobi Manshū*, March 1926, 25.

129. See, for instance, *Chōsen shakai jigyō* 13, no. 5 (May 1935): 61–67; and 13, no. 6 (June 1935): 42–54. Numerous smaller women's groups also operated in Japanese resident communities throughout the peninsula. In Seoul, the women's section of the Ryokki Renmei adopted its own distinctive approach to enlightening female settlers by organizing lectures and workshops to reform "life consciousness" based on the spirit of *kokutai* and by holding bazaars and using their proceeds to make *imon* visits to soldiers stationed in Korea (Takasaki 1982b, 69).

130. *Dōhōai* 14, no. 4 (April 1936): 16.

government and district commissioners, in cooperation with local civic organizations, launched a moral suasion drive targeting Korean female residents in five *hōmen* districts. They offered lectures on housekeeping to promote thrift, showed motion pictures on the topic of self-reliance, and distributed handbills urging local Korean families to switch to colored clothing. School pupils were even mobilized with the aid of school principals to ensure these messages were "thoroughly followed in each home."[131] The Dōminkai also undertook its own crusade to "educate and enlighten" Korean women. In May 1935, for instance, they assembled some 352 female factory workers from the Kanebō Spinning Company for watching a didactic film designed to "nurture the spirit of hard work."[132] For local housewives, the Dōminkai recruited Korean female educators and doctors to lecture on childcare, family management, thrift, and spiritual cultivation, and offered "life improvement" cooking classes that emphasized nutritional value.[133] Though ostensibly aimed at Korean women of all classes, most of their activities remained within the bounds of bourgeois lifestyles, often applying metropolitan norms and standards for housewifery.

In the course of the 1930s, women's participation in the moral suasion campaign became more visible, as they sat alongside male leaders at national-level symposiums and contributed their own opinions in print. Particularly notable was the role of middle-class Korean "new women" like Kim Hwal-lan (1899–1970) and Son Chŏng-gyu (1896–1950), who brought their modern education to bear on social reform.[134] The rising prominence of "new women" was part of a larger history, recently studied by Theodore Jun Yoo, of Korean women who crafted new identities outside the home while operating within the bounds of Japanese modernity.[135] Along with settler educators like Tsuda Setsuko and Fuchizawa Yoshie, these Korean women emerged as influential voices, especially

---

131. *Keijō ihō* 144 (September 1933): 43–44.

132. *Keijō ihō* 165 (June 1935): 43.

133. *Keijō ihō* 177 (June 1936): 34; 178 (July 1936): 31; and 170 (November 1935): 33.

134. From the mid-1930s, Korean women also began to outnumber Japanese members in the Patriotic Women's Association (Kawa 2001, 4–6).

135. Yoo 2009, Chapter 2.

when the Ugaki administration solicited their cooperation in launching a drive for "awakening Korean women" in early 1936.[136]

Their newfound influence became evident at the first women's forum held for this purpose in February 1936. At the eager solicitation of the educational bureau chief, Watanabe Toyohiko, the invited Korean teachers from local girls' schools candidly shared their views and tendered a variety of requests to the authorities, anxious to shape the official policy and discourse on gender. "The issue of women hinges above all on the problem of their education," Kim Hwal-lan argued, challenging the male-centered colonial school system and exposing its Achilles heel. "It is difficult to expect Korean women to understand the official ideology of 'good wife, wise mother' when they cannot even read the words and understand their meaning."[137] The Korean teachers were equally uninhibited in conveying their frustration with the ongoing, and rather arbitrary, official effort to restructure Korean lifeways. They agreed on the need to promote colored clothing as part of modernizing Korean customs, for instance, but saw nothing wrong with the cut of Korean traditional dress (*hanbok*), which they considered "perfect" from the perspectives of hygiene and labor. Tsuda Setsuko, the only Japanese female participant at the forum, concurred with the Korean teachers, explaining how Korean dress was so appealing that she herself wore it in summer and occasionally in winter as well.[138] One veteran Korean teacher went even further in taking the authorities to task for their single-minded pursuit of assimilation policy, as demonstrated by the inundation of school textbooks with "Japanese customs like the Boys' Festival, the *bon* [lantern festival], and the Girls' Festival," which would "make absolutely no sense to Korean children."[139]

Remarkably, however, the Korean teachers also directed the brunt of criticism at their own men. Undeterred by the presence of business tycoons like Han Sang-nyong at the meeting, Kim Hyŏn-sil lodged an unsparing attack on Korean men for showing gross lack of concern for

---

136. "Chōsen fujin kakusei undō kondankai," *Dōhōai* 14, no. 4 (April 1936): 13; *Chōsen kōron*, March 1936, 80.

137. "Chōsen fujin kakusei undō kondankai," *Dōhōai* 14, no. 4 (April 1936): 14.

138. Ibid., 30. There were other Japanese, including some Government-General employees, who argued for preserving Korean clothes (Lynn 2004, 81).

139. "Chōsen fujin kakusei undō kondankai," *Dōhōai* 14, no. 4 (April 1936): 27.

family affairs, squandering money on pleasure-seeking and keeping multiple wives.[140] Instead of imposing the burdens of family life solely on women, the teachers argued, the moral suasion campaign should make equal efforts to enlighten Korean men on family matters and "spiritually reform" their minds and attitudes—legitimate grievances that made Han Sang-nyong "feel ashamed."[141]

The forum was a telling demonstration of how women became empowered much as they were co-opted by the moral suasion drive; Korean women, in particular, appropriated the campaign to mount a double-barreled attack on Korean patriarchy and Japanese assimilation policy.[142] In displaying a shared commitment to reform, these women used their new leverage to address social concerns and advance their own agendas that simultaneously anticipated active state intervention in daily life. Their growing ties with the colonial government, which became increasingly formalized after 1937,[143] mirrored the relationship between women's groups and "social bureaucrats" in Japan. Women of both metropole and colony gained power and status by "assuming public roles, often in alliance with the state," whether in daily life improvement or in "diligence and thrift" campaigns, that empowered them as mothers and housewives.[144] Educated Korean women sought such a role no less eagerly than did their settler counterparts, who likewise (as we will see below) refused to remain on the sidelines of moral suasion campaigns.

## *Youth Guidance*

Another principal focus of the moral suasion drive was youth guidance, which had a long history of challenges. As late as 1930, barely 20 percent of school-aged Korean children were enrolled in ordinary schools, and youth groups with nationalistic and socialist leanings had proliferated beyond control.[145] Marxist and revolutionary thought that swept

140. Ibid., 23–24. An attack on Confucian patriarchy had already been launched by the first generation of "new women" in the 1920s (Kwon 1998, 381–405).

141. "Chōsen fujin kakusei undō kondankai," 29. Also see, ibid., 24–25, 32–33.

142. Such attacks reflected the hybrid identity of Korean women (Choi 1999).

143. See Chapter 8.

144. Garon 1997, 134.

145. In 1930, Korean youth groups totaled 1,247 with 92,522 members (Chōsen Sōtokufu Gakumukyoku Shakaika 1933, 108).

through Japanese campus life also reached Korean and Japanese expatriate students at Keijō Imperial University and higher schools. The colonial and metropolitan police authorities, almost in unison, suppressed this hothouse atmosphere of youth defiance, dealing a devastating blow to both organized nationalist activity in Korea and student radicalism in Japan in the first few years of the 1930s.[146] Capitalizing on the unfolding impact of Manchuria, the Ugaki administration from late 1932 launched full-scale efforts to shepherd Korean youth groups in "a healthy direction" while stamping out "undesirable" (*furyō*) groups. Detailed instructions urged local administrators to expand youth facilities, hold workshops on youth cultivation, and nurture "sound youth leaders,"[147] and especially encouraged sports as a means of "developing healthy minds and bodies."[148]

With the police crackdown on radicals in full swing, the colonial state also intensified its drive to co-opt young Korean nationalists and socialists who began to renounce resistance in greater numbers after 1931.[149] Local Japanese and Korean capitalists were called upon to assist former thought criminals and recent converts from socialism and communism by founding, at the behest of the governor of Kyŏnggi province, the Shōdōkai in November 1935.[150] As Yun Ch'i-ho noted rather grudgingly in his diary,[151] each member was asked to contribute from 500 to 1,000 yen for maintaining the society's activities, which ranged from providing medical assistance to helping converts find work or return to school.[152]

---

146. For the case of Japan, see Ambaras 2005, 161.

147. Chōsen Sōtokufu, *Shisei nijūgonenshi* 1935, 955.

148. Ibid., 954; Chōsen Sōtokufu Gakumukyoku Shakaika 1933, 107, 120.

149. Some 35 percent of Koreans imprisoned by the Peace Preservation Law had reportedly undergone "ideological apostasy" (*tenkō*) by the end of 1933 (Takasaki 1993, 126).

150. They included settler merchants such as Kobayashi Genroku of Chōjiya, Satō Hisatarō and Tojima Yūjirō of the KTA, and Korean entrepreneurs such as Pak Yŏng-ch'ŏl, Pak Hŭng-sik, and Kim Yŏn-su (*Dōhōai* 13, no. 12 [December 1935]: 62–63).

151. Taehan Min'guk Mun'gyobu Kuksa P'yŏnch'an Wiwŏnhoe 1987, 10:522 (entry for 26 November 1935).

152. Keikidō Keisatsu Buchō to Keimu Kyokuchō et al., 23 December 1937, 5–6. These activities were implemented in close coordination with a special supervisory facility for young former thought criminals created by the Korea Thought Criminals Protection Observation Law in 1936 (*Chōsen Sōtokufu kanpō*, 15 December 1936; *Dōhōai* 15, no. 2 [February 1937]: 6–12).

Youth guidance was not simply a matter of winning over Koreans, however. Efforts at thought control were also directed at the generation of settlers born and raised in Korea, who constituted fully one-third of the Japanese population by 1930.[153] Socialization of young settlers as "proper Japanese," a long-standing concern among local leaders and educators, gained renewed attention in the early 1930s.[154] In Seoul, members of local Japanese youth groups, organized into a citywide league by a former *kenpeitai* officer who also worked for the Dōminkai, were frequently mobilized along with school pupils for activities like National Spirit Promotion Week. But no group was more committed to youth education than the Ryokki Renmei (Green Flag League). The Ryokki Renmei grew out of an esoteric Buddhist study group formed in the mid-1920s by Japanese professors and right-leaning students at Keijō Imperial University.[155] When it formally came into being on National Foundation Day in February 1933, the league launched a movement to diffuse "Japanese spirit" and clarify the notion of Japanese *kokutai* (national polity). The movement was led by Tsuda Sakae (1895–1961), a professor at Keijō Imperial University and a member of the Kokuchūkai, an ultranationalist group of Nichiren followers.[156] Representing a small yet active segment of the settler intelligentsia, the Ryokki Renmei stood at the forefront of a new generation of brokers of empire, eager to direct the course of Japan's continental project from the Korean peninsula.

As an ever-faithful servant of the emperor, the Ryokki Renmei's activities served to lay bare the inseparable link between moral suasion and Japanization. Its professed objectives—"research on thought," "the training and nurturing of local leaders (*chūken jinbutsu*)," and "the creation of public welfare facilities"—echoed many colonial programs, but all

---

153. Tange 1943, 2–3.

154. For a detailed study of the education of Japanese children in colonial Korea that centered on this concern, see Cohen 2006, Chapter 3.

155. On the formation of the Ryokki Renmei, see Nagashima 2003, 57–87.

156. This group was led by Tanaka Chigaku (1861–1939), whose teachings influenced the very architect of the Manchurian Incident, Ishiwara Kanji. According to the study of Nagashima Hiroki, Tsuda Sakae drew fundamentally on the "*kokutai* science" of Satomi Kishio (1897–1974), a son of Tanaka Chigaku who founded the Kokuchūkai and first introduced Tsuda in his college years to Nichiren Buddhism (Nagashima 2003, 69, 72; Tsuda Sakae, "Tanaka Chigaku sensei o omou," *Ryokki* 4, no. 12 [December 1939]: 12).

were geared toward its unique goal to promote emperor-centered Japanism.[157] As demonstrated by its exclusively Japanese membership before 1937, this effort was initially directed not at Koreans but at second- or third-generation settlers. From the perspective of the Ryokki Renmei leaders, young settlers, whose perceived lack of awareness of Japan's *kokutai* had inspired the league's formation,[158] warranted an assimilation project of their own. More urgent a task than Japanizing Koreans was to nurture a new generation of settler leaders infused with "correct understanding of *kokutai*" at this critical stage of Japan's continental expansion.

For this purpose, the Ryokki Renmei shortly after its birth set up a "students' section" (*gakuseibu*), enrolling Japanese male students at Keijō Imperial University and other higher schools in Seoul. In addition to periodically holding workshops, the students' section annually organized assemblies and speeches on National Foundation Day to "foster awareness of Japanese spirit and *kokutai*," aiming especially at junior students.[159] To engage in these activities was not only a patriotic gesture but an intensely self-reflective endeavor for the league's young leaders like Morita Yoshio (1910–1992), a recent graduate of Keijō Imperial University. Morita's comments in the league's bulletin he edited provide a glimpse into the sensibilities of a Korean-born settler, situated at once within and apart from the two worlds of Japanese and Koreans. "Although I could feel like 'going to *naichi*,'" he mused, "I could never feel like 'returning to *naichi*'" for "there is no place other than Korea for me to return to." Distinguishing between "the ideal of the Japanese *minzoku*" and the reality of "our living in Korea," Morita asked fellow settlers, "Isn't understanding this [distinction] clearly the most important thing for [us] residents of Korea?"[160] Future settler leaders, as envisioned by the Ryokki Renmei, were those who maintained ties to the imperial core even as they remained grounded in Korean soil. Embodying the transcendental spirit of *kokutai* as a principle to follow on a daily basis

157. Takasaki 1982b, 64–65.
158. Chŏng and Yi 1999, 365–67.
159. Takasaki 1982b, 69.
160. *Ryokujin* 4 (October 1935): 94.

ensured this linkage.[161] And this would prevent them from falling into the interstitial and indeterminate zone between Japanese and Koreans, as Tsuda Sakae suggested in his lectures. By cultivating "correct awareness of Japan's *kokutai*," in other words, settlers could turn their liminality to advantage and achieve true authenticity as Japanese on colonial terrain, free from the influence of crass *kokutai* theorists at home.[162]

More notable was the league's focus on the education of young Japanese women, who frequently became a lightening rod for the criticism of Korea-born settlers.[163] The image of free-spirited settler women, doubling with the specter of the "Modern Girl," provoked worried discussion on a "marriage crisis" and chary commentaries on the social threats they represented.[164] In response to such concerns, the Ryokki Renmei established the Seiwa Onna Juku (Seiwa Women's Academy) under the direction of Sakae's mother, Yoshie, and his wife, Setsuko. Targeting graduates of local girls' higher schools, the academy offered a one-year curriculum designed to imbue young female settlers with proper attributes as "imperial women."[165] As one alumnus, Sawai Mariko, later recounted, some 30 students enrolled in the academy each year. They took classes in general education, such as history (including Korean history), literature, and psychology, taught by Keijō Imperial University professors, in addition to classes designed for female self-cultivation such as "home economics, tea ceremony, and *waka* [Japanese poetry]."[166] On occasion, Japanese students attended joint lectures with Korean students from a sister school, the Tokuwa Women's Academy

161. Morita Yoshio, "Gendaijin no kokutaikan no shokei to sono hihan," *Ryokki* 1, no. 8 (August 1936): 14.

162. Tsuda inherited much of Satomi Kishio's critique of "today's vulgar Japanists" and "armchair [*kannenteki*] *kokutai* advocates," along with his call for "practical realization" (*jissen*) of *kokutai* (*Ryokki* 1, no. 5 [May 1936]: inside cover).

163. See H. Lee 2008b.

164. For examples of "marriage crisis" discussions, see *Chōsen shakai jigyō* 13, no. 5 (May 1935): 61–67; and 13, no. 6 (June 1935): 42–54. The issue of Korea-born Japanese females became the topic of a 1936 discussion forum hosted by the Ryokki Renmei in which other settler leaders participated (*Ryokki* 1, no. 9 [September 1936]).

165. Takasaki 1993, 128.

166. They were slight variations on what were considered in prewar Japan "the three prerequisites for prospective brides: tea ceremony, flower arrangement, and sewing" (Satō 2003, 136).

(founded by Pak In-tŏk [1896–1980] in 1941), and engaged in "practical training" such as making lunches for local primary school pupils.[167]

Although Sawai saw the Seiwa Women's Academy as no more than a finishing school for future brides (*hanayome shugyō*), the teachers sought to ensure their students imbibed more than homemaking skills. Director of the academy Setsuko herself frequently stood at the podium, preaching the dual role of women as mothers and spiritual guardians of Japan's *kokutai*. In keeping with the motto of the Ryokki Renmei's women's section (*fujinbu*), which she also supervised, Setsuko taught her pupils that making a "family that grows with Japan" (*Nihon to tomoni nobiru katei*) was nothing less than a patriotic act of "becoming loyal and good subjects of the emperor."[168] "To create a family suffused with love, justice, and power means to assist and protect the emperor's power on heaven and earth forever [*tenjō mukyū*],"[169] she explained in the rhetoric of Japan's foundation myths and filial piety. In another lecture, Setsuko stressed the importance of making "a family that smells of Japan," and enjoined her students on New Year's Day to worship the emperor's portrait as a way to "heighten the feeling that 'we are Japanese.'"[170] To build and sustain an imagined community of Japanese across the sea required such mundane acts of daily self-affirmation as children of the emperor.

Inspired by Setsuko's sermon, one student penned in her essay a revelation that "women must not passively observe what men do," but rather "must actively engage in a movement as women." Having attended the Ryokki Renmei's general assembly, another student wrote how "My heart shook with deep emotion when we shouted 'Long Live the Emperor!' [*tennō heika banzai*]".[171] As Mariko's recollection suggests, however, not all Japanese students at the Seiwa Women's Academy were as ideologically awakened by the Ryokki Renmei as these model essays would have us believe. The league's "students' section," composed of several dozen members at the time of creation, also continued to attract

---

167. Sawai 1996, 118–20.

168. Tsuda Setsuko, "Nihon to tomo ni nobiru katei," *Ryokki* 2, no. 1 (January 1937): 14–19.

169. Tsuda Setsuko, "Josei to shite no hansei," *Ryokki* 1, no. 9 (September 1936): 8.

170. Tsuda Setsuko, "Nihon to tomo ni nobiru katei," *Ryokki* 2, no. 1 (January 1937): 17.

171. *Ryokki* 1, no. 7 (July 1936): 45–46.

only a narrow segment of Japanese male students.[172] It was after the outbreak of war in 1937, as we shall see in the next chapter, that the Ryokki Renmei attained recognition and influence beyond the settler community by offering itself as a central refuge for socialist and nationalist converts.

## *Religious Cultivation*

The moral suasion activities targeting women and youth had barely moved beyond their rough administrative contours when Ugaki launched yet another campaign in the name of *shinden kaihatsu* (religious cultivation) in the spring of 1935.[173] Ugaki specifically envisioned religious cultivation as complementing the ongoing campaign of rural revitalization,[174] with the hope "to nurture healthy faith" and combat "superstition" among Koreans.[175] At the root of his call for *shinden kaihatsu* was his strong faith in the role of religion in modern life, which he viewed "as vital as material stability and fulfillment." But efforts to cultivate a religious mind, like national or "Japanese spirit," ultimately converged on the promotion of emperor worship, which soon prevailed over a tangle of objectives the campaign put forth.

In launching the campaign, the colonial government enlisted the cooperation of established religions—long partners in the metropolitan state's crusade against radical thought—while keeping the activities of religious sects in check. In early 1935 the authorities invited leading Japanese and Korean Buddhist monks, Christian missionaries, and Shinto priests to a series of discussion forums, where they brainstormed about how to enlighten the Korean masses "mired in superstition and devoid

---

172. Some former students at Keijō Imperial University who attended the league's events later recounted how they "felt uncomfortable" or found the atmosphere "bizarre." Interviews and questionnaire survey with 25 members of the Keijō Teikoku Daigaku/Yoka Dōsōkai, distributed on 5 December 2002, Tokyo, Japan. Also see a special edition on students in *Ryokki* 1, no. 11 (November 1936).

173. The term *shinden kaihatsu* was evidently born out of a conversation between the Governor-General and Ōnishi Ryōkei, head priest of Kiyomizu Temple in Kyoto, as well as three settler followers of Buddhism: Kobayashi Genroku, Yamaguchi Tahee, and Kugimoto Tōjirō (Nakamura Kentarō 1969, 94).

174. Ugaki 1935, 162–63.

175. *Chōsen* (Chōsen Sōtokufu), April 1935, 103.

of religious devotion [*shinkōshin*]."[176] Buddhist leaders particularly welcomed the new public role assigned to them. In Ugaki's words, this was a golden opportunity for Korean Buddhists to "revive their past glory" and regain a moral authority that had been eclipsed since the mid-Chosŏn dynasty.[177] For Japanese Buddhists, it was a chance to spread their influence beyond the settler communities, where their missionary activity had stalled in the late nineteenth century.[178] Ueno Kōjin, supervisor of the Honganji congregation, described his mission of rekindling Buddhist faith as a means of "returning gratitude" to Koreans who had introduced the religion to his homeland.[179] "Japanese and Korean monks must set an example by actively harmonizing and assimilating with each other," argued Inoue Michio who headed the Sōtō-sect temple, to dispel the "biased view that cooperation would lead to a takeover of Korea's Buddhist institutions by Japanese monks."[180]

Like the other campaigns, the religious cultivation effort began with great fanfare but without a concrete program. Not surprisingly its initial activities were poorly coordinated. At Ugaki's instigation, in March 1935 Korea's Buddhist leaders embarked on a "religious revival campaign" by going on circuit lectures through the provinces.[181] But the lack of principles and official instructions led them to deliver only "self-seeking" lectures, one local magazine reported, inviting criticism from Korean villagers and making them even more confused about the meaning of *kokutai*.[182] Ugaki and his officials moved to tackle this problem in January 1936 by meeting with dozens of religious leaders, as well as school teach-

---

176. *Chōsen shinbun*, 2 February 1935; Chōsen Sōtokufu, *Shisei nijūgonenshi* 1935, 918–19.

177. Ugaki, "Chōsen Bukkyō honji jūji shōtai sekijō ni okeru sōtoku aisatsu" (6 March 1935), in Chōsen Sōtokufu, *Chōsen shisei ni kansuru yukoku* 1937, 848–49.

178. The priests at Nanzan Honganji, located at the heart of the Japanese settlement, had already launched their initiative by offering a summer school to train Korean Buddhists from 1932 on (*Chōsen oyobi Manshū*, August 1935, 36).

179. *Keijō nippō*, 28 January 1937.

180. Inoue Michio, "Chōsen Bukkyō no fukkō ni tsuite," *Chōsen oyobi Manshū*, April 1935, 50–51.

181. *Keijō nippō*, 1 March 1935.

182. *Chōsen kōron*, October 1935, 87–88. Attitudes of local Japanese and Korean scholars and religious leaders toward the *shinden kaihatsu* campaign were equally divergent, especially on the use of "folk beliefs" (*minkan shinkō*) such as shamanism. See Kawase 2002.

ers, social reformers, and other civilian leaders like Sin Sŏng-nin (Dōminkai), Niwa Seijirō (Christian Youth Association), and Tsuda Sakae (Ryokki Renmei).[183] Their deliberations provided the basis for what became the campaign's three main goals: to clarify the concept of *kokutai*; to promote revering the gods (*kami*) and worshipping the ancestors; and to nurture a spirit of gratitude, appreciation, and self-reliance. Local administrators and civil groups were furnished with detailed guidelines for implementing these objectives, from the use of mass media and other propaganda devices (including slogans, plays, movies, lectures, workshops, and National Spiritual Promotion Week) to mobilizing local school pupils, housewives, and even "past Korean heroes [*eiyū*]" for fostering people's religious sensibilities.[184] The Ryokki Renmei leaders were among the first to respond by incorporating *shinden kaihatsu* as a central objective,[185] with the result that, as Tsuda Sakae explained, the league's activity almost word for word came to "correspond with official policy."[186]

A jumble of instructions failed to conceal the haphazard nature of the campaign as well as its intended vagueness. The point of *shinden kaihatsu*, the education bureau chief Watanabe had explained earlier, was to "encourage Koreans to visit temples and churches, and listen to sermons on Buddhism or Christianity or whatever." The authorities seem to have hoped, rather naïvely, that cultivating a "habit" of going to churches or worshipping at shrines, regardless of their desire to do so "from the heart," would eventually "implant in the [Korean] minds the concept of revering the gods [*kami*]."[187] Their corporatist approach to thought control, in other words, was not to single out one religion for promotion or persecution so much as to bring them all under the rubric of moral suasion; the authorities appeared to care less about their doctrines than their practical utility for cultivating "spirituality" among the Korean people.[188]

---

183. *Chōsen* (Chōsen Sōtokufu), February 1936; *Dōhōai* 14, no. 2 (February 1936): 1.

184. *Chōsen oyobi Manshū*, February 1936, 7–8; *Dōhōai* 14, no. 2 (February 1936): 1.

185. *Ryokki* 1, no. 6 (June 1936): 2–3.

186. Tsuda Sakae, "Shinden kaihatsu no konponteki yōi," *Ryokki* 1, no. 5 (May 1936): 2–3.

187. *Chōsen oyobi Manshū*, August 1935, 5–6.

188. According to the historian Kawase Takaya (2002), the campaign represented a form of "strategic syncretism" aimed at mobilizing the people's energies for a variety of

Their lack of focus itself was a reflection of the characteristically diffuse nature of colonial power. Even in the midst of state efforts to centralize control over society, we are continually reminded of how Korean rule took shape through a string of makeshift and improvised strategies, launched by bureaucrats who were often no more certain than their civilian deputies about its precise goals and direction.

As residents of Korea would soon discover, however, religious cultivation, like national spirit promotion, ultimately placed Shinto on the pulpit from which to preach emperor's divinity. To school pupils who were already required to visit a local shrine on national holidays and all other public occasions, *shinden kaihatsu* in the name of the emperor was a fait accompli. But as the rest of the population were goaded to follow this ritual, it raised a fundamental question regarding the status of Shinto as religion—one that Shakuo Shunjō, who had been closely monitoring the moral suasion campaign since the 1930 symposium, was quick to address in his magazine. Where the *shinden kaihatsu* campaign seemed to equate religious faith (*shinkō*) with reverence for Shinto deities and ancestors, he noted, contradicted the official line that "Shinto was not a religion."[189] When pressed on this point, the educational bureau chief Watanabe responded, "we should leave such a question to experts, and in any case visit shrines and worship the sun goddess Amaterasu and the Meiji Emperor as Japanese *kokumin*."[190] While maintaining their stance of religious neutrality, in other words, the colonial authorities followed political leaders in Tokyo in insisting that Shinto worship was a patriotic state ritual that did not conflict with private religious belief.[191]

Nearly all Buddhists, long accustomed to coexistence with Shinto, accepted this reasoning, but some Christian missionaries, predictably, did not.[192] In a highly publicized case in November 1935, the American principals of three Presbyterian mission schools in South P'yŏngyang

---

state goals, and may have served as a precursor for the wartime campaign for national spiritual mobilization (see Chapter 8).

189. *Chōsen oyobi Manshū*, February 1936, 8.

190. *Chōsen oyobi Manshū*, August 1935, 5.

191. Watanabe issued a note to provincial governors clarifying this official stance (*Heijō Mainichi shinbun*, 25 February 1936).

192. For more details on the opposition of Presbyterians to Shinto worship in P'yŏngyang, see Clark 2003, 209–21.

province (a traditional stronghold of Christianity) refused to worship at Heijō Shrine prior to the provincial conference of middle school principals—an act the *Keijō nippō* condemned as "near treason."[193] When the provincial government responded by proclaiming that it would "severely punish" those who resisted Shinto worship,[194] Niwa Seijirō, a representative of Japanese settler Christians, stepped in to mediate. Having earlier declared that "we object neither to visiting shrines nor to the global diffusion of Japanese spirit,"[195] Niwa defended the official line that worshipping God and worshipping Japanese ancestors were not incongruous acts.[196] When attempts at persuasion and repeated warnings made only one school comply, the authorities forcibly dismissed the Western principals of all three schools and replaced them with Koreans,[197] paving the way for more stringent measures to deal with intransigent ministers in the ensuing years.

Shinto worship would be but one among many emperor-centered rituals to be promoted by local officials, schoolteachers, and civic groups who gathered beneath the rubric of *shinden kaihatsu*. In July 1935, the Seoul Federation of Moral Suasion Groups prepared a detailed explanation of the origins of the rising-sun flag, the "dignity" and "style" of the national flag, and "the proper methods of handling, hoisting, and storing the flag." It was distributed to every household and member of the Federation, as well as bureaucratic offices, schools, banks, and corporations in the city.[198] The practice of placing a Shinto altar at home, too, spread through official promotion. In the summer of 1935, the police bureau instructed 17,000 officers to install household shrines, and the educational bureau encouraged 15,000 primary and middle school teachers to follow suit. The Hirata department store, run by a settler merchant family in Seoul, was placed in charge of manufacturing Shinto altars; when the store became swamped with orders, the authorities

---

193. *Keijō nippō*, 21, 26, and 30 November 1935.

194. *Keijō nippō*, 15 January 1936; *Chōsen shinbun*, 15 January 1936.

195. *Chōsen oyobi Manshū*, August 1935, 38.

196. Niwa Seijirō, "Jinja fusanpai mondai to ichibu senkyōshi no gokai," *Keijō nippō*, 13 and 15 December 1935.

197. *Keijō nippō*, 21 January 1936; *Ōsaka Mainichi shinbun*, 7 March 1936, Korea edition; *Keijō nippō*, 14 March 1936.

198. Sin Yŏng-hong 1984, 216.

planned to mobilize local vocational school students, in the guise of "practical training," to "implant [in their heads] the concept of religious devotion."[199] Taking a cue from Seoul, provincial governments launched their own campaigns to build more village shrines and encourage local families to install Shinto altars, hoping to transform ordinary Korean homes into houses of worship.[200]

Although coercion was the ultimate backbone of the corporatist regime of moral suasion, the presence of settlers in urban areas also proved instrumental. Emperor-centered rituals spread not only through institutionalized campaigns run by bourgeois elites, but through grassroots initiatives launched by more humble merchants. One such settler was Ōkubo Masatoshi, who specialized in the sales of Japanese national flags in Seoul. Ōkubo headed the Korean branch of the Dai-Nihon Kokki Sen'yōkai (Greater Japan National Flag Hoisting Society), whose commitment to "Japanese spirit" (*Nihon damashii*) was conspicuously displayed by a tower he built for hoisting the rising-sun flag in the center of the city. Toward the end of each lunar year, Ōkubo also distributed relief bags to the city's poor containing what he called "energy rice," a towel, and knitted undershirts, each item dyed with slogans (such as thrift, punctuality, fire prevention, and hard work). These acts of philanthropy and patriotism—a combination key to the strategy of moral suasion—impressed the authorities enough to secure him an appointment as district commissioner, a role that further legitimated his influence as a broker of empire.[201]

Many local Japanese businesses integrated imperial rituals into job training as well. Takeshima Shintarō, the president of Chōsen Unsō (Korean Transportation Company), made it mandatory for his 1,500 employees to visit local shrines for spiritual cultivation;[202] Kanebō Service Station similarly encouraged its clerks to worship at a shrine "voluntarily" on the first and fifteenth of every month.[203] More idiosyncratic was Kobayashi Genroku of Chōjiya, who promoted the imperial cult

---

199. *Keijō nippō*, 23 October 1935.

200. In North Kyŏngsang, for instance, the provincial government planned to build one shrine in each *myŏn* (*Chōsen minpō*, 12 March 1936).

201. Sin Yŏng-hong 1984, 87–88.

202. *Chōsen kōron*, May 1935, 114.

203. *Chōsen kōron*, March 1937, 78.

by honoring the "Seventeen-Point Constitution" of Japan's ancient Prince Shōtoku and by reciting the words of Emperor Meiji, in addition to a Buddhist sutra, to his employees every morning.[204] A model imperial subjectivity was also demonstrated by the Hayaoki-kai (Get-Up-Early Society), a motley group of officials, students, housewives, shopkeepers, and clerks (including some Koreans) whose membership at one point totaled over 10,000. In addition to cleaning the stone altar and steps of Chōsen Shrine, their morning routine included singing the national anthem, bowing toward the Imperial Palace (in Tokyo), and shouting "Long Live the Emperor!" followed by a round of exercises (*kokumin taisō*), a recitation of the Meiji Emperor's rescripts, and a prayer for the imperial family.[205]

To what extent Koreans observed or understood these rituals remains unclear,[206] but the peninsula, like the metropole, increasingly fell into a pattern of performing them daily. Minami Jirō (1874–1955), who succeeded Ugaki as Governor-General in August 1936, gave further clarity and focus to the *shinden kaihatsu* campaign by foregrounding its goal of Japanization. Speaking to provincial governors in September 1936, Minami declared that his goal was to "raise awareness of *kokutai*" and "cultivate a sturdy national spirit" through Shinto worship,[207] a commitment manifested in the National Spirit Promotion Week that year. Across the peninsula, urban residents were mobilized through community councils, schools, and civic organizations to visit local shrines and to make a bow toward the Imperial Palace. Each household was required to hoist a Japanese flag "even when it rains," and the centrality of Japan's imperial institution in daily life was stressed for nurturing public morality.[208] Even prisoners participated in the spiritual

---

204. Murakami 1942, 471.

205. *Chōsen oyobi Manshū*, January 1937, 79–81.

206. According to the Korean social section chief of the Seoul Municipal Government, an increasing number of Korean residents visited Shinto shrines, but "Koreans do not truly understand the meaning of Shinto worship" (*Chōsen shakai jigyō* 12, no. 1 [January 1934]: 82). There was also a gap between the number of Korean visitors to Chōsen Shrine and the official assessment of their degree of "spiritual assimilation" in this period (Henry 2006, 421–22).

207. *Keijō nippō*, 25 September 1936.

208. *Dōhōai* 14, no. 12 (December 1936): 33; *Keijō ihō* 185 (February 1937): 32–34.

campaign within the confines of a penitentiary.[209] Alerting people to "Japan in crisis," the colonial government now urged local residents to make National Spirit Promotion Week an everyday routine. In the following years, the authorities would strengthen their cooperation with civilian volunteers, especially settler retailers and company owners who continued to render their services as unofficial purveyors of imperial rituals and paraphernalia.[210]

## *Conclusion*

The colonization of Manchuria had a far-reaching impact on Korea and its inhabitants. Rendered by the press and propagandists as a site of mutual benefit, Manchuria offered Japanese and Koreans an opportunity to reconstitute their relations on a new frontier of cooperative expansion. The building of Manchukuo boosted Korea's trade and fueled its manufacturing plants, reinforcing the peninsula's status as a military supply base and the crux of Japan's emergent yen-bloc economy. Moreover, an empire-wide call to prepare the nation for crisis led the colonial government to forge new institutional channels through which to reach deeper into the lives of its subjects.

All such developments were mediated by settler leaders—journalists, merchants, entrepreneurs, educators, ideologues, religious leaders—who, in their own ways and for their varying interests, came together to join in the construction of their nation's new continental empire. The brokers of empire were irrevocably transformed in the process. As they strove to turn their liminal location into a key locus for the pursuit of Japan's continental ambition, the circuits and boundaries of their activity and influence expanded through multiplying networks of exchange linking Japan, Korea, and the Chinese continent. Yet at the same time, they found themselves further enmeshed in the colonial state, their visions and activities increasingly woven into the framework of moral suasion. Ugaki's corporatist regime allowed many civilians to penetrate the ruling structure at its lowest level, which significantly enhanced the regime's own ability to "broadcast power," to borrow the term of Jeffrey

209. *Dōhōai* 14, no. 12 (December 1936): 28–31.
210. *Keijō ihō* 199 (June 1938): 52.

Herbst.[211] Put differently, the informal sphere in which the brokers of empire had been operating became more institutionalized, as they steadily expanded their role as local functionaries of the colonial regime. The paradoxical result was a combination of growing leverage and declining autonomy in the course of the 1930s.

The Manchurian impact on settler leaders' alliance with Korean elites was equally complicated. It had the effect of reinforcing their bourgeois unity even as it deepened settlers' ambivalence. For the prospect of mutual profit encouraged Koreans to redefine their terms of cooperation with the Japanese as an equal partnership in the colonial enterprise—a demand for full citizenship that, as we will see, increasingly spread to the rest of the local population.

The cascade of moral suasion campaigns launched under Ugaki signaled the beginning of sweeping changes that would engulf the peninsula after 1937. They set in motion a routine of increasingly regimented life in the colony that would revolve around daily public rituals to venerate the emperor. Wartime programs would also display the same pattern of official-civilian cooperation, building on Ugaki's corporatist strategy to deploy youth and women's groups, established religions, and community councils as vehicles of social control.[212] As the moral suasion network was transmuted into a fascistic structure for total war mobilization, the brokers of empire, too, were transformed more fully into organs of the colonial regime.

---

211. Herbst 2000.

212. This pattern was also observed in the promotion of the Manchurian venture in Japan (L. Young 1998, 161–74).

# EIGHT

## *Citizens and Subjects under Total War*

On New Year's Day, 1941, Governor-General Minami Jirō and his wife appeared on the front page of the *Keijō nippō*, clad in Korean traditional dress. By this carefully choreographed gesture of amity toward his Korean subjects, Minami apparently intended to demonstrate his personal devotion to fostering *naisen ittai* (unity between Japan and Korea), the wartime policy of the Government-General. If Minami temporarily donned Korean attire out of concern for public relations, Tsuda Setsuko of the Ryokki Renmei wore *hanbok* on a daily basis, in keeping with the motto of her organization to "take what is good and discard what is bad"[1] from Korean traditional customs. Whatever their differences, these two figures shared a wartime vision of ethnic engineering on an unparalleled scale. The goal to unify Koreans and Japanese in all manners of daily life and thought propelled what was arguably the most important partnership yet between the state and the settler community.

Launched at the peak of Japan's aggressive attempt to assert itself on the global stage, the policy of *naisen ittai* led to an unprecedented level of institutional integration of colony and metropole. By the time of the Pacific War, both regimes exercised a monopoly on violence through the ubiquitous police and the enlarged army. Both built an extensive framework for encompassing the entire population through "administered mass organizations"[2] and for blunting any collective resistance to state

1. Son et al. 1939, 2.
2. Kasza 1995.

policies. And in both countries, responsibilities for the day-to-day affairs of local communities devolved to men of influence from the middle strata.[3] In organizing the population for total war, the metropolitan and colonial states began to resemble each other, and so did the societies mobilized by them.

This blurring occurred as two distinct logics of governance intertwined. One was the compulsory unification of total war, or what historian Yamanouchi Yasushi has described as "enforced homogeneity," an attempt "to unite all the people under the slogan of a common destiny as citizens of a single national community."[4] The other was the culmination of a longer process of integrating Koreans culturally into the emperor-centered polity. During the last decade of Japanese rule, this long-standing colonial credo fused with the exigencies of war to generate a set of policies and practices collectively known as *kōminka* (imperialization), the accelerated transformation of the local populace into loyal subjects of the emperor. Targeting primarily but not exclusively Koreans, as we will see, imperialization may be heuristically seen as expediting processes launched since annexation to steer the colonial policy of assimilation: the making of loyal imperial subjects (*shinmin*) and dutiful citizens (*kokumin*), paired with an overall Japanization of lifestyle. As a final stage in this project, *kōminka* entailed a radical social experiment, "unmatched in world history,"[5] of assimilating 25 million Koreans into the Japanese nation (*minzoku*) in "form, mind, blood, and flesh."[6]

This grandiose project was carried out through an equally elaborate institutional apparatus. With the outbreak of war in 1937, the loosely connected civilian and semi-official actors who had been promoting *naisen yūwa*, moral suasion, and emperor worship coalesced into a single, highly centralized body under the banner of the Kokumin Seishin Sōdōin Undō (National Spiritual Mobilization Campaign). The settler-run Ryokki Renmei, with its ongoing mission to spread awareness of *kokutai*, played an especially critical role in the new organization as an ideological conduit between the peninsula and the metropole. But as the distinction

3. Amemiya 1998, 209–34.

4. Yamanouchi 1998, 3.

5. A recollection of one former colonial bureaucrat in Gakushūin Daigaku Tōyō Bunka Kenkyūjo 2000, 157.

6. *Sōdōin* 1, no. 2 (July 1939): 57–58.

between civilian and official agents further blurred in the course of total war, not a single broker of empire effectively operated outside of the state apparatus; rather, all settler leaders became fully absorbed into its local hierarchy.

Totalizing though its official design may have been, however, *naisen ittai* did not proceed as planned. Local reactions to the campaign betrayed a significant gap in perception between the authorities who insisted on imperial subjecthood, and Koreans who adopted wartime rhetoric to demand civic equality. Settlers, for their part, provided only ambivalent cooperation with imperialization policies, remaining reluctant as ever to accept their underlying premise of ethnic unity. Beneath the appearance of a united front, there accordingly emerged deep, if unspoken, fissures between Koreans and Japanese settlers, with each group trying to define the meaning of *naisen ittai* to elevate their own political standing. Not only did these developments expose and deepen the central tensions of empire; they also brought the liminality of settlers, once more, into sharp relief.

## *National Spiritual Mobilization*

In rousing Korea's residents for total war, the new colonial government under Minami continued to rely on the cooperation of the upper and middle classes. For a state authority that had labored long to win over the Korean intelligentsia, war itself proved to be the most effective force of conversion. Japan's resounding victories against China early in the conflict served as a breaking point for most nationalists and socialists, who had begun to vacillate in the wake of the Manchurian Incident of 1931. Having joined the Central Council a few years earlier, Ch'oe Rin set the tone by severing his already weakened ties to Ch'ŏndogyo (Religion of the Heavenly Way),[7] becoming the president of a pro-government paper, *Maeil sinbo*, in 1938. More public announcements of volte-face followed suit. Socialist converts to Japanism declared "a war on communism" by forming patriotic organizations to present a "united ideo-

7. Ch'ŏndogyo was launched in 1905 as a successor to the Tonghak (Eastern Learning), a religious movement rooted in the peasant rebellions of the nineteenth century. Ch'ŏndogyo followers played a central role in organizing the March First Movement of 1919.

logical front for national defense."[8] With or without official pressure, the entire spectrum of religious groups—Christians, Buddhists, Confucians, and Ch'ŏndogyo followers—unfurled their own patriotic drives by raising money, dispatching missions, and holding rallies and prayer meetings for the imperial army.[9] And where the impact of war did not suffice, the state moved to quash all voices of dissent, as it did with the two leading Korean dailies, *Tonga ilbo* and *Chosŏn ilbo*, which were finally ordered to shut down in August 1940.

Settler leaders, too, entered the fray. Using radio broadcasts, old and new brokers of empire—from journalist Kikuchi Kenjō and Kada Naoji of the Seoul Chamber of Commerce and Industry, to Tsuda Setsuko of the Ryokki Renmei—joined the bureaucrats in calling on their listeners to render "patriotic service to the nation on the home front" (*jūgo hōkoku*).[10] No more willing to brook dissent from their countrymen, the authorities, meanwhile, ferreted out Japanese teachers with "liberalist" inclinations and pressured them to resign,[11] and expelled from Korea journalists who dared to criticize Minami's policy of *naisen ittai* on the grounds of "libel against the Government-General."[12] In such a climate, Shakuo Shunjō, the feisty editor of the longest-running settler magazine, *Chōsen oyobi Manshū*, was finally forced to give up his decades-old struggle against the Governor-General's authoritarian rule. No longer able to "write my opinions or critique policies," which he viewed as tantamount to the loss of his "raison d'être," Shakuo announced his decision to lay down his pen in early 1941.[13]

Shakuo's departure from the colonial media symbolized the end of an era for the brokers of empire, and the beginning of their role as full-fledged partners of the wartime regime. Organized resistance in Korea all but disappeared after 1937,[14] and pro-government and fascistic movements multiplied to fill the void. In 1938 the Korea Central Young Men's

8. *Chōsen oyobi Manshū*, December 1939, 28–32.

9. *Chōsen kōron*, April 1938, 74–75; Im Chong-guk 1992, 297–308.

10. For a transcription of the radio broadcast, see Chōsen Hōsō Kyōkai 1938–1941.

11. Keijō Kōtō Shōgyō Gakkō 1990, 80–81.

12. Yi Hyŏng-sik 2008, 67, 74. Under the policy of "one paper per province," local Japanese-language newspapers were also abolished or consolidated, at a much faster pace than in the metropole.

13. Shakuo Shunjō, "Honshi haikan no ji," *Chōsen oyobi Manshū*, January 1941, 95–96.

14. *Chōsen oyobi Manshū*, January 1938, 39.

Christian Association led by Yun Ch'i-ho amalgamated with the Japanese YMCA led by Niwa Seijirō, exhorting its members to "arm [themselves] with the Bible" in spreading "Japanese spirit" and the gospel of *naisen ittai.*[15] The following year, merchants and manufacturers around the peninsula declared an Economic Patriotic Service Campaign to shore up Korea's role as "a military supply base" and to help implement state economic control.[16] Meanwhile, Japanese and Korean members of the Patriotic Women's Association and the army-backed Greater Japan National Defense Women's Association (Dai-Nihon Kokubō Fujinkai; founded in Osaka in 1932) vied to outdo each other in welcoming and sending off troops at train stations.[17] The settler intelligentsia, who had long stood behind the empire, now operated at the frontline of war propaganda. A leading voice in this effort, Mitarai Tatsuo (1895–1975) of the *Keijō nippō*, called on Korea's 25 dailies to unite in "guiding public opinion" and assisting the state in information control.[18] Two professors of Keijō Imperial Univeristy, Karashima Takeshi (1903–1967) and Tsuda Katashi (1906–1990; younger brother of Tsuda Sakae and director of the Ryokki Renmei) launched a more ambitious project to spread "the culture of the Imperial Way" and to foster "national literature" (*kokumin bungaku*) that embodied "Japanese spirit" by bringing together some 250 Korean and Japanese writers into the Chōsen Bunjin Kyōkai (Korea Writers' Association).[19] Through a flurry of patriotic activities, the entire settler leadership, along with the Korean upper class, was effectively transformed into an organ of the wartime colonial regime.

These joint Japanese-Korean organizations were brought under a single mass movement, christened the Kokumin Seishin Sōdōin Undō (National [or People's] Spiritual Mobilization Campaign). Launched in response to Prime Minister Konoe Fumimaro's (1891–1945) famed dec-

---

15. *Keijō nippō*, 5 August 1937; Keikidō, *Chian jōkyō* (September 1938), fuhyō, "Nihon Kirisutokyō Seinenkai Chōsen Rengōkai."

16. Kimura 2004, 112–13; *KG* 292 (May 1940): 141.

17. *Chōsen shinbun*, 29 September 1937. In March 1942 the two organizations were unified into the Korean branch of the Dai-Nihon Fujinkai (Greater Japan Women's Association) created in Tokyo a month earlier (Im Chong-guk 1992, 323).

18. *Chōsen oyobi Manshū*, March 1938, 81.

19. *Keijō Nippō*, 30 October 1939; *KSUY* 1943, 62. The association was later amalgamated along with other literary organizations into the Chōsen Bunjin Hōkokukai in 1943. For a study on *kokumin bungaku*, see Kim Yun-sik 1993, 7, 231–42.

laration of the "New Order in East Asia" in November 1938, the campaign aimed to engage the local population in two broad types of activity: war support (such as sending off soldiers and collecting donations for the army) and *kōminka* (especially diffusing Japanese language and emperor-centered rituals).[20] These activities gradually absorbed the existing colonial programs (rural revitalization, daily life reform, religious cultivation) and their local institutions into its administrative hierarchy.[21] But the ideological origins of the campaign, or Korea's "people's movement" (*kokumin undō*), as it was alternatively called,[22] dated much earlier, according to one of its settler directors who traced them to the activity of the Ilchinhoe, an organization notorious in public memory for having rallied for the annexation of Korea.[23] The call for *naisen ittai* signaled a final step toward realizing the goal of annexation to "amalgamate Japan and Korea into one body,"[24] prompting, indeed, a fundamental policy shift from the elimination of nationalism to the eradication of a nation. This shift became apparent as the various projects of assimilation—nationalization (*kokuminka*), Japanization (*Nihonjinka*), and imperialization (*kōminka*) whose rough outlines had emerged in the 1910s (see Chapter 2)—were now consolidated into one state-controlled program to mold all residents into a single, undifferentiated body: the emperor's people.

Although the National Spiritual Mobilization Campaign was largely a bureaucratic invention, the authorities sought to make it appear as civilian-led as possible. To that end, the colonial state enlisted a bevy of Japanese and Korean elites to form the Kokumin Seishin Sōdōin Chōsen Renmei (Korean League for National Spiritual Mobilization; hereafter the Korean League). Designed as a support organ for the Government-General,[25] the Korean League integrated into its member-

---

20. For details of this campaign and its objectives, see Uchida 2011b.

21. On the role of Korean public officials in soliciting "voluntary participation" of local residents in this campaign, see Matsumoto 2006. On the role of police officers, see Matsuda 2000, 204–10.

22. *CKSU* 1945, 21–22.

23. *CKSU* 1945, 1. The *naisen yūwa* campaign led by the Dōminkai and other organizations was also recognized as an ideological precursor to the wartime *naisen ittai* campaign. Ryokki Renmei, *Chōsen shisōkai gaikan*, 1939, 60–61.

24. *Chōsen gyōsei* 19, no. 7 (July 1940): 4.

25. *Sōdōin* 1, no. 1 (June 1939): 24; *CKSS* 1940, 26.

ship the entire array of civic and semi-official organizations that local elites had headed since the 1920s and early 1930s.[26] The brokers of empire and their Korean allies, joined by nationalist "converts,"[27] worked closely with high-ranking bureaucrats and army officers on the Korean League's board of directors, which was chaired by Vice Governor-General Ōno Rokuichirō (1887–1985). Its activities were supervised by the education bureau chief Shiobara Tokisaburō (1896–1964), Minami's right-hand man, who earned the sobriquet "the peninsula's Hitler" for his uncompromising stance on *kōminka*.

If the "civilian-led" Korean League served as the brain of the campaign, the key organs for enforcing its activities on the ground were patriotic neighborhood associations (J. *aikokuhan*; K. *aegukpan*) of ten to twelve households each.[28] The web of neighborhood associations ramified across the peninsula much faster than in the metropole, as the president of *Keijō nippō* proudly noted, providing "a precedent for Japan's *tonarigumi* (neighborhood association)"[29] that only began to be formed from 1940.[30] Through this mechanism, which encompassed individual

---

26. The Korean League, headquartered in Seoul, incorporated into its membership 61 civic and semi-official organizations, most of which were run by influential settlers and Korean elites: community councils and district commissioners; social work organizations and religious groups; chambers of commerce, newspaper agencies, and trade and professional associations; assimilationist and "pro-Japanese" organizations; and a host of "administered mass organizations" such as the Teikoku Gunjin Kōenkai (Imperial Soldiers' Assistance Association), the Teikoku Zaigō Gunjinkai (Imperial Local Reservists' Association), the Aikoku Fujinkai, and the Dai-Nihon Kokubō Fujinkai. A year before the National Spiritual Campaign was launched, these local groups had also made a ringing declaration of support to Japan's imperial army by forming the Korea Military Assistance League (see Chōsen Gunji Kōen Renmei 1939).

27. *Sōdōin* 1, no. 1 (June 1939): 54–55. They included brokers of empire (such as Ishihara Isojirō, Koezuka Shōta, Niwa Seijirō, Kada Naoji, Yanabe Eizaburō, and Maeda Noboru), and pro-Japanese bourgeois elites (such as Han Sang-nyong, Cho Pyŏng-sang, Wŏn Tŏk-sang, Pak Hŭng-sik, Pak Yŏng-ch'ŏl, and Kim Myŏng-chun). These elites were joined by former nationalists such as Kim Sŏng-su and Ch'oe Rin, and prominent Korean female educators such as Kim Hwal-lan and Son Chŏng-gyu.

28. In reality, the number ranged between seven and twenty households per group (Anzako 1995, 1–2).

29. Mitarai 1942, 27.

30. *CKSU* 1945, 43; Havens 1978, 40–41; Koezuka 1941, 120.

Korean *as well as* Japanese households,[31] Minami imagined "the will of the state pulsating energetically at every tip and cell" of the body politic.[32] "The true grand mission of each neighborhood assembly is to create one family community [*kyōdōtai*] as the basis for the state," explained Koezuka Shōta, a settler director of the Korean League. The formation of such "a patriotic neighborhood family" would have the effect of "injecting an awareness of true Japaneseness into one's soul," "unifying the state and the people," and "letting Japanese spirit spontaneously grow from within."[33] Once Japanese and Koreans embraced each other as "blood kin," the spiritual mobilizers hoped, a "family tree" of imperial subjects would sprout up in defense of a "family-empire."[34]

The use of patriotic neighborhood associations as grassroots organs of *kōminka* reflected Minami's personal credo. When explaining their significance to local deputies of the spiritual mobilization campaign in May 1939, Minami presented himself as the most faithful and abiding subject of the emperor, readily surrendering his autonomy to the august monarch. "Although my job is being the Governor-General, I am [also] a member of a patriotic neighborhood association, as is any resident of Korea. . . . Every morning without fail, I first make a bow toward the Imperial Palace, then recite the Oath as Subjects of the Imperial Nation, and on the first of every month I worship at a Shinto shrine."[35] Such a routine charted a method of imperialization by which "the onus of becoming Japanese,"[36] to borrow the words of Leo Ching, would be transferred from the colonizer to the colonized. No longer an indefinitely deferred goal of the colonial state, assimilation was redefined as the *telos* of the emperor's self-assimilating subjects.

Translating Minami's ideal into practice was another matter. The spiritual mobilizers, from neighborhood heads to schoolteachers and corporate managers, goaded (and in the case of Christians, harassed)

---

31. By late February 1939, there were 338,924 associations with 4,259,755 member families (Anzako 1995, 12).

32. *Chōsen* (Chōsen Sōtokufu), May 1938, 112.

33. Koezuka 1941, 117.

34. I borrow this metaphor of the "family tree" from L. Young 1998, 366.

35. Minami Jirō, "Renmei honrai no shimei: giron yorimo jikkō e," *Sōdōin* 1, no. 2 (July 1939): 59–60.

36. Ching 2001, 97.

local residents into performing the triad of imperial rituals, which became as routinized as fire drills and war donation drives. The effect was to exteriorize the process of *kōminka* by reducing it to a set of bodily practices and public rites—shortcuts for Koreans to "become Japanese"—without real regard for their ability to comprehend the meaning of their actions.[37] Tackling the ideological vacuity that soon became apparent was an afterthought. Although the authorities had no shortage of civilian volunteers to enlist for this purpose, the Ryokki Renmei emerged head and shoulders above the rest. After years of relative obscurity, this didactic organization was now catapulted into public prominence as the chief custodian of *kokutai* education, a status it maintained until the end of war.

## *Ideologue of* Naisen Ittai*: Ryokki Renmei*

As we saw in the previous chapter, the Ryokki Renmei had launched a movement to clarify the notion of *kokutai* and spread emperor ideology well before the state embarked on such an effort of its own. After 1937, the league redirected its focus to Korean youth, especially targeting recent converts from socialism and communism. While carrying out its own outreach activity, the Ryokki Renmei quickly attained the status of a de facto ideological arm of the colonial regime, and deepened its character as "an emperor-centered fascistic organization"[38] in the course of the war.

Several months before the colonial government launched the National Spiritual Moblization Campaign, the Ryokki Renmei unfurled its own "Green Life Movement" (*midori no seikatsu undō*). According to Tsuda Katashi who effectively led the organization from 1937 (while Sakae remained its nominal head), this was a "comprehensive cultural movement" to promote the construction of a "new Korea" through "daily life based on the spirit of green."[39] The "spirit of green," he explained, symbolized "life force," that which "makes everything expand and nurture": a spirit that "lies at the basis of all human thought . . .

---

37. For a similar process in wartime Taiwan, see ibid., 89–90.
38. Chŏng and Yi 1999, 365–67.
39. For details of the Green Life Movement, see Tsuda 1940, 143–56.

including Japanese spirit, Buddhism, and Western thought."[40] His explanation had unmistakable resonance with the notion of *kokutai* as expounded by the treatises *Kokutai no hongi* (Principles of the National Polity, 1937) and the *Shinmin no michi* (The Way of the Imperial Subject, 1941)—"that peculiar amalgamation of Shinto, Buddhist, neo-Confucian, and Western monarchist ideals"[41]—or with the succinct way one Korean member, Hyŏn Yŏng-sŏp, rendered "Japanese spirit": "plurality within absolute unity."[42] In short, what Tsuda referred to as the "spirit of green" was none other than Japan's *kokutai* itself. Highlighting the capacity of Japan's *kokutai* to "assimilate all those that have come its way" (in contrast to the Christian "West," which "hardly embraces pagans"), Tsuda claimed that "only by means of Japanese spirit can we unite the world."[43]

In building an emperor-centered "life community [*seikatsu kyōdōtai*], first in Japan and ultimately in the whole world," the Ryokki Renmei leaders endeavored to make young Koreans key partners in their project. "We must begin with the construction of a new East Asian Cooperative Community [*Tōa kyōdōtai*]," Tsuda argued, which depended on the cooperation of Koreans and Japanese who constituted the core of the dynamic yet eternal "Yamato *minzoku*."[44] Resorting to a Darwinian logic that Tessa Morris-Suzuki has aptly characterized as a "multicultural process of natural selection,"[45] the Ryokki Renmei leaders imagined the Japanese and Koreans as a divided nation coming to terms with its shared origins, and the cornerstone of a multiethnic empire that had begun to stretch across the Chinese continent. Only when the two peoples dissolved their separate identities into one *kokutai*, Katashi argued, could a new East Asian community come into being as the Yamato *minzoku* spread the Imperial Way to "all corners of the world" (*hakkō ichiu*). "The construction of a new Korea," and by extension the creation of a new global order, hinged on what he construed as a voluntary act of Korean

40. *Ryokki* 4, no. 12 (December 1939): 4–5.
41. Bix 2000, 314.
42. *Ryokki* 3, no. 2 (February 1938): 21.
43. Ryokki Renmei 1939, 47; Tsuda 1940, 152–53; *Ryokki* 5, no. 7 (July 1940): 5–8.
44. *Sōdōin* 1, no. 6 (November 1939): 45–48.
45. Morris-Suzuki 1998, 175.

national rebirth, an opportunity for "the peninsula's 23 million *kokumin* to make an unending contribution to world history."[46]

The Ryokki Renmei underwent rapid expansion after 1937 by creating its own network of moral suasion. In addition to a students' section and a women's academy, the Ryokki Renmei managed its own clinic, farm, lecture hall, library, and even a "sea house" designed to "promote health" on a beach in South Ch'ungch'ŏng.[47] To diffuse Japanese spirit, its Nihon Bunka Kenkyūjo (Japan Cultural Research Institute) also published a slew of periodicals and pamphlets, including "Korea's only ideological magazine permitted by the Newspaper Law."[48] And through countless lectures, seminars, and "several hundred small assemblies" it organized annually, the league aspired to reach out to "every strata of society." Actively enrolling Koreans in its ranks boosted its membership from several dozen at the time of creation to over 4,000 by 1941.[49]

During this period, the Ryokki Renmei manufactured some fanatical Korean ideologues of *naisen ittai*. The most famous by far was Hyŏn Yŏng-sŏp (1907–?), a son of a Central Council member and graduate of Keijō Imperial University, who joined the Ryokki Renmei in the spring of 1937. Hyŏn's book, *Chōsenjin no susumu beki michi* (The Way the Koreans Must Proceed), published in 1938 and reprinted eleven times within a year, was a searing denial of the author's past as much as an affirmation of his present. Intended as a form of "self-criticism," Hyŏn's book chronicled a spiritual journey of conversion, following a socialist youth to his final apostasy and "rebirth as Japanese." Its argument that Koreans were fated to become Japanese, and had no choice but to accept and welcome this destiny,[50] sent shock waves across the peninsula. So did Hyŏn's call for discarding the Korean vernacular, which he deemed an obstacle to the complete realization of *naisen yūwa*. "In order to live truly and permanently, Koreans must abandon them-

---

46. Tsuda 1939, 44–46; Tsuda 1940, 151.

47. For an overview of the Ryokki Renmei's activities, see *Ryokki* 3, no. 2 (February 1938): 14–17. For more on a farmers' academy (*nōseijuku*) opened in 1939 by the Ryokki Renmei, see the memoir of its manager (Yanagisawa Shichirō 1969).

48. *Ryokki* 1, no. 8 (August, 1936): 14; and 4, no. 12 (December 1939): 9.

49. Takasaki 1982b, 65–66.

50. Hyŏn 1940, 3, 185–204.

selves and dive into the Japanese state,"[51] Hyŏn argued. This required rigorous and self-conscious efforts to negate one's identity until one became "instinctively Japanese." More than a matter of mimicry, as historian Yi Sŭng-yŏp has perceptively noted, what was called for was an incessant attempt to "autonomously and willfully deceive oneself."[52] Such an act embodied the hope of young Koreans like Hyŏn to escape their colonized status by joining the ruling *minzoku* of a "new Japan" on its way to global supremacy. It also reflected their understanding of Korea's central position within Japan's far-flung empire. Hyŏn's colleague Yi Yŏng-gŭn (1910–?), for instance, opposed "treating Koreans, who are about to become imperialized as Japanese, on the same level as Manchurians and Chinese or Southern races." Clearly, Yi had internalized the message of Tsuda Katashi that Koreans should join the Japanese in guiding the East Asian community, whose concentric circles of ethnic brotherhood extended from the metropole to Korea, Taiwan, Manchukuo, and China, in that order.[53]

By 1940, the Green Life Movement was "in the process of reaching all of Korea as well as all of Japan," and was projected to soon envelop "Manchuria, China, and other parts of the world."[54] In 1943, when the authorities announced the decision to extend conscription and universal education to Korea, Tsuda Katashi offered a bold new timeline for *kōminka.* He now recast the 30 years since annexation as merely "the first half" of the process and dubbed the next 30 years as the "decisive" period for "imperializing the peninsula." This would further ensure that "the uppermost strata of [Korean] society 60 years from now will be dominated by children currently of age ten and below," offspring of "fathers and mothers who were born as pure imperial subjects." Accordingly, Tsuda called for the "complete realization of *naisen ittai* within two generations or 60 years."[55]

In expounding "the mission of unifying the world under the emperor's benevolent rule," the Ryokki Renmei was effectively joining the imperial chorus of theologians in Japan, including "university professors,

---

51. *Ryokki* 3, no. 2 (February 1938): 21.
52. Yi Sŭng-yŏp 2001, 32.
53. Ibid., 34–35; Tsuda 1939, 81.
54. *Ryokki* 5, no. 4 (April 1940): 42, 46.
55. *Ryokki* 8, no. 3 (March 1943): 16–18.

Zen and Nichiren Buddhist priests, and government bureaucrats,"[56] not to mention a long line of race theorists and anthropologists who had supplied intellectual justifications for the empire. Yet at the same time, the Ryokki Renmei leaders were careful to distinguish themselves from "a mere fascist or ultranationalist organization,"[57] and especially from metropolitan theorists whose understanding of *kokutai* they often dismissed as bastard Japanism. When Tsuda Katashi lamented that the Japanese at home who "should be the ones to lead the peninsula's people [*hantōmin*]" failed to comprehend the true meaning of *naisen ittai*, he was implicitly blaming *kokutai* theorists for making Korea "lecture" to their countrymen instead.[58] And out of desire to spread a more correct, "scientific" understanding of *kokutai*, his brother Sakae made a paean to his old master Tanaka Chigaku by crediting him with introducing to the world "Saint Nichiren," the thirteenth-century founder of Nichiren Buddhism, who allegedly clarified the meaning of *kokutai* "before Motoori Norinaga did."[59] By elevating the status of Tanaka vis-à-vis practitioners of National Learning (*kokugaku*), the Tsudas envisioned a place for themselves both above and apart from metropolitan thinkers of their generation.

Accompanying such expatriate posture, rooted in liminality, was an awareness, widespread among the colonial intelligentsia at the time,

---

56. Bix 2000, 326–27.

57. *Ryokki* 3, no. 2 (February 1938): 18–20. Although some scholars have characterized the Ryokki Renmei as "an emperor-centered fascist organization" (Chŏng and Yi 1999; Pak Sŏng-jin 1999), Nagashima Hiroki cautions against a simple characterization of the organization as fascist, pointing out its ideologically ambivalent roots in Satomi Kishio's *kokutai* science that defied a binary classification of "left-wing" and "right-wing" or "fascist" thought. Instead, he characterizes its orientation in terms of "restoration-renovation" (*fukkō-kakushin*). See Nagashima 2003, 58, 70–71. Noting the league's "entrepreneurial skills" in launching a variety of projects, one article likened the Ryokki Renmei to popular new religions such as Ōmotokyō and Hitonomichi Kyōdan (*Chōsen Gyōsei* 19, no. 2 [February 1940]: 98). Indeed, the league's aims (to "construct humankind's paradise" and to "complete an individual's human character"), in addition to its eclecticism and stress on daily mass life, very much resembled these new religions that mushroomed since the 1920s (see, for instance, Murayama Chijun's discussion of new religions in *Ryokki* 1, no. 5 [May 1936]: 8–14).

58. Tsuda 1939, 73.

59. *Ryokki* 4, no. 12 (December 1939): 14.

that Korea organizationally outpaced the imperial metropole.[60] Korea already possessed "a structure of centralized control more advanced" and "closer to the new era [meaning the New Order] than *naichi*," observed Katashi.[61] Just as the construction of Manchukuo stimulated the institutional growth of the state in Japan,[62] so wartime Korea offered a model for fashioning a new political system at home. Moreover, the Ryokki Renmei leaders saw themselves as "going a step ahead of the state" and leading the construction of the East Asian New Order, which they claimed they had anticipated "several years before" Tokyo.[63] By making Korea, indeed their own league, the chief locus from which to propagate the emperor-centered polity, they desired to make the Green Life Movement a mass campaign superior not only to that of Nazi Germany or Fascist Italy, but even to that of their home country.

Although the target of their activity shifted to Korean youth after 1937, the Ryokki Renmei leaders by no means lessened their effort to recruit fellow settlers. This remained a particular concern of director Morita Yoshio, himself a second-generation settler. Through the league's bulletin and pamphlets, Morita time and again urged local settlers to reach out to Koreans "to transform [them] into genuine Japanese for building a new Japan." Despite the fact that "many Japanese families are in [daily] contact with Koreans," he rued, "the Japanese still harbor a colonial spirit [*shokuminchi konjō*] and a conqueror-like desire to swagger." Morita reserved his harshest criticism for graduates of Keijō Imperial University, his alma mater, whom he considered "the least enthusiastic among the intelligentsia." "Just as Kenkoku [Jianguo] University in Manchukuo is the supreme cultural organ built on the ideal of ethnic harmony [*minzoku kyōwa*]," he argued, "Keijō Imperial University must be a supreme cultural organ of *naisen ittai*."[64] Moreover, Morita believed that the promotion of *naisen ittai* required parallel efforts to "instill the

60. *Ryokki* 5, no. 4 (April 1940): 35.

61. *Ryokki* 5, no. 10 (October 1940): 5.

62. L. Young 1998, Chapter 8.

63. *Ryokki* 5, no. 1 (January 1940): 75; no. 10 (October 1940): 6. Considering that the Tsudas launched their movement years before the official *kōminka* campaign, as historian Nagashima Hiroki suggests, it is more appropriate to see the colonial state following the Ryokki Renmei, rather than the other way around (2003, 75). See also Chŏng and Yi 1999, 366.

64. Ryokki Renmei 1939, 65–68.

spirit of imperial subjects" into Japanese expatriate children, "especially from primary school on."[65] His sentiment was echoed by Government-General bureaucrats. When interviewed by Ueda Tatsuo (Yi Yŏng-gŭn), a leading Korean member of the Ryokki Renmei, Shiobara Tokisaburō opined that education on *naisen ittai* "should not be something to be merely imposed on Korean youth, but must be similarly strengthened among Japanese youth in the peninsula."[66] Koiso Kuniaki (1880–1950), who succeeded Minami as the Governor-General in June 1942, concurred, worried that the "cultivation" (*shūyō*) of local settlers regarding *kōminka* was "still insufficient."[67]

While Morita appealed to young male settlers for greater awareness and leadership, female commanders of the Ryokki Renmei quickly found a variety of ways to engage local Japanese women in supporting the wartime regime. Under the slogan "Let us lend our hands to the completion of *naisen ittai*," the Seiwa Women's Academy, run by Tsuda Setsuko, directed its students to sew *imon* bags and pay consolation visits to Korean army volunteers, which became a daily or monthly routine. Setsuko also dispatched graduates of Seiwa to the Yamato Academy, set up in 1941 for teaching Japanese language to impoverished Korean children.[68] Korean students at Tokuwa Women's Academy, Seiwa's sister school, were invited to join the Japanese students in these endeavors "to truly assist his Majesty the Emperor under the same ideology [*shisō*]."[69]

The women's section (*fujinbu*) of the Ryokki Renmei, composed of older and mostly married Japanese women, carried the goal of the Academy further, seeing themselves as a "corps under the direct command [*chokuzoku butai*] of his imperial Majesty." Members of the women's section devoted their time to "the concrete realization of *naisen ittai*" by "investigating and researching Korean daily life" and remedying its "ig-

---

65. Since annexation, this concern had been discussed by local teachers and officials as one of the particular challenges of settler education (Cohen 2006, Chapter 3).

66. *Kokumin sōryoku* 3, no. 4 (April 1941): 20.

67. *Kokumin sōryoku* 4, no. 7 (July 1942): 11.

68. *Ryokki* 5, no. 4 (April 1940): 56–57; and 8, no. 1 (January 1943): 173. For the activities of the Yamato Academy, as chronicled in a diary left by a member of the Ryokki Renmei, see H. Lee 2008b.

69. *Ryokki* 6, no. 8 (August 1941): 166. In April 1943, the Ryokki Renmei absorbed the Tokuwa Women's Academy (Takasaki 1982b, 129, 140–41).

norance and lack of awareness," which Setsuko averred was "a duty assigned to us Japanese ladies." Their aim was not simply to "Japanize" (*naichika*) the Korean lifestyle, she explained, but also "to incorporate its good aspects into the life of a Japanese person [*naichijin*]."[70] Many members of the women's section were seen wearing Korean skirts (*ch'ima*) and blouses (*chŏgori*) on a daily basis, for instance—though not so much out of appreciation of Korean culture as out of purely economic concern for cost and labor efficiency.[71] All of their activity, however, was ultimately geared toward one ideological end: to "transform [Koreans] into practitioners of daily life [*seikatsusha*] who can measure up to the emperor's ideal of love, power, and justice, the way of Japan's *kokutai*."[72] This could be promoted even in the intimacies of the home. Thus one lecturer at the Seiwa Women's Academy explained at a roundtable forum how she "guided" a fifteen-year-old Korean housemaid by "teaching Japanese language and offering daily life guidance."[73]

While urging local Japanese women to cultivate greater "awareness as older sisters," the Ryokki Renmei equally emphasized the need to cooperate with "enlightened Korean female leaders and educators" in carrying out daily life reform.[74] The so-called new women, such as Kim Hwal-lan of Ewha Woman's College and Son Chŏng-gyu of Kyŏnggi Higher Women's School, had already taken the initiative in this direction by forming the Chosŏn Puin Munje Yŏn'guhoe (Korean Women's Problems Research Association), with an overall aim to "improve Korean family life" and "cultivate" Korean women.[75] They worked closely with settler leaders like Tsuda Setsuko through joint forums, where they discussed how to "promote *naisen ittai* by correctly organizing people's material lives in the areas of clothing, food, and shelter," a task that they

---

70. Ryokki Renmei 1939, 49; *Ryokki* 5, no. 4 (April 1940): 60; Son Chŏng-gyu et al. 1939, 2.

71. Im Chŏn-hye 1978, 143.

72. *Ryokki* 6, no. 5 (May 1941): 124.

73. *Ryokki* 6, no. 11 (November 1941): 98.

74. Son Chŏng-gyu et al. 1939, 4. Tsuda Setsuko advised Minami on this need for cooperation during their meeting in July 1938 (Im Chŏn-hye 1978, 140).

75. The association was formed under the aegis of the educational bureau in January 1937 (Cho Kihong, "Seikatsu kaizen ni tsuite," *Sōdōin* 1, no. 3 [August 1939]: 24; Im Chong-guk 1992, 270–71).

Figs. 12a–b Female leaders of the Ryokki Renmei at a roundtable forum (*left*), and Tsuda Setsuko (*right*). SOURCES: Ryokki Renmei, ed., *Ryokki* 7, no. 11 (November 1942): 845; no. 2 (February 1942): 333.

considered "to lie in the hands of women."[76] At one such roundtable forum convened in 1939, three female leaders (Son Chŏng-gyu, Tsuda Setsuko, and Cho Ki-hong of Sŏngsin Women's School) exchanged opinions on how to make Korean family life, "fraught with contradictions and irrational complexities," "more suitable for imperial subjects."[77] Their proposals for rationalizing the Korean home included careful meal planning, cutting back on condiments, better housekeeping, and fuel conservation—a mundane recipe for promoting the grand work of imperialization.[78]

Some Ryokki Renmei leaders desired to make women not only rational homemakers and agents of daily life reform, but central builders of the New Order. Tsuda Miyoko, wife of Katashi, demanded that the colonial authorities further integrate women in the construction of a "high-level national defense state." "The quality of citizens [*kokumin*], the improvement of physical strength, the growth of population, and the renovation of people's life . . . [all] fall on women's shoulders," Miyoko argued, at the same time noting that a growing number of

76. Son Chŏng-gyu et al. 1939, 2–3.

77. Ibid., 1–4.

78. Some of the ideas advanced by these female educators were incorporated into the National Spiritual Mobilization Campaign. They included the Chosŏn Puin Munje Yŏn'guhoe's proposal concerning Korean female dress (*CKSS* 1940, 37) and the Ryokki Renmei's proposal for revision of "standards for nuptial ceremonies" (*Ryokki* 5, no. 10 [October 1940]: 71).

women engaged in "productive labor" "for expanding industrial capacity." Inspired by Ichikawa Fusae and Oku Mumeo, leading Japanese feminists who actively collaborated with the wartime government, Miyoko hoped that the women of Korea would likewise strike a balance between family and work in contributing to the nation "without forgetting the particularity of women." And while urging "resolute action" to deal with "café waitresses, geisha, and prostitutes," as her counterparts did in the metropole, she called for the creation of "a women's board, something equivalent to the Nazi Frauenschaft (NSF)," which would allow women to "play a part in the execution of national policy." Whereas "the Meiji Restoration was achieved by the power of men," she concluded, "what we call the Shōwa Restoration today cannot be achieved without the mass participation of genuinely Japanese women."[79]

Moving in lockstep with if not ahead of the state, Ryokki Renmei leaders played a central role in shaping the ideological contours of the National Spiritual Moblization Campaign. By the early 1940s, when the movement was restructured as the Kokumin Sōryoku Undō (National Total Strength Campaign), a response to the rise of the Imperial Rule Assistance Association (Taisei Yokusankai) in Japan,[80] almost the entire leadership of the Ryokki Renmei had joined the executive board of the Korean League, occupying prominent positions in most bureaus.[81] When the league's headquarters were revamped in late 1942 by consolidating eleven existing subdivisions into five bureaus (General Affairs, Training, Public Welfare, Economics, and Propaganda), Tsuda Setsuko served on two planning committees, those for the Bureaus of General

---

79. Tsuda Miyoko, "Shintaisei no josei no yakuwari," *Ryokki* 5, no. 10 (October 1940): 62–65.

80. *CKSU* 1945, 42–44. But the Government-General was careful to stress that Korea's New Order movement was "not a political movement."

81. Since the formation of the Korean League, Tsuda Sakae served as an advisor to the Keijō [Municipal] League as well as a director of the Kyŏnggi Provincial League, and Hyŏn Yŏng-sŏp became one of the Korea League's managers (*Ryokki* 4, no. 8 [August 1938]: 60). When the Korean League came into being, the Ryokki Renmei also reorganized its headquarters and created a new post of a chief (*shukan*), which Tsuda Katashi assumed (Takasaki 1982b, 65).

Affairs and Training.[82] Her brother-in-law Katashi was aptly placed in charge of Propaganda (or the promotion of "the culture of the Imperial Way"), to be assisted by his colleague, Morita Yoshio.[83] Katashi's influence in particular was felt everywhere in the campaign. In consultation with the police bureau chief, and with his colleague Odaka Tomoo, Katashi authored "Outline of the Ideal of *Naisen Ittai* and Its Method of Realization" (1941),[84] which effectively served as a manual for local agents of the National Total Strength Campaign. As authorities on *kokutai*, Katashi and Odaka also lectured at training workshops for members of "promotional corps" (*suishintai*), mainly former Korean army volunteers, who helped take the campaign to the provinces.[85] By this time, if the Ryokki Renmei leaders appeared to direct the state campaign by proxy, their sermon on *kokutai* had indubitably become *the* orthodoxy.

## *Evaluating the Campaign*

To what extent did the Ryokki Renmei and other ideologues succeed in making local residents "voluntarily cooperate" with the wartime policy and internalize its message of unity?[86] Through its extensive network of patriotic neighborhood associations, it appears, the National Spiritual Mobilization Campaign did manage to mobilize residents across the social spectrum. *Hantō no jūgojin* (The Peninsula's Home Front Group, 1940), published by the Chōsen Gunji Kōen Renmei (Korea Military Assistance League), featured men and women of all ages and classes single-mindedly devoting themselves to supporting Japan's war effort. Included were touching anecdotes of Korean farmers rushing to the aid of Japanese families of conscripted or deceased soldiers by tending their paddy fields.[87] According to the local media, the sight of villagers sending off and welcoming soldiers at the train station became as familiar

---

82. *KSUY* 1943, 115–32. In the next two years, the five bureaus were restructured with some personnel changes, and Han Sang-nyong oversaw their entire operation as the general chief from 1943 to the end of the war (*CKSU* 1945, 163–67).

83. *KSUY* 1943, 117, 121, 133, 141. Three other Japanese in their 30s and 40s headed the other bureaus (*CKSU* 1945, 65–66; *KSUY* 1943, 4–5, 13–17).

84. Kokumin Sōryoku Chōsen Renmei Bōei Shidōbu 1941, 7.

85. *Kokumin sōryoku* 3, no. 4 (April 1941): 137.

86. For a detailed evaluation of the campaign, see Uchida 2011b.

87. Hayashi Katsuhisa 1940, 85–86, 96–97.

in Korea as in the metropole. So did women collecting donations and vituperating extravagance on street corners.[88] Local news reports especially highlighted the new visibility of Korean women, who "broke the old traditional customs and emerged onto the streets" to join Japanese women in war support activities. These scenes were jubilantly portrayed as evidence of "*naisen ittai* coming into reality."[89] Some statistics also seem to bear out the campaign's efficacy. In addition to increases in national defense donations, thanks to the efforts of local neighborhood heads, postal savings apparently met more than 100 percent of the target amount every year between 1938 and 1943.[90]

But how the spiritual mobilizers gauged their success in promoting *kōminka* depended on highly dubious measures. They ranged from tallying up the number of visitors to Shinto shrines, to making local residents memorize and recite the imperial oath; the latter was treated as a "litmus test" for measuring the loyalty to the emperor of non-Japanese-speaking Koreans,[91] even as a ticket to one's food ration.[92] Self-congratulatory records of success were also betrayed by persistent complaints from community leaders that educated, upper-class urbanites were harder to mobilize than "ignorant" farmers.[93] Moreover, abundant evidence of the use of coercion by neighborhood heads—especially as residents succumbed to war weariness—appears to further diminish the hasty official claim to mass imperialization of the peninsula.[94]

Along with lackluster participation, a lack of comprehension continued to bedevil the campaign—and the Koreans were not entirely to blame. While Tsuda Katashi on his lecture circuit conjured a new Korea awakened to a mission to lead Asia's destiny with Japan, local officials and neighborhood heads reported on their "uphill struggle" to communicate the vague and long-winded objectives of the National Spiritual

---

88. *Keijō nippō*, 23 August 1938.

89. For example, see *Chōsen kōron*, April 1938, 80–81.

90. Anzako 1995, 14.

91. Ibid.

92. Yi Okpun's testimony in H. Kang 2001, 113. This was enforced by both Japanese and Korean neighborhood heads. Testimony of a Korean female head in *Kokumin sōryoku* 3, no. 6 (June 1941): 13.

93. Keikidō Keisatsu Buchō to Keimu Kyokuchō (29 August 1941) and (30 June 1941); *Sōdōin* 1, no. 2 (July 1939): 17–18.

94. Keikidō Keisatsu Buchō to Keimu Kyokuchō (27 March 1941).

Mobilization Campaign.[95] The difficulty of Korea's spiritual mobilizers in reaching out to the public, one Japanese teacher complained, owed to their tendency to "seek credit for doing everything ahead of Japan" by hastily imposing activities on people without making them fully grasp their meaning.[96] In their frenzied attempts to mold Koreans into imperial subjects, they devised idiosyncratic practices such as the observance of a one-minute silence at noon, which "invited laughter" from metropolitan visitors, or introducing to the physical education curriculum "imperial subjects' calisthenics" (*kōkoku shinmin taisō*), which few pupils bothered to perform.[97] Given the paucity of Japanese-language speakers, it is also highly uncertain to what extent Korea's residents, even as they performed imperial rituals daily, understood their meaning.

The campaign's effort to foster *naisen ittai* by unifying the daily life customs of Japanese and Koreans—a central concern of the Ryokki Renmei—proved even more quixotic. Patriotic neighborhood associations encouraged the use of Japanese outside of schools,[98] but Korea remained a bilingual society, with Japanese speakers totaling less than 20 percent of the population in 1941,[99] a figure barely boosted by an official campaign hastily launched a year later.[100] The rate of intermarriage also remained low. From 1941 on, the colonial authorities awarded each interethnic couple a hanging scroll with the characters "*naisen ittai*" personally brushed in ink by Minami.[101] Although such unions increased over time, reaching 5,317 registered couples by the end of 1940, they remained a fraction of the total.[102] Both Japanese and Koreans resisted

---

95. For instance, see Keikidō Keisatsu Buchō to Keimu Kyokuchō (24 December 1940).

96. Keikidō Keisatsu Buchō to Keimu Kyokuchō (25 March 1941).

97. *Yomiuri shinbun*, 19 November 1945. Ultimately, though, the "imperial subjects' calisthenics" were exported to the metropole (Chŏng Kŭn-sik 2004, 77).

98. In South Chŏlla province, from 1938 local town and village spiritual mobilization leagues offered simple Japanese-language workshops to young Koreans aged between 15 and 30, with the goal of teaching an estimated 400,000 of these Koreans over a span of eight years (*Chōsen kōron*, November 1939, 94–95).

99. Anzako 1995, 14.

100. *Chōsen shakai jigyō* 20, no. 7 (July 1942): 22; Miyata 1985, 116–17. For more details on the Korean League's promotion of Japanese language, see Ch'oe Yuri 1997, 148–71.

101. *CKSU* 1945, 101–2.

102. Tange 1943, 50–51. The low rate of intermarriage was symbolized by the failure of *naisen kekkon* between members of the Yi royal family and the Japanese imperial and

intermarriage out of "mutual contempt and antagonism," Hyŏn Yŏng-sŏp noted, lamenting that even when they did marry, most created "unhappy" unions that ended in "tragedy."[103] His observation is corroborated by settler memoirs and testimonies, which chronicle widespread social stigma attached to the offspring of mixed parentage (*konketsuji*).[104] When considering how few Koreans understood Japanese, married Japanese, or wore colored dress, imperialization through daily life appears to have remained a lofty slogan at best.

The greatest limits of the *naisen ittai* campaign, some records suggest, lay not with the Koreans but with Japanese residents who refused to heed the message of ethnic unity—echoing the limits of its ideological precursor, the *naisen yūwa* campaign, of the 1920s (see Chapter 3). To be sure, some settlers did make "the realization of *naisen ittai*" a central objective of their neighborly duties. In the ethnically mixed neighborhood on Taihei Street in Seoul, for instance, Japanese families pooled money to take care of an impoverished Korean orphan, and one community head took special care "to encourage local Japanese and Korean children to play together so that they can be friends from a young age."[105] But it is doubtful whether other settlers were equally committed to embracing their Korean brethren. Evidence to the contrary includes one telling incident in Inch'ŏn that demonstrated how "patriotic" Koreans preaching *naisen ittai* could jar Japanese nerves. According to a police report, a Korean municipal official and head of his neighborhood association named Pak To-ŏn offended the sentiments of local Japanese residents by admonishing them for flaunting a sense of superiority, lecturing them on *naisen ittai* (including what the officer noted

aristocratic families in the 1930s, patterned after the politically arranged marriage between Yi Wang-ŭn and Nashinomotomiya Masako in 1920 (Suzuki Yūko 1992, 88–93).

103. *Chōsen oyobi Manshū*, April 1938, 65–67. On the other hand, according to the recent study of Su Yun Kim (2009), intermarriage for Koreans also represented the possibility of attaining "modern subjectivity."

104. Matsui Heizō's reminiscences in Keijō Nanzan Shōgakkō Dōsōkai 1996, 273. I also asked some former settlers who were in their 20s or early 30s when the war ended if they ever considered marrying a Korean. Of those who responded to my questionnaire, the majority (53) wrote "no" and others (9) stated "it was impossible or inconceivable [*arienai*]" (see Appendix 2). Similar results were obtained in Kimura Kenji's survey on former Japanese settlers in Sinŭiju (2001, 73–98).

105. *Kokumin sōryoku* 3, no. 6 (June 1941): 9–10.

as an "extreme claim" that "Empress Jingū was a descendant of a noble immigrant from Silla"), and going so far as to criticize the former Japanese prime ministers Hayashi Senjūrō and Konoe Fumimaro for "lacking in Japanese spirit." Unable to bear his "vitriolic" speech many Japanese attendees got up and left, assailing Pak for "going against his status as a Korean and an official" and "insulting the Japanese." The Korean residents, by contrast, evidently expressed support by giving him "enthusiastic applause."[106]

Given that the content of Pak's lecture did not deviate much from colonial orthodoxy, the reaction of settlers would have been a slap in the face of the Ryokki Renmei and other ideologues of *naisen ittai.* This incident was not atypical, according to one alumnus of Keijō Imperial University whose father worked for the Government-General. In the Japanese resident community in Seoul, Minami's successor Koiso Kuniaki was apparently made a "laughingstock" for trumpeting *naisen ittai* and evoking the "myth of shared ancestry" incessantly.[107] Nor were Japanese ideologues always united behind these theories. For instance, Mitarai Tatsuo of the *Keijō nippō* described the Japanese as "a mixed nation" (*fukugō minzoku*), highlighting the ability to embrace "multiplicity within unity" as "the most unique of Japanese uniqueness,"[108] but such a notion was spurned by the president of another newspaper agency. He argued that the "Yamato *minzoku*" must follow the example of the Germans in protecting the purity of their blood, and rejected intermarriage as a "completely misdirected" policy.[109] These contradictory attitudes reveal the profound, and persistent, unease settlers felt about the prospect of ethnic intermixing and more fundamentally about including Koreans in the category of "Japanese." Their ambivalence only intensified as the boundaries of metropolitan citizenship gradually widened in the course of war.

106. Keikidō Keisatsu Buchō to Keimu Kyokuchō and Keijō Chihō Hōin Kenjisei (24 July 1939).

107. Iijima Mitsutaka, personal correspondence, 2 August 2003, 8.

108. Mitarai Tatsuo, "Nihon no mukyūsei (jō)," *Kokumin sōryoku* 3, no. 4 (April 1941): 53–54.

109. Keikidō Keisatsu Buchō to Keimu Kyokuchō (25 March 1941). This sentiment was echoed by a few colonial bureaucrats, such as Yamana Sakio, who publicly opposed the idea of "mixing of Japanese and Korean blood" and intermarriages (Miyata 1985, 168).

## *Koreans into Japanese Citizens*

If the distinctions between "citizens" and "subjects" remained ambiguous in the Japanese notion of *kokumin*, in the settlers' attitudes toward Koreans, they could not be more patent. Settlers' desire for separation became clear as the colonial state moved to incorporate Koreans more fully into metropolitan citizenship (albeit in a secondary status), while promoting their imperial subjecthood. Specifically, existing colonial laws were revised to "allow" Koreans to volunteer for the Imperial Army (1938), receive metropolitan-level school education (1938),[110] and adopt Japanese family names (1940)—what the historian Miyata Setsuko has identified as the central stages of *kōminka*, which culminated in general conscription of Koreans (1944).[111] Effectively, these measures were taken to eliminate major differences that had existed between "metropolitan" and "colonial" citizenship within the empire, just as the Meiji government had taken similar steps toward the Okinawans and the Ainu, inhabitants of Japan's newly acquired "borderlands" in the late nineteenth century.[112] Though driven by official desire to mobilize Korean labor and resources for war, these revisions were enacted partly in response to elite Korean demands for citizenship, which had streamed into the Government-General's headquarters since the early 1930s (see Chapter 7).[113] After 1937, this process of negotiating the boundaries of citizenship, as it were, gained further momentum, as it spread from the elite to lower social classes. A new level of Korean quest for rights and equality, however, reignited assimilation anxiety among local settlers, who felt largely bypassed in the process.

---

110. After issuing a new Rescript on Education in 1938 to unify the colonial school systems for Japanese and Koreans at all levels, the Government-General, toward the close of war, announced its plan to introduce universal education from 1946.

111. Miyata 1985, 94. The political process of *naichi enchō* also reached a new stage when the Governor-General of Korea, along with governors of Taiwan and Karafuto, were brought under the jurisdiction of the Home Ministry in 1942 (Kusunoki 1991, 285, 285*n*1, 291). Takashi Fujitani (2007) suggests that through the extension of military service, the political status of Koreans was transformed from colonial subject into something akin to an ethnic minority within a multiethnic state like the United States.

112. Miyata et al. 1992, 154, 156–59, 205; Caprio 2009, Chapter 2. On the Ainu, see Howell 2004, 5–29; Morris-Suzuki 1998.

113. *Sōdōin* 1, no. 3 (August 1939): 10.

The first sign of contention surrounding citizenship emerged between the pool of early Korean applicants to the Chōsen Army's volunteer program, and settlers' ambivalent response to it. Most of the eager volunteers turned out to be small tenant farmers, much to the disappointment of Katsuo Nobuhiko, press chief of the Chōsen Army, who wished more middle- and upper-class Koreans had shown interest.[114] Moreover, the volunteers were often driven by highly personal motives—improved social standing, job prospects, fame and glory—rather than a sense of loyalty to the emperor.[115] Local settlers were anything but euphoric about the program's popularity among young Korean men, which the media and colonial officials celebrated as an "outpouring of patriotism" for the empire. To be sure, Japanese residents, from school principles to neighborhood heads, assisted the police in persuading Korean families to send their sons (especially primary school graduates) to the army. Even Japanese college students, as they testified after the war, were urged to encourage their elite Korean classmates to volunteer.[116] But the very idea of the native "right" to bear arms, a sore point of contention between the *colons* and the state in French Algeria,[117] deeply troubled Japanese settlers who remained doubtful of the Korean allegiance to the empire. Thus, a year before the Army volunteer program went into effect, when a group of Korean public officials lobbied the authorities for its swift implementation, the Japanese editor of the *Chōsen kōron* dismissed their action as "frivolous," reasoning that the majority of Koreans still did not understand the Japanese language and some had "no concept of awe toward the imperial house."[118]

Settler distrust of Koreans was, in fact, shared by many Chōsen Army officers, who remained wary of their "tenacious ethnic character." They were equally critical of the hasty optimism of Government-General bureaucrats, who were apt to see the volunteers, like visitors to Shinto

---

114. Miyata 1985, 65, 67–68; *Sōdōin* 1, no. 5 (October 1939): 8.

115. Ch'oe Yuri 1997, 190–92.

116. Iijima Mitsutaka, personal correspondence, 2 August 2003.

117. Lustick 1985, 67.

118. *Chōsen kōron*, September 1937, 1. And when the colonial government that same year unified the ethnically separate school systems at all levels, many settlers did not alter their stance of opposition to co-education. Responses to my questionnaire (see Appendix 2).

shrines, as "true specimens of *naisen ittai*," a claim often betrayed by the volunteers themselves who could barely speak Japanese and once in the training camp struggled to adjust to a Japanese lifestyle and diet.[119] Because the Koreans could not be trusted, as Kajiyama Toshiyuki (1930–1975) in a semi-autobiographical novel later described through the eyes of a young protagonist, when required "to present arms" in salute to the Governor-General at an annual ceremony, Japanese school students used real rifles, but Korean students were allowed to hold only wooden ones.[120]

Settlers' reaction to the name-changing (*sōshi kaimei*) campaign, launched two years later in 1940, seemed almost as divided as the Korean response, as the means (name change) and the end of including Koreans into Japan's family (*ie*) system, which lay at the basis of metropolitan citizenship, elicited mixed emotions.[121] For most of the 3.2 million families or 80 percent of the Korean households who adopted Japanese names by the 10 August deadline,[122] the decision was based on a variety of factors: official or peer pressure, the resolution of their family clan, or, as with the case of army volunteers, a pragmatic calculation of personal gain.[123] Those who played an active role in persuading these Korean families were the usual faces among the brokers of empire. In addition to calling on local Korean school students to cooperate with the campaign, the Ryokki Renmei published a handy manual for creating Japanese

119. Shiobara Tokisaburō, "Tokubetsu shiganhei seido ni tsuite," *Sōdōin* 1, no. 5 (October 1939), 5–6; Miyata 1985, 52–56, 71. To the army officers, the Army volunteer program was at best experimental and general conscription of Koreans was foreseeable only in the far-off future, a couple of decades at the least.

120. Kajiyama 1995, 58.

121. For a comprehensive study of this campaign, see Miyata et al. 1992.

122. At Han Sang-nyong's call, all 34 Korean members of the Kyŏnggi Provincial Assembly decided to adopt Japanese family names, a move followed by the neighborhood heads in Seoul (*Chōsen oyobi Manshū*, April 1940, 81; *Keijō ihō* 225 [August 1940]: 62).

123. As a way to cope with the pressure to adopt a Japanese surname, many Koreans internally continued to maintain their national identity and protect their surnames by retaining their old characters in the new names or choosing characters that reflected a Korean meaning (Gakushūin Daigaku Tōyō Bunka Kenkyūjo 2000, 61–62; H. Kang 2001, 120–22). On the decision-making of family clans, see Miyata et al. 1992, 138, 146. Among the pragmatic reasons to change one's surname included the desire to be treated "more favorably by the Japanese" and to reap "enormous social benefits" (*Keijō nippō*, 17 July 1940).

names, explaining name change as a path to completing *naisen ittai* as well as "elevating the status of women."[124] The league even opened a "consultation center" where Keijō Imperial University professors helped Korean visitors to select appropriate names by serving as their "godfathers," and offered "name divination" (*seimei handan*) on the side.[125] In commemoration of the campaign, the Dōminkai organized an elaborate "business card exchange ceremony" in Seoul and later published a roster of names adopted by its Korean attendees, many of whom worked for local Japanese stores and companies (where it had already become a customary practice to randomly assign Japanese names to Korean apprentices and employees).[126] More blunt methods were used by the Chōsen Transportation Company and the Railway Bureau, which apparently refused to handle packages with Korean names written on them.[127] But the most pivotal cooperation was provided by local Japanese schoolteachers, many of whom made their students literally beg their parents to change their names before they could enter the classroom.[128]

If these collaborators with the campaign understood name change as a means of expediting ethnic unity, other settlers recognized that it would merely backfire, especially in light of strong elite *yangban* opposition.[129] When Andō Toyoroku (1897–1990), manager of the Onoda cement factory in P'yŏngyang, learned that a Korean engineer was about to resign due to his clan's opposition to the campaign, Andō persuaded him to stay, and reassured other Korean employees that they need not change their names. And he personally entreated Minami to suspend the campaign, though to no avail.[130] According to the former settlers I

---

124. Ryokki Nihon Bunka Kenkyūjo 1940; Takenaka Yoshirō, response to questionnaire.

125. *Ryokki* 5, no. 4 (April 1940): 44, 62.

126. Dōminkai Honbu 1940. Testimonies at a roundtable meeting with graduates of the Nanzan Primary School, 21 July 2003, Tokyo.

127. Miyata et al. 1992, 113–14.

128. For example, see Richard E. Kim 1970, 99.

129. The imposition of the Japanese family system, the Korean elites feared, would undermine their aristocratic paternal lineage and destroy Korea's unique patriarchal family system based on matrimony and consanguinity (cemented through clan relationships), and the adoption of male heirs from other clan families would adulterate their noble blood (*Keijō nippō*, 9 November 1939 and 18 July 1940; Miyata et al. 1992, 131–37).

130. Andō 1984, 13, 137.

interviewed, voices of caution and dissent abounded within the Japanese resident community.[131] Aoki Etsuko, who taught Korean primary school students in wartime Seoul, recounted how she "felt it was an outrageous policy," and noted that both Japanese and Korean "teachers generally opposed the name-changing policy."[132] In criticizing the authorities for going too far, however, settlers were also stirred by a pervasive sense of unease about including Koreans into Japan's family tree. Settlers' ingrained fear of miscegenation was similar to that conveyed in a petition submitted to the Diet by two residents of Chiba prefecture, who deplored that if Koreans were permitted to adopt traditional Japanese names, it would lead to "a great invasion of the genealogy of the Japanese *minzoku*" and "mar the purity of Japan's *kokutai*."[133] Whatever their reasons for opposition, however, few settlers actually raised their voices in protest. Most of them, self-admittedly, did nothing but "nervously watch the Koreans to see if they would resist the new policy."[134] In the face of cultural violence being meted out to Koreans, if few settlers remained unperturbed, their concern for purity appears to have remained equally unshaken.

Among all the official measures and promises to incorporate Koreans into Japanese citizenship, local settlers expressed greatest resistance to the idea of extending conscription and suffrage, which loomed as the tide of war turned against Japan.[135] In May 1942 the metropolitan cabinet announced its decision to draft colonial soldiers, out of "unavoidable necessity" to "meet the military manpower shortage and stem

---

131. In my questionnaire I asked those former settlers who were old enough to remember how they felt about the Government-General's assimilation policy while growing up in wartime Korea. Of these settlers, 31 respondents wrote they did not particularly think anything of it (because they were only in primary or middle school), 23 felt it was an unrealistic policy (assimilation was impossible), and only 4 believed it was an ideal and rational policy. Other respondents specified what aspects of the assimilation policy they did or did not support, with many noting how the name change policy was considered "too extreme" by local settlers. Nine settlers did not respond to this question (see Appendix 2).

132. Interview with Aoki Etsuko, Tokyo, 21 December 2001.

133. Petition quoted in Miyata et al. 1992, 98–99.

134. Iijima Mitsutaka, personal correspondence, 13 December 2001, 36.

135. But the labor draft of ordinary Korean men and women (called "army civilians") began earlier in 1939 (Yamada, Koshō, and Higuchi 2005).

the attrition of the 'Yamato *minzoku*.'"[136] Young Koreans who had long desired conscription publicly expressed their "gratitude" by visiting Chōsen Shrine,[137] and many Japanese settlers joined the officials in celebrating the momentous decision made by their home government. Local women's groups helped to spread public understanding of the system and dispel any Korean anxiety about discrimination in the army through lectures, films, and traditional storyboards (*kamishibai*).[138] Some made enthusiastic calls for accelerating the imperialization of Koreans on this occasion. One 40-year Japanese resident of Seoul, with the help of Korean landlords and a Japanese capitalist in Manchukuo, planned to build an "imperial subjects training hall" for the purpose of "perfecting the peninsula's youth as fine Japanese in mind and body without further delay."[139]

For those who were already apprehensive about Korean army volunteers, however, the official announcement of a draft was far from an occasion for celebration. According to police reports, a cross-section of settlers—from a school principal and a chief of a civil defense unit in Taegu to a humble merchant in Kwangju—viewed conscription as "premature" and worried that it might "further embolden the Koreans." In exchange for military service, they predicted, the Koreans would "demand corresponding benefits" such as suffrage, universal education, and overseas allowance (*zaikin kahō*), demands that should be "completely repressed." "If Korean army reservists [*zaigō gunjin*] increased too much," some worried, "Japanese would have no choice but to take a step back from their leading position," which "would not bode well for the future life of Japanese settlers [*naichijin*]" on the peninsula.[140] Even more disquieting was the prospect, as entertained by a resident in Kwangju, that Korean conscripts "might join the enemy if the Greater East Asian War turned to the advantage of America and England."[141] Such fear of Korean "treachery" had already been voiced by Chōsen Army officers in their top-secret reports of 1939, which soberly acknowledged that the

---

136. Miyata 1985, 102–3; Utsumi 2001, 207.
137. See picture in Miyata et al. 1992, 33.
138. *Chōsen shakai jigyō* 21, no. 10 (October 1943): 16–17.
139. *Kokumin sōryoku* 4, no. 8 (August 1942): 90.
140. Shihōshō Keijikyoku 1942, 20–21.
141. Ibid.

"ethnic consciousness buried deep in their hearts and toadyism nurtured over many years cannot be dispelled so easily."[142] The image of "double-hearted" Koreans lying in wait to betray the colonial masters at the first opportunity, which had spread widely in the wake of the March First Movement, died hard in Japanese minds.

Settlers' ambivalence about extending citizenship to Koreans grew acute during the final years of war, when securing their loyalty and support became the official priority. In return for military and labor service, Tokyo decided to grant limited suffrage to the colonies by allowing a few representatives to sit in the Imperial Diet—a decision reached only after a good deal of wrangling between the colonial state, the Chōsen Army, and the metropolitan government.[143] According to their plan, to go into effect in 1946, 7 members from Korea and 3 from Taiwan, recommended by the Governor-Generals and appointed by imperial command, were to serve in the House of Peers. Moreover, 23 members from Korea and 5 members from Taiwan were to be elected to the House of Representatives by a limited electorate, that is, men over age 25 who paid 15 yen or more in direct state taxes.[144]

In drafting this final proposal, the authorities apparently gave little thought to the representation of Japanese settlers, who had thus far been disenfranchised by virtue of overseas residence.[145] Although the

---

142. Quoted in Miyata 1985, 100.

143. For more details on their deliberation and the final proposal adopted in April 1945, see Gakushūin Daigaku Tōyō Bunka Kenkyūjo 2000, 141, 170*nn*2–3, and 171*n*6; Okamoto Makiko 1996, 61–63. The passage of conscription made the issue of suffrage partly inevitable, for the revision of relevant laws (regarding family registration) to make Koreans eligible for military service simultaneously undermined the legal basis for denying them the right to vote (Ch'oe Yuri 1997, 225–29, 247).

144. The seven representatives from Korea to serve in the House of Peers included Yun Ch'i-ho, Kim Myŏng-chun, Pak Chung-yang (1874–1955), and Han Sang-nyong (Gakushūin Daigaku Tōyō Bunka Kenkyūjo 2000, 171*n*6, 172*n*7). Before this revision, a few Koreans (Pak Yŏng-hyo, Yun Tŏg-yŏng [1873–1940], and Yi Jin-ho) and one Taiwanese had been appointed to the House of Peers on the basis of "service to the state or learning and experience" (Tanaka Hiroshi 1974, 78–79).

145. The above provision in the final proposal differed from the two classified documents on suffrage drafted by the Government-General of Korea in 1938 and 1943, where settlers were still considered for representation. See Chōsen Sōtokufu Naimukyoku 1938, 17; and Chōsen Sōtokufu, "Gokuhi: sanseiken mondai" (1943). For the House of Peers, Ch'oe Yuri speculates that the Japanese government in the end decided to select only Koreans out of concern for Korean public opinion (1997, 237*n*162).

ethnicity of representatives was never specified (and never made public), the metropolitan and colonial governments prioritized allowing the Koreans to sit in the Diet, out of concern for securing cooperation for war and the loyalty of conscripts in particular.[146] The limited nature of the promised suffrage shows that it was a strategy of accommodation rather than a serious step toward fully enfranchising the colonial population, as long demanded by the Kungmin Hyŏphoe. Nonetheless, the official decision to enfranchise the Koreans would have deeply upset the Japanese resident community. By the time of the war, not a few settlers had come to believe that they were politically more disadvantaged than Koreans. One settler businessman in Seoul, for instance, grumbled over the declining power of Japanese residents in comparison to Koreans, who enjoyed more honorary posts in such institutions as the Central Council.[147] To remedy this perceived imbalance in political representation, Satoyoshi Motoki of *Chōsen kōron* proposed that the Korean-only Central Council should be completely restructured to allow for the appointment of powerful long-term settlers who had "devoted their lives to the development of Korea as forerunners of the empire's continental management."[148] Had it not come at a time of national emergency, one might surmise, the proposed suffrage may well have caused settler uproar, if not on the scale demonstrated a decade earlier by the *colons* in French Algeria, who successfully blocked the Blum-Viollet bill of 1936 that would have enfranchised over 20,000 Muslims.[149]

Though devoid of the political power and autonomy enjoyed by European settlers in Africa, in their impulse to exclude natives from citizenship, Japanese settlers showed themselves to be just as resolute. Nowhere did their defiance become more manifest than in their reactions to Governor-General Koiso's policy to further broaden the boundaries of inclusion. The decision to grant limited suffrage, indeed, was part of a more comprehensive package proposed by Koiso, during his two-year tenure in Korea (1942–1944), to "improve the treatment of

146. Gakushūin Daigaku Tōyō Bunka Kenkyūjo 2000, 149, 151.

147. Keikidō Keisatsu Buchō to Keimu Kyokuchō (30 June 1941).

148. Satoyoshi Motoki, "Chūsūin soshiki kaizenron," *Chōsen kōron*, May 1937, 2–3.

149. Lustick 1985, 71–75. In the case of British settlers in Rhodesia, they had "declared a unilateral independence rather than consider even moderate African advance in representation" as early as 1923 (Good 1976, 611).

overseas compatriots [*dōhō*]," a commitment made official when he became Japan's prime minister in July 1944. Koiso appointed a commission not only to investigate the issue of suffrage, but to review the existing legal constraints on Korean citizenship—the system of overseas allowance, restrictions on Korean travel to Japan, and a ban on the transfer of family registers—to an extent never contemplated by his predecessors.[150] In response to the news of Koiso's planned reforms, according to a classified 1945 Government-General report, Japanese settlers across the board opposed the idea of granting suffrage and other concessions, however limited in scope, to Koreans. Their reasoning always boiled down to this: it would "further embolden the Koreans to demand complete abolition of discrimination or make them more impudent" and would ultimately "jeopardize the status of Japanese [*naichijin*]."[151]

More than paranoia, such settler fear attested to an already widespread phenomenon among Koreans, who ascribed their own meanings to the rhetoric of *naisen ittai* to achieve parity. Their quest for citizenship gave rise to complex political alignments among the Korean ideologues of *naisen ittai*. For instance, advocates of "parallel cooperation" (*heikō teikei ron*) wished to preserve Korean cultural uniqueness, and some political autonomy, within the framework of pragmatic alliance with Japan, whereas proponents of "assimilation-unification" (*dōka ittai ron*), namely members of the Ryokki Renmei, called for complete absorption of Koreans into the Japanese ethnos.[152] As the hopes for independence faded in the course of war, Koreans of all social classes began, if unwittingly, to join these *naisen ittai* advocates, demanding rights and defining national interests, not against the empire but within its borders. By early 1941, one Kyonggi provincial report noted, *naisen ittai* was rendered into the local idiom by ordinary Koreans as "equality between Japanese and

---

150. Gakushūin Daigaku Tōyō Bunka Kenkyūjo 2000, 170–72.

151. Shihōshō Keijikyoku 1942, 20–21; Chōsen Sōtokufu, "Gokuhi: sanseiken mondai" 1943, 192.

152. Tsuda 1939, 35. For a detailed analysis of this conflict, see Yi Sŭng-yŏp 2001, 35–38; Matsuda 1997, 142–43; Cho Kyŏng-dal 2007. In both cases, as some scholars have noted, their fervent desire to become "Japanese superior to a Japanese" was an inversion rather than a renunciation of Korean nationalist sentiment. The stronger their desire to "escape from discrimination" and achieve parity with Japanese, the more radical their proposed measures of "self-negation" became (Miyata 1985, 157–64; Yi Sŭng-yŏp 2001, 34).

Koreans" (*naisen byōdō*). Not only did "wage earners harbor desire for additional allowance (*kahō*)," an imperial perquisite of expatriate Japanese, but "a growing number [of Korean residents] now raise their hands and ask questions, demanding the same rights [as the Japanese] at every meeting."[153] The following year, when the Japanese cabinet made the decision to conscript colonial soldiers, Koreans on the peninsula as well as in the metropole began calling for an "end to discrimination" in a whole host of areas—suffrage, education, travel, and family registers—as a "quid pro quo" (*kōkan jōken*) for bearing the "supreme duty of conscription."[154] Settlers' fear had become reality.

Within the lexicon of *naisen ittai*, and outside of the settlers' purview, indeed, unfolded a dynamic process of negotiation between a state that demanded unconditional loyalty and a colonized populace that made collaboration conditional.[155] Appropriating the colonizer's rhetoric to elevate the status of the colonized was a political strategy as old as the empire itself. And although such a strategy was inherently constrained by its rationale that resided within the colonizer's discourse, it assumed a life of its own as a mass phenomenon—as widespread, it seemed, as the nationalist movement of the 1920s. Its underlying "give-and-take" mentality deeply unsettled the colonial authorities, who typically argued, as Minami did in his 1942 speech to a Korean audience, that "before selfishly demanding rights, Koreans must first thoroughly master the essence of being loyal imperial subjects."[156] One 40-year resident of Korea added his own perverse logic: "*Naisen ittai* [for Koreans] is about understanding the spirit of imperial subjects as younger brothers of the

153. Keikidō Keisatsu Buchō to Keimu Kyokuchō (25 March 1941).

154. Shihōshō Keijikyoku 1942, 12–17, 22–23. Some demanded the abolition of Governor-General's rule as a way to eliminate the differences between Japan and Korea completely.

155. Takashi Fujitani in his forthcoming book argues that the conscription of Korean soldiers, based on this premise of unconditional loyalty, reflected a new governmentality: to apply the logic of a modern nation-state to colonial governance, and to expect its colonial subjects to "die for the country" without asking for anything in return (Korean Studies Colloquium Series Talk at Stanford University, 9 April 2010).

156. Quoted in Oguma 2002, 338. Also see *Sōdōin* 1, no. 3 (August 1939): 14–15. The aforementioned "Outline of the Ideal of *Naisen Ittai* and Its Method of Realization," compiled by Tsuda Katashi for the National Total Strength Campaign, was designed precisely to "root out" this Korean tendency to "make the elimination of discrimination a priority condition for the realization of *naisen ittai*."

Japanese [*naichijin*]," keeping in mind that "brotherhood has its order and its way."[157]

Settlers' insistence on hierarchy, the last gasp of a bygone era, was a feeble response to what they increasingly worried were signs of "Korean empowerment." Besides joining the army, qualified Koreans found relatively more opportunities in wartime than had hitherto been granted in bureaucratic appointment, enterprise, factories, and higher education, not least due to vacancies created by conscripted settlers. Settler anxiety about these developments was palpable in the Kyŏnggi provincial police reports (1941), which illustrate the reservoir of discontent the *naisen ittai* policy spawned among the Japanese population. One 30-year resident of Korea who served as a neighborhood head in Seoul fretted that "Korean intrusion into Japanese neighborhoods as a result of their economic expansion under the National Total Strength Campaign" was beginning to "oppress Japanese [residents]."[158] The campaign had made Koreans "intolerably insolent," observed another settler who served on the city assembly, arguing that "oppression, not cultural rule, must be the way to deal with Koreans, just like [we did] at the time of annexation."[159] Local Japanese women, for their part, groused that Koreans, from collectors of postal insurance bills to train conductors, addressed them casually as *okamisan*, *obasan*, or *kichibe*, instead of using more respectful terms like *okusan* or *ojōsan*.[160] Such abject sentiments apparently spread to children as well. As one former settler of Seoul later insisted, as if to set the historical record straight, "it was the Koreans who swaggered and bullied us during the period of *naisen ittai*."[161]

These voices, which portray Japanese as being increasingly hemmed in by Koreans, underscore the zero-sum mentality characteristic of settlers, their pathological tendency to view any perceived gain in Korean

---

157. Iwamoto Shōji, "Kaku aikokuhan hōmonki," *Kokumin sōryoku* 4, no. 2 (February 1942): 91–92.

158. Keikidō Keisatsu Buchō to Keimu Kyokuchō (30 June 1941).

159. Keikidō Keisatsu Buchō to Keimu Kyokuchō (29 August 1941).

160. *Chōsen oyobi Manshū*, August 1938, 80. Settler women displayed their own insensitivity toward Koreans. One Korean housewife later recalled asking local Japanese wives why they would address her as *okami-san* instead of *okusan* like other Japanese (H. Kang 2001, 136).

161. A roundtable conference with alumni of Nanzan Primary Shool, 21 July 2003, Tokyo.

status as their loss. This, I contend, was a warped reflection of settlers' own subaltern status in the empire, a condition that had persisted since the time of annexation. Especially because the dichotomy of "citizens" and "subjects" did not neatly map onto ethnic hierarchy,[162] Japanese settlers were apt to interpret every sign of Korean empowerment as sabotaging their own struggle for supremacy. And they were just as keen to appoint themselves as the gatekeepers to citizenship. As a disgruntled Japanese member of the Seoul City Assembly argued, those in a position to "control people's rights and freedom or levy duties" (i.e., police officers and tax office staff) "should all be Japanese."[163] An article in the *Chōsen kōron* made an even more blunt assertion. Irked by the Korean tendency to interpret *naisen ittai* in terms of equal rights, the author ventured his own definition: that is, "perfecting" the principle that "Japanese make the most of being Japanese and Koreans of being Korean . . . just as men and women are born with fundamentally separate rights and duties."[164] The two peoples, in other words, must be differentiated forever.

Since they had no legal prerogative to police the boundaries of citizenship, the settlers ensured their separation through mundane practices of exclusion. Koreans of all classes experienced these "viscerally" (*taikan teki*), explained journalist Sŏ Ch'un (1894–1943), such as when they were insulted as *yobo* at the local post office or in the train station.[165] Understandably, the Korean ideologues of *naisen ittai* experienced such discrimination with despair. No amount of proof would be enough to convince the ever-suspicious settlers of Korean loyalty, Hyŏn Yŏng-sŏp bewailed, explaining how hard it was even to rent a house from a landlord in Seoul unless he proved himself an "advocate of Japanese spirit."[166] And the higher the Koreans sought to climb the social ladder, the greater the barriers settlers placed in their way. Many Korean alumni

162. By contrast, the significant overlap between the citizen-subject dichotomy and the colonizer-colonized hierarchy ensured the supremacy of European settlers in colonial Africa (Mamdani 1996, 19).

163. Keikidō Keisatsu Buchō to Keimu Kyokuchō (29 August 1941).

164. MS-sei, "Dōchō tosetsu," *Chōsen kōron*, July 1939, 55.

165. Yi Sŭng-yŏp 2001, 39–40.

166. Hyŏn Yŏng-sŏp, "Keijō no seikatsu dansō," *Chōsen oyobi Manshū*, February 1939, 62.

of elite-track colonial schools later recounted their difficulty of landing prestigious jobs after graduation.[167] Through petty acts of prejudice and daily violence, local settlers refused to let the Koreans "forget" their Koreanness, even when they so desired, keeping the most ardent candidates for assimilation in an agony of perpetual self-loathing.[168]

## *Conclusion*

No period of Japanese colonial rule left a deeper imprint in Korean public memory than the wartime era of *naisen ittai*. In the name of unity, the Japanese empire undertook a project of ethnic engineering, with a totalizing scope never before seen. The military drive in Asia extended not only the territorial borders of Japan, but the ethnic boundaries of its citizenship that the Meiji constitution had left largely undefined. During World War II and in its wake, the European empires, too, moved toward opening avenues to citizenship,[169] and some even began to contemplate self-rule. But most had abandoned their lofty visions of cultural assimilation by the time Japan redoubled such efforts in its colonies. One of the few exceptions was Nazi Germany. Like wartime Japan, Germany treated its occupied territories as laboratories for ethnic restructuring. But the overriding policy of the Nazis toward "alien" ethnicities, as demonstrated by their treatment of Poles and Polish Jews, was to annihilate, not assimilate: theirs was an irredentist project of filling the colonized space with German "resettlers" from other parts of Eastern Europe.[170] The wartime aim of Japanese rulers, by contrast, was to eradicate a Korean nation by absorbing all its members into the domi-

---

167. Interviews with two graduates of the Keijō Industrial School, 10 May 2002, Seoul (see Appendix 2); Kim Hyŏng-gŭn, "Kankokujin sotsugyōsei no mune ni nokoru mono," in Keijō Kōtō Shōgyō Gakkō 1990, 209–11; Yi P'il-sŏk, "Onshi o omou," in ibid., 155–56.

168. Yi Sŭng-yŏp 2001, 34; Eckert 1991, 229. This psychology is akin to that Franz Fanon (1967) once described of an African man, who donned "a white mask" to escape the French association of blackness with evil, only to become "alienated from himself."

169. In the case of French Africa, the racial distinction between subject and citizen was abolished by the passage of a new citizenship law in 1946. Its effect was to empower African social and political organizations such as trade unions and students, who began to call for social and economic equality "all within a rhetoric of French citizenship" (Cooper 2003, 7).

170. Harvey 2005, 95–112.

nant category of "Japanese," albeit in ways that retained old colonial distinctions within the newly extended "family."[171]

In support of Japan's bid to create a new world order based in Asia, Governor-General Minami launched a mass movement to re-center Korea around the imperial throne, which at times preceded the fascistic movement in the metropole. Existing studies have highlighted the brutality of *naisen ittai*, but the process of mobilization began well before wartime. The National Spiritual Mobilization Campaign and the *kōminka* policies built, in significant measure, on the ideological and institutional scaffoldings erected by the brokers of empire and their Korean allies in the years leading to the outbreak of war. After 1937 these civilians operated as full-fledged agents of the colonial regime, channeling the will of the state down to each neighborhood, though with a mixed record of success. Never did Japanese of an age to remember the March First Movement imagine that they would live to see Koreans join the Imperial Army or compete with one another to send donations, with a level of enthusiasm that occasionally appeared to surpass that of the home islands.

Yet, the over-organized mechanism of the wartime campaign also compromised the intended goals of *naisen ittai*. Simply getting people involved, rather than making them fully grasp its meaning, became the foremost concern of local spiritual mobilizers; mobilization, in other words, became its own ideology. And contrary to the official design to create a uniform body of the emperor's people, *naisen ittai* policy was pulled in a variety of directions by the conflicting agendas of local actors on the ground. Even as Japanese and Korean residents together paid homage to the imperial house and engaged in home-front activities, they viciously collided over the meaning of *naisen ittai*, continuing a longstanding struggle between the Korean quest for equality and the settlers' pursuit of supremacy. Indeed, imperial subjecthood became externalized in ritualized acts of allegiance, while a contest for citizenship came to be fought within the inclusionary rhetoric of the wartime empire.

---

171. For instance, although the Koreans were pressured to adopt Japanese names, their clan names were kept in all official records and public documents, which allowed the Japanese to continue to discriminate against Koreans in employment and school admission. The authorities also did not lift a ban on the transfer of family registers between Japan and Korea.

As police records and memoirs remind us, the rising trend for Koreans to claim rights of citizenship in exchange for duties should not be automatically construed as an act of jettisoning the Korean nation or becoming "pro-Japanese."[172] For their part, Japanese settlers observed this phenomenon warily, prone to see ethnic motives behind every Korean action. From their vantage point, *naisen ittai* policy was a mixed blessing: while mitigating their old fear of Korean unrest, its promise of equality also stoked new fear about Korean empowerment. The mass inclusion of Koreans into the "Japanese," many settlers worried, threatened to undermine the colonial hierarchy, destabilize their nationality, and contaminate their purity. Given settlers' enduring concern about the lack of proper Japanese attributes among their children, one may easily surmise how "excessive displays of patriotism by Koreans" would have stirred anxiety about the authenticity of their own identity.[173] Settlers' paranoia was their liminality writ large.

If wartime agents like the Ryokki Renmei succeeded in producing some devoted Korean ideologues of *naisen ittai*, they seem to have failed utterly among Japanese residents. Even as they joined the officials in goading Koreans to assimilate and demonstrate their loyalty to the emperor, many settlers—including those fronting the campaign—never came to terms with the premise of ethnic unity, any more than they could accept the idea of Koreans as rights-bearing citizens. In their antagonistic response to *kōminka* policies, long-term settlers, in particular, showed themselves to be the most aggressive ideologues of assimi-

172. This was corroborated by one Korean school teacher, revealed only as "Kim" in a memoir written by a former settler. Kim privately conveyed to his Japanese colleague in the midst of war that there were, in fact, three types of Koreans. First, there were "completely pro-Japanese" Koreans including high-ranking bureaucrats, provincial administrators, upper-class salarymen, and the well-to-do. The second group were "completely anti-Japanese" Koreans who went in exile or underground to struggle for independence. And finally there were those who "resigned themselves to Japanese rule as something inevitable" or submitted to Japan for self-preservation "against their will." This last group included the majority of Koreans (from lower- and middle-level officials and wage earners down to "the ignorant masses"), but, in the eyes of Kim, they were all "imposters as pro-Japanese" (Iwasaki 1966, 179).

173. Uesugi Shigejirō, "Chōsenjin tono tsukiai," 1–2, enclosed in Hatae Kōzō, personal correspondence, July 2002.

lation as well as its most stalwart opponents. Settlers, to the end, represented the central paradox of Japanese colonial rule.

The finest irony of all was that many settlers, who had not a tad of faith in the idea of *naisen ittai*, became its most unthinking believers by the end of the war. Whether in home-front activities or in daily imperial rituals, the Japanese increasingly came to regard Korean participation as a manifestation of their presumed loyalty to the emperor, a fiction on which the entire apparatus of *naisen ittai* policy rested. Such complacency emerges poignantly from the reminiscences of Iwasaki Kiichi, who worked as a schoolteacher in Haenam in South Chŏlla province. By the end of the war, Iwasaki recalled, a student's ability to recite the "oath as subjects of the imperial nation" became an index of *kōminka*: "we completely believed that the docile students meekly obeyed this order, and even those who did not know Japanese had memorized this and came to recite it very well." Thus, he was "flabbergasted" to hear from one Korean person, in the wake of Japan's surrender, that when they were being forced to recite the oath, they were in fact saying "Kankoku" (Korea) instead of "*kōkoku*" (imperial nation) or "*kunkoku*" (sovereign's nation)—belatedly confirming the Chōsen Army's suspicion that Koreans might be internally praying for Japan's defeat at local shrines.[174] As also testified by my interviewees, while generally skeptical of Korean sincerity, most settlers seldom questioned whether their own students, colleagues, and employees acted in good faith. Blinded by confidence, they failed to see that Koreans closest to them could be "pro-Japanese in disguise, pro-Japanese out of resignation, and pro-Japanese at gunpoint,"[175] the veneer of submission that the majority of Koreans were forced to maintain under total war.

---

174. Iwasaki 1966, 212; Miyata et al. 1992, 183. In the wake of surrender, one newspaper article attributed the "failure of Japanese rule" to the "militaristic" imperialization policies, which made "the Korean people feel completely estranged from Japan already during the wartime" (*Yomiuri shinbun*, 19 November 1945).

175. Iwasaki 1966, 226–27; Matsuo 2002, 153; testimonies of Ikeda Masae, June 2003, Tokyo (see Appendix 2).

# *Conclusion*

From the emergence of imperial Japan in the late nineteenth century to the height of its global aggression during the Asia-Pacific War, settlers in Korea operated on the front lines of their nation's empire as merchants, adventurers, reformers, ideologues, community leaders, and semi-official agents. No aspect of the Japanese colonial experience remained unaffected by the presence of settlers. Yet for a long time, barely an outline of their lives existed in the historiographies of modern Japan and colonial Korea, neither of which has fully treated settlers as historical actors. The main aim of this book has been to reconstruct their life stories and examine what they tell us about Japan's modern transformation as nation and empire, settler colonialism as a form of domination, and the internal workings of colonial power more generally. That settlers played a pivotal role in each stage of Korean governance is one of the central contentions I have pressed in this book. That analyzing their activity helps us rethink the reach as well as limits of the colonial state, and deepen our understanding of the local operation of empire—especially the complex and multi-layered dynamics of cross-cultural encounter—is another.

The making of Japan as a modern nation-state entailed the creation of new peripheries on the home islands as well as overseas. I have traced these linkages through the lives of men and women who made Korea home while operating in the empire-wide context of Japanese modernity. Japanese settlers directly or indirectly shaped the construction and local administration of Korea as they mediated all the accompanying processes of modernity, from capitalism and press activity to the discourse on suffrage and autonomy, consumer culture, and techniques of social control. In brokering colonialism, settlers' activities in Korea affected, in turn, how modern Japan was made and remade abroad, much as it was engaged in a project to transform overseas territories in its own image. Whether in the trade of Korean rice, in the issue of the Colonial Ministry, or in the preparation for total war, just as metropolitan needs guided the Governor-General's rule, demands and methods of colonial governance, where voices of local settlers left their imprint, reverberated back home. Settler politics and anxieties about assimilation also deepened the tension inherent in the construction of a (putatively) homogeneous nation and a multiethnic empire—two concurrent projects that operated at the heart of imperial Japanese citizenship. Agents as well as products of the revolutionary era, settlers navigated the contemporaneous transformation of modern Japan and colonial Korea, as they inhabited the nexus of state and society, core and periphery, nation and empire.

I have conceptualized the role of influential settlers who operated in these liminal spaces as brokers of empire. Whether working with the Government-General and Korean capitalists, bridging the settler and Korean communities, or lobbying for the interests of the peninsula vis-à-vis the metropole, these settlers carved out a role for themselves as intermediaries, a role that became progressively institutionalized over time. I have traced the activities of the brokers of empire through three stages of Japanese rule: their emergence as subimperialists through the vortex of late Chosŏn politics around the turn of the century; their dynamic, and ambivalent, role as allies of Saitō's "cultural rule" in the 1920s; and their final metamorphosis into local agents of the wartime regime in the 1930s and 1940s. Rather than a coherent principle, as I have tried to show, a complex matrix of cultural anxieties, economic imperatives, and political opportunism underpinned each phase of settlers' activity. In their political and economic weakness in relation to the colonial state, the brokers of empire pursued their agendas more often by carefully aligning them with official policies than by openly defying them. They also often operated in tandem with Korean elites, who pursued their own interests, material stakes, and political payoffs. In this Janus-faced alliance, Japanese settlers flexibly adopted accommodative as well as oppositional stances toward the regime. In so doing, they complicated the process of governance and the dynamics of encounter beyond the institutional reach of the state, not unlike their cousins did in colonial Africa.

Yet the brokers of empire themselves did not hold a single vision of empire. They worked together to advance settler interests even as they competed with one another for leadership and influence. They shared ambivalence about assimilation policy but disagreed widely over its meaning. They held onto one another in times of crisis, while clashing over strategies for countering Korean dissent. Conflicting agendas as well as shared anxieties made up the internal dynamics of settler colonialism.

More broadly, settlers serve as a critical lens with which to look into the internal mechanism of colonial power. Tracing their documentary trails leads us to the edges and interstices of the empire—spaces where scholars have paid scant attention, yet where those who seemed marginal, in fact, affected some of the most important turning points in the empire. Several points in particular merit reiteration.

To focus on settlers, to look beneath and through the state, means, first of all, to deepen our understanding about the dispersal of power. Alongside the local administrators operated a diverse and amorphous complex of agents who constantly traversed the official and unofficial terrains of activity, performing a variety of services for the empire, while trying to make it serve their own interests. In the key areas of governance where settlers left a particularly strong imprint—the propagation of Pan-Asian ideals, the construction of knowledge about Korea, the domination of local economy and politics, the promotion of Manchurian trade, and the diffusion of emperor ideology—their activities and initiatives reveal how colonial power was often dispersed, not simply imposed but mediated and modified at the local level.[1] Moving in and out of the colonial state, and operating on a variety of levels, from policy-making to community control, the brokers of empire constantly interpolated themselves into official programs as political fixers and advisors, critics and propagandists, agents of capital and conduits of Japanese culture. And they consistently claimed that, as local men of influence and knowledge, they were uniquely suited to the role of guiding the course of empire.

---

1. Here I echo the key insights from micro-level analysis of colonial power in Mitchell 1991 and Cooper 2003.

In consolidating Japanese rule over Korea, these men and women for the most part operated in collaboration with the colonial regime. Assuming public roles as deputies of the state—opportunities that increased after 1919—granted them access to power and influence that were denied to them in the realm of formal politics. This political arrangement benefited both the state and its local agents: it reduced the costs of governance by displacing them onto local allies, who helped to maintain social control and order; and it empowered local agents by incorporating them into the ruling apparatus, while minimizing the growth of political demands on the state. This dynamic became particularly evident in the 1930s as the brokers of empire worked through the state-centered system of social control.

Yet collaboration did not always work so neatly. From beginning to end, the Japanese imperial project was filled with tension and conflict. Settlers and state, the two main empire-builders, worked together in advancing their nation's agenda to modernize and reform Korea, to exploit its resources and labor, and to entrench imperial control over the peninsula. But in demanding industries, agitating for suffrage, penetrating into Manchuria, and contradicting assimilation policy, settlers also articulated their own cultures, ideologies, and modes of dominance, indeed their own framework of power that was distinct, if not wholly independent, from the colonial government.

Nor did the settlers' attitudes to the imperial metropole remain unswerving. On the one hand, they stressed Korea's inseparable tie to Japan in extracting its natural resources, demanding more citizenship rights, and protecting themselves against opposition of the native majority. On the other hand, to avert metropolitan intervention in their pursuit of economic interests or to protect their privileges as members of a dominant class, they could just as easily loosen that tie by insisting on Korea's autonomy from Tokyo.

In addition to Korean nationalists, indeed, clamorous settlers were among the local-level forces that exerted pressures on the colonial and metropolitan authorities and complicated their strategies of governance. This point is again echoed by the case of settlers in colonial Africa, which I have cited occasionally throughout the book to both highlight the dependence of Japanese settlers on the state and isolate their agency from official policy-making, an exercise that allows us to probe the limits of colonial authority. Alliances as well as uneasy relationships abounded within the four-way dynamic of local settlers, Koreans, the colonial state, and the metropole that pushed and complicated Japan's imperialistic goals on the ground.

Documenting the lives of settlers, in turn, shows they were inextricably bound up with the activities of Koreans, however separate their worlds appeared to be. From the beginning of migration, settlers found themselves, willy-nilly, at the forefront of their nation's encounter with Korea. My analysis has highlighted how local encounters informed settlers' thoughts and actions, departing significantly from existing autobiographical accounts in which Koreans appear only as a backdrop to Japanese strivings. Particularly after the March First Movement of 1919 exposed the fragility of the Governor-General's rule, Korean nationalism emerged as a key determinant in shaping the course of empire. In the face of mounting nationalist activities, a central dilemma that confronted Japanese settlers throughout the 1920s was how to empower themselves without losing legitimacy, how to keep the political upper hand without completely excluding and thus antagonizing Koreans. And as the realms of political participation and public activism continued to expand in the 1930s, more Koreans entering the fray increasingly transformed a political calculus that had prevailed since annexation. In their pursuit of power and influence, the brokers of empire not only reached out to potential collaborators, but also engaged their critics and opponents in a search for common ground. Settler colonialism and Korean nationalism, each with its own shifting and internally diverse formations, were mutually constitutive processes, rather than isolated variables in a constellation of forces that reconfigured the Japanese empire.

As contemporary observers noted, settler leaders and Korean capitalist elites were cut from the same cloth. In the shared expediency of agitating together, Japanese and Korean elites often stood firm on issues affecting their communities and the peninsula as a whole, be it industry or local autonomy. Their relationship, however, remained as fractious as it was fraternal, for their fundamental goals were often drastically divergent. Stripped of their prerogative to manage their own affairs by the Governor-General, and with few legislative safeguards to protect their political standing in the colony, settlers sought at every opportunity to secure local supremacy. Korean elites, for their part, sought to establish a bourgeois identity outside the framework of Japanese dominance, even as they shared many values and goals of the colonizers. And in and out of local councils they waged "combat at close quarters" with the settlers, eager to displace them from the center stage of politics.

The two groups of allies, consequently, shared the dilemma of how far they could press their conflicting interests against each other before undermining their partnership with the colonial state, from which they derived their power and influence. Their competitive strivings translated into a focused battle for dominance and a broader struggle for citizenship, both of which intensified as the empire accelerated its efforts to make Koreans Japanese. Ultimately, the opposition of Japanese settlers to complete accommodation and the refusal of Korean elites to complete assimilation—i.e., the resistance of both sides to completely abandon their ideological positions as imperialists and nationalists—seemed to drive and sustain their alliance, which for most participants remained a partnership of convenience.

To recognize the fraught nature of settlers' alliance with Korean elites provides further insight into the dynamism of local nationalism as well. Scholars have long assumed that Korean political life attenuated as the colonial state flexed its muscles in the closing years of the 1920s. But the strength of nationalism seems more resilient (and the power of Japanese rule less paramount) when viewed from the perspective of local settlers. If organized resistance disappeared after 1937, the spirit of ethnic nationalism, in the eyes of many settlers, was merely deflected into new citizenship claims within the framework of *naisen ittai*. Throughout the colonial period, indeed, Korean nationalism expressed itself in one way or another. The brokers of empire confronted its ever shifting and conflicting guises through their interchanges with moderate nationalists, through their joint activities with capitalist elites, and through their struggles over citizenship with all levels of Korean society.

In sum, Japanese settlers' interactions with the state and civilians in Korea reveal a complex pattern of encounter in which all parties were transformed in fundamental, and often unexpected, ways. This book has focused on zones of contact that existed beside the main axis of confrontation between the state and the colonized, the story of which has dominated the conventional narrative on colonial Korea. One of the central insights to emerge from these encounters is that dynamic struggles took place as much within the hegemonic structure of colonial rule as outside it where the lines of division seemed most starkly drawn. Just as the activities of Koreans defied a simple dichotomy of collaboration and resistance, creating what historian Yun Hae-dong has called a "gray zone" of public activity and consciousness,[2] settlers' political actions always seemed to lie in the middle, a space of compromises and unspoken conflicts. It was in this fuzzy contact zone where the brokers of empire and their Korean allies worked together to advance what they perceived to be common interests—in areas from the marketplace to municipal politics—but finding themselves simultaneously locked in a prolonged struggle for local dominance. Meanwhile, in the divided realm of the print media, settler defenders and Korean critics of the Governor-General's rule actively sought a middle ground, for overt confrontation seemed to yield few gains for either party. As a result, and to some extent unbeknownst to both parties, there developed a degree of accommodation between the colonizer and the colonized. Unexpected consequences abounded in zones of colonial encounter.

The legacy of settler colonialism lives on, not only in the palimpsests of Japanese towns found throughout the Korean peninsula, but in the ongoing amnesia of the Japanese, in the contentious politics of memory, and in continuing discrimination against resident Koreans in Japan.[3] Above all, the legacy persists among the former residents of Korea who, having repatriated to the homeland, continue to live with a sense of their own otherness. On the one hand, a lingering sense of alienation about being neither "Korean" nor "mainland Japanese" has inspired second-generation repatriate writers such as Muramatsu Takeshi (1924–1993) to critically reflect on their colonial upbringing.[4] On the other hand, their marginality has found a new expression in the social category of *hikiagesha* or "evacuees," a secondary citizenship status to which settler repatriates were relegated in postwar Japan.[5]

Social stigma attached to the *hikiagesha*, paired with feelings of betrayal by their home government, has served to heighten a sense of vic-

---

2. Yun Hae-dong 2003.

3. For an examination of this link with the issue of resident Koreans through the scholarship of Hatada Takashi, see Kō Kiruhi (Ko Kil-hŭi) 2001.

4. Muramatsu Takeshi 1994 [1972], 235.

5. As Lori Watt (2009) has perceptively noted, this category emerged in the context of Japan's rebirth as a monoethnic nation following the implosion of its multiethnic empire. For a detailed discussion of how Japanese who grew up in Korea continued to struggle with their "cultural hybridity" after repatriation, see Cohen 2006, Chapter 4.

timhood as much as solidarity among the settler repatriates.[6] According to their memoirs and testimonies, if Japanese civilians were the first to set foot on the peninsula, so, too, were they the last to leave. Colonial bureaucrats and their families secretly fled in illegally chartered ships in the wake of surrender, leaving ordinary settlers to fend for themselves,[7] a narrative of a harrowing ordeal shared by repatriates from Manchuria.[8] Whether one could find safe and quick passage home in the ensuing months depended on which side of the 38th parallel—south occupied by the American forces and north by the Soviet troops—one happened to be at war's end.[9] Settlers were, indeed, the bookends of Japanese empire, who pioneered its construction and experienced its collapse as among the first to bear the impact of the emergent Cold War politics. Yet their hardship did not end there. Empire continued to haunt their return home, as Lori Watt has shown, where uncertain economic futures, and less-than-welcome treatment by the metropolitan residents, awaited them all.[10] Not only were repatriates seen as a nuisance adding pressure on precious food supply, they were often "mistaken for Koreans,"[11] the coup de grâce whereby the "colonized" was indelibly transposed onto their postcolonial identity of *hikiagesha*.

But that story of empire would remain incomplete without an awareness of settlers as witnesses, not mere spectators, to colonial violence—an awareness that few memoirs provide. The settlers' own liminal experience as neither ruler nor ruled has translated into an abiding concern to sever their life stories from the realm of colonial politics, as they continue to straddle the fine line dividing agents and victims of empire. The

6. Watt 2009, Chapter 4; Tamanoi 2009, Chapter 2. The repatriates' sense of victimhood was particularly demonstrated by their campaign in the 1950s and 1960s to demand compensation for "having unfairly borne the burden of war" from their government, which had effectively renounced the right to reclaim overseas assets by signing the Peace Treaty of 1951 (Morita 1964, 982–83).

7. My interviewees unanimously stressed this point (see Appendix 2).

8. Tamanoi 2009.

9. On Japanese repatriation from Korea, see Morita 1964; Morita and Osada 1979–1980; McWilliams 1988; and Watt 2009, 38–44. The American authorities used the same ships and trains used for repatriating Japanese to bring back Koreans, most of whom had been forcibly brought over to Japan as labor conscripts, on their return trip to the peninsula (McWilliams 1988, 12, 50).

10. Watt 2009, Chapters 2 and 3.

11. A response to my questionnaire from a graduate of Nanzan Primary School, anon.

effect of this has been to obscure their own responsibility for Japan's colonial past in Asia, contributing to the peculiar absence of settlers from public memory that opened this book's inquiry. The harshest criticism of this trend has come from the former settlers themselves, albeit a few. They call on fellow repatriates "not to indulge in nostalgia" or disavow their complicity with state violence by reasoning that they were "too young to know,"[12] lest their self-censorship perpetuate the cycle of Japanese amnesia that, in fact, began with second-generation settlers *before* 1945 (as when the March First Movement became a taboo topic by the 1930s).[13] Such an isomorphism between settler colonialism and the post-colonial present is one of the many legacies of empire that need to be further interrogated in the culture of silence and denial in Japan.

---

12. See, for instance, Keijō Nanzan Shōgakkō Dōsōkai 1996, 270, 272; Ikeda 1999.

13. During the twenty years of her life in Seoul, Sawai Mariko recounted, for instance, that she had never heard of the March First Movement, nor had she ever visited the Pagoda Park where it began (Sawai 1996, 36).

# *Appendixes*

## Appendix 1: Settler Leaders in Seoul, 1910–1930s

| Name | Occupation | Birthplace (year) | Arrival | RA | CC | SB | LC | CH | Other |
|---|---|---|---|---|---|---|---|---|---|
| ARRIVED BEFORE 1894 | | | | | | | | | |
| Kaitsu Mitsuo | public official | Shizuoka (1853) | 1878 | X | | | | | |
| Wada Tsuneichi | trader | Ōita (1862) | 1881 | X | X | | X | | |
| Nakamura Saizō | trader | Fukuoka (1855) | 1884 | X | X | | | | |
| Fuchigami Teisuke | real estate | Kagoshima (1869) | 1884 | X | X | | | | |
| Yamaguchi Tahee | draper | Kagoshima (1865) | 1885 | X | X | X | X | | |
| Matsunaga Tatsujirō | trader | Nagasaki (?) | 1885 | X | | | | | |
| Kojō Baien | doctor | Ōita (1860) | 1886 | X | | | X | | |
| Kajiwara Suetarō | trader | Ōita (1872) | 1887 | X | X | | | | |
| Kojō Kandō | entrepreneur | Ōita (1858) | 1887 | X | X | | X | | |
| Seki Shigetarō | trader | Saga (1856) | 1887 | X | X | | | | |
| Akiyoshi Tomitarō | real estate | Fukuoka (1861) | 1887 | X | X | | X | | |
| Mikami Yutaka | house rental | Fukuoka (1868) | 1887 | | | | X | X | |
| ARRIVED BETWEEN SINO- AND RUSSO-JAPANESE WARS (1894–1904) | | | | | | | | | |
| Kikuchi Kenjō | journalist | Kumamoto (1870) | 1894 | X | X | | | | |
| Ayukai Fusanoshin | scholar | Miyagi (1864) | 1894 | | | | | | X |
| Shin Tatsuma | western grocer | Fukuoka (1868) | 1894 | X | X | | | | |
| Saitō Hisatarō | entrepreneur | Nagasaki (1874) | 1894 | | | | | | |
| Terao Mōzaburō | contractor | Okayama (1870) | 1894 | | X | | X | | X |
| Sase Kumatetsu | *rōnin* | Aizu (1865) | 1894 | | | | | | X |
| Hayashida Kinjirō | trader/house rental | Nagasaki (1861) | 1894 | X | X | | | X | |
| Soga Tsutomu | contractor | Yamaguchi (1864) | 1894/5 | X | X | X | | | |
| Fujimura Tadasuke | public official | Yamaguchi (?) | 1894/5 | X | X | X | X | | X |

| | | | | | | | | | |
|---|---|---|---|---|---|---|---|---|---|
| Kugimoto Tōjirō | hardware merchant | Saga (1868) | 1895 | X | | | | | |
| Takagi Tokuya | western grocer | Gifu (1863) | 1895 | | X | | X | | |
| Masuda Miho | furniture maker | Fukuoka (1872) | 1896 | X | X | | X | | |
| Tomita Gisaku | entrepreneur | Hyōgo (1858) | 1898 | | | | X | | X |
| Miyoshi Wasaburō | trader/real estate | Ōsaka (1867) | 1899 | X | X | | X | | |
| Shinozaki Hansuke | stationer | Nagasaki (1882) | 1899 | | X | | X | | |
| Nakamura Kentarō | journalist | Kumamoto (1883) | 1899 | | | | | | X |
| Shiki Shintarō | contractor | Fukuoka (1869) | 1900 | | X | | X | | |
| Tokuhisa Yonezō | contractor | Yamaguchi (1868) | 1900 | X | | | X | | |
| Yamazaki Shikazō | moneylender | Yamaguchi (1879) | 1900 | | | | X | X | |
| Shakuo Shunjō | journalist | Okayama (1875) | 1900 | | | | | | X |
| Aoyagi Tsunatarō | journalist | Saga (1877) | 1901 | X | | | | | |
| Ikeda Chōbee | wholesale merchant | Fukui (1869) | 1902 | | X | X | | X | |
| Jinnai Mokichi | contractor | Nagasaki (1873) | 1902 | | X | | | | X |
| Shikkō Inotarō | rice miller | Saga (1870) | 1903 | X | X | | | | X |
| Shimizu Kiyoshi | corporate executive | Kumamoto (1871) | 1903 | X | X | X | X | | X |
| Narimatsu Midori | company employee | Ōita (1880) | 1903 | | | | X | | X |
| Fujita Yonesaburō | grocer | Osaka (1879) | 1903 | | X | | | | |
| ARRIVED 1904–1910 | | | | | | | | | |
| Yamato Yojirō | transportation | Ishikawa (1871) | 1904 | X | X | X | X | | X |
| Fujita Yasunoshin | contractor | Fukui (1866) | 1904 | | X | | | | |
| Kobayashi Genroku | clothier | Mie (1867) | 1904 | | | | | X | X |
| Ikeda Chōjirō | merchant | Fukuoka (1878) | 1904 | X | X | | X | X | X |
| Kenko Reizō | company owner | Niigata (1872) | 1904 | X | | | X | | |
| Tanaka Hanshirō | contractor | Kyoto (1871) | 1904 | X | | X | X | | |
| Arai Hatsutarō | contractor | Toyama (1873) | 1904 | | | | X | | X |
| Watanabe Sadaichirō | contractor | Tochigi (1872) | 1904 | | X | | | | X |

Appendix 1 (continued)

| Name | Occupation | Birthplace (year) | Arrival | RA | CC | SB | LC | CH | Other |
|---|---|---|---|---|---|---|---|---|---|
| Ōgaki Takeo | journalist | Ishikawa (1861) | 1904 | | X | | | | X |
| Fujii Kantarō | entrepreneur | Tokushima (1876) | 1904 | | | | X | | X |
| Adachi Jōjirō | corporate executive | Okayama (1868) | 1904 | | | | X | | X |
| Shiraishi Gen | transportation | Fukuoka (1873) | 1904 | | X | | | | |
| Sekine Kinsaku | furniture merchant | ? (1879) | 1904 | | X | | | | |
| Nakai Chūzō | merchant | Fukui (1870) | 1904 | | | | X | X | |
| Sawada Kiyoshi | restaurant | Kumamoto (1874) | 1904 | | | | X | | |
| Gondō Shirōsuke | journalist | ? (?) | 1904 | | | | | | X |
| Sugi Ichirobei | *rōnin* | Okayama (1870) | 1904/5 | | | X | | | X |
| Ogawa Shōhei | lawyer | Ōita (1876) | 1904/5 | X | X | X | X | X | |
| Takahashi Shōnosuke | lawyer | Gunma (1864) | 1905 | X | X | | | | X |
| Ōmura Momozō | public official | Fukui (1872) | 1905 | X | X | X | X | | X |
| Kudō Takeki | doctor | Kumamoto (1879) | 1905 | X | | | | X | X |
| Kojō Kamenosuke | pharmacy | Ōita (1873) | 1905 | | X | | | | |
| Tagawa Tsunejirō | iron works | Shimane (1884) | 1905 | | X | | | | |
| Fuchizawa Yoshie | educator | Iwate (1850) | 1905 | | | | | | X |
| Ōkubo Masahiko | lawyer | Ehime (1870) | 1905 | | | | X | | |
| Fukushima Seiichirō | grocer | Saitama (1873) | 1905 | | | | X | | |
| Asano Tasaburō | entrepreneur | Yamaguchi (?) | 1905 | | | | X | | |
| Kawamura Senjirō | transportation | Kagawa (1871) | 1905 | | | X | X | | |
| Sano Hikozō | hardware merchant | Mie (1878) | 1906 | | X | | | X | |
| Makiyama Kōzō | journalist/Dietman | Nagasaki (1882) | 1906 | X | | X | | | X |
| Kobayashi Fujiemon | mining/contractor | Nara (1869) | 1906 | X | X | | X | | X |
| Tennichi Tsunejirō | rice miller | Ishikawa (1875) | 1906 | X | X | | | | |

| | | | | | | | | | |
|---|---|---|---|---|---|---|---|---|---|
| Tojima Yūjirō | food processing | Shiga (1883) | 1906 | | X | | | X | |
| Aruga Mitsutoyo | bank president | Nagano (1892) | 1906 | | X | | | | X |
| Hiroe Sawajirō | tobacco manufacturing | Gifu (1885) | 1906 | | X | | | | |
| Tsujimoto Kasaburō | wholesale grocer | Osaka (1874) | 1906 | | X | | | X | |
| Nimiya Tsuneichi | iron works | Ehime (1885) | 1906 | | X | | | | |
| Kawai Naosaburō | corporate executive | Tokyo (1874) | 1906 | | X | | X | | |
| Kosugi Kinpachi | contractor | Ibaragi (1877) | 1906 | | | X | X | X | X |
| Tomii Jitsutarō | draper/house rental | Hyōgo (1876) | 1906 | | | | X | X | |
| Yamaguchi Hajime | public official | Gifu (1876) | 1906 | | X | | | | |
| Musha Renzō | corporate executive | Kyoto (1883) | 1906 | | X | | | | X |
| Ōmura Tomonojō | public official | Shimane (1871) | 1907 | X | | | X | | X |
| Takeuchi Kikutarō | charcoal manufacturing | Niigata (1869) | 1907 | X | X | | X | | |
| Hara Katsuichi | corporate executive | Yamaguchi (1856) | 1907 | | X | | X | | X |
| Kōchiyama Rakuzō | official → corporate executive | Yamaguchi (1880) | 1907 | | X | | X | | X |
| Takayama Takayuki | corporate executive | Toyama (1882) | 1907 | | | X | X | | X |
| Hattori Toyokichi | official → corporate executive | Mie (1865) | 1907 | | | X | X | | X |
| Sakurai Shōichi | official → bank director | Tokyo (1881) | 1907 | | | | X | | |
| Suzaki Seihichi | *kenpei* → transportation | Mie (1884) | 1907 | | | | | X | |
| Koezuka Shōta | milk manufacturing | Yamaguchi (1866) | 1908 | | | X | X | | X |
| Fuji Sadaichi | confectioner | Saga (1889) | 1908 | | X | | | | |
| Tsuzuki Yasuji | bicycle merchant | Aichi (1883) | 1909 | | X | | | X | |
| Saitō Onsaku | official → entrepreneur | Niigata (1858) | 1909 | | | | | | X |
| ARRIVED 1910–1920 | | | | | | | | | |
| Nitta Kōichi | house rental | Yamaguchi (1882) | 1910 | X | | X | X | | |
| Maeda Noboru | *kenpei* → youth corp leader | Tokyo? (1873) | 1910 | | | | | | X |
| Niwa Seijirō | YMCA leader | Kyoto (1865) | 1910 | | | | | | X |
| Nishizaki Gentarō | coal merchant, afforestation | Okayama (1880) | 1910 | | X | | | X | |

Appendix 1 (continued)

| Name | Occupation | Birthplace (year) | Arrival | RA | CC | SB | LC | CH | Other |
|---|---|---|---|---|---|---|---|---|---|
| Horiuchi Mansuke | silk fabrics merchant | Saitama (1885) | 1910 | | X | | | | X |
| Matsuura Saisei | rice merchant | Fukui (1888) | 1910 | | X | | | | |
| Yoshioka Sadajirō | knit wear merchant | Shiga (1886) | 1910 | | X | | | X | |
| Ishihara Isojirō | liquor store, credit association | Kyoto (1865) | 1910 | | | | X | | X |
| Tobe Gen | pawn shop/printing | Okayama (1885) | 1910 | | | | X | | |
| Suemori Tomiyoshi | real estate | Saga (1877) | 1910 | | | | | | X |
| Satō Torajirō | *rōnin* → company executive | Saitama (1864) | 1912 | | | | | | X |
| Motoyoshi Seiichi | confectioner | Ishikawa (1883) | 1913 | | X | | | | |
| Takai Ryūzaburō | bicycle import merchant | Shiga (1881) | 1913 | | X | | | X | |
| Matsumoto Masahiro | lawyer | Kōchi (1872) | 1913 | | | | X | | |
| Ishimori Hisaya | journalist | Miyagi (1891) | 1913 | | | | | | X |
| Arima Junkichi | journalist | Kagoshima (1879) | 1913 | | | | | | X |
| Hori Naoki | lawyer | Ōita (1887) | 1914 | | | | X | | |
| Takai Kenji | stationary/rubber/hardware | Kyoto (1883) | 1916 | | X | | X | | |
| Kada Naoji | official → corporate executive | Yamaguchi (1877) | 1917 | | X | | X | | |

SOURCES: Nakata 1904; Makiyama 1911; Kawabata 1913; Keijō Shinbunsha 1921; Nakamura Shiryō 1926; Keijō Shinbunsha 1930; Chōsen Hakurankai Keijō Kyōsankai 1930; Arima 1931; Morikawa 1935; Keijō Shinbunsha 1936; Abe Kaoru 1937.

NOTE: The list shows the first generation of settler leaders who arrived in Korea before or shortly after annexation and played an active role in the public realm during the first three decades (1910s–1930s) of the colonial period. For the purpose of highlighting the role of long-term settler leaders, the list does not contain those who were newly elected to the city council or the chamber of commerce in the 1930s. ABBREVIATIONS FOR HEADINGS: RA=residents' association; CC=chamber of commerce; SB=school board; LC=local council (either city or provincial council); CH=community head. The heading "Other" includes semi-official committees of the Government-General (such as the Industrial Commission and the Information Committee) and political or pro-government organizations (such as the Dōminkai). Each "X" indicates that the individual served as an executive member of that particular institution.

## Appendix 2: Oral Sources

In writing this book, I used oral and written testimonies of former Japanese settlers, which chronicle intimate details of their everyday life in the colony that are not captured by official and other published sources. In addition to reading private memoirs and school albums compiled by settler alumni associations, I conducted my own interviews, distributed written questionnaires, and received personal letters, which furnish information on some 90 Japanese men and women who lived in Seoul and other cities. With this database I built mainly during my fieldwork between December 2001 and July 2003, I have attempted to supplement my archival research on settler leaders wherever possible.[1]

### *Questionnaire Survey*

My oral history data, used mostly in the discussion of everyday life in Chapter 1 and the wartime in Chapter 8, is based on questionnaires that I distributed to former Japanese residents of colonial Korea. The questionnaire had two parts. The first part focused on settlers' daily life and encounters with Koreans, and the questions were divided into the following four categories: use of Korean language, everyday life, interaction with Koreans, and political awareness as colonists (including attitudes toward various colonial policies).[2] The second part focused on their interactions with Koreans and Korean culture after repatriation to Japan. The questionnaires also provided ample space in which the respondent could add more detailed explanations. I followed up by arranging personal interviews with many of the respondents.

The main respondents to my questionnaire were members of the following school alumni associations and organizations of Japanese repatriates from Korea based in eastern Japan: the Chūō Nikkan Kyōkai (Central Japan-Korea Association, whose precursor in the colonial period was the Central Korea Association), the Keijō Teikoku Daigaku Dōsōkai (alumni association of the Keijō Imperial University) and its branches in

1. I have made fuller use of my oral history research in a separate article on the cultural world of Japanese settler youth (Uchida, 2011), which is designed to complement this book focused on the political economy of adult settlers.

2. For creating the questionnaire, I used Kimura Kenji's survey on the former Japanese residents of Sinŭiju as a template (Kimura 2001b).

Kyūshū; the Rengyō no Kai (alumni association of all Japanese primary schools in Seoul); and the Higashi Nihon Dōsōkai (alumni association of middle, vocational, and teachers' schools in Seoul). They are mainly composed of former residents of Seoul, though some of them lived in other cities before 1945. Throughout the book, the names of respondents are withheld by mutual agreement, unless otherwise noted.

I distributed about a hundred questionnaires to members of these school alumni associations and received a total of 87 responses (76 males, 13 females).[3] In addition, I interviewed several individuals who did not belong to any of the above associations and asked them to fill out the same questionnaire. The biographical data of the 87 respondents can be summarized as follows:

BIRTH YEAR

Those who were born in the period from the mid-1910s to the mid-1920s, that is, those who were in their 20s at the end of colonial rule in 1945 formed the majority of respondents (46); 4 respondents were in their 30s; and 34 in their teens.

PLACE OF BIRTH

Two-thirds (57) of the respondents were born in Korea, and of these settlers, over 40 percent of them were born in Seoul. (Outside of Seoul, South Kyŏngsang province [Pusan] and Hwanghae province ranked the highest, and others were distributed more or less equally in other provinces.) There were 28 born in Japan, with the largest number in Kyushu (Fukuoka, Saga, and Ōita prefectures), followed by Kinki (Hyōgo and Osaka), and then Tokyo and other prefectures in the Kantō area.

YEARS OF RESIDENCE IN KOREA

The longest was 30 years, the shortest was 1.5 years, and the average was 17.3 years. With the exception of two respondents who repatriated to Japan in 1946, all respondents left Korea within several months of Japan's surrender in August 1945. When compared to the residents of Sinŭiju

3. The number of female respondents was much lower than their male counterparts, reflecting the relative absence of women in the university and vocational schools. I have supplemented my data with a published survey on the graduates of Seoul Women Teachers' School conducted by Sakimoto Kazuko (1999).

(Kimura 2001b, 84–85), it becomes evident that my respondents, most of whom lived in Seoul and other cities in the southern peninsula, repatriated much more quickly than those who lived in northern provinces.

OCCUPATION

The questionnaire treated "occupation" as employment or educational status.[4] The largest category was students (56), followed by company employees (15), and government/public officials (7). A few went onto Manchuria and Japan after graduating from high school. Many graduates of elite-track vocational schools found their first employment with *zaibatsu* firms such as Sumitomo and Noguchi, large Korea-based companies and banks such as the Chōsen Industrial Bank, and the Government-General of Korea. Many also entered the army during school attendance or soon after starting a job. The majority of my respondents received middle school education and higher, reflecting the overall higher educational background of overseas settlers as compared to that of metropolitan residents (Kimura 2001b, 85).

FAMILY OCCUPATION

The largest category was commerce/self-employed (27), followed by public officials/army/police (23), bank/company employees (14), and teachers (3). This more or less reflected the general occupational structure of Japanese settlers in Korea.

In sum, the majority of my respondents were born in Korea, and in their 20s when they repatriated to Japan, and were mostly students and some newly employed, whose families were engaged in commerce, business, and public service.

## *Interviews*

In order to supplement data gathered from the questionnaires, I conducted both personal interviews and group interviews (in the form of informal roundtable meetings) with former residents of Korea. Personal interviews covered settlers who lived all over Korea, from Pusan

---

4. In the event of a job change, I listed the respondent's occupation at the time of her or his repatriation (or the longest occupation held before repatriation).

in the south to Ch'ŏnjin in the north, but most of them lived in Seoul until the end of World War II. Group interviews were conducted with graduates of the Keijō Imperial University (15), Nanzan Primary School (7), and members of the Nikkan Chūō Kyōkai (6). They were followed up by individual interviews or written correspondence, which provided more personal and family details. Personal and group interviews together covered 55 individuals. I tape-recorded and transcribed most of these interviews. All personal interviews were conducted in confidentiality, and the names of interviewees are withheld by mutual agreement, unless otherwise noted.

Another source of my oral history data is a symposium on "Japanese Settlers and Modernity" (14 June 2003, Hitotsubashi University, Tokyo), organized by Yoshizawa Kayoko, then of Hitotsubashi University. The symposium was composed of two parts. The first part consisted of presentations on the history of Japanese settlers in Korea by historians Kimura Kenji, Takasaki Sōji, and myself. The second part centered on the life history of Ikeda Masae, a former Japanese female teacher in Kaesŏng and Seoul, whose memoir (Ikeda 1999) documents how she sent six of her former Korean pupils as *joshi teishintai* (women's volunteer labor corps) to a munitions factory in Toyama prefecture in Japan during the war. Her recollection and the discussions that followed at the symposium informed my understanding of settlers' wartime role and its postcolonial legacies.

I distributed twenty further questionnaires to Korean graduates of the Keijō Kōgyō Gakkō (Keijō Industrial School) at an annual school reunion held in Seoul (10 May 2002), and received five responses. I also conducted personal interviews with two of the respondents in Seoul and one in Tokyo, both in May 2002. My questionnaires and interviews focused on their daily interactions with Japanese and general patterns of Japanese and Korean residence and commercial life during the last decade of colonial rule. One interview was recorded with the consent of the interviewee, and other interviews were recorded in handwritten notes. All of my interviewees asked to remain anonymous. To supplement my oral data, I have used essays written by Korean graduates of colonial vocational schools in school alumni albums (such as Keijō Kōtō Shōgyō Gakkō 1990) and a published oral history (H. Kang 2001).

*Reference Matter*

# *Bibliography*

*Note: For Japanese-language works published in colonial Korea, I will refer to the place of publication by Japanese name as originally printed (e.g., Keijō for Seoul).*

ARCHIVE AND DOCUMENT ABBREVIATIONS

| | |
|---|---|
| *CKSS* | (Chōsen Sōtokufu). *Chōsen ni okeru kokumin seishin sōdōin.* Keijō: Chōsen Sōtokufu, 1940. |
| *CKSU* | Morita Yoshio, ed. *Chōsen ni okeru kokumin sōryoku undōshi.* Keijō: Kokumin Sōryoku Chōsen Renmei, 1945. |
| *CKZ* | *Keijō Shōgyō* (later *Shōkō*) *Kaigisho geppō: Chōsen Keizai Zasshi* |
| HYCTS | The Han'guk Yŏksa Chŏngbo Tonghap Sisŭtem (Korean History Data Integration System), Kuksa P'yŏnch'an Wiwŏnhoe (National History Compilation Committee), Kyŏnggi-do, Kwach'ŏn-si, South Korea |
| *KG* | *Keijō Shōkō Kaigisho geppō* (later *Keizai Geppō*) |
| KK-ARSS | Kokuritsu Kōbunshokan, Ajia Rekishi Shiryō Sentā (National Archives of Japan, Japan Center for Asian Historical Records), Tokyo, Japan. |
| *KSKN* | Itō Masataka, ed. *Keijō Shōkō Kaigisho nijūgonenshi.* Keijō: Keijō Shōkō Kaigisho, 1941. |
| *KSUY* | Kokumin Sōryoku Chōsen Renmei, ed. *Kokumin sōryoku undō yōran.* Keijō: Kokumin Sōryoku Chōsen Renmei, 1943. |
| *SMB* | *Saitō Makoto bunsho: Chōsen Sōtoku jidai kenkei shiryō.* 17 vols. Seoul: Koryŏ Sŏrim, 1990. |

| | |
|---|---|
| SMKB | Saitō Makoto Kankei Bunsho (Documents Related to Saitō Makoto), Kensei Shiryō Shitsu, Kokuritsu Kokkai Toshokan (Constitutional Documents Room, National Diet Library), Tokyo, Japan. |
| YB | Yūhō Bunko, Tōyō Bunka Kenkyūjo (Yūhō Archive, Research Institute for Oriental Cultures), Gakushūin University, Tokyo, Japan. |

PRIMARY SOURCES


Abe Kaoru, ed. 1925. *Sekirara no Chōsen.* Keijō: Minshū Jironsha.

———. 1929. *Kisha no mita Chōsen.* Keijō: Minshū Jironsha.

———. 1931. *Chōsen tōchi shinron.* Keijō: Minshū Jironsha.

———. 1932. *Chōsen mondai ronshū.* Keijō: Minshū Jironsha.

———. 1937. *Chōsen toyū taikan, Shōwa 12-nen ban.* Keijō: Minshū Jironsha.

Abe Mitsuie. 1919. "Chōsen tōchi iken." In *SMKB,* shokan no bu.

Abe Mitsuie to Saitō Makoto. 1 May 1921; 6 September 1921; 29 December 1921; 29 May 1922; 23 June 1922; 16 July 1922; 23 April 1923; 2 May 1923; 12 July 1925; 2 November 1929; and 11 November 1929. Correspondence. In *SMKB,* shokan no bu.

Aikoku Fujinkai, ed. 1908. *Okumura Ioko shōden.* Tokyo: Aikoku Fujinkai.

Andō Toyoroku. 1984. *Zaikaijin no Shōwashi: Kankoku waga kokoro no furusato.* Tokyo: Hara Shobō.

Aoyagi Tsunatarō [Nanmei, pseud.]. 1908. *Kankoku shokuminsaku.* Keijō: Nikkan Shobō.

——— [Nanmei, pseud.]. 1911. *Chōsen shūkyōshi.* Keijō: Chōsen Kenkyūkai.

———, ed. 1911–1918. *Chōsen Kenkyūkai kosho chinsho kankō.* 56 vols. Keijō: Chōsen Kenkyūkai.

——— [Nanmei, pseud.], ed. 1913. *Chōsen.* Vol. 1. Keijō: Chōsen Kenkyūkai.

———. 1916. *Shin Chōsen: zen.* Keijō: Chōsen Kenkyūkai.

——— [Nanmei, pseud.]. 1917. *Chōsen yonsennenshi.* Keijō: Chōsen Kenkyūkai.

———. 1923. *Chōsen tōchiron.* Keijō: Chōsen Kenkyūkai.

——— [Nanmei, pseud.]. 1924. *Chōsen bunkashi taizen.* Keijō: Chōsen Kenkyūkai.

——— [Nanmei, pseud.]. 1925. *Shin Chōsen.* Keijō: Keijō Shinbunsha.

——— [Nanmei, pseud.]. 1926a. *Chōsen shiwa to shiseki.* Keijō: Chōsen Kenkyūkai.

———. 1926b. *Sangyō no Chōsen.* Keijō: Chōsen Sangyō Chōsakai.

———. 1935. *Sekirara ni mita naisen shiron: zen.* Keijō: Tōa Dōmin Kyōkai.

Arakawa Gorō. 1906. *Saikin Chōsen jijō*. Tokyo: Shimizu Shoten.

Arima Junkichi, ed. 1931. *Chōsen shinshiroku*. Keijō: Chōsen Shinshiroku Kankōkai.

Aruga san no jiseki to omoide Hensankai, ed. 1953. *Aruga san no jiseki to omoide*. Tokyo: Aruga san no jiseki to omoide Hensankai.

*Asahi shinbun*

Ayukai Fusanoshin. 1913. "Shizen yori uketaru Chōsenjin no seijō." In *Chōsen*, vol. 1, ed. Aoyagi Tsunatarō [Nanmei, pseud.], 137–47. Keijō: Chōsen Kenkyūkai.

———. 1942. "Kaikodan." *Shomotsu Dōkōkai kaihō* 17 (September): 3.

Chiba Ryō. 1923. "Keijō chian no hiwa." *Chōsen* (Chōsen Sōtokufu), August, 127–28.

Chōjiya Shōten, ed. 1936. *Chōjiya shōshi*. Keijō: Chōjiya Shōten.

Chŏng Un-bok. 1908. "Aete Nihonjin shokun ni tsugu." *Chōsen* (Chōsen Zasshisha), May, 19–21.

*Chōsen* (Nikkan Shobō, March 1908–March 1909; Chōsen Zasshisha, April 1909–November 1911), 1908–1911.

Chōsen Bōeki Kyōkai, ed. 1937. *Shōwa-11 nendo jigyō hōkokusho*. July. Chōsen Bōeki Kyōkai Tsūhō (gōgai).

———, ed. 1938. *Shōwa-12 nendo jigyō hōkokusho*. July. Chōsen Bōeki Kyōkai Tsūhō (gōgai).

———, ed. 1943. *Chōsen bōekishi*. Keijō: Chōsen Bōeki Kyōkai.

Chōsen Gunji Kōen Renmei. 1939. *Gunji Kōen Renmei jigyō yōran*. Keijō: Chōsen Gunji Kōen Renmei.

*Chōsen gyōsei* (Chōsen Gyōseikai), January 1938 and November 1939.

Chōsen Hōsō Kyōkai, ed. 1938–1941. *Rajio kōen, kōza*, vols. 1–19. Keijō: Chōsen Hōsō Kyōkai.

*Chōsen jihō*, 1926–1927. Repr., Tokyo: Ryokuin Shobō, 1997.

*Chōsen jijō kimitsu tsūshin*, December 1924–February 1925.

*Chōsen Jitsugyō Kurabu kaihō* (Chōsen Jitsugyō Kurabu), September 1929–December 1930; *Chōsen Jitsugyō Kurabu*, January 1931–April 1939.

Chōsen Jōhō Iinkai. 1921a. *Chōsen Hyōron (KOREA REVIEW), Hawai Beikoku shinbun kankōbutsu oyobi tsūshin kiji tekiyō*. Jōhō Isan, no. 4. Keijō: Chōsen Sōtokufu.

———. 1921b. *Chōsen ni kansuru gaikokujin no hyōron*. Jōhō Isan, no. 7. Keijō: Chōsen Sōtokufu.

———. 1921c. *Chōsen ni kansuru kaigai kankōbutsu kiji tekiyō*. Jōhō Isan, no. 8. Keijō: Chōsen Sōtokufu.

Chōsen Kenkyūkai, ed. 1925. *Dai-Keijō*. Keijō: Chōsen Kenkyūkai.

———, ed. 1932. *Shin Chōsen no kenkyū*. Keijō: Senman Kenkyūkai.

Chōsen Kenpeitai Shireibu. 1933. *Hi: Chōsen dōhō ni taisuru Naichijin hansei shiroku*. Keijō.

*Chōsen kōron* (Chōsen Kōronsha), November 1913–November 1939.

*Chōsen minpō*

*Chōsen no jitsugyō* (Chōsen Jitugyō Kyōkai), 1905–1907.

*Chōsen oyobi Manshū* (Chōsen Zasshisha, December 1911–December 1922; Chōsen oyobi Manshūsha, January 1923–January 1941), 1912–1941.

*Chōsen shakai jigyō* (Chōsen Shakai Jigyō Kyōkai), December 1930–June 1935; *Dōhōai*, December 1935–December 1936; *Chōsen shakai jigyō*, July 1942–October 1943.

Chōsen Shinbunsha, ed. 1935. *Chōsen jinji kōshinroku, Shōwa 10-nendo*. Keijō: Chōsen Jinji Kōshinroku Hensanbu.

Chōsen Shōgyō Kaigisho Rengōkai. 1927. *Dai-10 kai Chōsen Shōgyō Kaigisho Rengōkai giji sokkiroku*. May. Keijō.

Chōsen Sōaikai. "Chōsen Sōaikai kaisoku" (n.d.). In *SMB*, vol. 12, 103–18.

Chōsen Sōtokufu. 1911–1944. *Chōsen Sōtokufu tōkei nenpō*.

———. 1912. *Saikin Chōsen jijō yōran*. 2 vols. Keijō: Chōsen Sōtokufu.

———. 1915, 1921. *Chōsen Sōtokufu shisei nenpō*.

———. 1920, 1936. *Chōsen Sōtokufu kanpō*. Repr., Seoul: Asea Munhwasa, 1985.

———. *Chōsen*, January 1921–May 1938.

———. 1921. *Chōsen ni okeru shinshisei*, October. Repr. in *Chōsen sōtokufu shiryō senshū: Saitō sōtoku no bunka tōchi*, ed. Yūhō Kyōkai, 35–94. Tokyo: Yūhō Kyōkai, 1970.

———, ed. 1921. *Sangyō Chōsa Iinkai kaigiroku*. Keijō: Chōsen Sōtokufu.

———, ed. 1922. *Sangyō Chōsa Iinkai giji sokkiroku*. Keijō: Chōsen Sōtokufu.

[Chōsen Sōtokufu]. "Senkyo seido no enkaku narabini genjō" (n.d.), ca. 1929. In *SMKB*, shokan no bu.

[Chōsen Sōtokufu]. "Chōsen ni okeru sansei ni kansuru seido no hōsaku" (one with no date and another dated 2 December 1929); "Chōsen ni okeru sanseiken seido no hōsaku" (n.d.); and a typed document, "Chōsen ni okeru sansei ni kansuru seido no hōsaku" (n.d.), *SMKB*.

———, ed. 1935. *Shisei nijūgonenshi*. Keijō: Chōsen Sōtokufu.

———, ed. 1937. *Chōsen shisei ni kansuru yukoku, kunji narabini enjutsu*. Keijō: Chōsen Sōtokufu.

———, ed. 1940. *Shisei sanjūnenshi*. Keijō: Chōsen Sōtokufu.

———. 1940. *Chōsen ni okeru kokumin seishin sōdōin* [*CKSS*]. Keijō: Chōsen Sōtokufu.

[Chōsen Sōtokufu]. 1943. "Gokuhi: sanseiken mondai—Chōsen ni okeru sansei seido hōsakuan." Classified report.

———. 1944. *Jinkō chōsa kekka hōkoku*, pt. 1. Keijō: Chōsen Sōtokufu.

Chōsen Sōtokufu Gakumukyoku Shakaika, ed. 1933. *Chōsen no shakai jigyō*. Keijō: Chōsen Sōtokufu Gakumukyoku Shakaika.

Chōsen Sōtoku Kanbō, Shomubu Chōsaka, ed. 1924. *Chōsen no dokuritsu shisō oyobi undō*. Chōsa Shiryō, no. 10. Keijō: Chōsen Sōtoku Kanbō, Shomubu Chōsaka.

———, ed. 1925. *Naisen mondai ni taisuru Chōsenjin no koe*. Keijō: Chōsen Sōtokufu.

Chōsen Sōtokufu Keimukyoku. December 1923. *Kantō chihō shinsai no Chōsen ni oyoboshitaru jōkyō*. In *SMKB*.

———, ed. 1930a. *Chian jōkyō*. Keijō: Chōsen Sōtokufu Keimukyoku.

———. 1930b. *Chōsen ni okeru shuppanbutsu gaiyō*. Keijō: Chōsen Sōtokufu Keimukyoku.

———, ed. 1930c. *Gokuhi: Kōtō Keisatsu kankei nenpyō*. Keijō: Chōsen Sōtokufu Keimukyoku.

———. 1934. *Chōsen shuppan keisatsu gaiyō, Shōwa 8-nen* (1933). Keijō: Chōsen Sōtokufu Keimukyoku.

———, ed. 1933, 1938. *Saikin ni okeru Chōsen chian jōkyō*. Repr., Tokyo: Gannandō Shoten, 1966.

———, ed. 1979. *Kōshū kōnichi gakusei jiken shiryō: Chōsen Sōtokufu Keimukyoku gokuhi bunsho*. Nagoya: Fubaisha.

Chōsen Sōtokufu Keimukyoku Hoanka, ed. 1927. *Chian jōkyō*. December. Repr., Tokyo: Fuji Shuppan, 1984.

Chōsen Sōtokufu Keimukyoku Toshoka. 1926. *Riōdenka no kōkyo ni saishi "onmon shinbunshi o tōshite mitaru" Chōsenjin no shisō keikō*. Repr. in *Nihon shokuminchika no Chōsen shisō jōkyō*, Chōsen Mondai Shiryō Sōsho 11, ed. Pak Kyŏng-sik, 247–330. Chōfu, Tokyo: Ajia Mondai Kenkyūjo, 1989.

———, ed. 1932. *Onmon shinbun sashiosae kiji shūroku*. Chōsa Shiryō 29 and 31. Keijō: Chōsen Sōtokufu Keimukyoku Toshoka.

———, ed. 1938. *Shōwa 12-nenchū ni okeru Chōsen shuppan keisatsu gaiyō*. Keijō.

Chōsen Sōtokufu Naimukyoku. 1922. *Kaisei chihō seido jisshi gaiyō*. Keijō.

———. 1938. "Chōsen senkyoken mondai." Classified report.

Chōsen Sōtokufu Shomu Chōsaka, ed. 1924. *Chōsen ni okeru naichijin*. Chōsen Sōtokufu Chōsa Shiryō 2. Keijō: Chōsen Sōtokufu.

Chōsen Sōtokufu Torishirabekyoku, ed. 1912. *Kosaku nōmin ni kansuru chōsa*. Keijō: Chōsen Sōtokufu Chōsakyoku.

*Chōsen suisan jihō*

Chōsen Zasshisha, ed. 1913. *Shin Chōsen oyobi shin Manshū: zen*. Keijō: Chōsen Zasshisha.

*Chosŏn ilbo*

Chōtori Kabushiki Kenkyūkai, ed. 1939. *Chōsen keizai no hatten to shōkenkai*. Keijō: Chōtori Kabushiki Kenkyūkai.

*Chungoe ilbo*

*Chūō Chōsen Kyōkai kaihō* (Chūō Chōsen Kyōkai), August 1926–September 1933.

Dai-Keijō Kōshokusha Meikan Kankōkai Hensankakari, ed. 1936. *Dai-Keijō kōshokusha meikan*. Keijō: Keijō Shinbunsha.

Dōkōkai Honbu. 1922. *Chōsen naisei dokuritsu seigan ni tsuite*. Tokyo: Dōkōkai Honbu.

*Dōmin* (Dōminkai), June 1924–January 1931.

Dōminkai. "Dōminkai sōritsu shushi" (15 April 1924). In *SMB*, vol. 12, 279–89.

———, ed. 1926. *Dōmin kaki daigaku: meishi kōenshū*. Taikyū [Taegu]: Dōminkai Kōshū Dōsōkai.

———, ed. 1927. *Dai-2 kai Dōmin kaki daigaku kōenshū*. Keijō: Dōminkai Shuppanbu.

———. "Seimeisho (teikoku Chōsen chūton shubihei zōha no ken)" (9 November 1931). In *SMB*, vol. 12, 834–38.

Dōminkai Honbu. 1940. *Kinen sōshi meishi kōkan meibo*. Keijō: Dōminkai.

*Dōminkai kaihō* (Dōminkai), May 1933–February 1934.

Fuchigami Teisuke. 1927. "Furuki omoidebanashi." In *Kyoryūmin no mukashi monogatari*, ed. Fujimura Tokuichi, 32–36. Keijō: Chōsen Futamukashikai.

"Fuhōshō no raireki," n.d. In *SMB*, vol. 8, 929–32.

Fujii Kamewaka. 1926. *Keijō no kōka*. Keijō: Chōsen Jijō Chōsakai.

Fujii Kantarō. 1922. "Kokusaku to imin jigyō no jūdaisei." December. Pamphlet.

———. 1922. "Sangyō Chōsa Iinkai ni taisuru kansō." *Chōsen* (Chōsen Sōtokufu), October, 65–66.

Fujimura Tokuichi, ed. 1927a. *Chōsen kōshokusha meikan*. Keijō: Chōsen Tosho Kankōkai.

———, ed. 1927b. *Kyoryūmin no mukashi monogatari*. Vol. 1. Keijō: Chōsen Futamukashikai.

———, ed. 1931. *Zensen fuyū kaigiin meikan*. Keijō: Chōsen Keisei Shinbunsha.

Fujita Bunpei, ed. 1978. *Keijō to Jinsen*. Higashi Osaka: Fujita Bunpei.

*Fuzan nippō*

[Gaimu Daijin Kanbō] Bunshoka, ed. 1898. *Nihon gaikō monjo.* Vol. 31. Tokyo: [Gaimu Daijin Kanbō] Bunshoka.

Gaimushō, ed. 1908. *Nihon gaikō monjo.* Vol. 41, no. 1. Repr., Tokyo: Nihon Kokusai Rengō Kyōkai, 1960.

Gakushūin Daigaku Tōyō unka Kenkyūjo, ed. *Jūgonen sensōka no Chōsen tōchi.* Mikōkai shiryō: Chōsen Sōtokufu kankeisha rokuon kiroku 1, supplement to *Tōyō bunka kenkyū* 2 (March 2000).

———. *Chōsen Sōtokufu, soshiki to hito.* Mikōkai shiryō: Chōsen Sōtokufu kankeisha rokuon kiroku 3, supplement to *Tōyō bunka kenkyū* 4 (March 2002).

Government-General of Chosen. 1912. *Annual Report on Reforms and Progress in Chosen (Korea), 1910–1911.* Keijō: Government-General of Chosen.

*Gunsan nippō*

Han Ik-kyo, ed. 1941. *Kan Sō Ryū kun o kataru.* Keijō: Kan Sōryū-shi Kanreki Kinenkai.

Hara Keiichirō, ed. 1950. *Hara Takashi nikki.* Vol. 8. Tokyo: Kangensha.

Hattori Tōru. 1931. *Chōsen oyobi Chōsenjin no keizai seikatsu.* Keijō: Teikoku Chihō Gyōsei Gakkai Chōsen Honbu.

Hayashi Katsuhisa, ed. 1940. *Hantō no jūgojin.* Keijō: Chōsen Gunji Kōen Renmei.

Hayashi Shōzō. 1964. *Kōya no ishi.* Tokyo: Kōyō Shobō.

*Hwangsŏng sinmun*

Hwasin Sasimnyŏnsa P'yŏnch'an Wiwŏnhoe, ed. 1966. *Hwasin sasimnyŏnsa.* Seoul: Hwasin Sanŏp Chusik Hoesa.

*Heijō Mainichi shinbun*

Hirai Mitsuo. 1924. "Naisen konzai no taisaku o ikan." *CKZ* 100 (April): 4–5.

*Hokusen nippō*

*Hokusen Nichinichi shinbun*

Hosoi Hajime. 1910. *Gendai Kanjō no fūun to meishi.* Keijō: Nikkan Shobō.

———. 1911. *Chōsen bunka shiron.* Keijō: Chōsen Kenkyūkai.

———, ed. 1922. *Senman sōsho.* Vol. 5. Tokyo: Jiyū Tōkyūsha.

———. 1924a. *Chōsen mondai no kisū.* Tokyo; Keijō: Ajia Bunka Renmei Honbu.

———. 1924b. *Chōsen bungaku kessakushū.* Tokyo: Hōkōsha.

Hosoi Hajime to Saitō Makoto. 1920. "Hantō tōchi no tōmen ōkyūsaku." Statement (*ikensho*). 13 April. In *SMB*, vol. 13, 503–47.

———. 1923. "Dai-Nihon shugi no karuritsu to Chōsen tōchi hōshin no henkō." Statement (*ikensho*). 17 September. In *SMB*, vol. 14, 563–664.

Hozumi Shinrokurō. 1973. *Waga shōgai o Chōsen ni.* Tokyo: Yūhō Kyōkai.

Hyŏn Yŏng-sŏp. 1940. *Chōsenjin no susumu beki michi.* Keijō: Ryokki Renmei.

Ikeda Masae. 1999. *Futatsu no urinara (waga sokoku): 21-seiki no kodomotachi e.* Osaka: Kaihō Shuppansha.

Imamura Raen. 1942. "Kin In Shoku [Kim Yun-sik] shi to Ayukai ou tono kōjō." *Shomotsu Dōkōkai kaihō* 17 (September): 15.

Imamura Tomo. 1927. "Nijūnen mae no Chōsen." In *Kyoryūmin no mukashi monogatari*, ed. Fujimura Tokuichi. Vol. 1, 158–212. Keijō: Chōsen Futamukashikai.

Ishimori Hisaya. "Hiwa, kawa: Chōsen monogatari" (n.d.). Unpublished essay. YB.

Itō Masataka, ed. 1941. *Keijō Shōkō Kaigisho nijūgonenshi* [*KSKN*]. Keijō: Keijō Shōkō Kaigisho.

Itō Usaburō, ed. 1927. *Chōsen oyobi Chōsen minzoku.* Vol. 1. Keijō: Chōsen Shisō Tsūshinsha. Handwritten original draft and published volume, microfilm. YB.

Iwasaki Kiichi. 1966. *Ondoru yawa.* Osaka: Kyōbunsha.

Jinsen-fu, ed. 1933. *Jinsen fushi.* Jinsen [Inch'ŏn]: Jinsen-fu.

*Kaebyŏk* (*Kaebyŏksa*), May 1922–June 1925.

Kageyama Yoshirō, ed. 1921. *Chōsen no bunka.* Osaka: Naigai Hyōronsha.

Kajiyama Toshiyuki. 1995. "Seeking Life amidst Death: The Last Day of the War." In *The Clan Records: Five Stories of Korea* (trans. Yoshiko Dykstra). Honolulu, HI: University of Hawai'i Press.

"Kan Sō Ryū [Han Sang-nyong] no gendō ni kansuru ken" (n.d). In *SMKB*, shokan no bu.

Kaneko Nanyō, ed. 1931. *Chōsen chihō jichi seido shikō kinen: Keijō fukai giin senkyoroku, Shōwa 6-nenchū aki.* Keijō: Kaneko Nanyō.

Kang, Hildi, ed. 2001. *Under the Black Umbrella: Voices from Colonial Korea, 1910–1945.* Ithaca, NY: Cornell University Press.

Kankoku Chūsatsu Kenpeitai Shireibu, ed. July 1910. *Daikan kyōkai ryakushi.* Keijō.

Kankoku Tōkanfu, ed. 1909. *Dai-3 ji Kankoku Tōkanfu tōkei nenpō.*

Kawabata Gentarō, ed. 1910. *Keijō to naichijin.* Keijō: Nikkan Shobō.

———, ed. 1913. *Chōsen zaijū naichijin jitsugyōka jinmei jiten.* Vol. 1. Keijō: Chōsen Jitsugyō Shinbunsha.

Kawai Asao. 1931. *Taikyū monogatari.* Taikyū: Chōsen Minpōsha.

Keijin Kyōfūkai hokki daihyōsha, Cho Sŏn-ku et al. "Chinjōsho" (26 August 1923). In *SMB*, vol. 16, 625–46.

Keijō Chihō Hōin Kenjisei, Kakibara Takurō to Chōsen Sōtokufu Hōmu Kyokuchō and Keijō Chihō Hōin Kenjichō. "Kōshi Kurabu iinkai no ken," no. 758 (16 September 1924). HYCTS.

Keijō Honmachi Keisatsu Shochō. "Keijō kisha naikō ni kansuru ken," no. 8296 (21 October 1924). HYCTS.

Keijō Honmachi Keisatsu Shochō to Keijō Chihō Hōin Kenjisei. "Keijō-fu kaikakushin enzetsukai ni kansuru ken," no. 2323 (24 April 1924). HYCTS.

———. "Zensen kōshokusha daikonshinkai no ken," no. 4062 (29 May 1924). HYCTS.

———. "Zensen kōshokusha konwakai ni kansuru ken," no. 4457 (11 June 1924). HYCTS.

———. "Kōshi Kurabu iinkai no ken," no. 6467 (19 August 1924). HYCTS.

———. "Zensen kōshokusha konwakai no ken," no. 4554 (15 June 1924). HYCTS.

———. "Zensen kōshokusha konwakai no ken," no. 4627 (16 June 1924). HYCTS.

———. "Kōshi Kurabu sōkai kaisai no ken," no. 8802 (15 November 1924). HYCTS.

———. "Shisō mondai kōenkai ni kansuru ken," no. 4827 (18 August 1925). HYCTS.

Keijō Honmachi Keisatsu Shochō to Keijō Chihō Hōin Kensatsusei. "Kokusuikaiin Shōtokukyū chinnyū ni kansuru ken," no. 2408 (5 May 1926). HYCTS.

———. "Keijō Bengoshi Shinbun Kisha Yūshi Renmei ni kansuru ken," no. 5150 (5 May 1926). HYCTS.

———. "Dai-3 kai kōshokusha taikai kaisai no ken," no. 2397 (12 May 1926). HYCTS.

———. "Takushokushō kansei hantai kiseikai uchiawasekai ni kansuru ken," no. 2403 (23 April 1929). HYCTS.

Keijō Honmachi Keisatsu Shochō to Keimukyokuchō, Keijō Chihō Hōin Kenjisei, Keikidō Keisatsubuchō, and funai kaku keisatsu shochō. "Takushokushō kansei hantai roku dantai kyōgikai ni kansuru ken," no. 2503 (25–26 April 1929). HYCTS.

*Keijō ihō* (Keijō-fu), September 1933–August 1940.

Keijō Kenpeibuntai, ed. 1910. *Isshinkai ryakushi.* Keijō.

Keijō Kenpeitai. "Keijō o chūshin to suru kannai naisenjin gakusei dōyō no tenmatsu," no. 250 (31 January 1930). HYCTS.

Keijō Kōtō Shōgyō Gakkō (dō Keizai Senmon Gakkō) Dōsōkai, Sūryōkai. 1990. *Hitotsubu no mugi: Keijō Kōtō Shōgyō Gakkō sōritsu 70-shūnen kinen bunshū.* Tokyo: Keijō Kōtō Shōgyō Gakkō (dō Keizai Senmon Gakkō) Dōsōkai, Sūryōkai.

Keijō Nanzan Shōgakkō Dōsōkai, ed. 1996. *Keijō Nanzan Shōgakkō 70-nen kinenshi: sakamichi to popura to aoisora to.* Tokyo: Keijō Nanzan Shōgakkō Dōsōkai.

*Keijō nippō*

Keijō Ryūzan Keisatsu Shochō to Keijō Chihō Hōin Kenjisei. "Dai-Nihon Kokusuikai Chōsen Honbu no kōdō ni kansuru ken," no. 1167 (7 May 1926). HYCTS.

Keijō Seidaimon Keisatsu Shochō to Keimukyokuchō et al. "Dōkaigiin senkyo ni kansuru kannai senkyo yūkensha no kansō," no. 1166 (February 17, 1933). HYCTS.

*Keijō shinbun*

Keijō Shinbunsha, ed. 1921. *Keijō-fu chōnai no jinbutsu to jigyō annai.* Keijō: Keijō Shinbunsha.

———, ed. 1930. *Chōsen no jinbutsu to jigyō.* Keijō: Keijō Shinbunsha.

———, ed. 1936. *Dai-Keijō kōshokusha meikan.* Keijō: Keijō Shinbunsha.

*Keijō shinpō*, 1907–1912. Repr. in *Kyŏngsŏng sinbo.* Seoul: Han'guk T'onggye Sŏ-jŏk, 2003.

Keijō Shōgyō Kaigisho, ed. *Keijō Shōgyō Kaigisho geppō: Chōsen Keizai Zasshi* [*CKZ*]. Keijō: Keijō Shōgyō Kaigisho, August 1923–October 1930.

Keijō Shōkō Kaigisho, ed. *Keijō Shōkō Kaigisho geppō: Chōsen Keizai Zasshi* [*CKZ*]. Keijō: Keijō Shōkō Kaigisho, November 1930–January 1932; *Keijō Shōkō Kaigisho geppō* (later *Keizai Geppō*) [*KG*], February 1932–March 1940.

———, ed. March 1937. *Keijō ni okeru kōjō chōsa.* Keijō: Keijō Shōkō Kaigisho.

Keijō Shōro Keisatsu Shochō to Keimu Kyokuchō and Keikidō Keisatsubuchō. "Minzokushugi bokkō ni kansuru ken," no. 13545 (30 December 1925). HYCTS.

——— to Keijō Chihō Hōin Kenjisei. "Keijō Bengoshi Shinbun Kisha Yūshi Renmei ni kansuru ken," no. 5150 (5 May 1926). HYCTS.

——— to Keijō Chihō Hōin Kenjisei. "Fuon gendōsha ni kansuru ken," no. 46-4 (15 April 1942). HYCTS.

Keijō-fu. 1927. *Keijō funai shakai jigyō gaikyō.* Keijō: Keijō-fu.

———. 1929. *Keijō shakai jigyō benran.* Keijō: Keijōfu.

———. 1934. *Keijō fushi.* Vol. 1 (1934), vol. 2 (1936), vol. 3 (1941). Keijō: Keijō-fu.

———, ed. 1936. *Keijō fusei ippan.* Keijō: Keijō Fuchō.

Keijō-fu Shakaika. 1934. *Keijō-fu shakai jigyō yōran.* Keijō: Keijō-fu.

Keijō Kyoryūmindan Yakusho. 1912. *Keijō hattatsushi.* Keijō: Keijō Kyoryūmindan Yakusho.

Keikidō. September 1938. *Chian jōkyō.* fuhyō, "Nihon Kirisutokyō Seinenkai Chōsen Rengōkai." HYCTS.

Keikidō to Keijō Chihō Hōin Kenjisei. "Nisshi shōtotsu jiken ni kansuru kannai jōkyō (dai-11 hō)," no. 8402-10 (2 October 1931). HYCTS.

——— to Keijō Chihō Hōin Kenjisei. "Nisshi shōtotsu jiken ni kansuru kannai jōkyō (dai-12 hō)," no. 8402-11 (3 October 1931). HYCTS.

Keikidō Keisatsubu, ed. May 1928. *Chian gaikyō.* Repr. in *Nihon shokuminchika no Chōsen shisō jōkyō,* ed. Pak Kyŏng-sik. Chōfu: Ajia Mondai Kenkyūjo, 1989.

———, ed. May 1929. *Chian jōkyō sono 1.* Repr. in *1920–30-nendai minzoku undō,* ed. Pak Kyŏng-sik. Kawasaki: Ajia Mondai Kenkyūjo, 1982.

———, ed. July 1931. *Chian jōkyō.* Repr. in *Nihon shokuminchika no Chōsen shisō jōkyō,* ed. Pak Kyŏng-sik. Chōfu: Ajia Mondai Kenkyūjo, 1989.

Keikidō Keisatsu Buchō to Keimu Kyokuchō et al. "Shōdōkai dai-3 kai kaiin sōkai kaisai ni kansuru ken," no. 5520 (23 December 1937). HYCTS.

———. "Jinsen furiin no shitsugen mondai ni kansuru ken," no. 1810 (24 July 1939). HYCTS.

———. "Saikin ni okeru dōnai no minjō ni kansuru ken," no. 3201-2 (19 December 1940). HYCTS.

———. "Kokumin sōryoku undō ni tomonau minjō ni kansuru ken," no. 141-3 (25 March 1941). HYCTS.

———. "Jikyoku ni taisuru bumin no gendō ni kansuru ken," no. 413–23 (27 March 1941). HYCTS.

———. "Jikyoku ka no minjō ni kansuru ken," no. 1743 (30 June 1941), and no. 2426 (29 August 1941). HYCTS.

Keishō Hokudō Keisatsubu [Pak Chung-yang], ed. 1934. *Kōtō keisatsu yōshi.* Taegu: Keishō Hokudō Keisatsukyoku. Repr., Seoul: Yŏgang Ch'ulp'ansa, 1970.

Kikuchi Kenjō. 1910a. *Daiinkun den: Chōsen saikin gaikōshi.* Keijō: Nikkan Shobō.

———. 1910b. *Daiinkun den.* Trans. into Korean as *Chosŏn ch'oegŭn oegyosa Taewŏn'gun chŏn: pu wangbi no ilsaeng.* Keijō: Nikkan Shobō. Repr., Tokyo: Perikansha, 1998.

———, ed. 1922. *Kakushu no Chōsen hyōron.* Tokyo: Jiyū Tōkyūsha.

———. 1925. *Chōsen shokokuki.* Keijō: Tairiku Tsūshinsha.

———. 1931. *Chōsen zakki.* 2 vols. Keijō: Keimeisha.

——— [Chōfū Sanjin, pseud.]. 1936. *Kindai Chōsen rimenshi: kindai Chōsen no yokogao.* Keijō: Chōsen Kenkyūkai.

———. 1940 [1937]. *Kindai Chōsenshi.* Vol. 2. Tokyo: Tairiku Kenkyūsho.

Kikuchi Kenjō to Saitō Makoto. 5 December 1920; 2 February 1923. Correspondence. In *SMKB*, shokan no bu.

———. 1929. "Chōsen tōchi iken." Statement (*ikensho*). September. In *SMKB*, shokan no bu.

Kikuchi Kenjō to Tokutomi Inoichirō (Sohō). October 1895. Correspondence. Repr., in *Tokutomi Sohō kankei monjo*, ed. Sakeda Masatoshi et al., 222. Kindai Nihon Shiryō Sensho 7-3. Tokyo: Yamakawa Shuppan, 1987.

Kim Yŏng-han. 1920. "Chōsen Judō Shinkōkai keika jōkyō hōkokusho." 17 April. In *SMB*, vol. 9, 159–69.

Kin Shuntaku [Kim Ch'un-t'aek]. 1914. Kin Manjū [Kim Man-jung], *Shashi nanseiki [Sassi namjŏnggi]*; *Kyū unmu [Kuunmong]: genbun wayaku taishō*. Trans. Chōsen Kenkyūkai. Chōsen Kenkyūkai Kosho Chinsho Kankō 1. Keijō: Chōsen Kenkyūkai.

Kitagawa Kichisaburō. 1927. "Nyūkyō tōjitsu no konwaku." In *Kyoryūmin no mukashi monogatari*, ed. Fujimura Tokuichi, 47–56. Keijō: Chōsen Futamukashikai.

Kitagawa Yoshiaki, ed. 1934. *Yamaguchi Tahee ou*. Keijō: Yamaguchi Tahee ou Hyōshōkai.

Kobayashi Genroku. "Chōsen angya no nengan." *Chōsen bukkyō* (Chōsen Bukkyōsha) 21 (January 1926): 9.

Koezuka Shōta. "Jōkai hayawakari dokuhon." *Kokumin sōryoku* 3, no. 5 (May 1941): 109–130.

Kokumin Kyōkai [Kungmin Hyŏphoe] Sendenbu, ed. 1931. *Kokumin Kyōkai undōshi*. Keijō: Kokumin Kyōkai Honbu.

*Kokumin sōryoku* (Kokumin Sōryoku Chōsen Renmei), April 1941-August 1942.

Kokumin Sōryoku Chōsen Renmei, ed. 1943. *Kokumin sōryoku undō yōran* [*KSUY*]. Keijō: Kokumin Sōryoku Chōsen Renmei.

Kokumin Sōryoku Chōsen Renmei Bōei Shidōbu. 1941a. *Hi: naisen ittai no gugen*. Keijō: Kokumin Sōryoku Chōsen Renmei Bōei Shidōbu.

———. 1941b. *Naisen ittai no rinen oyobi sono gugen hōsaku yōkō* (June).

Kokuryūkai, ed. 1966. *Tōa senkaku shishi kiden: jō*. Tokyo: Hara Shobō.

Kōtō Hōin Kenjikyoku Shisōbu, ed. *Shisō geppō* 2, no. 8 (November 1932).

Kudō Masumi. 1983. *Hatō o kugutte: nanajūnen no kyūseki*. Tokyo: Hara Shobō.

Kudō Takeki. 1929. *Igakujō yori mitaru naisen no kankei*. Keijō: Dōminkai Shuppanbu.

Kŭm Pyŏng-dong, ed. 1999. *Shiryō zasshi ni miru kindai Nihon no Chōsen ninshiki: Kankoku heigōki zengo*. Vol. 3. Tokyo: Ryokuin Shobō.

Kuzuu Yoshihisa. 1930. *Nikkan gappō hishi*. Tokyo: Kokuryūkai Shuppanbu.

Kye Hun-mo, ed. 1979. *Han'guk ŏllon yŏnp'yo.* Seoul: Kwanhun K'ŭllŏp Sinyŏng Yŏn'gu Kigŭm.

*Kyōshō no michi* (Kyōshōsha) 1 (September 1923).

Lee, Peter H., ed. 1996. *Sourcebook of Korean Civilization.* Vol. 2: From the Seventeenth Century to the Modern Period. New York: Columbia University Press.

*Maeil sinbo*

Makiyama Kōzō, ed. 1911. *Chōsen shinshi meikan.* Keijō: Nihon Denpō Tsūshinsha Keijō Shikyoku.

*Mankan no jitsugyō* (Mankan Jitsugyō Kyōkai), 1908–1910.

Mansen Shōgyō Kaigisho Rengōkai, ed. September 1918. *Mansen Shōgyō Kaigisho Rengōkai sokkiroku.*

*Manshū Nichinichi shinbun*, 4–8 June 1938.

Maruyama Tsurukichi. 1955. *Nanajūnen tokoro dokoro.* Tokyo: Nanajūnen Tokoro Dokoro Kankōkai.

Matsui Shigeru. 1952. *Matsui Shigeru jiden.* Tokyo: Matsui Shigeru Sensei Jiden Kankōkai.

Matsuo Shigeru. 2002. *Watashi ga hantō de shitakoto.* Tokyo: Sōshisha.

Matsuyama Tsunejirō. 1924. "Chōsen ni okeru sanseiken mondai." Pamphlet. 11 January.

Min Wŏn-sik. "Shin Nihonshugi" (October 1919). Repr. in *Banzai sōjō jiken (San'ichi undō): ko shishaku Sakatani Yoshirō hakushi 'Chōsen mondai zassan' no uchi*, ed. Kondō Ken'ichi, vol. 2, 123–25. Tokyo: Yūhō Kyōkai Chōsen Shiryō Hensankai, 1964.

Mitarai Tatsuo. 1942. *Minami sōtoku no Chōsen tōchi.* Keijō: Keijō Nippōsha.

Mitsui Kōzaburō. 1913. *Aikoku Fujinkai shi.* Tokyo: Aikoku Fujinkaisha.

Miyakawa Gorōsaburō to Saitō Makoto. 1923. "Chōsen tōchisaku: kenpakusho." Petition. 16 February. In *SMB*, vol. 14, 295–370.

Miyamoto Nobuharu, ed. 1921. *Keijō-fu chōnai no jinbutsu to jigyō annai, zen.* Keijō: Keijō Shinbunsha.

Morikawa Kiyoto, ed. 1935. *Chōsen Sōtokufu shisei nijūgoshūnen kinen hyōshōsha meikan.* Keijō: Hyōshōsha Meikan Kankōkai.

Morita Yoshio, ed. 1945. *Chōsen ni okeru kokumin sōryoku undōshi* [*CKSU*]. Keijō: Kokumin Sōryoku Chōsen Renmei.

———, ed. 1964. *Chōsen shūsen no kiroku: Beiso ryōgun no shinchū to Nihonjin no hikiage.* Tokyo: Gannandō Shoten.

Morita Yoshio and Osada Kanako, eds. 1979–1980. *Chōsen shūsen no kiroku: shiryō hen.* 3 vols. Tokyo: Gannandō Shoten.

Murakami Seito, ed. 1942. *Nihon hyakkaten sōran.* Tokyo: Hyakkaten Shinbunsha.

Muramatsu Takeshi. 1972. *Chōsen shokuminsha: aru Meijijin no shōgai*. Tokyo: Sanseidō. Repr. in *Umi no taryon: Muramatsu Takeshi chosakushū*. Tokyo: Kōseisha, 1994.

Naikaku Tōkeikyoku, ed. 1890, 1900. *Nihon teikoku tōkei nenkan*. Tokyo: Naikaku Tōkeikyoku.

Nakai Kinjō. 1915. *Chōsen kaikoroku*. Tokyo: Tōgyō Kenkyūkai Shuppanbu.

Nakamura Kentarō. 1969. *Chōsen seikatsu gojūnen*. Kumamoto: Seichōsha.

Nakamura Shiryō, ed. 1925, 1931, 1935, 1942. *Chōsen ginkō kaisha yōroku*. Keijō: Tōa Keizai Jihōsha.

———, ed. 1926. *Keijō, Jinsen shokugyō meikan*. Keijō: Tōa Keizai Jihōsha.

Nakata Kōnosuke, ed. 1904. *Zaikan jinshi meikan*. Moppo [Mokp'o]: Moppo Shinpōsha.

"Nikkan gappōron ni taisuru Kanjin no gendō," Otsuhi, no. 2711 (7 December 1909). Ref. code: B03050610300. KK-ARSS.

Nikkan Tsūshō Kyōkai. 1895. *Nikkan Tsūshō Kyōkai hōkoku*, no. 2. Tokyo: Nikkan Tsūshō Kyōkai. Repr., Seoul: Asea Munhwasa, 1983.

Ōgaki Takeo [Taewŏn Changbu]. 1906. "Widaehan kungmin enan samgae t'ŭksŏng i yuhamŭl kyŏnham." *Taehan Chaganghoe wŏlbo* 2 (25 August): 1–5.

———. 1907. "Ponhoe ŭi changnae." *Taehan Chaganghoe wŏlbo* 11 (25 May).

———. 1909. "Kankoku kokujō ippan." Appended to a resident-general's report to the Foreign Ministry Political Affairs Bureau. "Ōgaki Takeo no kōdō." Otsuhi, no. 2891. 28 December. Ref. code: B03056103 00. KK-ARSS.

———. 1919. "Chōsen no genjō oyobi sōjō no geiin ni tsuite." In *SMB*, vol. 9, 117–19.

———. 1927. "Kontontaru seijō to sono rimen." In *Kyoryūmin no mukashi monogatari*, ed. Fujimura Tokuichi, 108–13. Keijō: Chōsen Futamukashikai.

Ōgaki Takeo to Kurachi Tetsukichi. 1911. "Chinjōsho." Petition. 12 January. Ref. code: B03030229100. KK-ARSS.

Ōgaki Takeo et al. 1927. "Chōsen zaijūsha ni taisuru sanseiken fuyo ni kansuru ken" (petitioners: Ōgaki Takeo and 56 others; cosigned by a Diet member, Matsumoto Tsunejirō). Petition. In *Dai-52 kai Teikoku gikai shūgiin seigan bunshohyō* 519: 264.

Ogino Katsushige, ed. 1927. *Chōsen oyobi Manmō ni okeru Hokuriku dōjinshi*. Keijō: Hokuriku Dōjinshi Hensansha.

Ogura Seitarō, ed. 1943. *Chōsen sangyō nenpō, Shōwa-18 nenban*. Keijō: Tōyō Keizai Shinpōsha.

Oka Ryōsuke. 1915. *Keijō hanjōki*. Keijō: Hakubunsha.

Okada Mitsugu, ed. 1936. *Keijō no enkaku.* Keijō: Keijō Kankō Kyōkai.

Okamoto Ryūnosuke. Hirai Komajirō, ed. 1912. *Fūun kaikoroku.* Tokyo: Bukyō Sekaisha.

Okamoto Tatsuaki and Matsuzaki Tsugio, eds. 1989. *Kikigaki Minamata minshū-shi.* Tokyo: Sōfūkan.

Ōkurashō Kanrikyoku, ed. 1948–1950. *Nihonjin no kaigai katsudō ni kansuru rekishiteki chōsa.* Tokyo: Ōkurashō Kanrikyoku. Vol. 7, no. 6 (Chōsen-hen).

Ōmura Tomonojō, ed. 1911. *Kokukan sensei jikki.* Keijō: Chōsen Kenkyūkai.

———. 1922. *Keijō kaikoroku.* Keijō: Chōsen Kenkyūkai.

*Osaka Asahi shinbun*

*Ōsaka Mainichi shinbun*

Ōtaniha Honganji Chōsen Kaikyō Kantokubu, ed. 1927. *Chōsen kaikyō gojūnenshi.* Keijō: Ōtaniha Honganji Chōsen Kaikyō Kantokubu.

Ozaki Shinji. 1995. *Mou boku wa Keijōkko niwa modorenai.* Tokyo: Sekai Nippōsha.

Ōzorasha, ed. 2008. *Shashinchō: Chōsen.* Vol. 6 of *Ajia shashinshū.* Tokyo: Ōzorasha.

"Pak Hŭng-sik." 1981. In *Chaegye hoego* vol. 2: *wŏllo kiŏbin p'yŏn II.* Seoul: Han'guk Ilbosa.

Pak Yŏng Ch'ŏl. 1929. *Gojūnen no kaiko.* Keijō: Ōsakayagō Shoten.

*Pyŏlgŏn'gon* (Kaebyŏksa), 1 July 1930.

*Ryokki* (Ryokki Renmei), January 1936–March 1943.

Ryokki Nihon Bunka Kenkyūjo, ed. 1940. *Uji sōsetsu no shin seishin to sono tetsuzuki.* Keijō: Ryokki Renmei.

Ryokki Renmei, ed. 1939. *Chōsen shisōkai gaikan.* Keijō: Ryokki Renmei.

*Ryokujin* (Ryokujin Hakkōsho), September 1935–October 1935.

Saitō Makoto. 1920. "A Message from the Imperial Japanese Government to the American People: Home Rule for Korea?" *The Independent,* 31 January, 167–69.

*Saitō Makoto bunsho: Chōsen Sōtoku jidai kenkei shiryō* [*SMB*]. 1990. 17 vols. Seoul: Koryŏ Sŏrim.

Sakeda Masatoshi et al., eds. 1987. *Tokutomi Sohō kankei monjo.* Kindai Nihon Shiryō Sensho 7-3. Tokyo: Yamakawa Shuppan.

*Samch'ŏlli* (*Samch'ŏllisa*), July 1931.

Sasaki Taihei, ed. 1930. *Chōsen no jinbutsu to jigyō.* Keijō: Keijō Shinbunsha.

Sase Kumatetsu. 1927. "Isshinkai to Tōgakutō." In *Kyoryūmin no mukashi monogatari,* ed. Fujimura Tokuichi, 67–74. Keijō: Chōsen Futamukashikai.

Sawai Rie. 1996. *Haha no "Keijō," watashi no Souru.* Tokyo: Sōfūkan.

*Seisen nippō*

Shakuo Shunjō, ed. 1914. *Chōsen oyobi Manshū no kenkyū.* Keijō: Chōsen Zasshisha.

———, ed. 1930. *Chōsen no kenkyū.* Seoul: Chōsen oyobi Manshū sha.

Shibusawa Seien Kinenzaidan Ryūmonsha, ed. 1955–1971. *Shibusawa Eiichi denki shiryō.* Vol. 31. Tokyo: Shibusawa Eiichi denki shiryō Kankōkai.

Shihōshō Keijikyoku (Tokyo). "Chōsen ni taisuru chōheisei shikō no kakugi kettei kōhyō ni kansuru hankyō chōsa." Shihōshō Keijikyoku (Tokyo), *Shisō geppō* 95 (June 1942): 12–23.

*Shomotsu Dōkōkai kaihō* (Shomotsu Dōkōkai), vol. 17 (September 1942).

Shōmu Kenkyūkai. "Shōmu Kenkyūkai kisoku" (n.d.). In *SMB*, vol. 8, 681–714.

"Shōmusha gaisetsu" (n.d.). In *SMB*, vol. 8, 721–31.

*Sidae ilbo*

Sōaikai Sōhonbu Bunkabu, ed. 1923. *Sōaikai jigyō bengai.* Tokyo: Sōaikai Honbu.

*Sōdōin* (Kokumin Seishin Sōdōin Chōsen Renmei), June 1939–October 1940.

Soejima Michimasa. 1925. "Chōsen tōchi no konpongi." *Keijō nippō*, 26–28 November.

Son Chŏng-gyu et al., ed. 1939. *Gendai Chōsen no seikatsu to sono kaizen.* Keijō: Ryokki Renmei.

Song Chin-u. 1927. "Sekai no taisei to Chōsen no shōrai." In *Chōsen oyobi Chōsen minzoku*, ed. Itō Usaburō, n.p. Vol. 1. Keijō: Chōsen Shisō Tsūshinsha.

Sugimoto Masasuke and Oda Shōgo, eds. 1927. *Chōsenshi taikei: saikin seishi.* Keijō: Chōsenshi Gakkai.

Suzuki Takeo. 1939. *Tairiku heitan kichiron kaisetsu.* Keijō: Ryokki Renmei.

*Taehan Chaganghoe wŏlbo* (*Taehan Chaganghoe*), August 1906–June 1907.

Taehan Hyŏphoe, ed. 1907. *Taehan Hyŏphoe.* Keijō.

*Taehan Maeil sinbo*

Taehan Min'guk Mun'gyobu Kuksa P'yŏnch'an Wiwŏnhoe, ed. 1987. *Yun Ch'iho ilgi.* Vols. 8–10. Repr., Seoul: Kuksa P'yŏnch'an Wiwŏnhoe.

Tairiku Kenkyūsha, ed. 1934. *Mansen mondai no kisū.* Keijō: Tairiku Kenkyūsha.

Takahara Kiji, ed. 1935. *Kyojin Kashii ou no henrin: dōzō jomakushiki ni saishite.* Fuzan [Pusan].

Takushokushō Chōsen Jogai Dōmei. 1929. "Takushokushō shinsetsu ni tsuki Chōsen kankatsugai o yōsei." Petition. April. In *SMKB*.

Tanaka Ichinosuke (Reisui), ed. 1936. *Zensen shōkō kaigisho hattatsushi.* Fuzan: Fuzan Nippōsha.

Tanaka Hanshirō et al. to Takahashi Shōnosuke. 1913. "Kengi an." 4 October. In *SMB*, vol. 13, 37–41.

Tange Ikutarō, ed. 1943. *Chōsen ni okeru jinkō ni kansuru shotōkei.* Keijō: Chōsen Kōsei Kyōkai.

Tarui Tōkichi. 1893. *Daitō gappōron.* Repr., Tokyo: Chōryō Shorin: Wakatsuki Shoten, 1975.

Teikoku Tetsudō Kyōkai, ed. 1926. *Chōsen ni okeru tetsudō fukyū sokushin ni tsuki kengi.* Tokyo: Teikoku Tetsudō Kyōkai.

*T'onggambu munsŏ.* 1998. 11 vols. Repr., Kwachŏn-si, Kyŏnggi-do, Korea: Kuksa P'yŏnch'an Wiwŏnhoe.

Tōkanfu. 1907. *Kankoku shisei nenpō, Meiji 39/40-nen.* Keijō: Tōkanfu.

———. 1909. *Dai-2 ji Tōkanfu tōkei nenpō.* Keijō: Tōkanfu.

Tōkanfu Sōmubu, ed. 1906–1907. *Kankoku jijō yōran.* Vol. 1. Keijō: Keijō Nippōsha.

*Tōkyō Asahi shinbun*

Tomita Seiichi. 1936. *Tomita Gisaku den.* Chinnanho [Chinnamp'o]: Tomita Seiichi.

*Tonga ilbo*

Tsuda Katashi. 1939. *Naisen ittai ron no kihon rinen.* Keijō: Ryokki Renmei.

———. 1940. *Shin seikatsu sengen.* Keijō: Ryokki Renmei.

Ugaki Kazushige. 1935. *Chōsen o kataru.* Tokyo: Jitsugyō no Nihonsha.

Wada Tsuneichi. 1927. "Gensantsu no kaikō to waga gaimushō no hōshin." In *Kyoryūmin no mukashi monogatari*, vol. 1, ed. Fujimura Tokuichi, 11–18. Keijō: Chōsen Futamukashikai.

Wakō Kyōen. 1927. *Wakō Kyōen jigyō yōran.* Keijō: Wakō Kyōen Shuppanbu.

Watanabe Manabu and Umeda Masashi, eds. 1980. *Bōkyō Chōsen.* Tokyo: Kokusho Kankōkai.

Yamagata Isoo. 1916. "Chōsen ni okeru gaikoku senkyōshi." In *Shin Chōsen: zen*, ed. Aoyagi Tsunatarō, 195–200. Keijō: Chōsen Kenkyūkai.

Yamamoto Shirō, ed. 1984. *Terauchi Masatake kankei monjo: shushō izen.* Kyoto: Kyōto Joshi Daigaku.

Yamanashi Hanzō Rikugun Jikan to Saitō Makoto. 1919. "Chōsen minzoku undō ni taisuru taisaku." Statement (*ikensho*). 27 August. In *SMB*, vol. 9, 143–58.

Yanagisawa Shichirō. 1969. *Karano ni ikite.* Yokohama: Izumien.

Yang Chŏng-mo, ed. 1982. *Pusan Sangŭisa, 1889-yŏn–1982-yŏn.* Pusan: Pusan Sanggong Hoeŭiso.

Yasuda Yasunori. 1927. *Chōsen kyōiku ni anju shite.* Keijō: Ōsakayagō Shoten.

Yi Jin-ho et al., eds. 1934. *Watanabe ou kinen, Chōsen o kataru sono ichi: Chōsen no chi to hito tono saininshiki.* Keijō: Yi Hŭi-wan.

Yi Kwang-su. "Minjok Kaejoron." *Kaebyŏk*, May 1922, 18-72.

———. "Minjokchŏk Kyŏngnyun." *Tonga ilbo*, 2–6 January 1924.

*Yomiuri shinbun*

*Yudo* (Yudo Chinhŭnghoe), vol. 2 (n.d.).

Yūhō Kyōkai, ed. 1970. *Chōsen Sōtokufu shiryō senshū: Saitō sōtoku no bunka tōchi*. Tokyo: Yūhō Kyōkai.

———, ed. 1983. *Shiryō senshū: Chōsen ni okeru nōson shinkō undō*. Tokyo: Yūhō Kyōkai.

———, ed. 1984. *Watanabe Toyohiko kōjutsu: Chōsen Sōtokufu kaikodan*. Tokyo: Yūhō Kyōkai.

———, ed. 1986. *Hozumi Shinrokurō kōjutsu: rekidai sōtoku tōchi tsūkan*. Tokyo: Yūhō Kyōkai.

Zaisen Mindan Giin Rengōkai. 1912. "Chinjōsho." Petition. 25 November. In *SMB*, vol. 13, 43–44.

Zenkoku Shinbun Tōkyō Rengōsha, ed. 1912. *Nihon shokuminchi yōran*. Tokyo: Nihon Keizai Shinshisha.

"Zenra Nandō hyōgikaiin naisenjin atsureki no tenmatsu" (n.d.). In *SMB*, vol. 4, 381–419.

Zensen Naichijin Jitsugyōka Yūshi Konwakai. December 1920. *Zensen Naichijin Jitsugyō Yūshi Konwakai sokkiroku*. Keijō: Keijō Shōgyō Kaigishonai Konwakai Jimusho.

SECONDARY SOURCES

Abernethy, David. 2000. *The Dynamics of Global Dominance: European Overseas Empires, 1415–1980*. New Haven, CT: Yale University Press.

Ambaras, David R. 2005. *Bad Youth: Juvenile Delinquency and the Politics of Everyday Life in Modern Japan*. Berkeley, CA: University of California Press.

Amemiya Shōichi. 1998. "Self-Renovation of Existing Social Forces and Gleichschaltung: The Total-War System and the Middle Classes." In *Total War and "Modernization,"* ed. Yamanouchi et al., 209–38. Ithaca, NY: East Asia Program, Cornell University.

Anderson, Benedict R. 1983. *Imagined Communities: Reflections on the Origin and Spread of Nationalism*. London: Verso.

Anzako Yuka. 1995. "Chōsen ni okeru sensō dōin seisaku no tenkai: 'kokumin undō' no soshikika o chūshin ni." *Kokusai kankeigaku kenkyū* 21 bessatsu (March): 1–19.

Aoi Akihito. 2005. *Shokuminchi jinja to teikoku Nihon*. Tokyo: Yoshikawa Kōbunkan.

Aoki Atsuko. 2006. "Aru Nihonjin no Chōsen taiken: 'Jōkō Yonetarō nikki' shiryō shōkai." *Tōyō bunka kenkyū* 8 (March): 169–88.

Asano Toyomi. 2008. *Teikoku Nihon no shokuminchi hōsei: hōiki tōgō to teikoku chitsujo.* Nagoya: Nagoya Daigaku Shuppankai.

Asano Toyomi and Matsuda Toshihiko, eds. 2004. *Shokuminchi Teikoku Nihon no hōteki kōzō.* Tokyo: Shinzansha.

Askew, David. 2003. "Empire and the Anthropologist: Torii Ryūzō and Early Japanese Anthropology." *Japanese Review of Cultural Anthropology* 4: 133–154.

Atkins, E. Taylor. 2010. *Primitive Selves: Koreana in the Japanese Colonial Gaze, 1910–1945.* Berkeley, CA: University of California Press.

Auerback, Micah. 2007. "Japanese Buddhism in an Age of Empire: Mission and Reform in Colonial Korea, 1877–1931." Ph.D. diss., Princeton University.

Azuma, Eiichiro. 2005. *Between Two Empires: Race, History, and Transnationalism in Japanese America.* New York: Oxford University Press.

———. 2008. "'Pioneers of Overseas Japanese Development': Japanese American History and the Making of Expansionist Orthodoxy in Imperial Japan." *Journal of Asian Studies* 67, no. 4 (November): 1187–1226.

Bakhtin, Mikhail M. 1981. *The Dialogic Imagination: Four Essays.* Ed. Michael Holquist; trans. Caryl Emerson and Michael Holquist. Austin, TX: University of Texas Press.

Baldwin, Frank. 1979. "Participatory Anti-Imperialism: The 1919 Independence Movement." *Journal of Korean Studies* 1: 123–62.

Banerjee, Sukanya. 2010. *Becoming Imperial Citizens: Indians in the Late-Victorian Empire.* Durham, NC: Duke University Press.

Bayliss, Jeffrey P. 2008. "Minority Success, Assimilation, and Idenity in Prewar Japan: Pak Ch'un-gŭm and the Korean Middle Class." *Journal of Japanese Studies* 34, no. 1 (Winter): 33–68.

Bix, Herbert P. 2000. *Hirohito and the Making of Modern Japan.* New York: HarperCollins Publishers.

Botsman, Daniel V. 2005. *Punishment and Power in the Making of Modern Japan.* Princeton, NJ: Princeton University Press.

Brandt, Kim. 2007. *Kingdom of Beauty: Mingei and the Politics of Folk Art in Imperial Japan.* Durham, NC: Duke University Press.

Berman, Bruce. 1990. *Control and Crisis in Colonial Kenya: The Dialectic of Domination.* Athens, OH: Ohio University Press; London: J. Currey.

Berman, Bruce, and John Lonsdale. 1992. *Unhappy Valley: Conflict in Kenya and Africa.* London: J. Currey; Nairobi: Heinemann Kenya; Athens, OH: Ohio University Press.

Bhabha, Homi. 1994. *The Location of Culture*. London: Routledge.

Brook, Timothy. 2000. "Collaborationist Nationalism in Occupied Wartime China." In *Nation Work: Asian Elites and National Identities*, ed. Timothy Brook and Andre Schmid, 159–90. Ann Arbor, MI: University of Michigan Press.

———. 2007. *Collaboration: Japanese Agents and Local Elites in Wartime China*. Cambridge, MA: Harvard University Press.

Brooks, Barbara J. 1998. "Peopling the Japanese Empire: The Koreans in Manchuria and the Rhetoric of Inclusion." In *Japan's Competing Modernities: Issues in Culture and Democracy, 1900–1930*, ed. Sharon A. Minichiello, 25–44. Honolulu, HI: University of Hawai'i Press.

———. 2005. "Reading the Japanese Colonial Archive: Gender and Bourgeois Civility in Korea and Manchuria before 1932." In *Gendering Modern Japanese History*, ed. Kathleen Uno and Barbara Molony, 295–325. Cambridge, MA: Harvard University Asia Center.

Brudnoy, David. 1970. "Japan's Experiment in Korea." *Monumenta Nipponica* 25, no. 1/2: 155–95.

Buettner, Elizabeth. 2000. "Problematic Spaces, Problematic Races: Defining 'Europeans' in Late Colonial India." *Women's History Review* 9, no. 2, special issue: Borders and Frontiers in Women's History: 277–98.

Byington, Mark E. 2003. "A History of the Puyo State, Its People, and Its Legacy." Ph.D. diss., Harvard University.

Cannadine, David. 2002. *Ornamentalism: How the British Saw Their Empire*. Oxford, UK: Oxford University Press.

Caprio, Mark E. 2009. *Japanese Assimilation Policies in Colonial Korea, 1910–1945*. Seattle, WA: University of Washington Press.

Chandra, Vipan. 1974. "An Outline Study of the Ilchin-hoe (Advancement Society) of Korea." *Occasional Papers on Korea* 2: 43–72.

———. 1988. *Imperialism, Resistance, and Reform in Late Nineteenth-Century Korea: Enlightenment and the Independence Club*. Berkeley, CA: Institute of East Asian Studies, University of California at Berkeley.

Chang Sŏng-man et al., eds. 2006. *Han'guk kŭndaesŏng yŏn'gu ŭi kil ŭl mutta*. Kyŏnggi-do, P'aju-si: Tol Pegae.

Charrad, Monira. 2001. *States and Women's Rights: The Making of Postcolonial Tunisia, Algeria, and Morocco*. Berkeley, CA: University of California Press.

Chen, Ching-chih. 1984. "Police and Community Control Systems in the Empire." In *The Japanese Colonial Empire, 1895–1945*, ed. Ramon H. Myers and Mark R. Peattie, 213–39. Princeton, NJ: Princeton University Press.

Chen, Edward I-te. 1970. "Japanese Colonialism in Korea and Formosa: A Comparison of the Systems of Political Control." *Harvard Journal of Asiatic Studies* 30: 127–40.

Ching, Leo T. S. 2001. *Becoming "Japanese": Colonial Taiwan and the Politics of Identity Formation.* Berkeley, CA: University of California Press.

Cho Kyŏng-dal. 2005. "15-nen sensōka no Chōsen minshū: shokuminchi kindairon hihan shiron." *Chōsen Shōgakkai gakujutsu ronbunshū* 25: 9–29.

———. 2007. "Nihon teikoku no bōchō to Chōsen chishikijin: Tōa kyōdōtai ron to naisen ittai ron o megutte." In *Bōchōsuru teikoku, kakusansuru teikoku: dainiji taisen ni mukau Nichiei to Ajia*, ed. Ishida Ken, 163–201. Tokyo: Tōkyō Daigaku Shuppankai.

———. 2008. *Shokuminchiki Chōsen no chishikijin to minshū: shokuminchi kindaiseiron hihan.* Tokyo: Yūshisha.

Cho Sŏng-gu. 1998. *Chōsen minzoku undō to Soejima Michimasa.* Tokyo: Kenbun Shuppan.

Ch'oe Byŏng-do. 2006. "Manju Tongp'o Munje Hyŏbŭihoe ŭi kyŏlsŏng mit haech'e e kwanhan yŏn'gu." *Han'guk kŭnhyŏndaesa yŏn'gu* 39 (December): 204–34.

Ch'oe Yuri. 1997. *Ilche malgi singminji chibae chŏngch'aek yŏn'gu.* Seoul: Kukhak Charyowŏn.

Choi, Kyeong-Hee. 1999. "Neither Colonial nor National: The Making of the 'New Woman' in Pak Wansŏ's 'Mother's Stake 1.'" In *Colonial Modernity in Korea*, ed. Gi-Wook Shin and Michael Robinson, 221–47. Cambridge, MA: Harvard University Asia Center.

Chŏn U-yong. 2001. "Chongno wa Ponjŏng: singmin tosi Kyŏngsŏng ŭi tu ŏlgul." *Yŏksa wa hyŏnsil* 40 (June): 163–93.

———. 2005. "Singminji tosi imiji wa munhwa hyŏnsang – 1920-yŏndae ŭi Kyŏngsŏng." *Han-Il yŏksa kongdong yŏn'gu pogosŏ* 5: 131–67.

Chŏng Ae-yŏng. 1999. "Nisshin, Nichiro sensōki no taigaikō undō to Nakai Kitarō." *Nihon shokuminchi kenkyū* 11 (June): 52–65.

Chŏng Hye-kyŏng and Yi Sŭng-yŏp. 1999. "Ilche ha Nokki Yŏnmaeng ŭi hwaltong." *Han'guk kŭnhyŏndaesa yŏn'gu* 10 (June): 329–69.

Chŏng Kŭn-sik. 2004. "Shokuminchi shihai, shintai kiritsu, 'kenkō'." In *Seikatsu no naka no shokuminchi shugi*, ed. Mizuno Naoki, 59–102. Kyoto: Jinbun Shoin.

Chou, Wan-yao. 1996. "The Kōminka Movement in Taiwan and Korea: Comparisons and Interpretations." In *The Japanese Wartime Empire, 1931–1945*, ed.

Peter Duus, Ramon H. Myers, and Mark R. Peattie, 46–68. Princeton, NJ: Princeton University Press.

Christy, Alan. 1993. "The Making of Imperial Subjects in Okinawa." *positions: east asia cultures critique* 1, no. 3 (Winter): 607–39.

Clark, Donald N. 2003. *Living Dangerously in Korea: The Western Experience 1900–1950*. Norwalk, Connecticut: EastBridge.

Cohen, Nicole Leah. 2006. "Children of Empire: Growing up Japanese in Colonial Korea, 1876–1946." Ph.D. diss., Columbia University.

Cohn, Bernard S. 1996. *Colonialism and Its Forms of Knowledge*. Princeton, NJ: Princeton University Press.

"Colonial Modernity and the Making of Modern Korean Cities." 2008. Special issue of *Korea Journal* 48, no. 3 (Autumn).

Comaroff, Jean, and John Comaroff. 1991. *Of Revelation and Revolution: Christianity, Colonialism, and Consciousness in South Africa*, 2 vols. Chicago, IL: University of Chicago Press.

Conklin, Alice L. 1997. *A Mission to Civilize: The Republican Idea of Empire in France and West Africa, 1895–1930*. Stanford, CA: Stanford University Press.

Conroy, Hilary. 1960. *The Japanese Seizure of Korea: 1868–1910: A Study of Realism and Idealism in International Relations*. Philadelphia: University of Pennsylvania Press.

Cook, Harold F. 1972. *Korea's 1884 Incident: Its Background and Kim Ok-kyun's Elusive Dream*. Seoul: Royal Asiatic Society, Korea Branch.

Coombes, Annie, ed. 2006. *Rethinking Settler Colonialism: History and Memory in Australia, Canada, Aotearoa New Zealand, and South Africa*. Manchester, UK: Manchester University Press.

Cooper, Frederick. 2005. *Colonialism in Question: Theory, Knowledge, History*. Berkeley, CA: University of California Press.

Cooper, Frederick, and Ann Laura Stoler, eds. 1997. *Tensions of Empire: Colonial Cultures in a Bourgeois World*. Berkeley, CA: University of California Press.

Crews, Robert. 2006. *For Prophet and Tsar: Islam and Empire in Russia and Central Asia*. Cambridge, MA: Harvard University Press.

Crosby, Alfred W. 1996. *Ecological Imperialism: Biological Expansion of Europe, 900–1900*. Cambridge, UK: Cambridge University Press.

Cumings, Bruce. 1984. "The Legacy of Japanese Colonialism in Korea." In *The Japanese Colonial Empire, 1895–1945*, ed. Ramon Myers and Mark R. Peattie, 478–96. Princeton, NJ: Princeton University Press.

Daughton, J. P. 2006. *An Empire Divided: Religion, Republicanism, and the Making of French Colonialism, 1880–1914*. New York: Oxford University Press.

De Boer, John C. 2006. "Circumventing the Evils of Colonialism: Yanaihara Tadao and Zionist Settler Colonialism in Palestine." *positions: east asia cultures critique* 14, no. 3 (Winter): 567–95.

Delissen, Alain. 2000. "Denied and Besieged: the Japanese Community of Korea, 1876–1945." In *New Frontiers: Imperialism's New Communities in East Asia, 1842–1953*, ed. Robert Bickers and Christian Henriot, 125–45. Manchester, UK: Manchester University Press.

Denoon, Donald. 1983. *Settler Capitalism: The Dynamics of Dependent Development in the Southern Hemisphere.* Oxford, UK: Clarendon Press; New York: Oxford University Press.

Deuchler, Martina. 1977. *Confucian Gentlemen and Barbarian Envoys: The Opening of Korea, 1875–1885*. Seattle, WA: University of Washington Press.

Dirks, Nicholas, B. 2002. "Annals of the Archive: Ethnographic Notes on the Sources of History." In *From the Margins: Historical Anthropology and Its Futures*, ed. Brian Keith Axel, 47–65. Durham, NC: Duke University Press.

Doak, Kevin M. 2007. *History of Nationalism in Modern Japan: Placing the People.* Leiden: Brill.

Duara, Prasenjit. 2003. *Sovereignty and Authenticity: Manchukuo and the East Asian Modern.* Lanham: Rowman and Littlefield.

Dudden, Alexis. 2005. *The Japanese Colonization of Korea: Discourse and Power.* Honolulu, HI: University of Hawai'i Press.

Duncan, John. 1998. "Proto-nationalism in Premodern Korea." In *Perspectives on Korea*, ed. Sang-Oak Lee and Duk-Soo Park, 198–221. Sydney: Wild Peony.

Duus, Peter. 1984. "Economic Dimensions of Meiji Imperialism: The Case of Korea, 1895–1910." In *The Japanese Colonial Empire, 1895–1945*, ed. Ramon H. Myers and Mark R. Peattie, 128–71. Princeton, NJ: Princeton University Press.

———. 1995. *The Abacus and the Sword: The Japanese Penetration of Korea, 1895–1910*. Berkeley, CA: University of California Press.

Eckert, Carter J. 1991. *Offspring of Empire: The Kochang Kims and the Colonial Origins of Korean Capitalism, 1876–1945*. Seattle, WA: University of Washington Press.

———. 1996. "Total War, Industrialization, and Social Change in Late Colonial Korea." In *The Japanese Wartime Empire, 1931–1945*, ed. Peter Duus, Ramon H. Myers, and Mark R. Peattie, 3–39. Princeton, NJ: Princeton University Press.

Eckert, Carter J., Ki-baik Lee, Young Ick Lew, Michael Robinson, and Edward W. Wagner. 1990. *Korea, Old and New: A History*. Seoul: Ilchokak.

Elkins, Caroline. 2005. *Imperial Reckoning: The Untold Story of Britain's Gulag in Kenya.* New York: H. Holt.

Elkins, Caroline, and Susan Pedersen, eds. 2005. *Settler Colonialism in the Twentieth Century: Projects, Practices, Legacies.* New York: Routledge.

Eskildsen, Robert. 2002. "Of Civilization and Savages: The Mimetic Imperialism of Japan's 1874 Expedition to Taiwan." *American Historical Review* 107, no. 2 (April): 388–418.

Esselstrom, Erik. 2009. *Crossing Empire's Edge: Foreign Ministry Police and Japanese Expansionism in Northeast Asia.* Honolulu, HI: University of Hawai'i Press.

Evans, Julie et al., eds. 2003. *Equal Subjects, Unequal Rights: Indigenous Peoples in British Settler Colonies, 1830–1910.* Manchester, UK; New York: Manchester University Press.

Fabian, Johannes. 1983. *Time and the Other: How Anthropology Makes Its Object.* New York: Columbia University Press.

Fage, J. D., and Roland Oliver, eds. 1986. *The Cambridge History of Africa.* Vol. 7. Cambridge, UK: Cambridge University Press.

Fanon, Frantz. 1967. *Black Skin, White Masks.* New York: Grove.

Fieldhouse, D. K. 1973. *Economics and Empire, 1880–1914.* Ithaca, NY: Cornell University Press.

———. 1976. "Imperialism and the Periphery." In *The "New Imperialism": Analysis of Late Nineteenth-Century Expansion*, ed. Harrison M. Wright, 181–200. 2nd ed. Lexington, Massachusetts and Toronto: D. C. Heath and Company.

Fujikane, Candace, and Jonathan Y. Okamura, eds. 2008. *Asian Settler Colonialism: From Local Governance to the Habits of Everyday Life in Hawai'i.* Honolulu, HI: University of Hawai'i Press.

Fujitani, Takashi. 1996. *Splendid Monarchy: Power and Pageantry in Modern Japan.* Berkeley, CA: University of California Press.

———. 2007. "Right to Kill, Right to Make Live: Koreans as Japanese and Japanese as Americans during WWII." *Representations* 99 (Summer): 13–39.

———. 2011. *Race for Empire: Koreans as Japanese and Japanese as Americans in World War II.* Berkeley, CA: University of California Press.

Furukawa Noriko. 1993. "Shokuminchiki Chōsen ni okeru shotō kyōiku: shūgaku jōkyō no bunseki o chūshin ni." *Nihonshi kenkyū* 370 (June): 31–56.

Gann, Lewis H. 1984. "Western and Japanese Colonialism: Some Preliminary Comparisons." In *The Japanese Colonial Empire, 1895–1945*, ed. Ramon H. Myers and Mark R. Peattie, 497–525. Princeton, NJ: Princeton University Press.

Garon, Sheldon. 1997. *Molding Japanese Minds: The State in Everyday Life.* Princeton, NJ: Princeton University Press.

Gluck, Carol. 1985. *Japan's Modern Myths: Ideology in the Late Meiji Period.* Princeton, NJ: Princeton University Press.

Goldstein, Alyosha and Alex Lubin, eds. 2008. "Settler Colonialism." *South Atlantic Quarterly special issue* 107, no. 4 (Fall).

Good, Kenneth. 1976. "Settler Colonialism: Economic Development and Class Formation." *Journal of Modern African Studies* 14, no. 4 (December): 597–620.

Gordon, Andrew. 1991. *Labor and Imperial Democracy in Prewar Japan.* Berkeley, CA: University of California Press.

———. 2003. *A Modern History of Japan: From Tokugawa Times to the Present.* New York: Oxford University Press.

Goswami, Manu. 2004. *Producing India: From Colonial Economy to National Space.* Chicago, IL: University of Chicago Press.

Gragert, Edwin H. 1994. *Landownership under Colonial Rule: Korea's Japanese Experience, 1900–1935.* Honolulu, HI: University of Hawai'i Press.

Han Kee-hyung [Han Ki-hyŏng]. 2005. "Kŭndae ch'ogi Han'gugin ŭi Tong Asia insik: 'Ch'ŏngch'un' kwa 'Kaebyŏk' ŭi charyo rul chungsim ŭro." *Taedong munhwa yŏn'gu* 50 (January): 167–98.

Harvey, Elizabeth. 2005. "Management and Manipulation: Nazi Settlement Planners and Ethnic German Settlers in Occupied Poland." In *Settler Colonialism in the Twentieth Century: Projects, Practices, Legacies,* ed. Caroline Elkins and Susan Pedersen, 95–112. New York: Routledge.

Hashiya Hiroshi. 2004. *Teikoku Nihon to shokuminchi toshi.* Tokyo: Yoshikawa Kōbunkan.

Hatada Takashi, ed. 1969. *Nihonjin no Chōsenkan.* Tokyo: Keisō Shobō.

———. 1975. "Chōsen seisaku to teitairon." *Kikan sanzenri* 3 (August): 42–47.

———. 1983. *Chōsen to Nihonjin.* Tokyo: Keisō Shobō.

Hatano Masaru. 1993. "Nikkan heigō undō: Uchida Ryōhei to taigai kōha seron no ugoki o chūshin ni." *Ningen kagaku: Jōban Daigaku Ningen Kagakubu kiyō* (March): 61–84.

Hatsuse Ryūhei. 1980. *Dentōteki uyoku: Uchida Ryōhei no kenkyū.* Fukuoka: Kyūshū Daigaku Shuppankai.

Havens, Thomas R. H. 1978. *Valley of Darkness: The Japanese People and World War II.* New York: W. W. Norton and Company.

Hayashi Yūsuke. 1999. "Undō dantai toshite no Isshinkai: minshū tono sesshoku yōsō o chūshin ni." *Chōsen gakuhō* 172 (July): 43–67.

Henderson, Gregory. 1968. *Korea: Politics of the Vortex.* Cambridge, MA: Harvard University Press.

———. 1973. "Japan's Chōsen: Immigrants, Ruthlessness and Developmental Shock." In *Korea Under Japanese Colonial Rule: Studies of the Policy and Techniques of Japanese Colonialism*, ed. Andrew C. Nahm, 261–69. Kalamazoo, MI: Western Michigan University.

Henry, Todd A. 2005. "Sanitizing Empire: Japanese Articulations of Korean Otherness and the Construction of Early Colonial Seoul, 1905–19." *Journal of Asian Studies* 64, no. 3 (August): 639–75.

———. 2006. "Keijō: Japanese and Korean Constructions of Colonial Seoul and the History of Its Lived Spaces, 1910–1937." Ph.D. diss., University of California at Los Angeles.

———. 2008. "Re-Spatializing Chosŏn Royal Capital: The Politics of Urban Reforms in Early Colonial Seoul, 1905–19." In *Sitings: Critical Approaches to Korean Geography*, ed. Timothy R. Tangherlini and Sallie Yea, 15–38. Honolulu, HI: University of Hawai'i Press.

Herbst, Jeffrey. 2000. *States and Power in Africa: Comparative Lessons in Authority and Control.* Princeton, NJ: Princeton University Press.

Hino Hideko. 1981. "Yosano Tekkan to Chōsen." *Kikan sanzenri* 28 (Winter): 210–19.

Hishiki Masaharu. 1993. "Higashi Nishi Honganji kyōdan no shokuminchi fukyō." In *Tōgō to shihai no ronri*, ed. Ōe Shinobu et al., 157–75. Iwanami Kōza Kindai Nihon to Shokuminchi 4. Tokyo: Iwanami Shoten.

Ho, Samuel Pao-San. 1984. "Colonialism and Development: Korea, Taiwan, and Kwantung." In *The Japanese Colonial Empire, 1895–1945*, ed. Ramon H. Myers and Mark R. Peattie, 347–98. Princeton, NJ: Princeton University Press.

Hong Jong-uk. 2004. "1930-nendai ni okeru shokuminchi Chōsenjin no shisōteki mosaku." *Chōsenshi kenkyūkai ronbunshū* 42 (October): 159–86.

Hong Kal. 2005. "Modeling the West, Returning to Asia: Shifting Identities in Japanese Colonial Expositions in Korea." *Comparative Studies in Society and History* 47, no. 3 (July): 507–31.

Hong Sun-gwŏn. 2006a. "1910–20-yŏndae 'Pusan puhyŏbŭihoe' ŭi kusŏng kwa chibang chŏngch'i." *Yŏksa wa kyŏnggye* 60 (September): 177–219.

———. 2006b. *Ilche sigi chae Pusan Ilbonin sahoe chuyo inmul chosa pogo.* Seoul: Sŏnin.

Hong Sun-gwŏn et al. 2008. *Pusan ŭi tosi hyŏngsŏng kwa Ilbonindŭl.* Seoul: Sŏnin.

Hori Kazuo. 1995. *Chōsen kōgyōka no shiteki bunseki: Nihon shihonshugi to shokuminchi keizai.* Tokyo: Yūhikaku.

Howell, David. 2004. "Making 'Useful Citizens' of Ainu Subjects in Early Twentieth Century Japan." *Journal of Asian Studies* 63, no. 1 (February): 5–29

Huffman, James L. 1997. *Creating a Public: People and Press in Meiji Japan.* Honolulu, HI: University of Hawai'i Press.

Hur, Nam-Lin. 1999. "The Sōtō Sect and Japanese Military Imperialism in Korea." *Japanese Journal of Religious Studies* 26, no. 1/2 (Spring): 107–34.

Ikegawa Hidekatsu. 1985. "Ōgaki Takeo no kenkyū: Daikan Jikyōkai tono kanren o chūshin ni shite." *Chōsen gakuhō* 117 (October): 525–67

———. 1986. "Ōgaki Takeo ni tsuite." *Chōsen gakuhō* 119/120 (July): 65–84.

———. 1996. "Daikan teikoku makki kakudantai ni mirareru Nihonjin komon ni tsuite: Saeki Gōhei." *Chōsen gakuhō* 158 (January): 35–128.

Im Chŏn-hye. 1978. "Chōsen tōchi to Nihon no onna tachi." In *Onna to kenryoku*, ed. Morosawa Yōko, 87–144. Tokyo: Heibonsha.

Im Chong-guk. 1992. *Shin'nichiha: Richō matsu kara kyōni itaru baikoku baizokushatachi no shōtai.* Tokyo: Ochanomizu Shobō.

Im Tae-sik. 1997. "Ilche ha Kyŏngsŏng-bu 'yuji'chiptan ŭi chonjae hyŏngt'ae." *Sŏulhak yŏn'gu* 8 (February): 99–125.

Inaba Tsugio. 1997. *Kyū Kanmatsu "Nichigo gakkō" no kenkyū.* Fukuoka: Kyūshū Daigaku Shuppankai.

———. 1999. *Kyū Kankoku no kyōiku to Nihonjin.* Fukuoka: Kyūshū Daigaku Shuppankai.

Inoue Kazue. 2006. "Shokuminchiki Chōsen ni okeru seikatsu kaizen undō." In *1930-nendai no Higashi Ajia keizai: Higashi Ajia shihonshugi keiseishi II*, ed. Nakamura Satoru, 105–34. Tokyo: Nihon Hyōronsha.

Inoue Manabu. 1969. "Kien: Ayukai Fusanoshin ni tsuite (jō)." *Chōsen kenkyū* 82 (February): 50–63.

Isoda Kazuo. 1999. *"Kōkoku no sugata" o otte: kyōkasho ni miru shokuminchi kyōiku bunkashi.* Tokyo: Kōseisha.

Itagaki Ryūka. 2004. "'Shokuminchi kindai o megutte': Chōsenshi kenkyū ni okeru genjō to kadai." *Rekishi hyōron* 654 (October): 35–45.

———. 2008. *Chōsen kindai no rekishi minzokushi: Keihoku Sanju no shokuminchi keiken.* Tokyo: Akashi Shoten.

Janelli, Robert L. 1986. "The Origins of Korean Folklore Scholarship." *Journal of American Folklore* 88, no. 391 (January–March): 24–49.

Kagaya Shinko. 2001. "No Performances in Gaichi." *Asian Theatre Journal* 18, no. 2 (Fall): 257–69.

Kajimura Hideki. 1977. *Chōsenshi.* Tokyo: Kōdansha.

———. 1992. *Chōsenshi to Nihonjin*. Kajimura Hideki Chosakushū 1. Tokyo: Akashi Shoten.

Kaneko Fumio. 1986. "1920-nendai ni okeru Chōsen sangyō seisaku no keisei: Sangyō Chōsa Iinkai o chūshin ni." In *Kindai Nihon no keizai to seiji*, ed. Hara Akira, 175–200. Tokyo: Yamakawa Shuppansha.

———. 1993. "Shokuminchi tōshi to kōgyōka." In *Shokuminchika to sangyōka*, ed. Ōe Shinobu et al., 27–50. Iwanami Kōza Kindai Nihon to Shokuminchi 3. Tokyo: Iwanami Shoten.

Kang Jae-ho. 2001. *Shokuminchi Chōsen no chihō seido*. Tokyo: Tōkyō Daigaku Shuppankai.

Kang Man-gil. 1975. *Han'guk sangŏp ŭi yŏksa*. Seoul: Sejong Taewang Kinyŏm Saŏphoe.

Kang Tong-jin. 1979. *Nihon no Chōsen shihai seisakushi kenkyū: 1920-nendai o chūshin to shite*. Tokyo: Tōkyō Daigaku Shuppankai.

Kasuya Ken'ichi. 1992. "Chōsen Sōtokufu no bunka seiji." In *Teikoku tōchi no kōzō*, Iwanani Kōza: Kindai Nihon to Shokuminchi 2, ed. Ōe Shinobu et al., 121–46. Tokyo: Iwanami Shoten.

Kasza, Gregory J. 1995. *The Conscription Society: Administered Mass Organizations*. New Haven, CT: Yale University Press.

Katō Kiyofumi. 1998. "Seitō naikaku kakuritsuki ni okeru shokuminchi shihai taisei no mosaku: Takushokushō secchi mondai no kōsatsu." *Higashi Ajia kindaishi* 1 (March): 39–57.

Kawa Kaoru. 2001. "Sōryokusenka no Chōsen josei." *Rekishi hyōron* 612 (April): 2–17.

Kawai Kazuo. 1986. *Chōsen ni okeru sanmai zōshoku keikaku*. Tokyo: Miraisha.

——— et al., eds. 2000. *Kokusaku-gaisha Tōtaku no kenkyū*. Tokyo: Fuji Shuppan.

Kawakita Akio. 1995. "1920-nendai Chōsen no kōgyōka rongi ni tsuite." In *Kindai Higashi Ajia no shosō*, ed. Kagoshima Keizai Daigaku Chiiki Sōgō Kenkyūjo, 163–93. Tokyo: Keisō Shobō.

Kawamura Minato. 2000. *Souru toshi monogatari*. Tokyo: Heibonsha.

Kawase Takaya. 2001. "Shokuminchiki Chōsen ni okeru Nihon kirisutokyō no shokuminchi dendō." *Shisōshi kenkyū* 1 (March): 141–53.

———. 2002. "Shokuminchiki Chōsen ni okeru 'shinden kaihatsu undō' seisaku." *Kankoku Chōsen no bunka to shakai* 1 (October): 103–28.

Kawashima, Ken. 2009. *The Proletarian Gamble: Korean Workers in Interwar Japan*. Durham, NC: Duke University Press.

Keller, Richard. 2007. *Colonial Madness: Psychiatry in French North Africa*. Chicago, IL: University of Chicago Press.

Kennedy, Dane. 1987. *The Islands of White: Settler Society and Culture in Kenya and Southern Rhodesia, 1890–1939*. Durham, NC: Duke University Press.

Ki Yu-jŏng. 2007. "1920-yŏndae Kyŏngsŏng ŭi 'yuji ch'ŏngch'i' wa Kyŏngsŏng puhyŏbŭihoe." *Sŏulhak yŏn'gu* 28 (February): 1–34.

———. 2009. "Singminji tae moguk kan kyŏngje mach'al kwa ch'aejo Ilbonin sahoe ŭi taeŭng." *Sahoe wa yŏksa* 82 (June): 323–59.

Kim Chin-gyun and Chŏng Kŭn-sik, eds. 1997. *Kŭndae chuch'e wa singminji kyuyul kwŏllyŏk*. Seoul: Munhak kwahaksa.

Kim Chin-song et al. 1999. *Sŏul e ttansŭhol ŭl hŏhara*. Seoul: Hyŏnsil Munhwa Yŏn'gu.

Kim Chŏk-pong. 1994. *Aeguk munhwa undong tanch'e hakhoe wa kŭ hwaltong*. P'yŏngyang: Sahoe Kwahak Ch'ulp'ansa.

Kim Chu-yong. 2004. "Manju Pominhoe ŭi sŏlrip kwa 'Sŏn-Man ilch'ehwa.'" *Han-Il kwan'gyesa yŏn'gu* 21 (October): 187–224.

Kim Hang-gu. 1999. "Taehan Hyŏphoe ŭi chŏngch'i hwaltong yŏn'gu." *Tongsŏ sahak* 5, no. 1: 183–212.

Kim, Hwansoo. 2007. "Strategic Alliances: The Dynamic Relationship between Korean and Japanese Buddhism, 1877–1912." Ph.D. diss., Harvard University.

Kim In-ho. 2000. *Singminji Chosŏn kyŏngje ŭi chongmal*. Seoul: Sin Sŏwŏn.

Kim, Key-Hiuk. 1980. *The Last Phase of the East Asian World Order: Korea, Japan and the Chinese Empire, 1860–1882*. Berkeley, CA: University of California Press.

Kim Kyu-hwan. 1959. "Shokuminchika Chōsen ni okeru genron oyobi genron seisakushi." Ph.D. diss., University of Tokyo.

Kim, Kyu Hyun. 2007. *The Age of Visions and Arguments: Parliamentarianism and the National Public Sphere in Early Meiji Japan*. Cambridge, MA: Harvard University Asia Center.

Kim Myŏng-su. 2000. "Hanmal Ilch'eha Han Sang-nyong ŭi kiŏp hwaltong yŏn'gu." *Yŏnse kyŏngje yŏn'gu* 7, no. 2 (September): 173–218.

Kim Nang-nyŏn. 2003. *Ilche ha Han'guk kyŏngje*. Seoul: Haenam.

Kim Paeg-yŏng. 2003. "Wangjo sudoro put'ŏ singmin tosi ro." *Han'guk hakpo* 29, no. 3: 76–102.

——— [Kim Baek Yung]. 2008. "Ruptures and Conflicts in the Colonial Power Bloc: the Great Keijo Plan of the 1920s." *Korea Journal* 48, no. 3 (Autumn): 1–40.

Kim Puja. 2005. *Shokuminchiki Chōsen no kyōiku to jendā*. Yokohama: Seori Shobō.

Kim, Richard E. 1970. *Lost Names: Scenes from a Korean Boyhood.* New York: Praeger.

Kim, Su Yun. 2009. "Romancing Race and Gender: Intermarriage and the Making of 'Modern Subjectivity' in Colonial Korea, 1910–1945." Ph.D. diss., University of California at San Diego.

Kim Tong-myŏng. 2006. *Chibae wa chŏhang, kŭrigo hyŏmnyŏk: singminji Chosŏn esŏ ŭi Ilbon chegukchuŭi wa Chosŏnin ŭi chŏngch'i undong.* Seoul: Kyŏngin Munhwasa.

Kim Yun-sik. 1993. "1940-nen zengo zai Souru Nihonjin no bungaku katsudō: 'kokumin bungaku' shi to kanren shite." In *Bunka no naka no shokuminchi*, ed. Ōe Shinobu et al., 231–42. Iwanami Kōza Kindai Nihon to Shokuminchi 7. Tokyo: Iwanami Shoten.

Kinmonth, Earl H. 1981. *The Self-Made Man in Meiji Japanese Thought: From Samurai to Salary Man.* Berkeley, CA: University of California Press.

Kimura Kenji. 1989. *Zaichō Nihonjin no shakaishi.* Tokyo: Miraisha.

———. 1993. "Zaigai kyoryūmin no shakai katsudō." In *Bōchō suru teikoku no jinryū*, ed. Ōe Shinobu et al., 27–76. Iwanami Kōza Kindai Nihon to shokuminchi 5. Tokyo: Iwanami Shoten.

———. 1996. "Chōsen kyoryūchi ni okeru Nihonjin no seikatsu taiyō." *Ikkyō ronsō* 115, no. 2 (February): 42–62.

———. 1997. "Chōsen ni okeru shōgyō kaigisho rengōkai no ketsugi jikō." In *Kindai Ajia no Nihonjin keizai dantai*, ed. Namikata Shōichi, 39–64. Tokyo: Dōbunkan Shuppan.

———. 2001a. "Kindai Nihon no imin, shokumin katsudō to chūkansō." In *Teikokushugi to shokuminchi*, ed. Yanagisawa Asobu and Okabe Makio, 166–78. Tokyo: Tōkyōdō Shuppan.

———. 2001b. "Shokuminchika Shingishū zaijū Nihonjin no ibunka sesshoku." In *Kōsaku suru kokka, minzoku, shūkyō: imin no shakai tekiō*, ed. Togami Muneyoshi, 73–98. Tokyo: Fuji Shuppan.

———. 2002. "Settling into Korea: The Japanese Expansion into Korea from the Russo-Japanese War to the Early Period of Annexation." In "Japanese Settler Colonialism and Capitalism in Japan: Advancing into Korea, Settling Down, and Returning to Japan, 1905–1950." *Occasional Papers in Japanese Studies* (Edwin O. Reischauer Institute of Japanese Studies, Harvard University), no. 2002-03 (June): 1–10.

———. 2004. "Chōsen ni okeru keizai tōsei no shinkō to keizai dantai." In *Senjika Ajia no Nihon keizai dantai*, ed. Yanagisawa Asobu and Kimura Kenji, 95–134. Tokyo: Nihon Keizai Hyōronsha.

———. 2005. "Senjika shokuminchi Chōsen ni okeru keizai dantai to chūshō shōgyōsha." Ph.D. diss., Tokyo Kokusai Daigaku Daigakuin.

Kimura Kenji and Sakamoto Yūichi. 2007. *Kindai shokuminchi toshi Pusan.* Tokyo: Sakurai Shoten.

Kō Kiruhi [Ko Kil-hŭi]. 2001. *"Zaichō Nihonjin nisei" no aidentitī keisei: Hatada Takashi to Chōsen, Nihon.* Tokyo: Kiri Shobō.

Ko Sŏng-bong. 2006. *Shokuminchi no tetsudō.* Tokyo: Nihon Keizai Hyōronsha.

Kobayashi Hideo et al., eds. 1994. *Shokuminchi e no kigyō shinshutsu: Chōsen kaisharei no bunseki.* Tokyo: Kashiwa Shobō.

Kokushi Daijiten Henshū Iinkai, ed. 1988. *Kokushi daijiten.* Vol. 9. Tokyo: Yoshikawa Kōbunkan.

Komagome Takeshi. 1996. *Shokuminchi teikoku Nihon no bunka tōgō.* Tokyo: Iwanami Shoten.

———. 2000. "'Teikokushi' kenkyū no shatei." *Nihonshi kenkyū* 452 (April): 224–31.

Kong Che-uk. 2006. "Ŭibok t'ongje wa 'kungmin' mandŭlgi." In *Singminji ŭi ilsang, chibae wa kyunyŏl,* ed. Kong Che-uk and Chŏng Kŭn-sik, 135–92. Seoul: Munhwa Kwahaksa.

Kong Che-uk and Chŏng Kŭn-sik, eds. 2006. *Singminji ŭi ilsang, chibae wa kyunyŏl.* Seoul: Munhwa Kwahaksa.

Kublin, Hyman. 1959. "The Evolution of Japanese Colonialism." *Comparative Studies in Society and History* 2, no. 1 (October): 67–84.

Kurose Yūji. 2003. *Tōyō Takushoku Kaisha: Nihon teikokushugi to Ajia Taiheiyō.* Tokyo: Nihon Keizai Hyōronsha.

Kusunoki Seiichirō. 1991. "Gaichi sanseiken mondai." In *Kindai Nihonshi no shinkenkyū* 9, ed. Tezuka Yutaka, 256–94. Tokyo: Hokujusha.

Kwon, In-sook. 1998. "'The New Women's Movement' in 1920s Korea." *Gender & History* 10, no. 3 (November): 381–405.

Kyō Shōichi. 1988. "Tenyūkyō to 'Chōsen mondai.'" *Shigaku zasshi* 97, no. 8 (August): 1–37.

Lamley, Harry. 1970–71. "Assimilation Efforts in Colonial Taiwan: The Fate of the 1914 Movement." *Monumenta Serica* 29: 496–520.

Larsen, Kirk W. 2008. *Tradition, Treaties, and Trade: Qing Imperialism and Chosŏn Korea, 1850–1910.* Cambridge, MA: Harvard University Asia Center.

Lee, Chulwoo. 1999. "Modernity, Legality, and Power in Korea Under Japanese Rule." In *Colonial Modernity in Korea,* ed. Gi-Wook Shin and Michael Robinson, 21–51. Cambridge, MA: Harvard University Asia Center.

Lee, Helen J. S. 2003. "Popular Media and the Racialization of Koreans Under Occupation." Ph.D. diss., University of California, Irvine.

———. 2008a. "Ch'eguk ŭi ttal rosŏ chungnŭndanŭn kŏt." *Asea yŏn'gu* 51, no. 2 (2008): 80–105.

———. 2008b. "Writing Colonial Relations of Everyday Life in Senryū." *positions: east asia cultures critique* 16, no. 3 (Winter): 601–28.

Lewis, Michael. 2000. *Becoming Apart: National Power and Local Politics in Toyama, 1868–1945*. Cambridge, MA: Harvard University Asia Center.

Lo, Ming Cheng. 2002. *Doctors Within Borders: Profession, Ethnicity, and Modernity in Colonial Taiwan*. Berkeley, CA: University of California Press.

Lustick, Ian. 1985. *State-Building Failure in British Ireland and French Algeria*. Berkeley, CA: Institute of International Studies, University of California, Berkeley.

Lynn, Hyung Gu. 2001. "Limits of the Colonial State: Interest Intersections and the State in Colonial Korea, 1919–1942." Ph.D. diss., Harvard University.

———. 2004. "Fashioning Modernity: Changing Meanings of Clothing in Colonial Korea." *Journal of International and Area Studies* 11, no. 3 (Spring): 75–93.

———. 2005. "Malthusian Dreams, Colonial Imaginary: The Oriental Development Company and Emigration to Korea." In *Settler Colonialism in the Twentieth Century: Projects, Practices, Legacies*, ed. Caroline Elkins and Susan Pedersen, 25–40. London: Routledge.

———. 2008. "Chūō Chōsen Kyōkai to seisaku kettei kaitei." In *Nihon no Chōsen, Taiwan shihai to shokuminchi kanryō*, ed. Matsuda Toshihiko, 325–39. Kokusai Kenkyū Shūkai hōkokusho vol. 30. Kyoto: Kokusai Nihon Bunka Kenkyū Sentā.

Mabuchi Sadatoshi. 1987. "Terauchi Masatake to budan seiji." *Kikan sanzenri* 49 (February): 66–73.

Mamdani, Mahmood. 1996. *Citizen and Subject: Contemporary Africa and the Legacy of Late Colonialism*. Princeton, NJ: Princeton University Press.

Manela, Erez. 2007. *The Wilsonian Moment: Self-Determination and the International Origins of Anticolonial Nationalism*. Oxford, UK; New York: Oxford University Press.

Maruko Siniawer, Eiko. 2008. *Ruffians, Yakuza, Nationalists: The Violent Politics of Modern Japan, 1860–1960*. Ithaca, NY: Cornell University Press.

Matsuda Toshihiko. 1995. *Senzenki no Zainichi Chōsenjin to sanseiken*. Tokyo: Akashi Shoten.

———. 1997. "Shokuminchi makki Chōsen ni okeru aru tenkōsha no undō." *Jinbun gakuhō* 79 (March): 131–62.

———. 2000. "Sōryokusenki no shokuminchi Chōsen ni okeru keisatsu gyōsei: keisatsukan ni yoru 'jikyoku zadankai' o jiku ni." *Nihonshi kenkyū* 452 (April): 195–223.

Matsumoto Takenori. 1991. *Shokuminchi Chōsen no suiri kumiai jigyō.* Tokyo: Miraisha.

———. 1998. *Shokuminchi kenryoku to Chōsen nōmin.* Tokyo: Shakai Hyōronsha.

———. 2005. *Chōsen nōson no 'shokuminchi kindai' keiken.* Tokyo: Shakai Hyōronsha.

———. 2006. "Senjiki Chōsen ni okeru Chōsenjin chihō shokuin no 'tainichi kyōryoku'." In *Shihai to bōryoku*, ed. Kurasawa Aiko et al., 221–48. Iwanami Kōza Ajia Taiheiyō Sensō 7. Tokyo: Iwanami Shoten.

Matsusaka, Yoshihisa Tak. 2001. *The Making of Japanese Manchuria, 1904–1932.* Cambridge, MA: Harvard University Asia Center.

McNamara, Dennis L. 1996. *Trade and Transformation in Korea, 1876–1945.* Boulder, CO: Westview Press.

McWilliams, Wayne C. 1988. *Homeward Bound: Repatriation of Japanese from Korea after World War II.* Asian Studies Monograph Series. Hong Kong: Asian Research Service.

Memmi, Albert. 1965. *The Colonizer and the Colonized.* Trans. Howard Greenfeld. New York: Orion Press.

Metzler, Mark. 2005. *Lever of Empire: The International Gold Standard and the Crisis of Liberalism in Prewar Japan.* Berkeley, CA: University of California Press.

Mitchell, Timothy. 1988. *Colonising Egypt.* Cambridge, UK: Cambridge University Press.

———. 1991. "The Limits of the State: Beyond Statist Approaches and Their Critics." *American Political Science Review* 85, no. 1 (March): 77–96.

Miyata Setsuko. 1985. *Chōsen minshū to "kōminka" seisaku.* Tokyo: Miraisha.

Miyata Setsuko, Kim Yŏng-dal, and Yang T'ae-ho. 1992. *Sōshi kaimei.* Tokyo: Akashi Shoten.

Mizoguchi Toshiyuki and Umemura Mataji, eds. 1988. *Kyū Nihon shokuminchi keizai tōkei: suikei to bunseki.* Tokyo: Tōyō Keizai Shinpōsha.

Mizoguchi Toshiyuki and Yamamoto Yūzō. 1984. "Capital Formation in Taiwan and Korea." In *The Japanese Colonial Empire, 1895–1945*, ed. Ramon H. Myers and Mark R. Peattie, 399–419. Princeton, NJ: Princeton University Press.

Mizuno Naoki. 2008. *Sōshi kaimei: Nihon no Chōsen shihai no nakade.* Tokyo: Iwanami Shoten.

Moon, Yumi. 2005. "The Populist Contest: The Ilchinhoe Movement and the Japanese Colonization of Korea, 1896–1910." Ph.D. diss., Harvard University.

———. 2010. "Populist Collaborators: The Ilchinhoe and the Japanese Colonization of Korea, 1896–1910." Unpublished manuscript.

Moriyama Shigenori. 1992. *Nikkan heigō*. Tokyo: Yoshikawa Kōbunkan.

———. 1997. "Kaisetsu." In *Gendai Kanjō no fūun to meishi*, Hosoi Hajime, 472–83. Keijō: Nikkan Shobō, 1910. Repr. Tokyo: Perikansha.

Morris-Suzuki, Tessa. 1998. "Becoming Japanese: Imperial Expansion and Identity Crises in the Early Twentieth Century." In *Japan's Competing Modernities: Issues in Culture and Democracy 1900–1930*, ed. Sharon A. Minichiello, 157–80. Honolulu, HI: University of Hawai'i Press.

Moskowitz, Karl. 1974. "The Creation of the Oriental Development Company: Japanese Illusions Meet Korean Reality." *Occasional Papers on Korea* 2: 73–121.

Munasinghe, Viranjini. 2006. "Theorizing World Culture Through the New World: East Indians and Creolization." *American Ethnologist* 33, no. 4 (November): 573–75.

Myers, Ramon H. and Mark Peattie, eds. 1984. *The Japanese Colonial Empire, 1895–1945*. Princeton, NJ: Princeton University Press.

Nada Isao. 2003. "Shokuminchiki ni okeru Chōsen zaikai no kōgyōka ninshiki to senji keizai taisei." *Sensō to heiwa* (Osaka Kokusai Heiwa Kenkyūjo) 12 (March): 33–45.

Nagashima Hiroki. 2003. "Shōwa senzenki no Chōsen ni okeru 'uha' gakusei undō shiron: Tsuda Sakae to Keijō Teidai Yoka Risshōkai, Ryokki Renmei no setsuritsu katei o meguru kisoteki kōsatsu." *Kyūshū shigaku* 135 (February): 57–87.

Nakamura Satoru and An Pyŏng-jik. 1993. *Kindai Chōsen kōgyōka no kenkyū*. Tokyo: Nihon Hyōronsha.

Nakao Katsumi, ed. 2000. *Shokuminchi jinruigaku no tenbō*. Tokyo: Fūkyōsha.

———. 2004. "Jinruigaku to shokuminchi kenkyū: Higashi Ajia no shiten kara." *Shisō* 957: 92–107.

Namiki Masato. 1993. "Shokuminchiki Chōsenjin no seiji sanka ni tsuite: kaihōgoshi tono kanren ni oite." *Chōsenshi Kenkyūkai ronbunshū* 31 (October): 29–59.

———. 2003. "Chōsen ni okeru 'shokuminchi kindaisei,' 'shokuminchi kōkyōsei,' tainichi kyōryoku: shokuminchi seijishi, shakaishi kenkyū no tame no yobiteki kōsatsu." *Kokusai kōryū kenkyū: Kokusai Kōryū Gakubu kiyō* (Ferisu Jogakuin Daigaku) 5 (March): 1–42.

Oguma Eiji. 1998. *"Nihonjin" no kyōkai: Okinawa, Ainu, Taiwan, Chōsen, shokuminchi shihai kara fukki undō made.* Tokyo: Shin'yōsha.

———. 2002. *A Genealogy of "Japanese" Self-Images.* Trans. David Askew. Melbourne: Trans Pacific Press.

Oh, Se-Mi. 2008. "Consuming the Modern: The Everyday in Colonial Seoul, 1915–1937." Ph.D. diss., Columbia University.

Okamoto Makiko. 1996. "Ajia, Taiheiyō sensō makki ni okeru Chōsenjin, Taiwanjin sanseiken mondai." *Nihonshi kenkyū* 401 (January): 53–67.

———. 1998. "Seitō seijiki ni okeru bunkan sōtokusei." *Nihon shokuminchi kenkyū* 10 (July): 1–18.

———. 2000. "Sōtoku seiji to seitō seiji: nidai seitōki no Sōtoku jinji to Sōtokufu kansei, yosan." *Chōsenshi Kenkyūkai ronbunshū* 38 (October): 31–60.

———. 2008. *Shokuminchi kanryō no seijishi: Chōsen, Taiwan Sōtokufu to teikoku Nihon.* Tokyo: Sangensha.

Oka, Yoshitake. 1982. "Generational Conflict after the Russo-Japanese War." In *Conflict in Modern Japanese History*, ed. Tetsuo Najita and J. Victor Koschmann, 198–200. Princeton, NJ: Princeton University Press.

Osterhammel, Jürgen. 2005. *Colonialism: A Theoretical Overview.* Trans. Shelly L. Frisch. 2nd edition. Princeton, NJ: Markus Wiener Publishers.

Pai, Hyung-il. 1994. "The Politics of Korea's Past: The Legacy of Japanese Colonial Archaeology in the Korean Peninsula." *East Asian History* 7: 25–48.

———. 1999. "Japanese Anthropology and the Discovery of 'Prehistoric Korea.'" *Journal of East Asian Archaeology* 1: 353–82.

———. 2000. *Constructing "Korean" Origins: A Critical Review of Archaeology, Historiography, and Racial Myth in Korean State-Formation Theories.* Cambridge, MA: Harvard University Asia Center.

Palais, James B. 1975. *Politics and Policy in Traditional Korea.* Cambridge, MA: Council on East Asian Studies, Harvard University.

Pak Ch'an-sŭng. 1992. *Han'guk kŭndae chŏngch'i sasangsa yŏn'gu: minjokchuŭi up'a ŭi sillyŏk yangsŏng undongnon.* Seoul: Yŏksa Pip'yŏngsa.

———. 2007. *Minjokchuŭi ŭi sidae: Ilche ha ŭi Han'guk minjokchuŭi.* Seoul: Kyŏngin Munhwasa.

Pak Chong-gŭn. 1982. *Nisshin sensō to Chōsen.* Tokyo: Aoki Shoten.

Pak Sŏng-jin. 1999. "Ilche malgi Nokki Yŏnmaeng ŭi naesŏn ilch'eron." *Han'guk kŭnhyŏndaesa yŏn'g'u* 10 (June): 370–97.

Pang Ki-jung. 2002. "1930-yŏndae Mulsan Changnyŏ Undong kwa minjŏk chabonjuŭi kyŏngje sasang." *Tongbang hakchi* 115: 47–108.

———, ed. 2004. *Ilche p'asijŭm chibae chŏngch'aek kwa minjung saenghwal.* Seoul: Hyean.

Park, Hyun Ok. 2000. "Korean Manchuria: The Racial Politics of Territorial Osmosis." *South Atlantic Quarterly* 99, no. 1 (Winter): 193–215.

Park, Soon-Won. 1999. *Colonial Industrialization and Labor in Korea: The Onoda Cement Factory.* Cambridge, MA: Harvard University Asia Center.

Pearson, David. 2001. *The Politics of Ethnicity in Settler Societies: States of Unease.* New York: Palgrave.

Peattie, Mark R. 1984a. "Introduction." In *The Japanese Colonial Empire, 1895–1945*, ed. Ramon H. Myers and Mark R. Peattie, 3–51. Princeton, NJ: Princeton University Press.

———. 1984b. "Japanese Attitudes toward Colonialism, 1895–1945." In *The Japanese Colonial Empire, 1895–1945*, ed. Ramon H. Myers and Mark R. Peattie, 80–127. Princeton, NJ: Princeton University Press.

———. 1988a. "The Japanese Colonial Empire, 1895–1945." In *The Cambridge History of Japan* vol. 6, *The Twentieth Century*, ed. Peter Duus, 217–70. New York: Cambridge University Press.

———. 1988b. *Nan'yō: The Rise and Fall of the Japanese in Micronesia, 1885–1945.* Honolulu, HI: University of Hawai'i Press.

Penvenne, Jeanne Marie. 2005. "Settling against the Tide: The Layered Contradictions of Twentieth-Century Portuguese Settlement in Mozambique." In *Settler Colonialism in the Twentieth Century: Projects, Practices, Legacies*, ed. Caroline Elkins and Susan Pedersen, 79–94. New York and London: Routledge.

Pratt, Mary Louise. 1992. *Imperial Eyes: Travel Writing and Transculturation.* London and New York: Routledge.

Prochaska, David. 1990. *Making Algeria French: Colonialism in Bône, 1870–1920.* Cambridge, UK: Cambridge University Press.

Pyle, Kenneth B. 1969. *The New Generation in Meiji Japan: Problems of Cultural Identity, 1885–1895.* Stanford, CA: Stanford University Press.

———. 1973. "The Technology of Japanese Nationalism: The Local Improvement Movement, 1900–1918." *Journal of Asian Studies* 33 (November): 51–65.

Richards, Thomas. 1996. *Imperial Archive: Knowledge and the Fantasy of Empire.* London; New York: Verso.

Roberts, Andrew. 1986. "The Imperial Mind" and "Portuguese Africa." In *The Cambridge History of Africa* vol. 7, ed. J. D. Fage and Roland Oliver, 24–76, 494–543. Cambridge, UK: Cambridge University Press.

Roberts, Richard L. 1996. *Two Worlds of Cotton: Colonialism and the Regional Economy in the French Soudan, 1800–1946.* Stanford, CA: Stanford University Press.

Roberts, Sophie. 2010. "French Colonialism, Algerian Jews, and the Limits of Citizenship: French Anti-Semitism, Social Change, and the Jews of Algeria, 1870–1944." Ph.D. diss., University of Toronto.

Robinson, Michael E. 1982–83. "Ideological Schism in the Korean Nationalist Movement, 1920–1930." *Journal of Korean Studies* 4: 241–68

———. 1984. "Colonial Publication Policy and the Korean Nationalist Movement." In *The Japanese Colonial Empire, 1895–1945*, ed. Ramon H. Myers and Mark R. Peattie, 312–43. Princeton, NJ: Princeton University Press.

———. 1988. *Cultural Nationalism in Colonial Korea, 1920–25*. Seattle, WA: University of Washington Press.

———. 1993. "Enduring Anxieties: Cultural Nationalism and Modern East Asia." In *Cultural Nationalism in East Asia: Representation and Identity*, ed. Harumi Befu, 167–86. Berkeley, CA: Institute of East Asian Studies, University of California.

Robinson, Ronald. 1972. "Non-European Foundations of European Imperialism: Sketch for a Theory of Collaboration." In *Studies in the Theory of Imperialism*, ed. Roger Owen and Bob Sutcliffe, 117–40. London: Longman.

Robinson, Shira Nomi. 2005. "Occupied Citizens in a Liberal State: Palestinians under Military Rule and the Colonial Formation of Israeli Society, 1948–1966." Ph.D. diss., Stanford University.

Ruedy, John. 2005. *Modern Algeria: The Origins and Development of a Nation*. 2nd edition. Bloomington, IN: Indiana University Press.

Russell, Lynette, ed. 2001. *Colonial Frontiers: Indigenous-European Encounters in Settler Societies*. Manchester, UK: Manchester University Press.

Saaler, Sven, and J. Victor Koschmann, eds. 2007. *Pan-Asianism in Modern Japanese History: Colonialism, Regionalism, and Borders*. New York: Routledge.

Said, Edward W. 1978. *Orientalism*. New York: Pantheon Books.

Sakai, Naoki, Brett de Bary, and Iyotani Toshio, eds. 2005. *Deconstructing Nationality*. Ithaca, NY: East Asia Program, Cornell University.

Sakano Tōru. 2005. *Teikoku Nihon to jinruigakusha: 1884–1952-nen*. Tokyo: Keisō Shobō.

Sakimoto Kazuko. 1999. "'Kōminka' seisakuki no zaichō Nihonjin: Keijō Joshi Shihan Gakkō o chūshin ni." *Kokusai kankeigaku kenkyū* (Tsudajuku Daigaku) 25 (March): 79–94.

Sakurai Ryōju. 1998. "Kaisetsu." In *Daiinkun den*, Kikuchi Kenjō, 399–411. Keijō: Nikkan Shobō, 1910. Repr. Tokyo: Perikansha.

Sakurai Yoshiyuki. 1964. *Meiji to Chōsen*. Tokyo: Sakurai Yoshiyuki Sensei Kanreki Kinenkai.

Sand, Jordan. 2005. *House and Home in Modern Japan: Architecture, Domestic Space, and Bourgeois Culture, 1880–1930*. Cambridge, MA: Harvard University Asia Center.

Sasa Hiroo. 1977. "Kumamoto Kokkentō to Chōsen ni okeru shinbun jigyō." *Kokushikan Daigaku Jinbungakkai kiyō* 9: 21–38.

Satia, Priya. 2008. *Spies in Arabia: The Great War and the Cultural Foundations of Britain's Covert Empire in the Middle East.* Oxford, UK: Oxford University Press.

Satō, Barbara H. 2003. *The New Japanese Woman: Modernity, Media, and Women in Interwar Japan.* Durham, NC: Duke University Press.

Satogami Ryūhei. 1996. "Kindai Nihon no Chōsen ninshiki." In *Kindai Nihon no Ajia ninshiki*, ed. Furuya Tetsuo, 243–98. Tokyo: Ryokuin Shobō.

Scalapino, Robert A., and Lee Chong-Sik. 1972. *Communism in Korea.* Vol. 1. Berkeley, CA: University of California Press.

Schmid, Andre. 1997. "Rediscovering Manchuria: Sin Ch'aeho and the Politics of Territorial History in Korea." *Journal of Asian Studies* 56, no. 1 (February): 26–46.

———. 2002. *Korea Between Empires, 1895–1919*. New York: Columbia University Press.

Seraphim, Franziska. 2006. *War Memory and Social Politics in Japan, 1945–2005*. Cambridge, MA: Harvard University Asia Center.

Shafir, Gershon. 1996. *Land Labor and the Origins of the Israeli-Palestinian Conflict, 1882–1914*. Berkeley, CA: University of California Press.

Shibazaki Rikie. 1983. "Tokutomi Sohō to *Keijō nippō*." *Nihon Rekishi* 425 (October): 65–83.

Shimizu, Akitoshi. 1999. "Colonialism and the Development of Modern Anthropology in Japan." In *Anthropology and Colonialism in Asia and Oceania*, ed. Jan van Bremen and Akitoshi Shimizu, 115–71. Richmond, Surrey, UK: Curzon Press.

Shin, Gi-Wook, and Do-Hyun Han. 1999. "Colonial Corporatism: The Rural Revitalization Campaign, 1932–1940." In *Colonial Modernity in Korea*, ed. Gi-Wook Shin and Michael Robinson, 70–96. Cambridge, MA: Harvard University Asia Center.

Shin, Gi-Wook, and Michael Robinson, eds. 1999. *Colonial Modernity in Korea.* Cambridge, MA: Harvard University Asia Center.

Shin Mi-sen [Sin Mi-sŏn]. 1995. "Zaichō Nihonjin no ishiki to kōdō." *Nihon gakuhō* 14 (March): 43–62.

Sin Kyu-sŏp. 2000. "Zaiman Chōsenjin no 'Manshūkokkan oyobi 'Nihon teikokuzō." *Chōsenshi Kenkyūkai ronbunshū* 38 (October): 93–121.

Sin Myŏng-jik. 2003. *Modŏn ppoi, Kyŏngsŏng ŭl kŏnilda: manmun manhwa ro ponŭn kŭndae ŭi ŏlgul.* Seoul: Hyŏnsil Munhwa Yŏn'gu.

Sin Yong-ha. 1998. *Ilche singminji kŭndaehwaron pip'an.* Seoul: Munhak kwa Chisŏngsa.

Sin Yŏng-hong. 1984. *Kindai Chōsen shakai jigyōshi kenkyū: Keijō ni okeru hōmen iin seido no rekishiteki tenkai.* Tokyo: Ryokuin Shobō.

Sinha, Mrinalini. 2001. "Britishness, Clubbability, and the Colonial Public Sphere: The Genealogy of an Imperial Institution in Colonial India." *Journal of British Studies* 40, no. 4 (October): 489–521.

Smith, Kerry. 2001. *A Time of Crisis: Japan, the Great Depression, and Rural Revitalization.* Cambridge, MA: Harvard University Asia Center, 2001.

Smith, Woodruff D. 1978. *The German Colonial Empire.* Chapel Hill, NC: University of North Carolina Press.

Spurr, David. 1993. *The Rhetoric of Empire: Colonial Discourse in Journalism, Travel Writing, and Imperial Administration.* Durham, NC: Duke University Press.

Sŏ Hyŏn-ju. 2000. "Kyŏngsŏng chiyŏk ŭi minjokpyŏl kŏjuji pulli ŭi ch'ui, 1927-yŏn–1942-yŏn." *Kuksagwan nonch'ong* 94 (December): 223–59.

———. 2001. "Kyŏngsŏng-bu ŭi chŏngch'ongdae wa chŏnghoe." *Sŏulhak yŏn'gu* 16 (March): 109–76.

Sŏn Chae-wŏn. 1998. "Shokuminchiki Chōsen ni okeru koyō seido." *Nihon shokuminchi kenkyū* 10 (July): 19–32.

Son Chŏng-mok. 1992. *Han'guk chibang chedo, chach'isa yŏn'gu.* Seoul: Ilchisa.

———. 1996. *Ilche kangjŏmgi tosihwa kwajŏng yŏn'gu.* Seoul: Ilchisa.

Song Kyu-jin. 2001. *Ilche ha ŭi Chosŏn muyŏk yŏn'gu.* Seoul: Koryŏ Taehakkyo Minjok Munhwa Yŏn'guwŏn.

Song Yŏn-ok. 1993. "Chōsen shokuminchi shihai ni okeru kōshōsei." *Nihonshi kenkyū* 371 (July): 52–66.

———. 2002. "Henkyō e no josei jinkō idō: teikoku kara shokuminchi Chōsen e." In *Henkyō no mainoritī: shōsū gurūpu no ikikata*, ed. Teratani Hiromi et al., 59–88. Tokyo: Eihōsha.

Stasiulis, Daiva, and Nira Yuval-Davis, eds. 1995. *Unsettling Settler Societies: Articulations of Gender, Race, Ethnicity and Class.* London and Thousand Oaks, CA: Sage.

Stoler, Ann Laura. 1989."Rethinking Colonial Categories: European Communities and the Boundaries of Rule." *Comparative Studies in Society and History* 31, no. 1 (January): 134–61.

———. 2002a. *Carnal Knowledge and Imperial Power: Race and the Intimate in Colonial Rule.* Berkeley, CA: University of California Press.

———. 2002b. "Colonial Archives and the Arts of Governance." *Archival Science* (Kluwer Academic Publishers, Netherlands) 2: 87–109.

———. 2008. *Along the Archival Grain: Epistemic Anxieties and Colonial Common Sense.* Princeton, NJ: Princeton University Press.

Stora, Benjamin. 2001. *Algeria, 1830–2000: A Short History.* Trans. Jane Marie Todd. Ithaca, NY: Cornell University Press.

Suga Kōji. 2004. *Nihon tōchika no kaigai jinja: Chōsen Jingū Taiwan Jinja to saijin.* Tokyo: Kōbundō.

Suh, Dae-Sook. 1967. *The Korean Communist Movement, 1918–1948.* Princeton, NJ: Princeton University Press.

Suzuki Yūko. 1992. *Jūgun ianfu, naisen kekkon: sei no shinryaku, sengo sekinin o kangaeru.* Tokyo: Miraisha.

Takahashi Yasutaka. 1993. "Shokuminchi no tetsudō to kaiun." In *Shokuminchika to sangyōka*, ed. Ōe Shinobu et al., 263–89. Iwanami Kōza Kindai Nihon to Shokuminchi 3. Tokyo: Iwanami Shoten.

———. 1995. *Nihon shokuminchi tetsudō shiron.* Tokyo: Nihon Keizai Hyōronsha.

Takasaki Sōji. 1982a. "Aru 'Chōsentsū' no ikita michi." *Kikan sanzenri* 30 (May): 104–15.

———. 1982b. "Ryokki Renmei to 'kōminka' undō." *Kikan sanzenri* 31 (August): 64–72.

———. 1993. "Chōsen no shinnichiha: Ryokki Renmei de katsuyaku shita Chōsenjin tachi." In *Teikō to kutsujū*, ed. Ōe Shinobu et al., 123–48. Iwanami Kōza Kindai Nihon to Shokuminchi 6. Tokyo: Iwanami Shoten.

———. 2002. *Shokuminchiki Chōsen no Nihonjin.* Tokyo: Iwanami Shoten.

Takayanagi Toshio. 1997. "Kaidai, 'Chōsen Jiron' ni miru Nihonjin no Chōsenkan henkaku undō no kyūseki." In *"Chōsen Jiron" bessatsu: kaidai, sōmokuji, sakuin.* Tokyo: Ryokuin Shobō.

Tamanoi, Mariko. 2009. *Memory Maps: The State and Manchuria in Postwar Japan.* Honolulu, HI: University of Hawai'i Press.

Tanaka Hiroshi. 1974. "Nihon no shokuminchi shihaika ni okeru kokuseki kankei no keii." *Aichikenritsu Daigaku Gaikokugo Gakubu kiyō* 9 (December): 61–96.

Tanaka Ryūichi. 2007. *Manshūkoku to Nihon no teikoku shihai.* Tokyo: Yūshisha.

Tanaka, Stefan. 1993. *Japan's Orient: Rendering Pasts into History.* Berkeley, CA: University of California Press.

To Myŏn-hoe. 2001. "Singmin juŭi ka nurak toen 'singminji kŭndaesŏng.'" *Yŏksa munje yŏn'gu* 7: 251–72.

Toyoda Shōichi. 1963. *Keiryū yume no makura: Keijō Ryūzan shōshi.* Iwakura, Japan: Ōkawa Reizō.

Tsurumi, Patricia. 1984. "Colonial Education in Korea and Taiwan." In *The Japanese Colonial Empire, 1895–1945*, ed. Ramon H. Myers and Mark R. Peattie, 275–311. Princeton, NJ: Princeton University Press.

U Kai Zai [U K'wae-je]. 2001. Trans. Suzuki Yōji. "Dentō bunka no rikai to Kannichi ryōkoku kankei: Chōsen Kenkyūkai no kosho chinsho kankō o chūshin ni." *Chōsen Gakuhō* 178 (January): 181–205.

Uchida, Jun. 2003a. "Shokuminchiki Chōsen ni okeru dōka seisaku to zaichō Nihonjin: Dōminkai o jirei to shite." *Chōsenshi Kenkyūkai ronbunshū* 41 (October): 173–201.

———. 2003b. Review of Takasaki Sōji, *Shokuminchiki Chōsen no Nihonjin* (2002). In *Kankoku Chōsen no bunka to shakai* 2 (October): 278–86.

———. 2005. "'Brokers of Empire': Japanese Settler Colonialism in Korea, 1910–1937." Ph.D. diss., Harvard University.

———. 2008. "'A Scramble for Freight': The Politics of Collaboration along and across the Railway Tracks of Colonial Korea." *Comparative Studies in Society and History* 51, no. 1 (January): 117–50.

———. 2011a. "A Sentimental Journey: Mapping the Interior Frontier of Japanese Settlers in Colonial Korea." *Journal of Asian Studies* 70, no. 3 (August), forthcoming.

———. 2011b. "Between Collaboration and Conflict: State and Society in Wartime Korea." In *Tumultuous Decade: Japan's Challenge to the International System, 1931–41*, ed. Masato Kimura and Tosh Minohara. Toronto, ON: University of Toronto Press, forthcoming.

Unno Fukuju. 1995. *Kankoku heigō.* Tokyo: Iwanami Shoten.

Wakatsuki Yasuo. 1995. *Sengo hikiage no kiroku.* Tokyo: Jiji Tsūshinsha.

Walraven, Boudewijn. 1999. "The Natives Next-door: Ethnology in Colonial Korea." In *Anthropology and Colonialism in Asia and Oceania*, ed. Jan van Bremen and Akitoshi Shimizu, 219–44. Richmond, Surrey, UK: Curzon Press.

Watt, Lori. 2009. *When Empire Comes Home: Repatriation and Reintegration in Postwar Japan.* Cambridge, MA: Harvard University Asia Center.

Wehler, Hans-Ulrich. 1985. *The German Empire, 1871–1918.* Trans. Kim Traynor. Dover, NH: Berg Publishers.

Weiner, Michael. 1995. "Discourses of Race, Nation, and Empire in Pre-1945 Japan." *Ethnic and Racial Studies* 18, no. 3 (July): 433–56.

White, Richard. 1991. *The Middle Ground: Indians, Empires, and Republics in the Great Lakes Region, 1650–1815*. Cambridge, UK: Cambridge University Press.

Wolfe, Patrick. 1999. *Settler Colonialism and the Transformation of Anthropology: The Politics and Poetics of an Ethnographic Event.* London and New York: Cassell.

Yamada Kanto. 2000. "Nihonjin keisatsukan ni taisuru Chōsengo shōrei seisaku." *Chōsenshi Kenkyūkai ronbunshū* 38 (October): 123–49.

Yamada Shōji, Koshō Tadashi, and Higuchi Yūichi. 2005. *Chōsen senji rōdō dōin.* Tokyo: Iwanami Shoten.

Yamanouchi, Yasushi. 1998. "Total-War and System Integration: A Methodological Introduction." In *Total War and 'Modernization,'* ed. Yasushi Yamanouchi, J. Victor Koschmann, and Ryūichi Narita, 1–42. Ithaca, NY: East Asia Program, Cornell University.

Yamato Kazuaki. 1988. "Shokuminchiki Chōsen chihō gyōsei ni kansuru ichi shiron – mensei no kakuritsu katei o chūshin ni." *Reikishi hyōron* (Rekishi Kagaku Kyōgikai) 458: 40–61.

Yamazaki Tanshō. 1943. *Gaichi tōchi kikō no kenkyū.* Tokyo: Takayama Shoin.

Yanagisawa Asobu and Okabe Makio, eds. 2001. *Teikokushugi to shokuminchi*, Tenbō Nihon Rekishi 20. Tokyo: Tōkyōdō Shuppan.

Yi Chae-hang, ed. 1984. *Sanggong Hoeŭiso paengnyŏnsa.* Seoul: Taehan Sanggong Hoeŭiso.

Yi Chong-min. 2004. "Keihanzai no torishimari hōrei ni miru minshū tōsei." In *Shokuminchi teikoku Nihon no hōteki kōzō*, ed. Asano Toyomi and Matsuda Toshihiko, 319–52. Tokyo: Shinzansha.

Yi Hae-ch'ang. 1971. *Han'guk sinmunsa yŏn'gu.* Seoul: Sŏngmun'gak.

Yi Hŭi-jŏng. 2008. *Han'guk kŭndae sosŏl ŭi hyŏngsŏng kwa 'Maeil sinbo.'* Seoul: Somyŏng Ch'ulp'an.

Yi Hyeong-nang. 1996. "Shokuminchi Chōsen ni okeru beikoku kensa seido no tenkai katei." *Ikkyō ronsō* 115, no. 2 (February): 552–62.

Yi Hyŏn-jong. 1970. "Taehan Hyŏphoe e kwanhan yŏn'gu." *Asea yŏn'gu* 13, no. 3: 17–56.

Yi Hyŏng-sik. 2007. "Senzenki ni okeru Chūō Chōsen Kyōkai no kiseki." *Chōsen gakuhō* 204 (July): 101–40.

———. 2008. "Minami Jirō sōtoku jidai ni okeru Chūō Chōsen Kyōkai." *Nihon rekishi* 720 (May): 62–79.

Yi Sŭng-yŏp. 2001. "Chōsenjin naisen ittai ronja no tenkō to dōka no ronri." *Nijusseiki kenkyū* 2 (December): 25–46.

———. 2003. "Zensen kōshokusha taikai: 1924–1930." *Nijusseiki kenkyū* 4 (December): 95–120.

———. 2005. "3.1 undōki ni okeru Chōsen zaijū Nihonjin shakai no taiō to dōkō." *Jinbun gakuhō* 92 (March): 119–44.

——— [Lee Seung-yup]. 2008. "Japanese Resident Society in Colonial Korea during the Military Rule Period, 1910s." Paper presented at the Association for Asian Studies Annual Meeting, Atlanta.

Yi Yŏng-mi. 2005. *Kankoku shihōseido to Ume Kenjirō.* Tokyo: Hōsei Daigaku Shuppankyoku.

Yŏm Pok-kyu. 2004. "Singminji kŭndae ŭi konggan hyŏngsŏng—kŭndae Sŏul ŭi tosi kyehoek kwa tosi konggan ŭi hyŏngsŏng, pyŏnyong, hwakchang." *Munhwa kwahak* 39 (September): 197–219.

Yoo, Theodore Jun. 2008. *The Politics of Gender in Colonial Korea: Education, Labor, and Health, 1910–1945*. Berkeley, CA: University of California Press.

Yoshino Makoto. 1978. "Richō makki ni okeru beikoku yushutsu no tenkai to bōkokurei." *Chōsenshi Kenkyūkai ronbunshū* 15 (March): 101–31.

Young, Crawford. 1994. *The African Colonial State in Comparative Perspective.* New Haven, CT: Yale University Press.

Young, Louise. 1998. *Japan's Total Empire: Manchuria and the Culture of Wartime Imperialism.* Berkeley, CA: University of California Press.

Yun Chŏng-uk. 1996. *Shokuminchi Chōsen ni okeru shakai jigyō seisaku.* Osaka: Ōsaka Keizai Hōka Daigaku Shuppanbu.

Yun Hae-dong. 1992. "Ilche ha Mulsan Changnyŏ Undong ŭi paegyŏng kwa kŭ inyŏm." *Han'guksa non* 27: 281–353.

———. 2003. *Singminji ŭi hoesaek chidae: Han'guk ŭi kŭndaesŏng kwa singminjuŭi pip'an.* Seoul: Yŏksa Pip'yŏngsa.

# *Index*


Abe Kaoru 阿部薰, 281–82, 314
Abe Mitsuie 阿部充家 (1862–1936), 151, 154, 172, 212, 249, 264, 287, 296*n*120
Abernethy, David, 133
accommodation, Korean: official policy of, 101, 147–48, 163–64, 185–86, 220, 254, 304, 315, 385; settlers' attitude to, 21, 185–86, 220, 223–24, 254, 279, 399. *See also* collaboration; Korean elites
acculturation, 85, 89–90, 148
Adachi Kenzō 安達謙蔵 (1864–1948), 50, 274*n*37
"administered mass organizations," 355, 361*n*26
Aeguk Kyemong Undong 愛國啓蒙運動 (Patriotic Enlightenment Movement), 103–11, 164, 190
Africa: colonial states in, 14–15, 21–23, 230*n*7; settler colonies in, 18–19, 83; "scramble for," 40; missionaries in, 39; colonial pioneers in, 41, 132; Indians in East, 61; indigenous elites in, 116*n*80, 118, 123–24, 231, 264*n*2, 302*n*144, 390*n*168; *évolué*, 116*n*80, 231*n*15. *See also* Algeria; Kenya; South Africa; Southern Rhodesia; settlers, in Africa
Agricultural and Residential Land Certification Law, 61–62
Aikoku Fujinkai 愛国婦人会 (Patriotic Women's Association), 57, 77*n*159, 310, 337, 338*n*134, 359, 361*n*26
Akashi Motojirō 明石元二郎 (1864–1919), 130, 191
Akiyama Masanosuke 秋山雅之介 (1866–1937), 191
Algeria, French: as settler colony, 18–19, 133, 146; comparability with Korea, 18, 19*n*38; colonial administrators in, 125; self-rule in, 265*n*4; Assembly, 283. *See also colons*
Alsace-Lorraine, German, 133, 146
Amaterasu, sun goddess 天照大神, 79, 120, 196, 198, 204*n*63, 349
An Chung-gŭn 安重根 (1879–1910), 111
Andō Toyoroku 安藤豊禄 (1897–1990), 381
annexation of Korea, 12, 26, 39*n*16, 94, 98, 111; Ilchinhoe's campaign for, 108, 111–14, 360; and settlers, 52, 56, 94, 101, 112–15; treaty of, 114–15, 121; and assimilation policy, 116, 118, 181, 195, 197–98, 360; imperial rescript on, 298
anthropology, 117, 195, 200*n*45, 203, 367. *See also* ethnography
anticolonial empire, 299, 302
Aoyagi Tsunatarō 青柳綱太郎 (pen name: 南冥 Nanmei) (1877–1932), 52,

120, 126–27, 191–208 *passim*, 212, 218–20, 223, 225, 281, Appendix 1
Arai Hatsutarō 荒井初太郎 (1873–?), 245, Appendix 1
Aruga Mitsutoyo 有賀光豊 (1873–1949), 149, 242*n*70, 249*n*96, 257*n*131, 296, Appendix 1
Asian ethnic league 亜細亜民族連盟 (*Ajia minzoku renmei*), 321
Askew, David, 200*n*45
*assimilados* ("assimilated citizens"), in Portuguese Africa, 231*n*15
assimilation, French policy of, 19*n*38, 116, 284; and citizenship, 24*n*56, 184*n*145, 390*n*169. *See also* Algeria
assimilation 同化 (*dōka*), Japanese policy of, 79*n*168, 83, 116–20, 127, 285, 356, 360; settlers' attitudes to, 21, 88–89, 117–20, 132–36, 152, 195–201 *passim*, 206, 210, 218–26 *passim*, 382*n*131; and Saitō's cultural rule, 144–48, 185–86, 296*n*121, 304; and Buddhism, 39–40, 179–80, 330*n*97, 347; and education, 58, 120*n*99; and Korean elites, 123–24, 294–95, 389–90, 399; Hara on, 146–47, 280; Korean rejection of, 201, 212, 339–40; limits of, 217–20, 222–26, 304; Japanese critics of, 285–86; Korean appropriation of, 280, 289, 319–20, 386; and moral suasion, 328*n*91, 332–34, 352*n*206. *See also isshi dōjin*; *kōminka*; *naichi enchō*; *naisen ittai*; *naisen yūwa*
Atkins, E. Taylor, 200*n*46
Ayukai Fusanoshin 鮎貝房之進 (1864–1946), 55, 88, 91, 117–18, 156, 191, 197, 202*n*55, Appendix 1

Berman, Bruce, 226, 256*n*122
Botsman, Daniel, 123*n*114
brokered colonialism, 30, 395
brokers of empire: definition, 5–8; characteristics of, 25–26, 93–95, 395–96; and Korean elites, 7, 16–18, 27–28, 398–400 (*see also under* collaboration); emergence of, 50, 91–92, 139; subgroups of, 92–93, Appendix 1; as intermediaries of cultural rule, 153–64, 177–82 (*see also* Dōminkai); as pundits on Korea (*see* Chōsen Kenkyūkai); interchange with Korean nationalism, 207–25; as partners in economic policy-making, 233–40, 325–26; campaign for Korean industries, 240–52, 254–59; campaign for local autonomy and suffrage, 272–78; debates on suffrage, 281–87; opposition to Colonial Ministry, 297–301; support for Manchurian colonization, 307–8, 310–18 (*see also* Chōsen Bōeki Kyōkai); agents of moral suasion, 327–38, 341–53; organs of the wartime regime, 358–61, 363–73, 380–81
Brook, Timothy, 17*n*31, 281
Brooks, Barbara, 79*n*168, 318*n*44
Buddhism, Japanese: settler followers of, 2, Table 3, 77, 79*n*171, 179, 346*n*173; priests and missionaries, 10, 39–40, 62, 346; teachers, 55–56; and assimilation, 330*n*97; and moral suasion, 331*n*100, 346–48; Nichiren, 342, 363–64, 367 (*see also* Ryokki Renmei)

Campaign to Increase Korean Rice Production 朝鮮産米増殖計画 (*Chōsen sanmai zōshoku keikaku*), 176, 242; impact on the metropole, 256
Caprio, Mark E., 16*n*29, 18*n*34, 19*n*38, 120*n*99
Central Council 中枢院 (J. Chūshūin, K. Chungch'uwŏn), 124, 149, 153, 160, 167–68, 201–2, 279, 288–91, 319, 357, 365, 385
chambers of commerce: as settler institutions, 7, 68–69, 266–67; cooperation of Japanese and Koreans through, 230–32, 255–56, 258; Korean capitalists in, 261–62; Korean Federation of, 240, 246, 248; National Federation of, 248; civilian elites in, 268, 272; trips to Manchuria, 322; under war, 361*n*26
Charter Oath, 131

China: Japan's war against, 44–47, 357; Chinese merchants in Korea, 44–45, 47, 69*n*125, 71; "Chinese imperialism," 44–47; Pan-Asian alliance with, 106, 108, 366; Korean political exiles in, 148, 311; and *Tōyōshi*, 195; Korea's trade with, 256, 325–26; conflict over Korean migrants in Manchuria, 310–13. *See also* Qing dynasty
Ching, Leo T. S., 200*n*45, 362
Cho Pyŏng-sik 趙秉式 (1823–1907), 51
Cho Chin-t'ae 趙鎮泰 (1853–1933), 149, 232, 233, 246–47
Cho Chung-ŭng 趙重應 (1860–1919), 178
Cho Man-sik 曺晩植 (1882–1950?), 253, 287
Cho Pyŏng-sang 曺秉相 (1891–?), 276*n*44, 289, 301, 313, 319, 361*n*27
Ch'oe Nam-son 崔南善 (1890–1957), 161*n*53, 204, 211–12
Ch'oe Rin 崔麟 (1878–?), 287, 357, 361*n*27
Chōjiya 丁子屋, 1–2, 38, 179–80, 335, 351. *See also* Kobayashi Genroku
Chŏn Sŏng-uk 全聖旭 (1877–?), 268*n*18, 276*n*44, 330
Ch'ŏndogyo 天道教 (Religion of the Heavenly Way), 357–58
Chŏng Un-bok 鄭雲復 (1870–1920), 108, 321
Chongno 鐘路, 72, 75, 82, 84, 86
Chōsen Army 朝鮮軍, 70, 326; volunteer program, 369, 373, 378–80; skepticism toward Korean soldiers, 383, 393; debate on suffrage, 384. *See also* Imperial Army
Chōsen Bank 朝鮮銀行, 99*n*8, 246, 322
Chōsen Bōeki Kyōkai 朝鮮貿易協会 (Korea Trade Association), 322–26
Chōsen Bukkyōdan 朝鮮仏教団 (Korean Buddhist Association), 179–80
Chōsen Bunjin Kyōkai 朝鮮文人協会 (Korea Writers' Association), 359
Chōsen Bussan Kyōkai 朝鮮物産協会 (Association for Korean Products), 254
Chōsen Gunji Kōen Renmei 朝鮮軍事後援連盟 (Korea Military Assistance League), 361*n*61, 373
*Chōsen gunsho taikei* 朝鮮群書大系 (A Compendium of Various Korean Writings), 194*n*18
Chōsen Industrial Bank 朝鮮殖産銀行, 239*n*56, 242*n*70, 246, 275, 296, 411
Chōsen Kenkyūkai 朝鮮研究会 (Korea Research Association; KRA), 191–206 *passim*, 208, 218, 281*n*65
Chōsen Kosho Kankōkai 朝鮮古書刊行会 (Society for the Publication of Korean Antique Books), 194*n*18
*Chōsen kōron* 朝鮮公論, 124, 213–14, 224, 253, 273, 320, 379, 385, 389
Chōsen Kyōkai 朝鮮協会 (Korea Association), 59*n*90
Chōsen Nogi Society 朝鮮乃木会, 178
*Chōsen oyobi Manshū* 朝鮮及満洲, 87–88, 130, 209, 220, 358. *See also* Shakuo Shunjō
*Chōsen oyobi Chōsen minzoku* 朝鮮及朝鮮民族 (Korea and the Korean People), 211–12
Chōsen Shakai Jigyō Kyōkai 朝鮮社会事業協会 (Korea Social Work Association), 336
*Chōsen shisō tsūshin* 朝鮮思想通信 (Korean Thought News), 211–15
Chōsen Shōgyō Kaigisho Rengōkai 朝鮮商業会議所連合会 (Korean Federation of Chambers of Commerce), 240–41, 246, 248
Chōsen Shrine 朝鮮神宮, 72*n*140, 204*n*63, 307, 332, 352, 383
Chōsen Suisankai 朝鮮水産会 (Korea Marine Products Association), 324
Chōsen Tetsudōmō Sokusei Kiseikai 朝鮮鉄道網速成期成会 (Association for the Rapid Construction of Korean Railroads), 249–50
*Chōsenjin no susumu beki michi* 朝鮮人の進むべき道 (The Way the Koreans Must Proceed), 365–66. *See also* Hyŏn Yŏng-sŏp

Chosŏn Korea, dynasty, 26, 39, 44, 70, 160, 162, 310*n*8, 347; and colonial state, 115–16; settler discourse on, 192–93, 199–200

*Chosŏn ilbo* 朝鮮日報, 207, 209*n*83, 215–16, 221, 225, 253, 258

Chosŏn Mulsan Changnyŏ Undong 朝鮮物産奨励運動 (Korean Production Movement), 253–55

Chosŏn Puin Munje Yŏn'guhoe 朝鮮婦人問題研究会 (Korean Women's Problems Research Association), 370–71

Christianity, in Korea: Western missionaries, 39, 55, 151, 156, 180, 349–50; Japanese followers of, 39*n*18, 156, 181, 274; and anticolonial activities, 150, 163; Korean leaders of, 151, 156; collaboration with the state, 346, 348, 358–59; and *kokutai*, 364

*chūken jinbutsu* 中堅人物 ("mainstay" or leader), 328, 330, 342

Chūō Chōsen Kyōkai 中央朝鮮協会 (Central Korea Association), 249–50, 295*n*118, 299

citizen-subjects, 24, 123*n*113, 144*n*5. *See also kokumin*

citizenship: colonial, 7, 123, 144–45, 148, 185, 288, 378; Japanese/metropolitan, 14, 29, 122, 284, 377–78, 380, 382, 395; and colonialism, 97–98; settlers' quest for, 97–98, 127–33, 135, 137–38, 284, 288, 397; Korean quest for, 279–81, 288–89, 318–22, 378, 386–87, 392, 399; conflict between settlers and Koreans over, 288–93, 303–4, 391, 399; incorporation of Koreans into metropolitan, 378–90 *passim*; of settler repatriates, 400; in European empires, 24, 123, 231*n*15, 385, 390. *See also under* laws; suffrage

civil society, 6, 23–24, 123, 265

city 府 (J. *fu*; K. *pu*), 266; council 府協議会, 7, 266–70, 272, 283, 292; assembly 府会, 179, 296*n*122, 319, 388–89

civilization 文明化 (*bunmeika*), 118, 120

class: and nation, 237*n*47; and race/ethnicity, 262

coevalness, denial of, 200, 200*n*46

Cohen, Nicole L., 16*n*29, 25*n*62, 90

collaboration: definition and usage of, 17*n*31, 263*n*1; of settlers and Korean bourgeois elites, 17–18, 27–29, 158–64, 230–33, 237*n*47, 246, 250, 255–59, 261–62, 398–400 (*see also* Dōminkai); among "men on the spot," 47–50; of settlers with the state, 145–46, 153–77, 186–87, 190–204, 207–9, 359, 363–73, 376, 379–81; partnership of businessmen with the state, 230–34, 239, 325–26; political alliance of settlers and Koreans, 263–64, 272–73, 276–81, 297–304; of civilian elites with moral suasion, 328–40, 346–53 *passim*; of civilian elites with the wartime regime, 357–63, 373–74. *See also* middle ground

*colons*, in Algeria: size of 3, 20; political power of, 12*n*19, 23–24, 258*n*134, 269, 274; conflict with the state, 13*n*23, 21, 379, 385; social composition of, 20, 37, 66; ambivalence toward metropole, 21, 284; control over land, 22; separation from natives, 87, 184. *See also pieds noirs*

Colonial Affairs: Bureau of, 拓殖局 (Takushokukyoku), 297; Ministry of, 拓務省 (Takumushō), 294*n*113, 299–300, 322*n*60

colonial archive, 2, 189–90, 198–99, 203, 206–7, 212, 221, 224–26

colonial corporatism, 28, 328, 328*n*90, 351, 353–54. *See also* moral suasion

colonial encounter, 15–17, 25, 82, 85, 88, 394, 400. *See also* contact zone; middle ground

colonial "middle," 16–17

colonial modernity, 15–16, 237

colonial power, 6, 8, 12, 14, 16, 29–30, 349, 394, 396

colonial state, in Korea: nature and power of, 6, 14–15, 23, 115–16, 137, 264–66, 270, 272; limits and

internal workings of, 5*n*8, 303, 396–97; ability to "broadcast power," 15, 353; and settlers (*see under* settlers, Japanese in Korea); as arbiter between settlers and Koreans, 125–26, 290–91, 302, 304; co-optation of Koreans, 123–24, 149–50, 158–64, 287, 341; inclusion of civilian elites into governance, 149–50, 153–58, 186, 228, 233–40, 266–68, 325–26, 328–29, 360–61, 372–73 (*see also* moral suasion); and the metropole, 228–30, 247, 252, 261, 355–56; control over economy, 229–30
colony of settlement or "settlement colony" 移住植民地 (*ijū shokuminchi*), Korea as 7, 9, 18, 58; European, 133, 265
Colonization, Ministry of 拓殖省 (Takushokushō), 297–99, 395
colored clothing, promotion of 色服奨励 (*irofuku shōrei*). *See under* moral suasion
"combat at close quarters" 接近戦 (*sekkinsen*), 288 97, 399
Communist Party, Korean, 293
community councils 町/洞会 (J. *chō/dōkai*; K. *chŏng/tonghoe*), 329, 332, 352, 361*n*26
Confucianism: Koreans as faithful followers of, 38, 86, 118; anti-colonial resistance by literati, 99; effort to co-opt literati, 107, 124, 158, 160, 162; etymology of *dōka*, 116, 121; myth of Kija, 205; in Japan, 208; and Kungmin Hyŏphoe, 280*n*62; and moral suasion, 332, 340*n*140; and war support, 358; and *kokutai*, 364. *See also* Yudo Chinhŭnghoe
conscription: of settlers, 24, 90, 122; of Koreans, 290–91, 319, 366, 378, 380*n*119, 382–84, 387
contact zone, 16, 84, 400
continental empire, 308–9, 318, 353. *See also* Manchuria
continental advance supply base, Korea as, 323*n*68, 325, 353, 359
cultural rule 文化政治 (*bunka seiji*), 144–50; setters' reaction to, 152–53; settlers as intermediaries of, 145–46, 153–82, 186; co-optation of local elites into, 149, 228, 267; as a template for Manchukuo, 185–86; critique of, 213–14; limits of, 220, 296, 304. *See also* Saitō Makoto; *naisen yūwa*

Dai-Ichi Bank 第一銀行 (First National Bank), 40*nn*23–24, 99*n*8, 233*n*24. *See also* Chōsen Bank
Dai-Nihon Fujinkai 大日本婦人会 (Greater Japan Women's Association), 359*n*17
Dai-Nihon Kaigai Kyōikukai 大日本海外教育会 (Greater Japan Overseas Education Association), 55
Dai-Nihon Kokki Sen'yōkai 大日本国旗宣揚会 (Greater Japan National Flag Hoisting Society), 351
Dai-Nihon Kokubō Fujinkai 大日本国防婦人会 (Greater Japan National Defense Women's Association), 359, 361*n*26
Dai-Nihon Kokusuikai 大日本国粋会 (Greater Japan National Essence Association), 182–83, 244
"deputies of the state," 329, 397
Diet, in Japan, 99, 110, 146; and settler lobbyists from Korea, 128–29, 241, 249–50; and Korean governance, 204*n*63, 299, 382; and suffrage in Korea, 273–79 *passim*, 282–83, 292, 296–97, 322*n*60, 384–85; settlers as members of, 93, 104, 166–67, 182*n*134, 244–45, 249, 273–74, 277–78, 296. *See also* "Korea lobby"
Dirks, Nicholas, 198
district commissioners 方面委員 (*hōmen iin*), 329–30, 335, 338, 351, 361*n*26
Doak, Kevin, 138
*dōbun dōshu* 同文同種 (same script, same race), 116, 195, 201
*dōgen dōshu* 同源同種 (same origin, same race), 284, 286

*dōhō* 同胞 (brethren, compatriot): Koreans as, 177, 290, 335, 376; Koreans in Manchuria as, 171, 311–16, 318*n*44
Dōminkai 同民会 (Association of One People): assimilation campaign, Table 5, 165–86 *passim*, 230*n*9, 293–96, 298, 311; leaders of, 276, 284, 298, 301, 315, 342; and moral suasion, 330–35 *passim*, 338, 348; wartime role of, 360*n*23, 381
Duara, Prasenjit, 169, 186*n*149
Dudden, Alexis, 30
Duus, Peter, 8, 12, 60*n*98, 99, 137

East Asian league or cooperative community 東亜共同体 (Tōa Kyōdōtai), 315–16, 364–66
"East Asian Modern," 169
Eckert, Carter J., 233, 262, 317
education: as force of colonization, 55–58; and Korean assimilation, 40*n*21, 117–19, 120*n*99, 146, 201–2; of Korean women, 57, 338–40, 370–71; of young settlers, 71, 90, 124, 266, 342–46, 369; and Korean self-strengthening, 105, 280; mixed, 136*n*160, 321, 316, 319, 321, 330, 378, 379*n*118; official-civilian committee on, 149, Fig. 4; Dōminkai's promotion of Korean, 153, 172–74, 183, 338; critique of official policy of, 214, 218–19; Korean demands for, 288, 290, 319, 383, 387–88; universal, 290, 366, 378*n*110, 383; youth, 340–41
emperor, Japanese, 1–2, 335; settlers' identification with, 77, 80, 90, 131, 139; and the Governor-General, 115, 297*n*125; Japan as polity centered on, 116–17, 356, 368; and colonial citizenship, 144*n*5; promotion of the ideology and worship of, 159 (Table 5: Dōkōkai), 326, 343–46, 349–52, 356, 363–70 *passim*, 396; in Korean history, 196–97, 284; Korean loyalty to, 374, 379, 392–93. *See also kōminka*; Ryokki Renmei; *shinmin*
emperor, Korean, 98–99, 103, 111, 143, 182, 199, 202
Eskildsen, Robert, 30*n*66
ethnic nationalism 民族主義 (*minzoku shugi*), 138, 219, 237*n*47, 321, 399
ethnography, colonial, 160*n*53, 195, 198–99, 200–204 *passim*
extraterritoriality, 36, 43, 99–100, 122

Fabian, Johannes, 200*n*46
factionalism, in Korean history, 199–200, 202, 205
family 家 (*ie*), 112; state, 116; registration (*koseki*), 122, 132, 273, 386–87; Japanese and Koreans as one, 195, 285, 362; as locus of moral suasion, 337–38, 340, 345; Koreans into the Japanese system of (*see* name-changing campaign). *See also under* laws; citizenship
fascism, and wartime Korea, 354, 358–59, 363, 368, 391
Feet-Washing Movement 洗足運動, 181
Fieldhouse, David, 44
fiscal self-sufficiency, principle of, 230*n*7, 235, 276
"Flogging Ordinance," 122, 213
Foreign Affairs, Ministry of (Japan), 38, 49–50, 72, 311
foundation myths, Japanese, 196, 345. *See also* Amaterasu
"Four Great Points for Korean Industrial Development" (朝鮮産業開発四大要項), 240–43, 252. *See also under* railways
freedom and popular rights, movement for 自由民権運動 (*jiyūminken undō*): and Korean reform, 10, 37, 93, 104–5, 108–9; and settlers' quest for citizenship, 97–98, 129–31, 136
Fuchizawa Yoshie 渕沢能恵 (1850–1936), 56–57, 337–38, Appendix 1
Fujii Kantarō 藤井寛太郎 (1876–?), 234–35, 237–38, 242*n*70, 249*n*96, 315–16, Appendix 1
Fujitani, Takashi, 77*n*154, 378*n*111
Fukumoto Nichinan 福本日南 (1857–1921), 191

Fukuzawa Yukichi 福沢諭吉 (1835–1901), 53, 57, 105

Garon, Sheldon, 327*n*87
*geisha*, 66*n*119, Table 3, 70, 78–79, 82, 184, 372
*genrō* 元老 (elder statesmen), 92, 146
Girei Junsoku 儀礼準則 (Regulations on Rituals), 333–34
god 神 (*kami*), 196, 330, 348. *See also* Shinto
Goken Undō 護憲運動 (Movement to Protect Constitutional Government), 129–30
"good wife, wise mother" 良妻賢母 (*ryōsai kenbo*), ideology of, 337, 339
Government-General 総督府, Korea: nature/power of, 14–15, 115–16, 398; and *isshi dōjin* policy, 121–22, 145; and Korean elites, 123–24, 293; conflict with settlers, 128, 133, 138, 220, 228; compilation of Korean history, 202; economic policies of, 229–30, 247, 256–57, 260; suppression of politics, 265–66; and local elites, 267, 302; on Korean self-rule, 287, 296*n*121; and Manchuria, 316–17, 322, 324; wartime policies of, 355, 378*n*110, 384
Governor-General's rule 総督政治 (*sōtoku seiji*): as "military dictatorship," 5*n*8, 15, 213; and colonial citizenship, 123; critique of, 124–25, 131, 134, 157, 192, 207–8, 213–14, 218
Great Kantō Earthquake, impact in Korea, 164–65, 181, 214, 218, 244, 277, 330
Green Life Movement 緑の生活運動 (*midori no seikatsu undō*), 363–64, 366–68. *See also* Ryokki Renmei
*gumin* 愚民 (foolish commoners), 119, 126

Hagino Yoshiyuki 萩野由之 (1860–1924), 191, 196
Hagitani Kazuo 萩谷籌夫 (1869–1935), 156, 206
Hamaguchi Osachi 浜口雄幸 (1870–1931), 246, 299
*hanbok* 韓服 (Korean traditional dress), 85, 88, 334, 336*n*126, 339, 355
Han, Do-Hyun, 328
Han Man-hŭi 韓萬熙, 292, 317
Han Sang-nyong 韓相龍 (1880–1949), 149, 155, 232–33, 236–39, 258, 294–95, 304, 339–40, 361*n*27, 373*n*82, 380*n*122, 384*n*144
*Hantō no jūgojin* 半島の銃後陣 (The Peninsula's Home Front Group), 373
Hara Takashi 原敬 (1856–1921), 146, 186*n*149, 280
Hasegawa Yoshimichi 長谷川好道 (1850–1924), 136
Hawai'i, 19*n*39, 36, 41, 59
Hayashi Gonsuke 林權助 (1860–1939), 50–52
Hayashi Senjūrō 林銑十郎 (1876–1943), 377
Hayashi Shōzō 林省三, 180–82
hegemony, 5, 11, 16, 30, 84, 106, 147*n*8, 172, 181, 205*n*66, 237, 399
Henry, Todd A., 16, 72*n*140, 328*n*91
Herbst, Jeffrey, 15*n*26, 353
Higashi Honganji 東本願寺 (Eastern Temple of the Original Vow), 39, 55–56
*hikiagesha* 引揚者 (repatriates), from Korea, 3–4, 400–402, Appendix 2
Hiroe Sawajirō, 廣江澤次郎, 38, Appendix 1
*hisenkyoken* 被選挙権 (right to run for office), 273
Hoan Kisoku 保安規則 (Security Regulations), 100
Hōjō Tokiyuki 北条時敬 (1858–1929), Table 5, 166, 168
Hokkaido 北海道, 9, 18*n*34, 37, 59, 120*n*99
Home Ministry (Japan), 89, 301, 378*n*111
homogeneous nation 単一民族国家 (*tan'itsu minzoku kokka*), 117*n*86, 215–16, 395
Honmachi 本町, 71–78, 82, 84, Fig. 1

Hosoi Hajime 細井肇 (1886–1934), 154–55, 162, 165, 189, 191, 193–94, 197, 199, 203, 205–8, 217–18, 222
House of Peers 参議院, Korean appointment to, 278, 282, 296*n*123, 384
House of Representatives 衆議院: settler members of, 273–74; Korean election to, 278–79, 296*n*123, 384
Hozumi Shinrokurō 穂積真六郎 (1889–1970), 283
Hozumi Yatsuka 穂積八束 (1860–1912), 117*n*86, 218
*hyanggyo* 郷校 (county school), Table 5, 160
Hyŏn Yŏng-sŏp 玄永燮 (1907–?), 364–66, 372*n*81, 376, 389

Ichikawa Fusae 市川房枝 (1893–1981), 372
*ikkaku senkin* 一攫千金 (get-rich-quick), 37, 126, 228
Ikeda Chōjirō 池田長次郎 (1878–?), 112*n*62, 292, Appendix 1
*Ilchinhoe* 一進会 (Advancement Society), 103–6, 108–10; annexation campaign of, 111–13, 294, 360; leaders of, 84*n*193, 118, 158, 236, 321; Japanese advisors of, 104, 106 (*see also* Uchida Ryōhei); settler supporters of, 94, 104, 154, 178; former members of, Table 5 (Dōkōkai), 163
Immigration Act, in the United States, 170
Imperial Army, Japanese, 308, 358, 361*n*26, 378, 391. *See also* Chōsen Army
imperial democracy, 129
Imperial Palace, Japanese, 333, 352, 362
Imperial Rule Assistance Association 大政翼賛会 (Taisei Yokusankai), 372
imperial subjecthood, 169, 281, 357, 378, 391
imperialism, 8–9, 30*n*65, 36, 40, 61, 91, 105, 170, 182, 217; Chinese, 44–45; anti-, 169, 216, 218; social, 315, 318; "surrogate," 317
imperialization. *See kōminka*
import tariffs: in Korea, 36, 43, 69, 232, 240–42, 252, 327*n*85; in Manchuria, 323
Inaba Iwakichi 稲葉岩吉 (1876–1940), 204
"in-between." *See* liminality
India, British, 37, 123, 133, 145*n*5, 156*n*38, 193*n*15, 222, 250, 253; Macaulay on, 285
industry control laws, 325, 327*n*85
industrial research committee, 325–26. *See also* Sangyō Chōsa Iinkai
industrialization 産業化 (*sangyōka*) or 工業化 (*kōgyōka*), 234, 252, 260–61, 323*n*68, 325*n*80. *See also* Korean industries
Inoue Kaoru 井上馨 (1836–1915), 40*n*23
Inoue Tetsujirō 井上哲次郎 (1856–1944), 117*n*86
interculturation, 85–87
intermarriage: Japanese promotion of, 170, 242; failure of, 375–76; in Roman Empire, 219; settler rejection of, 377
interpenetration: between state and society, 309, 329; racial, 121*n*103
Inukai Tsuyoshi 犬養毅 (1855–1932), 130, 167
Ireland: British colonization of, 19*n*38, 21*n*46, 59, 66; and Korean rule, 146*n*6, 283–85; and Korean nationalism, 217, 287
irredentism: Korean, 313–14; German, 390
Ishimori Hisaya 石森久彌 (1891–?), 213–14, 224, 320, Appendix 1
*isshi dōjin* 一視同仁 (impartiality and equal favor): etymology of *dōka*, 116; as administrative neutrality 121, 169, 298; settler opposition to, 132, 145; Korean demand for, 162, 279
Itagaki Ryūta 板垣竜太, 16*n*28
Itō Hirobumi 伊藤博文 (1841–1909): as Prime Minister, 53–54, 105; as Resident-General of Korea, 79*n*169, 84*n*193, 98–100, 107, 114, 234; set-

tlers' attack on, 100–103, 130; attitude to reformers, 109–11
Itō Usaburō 伊藤卯三郎 (pen name: Kandō 韓堂), 211
Itsubi Gijuku 乙未義塾, 55, 88

Japanese clubs 日本人会 (*Nihonjinkai*), 69*n*128
Japanese consulate: in Korea, 39; in Kando, 311; police, 38*n*13, 45, 311*n*12, 318
Japanese spirit 日本精神 (*Nihon seishin*) or 日本魂 (*Nihon damashii*), 119, 342–43, 346, 350–51, 359, 362–65, 377, 389
Japanism, 120, 279, 321, 343, 357, 367
Japanization 日本化 (*Nihonka*) or 日本人化 (*Nihonjinka*), 7, 57, 118, 120, 131, 134–35, 144, 148, 184, 197, 333, 342, 356, 360, 370. *See also* assimilation
Jilin 吉林, 314, 316
Jingū, Empress 神功皇后, 196, 204, 377
Jinnai Mokichi 陣内茂吉 (1873–?), 252, 316, Appendix 1
*jinshu* 人種 (race), 117, 170
Jiyū Tōkyūsha 自由討究社 (Freedom Investigation Company), 154
Jōhō Iinkai 情報委員会 (Information Committee), 155–58
Jōhō Gakari 情報係 (Information Section), 157
June Tenth Movement, 183

Kabo reforms, 48, 61*n*106, 84
Kada Naoji 賀田直治 (1877–?), 235, 238, 325, 358, 361*n*27, Appendix 1
*Kaebyŏk* 開闢, 211, 213–14
*kaekchu* 客主 (inland market broker), 42
Kaisharei 会社令 (Company Law), 126, 148, 229–30, 232
Kajimura Hideki 梶村秀樹 (1935–1989), 12
Kajiyama Toshiyuki 梶山季之 (1930–1975), 380
Kakp'a Yuji Yŏnmaeng 各派有志連盟 (League of All Parties of Local Notables), 165
*kalbo* (prostitute), 79
*kan* 官 (officials): boundaries of *min* and, 6, 137, 186; collaboration with *min*, 48; conflict with *min*, 97; "placing officials above the people" (*kanson minpi*), 126. *See also min*
Kanazawa Shōzaburō 金沢庄三郎 (1872–1967), 195
Kando 間道 (Ch. Jiandao), Koreans in, 310–18 *passim*; trade in 322
Kang Pyŏng-ok 康秉鈺 (1880–1928), 289–90
Kanghwa treaty, 36, 43
*Kanjō shinpō* 漢城新報, 49–50, 196
Karashima Takeshi 辛島驍 (1903–1967), 359
Kashii Gentarō 香椎源太郎 (1867–?), 94, 234, 241
Katō Keizaburō 加藤敬三郎 (1873–1939), 322
Katō Takaaki 加藤高明 (1860–1926), 167, 246, 285*n*81
Katsura Tarō 桂太郎 (1848–1913), 101–2, 111, 113
Keijin Fugeki Kumiai 敬神巫覡組合 (Guild of Pious Shamans; alias. Keijin Kyōfūkai 敬神矯風会), 161–62. *See also* shamans
Keijō 京城 (Seoul): colonial city of, 70–76, 248; Ginza of, 73; Shibusawa of, 227
Keijō Imperial University, 341–44, 346*n*172, 365, 368, 377, 381, 410, 412
Keijō Kyoryūmindan 京城居留民団 (Seoul Residents' Association), 71, 136*n*160, 273
*Keijō nippō* 京城日報, 102, 151, 155*n*32, 210, 215–17, 225, 355; attack on Central Council, 290–91; attack on Presbyterians, 350. *See also* Soejima Michimasa; Mitarai Tatsuo
*Keijō shinpō* 京城新報, 100–103, 190–91, 196. *See also* Minegishi Shigetarō
Keijō Shrine 京城神社, 72*n*140, 79–81, 83*n*190, Fig. 2a-b, 332
*kenpeitai* 憲兵隊 (armed police or gendarmerie), 115, 130, 152, 178, 184, 342

Kenseikai 憲政会 (later Minseitō 民政党), 274, 278
Kenya, British: as settler colony, 18–19; settlers in, 20–23, 26*n*63, 66*n*117, 250, 264*n*2, 267*n*9, 274; separation of settlers and natives, 76, 121*n*103, 133; administrators of, 125–26; native bourgeoisie in, 302*n*144
Kija 箕子, 205
Kikuchi Kenjō 菊池謙譲 (1870–1953), 48–52, 57, 94, 113, 130, 149, 358, Appendix 1; as advisor to Saitō, 155, 294, 302; and pro-Japanese organizations, 158, 160, 163; on Koreans, 189, 191–92, 196, 199–200, 204*n*61, 313–14, 321–22
Kim Hong-jip 金弘集 (1842–1896), 48, 56*n*78
Kim Hwal-lan 金活蘭 (1899–1970), 338–39, 361*n*27, 370
Kim Ka-jin 金嘉鎮 (1846–1922), 108
Kim Man-jung 金萬重 (1637–1692), 199
Kim Myŏng-chun 金明濬, 361*n*27, 384*n*144
Kim Sŏng-su 金性洙 (1891–1955), 154, 253, 287, 361*n*27
Kim Tong-myŏng 金東明, 224*n*136, 284*n*75, 293*n*108
Kim Yun-sik 金允植 (1903–1950), 56*n*78, 107, 188, 194*n*18
Kimura Kenji 木村健二, 12, 16*n*29, 47, 376*n*104, 409*n*2, 412
*kisaeng* 妓生 (female Korean entertainer), 79, 82
Kita Sadakichi 喜田貞吉 (1871–1939), 195
Kizokuin 貴族院 (Peerage), 282
Kobayashi Genroku 小林源六 (1867–1940), 1–3, 38–39, 94, 179–80, 249*n*96, 330*n*97, 335, 341*n*150, 346*n*173, 351–52, Appendix 1
Kōchiyama Rakuzō 河内山楽三 (1880–?), 234*n*29, 239*n*56, 249*n*96, Appendix 1
Koezuka Shōta 肥塚正太 (1866–?), 276*n*44, 361*n*27, 362, Appendix 1
Koguryŏ 高句麗, kingdom of, 196, 313
Koiso Kuniaki 小磯国昭 (1880–1950), 369, 377, 385–86
*Kojiki* 古事記, 196
Kōjō Kaikan 向上会館, 177, 179
Kojō Kandō 古城管堂 (1858–1934), 271, Appendix 1
Kojong 高宗, King (after 1897, Emperor) (1852–1919), 46–47, 50–51, 99, 107, 111, 143, 196, 199, 202, 314*n*23
Kōkaisha 黄海社, 244
*kokka* 国家 (state): thought of (*kokkateki shisō*), 109, 215; nationalism (*kokka shugi*), 134, 138, 219; multiethnic, 169, 215; homogeneous, 216; and Korea, 198, 280
Kokubun Shōtarō 国分象太郎, 201
Kokuchūkai 国柱会, 342
*kokumin* 国民 (nation, people, citizen): as "citizen-subjects," 24, 123*n*113, 144*n*5, 378; members of the "Japanese nation," 36, 48, 146; settlers' awareness as, 96, 100, 131–32; nationalization (*kokuminka*), 120, 360; and the Meiji Constitution, 123*n*113, 132*n*144; Japanese perception of Koreans as, 132, 135, 169, 349, 365; and literature, 194, 359; Korean demand for recognition as, 279, 281, 320, 356, 371; assimilation of Koreans as, 356. *See also* Kokumin Seishin Sōdōin Undō
Kokumin Seishin Sakkō Shōsho 国民精神作興証書 (Imperial Rescript on the Promotion of the National Spirit), 330, 332
Kokumin Seishin Sōdōin Chōsen Renmei 国民精神総動員朝鮮連盟 (Korean League for National Spiritual Mobilization), 360–62, 372, 375*n*100
Kokumin Seishin Sōdōin Undō 国民精神総動員運動 (National [or People's] Spiritual Mobilization Campaign), 356, 359–62, 372–77, 391
Kokumin Sōryoku Undō 国民総力運動 (National Total Strength Campaign), 372–73, 387–88
*kokutai* 国体 (national polity), 176, 219,

342, 382; theorists of, 117, 344; promotion of 337*n*129, 342–45, 356, 363–64, 367, 370, 373 (*see also* Ryokki Renmei); and religious cultivation, 347–48, 352
*Kokutai no hongi* 国体の本義 (Principles of the National Polity), 364
Kokuryūkai 黒龍会 (Black Dragon or Amur River Society), 104, 181, 200*n*44, Table 5 (Dōkōkai)
Komagome Takeshi 駒込武, 259
Komine Gensaku 小峰源作, 161, 162*n*57
*kōminka* 皇民化 (imperialization): policies of, 29, 356–57, 360; promotion of Japanese language, 369, 370, 375; promotion of intermarriage, 375–76; extension of military service, 378–80; name-changing campaign, 380–82; extension of conscription and suffrage, 382–86; and *dōka*, 120, 360; as goal of National Spiritual Mobilization Campaign, 360, 362–63; and Ryokki Renmei, 363–73, 380–81; among settler children, 368–69; limits and failure of, 374–77, 393; settlers' response to, 379–90, 392–93. *See also naisen ittai*
Kōminkai 皇民会 (Imperial Subjects' Association), 166, 182
Komura Jutarō 小村寿太郎 (1855–1911), 53–54, 59
Konoe Atsumaro 近衛篤麿 (1863–1904), 51, 56, 59*n*90
Konoe Fumimaro 近衛文麿 (1891–1945), 359–60, 377
Korea Business Club 朝鮮実業倶楽部 (Chōsen Jitsugyō Kurabu), 239–40
"Korea lobby" (or "Korea hands"), in the Diet, 13, 58, 59*n*90, 249–50, 259, 274–75, 279
"Korea-made products," promotion of, 254
Korean assembly, 273, 283, 286*n*85, 291–92, 294–96. *See also* suffrage
Korean court, 46–54, 115, 162, 199
Korean elites: relations with settlers, 7, 17–18, 27–28, 38, 302, 395, 398–99; official effort to co-opt, 123–24, 149, 158–65 *passim*; promotion of *naisen yūwa*, 165–68, 171–77, 184–85; economic cooperation with settlers, 230–33, 240, 246–47, 250, 255–59; inclusion into economic policy-making, 233–40, 325–26; bourgeois nationalism of, 236–37, 239*n*58, 255*n*119, 262, 280–81, 292–93, 304; as collaborators to the state, 263–64, 303; political alliance with settlers, 264, 272–73, 276–77, 279, 297–301, 303–4 (*see also* Zen-Sen Kōshokusha Taikai); demand for suffrage and citizenship, 278–81, 318–21 (*see also* Kungmin Hyŏphoe); political participation of, 124, 149, 266, 268–70, 296, 288–91, 385 (*see also* Central Council); on Korean self-rule, 288, 291–92, 294–95; in the Manchurian venture, 307–8, 317, 319; cooperation with wartime policies, 357, 359–61, 380*n*122; opposition to name-changing, 381
Korean exchange students, 148, 154, 275
Korean industries: as goal of national self-strengthening, 164, 280–81; Dōminkai's promotion of, 168, 172, 174–75, 177, 183; bourgeois campaign for, 228, 240–52, 260 (*see also under* railways); official regulation of, 229, 325, 327*n*85; Saitō's policy on, 228, 230, 260; official-civilian committees on, 228, 233–40, 325–26; and Korean Production Movement, 253–54; and promotion of "Korea-made products," 254–55; and local "economic nationalism," 256–59; Korean industrialization, 234, 252, 260–61, 325*n*80; and suffrage, 273, 275–77; and Manchuria, 326, 353; Ugaki's policy to promote, 323*n*68, 327*n*85
Korean nationalism: rise of, 7, 143–45, 207, 293, 398; Saitō's policy toward, 148, 154; impact on settlers' modus operandi, 27, 153, 264*n*2, 398; Japanese efforts to counter, 155, 157, 169–

72, 201–2; moderate or "cultural" nationalists, 154, 164, 172, 183*n*141, 221–26, 253–55, 280, 284, 287; radicals (socialists and communists), 164, 182–83, 220, 255*n*119, 287, 293, 308, 341, 346, 357; unity between moderates and radicals, 216, 293 (*see also* Sin'ganhoe); of the bourgeoisie, 235–37, 239*n*58, 255*n*119, 262, 280–81, 292–93, 304; the impact of Manchurian invasion on, 318–22; official suppression and demise of, 341, 357–58; Japanese fear of the tenacity of, 320–21, 379–80, 383–84, 386–87, 399. *See also* Aeguk Kyemong Undong; March First Movement

Korean rice, campaign to protect 鮮米擁護運動 (*Senmai yōgo undō*), 256–59

Korean royal household, 51, 57, 192, 234

"Korean stagnation," theory on 朝鮮停滞論 (*Chōsen teitairon*), 197–98

Korean studies 朝鮮研究 (*Chōsen kenkyū*), 154, 189–90. *See also* Chōsen Kenkyūkai; colonial archive

"Korean-centered(ness)" 朝鮮人本位 (*Chōsenjin hon'i*), 152, 236, 255*n*119, 262, 294

"Koreanization," settler fear of, 87–90, 134–35

Kōshi Club 甲子俱楽部: suffrage campaign, 276–83, 295–96, 303, Table 5; conflict with Korean views, 288, 292–93; opposition to Colonial Ministry, 298–302 *passim*; and Manchuria, 307, 311, 319

Kugimoto Tōjirō 釘本藤次郎 (1868–1933), 88, 134, 238, 244, 248, 346*n*173, Appendix 1

Kungmin Hyŏphoe 国民協会 (People's Association), Table 5; leaders of, 167–68, 211; and assimilation campaign, 184, 293; suffrage campaign, 278–81, 284, 297*n*123, 321–22, 385; and nationalism, 294; opposition to Colonial Ministry, 297–302 *passim*; and moral suasion, 335

Kuroita Katsumi 黒板勝美 (1874–1946), 176

Ku Wan-hŭi 具完喜, 51

Kwangju student demonstrations, 176, 315

Kwantung Army 関東軍, 307, 310, 312–13, 317

*kyōson kyōei* 共存共栄 (coexistence and coprosperity), 171, 181, 237, 330

laws, in colonial Korea: on landownership, 61–62; overall administration of, 121–23; issued by Governor-General, 116, 131, 135, 341*nn*149–52, 365 (*see also* Kaisharei); and family registration, 122, 132, 384*n*143; based on principle of residence (属地法 *zokuchi-hō*), 121*n*105, 122, 273, 384; based on principle of the person or nationality (属人法 *zokujin-hō*), 121*n*105, 273; and nationality, 121*n*105, 122, 132; and colonial citizenship, 122–23, 144*n*5; and metropolitan laws, 121–23, 144*n*5, 147, 277–78, 282, 325, 327*n*85; revision of, 378, 384*n*143

Lee, Helen, 16*n*29, 87*n*208

Lenin, 9; -ism, 217

life improvement 生活改善 (*seikatsu kaizen*), 332–33, 336–40. *See also* colored clothing

liminality, 25, 29, 90, 98, 132, 138–39, 185, 200, 261, 301, 316, 321, 344, 353, 357, 367, 392, 395, 401

Lo, Ming Cheng, 25*n*62

local autonomy 地方自治 (*chihō jichi*): in Japan, 68, 109, 128–29; of settlers in Korea, 21, 100, 128–29, 252, 272; demand for Korea's, 264, 271–73, 276, 285. *See also* self-rule; suffrage; Zen-Sen Kōshokusha Taikai

"local economic nationalism," 252–59, 256*n*122. *See also* Korean rice, campaign to protect

Lustick, Ian, 21

Machida Kōsaku 町田耕作 (pen name: 天民 Tenmin), 286

Maeda Noboru 前田昇 (1873–?), 330, 361*n*27, Appendix 1
*Maeil sinbo* 每日申報, 166, 190, 202, 210, 357
Makiyama Kōzō 牧山耕蔵 (1882–1961), 124, 182*n*134, 249, 273–75, 279, Appendix 1
Mamdani, Mahmood, 24*n*56, 123*n*112
Manchukuo 満州国, 2, 160*n*50, 169, 186, 308, 313–18, 323, 325–26, 366, 368, 383
Manchuria: Japan's conflict with Russia over, 1, 9, 50, 58; Korean migrants in, 28, 62, 241, 310–18; Japanese emigration to, 59, 60*n*97; Korean political activities in, 155, 311; and settlers' activities and influence in, 177, 202, 232, 322–27, 366; Korean irredentism in, 196, 313–14; as joint Japanese-Korean venture, 308, 315–19; Korea's trade with, 256, 322–26; Japanese repatriates from, 401. *See also* South Manchurian Railway Company
Manchurian Incident, 11, 308, 310, 321, 342*n*156, 357; impact on Korean *tenkō*, 318*n*41, 341*n*149, 357
Mansenshi 満鮮史 (Manchuria-Korea history), 313
March First Movement: as turning point in empire, 11, 15, 143–44, 265, 268, 398; causes for, 150–52; settlers' responses to, 152–53, 168*n*80, 178, 186, 391, 402; and discourse on Koreans, 188–89, 206, 384; and Korean elites, 281, 291; and Ch'ŏndogyo, 357*n*7. *See also* Korean nationalism
Maruyama Tsurukichi 丸山鶴吉 (1883–1956), 152, 166, 181, 235–36, 253–54
Matsuda Toshihiko 松田利彦, 280, 296*n*121
Matsui Fusajirō 松井房次郎, 257–58
Matsuyama Tsunejirō 松山常次郎 (1884–1961), 235, 244, 274, 277–79, 282
Megata Tanetarō 目賀田種太郎 (1853–1926), 192
Meiji Constitution, 123, 132*nn*144–45, 390
Meiji Emperor, 131, 204*n*63, 298, 335, 349, 352
Memmi, Albert, 7
"men on the spot," 26, 47–52, 200. *See also* subimperialists
middle ground, 153, 217, 220–26 *passim*, 400
migrants, Japanese in Korea: government support for, 9, 41, 59; as trailblazers, 36–39, 58, Map 1; journalists and *rōnin*, 45, 49–50, 100–103, 111–14; Buddhists, 39–40, 56; prostitutes and geisha, 38, 39, 66*n*119, 70, 72*n*138, 78–79, 82, 184; merchants, 40–47, 52–54; teachers, 55–58; farmers, 59–61, 209; land grab and settlement of, 61–64; official regulation of, 100–101, 125–27; fall in the number of, 144; Korean criticism of, 235, 237–38; settlers' call for more, 238, 241, 315; comparison with Koreans in Manchuria, 314–15. *See also* settlers, Japanese in Korea
migrants, Japanese in the United States, 36, 41, 59, 170
Mikami Sanji 三上参次 (1865–1939), 191
military rule 武断政治 (*budan seiji*), 12, 115–16, 134, 137, 148, 157, 189, 210, 213–14
*Mimana* 任那, 89, 196, 204, 284
*min* 民 (civilians or people): and *kan*, 6, 48, 97, 137, 186; commoners (*shomin*), 4; "foolish commoners" (*gumin*), 119, 126. *See also kan*
Min Wŏn-sik 閔元植 (1887–1921), Table 5, 279
Minami Jirō 南次郎 (1874–1955), 29, 325*n*79; and *shinden kaihatsu*, 352–53; and *naisen ittai* policy, 355, 357–58, 361–62, 370*n*74, 375, 381, 387, 391. *See also kōminka*
Minegishi Shigetarō 峰岸繁太郎, 100–102, 112, 114, 190

*mindo* 民度 (cultural level), 21, 119, 122, 128, 201, 296*n*121
*min'i chōtatsu* 民意調達 ("solicit public opinion"), 149–50, 186, 267. *See also* cultural rule
*minjok* 民族 (K. ethnic group or ethnos), Korean, 138, 161, 205, 212, 280, 313–14, 322; consciousness, 215; interests, 236; bourgeoisie, 237*n*47; rights, 255*n*119; Puyŏ, 314
*minzoku* 民族 (J. ethnic group or ethnos): Japanese/Yamato, 100, 135, 181, 204, 218, 313–14, 316, 343, 356, 364, 366, 377, 382–83; definition of, 117, 201*n*48; *kongō* (mixed), 117, 377; and Meiji Constitution, 132*n*144; ethnic nationalism, 138, 219; Asian, 168, 321; as states, 169, 215, 216, 286; Korean, 189, 201, 207, 211, 314, 316, 322; relations of Japanese and Korean, 195, 197–98, 223, 286; and *kokutai,* 219
Mitarai Tatsuo 御手洗辰雄 (1895–1975), 359, 377
Miura Gorō 三浦梧楼 (1847–1926), 48–50. *See also* Queen Min
Miyakawa Gorōsaburō 宮川五郎三郎, 207–8
Miyata Setsuko 宮田節子, 378
Miyazaki Tōten 宮崎滔天 (1871–1922), 108
Mizuno Rentarō 水野錬太郎 (1868–1949), 154*n*29, 156, 267*n*12
Moon, Yumi, 104, 112*n*63
moral suasion 教化 (*kyōka*), campaign, 28, 309, 327–54; promotion of colored clothing, 2, 332–39 *passim*, 376; and women, 336–40; and youth, 340–46; and *shinden kaihatsu* (religious cultivation), 348–53; as basis for war mobilization, 354, 356, 365. *See also* colonial corporatism
Morita Yoshio 森田芳夫 (1910–1992), 343–44, 368–69, 373
Morris-Suzuki, Tessa, 123, 364
Mozambique, Portuguese, 20*n*44, 66*n*117
Mukden 奉天 (Fengtian), 323–24
multiethnic state 混合民族国家 (*kongō minzoku kokka*): Korea as, 169, 178, 181–82, 185–86, 318, 378*n*111; in the world, 215–16
multiethnic empire, Japan as, 29, 364, 395, 400*n*5
Muramatsu Takeshi 村松武司 (1924–1993), 400
Murayama Chijun 村山智順 (1891–1968), 161*n*53, 202*n*55, 367*n*57
Mutō Nobuyoshi 武藤信義 (1868–1933), 313
Mutsu Munemitsu 睦奥宗光 (1844–1897), 45–46
Myŏngsin Women's School (later Sungmyŏng Women's Higher Ordinary School), 57

Nagamori plan, 59
Nagashima Hiroki 永島広紀, 342*n*156, 367*n*57, 368*n*63
*naichi enchō* 内地延長 (extending the mainland): policy of, 21, 146–47, 222, 247, 277; and pro-government organizations, Table 5, 276–80 *passim*; and Korean industrialization, 241; and suffrage, 264, 281*n*65, 283–87, 295–96; Korean rejection of, 292, 294, 304; as rationale for opposition to Colonial Ministry, 297–300. *See also* assimilation, Japanese policy of
*naisen ittai* 内鮮一体 (unity between Japan and Korea): wartime policy of, 12, 29, 355–60, 390–91; ideologues of, 321*n*59, 363–73, 386; success and limits of, 374–77, 379–80; name change as a means of, 381; Korean interpretation of, 386–87, 399; settler resistance to, 387–90, 392–93. *See also kōminka*; Ryokki Renmei
*naisen yūwa* 内鮮融和 (harmony between Japanese and Koreans): ideology of, 2, 27, 224, 238, 277; as framework for colonial citizenship, 144–45, 148, 185; as Saitō's policy of assimilation, 144–48, 185–86, 230, 242; campaign for, 165–77, 220; and vision of multieth-

nic Korea, 169, 178, 181, 185–86; grassroots agents of, 177–82, 356; limits of, 182–85; rhetorical appropriation of, 209, 217; and Korean organizations, 291, 298, 302; impact of Manchuria on, 315, 319; as precursor to *naisen ittai*, 360*n*23, 365, 376. *See also* assimilation, Japanese policy of; Dōminkai
Nakai Kitarō 中井喜太郎 (1864–1924), 59*n*90, 71
Nakamura Kentarō 中村健太郎 (1883–?), 166, 179, 204*n*61, 330, Fig. 5, Appendix 1
Nakamura Saizō 中村再蔵 (1855–?), 92, Appendix 1
Nakanishi Inosuke 中西伊之助 (1887–1958), 182
Namch'on 南村 ("South Village"), 72
name-changing 創氏改名 (*sōshi kaimei*), campaign, 29, 378, 380–82
Namiki Masato 並木正人, 175, 293
Namsan 南山 (South Mountain), 38, 71, 73, 82, 178
Narimatsu Midori 成松緑 (1880–?), 245, 276*n*44, Appendix 1
national defense, 31, 249, 286, 325, 358–39; funds, 332, 374; -state, 371
National Foundation Day, 342–43
National Learning 国学 (*kokugaku*), 367
national spirit 国民精神 (*kokumin seishin*): promotion of, 309, 331–32, 349; Imperial Rescript on, 330; National Spirit Promotion Week, 332–33, 348, 352–53; through Shintō worship, 352. *See also* Kokumin Seishin Sōdōin Undō
nationalism: state, 138, 219; ethnic, 138, 219, 237*n*47, 321, 399; anti-colonial, 169, 170, 262; debate on, 215–16; economic, 228, 253; bourgeois, 237*n*47; "local economic," 256–59. *See also* Korean nationalism
nationalization 国民化 (*kokuminka*), 120, 360
Natsume Sōseki 夏目漱石 (1867–1916), 102
Nazi Germany, 17*n*31, 368, 377, 390
"new women," Korean, 338–40, 370–71
New Order, in East Asia, 360, 368, 371, 372*n*80
*Nihon shoki* 日本書紀, 196, 208
Nishimura Yasukichi 西村保吉 (1865–1942), 234*n*29, 246, 261
Nishizaki Tsurukichi 西崎鶴吉, 94
*Nissen dōsoron* 日鮮同祖論 (theory on shared ancestry of Japanese and Koreans), 117, 161*n*53, 195, 224, 377
Niwa Seijirō 丹羽清次郎 (1865–1957), 156, 348, 350, 359, 361*n*27, Appendix 1
Nogi Maresuke 乃木希典 (1849–1912), 178
Noguchi Shitagau 野口遵 (1873–1944), 323*n*68

"Oath as Subjects of the Imperial Nation" 皇国臣民ノ誓詞 (*kōkoku shinmin no seishi*), 362, 374, 393
Oda Shōgo 小田省吾 (1871–?), 191, 208
Odaka Tomoo 尾高朝雄 (1899–1956), 373
Ōgaki Takeo 大垣丈夫 (1862–1929), 91, 97–98, 191*n*11, 208, 249*n*96, Appendix 1; as advisor to Taehan Chagang-hoe, 105–14; collaboration with Saitō's regime, 155–56, 158–64, 187, 206; as leader of Kōshi Club, 276, 278; on Korean self-rule, 284–86
Ōi Kentarō 大井憲太郎 (1843–1922), 108*n*46
Ōike Chūsuke 大池忠助 (1856–1930), 78, 94
Okamoto Ryūnosuke 岡本柳之助 (1852–1912), 45–46, 48–49
Ōkawa Shūmei 大川周明 (1886–1957), 176
Okinawa, 18*n*34, 120*n*99, 136*n*157, 146, 186*n*149, 314, 378
Oku Mumeo 奥むめお (1895–1997), 372
Ōkubo Masatoshi 大久保真敏, 351
Okumura Enshin 奥村円心 (1843–1913), 56

Okumura Ioko 奥村五百子 (1845–1907), 56–57
Ōkura Kihachirō 大倉喜八郎 (1837–1928), 40
Ōmiwa Chōbee 大三輪長兵衛 (1835–1908), 53
Ōmura Momozō 大村百蔵 (1872–?), 247*n*87, 275, 276*n*44, 288–89, Appendix 1
Ōmura Takuichi 大村卓一 (1872–1946), 248–49
Ōmura Tomonojō 大村友之丞 (1871–?), 89, 135–36, 246, 247*n*87, Appendix 1
Ōno Rokuichirō 大野緑一郎 (1887–1985), 361
organic regulations 官制 (*kansei*), of the Governor-General of Korea, 297, 299
Oriental Development Company (ODC) 東洋拓殖会社 (Tōyō Takushoku Kaisha): farm colonization program, 11*n*19, 59–60, 126; as money lender, 62; criticism of, 102, 151, 209, 222, 235; as agent of state economic projects, 231–33, 246, 317
Orientalism, 206

Pai, Hyung Il, 189, 201*n*47
Pak Che-sun 朴齊純 (1858–1916), 50–51
Pak Ch'un-gŭm 朴春琴 (1891–1973), 296, 296*n*123, 320
Pak Chung-yang 朴重陽 (1874–1955), 384*n*144
Pak Hŭng-sik 朴興植 (1903–1994), 237*n*47, 325, 341*n*150, 361*n*27
Pak In-tŏk 朴仁德 (1896–1980), 344–45
Pak Sang-hŭi 朴尚僖, 288–89
Pak Sŭng-ŏk 朴承億, 322*n*65
Pak Ŭn-sik 朴殷植 (1859–1925), 107, 201
Pak Yŏng-ch'ŏl 朴栄喆 (1879–1939), 298, 301, 361*n*27
Pak Yŏng-hyo 朴泳孝 (1861–1939), 201, 223, 235, 296
Pan-Asianism: and Korean reform, 104, 106, 108, 321; advocates of, 108, 166, 171, 176, 181; and *naisen yūwa*, 27, 145, 170–71, 178; and Manchuria, 315, 316*n*30
"parallel development of agriculture and manufacturing" 農工並進 (*nōkō heishin*), 247
Park, Hyun Ok, 316, 318*n*43
"party of twenty" 二十年党 (*nijūnen-tō*), 94*n*232, 276
patriotic neighborhood associations 愛国班 (J. *aikokuhan*; K. *aegukpan*), 361–62, 373, 376; heads of, 362, 374, 379–80, 388
Peace Preservation Law, 122, 341*n*149
Peattie, Mark R., 11–12
*pieds noirs*, 20, 37*n*6. *See also* Algeria; *colons*
pleasure quarters 遊郭 (*yūkaku*), 71, 77–79
*pobusang* 褓負商 ("pack and back" peddlers), 162–63
political merger 政合邦 (*seigappō*), 108, 112–13, 321
press: as instrument of settler colonialism, 13, 26–27, 98, 100–103, 114, 117, 125–26, 210–11, 266, 285–86, 290, 295; censorship, 100, 129, 134, 148, 190–91, 207, 210, 214, 220–22, 358; as vanguard of Korean nationalism, 112, 164–65, 207–10, 224–25, 235, 239, 280, 308, 320; as medium of dialogue between settlers and Koreans, 207–17; portrayal of Koreans in Manchuria, 310–13
Prochaska, David, 72*n*141, 83*n*186, 87
pro-government or "pro-Japanese" organizations, 27, 158–66, Table 5, 168, 183–84, 211, 293, 297–98, 330, 358–59, 361*n*26
prostitutes, 3, 37–39, 70, 72*n*138, 79, 372
protectorate rule, 10, 58, 98–103, 106, 108–11, 114, 286. *See also* Itō Hirobumi
province 道 (J. *dō*; K. *tong*): councils 道協議会, 27, 177, 267, 269–71,

Fig. 11, 288–90, 303; assembly 道会, 258, 296*n*122, 319, 380*n*122
public officials 公職者 (*kōshokusha*), Table 3, 128, 272, 276, 281, 411; Korean, 168, 288–89, 291, 293–94, 296, 360*n*21, 379. *See also* Zen-Sen Kōshokusha Taikai
Pukch'on 北村 ("North Village"), 72

Qing dynasty, 10, 41, 310. *See also* China
Queen Min 閔妃 (1851–1895): assassination of, 48–50, 55, 56*n*78, 94, 166; contest with the Taewŏn'gun, 199–200

railways, in Korea: Japanese construction of, 40, 115; Korean concessions for, 48, 52–54; settlers' lobbying for, 52–54, 69, 228, 234–35, 238, 240–52 *passim*, 261, 275; and growth of settler communities, 64, 70, 92–93, 243; bureau of, 168, 248, 381; Korean Railways, 244, 248; in Manchuria, 310, 312, 317, 325. *See also* South Manchurian Railway Company
"recalcitrant Koreans" 不逞鮮人 (*futei Senjin*), 150, 161, 207, 210, 286
religious devotion 信仰心 (*shinkōshin*), 309, 330, 347, 351
repatriates. *See hikiagesha*
residents' associations 居留民団 (*kyoryūmindan*), 69–70, 128–29, 266, 271
Rhodes, Cecil (1853–1902), 41, 132
Rikken Seiyūkai 立憲政友会, 102, 109*n*50, 110, 129, 182*n*133, 273–74, 279, 297
*risshin shusse* 立身出世 (rising in the world), 37
Risshō Academy 立正学院, 178
Robinson, Michael E., 15, 147*n*8, 164, 221–22, 255*n*119
Roman Empire, 218–19
Ronald Robinson, 263*n*1
*rōnin* 浪人 (adventure-seekers), 37, 45–46, 49–51, 91, 95, 110–11, 167, 178, 181, 303
Rural Revitalization Campaign 農村振興運動, 259*n*140, 331, 346, 360
Russia, Tsarist, 9, 41, 44, 47–48, 50–51, 53, 56, 314
Russo-Japanese War, 1, 44, 171, 178, 307; settlers' support for, 10, 41, 46, 124, 337; impact on migration, 42, 46–47, 55, 58, 61–62, 68*n*123, 80, 92–93, 99; and railways, 54; aftermath of, 91, 97–98; and Manchuria, 312
Ryokki Renmei 緑旗連盟 (Green Flag League): and moral suasion, 332, 337, 348; students' section, 343–46; Seiwa Women's Academy, 344–45; women's section, 345, 369–72; as ideologue of *naisen ittai*, 355–56, 358–59, 363–73, 375, 377; and name-changing campaign, 380–81; Korean members of, 365–66, 386, 389–90

*sadae* 事大 ("serving the great"), Japanese discourse on, 198–99, 204–5, 217, 384
Said, Edward W., 188*n*2, 206
Saigō Takamori 西郷隆盛 (1828–1877), 37
Saionji Kinmochi 西園寺公望 (1849–1940), 102
Saitō Hisatarō 斉藤久太郎 (1874–?), 257, 259, Appendix 1
Saitō Makoto 斎藤実 (1858–1936), 27, 144–55, 157, 160, 165–66, 186, 189, 207; economic policy of, 228, 230, 233; local political reform by, 267–70; on Korean suffrage and self-rule, 285, 295–96, 304; opposition to Colonial Ministry, 297, 299–300; as Prime Minister, 274, 308*n*4. *See also* cultural rule; *naisen yūwa*
Sakatani Yoshirō 阪谷芳郎 (1863–1941), 249, 299
*Samguk sagi* 三国史記 (History of the Three Kingdoms), 208
Sangmusa 商務社 (Commercial Affairs Company), 163
Sangyō Chōsa Iinkai 産業調査委員会 (Industrial Commission), 228, 233–40,

242, 244, 255*n*119, 262, 325. *See also* industrial research committee
Sasa Masayuki 佐々正之 (1862–1928), 166
Sasa Tomofusa 佐々友房 (1854–1906), 166
Sase Kumatetsu 佐瀬熊鐵 (1866–1929), 104, Appendix 1
*Sassi namjŏnggi* 謝氏南征記 (Record of Lady Sa's Journey to the South), 199
Satō Torajirō 佐藤虎次郎 (1864–1928), 166–67, 182, 284–85, Fig. 5, Appendix 1
Satomi Kishio 里見岸雄 (1897–1974), 342*n*156, 344*n*162, 367*n*57
Satoyoshi Motoki 里吉基樹, 385
Satsuma-Chōshū clique, 129–30, 213
Sawai Mariko 沢井真理子, 344, 402*n*13
Schmid, Andre, 120*n*100, 196, 204–5, 222*n*130
school board, 268, 272
Scotland, 19*n*38, 284–85
*Seikanron* 征韓論 ("conquest of Korea" debates), 96
Seimu 成務, Emperor (legendary 13th emperor of Japan), 284
Seiwa Onna Juku 清和女塾 (Seiwa Women's Academy). *See under* Ryokki Renmei
Seiyūkai. *See* Rikken Seiyūkai
Sekiya Teisaburō 関谷貞三郎 (1875–1950), 118–19
self-reliance 自力更生 (*jiriki kōsei*), 331, 338, 348
self-rule 自治 (*jichi*): Itō's policy of Korean, 98–100; end of Japanese settler, 128–29, 265, 283; in European empires, 146, 265, 284, 390; settler views on Korean, 223, 283–87, 295*n*118; Korean demands for, 264, 266, 271, 287, 320; Korean elite support for, 288, 292–95; official views on Korean, 296, 304. *See also* local autonomy; suffrage; Zen-Sen Kōshokusha Taikai
self-strengthening 実力養成 (*jitsuryoku yōsei*): in late Chosŏn Korea, 93, 103–4 (*see also* Aeguk Kyemong Undong); Japanese appropriation of, 145, 155, 172, 209–10, 217, 254; as mutual emphasis of capitalists and nationalists, 255*n*119, 280–81
*senkyoken* 選挙権 (right to vote), 273
Senmai Kyōkai 鮮米協会 (Korean Rice Association), 256, 257*n*131
Senmai Yōgo Kiseikai 鮮米擁護期成会 (Society for the Protection of Korean Rice), 257–59
Senshinkai 洗心会 (Washing-Minds Society), 178
Seoul Chamber of Commerce 京城商業会議所 (after 1930, Seoul Chamber of Commerce and Industry 京城商工会議所), 74*n*146, 152, 275; leaders of, 89, 135, 232*n*17, 244, 316, 358
Seoul City Council 京城府協議会, 268*n*18, 272, 283, 292
Seoul City Assembly 京城府会, 179, 389
*Seoul Press*, 156
settler colonialism: in British white dominions, 18; in Africa, 18–19; Israel as a form of, 18*n*35; in Hawai'i, 19*n*39; in Korea, 25–29, 250, 394, 396, 398, 400–402. *See also under settlers*
settler colonies. *See under* Africa
settlers, in Africa: power of, 7, 21–24, 123, 151, 264*n*2, 385, 389*n*162; and the state, 13*n*23, 15*n*26, 17*n*31, 21–23; social composition of, 20, 65–66*n*117; and natives, 20–21, 24, 83, 88, 124, 231, 264*n*2, 385. *See also* Algeria; *colons*; Kenya; South Africa; Southern Rhodesia
settlers, Japanese in Korea: population and social composition of, 3, 20, 64–67, Map 2, Tables 1–4; and the colonial state, 10–15, 23, 25, 91, 94, 115, 137–38, 396–97 (*see also under* collaboration); and Korean elites (*see under* collaboration); comparison with settlers in Africa, 19–25; mentality of,

20–21, 47, 93, 95, 139, 227–28; opposition to Korean policy, 21–22, 99–103, 114, 124–27, 132–34; attitudes toward the metropole, 21, 264, 284, 301, 304, 397; economic and political power of, 22–25, 228–29, 265–66, 268–70, 273; legal ambiguity of, 24–25, 122–23, 273; women, 56–57, 77, 86, 310, 337–38, 344–45, 359, 369–72, 383, 388; institutions of self-government, 68–70; Seoul as a city of, 70–76; everyday life and culture of, 76–87; education of Korea-born, 71, 88, 90, 342–44, 369; discrimination against Koreans, 83, 85, 151, 171, 184, 301, 389–90; anxiety about assimilation, 87–90, 134–35, 377–78, 382, 395; debates on *dōka*, 117–20; struggle for autonomy and citizenship, 127–32, 136–39; response to March First Movement, 143–44, 150–53; ambivalent cooperation with wartime policies, 357, 376–90, 392–93. *See also* brokers of empire; migrants, Japanese in Korea

Shakuo Shunjō 釋尾春芿 (1875–?): on Koreans, 119–20, 191, 194, 197, 205, 222, 320, 322; on Governor-General's rule, 130–36, 267; and Song Chin-u, 220–22, 225–26; and Central Korea Association, 249*n*96; on suffrage and self-rule, 282, 286; on migration in Manchuria, 315; on moral suasion, 330*n*97, 331*n*100, 349; departure from media, 358

shamans (K. *mudang* 巫堂, J. *fugeki* 巫覡), regulation of, 160–62, 347*n*182

Shibukawa Genji 渋川玄耳 (1872–1926), 102

Shibusawa Eiichi 渋沢栄一 (1840–1931), 40, 59, 167, 233, 249–50; Korea's "Shibusawa," 227, 233

Shidehara Taira 幣原坦 (1870–1953), 191

Shiki Shintarō 志岐信太郎 (1869–?), 241, 247, Appendix 1

Shimada Saburō 島田三郎 (1852–1923), 285

Shimooka Chūji 下岡忠治 (1870–1925), 176, 242*n*70, 246–48, 250, 254

Shin, Gi-Wook, 15, 147*n*8, 328

Shin Tatsuma 進辰馬 (1868–?), 54, 84, Appendix 1

*shinden kaihatsu* 心田開発 (religious cultivation). *See under* moral suasion

Shinmachi 新町, 72, 78–79

*shinmin* 臣民 ("subjects of the monarch" or imperial subjects): and assimilation, 115, 119, 169, 218, 326, 356; distinction from "Japanese," 131–32, 319; and Meiji Constitution, 123*n*113, 132*n*144, 138; Japanese settlers as, 124, 368–69; official treatment of Japanese and Koreans as equal, 135–36, 299; and *naisen ittai*, 362, 366, 371, 375, 383, 387. *See also kōminka*

*Shinmin no michi* 臣民の道 (The Way of the Imperial Subject), 364

Shinto: state, 39, 364; shrines, 69, 77, 79, 90, 310, Table 3; and Korean assimilation, 83, 268; and shamanism, 161; and *kōminka*, 325–26, 333, 362, 374, 379–80; and *shinden kaihatsu*, 346, 349–52

Shiobara Tokisaburō 塩原時三郎 (1896–1964), 361, 369

*shishi* 志士 ("loyalist" or "patriot"), 54, 105, 221*n*127

Shōdōkai 昭道会, 341

Shōmu Kenkyūkai 商務研究会 (Commercial Affairs Research Association), 162–63

*Sidae ilbo* 時代日報, 207

Silla 新羅, 196, 284, 379

Sin Ch'ae-ho 申采浩 (1880–1936), 204, 212*n*98, 237, 313

Sin Sŏng-nin 申錫麟 (1865–?), 166–67, 348, Fig. 5

Sin Ŭng-hŭi 申應熙 (1859–1928), 276*n*44

Sin'ganhoe 新幹会, 216*n*117, 220*n*126, 293, 333*n*109

Sino-Japanese War: First (1894–95), 44, 55, 92, 104; Second (1937–1945), 28, 323, 325

"Six Great Points (for Korean Industrial Development)" 朝鮮産業発達六大要項, 252
Sŏ Ch'un 徐椿 (1894–1943), 389
Sōaikai 相愛会 (Mutual Love Association), Korean branch, Table 5, 167*n*78, 296
Sŏbuk Hakhoe 西北学会 (Northwest Educational Association), 103–4, 111–12, 321
Social Darwinism, idea of, 168, 198, 205, 364
social imperialism, 315, 318
social work 社会事業 (*shakai jigyō*): as medium of settler colonialism, 3, 26, 145, 153, 172, 184*n*142, 333; and moral suasion, 328–33 *passim*
*sŏdang* 書堂 (private elementary school), 174
Soejima Michimasa 副島道正 (1871–1948), 285–87
sojourners 出稼人 (*dekaseginin*), 10, 37–38, 91, 95, 128
Sŏk Chin-hyŏng 石鎮衡 (1877–1946), 290
Son Ch'i-ŭn 孫致殷, 292
Son Chŏng-gyu 孫貞圭 (1896–1950), 338, 361*n*27, 370–71
Sone Arasuke 曾禰荒助 (1849–1910), 111–13
Song Chin-u 宋鎮禹 (1890–1945), 210, 212, 220–22, 287
Song Pyŏng-jun 宋秉畯 (1857–1925), 84*n*193, 104, 113*n*68, 118, 158, Table 5, 233, 236, 282
Song Tal-byŏng 宋達燮, 184–85
South Africa, 15*n*26, 18, 19*n*37, 20*n*43, 22, 24, 66*n*117, 123*n*112
South Manchurian Railway Company (SMRC) 南満州鉄道株式会社, 248, 259*n*141, 317, 323, 325
Southern Rhodesia, 13*n*23, 19*n*37, 20–23, 65*n*117, 76, 264*n*2
state nationalism 国家主義 (*kokka shugi*), 138, 219
subaltern, Japanese settlers as, 24–25, 36, 93, 286, 301, 389. *See also* liminality
subimperialists, Japanese settlers as, 26, 44, 114, 395
suffrage: denial to settlers in Korea, 24, 122–23, 273; joint settler-Korean campaign for, 264, 276–79; settlers' advocacy of, 275–78; Korean campaign for, 278–81, 301, 319; settler anxiety about Korean demand for, 281, 294, 321–22, 382–83, 386–87; Japan's universal male, 278–79, 282; settler debates on, 281–87; disagreements between settlers and Koreans over, 289, 292, 303–4; Saitō's opinion on, 295–96; official promise of limited, 384–86. *See also* citizenship; Kōshi Club; Kungmin Hyŏphoe; self-rule; Zen-Sen Kōshokusha Taikai
Sugi Ichirobei 杉一郎平 (1870–?), 178–79, Appendix 1
Sugimura Fukashi 杉村濬 (1848–1906), 46
Sukchong 肅宗, King (1661–1720), 199
Sunjong 純宗, Emperor (1874–1926), 111, 182, 199, 202
Susano-o (no mikoto) 素戔嗚尊 (younger brother of the sun goddess Amaterasu), 196, 204*n*63

Tada Eikichi 多田栄吉 (1879–?), 257
Taedong Samunhoe 大東斯文会 (Great Eastern Way Society), Table 5, 160
Taehan Chaganghoe 大韓自強会 (Great Korea Self-Strengthening Association), 103, 105, 107–10. *See also* Taehan Hyŏphoe
Taehan Hyŏphoe 大韓協会 (Great Korea Association), 105*n*28, 107–13. *See also* Taehan Chaganghoe
*Taehan Maeil sinbo* 大韓毎日申報, 103, 190
Taewŏn'gun 大院君 (1821–1898), 46, 48–50, 56, 199–200, 208
Tagawa Tsunejirō 田川常次郎 (1884–?), 245, Appendix 1
Taishō Shinbokukai 大正親睦会 (Taishō Friendship Society), 158, 168*n*79, 298, Table 5

Taiwan: colonization of, 30*n*66, 36, 66, 118*n*92; Korean Studies and, 195, 202; assimilation policy in, 120*n*99, 132, 146; Japanese residents in, 132, 157, 314; economy, 230, 241, 256, 258; and suffrage, 122, 283, 285, 384; vis-à-vis Korea, 299; and East Asian community, 366; amalgamation into metropole, 378*n*111
Takahashi Shōnosuke 高橋章之助 (1864–?), 104, 276, Appendix 1
Takahashi Tōru 高橋亨 (1878–1967), 191
Takasaki Sōji 高崎宗司, 12, 412
Takashima Heizaburō 高島平三郎 (1865–1946), 169
Takayama Takayuki 高山孝之 (1882–?), 182–83, Appendix 1
Takekoshi Yosaburō 竹越与三郎 (1865–1950), 58–59
Takushokushō Kansei Hantai Dōmeikai 拓殖省官制反対同盟会 (Alliance for Opposition to the Organic Regulations on the Colonial Ministry), 298–302
Tanaka Chigaku 田中智学 (1861–1939), 342*n*156, 367
Tanaka Giichi 田中義一 (1864–1929), 296*n*121, 297; "Tanaka plan," 297–302 (*see also* Colonization, Ministry of)
Tan'gun 檀君, 195, 205, 211–12
Tarui Tōkichi 樽井藤吉 (1850–1922), 106
Teikoku Tetsudō Kyōkai 帝国鉄道協会 (Imperial Railway Association), 249
*tenkō* 転向 (ideological conversion or apostasy), 318*n*41, 341, 346, 357–58, 361, 363, 365
Terao Mōzaburō 寺尾猛三郎 (1870–?), 276*n*44, Appendix 1
Terauchi Masatake 寺内正毅 (1852–1919): as War Minister, 53, 113; military rule, 26, 115–16, 190–91, 201–2, 210, 267; and assimilation (*isshi dōjin*) policy, 116, 121–24; regulation of migrants, 125–27; abolition of settlers' self-government, 128–29, 266, 276; and Satsuma-Chōshū clique, 129–30; criticism of, 130–34, 136, 150, 213–14
thought guidance 思想善導 (*shisō zendō*), 153, 168, 174, 328, 330, 337
Three Kingdoms period (57 BCE–668 CE), 194, 208
Tōa Dōbunkai 東亜同文会 (East Asia Common Culture Society), 51, 55, 59*n*90
Tōa Kyōshōkai 東亜共昌会 (East Asian Coprosperity Society), 178
Tōgō Minoru 東郷実 (1881–1959), 58
Tokutomi Sohō 徳富蘇峰 (1863–1957), 48, 105, 167
Tokuwa Women's Academy 徳和女塾, 344–45, 369
Tominaga Fumikazu 富永文一 (1891–1959), 267–68
Tomita Gisaku 富田儀作 (1858–1930), 94, 149, 233, 249*n*96, 254, Appendix 1
*Tonga ilbo* 東亜日報: as vanguard of nationalism, 207, 209–10, 216, 280, 321*n*57; on Japanese industrial policy, 238, 252–54; demise of, 358. *See also* Song Chin-u
Tonghak 東学 (Eastern Learning): uprising, 45–46, 162; and Ilchinhoe, 104*n*23; and Ch'ŏndogyo, 357*n*7
total war, 11, 15, 28, 354, 356–57, 393, 395
township 面 (J. *men*; K. *myŏn*): local government in, 266*n*7, 267–69, 293*n*107, 296*n*122; and spiritual mobilization, 375*n*98
Tōyama Mitsuru 頭山満 (1855–1944), 104, 167, 200*n*44
Tōyō Takushoku Kabushiki Kaisha 東洋拓殖株式会社 (Oriental Development Company; ODC), 59–62, 126, 232–33, 246, 317; criticism of, 102, 151, 209, 222, 235
Tōyōshi 東洋史 (Eastern History), 195, 196*n*24
Triple Intervention, 47, 52

Tsuda Katashi 津田剛 (1906–1990), 359, 363–68 *passim*, 372–74, 387*n*156
Tsuda Miyoko 津田美代子, 371–72
Tsuda Sakae 津田栄 (1895–1961), 332, 342, 344, 348, 372*n*81
Tsuda Setsuko 津田節子 (1902–1972), 337–39, 344–45, 355, 358, 369–73
Tumen river, 310, 314
"Twelve-Year Plan on Korean Railroads" 朝鮮鉄道十二年計画, 250, Map 4

Uchida Ryōhei 内田良平 (1874–1937), 104, 106, 110, 111–13, Table 5, 167, 170, 200*n*44
Ugaki Kazushige 宇垣一成 (1868–1956), 308*n*4; industrial policy of, 323*n*68, 325*n*79, 327*n*85; and moral suasion, 28, 309, 327–28, 331–34, 338–39, 341, 346–48, 353–54
ultranationalists, 48–49, 99, 112–14, 167. *See also* Uchida Ryōhei

Wada Tsuneichi 和田常一 (1862–?), 38, 53, 92, Appendix 1
Wakatsuki Reijirō 若槻礼次郎 (1866–1949), cabinet, 296*n*121
Wakō Kyōen 和光教園, 177
Wanbaoshan 万宝山, Incident, 312, 318*n*41
war relief 慰問 (*imon*), 310, 337*n*129, 369
war support, 333, 337, 359–60, 373–74, 391
Watanabe Benzō 渡辺弁三, 180
Watanabe Sadaichirō 渡辺定一郎 (1872–?), 182*n*134, 244–48, 249*n*96, 259*n*142, 274–75, 277, 323, Fig. 10, Appendix 1
Watanabe Toyohiko 渡辺豊日子, 271, 339, 348–49
Watt, Lori, 4, 400*n*5, 401
Wilson, Woodrow (1856–1924), Fourteen Points of, 143, 169
Wŏn Tŏk-sang 元悳常 (1883–?), 246, 247*n*87, 361*n*27
World War I, aftermath of, 145, 169, 216, 253. *See also* nationalism
World War II, 17*n*31, 390, 412

Xinjing 新京 (Changchun), 312, 324

Yalu river, 310, 314, 326
Yamagata Aritomo 山県有朋 (1838–1922), 51–53
Yamagata Isaburō 山県伊三郎 (1858–1927), 119, 204*n*63, 275
Yamagata Isoo 山県五十雄 (1869–1959), 156
Yamaguchi Tahee 山口太兵衛 (1865–1934), 43, 46–47, 53–54, 91–94, 227, 233, 243, 346*n*173, Appendix 1
Yamaji Aizan 山路愛山 (1865–1917), 191, 195
Yamamoto Miono 山本美越乃 (1874–1941), 294, 295*n*118
Yamanashi Hanzō 山梨半造 (1864–1944), 156*n*34, 290–91
Yamanouchi Yasushi 山之内靖, 356
Yamato Academy 大和塾, 369
Yamato Yojirō 大和與次郎 (1871–?), 330, Appendix 1
Yanaihara Tadao 矢内原忠雄 (1893–1961), 18*n*35, 285
*yangban* 兩班 (officials of the "two orders"), elites, 71, 84, 87; efforts to co-opt, 107, 115, 123–24, 152, 158; as metaphor of Korean disunity, 205; opposition to name change, 381
yen-bloc, 325, 353
Yi Chae-gŭk 李載國, 168
Yi Chi-yong 李址鎔 (1870–?), 163
Yi Chŏng-suk 李貞淑 (1858–1935), 57
Yi Jin-ho 李軫鎬 (1867–1943), 246, 384*n*144
Yi Kwang-su 李光洙 (1892–1950), 154, 183*n*141, 208, 253
Yi Sang 李箱 (1910–1937), 76
Yi Sŭng-yŏp 李昇燁, 16, 366
Yi Wan-yong 李完用 (1858–1926), 53, 111, 113, 232*n*17, 233, 282
Yi Wŏn-sŏk 李元錫, 179

Yi Yong-gu 李容九 (1868–1912), 104, 113*n*68, 321
Yi Yŏng-gŭn 李泳根 (Ueda Tatsuo 上田龍男) (1910–?), 366, 369
*yobo*: "-ization," 87, 134; Japanese use of, 151, 171, 389
*yŏgak* 旅閣 (coastal trade broker), 42
Yŏnjŏnghoe 研政会 (Political Study Club), 287
*yoron* 世論 (public opinion), age of, 102–3
Yosano Akiko 与謝野晶子 (1878–1942), 55
Yosano Tekkan 与謝野鉄幹 (1873–1935), 55, 56*n*78
Yoshida Masakazu 吉田雅一 (1876–?), 324
Yoshida Tōgo 吉田東伍 (1864–1918), 191
Yoshino Sakuzō 吉野作造 (1878–1933), 181
Young, Louise, 309*n*5
Yu Kil-chun 兪吉濬 (1856–1914), 194*n*18
Yuan Shikai 袁世凱 (1859–1916), 45
Yudo Chinhŭnghoe 儒道振興会 (Society for the Promotion of the Confucian Way), Table 5, 160, 162*n*59, 168*n*79
Yuminhoe 維民会, 235–36, 238
Yun Ch'i-ho 尹致昊 (1865–1945), 151, 156, 184, 341, 359, 384*n*144
Yun Hae-dong, 237*n*47, 400
Yun Tŏg-yŏng 尹德榮 (1873–1940), 384*n*144

*zaibatsu* 財閥, 40, 233*n*24, 261*n*145, 323*n*68, 411
*zaikin kahō* 在勤加俸 (overseas allowance), 77, 122*n*108, 319, 383, 386
Zenkoku Shōgyō Kaigisho Rengōkai 全国商業会議所連合会 (National Federation of Chambers of Commerce), in Japan, 248
Zen-Sen Kōshokusha Taikai 全鮮公職者大会 (All-Korea Public Officials' Convention), 272–78, 282, 288–96 *passim*, 303. *See also* Kōshi Club

*Harvard East Asian Monographs*
(titles now in print)

7. Chao Kuo-chün, *Economic Planning and Organization in Mainland China: A Documentary Study, 1949–1957*
13. S. M. Meng, *The Tsungli Yamen: Its Organization and Functions*
31. Madeleine Chi, *China Diplomacy, 1914–1918*
36. Peter Frost, *The Bakumatsu Currency Crisis*
38. Robert R. Campbell, *James Duncan Campbell: A Memoir by His Son*
39. Jerome Alan Cohen, ed., *The Dynamics of China's Foreign Relations*
40. V. V. Vishnyakova-Akimova, *Two Years in Revolutionary China, 1925–1927*, trans. Steven L. Levine
41. Meron Medzini, *French Policy in Japan during the Closing Years of the Tokugawa Regime*
46. W. P. J. Hall, *A Bibliographical Guide to Japanese Research on the Chinese Economy, 1958–1970*
47. Jack J. Gerson, *Horatio Nelson Lay and Sino-British Relations, 1854–1864*
48. Paul Richard Bohr, *Famine and the Missionary: Timothy Richard as Relief Administrator and Advocate of National Reform*
50. Britten Dean, *China and Great Britain: The Diplomacy of Commercial Relations, 1860–1864*
51. Ellsworth C. Carlson, *The Foochow Missionaries, 1847–1880*
53. Richard M. Pfeffer, *Understanding Business Contracts in China, 1949–1963*
55. Ranbir Vohra, *Lao She and the Chinese Revolution*
60. Noriko Kamachi, John K. Fairbank, and Chūzō Ichiko, *Japanese Studies of Modern China Since 1953: A Bibliographical Guide to Historical and Social-Science Research on the Nineteenth and Twentieth Centuries, Supplementary Volume for 1953–1969*
61. Donald A. Gibbs and Yun-chen Li, *A Bibliography of Studies and Translations of Modern Chinese Literature, 1918–1942*
62. Robert H. Silin, *Leadership and Values: The Organization of Large-Scale Taiwanese Enterprises*
63. David Pong, *A Critical Guide to the Kwangtung Provincial Archives Deposited at the Public Record Office of London*

69. Eric Widmer, *The Russian Ecclesiastical Mission in Peking during the Eighteenth Century*
73. Jon Sigurdson, *Rural Industrialism in China*
74. Kang Chao, *The Development of Cotton Textile Production in China*
75. Valentin Rabe, *The Home Base of American China Missions, 1880–1920*
78. Meishi Tsai, *Contemporary Chinese Novels and Short Stories, 1949–1974: An Annotated Bibliography*
80. Endymion Wilkinson, *Landlord and Labor in Late Imperial China: Case Studies from Shandong by Jing Su and Luo Lun*
84. J. W. Dower, *Empire and Aftermath: Yoshida Shigeru and the Japanese Experience, 1878–1954*
85. Martin Collcutt, *Five Mountains: The Rinzai Zen Monastic Institution in Medieval Japan*
86. Kwang Suk Kim and Michael Roemer, *Growth and Structural Transformation*
89. Sung Hwan Ban, Pal Yong Moon, and Dwight H. Perkins, *Rural Development*
92. Edward S. Mason, Dwight H. Perkins, Kwang Suk Kim, David C. Cole, Mahn Je Kim et al., *The Economic and Social Modernization of the Republic of Korea*
93. Robert Repetto, Tai Hwan Kwon, Son-Ung Kim, Dae Young Kim, John E. Sloboda, and Peter J. Donaldson, *Economic Development, Population Policy, and Demographic Transition in the Republic of Korea*
94. Parks M. Coble, Jr., *The Shanghai Capitalists and the Nationalist Government, 1927–1937*
96. Richard Wich, *Sino-Soviet Crisis Politics: A Study of Political Change and Communication*
97. Lillian M. Li, *China's Silk Trade: Traditional Industry in the Modern World, 1842–1937*
98. R. David Arkush, *Fei Xiaotong and Sociology in Revolutionary China*
100. James Reeve Pusey, *China and Charles Darwin*
101. Hoyt Cleveland Tillman, *Utilitarian Confucianism: Chen Liang's Challenge to Chu Hsi*
102. Thomas A. Stanley, *Ōsugi Sakae, Anarchist in Taishō Japan: The Creativity of the Ego*
103. Jonathan K. Ocko, *Bureaucratic Reform in Provincial China: Ting Jih-ch'ang in Restoration Kiangsu, 1867–1870*
104. James Reed, *The Missionary Mind and American East Asia Policy, 1911–1915*
105. Neil L. Waters, *Japan's Local Pragmatists: The Transition from Bakumatsu to Meiji in the Kawasaki Region*
106. David C. Cole and Yung Chul Park, *Financial Development in Korea, 1945–1978*
107. Roy Bahl, Chuk Kyo Kim, and Chong Kee Park, *Public Finances during the Korean Modernization Process*
108. William D. Wray, *Mitsubishi and the N.Y.K., 1870–1914: Business Strategy in the Japanese Shipping Industry*
109. Ralph William Huenemann, *The Dragon and the Iron Horse: The Economics of Railroads in China, 1876–1937*
111. Jane Kate Leonard, *Wei Yüan and China's Rediscovery of the Maritime World*
117. Andrew Gordon, *The Evolution of Labor Relations in Japan: Heavy Industry, 1853–1955*

119. Christine Guth Kanda, *Shinzō: Hachiman Imagery and Its Development*
121. Chang-tai Hung, *Going to the People: Chinese Intellectual and Folk Literature, 1918–1937*
123. Richard von Glahn, *The Country of Streams and Grottoes: Expansion, Settlement, and the Civilizing of the Sichuan Frontier in Song Times*
124. Steven D. Carter, *The Road to Komatsubara: A Classical Reading of the Renga Hyakuin*
126. Bob Tadashi Wakabayashi, *Anti-Foreignism and Western Learning in Early-Modern Japan: The "New Theses" of 1825*
127. Atsuko Hirai, *Individualism and Socialism: The Life and Thought of Kawai Eijirō (1891–1944)*
129. R. Kent Guy, *The Emperor's Four Treasuries: Scholars and the State in the Late Chien-lung Era*
130. Peter C. Perdue, *Exhausting the Earth: State and Peasant in Hunan, 1500–1850*
131. Susan Chan Egan, *A Latterday Confucian: Reminiscences of William Hung (1893–1980)*
132. James T. C. Liu, *China Turning Inward: Intellectual-Political Changes in the Early Twelfth Century*
134. Kate Wildman Nakai, *Shogunal Politics: Arai Hakuseki and the Premises of Tokugawa Rule*
137. Susan Downing Videen, *Tales of Heichū*
138. Heinz Morioka and Miyoko Sasaki, *Rakugo: The Popular Narrative Art of Japan*
139. Joshua A. Fogel, *Nakae Ushikichi in China: The Mourning of Spirit*
140. Alexander Barton Woodside, *Vietnam and the Chinese Model: A Comparative Study of Vietnamese and Chinese Government in the First Half of the Nineteenth Century*
141. George Elison, *Deus Destroyed: The Image of Christianity in Early Modern Japan*
144. Marie Anchordoguy, *Computers, Inc.: Japan's Challenge to IBM*
146. Mary Elizabeth Berry, *Hideyoshi*
147. Laura E. Hein, *Fueling Growth: The Energy Revolution and Economic Policy in Postwar Japan*
148. Wen-hsin Yeh, *The Alienated Academy: Culture and Politics in Republican China, 1919–1937*
149. Dru C. Gladney, *Muslim Chinese: Ethnic Nationalism in the People's Republic*
150. Merle Goldman and Paul A. Cohen, eds., *Ideas Across Cultures: Essays on Chinese Thought in Honor of Benjamin L Schwartz*
151. James M. Polachek, *The Inner Opium War*
152. Gail Lee Bernstein, *Japanese Marxist: A Portrait of Kawakami Hajime, 1879–1946*
154. Mark Mason, *American Multinationals and Japan: The Political Economy of Japanese Capital Controls, 1899–1980*
155. Richard J. Smith, John K. Fairbank, and Katherine F. Bruner, *Robert Hart and China's Early Modernization: His Journals, 1863–1866*
157. William Wayne Farris, *Heavenly Warriors: The Evolution of Japan's Military, 500–1300*
159. James B. Palais, *Politics and Policy in Traditional Korea*
161. Roger R. Thompson, *China's Local Councils in the Age of Constitutional Reform, 1898–1911*

162. William Johnston, *The Modern Epidemic: History of Tuberculosis in Japan*
163. Constantine Nomikos Vaporis, *Breaking Barriers: Travel and the State in Early Modern Japan*
164. Irmela Hijiya-Kirschnereit, *Rituals of Self-Revelation: Shishōsetsu as Literary Genre and Socio-Cultural Phenomenon*
165. James C. Baxter, *The Meiji Unification through the Lens of Ishikawa Prefecture*
166. Thomas R. H. Havens, *Architects of Affluence: The Tsutsumi Family and the Seibu-Saison Enterprises in Twentieth-Century Japan*
167. Anthony Hood Chambers, *The Secret Window: Ideal Worlds in Tanizaki's Fiction*
168. Steven J. Ericson, *The Sound of the Whistle: Railroads and the State in Meiji Japan*
169. Andrew Edmund Goble, *Kenmu: Go-Daigo's Revolution*
170. Denise Potrzeba Lett, *In Pursuit of Status: The Making of South Korea's "New" Urban Middle Class*
171. Mimi Hall Yiengpruksawan, *Hiraizumi: Buddhist Art and Regional Politics in Twelfth-Century Japan*
173. Aviad E. Raz, *Riding the Black Ship: Japan and Tokyo Disneyland*
174. Deborah J. Milly, *Poverty, Equality, and Growth: The Politics of Economic Need in Postwar Japan*
175. See Heng Teow, *Japan's Cultural Policy toward China, 1918–1931: A Comparative Perspective*
176. Michael A. Fuller, *An Introduction to Literary Chinese*
177. Frederick R. Dickinson, *War and National Reinvention: Japan in the Great War, 1914–1919*
178. John Solt, *Shredding the Tapestry of Meaning: The Poetry and Poetics of Kitasono Katue (1902–1978)*
179. Edward Pratt, *Japan's Protoindustrial Elite: The Economic Foundations of the Gōnō*
180. Atsuko Sakaki, *Recontextualizing Texts: Narrative Performance in Modern Japanese Fiction*
181. Soon-Won Park, *Colonial Industrialization and Labor in Korea: The Onoda Cement Factory*
182. JaHyun Kim Haboush and Martina Deuchler, *Culture and the State in Late Chosŏn Korea*
183. John W. Chaffee, *Branches of Heaven: A History of the Imperial Clan of Sung China*
184. Gi-Wook Shin and Michael Robinson, eds., *Colonial Modernity in Korea*
185. Nam-lin Hur, *Prayer and Play in Late Tokugawa Japan: Asakusa Sensōji and Edo Society*
186. Kristin Stapleton, *Civilizing Chengdu: Chinese Urban Reform, 1895–1937*
187. Hyung Il Pai, *Constructing "Korean" Origins: A Critical Review of Archaeology, Historiography, and Racial Myth in Korean State-Formation Theories*
188. Brian D. Ruppert, *Jewel in the Ashes: Buddha Relics and Power in Early Medieval Japan*
189. Susan Daruvala, *Zhou Zuoren and an Alternative Chinese Response to Modernity*
191. Kerry Smith, *A Time of Crisis: Japan, the Great Depression, and Rural Revitalization*
192. Michael Lewis, *Becoming Apart: National Power and Local Politics in Toyama, 1868–1945*

193. William C. Kirby, Man-houng Lin, James Chin Shih, and David A. Pietz, eds., *State and Economy in Republican China: A Handbook for Scholars*
194. Timothy S. George, *Minamata: Pollution and the Struggle for Democracy in Postwar Japan*
195. Billy K. L. So, *Prosperity, Region, and Institutions in Maritime China: The South Fukien Pattern, 946–1368*
196. Yoshihisa Tak Matsusaka, *The Making of Japanese Manchuria, 1904–1932*
197. Maram Epstein, *Competing Discourses: Orthodoxy, Authenticity, and Engendered Meanings in Late Imperial Chinese Fiction*
199. Haruo Iguchi, *Unfinished Business: Ayukawa Yoshisuke and U.S.-Japan Relations, 1937–1952*
200. Scott Pearce, Audrey Spiro, and Patricia Ebrey, *Culture and Power in the Reconstitution of the Chinese Realm, 200–600*
201. Terry Kawashima, *Writing Margins: The Textual Construction of Gender in Heian and Kamakura Japan*
202. Martin W. Huang, *Desire and Fictional Narrative in Late Imperial China*
203. Robert S. Ross and Jiang Changbin, eds., *Re-examining the Cold War: U.S.-China Diplomacy, 1954–1973*
204. Guanhua Wang, *In Search of Justice: The 1905–1906 Chinese Anti-American Boycott*
205. David Schaberg, *A Patterned Past: Form and Thought in Early Chinese Historiography*
206. Christine Yano, *Tears of Longing: Nostalgia and the Nation in Japanese Popular Song*
207. Milena Doleželová-Velingerová and Oldřich Král, with Graham Sanders, eds., *The Appropriation of Cultural Capital: China's May Fourth Project*
208. Robert N. Huey, *The Making of 'Shinkokinshū'*
209. Lee Butler, *Emperor and Aristocracy in Japan, 1467–1680: Resilience and Renewal*
210. Suzanne Ogden, *Inklings of Democracy in China*
211. Kenneth J. Ruoff, *The People's Emperor: Democracy and the Japanese Monarchy, 1945–1995*
212. Haun Saussy, *Great Walls of Discourse and Other Adventures in Cultural China*
213. Aviad E. Raz, *Emotions at Work: Normative Control, Organizations, and Culture in Japan and America*
214. Rebecca E. Karl and Peter Zarrow, eds., *Rethinking the 1898 Reform Period: Political and Cultural Change in Late Qing China*
215. Kevin O'Rourke, *The Book of Korean Shijo*
216. Ezra F. Vogel, ed., *The Golden Age of the U.S.-China-Japan Triangle, 1972–1989*
217. Thomas A. Wilson, ed., *On Sacred Grounds: Culture, Society, Politics, and the Formation of the Cult of Confucius*
218. Donald S. Sutton, *Steps of Perfection: Exorcistic Performers and Chinese Religion in Twentieth-Century Taiwan*
219. Daqing Yang, *Technology of Empire: Telecommunications and Japanese Expansionism in Asia, 1883–1945*
220. Qianshen Bai, *Fu Shan's World: The Transformation of Chinese Calligraphy in the Seventeenth Century*

221. Paul Jakov Smith and Richard von Glahn, eds., *The Song-Yuan-Ming Transition in Chinese History*
222. Rania Huntington, *Alien Kind: Foxes and Late Imperial Chinese Narrative*
223. Jordan Sand, *House and Home in Modern Japan: Architecture, Domestic Space, and Bourgeois Culture, 1880–1930*
224. Karl Gerth, *China Made: Consumer Culture and the Creation of the Nation*
225. Xiaoshan Yang, *Metamorphosis of the Private Sphere: Gardens and Objects in Tang-Song Poetry*
226. Barbara Mittler, *A Newspaper for China? Power, Identity, and Change in Shanghai's News Media, 1872–1912*
227. Joyce A. Madancy, *The Troublesome Legacy of Commissioner Lin: The Opium Trade and Opium Suppression in Fujian Province, 1820s to 1920s*
228. John Makeham, *Transmitters and Creators: Chinese Commentators and Commentaries on the Analects*
229. Elisabeth Köll, *From Cotton Mill to Business Empire: The Emergence of Regional Enterprises in Modern China*
230. Emma Teng, *Taiwan's Imagined Geography: Chinese Colonial Travel Writing and Pictures, 1683–1895*
231. Wilt Idema and Beata Grant, *The Red Brush: Writing Women of Imperial China*
232. Eric C. Rath, *The Ethos of Noh: Actors and Their Art*
233. Elizabeth Remick, *Building Local States: China during the Republican and Post-Mao Eras*
234. Lynn Struve, ed., *The Qing Formation in World-Historical Time*
235. D. Max Moerman, *Localizing Paradise: Kumano Pilgrimage and the Religious Landscape of Premodern Japan*
236. Antonia Finnane, *Speaking of Yangzhou: A Chinese City, 1550–1850*
237. Brian Platt, *Burning and Building: Schooling and State Formation in Japan, 1750–1890*
238. Gail Bernstein, Andrew Gordon, and Kate Wildman Nakai, eds., *Public Spheres, Private Lives in Modern Japan, 1600–1950: Essays in Honor of Albert Craig*
239. Wu Hung and Katherine R. Tsiang, *Body and Face in Chinese Visual Culture*
240. Stephen Dodd, *Writing Home: Representations of the Native Place in Modern Japanese Literature*
241. David Anthony Bello, *Opium and the Limits of Empire: Drug Prohibition in the Chinese Interior, 1729–1850*
242. Hosea Hirata, *Discourses of Seduction: History, Evil, Desire, and Modern Japanese Literature*
243. Kyung Moon Hwang, *Beyond Birth: Social Status in the Emergence of Modern Korea*
244. Brian R. Dott, *Identity Reflections: Pilgrimages to Mount Tai in Late Imperial China*
245. Mark McNally, *Proving the Way: Conflict and Practice in the History of Japanese Nativism*
246. Yongping Wu, *A Political Explanation of Economic Growth: State Survival, Bureaucratic Politics, and Private Enterprises in the Making of Taiwan's Economy, 1950–1985*
247. Kyu Hyun Kim, *The Age of Visions and Arguments: Parliamentarianism and the National Public Sphere in Early Meiji Japan*

248. Zvi Ben-Dor Benite, *The Dao of Muhammad: A Cultural History of Muslims in Late Imperial China*
249. David Der-wei Wang and Shang Wei, eds., *Dynastic Crisis and Cultural Innovation: From the Late Ming to the Late Qing and Beyond*
250. Wilt L. Idema, Wai-yee Li, and Ellen Widmer, eds., *Trauma and Transcendence in Early Qing Literature*
251. Barbara Molony and Kathleen Uno, eds., *Gendering Modern Japanese History*
252. Hiroshi Aoyagi, *Islands of Eight Million Smiles: Idol Performance and Symbolic Production in Contemporary Japan*
253. Wai-yee Li, *The Readability of the Past in Early Chinese Historiography*
254. William C. Kirby, Robert S. Ross, and Gong Li, eds., *Normalization of U.S.-China Relations: An International History*
255. Ellen Gardner Nakamura, *Practical Pursuits: Takano Chōei, Takahashi Keisaku, and Western Medicine in Nineteenth-Century Japan*
256. Jonathan W. Best, *A History of the Early Korean Kingdom of Paekche, together with an annotated translation of* The Paekche Annals *of the* Samguk sagi
257. Liang Pan, *The United Nations in Japan's Foreign and Security Policymaking, 1945–1992: National Security, Party Politics, and International Status*
258. Richard Belsky, *Localities at the Center: Native Place, Space, and Power in Late Imperial Beijing*
259. Zwia Lipkin, *"Useless to the State": "Social Problems" and Social Engineering in Nationalist Nanjing, 1927–1937*
260. William O. Gardner, *Advertising Tower: Japanese Modernism and Modernity in the 1920s*
261. Stephen Owen, *The Making of Early Chinese Classical Poetry*
262. Martin J. Powers, *Pattern and Person: Ornament, Society, and Self in Classical China*
263. Anna M. Shields, *Crafting a Collection: The Cultural Contexts and Poetic Practice of the* Huajian ji 花間集 *(Collection from among the Flowers)*
264. Stephen Owen, *The Late Tang: Chinese Poetry of the Mid-Ninth Century (827–860)*
265. Sara L. Friedman, *Intimate Politics: Marriage, the Market, and State Power in Southeastern China*
266. Patricia Buckley Ebrey and Maggie Bickford, *Emperor Huizong and Late Northern Song China: The Politics of Culture and the Culture of Politics*
267. Sophie Volpp, *Worldly Stage: Theatricality in Seventeenth-Century China*
268. Ellen Widmer, *The Beauty and the Book: Women and Fiction in Nineteenth-Century China*
269. Steven B. Miles, *The Sea of Learning: Mobility and Identity in Nineteenth-Century Guangzhou*
270. Man-houng Lin, *China Upside Down: Currency, Society, and Ideologies, 1808–1856*
271. Ronald Egan, *The Problem of Beauty: Aesthetic Thought and Pursuits in Northern Song Dynasty China*
272. Mark Halperin, *Out of the Cloister: Literati Perspectives on Buddhism in Sung China, 960–1279*

273. Helen Dunstan, *State or Merchant? Political Economy and Political Process in 1740s China*
274. Sabina Knight, *The Heart of Time: Moral Agency in Twentieth-Century Chinese Fiction*
275. Timothy J. Van Compernolle, *The Uses of Memory: The Critique of Modernity in the Fiction of Higuchi Ichiyō*
276. Paul Rouzer, *A New Practical Primer of Literary Chinese*
277. Jonathan Zwicker, *Practices of the Sentimental Imagination: Melodrama, the Novel, and the Social Imaginary in Nineteenth-Century Japan*
278. Franziska Seraphim, *War Memory and Social Politics in Japan, 1945–2005*
280. Cynthia J. Brokaw, *Commerce in Culture: The Sibao Book Trade in the Qing and Republican Periods*
281. Eugene Y. Park, *Between Dreams and Reality: The Military Examination in Late Chosŏn Korea, 1600–1894*
282. Nam-lin Hur, *Death and Social Order in Tokugawa Japan: Buddhism, Anti-Christianity, and the* Danka *System*
283. Patricia M. Thornton, *Disciplining the State: Virtue, Violence, and State-Making in Modern China*
284. Vincent Goossaert, *The Taoists of Peking, 1800–1949: A Social History of Urban Clerics*
286. Charo B. D'Etcheverry, *Love after* The Tale of Genji*: Rewriting the World of the Shining Prince*
287. Michael G. Chang, *A Court on Horseback:Imperial Touring & the Construction of Qing Rule, 1680–1785*
288. Carol Richmond Tsang, *War and Faith:* Ikkō Ikki *in Late Muromachi Japan*
289. Hilde De Weerdt, *Competition over Content: Negotiating Standards for the Civil Service Examinations in Imperial China (1127–1279)*
290. Eve Zimmerman, *Out of the Alleyway: Nakagami Kenji and the Poetics of Outcaste Fiction*
291. Robert Culp, *Articulating Citizenship: Civic Education and Student Politics in Southeastern China, 1912–1940*
292. Richard J. Smethurst, *From Foot Soldier to Finance Minister: Takahashi Korekiyo, Japan's Keynes*
293. John E. Herman, *Amid the Clouds and Mist: China's Colonization of Guizhou, 1200–1700*
294. Tomoko Shiroyama, *China during the Great Depression: Market, State, and the World Economy, 1929–1937*
295. Kirk W. Larsen, *Tradition, Treaties and Trade: Qing Imperialism and Chosŏn Korea, 1850–1910*
296. Gregory Golley, *When Our Eyes No Longer See: Realism, Science, and Ecology in Japanese Literary Modernism*
297. Barbara Ambros, *Emplacing a Pilgrimage: The Ōyama Cult and Regional Religion in Early Modern Japan*
298. Rebecca Suter, *The Japanization of Modernity: Murakami Haruki between Japan and the United States*

299. Yuma Totani, *The Tokyo War Crimes Trial: The Pursuit of Justice in the Wake of World War II*
301. David M. Robinson, ed., *Culture, Courtiers, and Competition: The Ming Court (1368–1644)*
302. Calvin Chen, *Some Assembly Required: Work, Community, and Politics in China's Rural Enterprises*
303. Sem Vermeersch, *The Power of the Buddhas: The Politics of Buddhism During the Koryŏ Dynasty* (918–1392)
304. Tina Lu, *Accidental Incest, Filial Cannibalism, and Other Peculiar Encounters in Late Imperial Chinese Literature*
305. Chang Woei Ong, *Men of Letters Within the Passes: Guanzhong Literati in Chinese History, 907–1911*
306. Wendy Swartz, *Reading Tao Yuanming: Shifting Paradigms of Historical Reception (427–1900)*
307. Peter K. Bol, *Neo-Confucianism in History*
308. Carlos Rojas, *The Naked Gaze: Reflections on Chinese Modernity*
309. Kelly H. Chong, *Deliverance and Submission: Evangelical Women and the Negotiation of Patriarchy in South Korea*
310. Rachel DiNitto, *Uchida Hyakken: A Critique of Modernity and Militarism in Prewar Japan*
311. Jeffrey Snyder-Reinke, *Dry Spells: State Rainmaking and Local Governance in Late Imperial China*
312. Jay Dautcher, *Down a Narrow Road: Identity and Masculinity in a Uyghur Community in Xinjiang China*
313. Xun Liu, *Daoist Modern: Innovation, Lay Practice, and the Community of Inner Alchemy in Republican Shanghai*
314. Jacob Eyferth, *Eating Rice from Bamboo Roots: The Social History of a Community of Handicraft Papermakers in Rural Sichuan, 1920–2000*
315. David Johnson, *Spectacle and Sacrifice: The Ritual Foundations of Village Life in North China*
316. James Robson, *Power of Place: The Religious Landscape of the Southern Sacred Peak (Nanyue 南嶽) in Medieval China*
317. Lori Watt, *When Empire Comes Home: Repatriation and Reintegration in Postwar Japan*
318. James Dorsey, *Critical Aesthetics: Kobayashi Hideo, Modernity, and Wartime Japan*
319. Christopher Bolton, *Sublime Voices: The Fictional Science and Scientific Fiction of Abe Kōbō*
320. Si-yen Fei, *Negotiating Urban Space: Urbanization and Late Ming Nanjing*
321. Christopher Gerteis, *Gender Struggles: Wage-Earning Women and Male-Dominated Unions in Postwar Japan*
322. Rebecca Nedostup, *Superstitious Regimes: Religion and the Politics of Chinese Modernity*
323. Lucien Bianco, *Wretched Rebels: Rural Disturbances on the Eve of the Chinese Revolution*
324. Cathryn H. Clayton, *Sovereignty at the Edge: Macau and the Question of Chineseness*
325. Micah S. Muscolino, *Fishing Wars and Environmental Change in Late Imperial and Modern China*

326. Robert I. Hellyer, *Defining Engagement: Japan and Global Contexts, 1750–1868*
327. Robert Ashmore, *The Transport of Reading: Text and Understanding in the World of Tao Qian (365–427)*
328. Mark A. Jones, *Children as Treasures: Childhood and the Middle Class in Early Twentieth Century Japan*
329. Miryam Sas, *Experimental Arts in Postwar Japan: Moments of Encounter, Engagement, and Imagined Return*
330. H. Mack Horton, *Traversing the Frontier: The* Man'yōshū *Account of a Japanese Mission to Silla in 736–737*
331. Dennis J. Frost, *Seeing Stars: Sports Celebrity, Identity, and Body Culture in Modern Japan*
332. Marnie S. Anderson, *A Place in Public: Women's Rights in Meiji Japan*
333. Peter Mauch, *Sailor Diplomat: Nomura Kichisaburō and the Japanese-American War*
334. Ethan Isaac Segal, *Coins, Trade, and the State: Economic Growth in Early Medieval Japan*
335. David B. Lurie, *Realms of Literacy: Early Japan and the History of Writing*
336. Lillian Lan-ying Tseng, *Picturing Heaven in Early China*
337. Jun Uchida, *Brokers of Empire: Japanese Settler Colonialism in Korea, 1876–1945*
338. Patricia L. Maclachlan, *The People's Post Office: The History and Politics of the Japanese Postal System, 1871–2010*
339. Michael Schiltz, *The Money Doctors from Japan: Finance, Imperialism, and the Building of the Yen Bloc, 1895–1937*
340. Daqing Yang, Jie Liu, Hiroshi Mitani, and Andrew Gordon, eds., *Toward a History beyond Borders: Contentious Issues in Sino-Japanese Relations*
341. Sonia Ryang, *Reading North Korea: An Ethnological Inquiry*
342. Susan Huang, *Picturing the True Form: Daoist Visual Culture in Traditional China*
343. Barbara Mittler, *A Continuous Revolution: Making Sense of Cultural Revolution Culture*
344. Hwansoo Ilmee Kim, *Empire of the Dharma: Korean and Japanese Buddhism, 1877–1912*
345. Satoru Saito, *Detective Fiction and the Rise of the Japanese Novel, 1880–1930*
346. Jung-Sun N. Han, *An Imperial Path to Modernity: Yoshino Sakuzō and a New Liberal Order in East Asia, 1905–1937*
347. Atsuko Hirai, *Government by Mourning: Death and Political Integration in Japan, 1603–1912*
348. Darryl E. Flaherty, *Public Law, Private Practice: Politics, Profit, and the Legal Profession in Nineteenth-Century Japan*
349. Jeffrey Paul Bayliss, *On the Margins of Empire: Buraku and Korean Identity in Prewar and Wartime Japan*
350. Barry Eichengreen, Dwight H. Perkins, and Kwanho Shin, *From Miracle to Maturity: The Growth of the Korean Economy*
351. Michel Mohr, *Buddhism, Unitarianism, and the Meiji Competition for Universality*
352. J. Keith Vincent, *Two-Timing Modernity: Homosocial Narrative in Modern Japanese Fiction*

353. Suzanne G. O'Brien, *Customizing Daily Life: Representing and Reforming Customs in Nineteenth-Century Japan*
354. Chong-Bum An and Barry Bosworth, *Income Inequality in Korea: An Analysis of Trends, Causes, and Answers*
355. Jamie L. Newhard, *Knowing the Amorous Man: A History of Scholarship on* Tales of Ise
356. Sho Konishi, *Anarchist Modernity: Cooperatism and Japanese-Russian Intellectual Relations in Modern Japan*
357. Christopher P. Hanscom, *The Real Modern: Literary Modernism and the Crisis of Representation in Colonial Korea*
358. Michael Wert, *Meiji Restoration Losers: Memory and Tokugawa Supporters in Modern Japan*
359. Garret P. S. Olberding, ed., *Facing the Monarch: Modes of Advice in the Early Chinese Court*
360. Xiaojue Wang, *Modernity with a Cold War Face: Reimagining the Nation in Chinese Literature Across the 1949 Divide*
361. David Spafford, *A Sense of Place: The Political Landscape in Late Medieval Japan*
362. Jongryn Mo and Barry Weingast, *Korean Political and Economic Development: Crisis, Security, and Economic Rebalancing*
363. Melek Ortabasi, *The Undiscovered Country: Text, Translation, and Modernity in the Work of Yanagita Kunio*
364. Hiraku Shimoda, *Lost and Found: Recovering Regional Identity in Imperial Japan*
365. Trent E. Maxey, *The "Greatest Problem": Religion and State Formation in Meiji Japan*
366. Gina Cogan, *The Princess Nun: Bunchi, Buddhist Reform, and Gender in Early Edo Japan*
367. Eric C. Han, *Rise of a Japanese Chinatown: Yokohama, 1894–1972*